THE ARABIC VERSION OF THE *NICOMACHEAN ETHICS*

ARISTOTELES SEMITICO-LATINUS

founded by H.J. Drossaart Lulofs

is prepared under the supervision of the ROYAL NETHERLANDS ACADEMY OF ARTS AND SCIENCES as part of the CORPUS PHILOSOPHORUM MEDII AEVI project of the UNION ACADÉMIQUE INTERNATIONALE.

The Aristoteles Semitico-Latinus project envisages the publication of the Syriac, Arabic and Hebrew translations of Aristotle's works, of the Latin translations of those translations, and of the mediaeval paraphrases and commentaries made in the context of this translation tradition.

VOLUME 17

TUTA SUB AEGIDE PALLAS · 1683 ·

THE ARABIC VERSION OF THE *NICOMACHEAN ETHICS*

EDITED BY

ANNA A. AKASOY AND ALEXANDER FIDORA

WITH AN INTRODUCTION AND
ANNOTATED TRANSLATION BY

DOUGLAS M. DUNLOP

TUTA SUB AEGIDE PALLAS · 1683 ·

BRILL
LEIDEN · BOSTON
2005

This book is printed on acid-free paper

Library of Congress Cataloging-in-Publication Data

A C.I.P. record for this book is available from the Library of Congress.

ISSN 0927-4103
ISBN 90 04 14647 4

PRINTED IN THE NETHERLANDS

CONTENTS

Preface vii

Introduction 1

Text and Translation

Book I 112
Book II 154
Book III 184
Book IV 236
Book V 288
Book VI 332
'Seventh Book' 334
Book VII 370
Book VIII 424
Book IX 480
Book X 528

Selective Bibliography 585

Graeco-Arabic Glossary 593

Reversed Glossary 611

Index Nominum 617

PREFACE

The present edition of the Arabic version of Aristotle's *Nicomachean Ethics* looks back on a long history: the only extant Arabic manuscript of this work was discovered in Fez, in two parts, the first found by Arthur J. Arberry in the winter of 1951-1952, the second by Douglas M. Dunlop in the summer of 1959.

Both scholars continued working on the text of the Arabic *Nicomachean Ethics*, a book which is beyond any doubt among the most important of Aristotle's writings: Arberry prepared an edition of the Arabic text at the same time as Dunlop translated it into English, using, as can be seen from his introduction and translation, material he obtained from Arberry. Unfortunately, both scholars died before concluding their work, in 1969 and 1987 respectively.

While Arberry's edition seems to have gone missing, Dunlop's introduction and English translation were handed over to Malcolm C. Lyons, from Cambridge University. Professor Lyons offered Brill the typescript for publication only a few months after Dunlop's death, in December 1987. Although Brill accepted the book for the Islamic Theology and Philosophy series, technical difficulties prevented its publication. Since then, it has remained with Hans Daiber, co-editor of the series, and now also co-editor of the Aristoteles Semitico-Latinus series. It was he who encouraged us to take over Dunlop's material, and to publish a new, critical edition of the Arabic text together with Dunlop's introduction and English translation.

* * *

As the present book is, therefore, not only ours, but also and in the first place Dunlop's, we would like to recall some dates concerning the life and works of this eminent orientalist.

Douglas Morton Dunlop was born on 25 February, 1909 in Scotland as the only son of Reverend H. Morton Dunlop and Helen Oliver. He studied at Glasgow University, University College

Oxford, Edinburgh University, Trinity College Glasgow and Bonn University, where he worked with Paul Kahle from 1937-1939. He graduated from Oxford in 1939, taking his DLitt. at Glasgow in 1955.

In 1939 he became Assistant Professor of Hebrew at Glasgow University, serving as a fireman from 1942 to 1944. He became Assistant Professor of Oriental Languages in 1947, moving to St. Andrews to take up the post of Lecturer in Semitic Languages in 1948. In 1950 he took a lectureship in Islamic History at Cambridge, where he spent twelve years before being appointed as Visiting Professor of History at Columbia University; he was made permanent in 1963, Emeritus Professor in 1977.

His most outstanding publications include: *The History of the Jewish Khazars* (Princeton 1954); *Arabic Science in the West* (Karachi 1958); al-Fārābī, *Fuṣūl al-madanī / Aphorisms of the Statesman* (Cambridge 1961); *Arab Civilization to AD 1500* (Harlow 1971); Abū Sulaimān al-Sijistānī, *Muntakhab ṣiwan al-ḥikmah* (The Hague 1979); he also published several papers and reviews in British and foreign orientalist publications, as well as encyclopaedia articles.

Dunlop travelled in Turkey and Syria in 1938, returning to Syria a year later; in the summer of 1959 he visited Fez in Morocco where he discovered the second part of the *Nicomachean Ethics*. Although Professor Dunlop had wide research interests—witness his publications, listed below—there can be no doubt that this text held a particular fascination for him for the rest of his life.

Douglas Morton Dunlop died on 3 June, 1987, leaving among his papers a near-complete introduction and a full English translation of the Arabic *Nicomachean Ethics*.

* * *

In editing Dunlop's introduction and English translation of the *Nicomachean Ethics*, we have respected, as much as possible, his text. We have only corrected evident mistakes and occasionally updated some of his bibliographical references. Some of Dunlop's remarks concerning the Arabic text have been deleted from the English translation and taken into account in our edition of the Arabic text. More recent literature on the *Nicomachean Ethics* in the

Arabic tradition than that known to Dunlop can be found in the selective bibliography at the end of this volume.

Our critical edition of the Arabic translation gives a more reliable text than that offered by Badawi in his 1979 Kuwait edition.[1] The aim of this edition is a reconstruction of the translator's autograph. Due to the limited textual tradition the basis of our edition is constituted nearly exclusively by the unique manuscript of the Arabic version of the *Nicomachean Ethics* (Ms. Fez, Qarawīyīn L 2508/80 and L 3043/80). We have followed the text of this manuscript except where it contained obvious grammatical errors, and corruptions of the original translation have been emended in harmony with the Greek text. The text of the manuscript has not been corrected where a discrepancy with respect to the Greek text can be explained as a deliberate interpretation of the translator (even if the wording distorts the original sense).

An unfortunate circumstance of the history of this edition is the deterioration of the Fez manuscript in the years since its discovery by Arberry and Dunlop. As is evident from Dunlop's translation and his references to Arberry's lost transcription, some parts of the manuscripts were not then so damaged by worms and misguided conservation treatment as they are now.[2] In these cases we have tried to reconstruct the Arabic text on the basis of Dunlop's translation and recorded the illegible parts in the apparatus. In other cases where a reconstruction of the Arabic text has not been possible, we have recorded the part of the English translation without legible Arabic equivalent in the apparatus. The apparatus includes furthermore all the diverging readings in Badawi's edition except for 1) parts which have been declared illegible by Badawi but appeared clear to us, 2) parts which were retranslated by Badawi from the Greek, 3) minor changes (such as *tā'* and *yā'* at the beginning of imperfect verbs in the third person singular). Hamza, tashdīd and in rare cases vocalisation have been added in the Arabic text according to classical use without

---

[1] For Badawi's *ratio edendi*, which differs from ours, cf. ʿAbdurraḥmān Badawi, "Averroès face au texte qu'il commente", in: Jean Jolivet (ed.), *Multiple Averroès: Actes du Colloque International organisé à l'occasion du 850e anniversaire de la naissance d'Averroès, Paris 20-23 septembre 1976*, Paris 1978, pp. 59-89.

[2] The photographs of the Fez manuscript which were brought by Arberry to Cambridge are not among his papers at Cambridge University Library and Pembroke College, but they should preserve the text in a better state.

being noted in the apparatus. The writing of words like هاؤلاء and لاكن has also been adjusted to هؤلاء and لكن.

Abbreviations in the *apparatus criticus*:

F = Fez manuscript (Qarawīyīn L 2508/80 and L 3043/80)

Bad = Abdarrahman Badawi's edition of the Arabic version of the *Nicomachean Ethics* (*Kitāb al-akhlāq*, Kuwait 1979)

Dun = Dunlop's translation and reconstructed Arabic wording

Arberry = emendations by Arberry, mentioned by Dunlop in the typescript

Ax = Dorothy G. Axelroth, *An Analysis of the Arabic Translation of Book Ten of Aristotle's Nicomachean Ethics*, PhD thesis, The Dropsie College, Philadelphia 1968.

* = in accordance with the Greek text
add. = added
corr. = correction of a miswritten skeleton
del. = deleted
mrg. = margin
om. = omitted
prop. = proposed
read. = correction of a pointing
suppl. = supplied
w.p. = without points

In the Arabic text square brackets indicate the page numbers of the manuscript. The first number gives the page number, the second number the part of the manuscript. Part one in our count corresponds to the first part of the manuscript (L 2508/80), parts two and three to the second part (L 3043/80). Passages of Arabic text in square brackets are additions to the text as suggested by Dunlop. In the English translation, these additions to the Arabic are also set in square brackets, whereas additions to the English translation only have been placed in round brackets. Suspension points [...] signify an illegible passage in the manuscript.

The selective Graeco-Arabic Glossary at the end of our book lists the key philosophical terms of the *Nicomachean Ethics* in Greek and their Arabic equivalents. It is accompanied by a reversed Arabic-Greek Glossary.

* * *

Our work on this volume started within the interdisciplinary research network "The Culture of Knowledge and Social Change" (Wissenskultur und gesellschaftlicher Wandel), founded by the Deutsche Forschungsgemeinschaft (DFG) in 1999 at the Johann Wolfgang Goethe University, Frankfurt am Main. We are very grateful for the support received from two projects within this network: namely, the project directed by Professor Johannes Fried, on Frederick II and his Sicilian court, where Anna Akasoy was a research assistant, and the project directed by Professor Matthias Lutz-Bachmann and Alexander Fidora, on the epistemological changes in medieval philosophy. We are indebted to our Frankfurt colleagues from this network, as well as from the Departments of History, Oriental Studies and Philosophy.

Of course, there have been many other friends and colleagues who offered us their help: In the first place, Charles Burnett and Peter Pormann from the Warburg Institute (London); Bennacer el-Bouazzati (Rabat); ʿAlī al-Ghazīwī from the Qarawīyīn Library (Fez); Jordi Cors Meya from the Universitat Autònoma de Barcelona (Barcelona); Dimitri Gutas from Yale University (New Haven); Steven Harvey from Bar Ilan University (Ramat Gan); Jean L. Lauand from the Universidade de São Paulo (São Paulo); Rafael Ramón Guerrero from the Universidad Complutense (Madrid).

Our greatest debt is with Jaap Mansfeld (Utrecht) and Hans Daiber (Frankfurt) from the Aristoteles Semitico-Latinus comité.

They all have gone through our texts—some of them more than once—saving us from many errors and inaccuracies.

Anna Akasoy / Alexander Fidora
(London – Frankfurt – Barcelona)

Bibliography Douglas M. Dunlop (1909-1987)

"Another 'Prophetic' Letter", in: *Journal of the Royal Asiatic Society* (1940), pp. 54-60.

"The Spanish Historian Ibn Ḥubaish", in: *Journal of the Royal Asiatic Society* (1941), pp. 359-362.

"The Dhunnunids of Toledo", in: *Journal of the Royal Asiatic Society* (1942), pp. 77-96.

"Muḥammad b. Mūsā al-Khwārizmī", in: *Journal of the Royal Asiatic Society* (1943), pp. 248-250.

"Hafiz-I Abru's Version of the Timurid Embassy to China in A.D. 1420", in: *Glasgow University Oriental Society Transactions* 11 (1944), pp. 15-19.

"A Spanish Muslim Saint: Abu 'l-Abbas al-Mursi", in: *Moslem World* 35 (1945), pp. 181-196.

"The Karaits of Eastern Asia", in : BSOAS 13 (1946), pp. 276-289.

"Notes on the Dhunnunids of Toledo", in: *Journal of the Royal Asiatic Society* (1954), pp. 17-19.

"Al-failasūf al-ʿArabī Ibn Bājjah", in: *Arabic Listener* 5/7 (1944).

"Ibn Bājjah's *Tadbīru'l-Mutawaḥḥid* (*Rule of the Solitary*)", in: *Journal of the Royal Asiatic Society* (1945), pp. 61-81.

"Ḥāfiẓ-i Abrū's Version of the Timurid Embassy to China in A.D. 1420", in: *Glasgow University Oriental Society Transactions* 11 (1946), pp. 15-19.

"Scotland According to al-Idrīsī", in: *Scottish Historical Review* 26 (1947), pp. 114-118.

"Aspects of the Khazar Problem", in: *Glasgow University Oriental Society Transactions* 13 (1949), pp. 33-44.

"A Note on Colcodea in Renderings from the Arabic", in: *Jewish Quarterly Review* 39 (1949), pp. 403-408.

"Zeki Validi's Ibn Faḍlān", in: *Die Welt des Orients* 1 (1949), pp. 307-312.

"David Colville, a Successor of Michael Scot", in: *Bulletin of Hispanic Studies* 28 (1951), pp. 38-42.

"The Existence and Definition of Philosophy from an Arabic Text Ascribed to al-Fārābī", in: *Iraq* 13 (1951), pp. 76-94.

"St. Andrews Arabic Alchemy MS", in: *St. Andrews University Chemical Society* (April 1951).

"A Christian Mission to Muslim Spain in the 11th Century", in: *al-Andalus* 17 (1952), pp. 259-310.

"Dīwān Attributed to Ibn Bājjah (Avempace)", in: BSOAS 14 (1952), pp. 463-477.

"Al-Fārābī's *Aphorisms of the Statesman*", in: *Iraq* 14 (1952), pp. 93-117.

"John Mesue and his Work", in: *Bulletin of the British Society for the History of Science* 1 (1952), p. 213.

"An 11th Century Spanish Account of the Northern Nations", in: BSOAS 15 (1953), pp. 159-161.

"Ḥafṣ b. Albar – the Last of the Goths?", in: *Journal of the Royal Asiatic Society* (1954), pp. 137-151.

The History of the Jewish Khazars (Princeton Oriental Studies; 16), Princeton 1954 (reprinted New York 1967).

"The *Ǧawāmiʿ Al-ʿUlūm* of Ibn Farīġūn", in: *Zeki Velidi Togan'a Armağan, Symbolae in honorem A. Z. V. Togan*, Istanbul 1950-1955, pp. 348-353.

"Al-Fārābī's Introductory Sections on Logic", in: *The Islamic Quarterly* 2 (1955), pp. 264-282.

"R-slanda in al-Idrīsī", in: *The Scottish Historical Review* 34 (1955), pp. 95-96.

"Sobre Ḥafṣ Ibn Albar al-Qūṭī al-Qurṭubī", in: *al-Andalus* 20 (1955), pp. 211-213. [Reply to García Gómez' review of his article in JRAS 1954]

"Philosophical Predecessors and Contemporaries of Ibn Bajjah", in: *The Islamic Quarterly* 2 (1955), pp. 100-116.

"Arabic Medicine in England", in: *Journal of the History of Medicine and Allied Sciences* 11 (1956), pp. 166-182.

"Al-Fārābī's *Eisagoge*", in: *The Islamic Quarterly* 3 (1956), pp. 117-138.

"Al-Fārābī's Introductory *Risālah* on Logic", in: *The Islamic Quarterly* 3 (1956), pp. 224-235.

"The 'Arabian Tailor', Henry Wild", in: BSOAS 19 (1957), pp. 579-581.

"Biographical Material from the *Ṣiwān al-Ḥikmah*", in: *Journal of the Royal Asiatic Society* (1957), pp. 82-89.

"The British Isles According to Medieval Arabic Authors", in: *Islamic Quarterly* 4 (1957), pp. 11-28.

"Remarks on the Life and Works of Ibn Bājjah (Avempace)", in: Zeki Velidi Togan (ed.), *Proceedings of the Twenty-Second Congress of Orientalists*, Held in Istanbul, September 15th to 22nd 1951, Leiden 1957, vol. II, pp. 188-196.

"Sources of Gold and Silver in Islam According to al-Hamdānī (10th Century A.D.)", in: *Studia Islamica* 8 (1957), pp. 29-49.

Arabic Science in the West (Pakistan Historical Society Publication; 35), Karachi 1958.

"City of Wrong, a Friday in Jerusalem", in: *Revista del Instituto Egipcio de Estudios Islámicos en Madrid* 6 (1958), pp. 143-144.

"Al-Fārābī's Paraphrase of the *Categories* of Aristotle", in: *The Islamic Quarterly* 4 (1957-1958), pp. 168-197 and 5 (1959), pp. 21-54.

"Ibn Idharī's Account of the Party Kings (*Mulūk at-Tawa'if*)", in: *Glasgow University Oriental Society Transactions* 17 (1958), pp. 19-28.

"The Translations of al-Biṭrīq and Yaḥyā (Yuḥannā) b. al-Biṭrīq", in: *Journal of the Royal Asiatic Society* (1959), pp. 140-150.

"A Little-known Work on Politics by Lisān ad-Dīn b. al-Khaṭīb", in: *Miscelánea de Estudios Árabes y Hebráicos* 8 (1959), pp. 47-54.

"A Source of Al-Masʿūdī: the *Madīnat al-Fāḍilah* of Al-Fārābī", in: S. Maqbul Ahmad / A. Rahman (eds), *Al-Masʿūdī Millenary Commemoration Volume*, Aligarh 1960, pp. 69-71.

"The Work of Translation at Toledo", in: *Babel* 6 (1960), pp. 55-59.

al-Fārābī, *Fuṣūl al-madanī (Aphorisms of the Statesman)*, edited with an English translation, introduction and notes by Douglas M. Dunlop (University of Cambridge Oriental Publications; 5), Cambridge 1961.

"Averroes (Ibn Rushd) on the Modality of Propositions", in: *Islamic Studies* 1 (1962), pp. 23-34.

"The *Nicomachean Ethics* in Arabic, Books I-VI", in: *Oriens* 15 (1962), pp. 18-34.

"Some Remarks on Weil's History of the Caliphs", in: Bernard Lewis / P. M. Holt (eds.), *Historians of the Middle East*, London 1962, pp. 315-329.

"The Arabic Manuscripts of the Academia de Ciências de Lisboa", in: *Actas del Primer Congreso de Estudios Árabes e Islámicos*, Córdoba 1964, pp. 285-291.

"Al-Harith b. Sa'id al Kadhdhab, a Claimant to Prophecy in the Caliphate of 'Abd al-Malik", in: *Studies in Islam* 1 (1964), pp. 12-18.

"A New Source of Information on the Battle of Talas or Aṭlakh", in: *Ural-Altaische Jahrbücher*, Pars Altaica 36 (1964), Wiesbaden 1965, pp. 326-330.

"The Khazars", in: Cecil Roth (ed.), *The World History of the Jewish People*, Second Series: *The Medieval Period*, Vol. II: *The Dark Ages. Jews in Christian Europe 711-1096*, Tel Aviv 1966, pp. 325-356.

"A Letter of Hārūn ar-Rashīd to the Emperor Constantine VI", in: Matthew Black / Georg Fohrer (eds.), *In memoriam Paul Kahle*, Berlin 1968, pp. 106-115.

Arab Civilization to A.D. 1500, Harlow 1971.

"Observations on the Medieval Arabic Version of Aristotle's *Nicomachean Ethics*", in: *Oriente e occidente nel medioevo, Filosofia e scienza* (Convegno internazionale, 9-15 aprile 1969), Rome 1971, pp. 229-250.

"The *Mudhākarāt fī ʿilm an-Nujūm* (*Dialogues on Astrology*) Attributed to Abū Maʿshar al-Balkhī (Albumasar)", in: Clifford E. Bosworth (ed.), *Iran and Islam. In memory of the late Vladimir Minorsky*, Edinburgh 1971, pp. 229-246.

"A Diplomatic Exchange between al-Ma'mūn and an Indian King", in: Sami A. Hanna (ed.), *Medieval and Middle Eastern Studies in Honor of Aziz Suryal Atiya*, Leiden 1972, pp. 133-143.

"Arab Relations with Tibet in the Eighth and Early Ninth Centuries A.D.", in: *Islâm Tetkikleri Enstitüsü Dergisi* 5 (1973), pp. 301-318.

"H. M. Baratz and his View of Khazar Influence on the Earliest Russian Literature, Juridical and Historical", in: Saul Lieberman (ed.), *Salo Wittmayer Baron Jubilee Volume on the Occasion of his Eightieth Birthday*, 3 vols., Jerusalem 1974, vol. I, pp. 345-367.

"A Masterpiece of Translation from the School of Ḥunain: Aristotle's *Nicomachean Ethics*", Ephrem-Hunayn Festival, 4-7/2/1974, Baghdad 1974, pp. 471-488.

"The Manuscript Taimur Pasha 290 Aḫlāq and the *Summa Alexandrinorum*", in: *Arabica* 21 (1974), pp. 252-263.

"Addenda et corrigenda to Arabica XXI, pp. 252-263", in: *Arabica* 23 (1976), pp. 313-314.

"Philosophical Discussions in Sijistan in the 10th Century A.D.", in: *Akten des 7. Kongresses für Arabistik und Islamwissenschaft*, Göttingen 1976, pp. 108-114.

Abū Sulaimān al-Sijistānī, *Muntakhab ṣiwan al-ḥikmah*, ed. Douglas M. Dunlop, The Hague 1979.

"Relations Between Norway and the Maghrib in the 7th/13th Century", in: *Journal of the Ancient Near Eastern Society Columbia University* 11 (1979), pp. 41-44.

"The Arabic Translation of the *Summa Alexandrinorum*", in: AHDLMA 49 (1983), pp. 253-263.

"Remarks on a Text of Avempace", in: Renato Traini (ed.), *Studi in onore di Francesco Gabrieli nel suo ottantesimo compleanno*, vol. I, Rome 1984, pp. 291-300.

"Divine Ascriptions in the *Summa Alexandrinorum*", in: *Hamdard Islamicus* 6/3 (1983), pp. 43-45. [Also in: *Essays on Islam*, Felicitation volume in honor of Dr. Muhammad Hamidullah, ed. Hakim Mohamed Said, Karachi 1992, pp. 102-105.]

INTRODUCTION

I

The interest of the Arabs in the *Nicomachean Ethics* of Aristotle begins more than a thousand years ago, and has continued until modern times.[1] Yet while much of Aristotle is known in medieval Arabic versions, often the work of Christian subjects of the Caliphate in the early ʿAbbāsid period, no medieval translation of the *Ethics*[2] has come to light until recently. The fortunate recovery of an ancient manuscript containing the bulk of the *Nicomachean Ethics* in Arabic[3] has therefore attracted a good deal of attention in scholarly circles and has thrown light on the transmission of that part of the Aristotelian corpus concerning whose fortune in Arabic we are perhaps least well informed. For while we have rather frequent references to the *Nicomachean Ethics* in the writings of al-Kindī, al-Fārābī, Ibn Bājjah and others,[4] a text from which they might be supposed to have quoted has hitherto been conspicuously absent. Also though the *Nicomachean Ethics*, the *Eudemian Ethics* and the *Magna Moralia* are mentioned separately in the Arabic biographies of Aristotle, there is no definite evidence that any of these except the first was ever translated into Arabic, and the only notice which we have regarding the translation of the *Nicomachean Ethics*[5] is obscure and, in the two forms in which it is found, contradictory.

This situation is substantially changed now that we have the *Nicomachean Ethics* more or less *in extenso* in an Arabic manuscript dated Shaʿbān 619 A.H. / October 1222 A.D.,[6] with the strong

---

[1] Cf. for example the modern Arabic translation of the *Nicomachean Ethics* by Lutfi as-Saiyid Pasha.

[2] In what follows 'the *Ethics*' or more frequently 'EN' is used as an abbreviation of the *Nicomachean Ethics* (*Ethica Nicomachea*).

[3] With the exception of most of Book VI and some other places where the MS. is defective. For a list of these, see pp. 98f.

[4] See below, III.

[5] That of Ibn an-Nadīm, repeated by al-Qifṭī, for which see below, pp. 26f.

[6] The date 629/1232 sometimes given is incorrect, see below, p. 3, n. 9.

presumption, amounting to virtual certainty, that the translation is much earlier, going back to the 3rd/9th or at least the 4th/10th century.[7] As a translation of Aristotle into Arabic, it is a remarkable performance, showing nearly everywhere a firm grasp of the intricacies of the thought of Aristotle. It is capable of retranslation into another language, e.g. English, in a way that cannot be said of the medieval Arabic version of Aristotle's *Poetics* or his *Rhetoric*.[8] Where the Arabic translator fails to follow the argument, it is often through a misreading of the Greek text, which may not be due to him (for a discussion of the kind of text which he had in front of him, see below, VIII), or because a reference to the public life of the Greeks, or to Greek history, eludes him, not that his knowledge of the language which he is translating or his perception of ethical distinctions is at fault. It has to be allowed that in spite of some blemishes this translation is a remarkable achievement. At the same time—to say nothing here of the possibilities for the criticism of the Greek original which the new text may offer—, while of course much new light is thrown on Aristotle's *Nicomachean Ethics* among the Arabs by its recovery, not all the connected problems are thereby solved. Several indeed appear so intractable as to defy a solution in the present state of our knowledge.

II

The existence of the manuscript was first made generally known by the late Professor Arthur J. Arberry of Cambridge University, who described his finding of it as follows:

> The most interesting experience I had during my visit to Morocco in the winter of 1951-1952 [...] was the discovery, in the famous Qarawīyīn Library in Fez, of a manuscript containing one half, the second half, of an Arabic translation of the *Nicomachean Ethics*. The shortness of my stay in that ancient and fascinating Moorish city [...] made it impossible for me to do more at the time than take note of the existence of this precious codex; but later the authorities of the Institut des Hautes Études Marocaines in Rabat [...] procured for me a micro-

[7] For a discussion of this, see pp. 27f. and 94f.

[8] For the *Rhetoric* see the remarks of Malcolm C. Lyons in Aristotle, *Ars Rhetorica: The Arabic Version*, a new edition, with commentary and glossary by Malcolm C. Lyons, 2 vols., Cambridge 1982, vol. I, p. XXV.

> film of the manuscript. It is now my high privilege to publish this preliminary note, in anticipation, I hope, of a full edition later on. The manuscript, which is unbound and in fairly good condition, gives us in folios 1-42 the text of Books VII to X of the *Nicomachean Ethics*. The script is an excellently legible *Maghribī*, and the copy is dated Wednesday, 27 Shaʿbān 629 = 18 June 1232[9].[10]

Arberry had photographs made from the microfilm of Books VII to X, together with other material from the same manuscript, and completed a transcript of the Arabic text of this last part of the *Nicomachean Ethics*, with notes and an introduction, which, as he mentions, he intended eventually to publish. It is this transcript which forms the basis of this English translation, for shortly before his last illness Arberry very generously and considerately passed over to me his materials on the Arabic *Ethics*. This material included photocopies of a number of pages of the Fez manuscript. Photocopies of other pages of the manuscript were at one time in the possession of Dr. Richard Walzer, but appear to have gone missing, and I was never able to see them.

The manuscript brought to light and used by Arberry was formerly No. L 3043/80 of the Qarawīyīn Library. It is of some interest to find on a separate page, before the beginning of Book VIII of the Arabic, i.e. Book VII of the Greek original, the following notice, written in a modern *Maghribī* hand with European numerals and undated, of an earlier discovery of the manuscript:

> The *Book of Ethics* of Aristotle called *Nīqūmākhiyā* from the first of the Eighth Book to the last of the Eleventh Book. And at the end of the *Book of Ethics* is a special book of introduction to the science of ethics, not related to a theme, which is thought to be *On Philosophy* by Nicolaus. The whole was written in the year 619. It was found among

---

[9] This was a mistake which has been followed by others, Malcolm C. Lyons, "A Greek Ethical Treatise", in: *Oriens* 13-14 (1961), pp. 35-57, here p. 35; René A. Gauthier and Jean Y. Jolif in Aristotle, *L'Éthique à Nicomaque*, ed. and transl. René A. Gauthier and Jean Y. Jolif, 2 vols., Louvain/Paris ^{2}1970, vol. I/1, p. 108, n. 77; and Douglas M. Dunlop, "The *Nicomachean Ethics* in Arabic, Books I-VI", in: *Oriens* 15 (1962), pp. 18-34, here p. 18, cf. also p. 19 where the other date is referred to.

[10] Cf. Arthur J. Arberry, "The *Nicomachean Ethics* in Arabic", in: BSOAS 17 (1955), pp. 1-9, here p. 1. Arberry referred briefly to the Fez MS. in his article "An Arabic Treatise on Politics" [i.e. the *Kitāb as-saʿādah wa'l-isʿād* of al-ʿĀmirī], in: *The Islamic Quarterly* 2 (1955), pp. 9-22, here pp. 18-19.

the debris (*khurūm*) of the Library. Number of leaves: Ethics 40, Introduction 27. Total 67.

For the first half of the Arabic text I have relied for the most part on photographs of what was then a separate manuscript, Qarawīyīn No. L 2508/80. I was shown this on a visit to Fez in the summer of 1959 by the learned Librarian of the Qarawīyīn Library, al-ʿĀbid al-Fāsī. It contained much of Books I-VI of the *Nicomachean Ethics* and was evidently the first part of the manuscript seen by Arberry. Through the good offices of John Isherwood, Esq., then H. M. Consul in Fez, in liaison with the authorities of the Qarawīyīn Library, I was able to have the above-mentioned photographs made and drew attention to the new development in an article published in *Oriens* in 1962.[11] Some time later Dr. Lawrence V. Berman kindly sent me a Xerox copy of the complete text in 11 Books, i.e. including the intrusive 'Seventh Book'. Dr. Berman, then of Dropsie College, Philadelphia, later Professor at Stanford University, had visited Fez in 1962. Later still I received a microfilm of both parts of the manuscript with the exception of the 'Seventh Book', which in the meantime had passed from the Qarawīyīn to the Bibliothèque Générale, Rabat, through the kindness of Michael Scott, Esq., Tangier. To these gentlemen and to the public authorities concerned I should like to offer my grateful thanks for their assistance, without which the present work would have been impossible.

Berman in 1962 first distinctly showed the existence in the Fez manuscript of a number of pages of an additional 'Seventh Book' which having been inserted between Books VI and VII of the Greek text brought up the number of Books of the Arabic *Nicomachean Ethics* to eleven.[12] This part of the Fez manuscript had already been isolated by Lyons in his article referred to above and characterised by him as "what may well be one of the oldest extant summaries of Aristotle's *Ethics*",[13] but not identified as belonging to a 'Seventh Book' of the *Ethics*, probably because the heading of the 'Seventh Book' is illegible in the manuscript.[14] Berman was able to use the so-called *zimām* numeral letters to arrange the pages of the manuscript,

---

[11] Dunlop, "The *Nicomachean Ethics* in Arabic, Books I-VI", *loc. cit.*

[12] Lawrence V. Berman, "A Note on the Added Seventh Book of the *Nicomachean Ethics* in Arabic", in: JAOS 82 (1962), pp. 555-556, here p. 555.

[13] Lyons, "A Greek Ethical Treatise", *loc. cit.*, p. 57.

[14] Or nearly so. See below, p. 99.

with help from the Librarian, who knew these *zimām* numerals as *al-qalam al-Fāsī*, 'the Fez notation'.[15]

Meanwhile there had appeared in Rabat, 1380/1960, an official publication of the Moroccan Ministère de l'Éducation Nationale, de la Jeunesse et des Sports (Wizārat at-Tahdhīb al-Waṭanī wa'sh-Shabībah wa'r-Riyāḍah) entitled *Liste des manuscrits précieux, exposés à la Bibliothèque de l'Université Quaraouyine à Fès, à l'occasion du onzième centenaire de la fondation de cette Université* (*Qā'imah li-nawādir al-makhṭūṭāt al-ʿarabīyah al-maʿrūḍah fī maktabat Jāmiʿat al-Qarawīyīn bi-Fās bi-munāsabat murūr miʾah wa-alf sanatin ʿalā taʾsīs hādhihi 'l-Jāmiʿah*). Here the two manuscripts numbered L 2508/80 and L 3043/80 are brought together as forming a single work, which of course they do, with the following notice (p. 73, under the heading 'Philosophy'):

> No. 321. The *Book of Ethics*, called also *Nīqūmākhīya*, by the *shaikh* of the philosophers and ancient thinkers, Aristotle, who died in the year 322 B.C., containing 11 Books. And there follows the last Book an introductory treatise on ethics, thought to be by Nicolaus, as in the heading of the said introduction. The whole is in correct *Maghribī* script. All the copying was complete in A.H. 619.

The manuscript is on stout paper, the size of its two parts being respectively 21 by 15 centimetres and 16 by 10 centimetres, the difference being of course due to cutting. Of 223 pages in the complete manuscript the *Nicomachean Ethics* occupies 193 pages, the remainder being a work on ethics attributed to a certain Nicolaus. There are 23 lines to a page.[16] On the title-page (fol. 1a), in a different hand from the text of the manuscript, we read:

> The First Discourse of the Book of Aristotle (*Arisṭū*) on Ethics,[17] and it is that which is called *Naiqūmākhiyā* [sic] (*al-Maqāla al-ūlā min*

---

[15] Berman, "A Note on the Added Seventh Book", *loc. cit.*, p. 555, n. 6. For the *zimām* numerals, see Franz Rosenthal in Ibn Khaldūn, *The Muqaddimah. An Introduction to History*, translated from the Arabic by Franz Rosenthal (Bollingen Series; 43), 3 vols., New York 1958, vol. III, p. 197, n. 882 and the references there given.

[16] Cf. Lawrence V. Berman, "Excerpts from the Lost Arabic Original of Ibn Rushd's *Middle Commentary* on the *Nicomachean Ethics*", in: *Oriens* 20 (1967), pp. 31-59, here pp. 32-33 for these and other details. Berman's "111 leaves" corresponds to "223 pages", which will include title-page.

[17] This is also the heading of the text on fol. 1b, but on the title page *Arisṭū* is followed by the 'guarding *alif*' (*alif al-wiqāyah*).

kitāb Arisṭū fī 'l-akhlāq wa-huwa al-musammā bi-Nīqūmākhīyā).

This is followed by the name ʿAlī b. Harīdūs and two partially illegible (and hardly translatable) lines of poetry:

> *la'in mariḍa 'l-ḥabību* [...] / [...] *kalīlun fīhā bukhāruhu*
> *ṣafā launun wa-rāqa 'l-ʿainu ḥusnan / faj'atan ka'annahu fī* [...] *nuḍāruhu*

ʿAlī b. Harīdūs is presumably a former owner of the book, and his name is perhaps the same as that of the Harūdus (Haraudas) family, originally of Guadix near Granada.[18]

The date of copying is given by a colophon at the end of the Eleventh Book:

> Completed the Eleventh Discourse of the Book of Aristotle on Ethics, and it is that which is called *Nīqūmākhiyā*. And praise to God and blessing on His servants whom He has chosen. And that on Wednesday, the 27th of the honoured Shaʿbān of the year 619 [i.e. 6th October, A.D. 1222].

III

Notices of the *Nicomachean Ethics* in Arabic, though not infrequent, tend to be obscure and are in part contradictory. Earliest mention of the work appears to be in a short *Letter on the Number of the Books of Aristotle and What Is Needed to Acquire Philosophy* (*Risālah fī kammīyat kutub Arisṭūṭālīs wa-mā yuḥtāju ilaihi fī taḥṣīl al-falsafah*) of al-Kindī.[19] Al-Kindī's dates are approximately 185/801 to 252/866. His *Risālah* mentions the *Nicomachean Ethics* in two

---

[18] Cf. Abū Jaʿfar ibn az-Zubair, *Ṣilat aṣ-ṣilah*, ed. Évariste Lévi-Provençal, Paris 1937, p. 92; Ibn al-Abbār, *at-Takmilah li-Kitāb aṣ-ṣila*, ed. ʿIzzat al-ʿAṭṭār al-Ḥusainī, 2 vols., Cairo 1956, vol. I, p. 154.

[19] Ed. by Muḥammad ʿAbd al-Hādī Abū Rīdah, *Rasā'il al-Kindī al-falsafīyah*, 2 vols., Cairo 1369/1950-1372/1953, vol. I, pp. 363-384 (Arabic text and notes); also ed. by Michelangelo Guidi and Richard Walzer, "Studi su al-Kindi I. Uno scritto introduttivo allo studio di Aristotele", in: *Atti dell'Accademia Nazionale dei Lincei. Memorie. Classe di Scienze Morali, Storiche e Filologiche* 6/5 (1940), pp. 375-419 (Arabic text, Italian transl. and notes). Richard J. McCarthy in his bibliography of al-Kindī (*At-taṣānīf al-mansūbah ilā Failasūf al-ʿarab, baḥth bi-munāsabat iḥtifālāt Baghdād wa'l-Kindī*, Baghdad 1382/1962, pp. 65-66) has noted that there are many discrepancies between the two editions ("about 260 differences"). Yet both texts were made from the same MS.

places, first, at the end of the enumeration of the works of Aristotle,[20] following upon the *Metaphysics* (*Mā ba'd aṭ-ṭabī'ah*).[21] Here we have:

> After all these he composed books which, though they are of the same kind as the discussion of the soul, appear in perfection, and the discussion is clear in them only after the discussion of what has no need for bodies at all [sc. psychology and metaphysics]. They are the choice fruit of the knowledge of these books [sc. Aristotle's works on the subjects indicated], by which comprehension of them takes place.[22] They are his books on ethics, I mean the ethical qualities and government of the soul, that it may preserve in human virtue and be one with it, which is the aim of the man of balanced nature in his present life and his means of salvation in the world to come, for which there is no substitute, no equivalent for its benefit and no well-being with its loss.
>
> Among them is his large *Book on Ethics* [written] to his son Nīqūmākhus, and it is that which is called *Nīqūmākhiyā*, and is in 11 discussions (*qaul*). And among them is another book, less than the number of these discourses (*maqālāt*) [and] resembling the meanings of his book [written] to Nīqūmākhus. He wrote it to one of his brethren.
>
> Apart from these three [sic] treatises (*maqālāt*) there are many books by him on minor matters, and letters (*rasā'il*) on various minor matters also.[23]

In this passage al-Kindī evidently refers to the *Nicomachean Ethics* and the *Eudemian Ethics*. The latter work is fairly described as containing a smaller number of books than the *Nicomachean Ethics* and similar subject matter, while Eudemus, contemporary with Aristotle (actually his pupil), is somewhat inappropriately characterised as 'one of his brethren'. It is remarkable that here in what seems to be the first notice of the *Nicomachean Ethics* in Arabic it is mentioned as containing 11 Books. It is remarkable also that al-Kindī's text here speaks of three works of Aristotle on ethics, though previously he has noticed only two. Al-Kindī's editor Abū Rīdah suggests[24] two theoretical possibilities to account for the discrepancy:

---

[20] al-Kindī, *Rasā'il*, *op. cit.*, vol. I, p. 369.

[21] Al-Kindī's text, *Rasā'il*, *op. cit.*, vol. I, p. 368, has: *Ma ba'd aṭ-ṭabī'īyāt*, presumably the original and more correct form. Later the other form was in use and is found in most of the books.

[22] I.e. *al-muntakhabah taqa'u*, the reading of Abū Rīdah; *al-muntijah naf'*, Guidi and Walzer, but the expression seems strange.

[23] al-Kindī, *Rasā'il*, *op. cit.*, vol. I, p. 369.

[24] al-Kindī, *Rasā'il*, *op. cit.*, vol. I, p. 369, n. 2.

either the reference to three works is an addition to the original text, or something, perhaps a reference to Aristotle's *Magna Moralia*, has fallen out. Of these suggestions the second is decidedly preferable, since the Arabic tradition, apparently following late Greek sources, regularly speaks of three ethical works of Aristotle.[25]

Al-Kindī refers to the ethical works a second time at the end of the *Risālah*, in a passage where he is concerned with their aim or tendency (*gharaḍ*, plur. *aghrāḍ*):

> As for [Aristotle's] aim in his ethical-political books (*fī kutubihi al-khulqīyah as-siyāsīyah*), the first of his books is [written] to his son Nīqūmākhus, and he entitled it by his name Nīqūmākhus, on the ethical qualities and government of the soul,[26] by the excellent ethical qualities and avoidance of the vicious [qualities]. In it he classified government according to its types, I mean special, general[27] and political government with what distinguishes them,[28] and [gave] a detailed account of the ethical qualities and passions[29] which attach to each, and the explanation that happiness is virtue in all times—virtue in the soul and body and what is outside of both also.
>
> As for his aim in his second book, and it is that which is called *Būlīṭīqī*,[30] i.e. the Statesman (*al-Madanī*), which he wrote to one of his

[25] Cf. pp. 14f., 32, 53, n. 215.

[26] The phrase is repeated by al-Kindī from his earlier notice of Aristotle's ethical works (cf. p. 7).

[27] Abu Rīdah has *gharībah*, 'strange' or 'foreign' government; Guidi and Walzer read *murabbiyah*, translating "il governo dell'educatore". Neither of these terms seems to occur elsewhere in similar contexts. For 'general', *al-ʿāmmah*, cf. al-Yaʿqūbī's *tadbīr al-ʿāmmah wa 'l-khāṣṣah*, below, pp. 10f.

[28] I.e. with *bihi* inserted after *tanfaṣilu*.

[29] Text is *al-akhlāq wa 'l-ālām*, which will stand, cf. EN 1155b 10 *al-akhlāq wa 'l-āfāt*, where *al-āfāt* is one of several expressions used for Greek πάθος, plur. πάθη, in EN (cf. e.g. 1147a 14-15, 1156a 32). EN has *ālām* = πάθη at 1168b 20, and elsewhere this rendering is common. Cf. Lyons in Aristotle, *Ars Rhetorica*, *op. cit.*, Glossary, s. vv. πάθος, *alam*. Otherwise we might read, for *al-akhlāq*, *al-afʿāl* to get the familiar parallelism, frequently rendered by EN: *ʿawāriḍ*, 'passions', as opposed to *afʿāl*, 'actions' (1106b 16-17, 24-25, 1107a 4-5, 1111b 1; the sing. *ʿāriḍ* at 1107a 9). Occasionally we also have *infiʿālāt*, 1104b 14, cf. 1145b 5, and *shahawāt*, 1095a 4, cf. 1095a 8.

[30] There is little likelihood that the *Politics* of Aristotle or the *Politicus* of Plato is the third work intended by al-Kindī in his earlier notice (quoted above, p. 7). The latter, the *Politicus*, is of course suggested by the identification of *Būlīṭīqī* with *al-Madanī*, cf. *Fuṣūl al-madanī* the alternative title of al-Fārābī's *Kitāb al-fuṣūl al-muntazaʿah* which undoubtly has affinities with the *Politicus* of Plato (see Douglas M. Dunlop in al-Fārābī, *Fuṣūl al-madanī [Aphorisms of the Statesman]*, edited with an English translation, introduction and notes by Douglas M. Dunlop [University of Cambridge Oriental Publications; 5], Cambridge 1961, pp. 17-18). But again in

> brethren, it deals with the like of what he said in the first [book]. He spoke in it more of political government. Some of its discourses (*maqālāt*) are exactly the same as some of the discourses of the first [book].[31]

We note that in this second passage the same two books are mentioned as in the first passage from the *Risālah*, viz. the *Nicomachean Ethics* and the *Eudemian Ethics*, the latter here confused with a *Kitāb Būlīṭīqī*, which should be the *Politics* of Aristotle.[32]

In regard to the date of the *Risālah* in which these first notices of the *Nicomachean Ethics* in Arabic appear, the earlier editors Guidi and Walzer conjectured that it was written during the Caliphate of al-Ma'mūn (198/813-218/833), on the ground that no mention is made in it of the so-called *Theology of Aristotle*, which was translated for al-Ma'mūn's successor al-Muʿtaṣim by ʿAbd al-Masīḥ b. Nāʿimah and later revised by al-Kindī himself.[33] The date of Ibn Nāʿimah's translation is given as about 220/835.[34] Guidi and Walzer also noted that the *Risālah* was later than al-Kindī's *al-Kitāb al-aʿẓam fī 't-ta'līf* (*Greatest Book on Harmony*), which is mentioned in the text.[35]

On the other hand, the *Theology of Aristotle* in the text published by Dieterici has the following heading:

> The first discourse (*mī'mar*, a Syriac word) of the book of Arisṭāṭālīs [sic], the philosopher, named *Uthūlūjiyā*, and it is a discussion of

---

another work of al-Fārābī, *Kitāb iḥṣā' al-ʿulūm (Catálogo de las ciencias)*, ed. Ángel González Palencia, Madrid/Granada ²1953, p. 96, the *Kitāb Būlīṭīqī* is apparently identified with the *Kitāb as-siyāsah* of Aristotle, i.e. the *Politics*, and this is Abū Rīdah's view of the meaning in the passage of al-Kindī where *Būlīṭīqī* is mentioned. The text as printed by González Palencia is not unequivocal: *hādhihi fī Kitāb Būlīṭīqī wa-huwa fī Kitāb as-siyāsah li-Arisṭūṭālīs*, which he translates: "Todo esto se contiene en el libro de *Política*, es decir, en el libro del *Gobierno* de Aristóteles." However this may be, what is said about the *Kitāb Būlīṭīqī* in al-Kindī has somehow been imported into the text and is not an addition to information already given about the *Nicomachean Ethics* and the *Eudemian Ethics* when first mentioned (p. 8f.). Evidently mention of the *Kitāb Būlīṭīqī* comes in a notice of the *Eudemian Ethics*, as the following words show.

[31] al-Kindī, *Rasā'il*, *op. cit.*, vol. I, p. 384.

[32] Cf. above, n. 30.

[33] Guidi and Walzer in al-Kindī, "Studi su al-Kindi", *loc. cit.*, p. 375.

[34] Carl Brockelmann, GAL I, p. 204; Georg Graf, *Geschichte der christlichen arabischen Literatur* (Studi e Testi; 133), 5 vols., Vatican City 1944-1953, vol. II, p. 228.

[35] Guidi and Walzer in al-Kindī, "Studi su al-Kindi", *loc. cit.*, p. 398, cf. p. 375.

> divinity (*ar-rubūbīyah*), the Commentary (*tafsīr*)[36] of Porphyry of Tyre, translated into Arabic by ʿAbd al-Masīḥ b. ʿAbd Allāh Nāʿimah of Ḥoms (Emesa). Abū Yūsuf Yaʿqūb b. Isḥāq al-Kindī—may God have mercy on him—corrected it for Aḥmad b. al-Muʿtaṣim bi'llāh.[37]

If this is right, then the work was translated not for the Caliph al-Muʿtaṣim (d. 227/842) but for his son Aḥmad b. al-Muʿtaṣim, the pupil of al-Kindī, who was alive at least as late as 862.[38] The possibility of a later date for the *Risālah* than the Caliphate of al-Ma'mūn evidently has to be taken into account.

In any case, whenever it was written, the *Risālah* is likely to be earlier than al-Kindī's correction or paraphrase (*tafsīr*)[39] of the *Theology of Aristotle*, which al-Kindī, like al-Fārābī, may have regarded as an authentic work of Aristotle. It was evidently translated into Arabic from Syriac,[40] as appears to have been the case also with the *Nicomachean Ethics*.[41] This together with the fact that both works are mentioned in connexion with a *tafsīr* of Porphyry (cf. below, p. 26f.) might suggest some link between the two.

A notice of the works of Aristotle in the *Historiae* (*Ta'rīkh*) of al-Yaʿqūbī (3rd/9th century) presents the same scheme as in al-Kindī's *Risālah*, but is much less developed. At the end of his list immediately after a mention of the *Metaphysics*, i.e. quite as in the *Risālah*, we find the following on the ethical works of Aristotle:

> As for his books on moral character (*khulq*), [his aim herein] [...][42] and the explanation of the ethical qualities of the soul, happiness in the soul and body, rule of the people and of the élite (*tadbīr al-ʿāmmah wa'l-*

---

[36] Similarly (i.e. not *bi-tafsīr* or with another particle) Steinschneider, *Die arabischen Übersetzungen aus dem Griechischen*, Leipzig 1893 (reprinted Graz 1960), p. 116.

[37] Pseudo-Aristotle, *Die sogenannte Theologie des Aristoteles aus arabischen Handschriften*, ed. Friedrich Dieterici, Leipzig 1882 (reprinted Frankfurt am Main 2000), p. 1. Dieterici himself gave "um 840" as the date of the translation (Pseudo-Aristotle, *Die sogenannte Theologie des Aristoteles aus dem Arabischen übersetzt*, transl. Friedrich Dieterici, Leipzig 1883 [reprinted Frankfurt am Main 2000], p. V).

[38] Cf. aṭ-Ṭabarī, *Ta'rīkh ar-rusul wa'l-mulūk (Annales)*, ed. Michael J. de Goeje *et al.*, 15 vols., Leiden 1879-1901, Tertia Series III, p. 1502, on the accession of al-Mustaʿīn.

[39] Cf. Ibn an-Nadīm, *Kitāb al-fihrist*, ed. Gustav Flügel, 2 vols., Leipzig 1871-1872, vol. I, p. 252, of the *Theology of Aristotle*: *wa-fassarahu al-Kindī*.

[40] Cf. Georg Graf, *Geschichte der christlichen arabischen Literatur*, *op. cit.*, vol. II, p. 228.

[41] Cf. below, pp. 26, 62, 106.

[42] The words in brackets are supplied by the editor to fill the lacuna, but something is still lacking before *wa'l-ibānah*, 'and the explanation'.

> *khāṣṣah*), a man's rule of his wife, government and the rule of cities and stories of the rulers of cities (*qiṣaṣ ahl at-tadbīr li'l-mudun*).[43]

This notice corresponds to the second passage quoted from the *Risālah fī kammīyat kutub Arisṭūṭālīs*. The date of al-Yaʿqūbī's book is given as 259/872, i.e. after the death of al-Kindī and too late to give any nearer indication than we had previously for the dating of the *Risālah*.

We now come to al-Fārābī (circa 260/874-339/950) who refers to the *Nicomachean Ethics* several times, notably in his *Harmony Between the Views of Plato and Aristotle* (*Kitāb al-jamʿ baina ra'yai al-ḥakīmain Aflātūn al-ilāhī wa-Arisṭūṭālīs*); elsewhere he speaks of Aristotle's *Kitāb al-akhlāq*.[44]

The title *Harmony Between the Views of Plato and Aristotle* sufficiently indicates the influence of later Greek thought, specifically Neoplatonism, on al-Fārābī. We hear of a work of Porphyry on the same subject, Περὶ τοῦ μίαν εἶναι τὴν Πλάτωνος καὶ 'Αριστοτέλους αἵρεσιν,[45] now lost. It may readily be thought of as lying behind the *Harmony* of al-Fārābī.

Several references to EN come in a section of the *Harmony* where al-Fārābī speaks of the ethical qualities of the soul (*akhlāq an-nafs*),[46] the first as follows:

> Aristotle in the *Nicomachean Ethics* (*Kitāb Nīqūmākhiyā*) makes clear that all ethical qualities are habits which alter, and that none of them is by nature, and that it is possible for a man to change from each one of them to another through habituation and use (*Arisṭū yaṣraḥu fī kitāb Nīqūmākhiyā anna 'l-akhlāq kullahā ʿādāt tataghaiyaru wa-annahu laisa shai' minhā bi'ṭ-ṭabʿ wa-anna 'l-insān yumkinuhu an yantaqila min kull wāḥid ilā ghairihi bi'l-iʿtiyād wa'd-durbah*).[47]

---

[43] al-Yaʿqūbī, *Ta'rīkh (Historiae)*, ed. Martijn Th. Houtsma, 2 vols., Leiden 1883, vol. I, p. 150.

[44] Cf. p. 15.

[45] Cited by Dieterici in al-Fārābī, *Philosophische Abhandlungen*, transl. Friedrich Dieterici, Leiden 1892 (reprinted Frankfurt am Main 1999), p. XIII and p. 196; from the *Suda*, s.v. Πορφύριος.

[46] Or perhaps translate simply 'morals'. The expression was already used by al-Kindī, cf. pp. 7, and recurs in a similar passage of the Qāḍī Ṣāʿid, see p. 32.

[47] Text: al-Fārābī, *Philosophische Abhandlungen aus Londoner, Leidener und Berliner Handschriften*, ed. Friedrich Dieterici, Leiden 1890 (reprinted Frankfurt am Main 1999), p. 16. Transl.: al-Fārābī, *Philosophische Abhandlungen*, *op. cit.*, p. 27.

For this Dieterici cited EN II, 1, 1-2 = 1103a 17-19, which in the Fez manuscript of the *Ethics* is quite different: *[al-faḍā'il] al-khulqīya tuktasabu min al-ʿādah* [...] *wa-min hādhā yatabaiyanu annahu laisa shai' min al-faḍā'il al-khulqīyah yakūn fīnā bi'ṭ-ṭabʿ ʿalā ḥāl min al-aḥwāl.* If al-Fārābī is quoting the version in the Fez manuscript, he gives the general sense only; there is no evidence here that he knew the version.

A little further on in the same passage we have:

> Aristotle in his book known as *Nīqūmākhiyā* speaks only about the rules of the city,[48] as we have explained in several places of our Commentary on that book. If the matter here also were, as Porphyry and many commentators after him said, that he is speaking about ethics, then his words are about ethical rules, and the expression of rules is always general and absolute, without reference to anything else (*Arisṭū fī kitābihi al-maʿrūf bi-Nīqūmākhiyā innamā yatakallamu ʿalā 'l-qawānīn al-madanīyah ʿalā mā baiyannā fī mawāḍiʿ min sharḥinā li-dhālika 'l-kitāb wa-lau kāna al-amr fīhi aiḍan ʿalā mā qālahu Furfūriyūs wa-kathīr mimman baʿdahu min al-mufassirīn annahu yatakallamu ʿalā 'l-akhlāq fa'inna kalāmahu ʿalā 'l-qawānīn al-khulqīyah wa'l-kalām al-qānūnī abadan yakūnu kullīyan wa-muṭlaqan lā bi-ḥasab shai' ākhar*).[49]

Unfortunately al-Fārābī's Commentary on the *Nicomachean Ethics* is at present lost, and the exact significance of what is here said is not clear. The reference in al-Fārābī's text to the Commentaries of Porphyry and many others is surprising, as he might be expected to know, apart from Porphyry, only of Themistius as commentator of the *Ethics*,[50] and it doubtless reflects the Greek original of the *Harmony*. Al-Fārābī will also have known the Commentary of Porphyry mentioned by Ibn an-Nadīm in the *Fihrist*.[51]

Later in the same discussion al-Fārābī repeats what he had previously said:

> Aristotle does not deny that for some people to pass from ethical quality to ethical quality[52] is possible more easily and for others with more difficulty, as he made clear in his book known as the 'little

---

[48] Cf. p. 87.
[49] al-Fārābī, text p. 17; transl. p. 27.
[50] Cf. Ibn an-Nadīm, *Fihrist*, *op. cit.*, vol. I, p. 252.
[51] See a discussion of this below, pp. 85ff.
[52] This subject is also mentioned by Maimonides, quoting al-Fārābī's Commentary on the *Nicomachean Ethics*. See p. 50.

> *Nīqūmākhiyā*'. For he has enumerated the causes of the difficulty of changing from ethical quality to ethical quality and the causes of its being easy, mentioning how many they are, what they are, what the tendency of each of these causes is, and what the indications and what the impediments are (*wa-laisa yunkiru Arisṭū anna baʿḍa 'n-nās yumkinu fīhi at-tanaqqul min khulq ilā khulq ashal wa-fī baʿḍihim aʿsar ʿalā mā ṣarraḥa bihi fī kitābihi al-maʿrūf bi-Nīqūmākhiyā aṣ-ṣaghīr fa'innahu ʿadda asbāb ʿusr at-tanaqqul min khulq ilā khulq wa-asbāb as-suhūlah kam hiya wa-mā hiya wa-ʿalā aiyi jihatin kullu wāḥidin min tilka 'l-asbāb wa-mā al-ʿalāmāt wa-mā al-mawāniʿ*).[53]

The whole discussion turns on EN II, 1, as already indicated, but here we are concerned specifically with changes of character. This is a subject mentioned in the *Nicomachean Ethics* with reference to changes in the state ("the bad king becomes a tyrant" [Ross], VIII, 10, 3), also incidentally in the discussion of "occasions of breaking off friendship" (Ross) at IX, 3, but nowhere treated systematically, or at least not in the manner indicated by al-Fārābī in the passage last quoted. At first sight we seem to have here in the 'little *Nīqūmākhiyā*' a different work.

An earlier reference to the 'little *Nīqūmākhiyā*' in the *Harmony* is in connexion with a logical point, the difference between contrary and contradictory:

> Plato, where he explains that the most just lies between justice and injustice,[54] intends to explain only political ideas and their gradations, not the contradiction of the expressions thereon. Aristotle has mentioned in the 'little *Nīqūmākhiyā*' on government something similar to what is explained by Plato (*wa-ammā Aflāṭūn ḥaithu baiyana anna 'l-aʿdal mutawassiṭ baina 'l-ʿadl wa'l-jaur fa'innahu innamā qaṣada bayān al-maʿānī as-siyāsīyah wa-marātibihā lā muʿānadat al-aqāwīl fīhā wa-qad dhakara Arisṭū fī Nīqūmākhiyā aṣ-ṣaghīr fī's-siyāsah shibhan bimā baiyanahu Aflāṭūn*).[55]

Dieterici, though with some hesitation ("vielleicht"), indicated the beginning of EN V, 9 as the passage here referred to.[56] A closer similarity is, however, with EN V, 5, 17 = 1133b 30-31, where we have the definition: 'Just dealing is intermediate between doing injustice and having injustice done one (*al-muʿāmalah al-ʿādilah fīmā*

[53] al-Fārābī, text p. 18; transl. p. 29.
[54] Cf. Plato, *Republic*, 359A.
[55] al-Fārābī, text p. 13; transl. p. 21.
[56] In al-Fārābī, transl. p. 208 (commentary).

baina an yajūra jā'ir wa-yujāru ʿalaihi).' It may not be unnecessary to add that the similarity is of the thought, not the language in which it is expressed.

There remains something more positive to say about the 'little *Nīqūmākhiyā*'. It is well known that the Neoplatonists had a listing of the ethical works of Aristotle which included a 'little *Nicomachean Ethics* addressed to Nicomachus, the son' (πρὸς Νικομάχον τὸν υἱὸν τὰ μικρὰ Νικομάχια) as well as a 'great *Nicomachean Ethics* addressed to Nicomachus, the father' (πρὸς Νικομάχον τὸν πατέρα τὰ μεγάλα Νικομάχια) and the *Eudemian Ethics*.[57] This listing passed somehow to the Arabs and is the basis of the list of Aristotle's books of al-Kindī.[58] It was known also to al-Fārābī.[59] While there is general agreement that in the threefold enumeration the *Nicomachean Ethics*, *Eudemian Ethics* and *Magna Moralia* are meant, opinions differ as to what is intended respectively by τὰ μεγάλα Νικομάχια and τὰ μικρὰ Νικομάχια. Some would identify the latter, τὰ μικρὰ Νικομάχια, with the *Magna Moralia*, on the ground presumably that the *Magna Moralia* is a smaller book than the *Nicomachean Ethics*, so that there would be no justification for identifying the 'Parva' with the 'Nicomachica', i.e. the 'Parva' is the *Magna Moralia*. But this is a paradox which lacks all support in the texts. Others have understood the title τὰ μικρὰ Νικομάχια to be for the *Nicomachean Ethics*.[60] There is paradox here also of course. Why should the substantially

---

[57] Elias, *In Porphyrii Isagogen et Aristotelis Categorias Commentaria*, ed. Adolf Busse (Commentaria in Aristotelem Graeca; 18), Berlin 1900, pp. 32-33, also cited by Franz Susemihl from *Comm. Porphyr. Prolegg. in Categ. Schol. in Arist. 9b 20* in his edition of *Ethica Eudemia* (Leipzig 1884, reprinted Amsterdam 1967), p. XVIII. See similarly the Prooemium of the same Elias (6th century A.D.) to his Commentary on the *Categories*, *loc. cit.*, p. 116, also cited by Susemihl from David (sc. the Armenian, to whom the work was formerly attributed) in *Categ. Schol. 25a 40 sqq.*, *loc. cit.*, p. XIX. I have followed Susemihl in writing Νικομάχια rather than Νικομάχεια (Busse).

[58] Cf. p. 7.

[59] See p. 15f.

[60] Adolf Stahr, as early as 1844, understood the title Νικομάχεια μικρά to be for the *Nicomachean Ethics*, though he was unable to provide an explanation (art. "Aristotle", in: William Smith (ed.), *Dictionary of Greek and Roman Biography and Mythology* I [1844], pp. 317-344, here p. 330). See also Jaap Mansfeld, *Prolegomena Mathematica. From Apollonius of Perga to the Late Neoplatonism. With an Appendix on Pappus and the History of Platonism*, Leiden 1998, pp. 18 (n. 54), 20, 124-125 (n. 67), where further examples of 'great' and 'small' and title are given.

larger *Nicomachean Ethics* be called τὰ μικρὰ Νικομάχια and the smaller work is called τὰ μεγάλα Νικομάχια (*Magna Moralia*)? The answer is supplied by a suggestion of Henry Jackson,[61] following which we can say that while the *Magna Moralia* is less than half the length of the *Nicomachean Ethics* (some 32 folios compared with 87 folios), each of the two Books of the *Magna Moralia* is considerably larger than any of the ten Books of the *Nicomachean Ethics*, and assuming that in both works each Book formed a single roll, the two rolls of the *Magna Moralia* would evidently have been the larger, whence the name. We thus have good ground to identify the 'little *Nīqūmākhiyā*' with the *Nicomachean Ethics*. There is one observable fact in the texts which may speak for the identity. As we saw, al-Fārābī in the *Harmony Between the Views of Plato and Aristotle* says that according to Aristotle some people are able to pass from ethical quality to ethical quality more easily than others and that this is treated at large in the 'little *Nīqūmākhiyā*'.[62] We shall find that Maimonides cites a similar passage, but states that al-Fārābī mentioned it in his Commentary on the *Nicomachean Ethics*.[63]

In a work *On the Meanings of Intellect* (*Maqālah fī maʿānī al-ʿaql*) al-Fārābī speaks several times of the Sixth Treatise (*al-maqālah as-sādisah*) of the *Book of Ethics* (*Kitāb al-akhlāq*) of Aristotle.[64] The reference here is certainly to the *Nicomachean Ethics*, Book VI, and such expressions in the *Maqālah fī maʿānī al-ʿaql* as *ʿaql* (νοῦς), *mutaʿaqqil* (φρόνιμος), etc. are familiar from the Arabic of the Fez manuscript. We cannot, however, compare the two texts in detail, since by far the larger part of Book VI is missing in the Fez manuscript.[65]

Al-Fārābī like al-Kindī has a listing of the works of Aristotle. This is in his *Letter on the Necessary Preliminaries before the Study of Philosophy* (*Risālah fīmā yanbaghī an yuqaddama qabl taʿallum al-falsafah*),[66] where there is a brief reference to Aristotle's books on

---

[61] Quoted by G. Cyril Armstrong in Aristotle, *Magna Moralia (with Metaphysics, X-XIV, and Oeconomica)*, ed. and transl. G. Cyril Armstrong, London 1958, p. 427-428.

[62] Above, pp. 12ff.

[63] See below, p. 50.

[64] al-Fārābī, text pp. 39 and 41; transl. pp. 61, 64, 65.

[65] See below, p. 1, n. 3.

[66] On the Προτέλεια τῆς συναναγνώσεως τῆς φιλοσοφίας cf. Jaap Mansfeld, *Prolegomena. Questions to Be Settled Before the Study of an Author*, Leiden 1994, p. 28.

practical philosophy:

> As for the books from which are learned the things which are put into operation in philosophy [i.e. the *aʿmāl al-falsafah* mentioned earlier by al-Fārābī],[67] from some of them is learned improvement of morals, from others the rule of cities and from others the rule of the household (*wa-ammā al-kutub allatī yutaʿallamu minhā al-umūr allatī tustaʿmalu fī 'l-falsafah fa-baʿḍuhā yutaʿallamu minhā iṣlāḥ al-akhlāq wa-baʿḍuhā yutaʿallamu minhā tadbīr al-mudun wa-baʿḍuhā yutaʿallamu minhā tadbīr al-manzil*).[68]

The passage reappears in a later work, the *Categories of the Nations* (*Ṭabaqāt al-umam*) of the Qāḍī Ṣāʿid, where the reference to the ethical works of Aristotle is more explicit.[69] The general dependence of this part of the *Ṭabaqāt al-umam* on al-Fārābī's *Risālah*, or rather on al-Fārābī's source,[70] is easily demonstrable.

In view of the quite numerous quotations already given, it might be thought that when al-Fārābī treats in a special work of the philosophy of Aristotle, he would have at least something to say about the *Nicomachean Ethics* under its own name, or perhaps as the *Book of Ethics* (*Kitāb al-akhlāq*). Al-Fārābī has such a work, the *Falsafat Arisṭūṭālīs* (*Philosophy of Aristotle*).[71] This is strictly speaking not an independent treatise, but the third and last part of a tripartite book, of which the first part is the *Attainment of Happiness* (*Kitāb taḥṣīl as-saʿādah*), often mentioned separately, and the second part, the *Philosophy of Plato* (*Falsafat Aflāṭūn*).[72] It is certainly remarkable that in the *Falsafah Arisṭūṭālīs*, the aim of which is to give an account of Aristotle's philosophy on the basis of notices of

---

[67] al-Fārābī, text p. 50; transl. p. 84.

[68] al-Fārābī, text p. 51; transl. p. 86. This list (and similar lists cited below) derive from accounts of the study of Aristotle's works in the introductory sections of Greek commentaries on Aristotle. See Simplicius, *Commentaire sur les Catégories*, ed. Ilsetraut Hadot, transl. Philippe Hoffmann, fasc. I, Leiden 1990, pp. 10-11, and Ilsetraut Hadot, "The Role of the Commentaries on Aristotle in the Teaching of Philosophy According to the Prefaces of the Neoplatonic Commentaries on the *Categories*", in: Henry Blumenthal and Howard Robinson (eds.), *Aristotle and the Later Tradition*, Oxford 1991, pp. 175-189.

[69] See p. 32. Ṣāʿid actually uses the phrase *aʿmāl al-falsafah* for the more cumbrous expression in al-Fārābī here, but cf. above, n. 67.

[70] Cf. below, pp. 32ff.

[71] Ed. Muhsin Mahdi, Beirut 1961 (transl. the same, *Alfarabi's Philosophy of Plato and Aristotle*, New York 1962).

[72] *Alfarabius de Platonis Philosophia*, ed. Franz Rosenthal and Richard Walzer (Plato arabus; 2), London 1943.

his own books, there is no mention of either *Kitāb Nīqūmākhiyā* or a *Kitāb al-akhlāq*, nor indeed of Aristotle's ethico-political writings in general. What we should expect is a mention of these, at the end of the list of works after the *Metaphysics*, where they appear in other listings.[73]

Ibn Abī Uṣaibiʿah's list of the works of al-Fārābī includes a *Book of the Two Philosophies of Plato and Aristotle* (*Kitāb al-falsafatain li-Aflāṭūn wa-Arisṭū*),[74] which, though it appears as a separate entry, is now generally accepted to be the second and third parts of the tripartite work mentioned in the previous paragraph. The very short notice in Ibn Abī Uṣaibiʿah's list merely gives the title as above, adding the words *makhrūm al-ākhir*, i.e. defective or incomplete at the end. Ibn Abī Uṣaibiʿah wrote towards the middle of the 7th/13th century. Two hundred years earlier the Qāḍī Ṣāʿid writing in 460/1068 indicated that the single copy of the *Falsafat Arisṭūṭālīs* which he had seen ended with the first part of the metaphysics and the proof of it through natural science (*intahā bihi al-qaul fī 'n-nuskhat al-wāṣilah ilainā ilā auwal al-ʿilm al-ilāhī wa'l-istidlāl bi'l-ʿilm aṭ-ṭabīʿī ʿalaihā*).[75] This corresponds sufficiently well with the end of the text as we have it at present,[76] though the last words suggest that the Qāḍī's text was somewhat longer than ours. In any case, the *Falsafat Arisṭūṭālīs* evidently then as now had no mention of the ethical works and apparently also, unlike the *Falsafat Aflāṭūn*, no formula of completion. From these indications it appears that the work is incomplete.

Professor Muhsin Mahdi, stressing slight differences between the titles of the second and third parts of the tripartite work, which may correspond to a difference of aim on the part of al-Fārābī, has argued that the third part, the *Falsafat Arisṭūṭālīs*, is complete.[77] It is possible

---

[73] Those of al-Kindī (pp. 7ff.), al-Yaʿqūbī (pp. 10f.) and Ibn an-Nadīm in the *Fihrist* (pp. 25f.).

[74] Ibn Abī ʿUṣaibiʿah, *ʿUyūn al-anbāʾ fī ṭabaqāt al-aṭibbāʾ*, ed. Imru'u l-Qais b. aṭ-Ṭahhan (August Müller), 2 vols., Cairo 1299/1882, vol. II, p. 138.

[75] Text: Abū Qāsim b. Ṣāʿid al-Andalusī, *Kitāb ṭabaqāt al-umam*, ed. Louis Cheikho, Beirut 1912, p. 53. Transl.: Abū Qāsim b. Ṣāʿid al-Andalusī, *Livre des catégories des nations (Kitâb Ṭabaqât al-Umam)*, transl. Régis Blachère, Paris 1935, p. 108.

[76] al-Fārābī, *Falsafat Arisṭūṭālīs*, *op. cit.*, p. 132 (transl. Muhsin Mahdi, *Alfarabi's Philosophy of Plato and Aristotle*, *op. cit.*, p. 130).

[77] al-Fārābī, *Falsafat Arisṭūṭālīs*, *op. cit.*, pp. 22-25.

that al-Fārābī considered Aristotle's ethical works as not strictly belonging to the philosophical inquiry as such, and hence sometimes left them aside altogether. This is so notably in his *Book of Enumeration of the Sciences* (*Kitāb iḥṣā' al-ʿulūm*), in which there is no mention of Aristotle's ethical writings.[78] On this view the case of the *Falsafat Arisṭūṭālīs* may be similar: the work is complete without mention of the ethical writings because ethics is strictly speaking no part of philosophy. But in both works the explanation of al-Fārābī's silence appears to be that as yet, i.e. at the time of writing,[79] he did not know any of the ethical writings of Aristotle, specifically the *Nicomachean Ethics*, except indirectly.[80] At some point, however, al-Fārābī evidently had a text of the *Ethics* and wrote a Commentary thereon, or rather on the first part of it,[81] the surviving fragments of which are of great interest, though the work as a whole is lost. There is a reference to it by al-Fārābī himself as previously mentioned,[82] and other references in Ibn Bājjah, Ibn Ṭufail, Ibn Rushd and Maimonides, for which see below. Another passage has been identified by Berman in a Paris codex of the Hebrew translation of the *Middle Commentary* of Ibn Rushd on the *Nicomachean Ethics* with practical certainty as by al-Fārābī, and with good deal of

---

[78] Somewhat obscured in the Latin translations of *Kitāb iḥṣā' al-ʿulūm*, which give *Ethica* (see al-Fārābī, *Kitāb iḥṣā' al-ulūm [Catálogo de las ciencias]*, *op. cit.*, pp. 112 and 114; *Etica*, p. 113, is a misreading of *Etiam*) from the Latin translation of Dominicus Gundisalvus, also *ethica* (see al-Fārābī, *Kitāb iḥṣā' al-ulūm*, p. 168) or *liber Ethice Aristotilis* (p. 170) from the Latin of Gerard of Cremona, for Arabic *as-siyāsah* (p. 93) or *kitāb as-siyāsah li-Arisṭūṭālīs* (p. 90). For Gundisalvus' translation see also the edition by Manuel Alonso, *De scientiis*, Madrid/Granada 1954.

[79] Muhsin Mahdi places the composition of the *Falsafat Arisṭūṭālīs* between 325/936 and 335/946, i.e. late in the life-time of al-Fārābī (d. Rajab 339 / December 950) (*Alfarabi's Philosophy of Plato and Aristotle*, *op. cit.*, p. 26).

[80] There is no certainty that the *Falsafat Arisṭūṭālīs* originally did contain, or if completed by al-Fārābī would have contained, a reference to the ethical writings.

[81] The sources describe this work as incomplete: *tafsīr qiṭʿah min Kitāb al-akhlāq li-Arisṭālīs* [sic], i.e. *Commentary on a Portion of the Book of Ethics of Aristotle*, Ibn an-Nadīm, *Fihrist*, *op. cit.*, vol. I, p. 263; *sharḥ ṣadr Kitāb al-akhlāq li-Arisṭūṭālīs*, i.e. *Commentary on the First Part of the Book of Ethics of Aristotle*, Ibn Abī Uṣaibiʿah, *ʿUyūn al-anbā'*, *op. cit.*, vol. II, p. 138; cf. *ṣadr sharḥihi li-Kitāb Nīqūmākhīyā* in Maimonides (cf. p. 50); *kalāmihi fīmā sharaḥahu min Kitāb al-akhlāq* ('his words in what he commented on of the *Book of Ethics*'), Ibn Bājjah, Bodleian MS., Pococke 206, fol. 126b, introducing the quotation from al-Fārābī discussed below, pp. 49 and 88ff. The translation 'Introduction' is here inappropriate for *ṣadr*.

[82] Cf. above, p. 12.

likelihood as from the beginning of al-Fārābī's *Commentary on the Ethics*. This passage also is considered below.[83]

We may now pass to al-ʿĀmirī (Abū 'l-Ḥasan Muḥammad b. Abī Dharr Yūsuf), a younger contemporary of al-Fārābī, whose *Kitāb as-saʿādah wa 'l-isʿād* (*Book of Happiness and Making Happy*) has only recently become known in the West.[84] The *Kitāb as-saʿādah wa 'l-isʿād* is a collection of material rather than a fully digested philosophical work. It consists for the most part of quotations from earlier writers, notably Plato and Aristotle, with al-ʿĀmirī's comments thereon, and, in spite of the similarity of title, is a very different production from the more independent and original *Kitāb at-tanbīh ʿalā sabīl as-saʿādah* (*Book of the Directive to the Way of Happiness*) and *Kitāb taḥṣīl as-saʿādah* (*Book of the Attainment of Happiness*) of al-Fārābī. Al-Fārābī appears to be twice mentioned in the *Kitāb as-saʿādah wa 'l-isʿād*, in a manner consistent with his being then alive—the words are *qāla baʿḍ al-ḥuddath*[85] *min al-mutafalsifīn* ('one of the recent philosophers says') in both places[86]—, so that the book may have been written before 339/950, the year of al-Fārābī's death. Arberry translated "a modern philosophaster", which makes al-ʿĀmirī's reference to his predecessor needlessly caustic.[87] The Arabic *mutafalsif* is rather 'one who philosophises', hardly different from *failasūf*, as can be seen from many instances.[88] Al-ʿĀmirī himself

---

[83] Cf. below, pp. 51f. and 93.

[84] For his work and personality see Arberry, "An Arabic Treatise on Politics", *loc. cit.*, and Minovi's Introduction to his edition of al-ʿĀmirī, *Kitāb as-saʿādah wa 'l-isʿād*, ed. Mojtaba Minovi (University of Tehran Publications; 435 / The Mahdavi Fund Series; 5), Wiesbaden 1377/1957. Al-ʿĀmirī's wandering life is mentioned in the *Kitāb al-imtāʿ wa 'l-muʾānasah* of Abū Ḥaiyān at-Tauḥīdī, ed. Ahmad Amin and Ahmad az-Zain, 3 vols., Beirut n.d., vol. II, pp. 15-16.

[85] *Sic* Minovi's printed text, p. 211. At p. 194 the word is unpointed.

[86] Ed. Minovi, p. 194 and p. 211. On the latter page a lozenge in the margin contains the words *Fuṣūl Fārābī manẓūr ast ẓāheran*, i.e. 'the *Fuṣūl* of al-Fārābī is apparently intended'. The quotation (*māddat as-siyāsah aḥwāl an-nās fī haiʾātihim wa-akhlāqihim qāla: wa-ṣūratuhā al-faḍīlah wa-hiya al-gharaḍ wa-ilaihā at-targhīb wa 't-tarhīb*, i.e. 'the matter of government is the conditions of the people in their guise and morals. He continued: And its form is virtue, the goal to which men are led through desire and fear') does not appear in the text of al-Fārābī's *Fuṣūl al-madanī*, *op. cit.*

[87] Arberry, "An Arabic Treatise on Politics", *loc. cit.*, pp. 15-16.

[88] The word of course is the active participle of the first derived form of the quadriliteral verb and not of form V of the regular verb, with the meaning 'give

dies at an advanced age in 381/992.[89] In the *Kitāb as-saʿādah wa'l-isʿād* he mentions the *Nicomachean Ethics* once by name:

> *qāla Arisṭūṭālīs fī Nīqūmākhiyā fī bāb al-kabīr al-himmah innahu lā faṣla al-battatan baina an yafḥaṣa fāḥiṣ ʿan al-haiʾah wa-baina an yafḥaṣa ʿan alladhī lahu al-haiʾah*, i.e. Aristotle said in the *Nicomachean Ethics* in the chapter on the magnanimous man that there is no distinction at all between an investigator investigating the state of character and investigating the man who has it.[90]

This evidently represents EN IV, 3, 2 = 1123a 35 - 1123b 1 of the Greek original, where Aristotle describes the great-souled man. The Greek here is translated quite differently in the Fez manuscript of the *Ethics*: *wa-lā farqa baina an yakūna naẓarunā fī kibr an-nafs au fī al-kabīr an-nafs*. In other passages, however, the wording accords closely with the text of the Fez manuscript, as can be seen from a few

---

oneself out as, think oneself, etc.', cf. *salṭana*, 'proclaim Sultan', and *tasalṭana*, 'become a Sultan'. Examples are al-Fārābī, *Kitāb al-jamʿ bain al-ḥakīmain Aflāṭūn wa-Arisṭū*, ed. Friedrich Dieterici, in: *Philosophische Abhandlungen aus Londoner, Leidener und Berliner Handschriften, op. cit.*, p. 16: *fa-ẓāhir anna hādhihi wa-ashbāhahā maʿānin laṭīfah daqīqah tanabbaha lahā al-mutafalsifūn*, i.e. 'it is thus clear that these and the like of them are refined and subtle contents to which the philosophers have directed attention'; and earlier al-Kindī, *Fī 'l-falsafah al-ūlā*, ed. Abū Rīdah, in: *Rasāʾil al-Kindī, op. cit.*, vol. I, p. 102: *huwa baiyin ʿindanā wa-ʿinda al-mubarrizīn min al-mutafalsifīn qablanā min ghair ahl lisāninā*, i.e. 'it is plain with us and with the leading philosophers before us, whose language was not ours'; again al-Fārābī, *Kitāb at-tanbīh ʿalā sabīl as-saʿādah*, Haidarabad 1346/1927, p. 17: *wa-qaum mimman yunsabu ilā 'l-ʿilm au yatafalsafu qad ʿaraḍa lahum dhālika*, i.e. 'and to some people who are connected with learning or philosophise, that has happened'; and the same, *Kitāb al-ḥurūf*, ed. Muḥsin Mahdī, Beirut 1969, p. 101: *fa-li-dhālika tasmaʿu al-mutafalsifīn yaqūlūna al-ḥadd yuʿarrifu jauhar ash-shaiʾ*, i.e. 'and therefore you hear the philosophers saying that the definition gives the substance of the thing'. Again, EN II, 4, 6 = 1105b 17-18: *laisat taṣiḥḥu anfusuhum bi-hādhā 't-tafalsuf.* Amélie-Marie Goichon gives from Naṣīr ad-Dīn aṭ-Ṭūsī (d. 672/1274) *mutafalasifa min al-'islāmīyīn*, "soi-disant philosophes musulmans", Ibn Sīnā, *Livre des directives et remarques (Kitāb al-išārāt wa't-tanbīhāt)*, transl. Amélie-Marie Goichon, Beirut/Paris 1951, p. 406, n. 1. Léon Gauthier, *Ibn Thofaïl, sa vie, ses œuvres* (Publications de l'École des Lettres d'Alger; 43), Paris 1909, p. 68, n., has "*motafalsif* (au pluriel: *motafalsifa*) qui pourrait se rendre exactement par *philosophisant*, s'applique à un faïlaçouf de second plan, par opposition aux grands maîtres: on s'en contente par modestie, pour soi et pour ses contemporains". But it is difficult to maintain the distinction. Hans Wehr and J. Milton Cowan, *A Dictionary of Modern Written Arabic*, Ithaca N.Y. 1961, give *mutafalsif*: 'philosophaster', 'philosophist'.

[89] See Minovi in his Introduction to al-ʿĀmirī, *Kitāb as-saʿādah wa'l-isʿād, op. cit.*, p. IV.

[90] *Ibid.*, pp. 200-201.

examples. We may consider al-ʿĀmirī (ed. Minovi, p. 124): *aṣ-ṣabr ʿalā samāʿ ash-shatīmah wa-tark al-ghaḍab li'l-aṣdiqāʾ wa-li'l-qarābah min akhlāq al-ʿabīd*, compared with EN IV, 5, 6 = 1126a 7-8: *aṣ-ṣabr ʿalā samāʿ ash-shatīmah wa-tark al-ghaḍab li'l-qarābāt wa'l-auliyāʾ min akhlāq al-ʿabīd*; or al-ʿĀmirī (ed. Minovi, p. 138): *aṣ-ṣadīq ākhar huwa huwa*, compared with EN IX, 4, 5 = 1166a 31-32: exactly the same, *aṣ-ṣadīq ākhar huwa huwa* (ἔστι γὰρ ὁ φίλος ἄλλος αὐτός); or again (ed. Minovi, p. 139):

> *al-maḥabba min al-ashyāʾ al-muḍṭarrah jiddan fī 'l-ʿumr fa-innahu laisa yumkinu aḥadan an yaslama min ghair al-aṣdiqāʾ wa-innahu laisa fī 'l-faqr wa-sūʾ al-ḥāl maljaʾ ākhar siwā al-aṣdiqāʾ wa-hum maʿūnat al-mashāʾikh fīmā yaḥtājūna ilaihi wa-hum maʿūnat ash-shabāb ʿalā 'l-afʿāl al-jaiyidah fa-inna 'l-ithnain idhā 'jtamaʿā kānā aʿwan ʿalā 'l-fahm wa-ʿalā 'l-fiʿl wa-hum maljaʾ al-aḥdāth li-an lā yukhṭiʾū. qāla: wa-mā al-manfaʿah bi-ḥusn al-ḥāl idhā 'ftuqida minhā iṣṭināʿ al-maʿrūf fa-innamā yakūnu dhālika mamdūḥan bi'l-aṣdiqāʾ*,

which closely resembles the wording of EN VIII, 1, 1-2 = 1155a 3-15, but alters the order:

> *fa-innahā* [sc. *al-maḥabba*] *faḍīlah mā min faḍāʾilinā wa-hiya min al-ashyāʾ al-muḍṭarrah jiddan fī 'l-ʿumr* [...] *al-manfaʿah bi-ḥusn hādhihi 'l-ḥāl idhā 'ntaqaṣa minhā iṣṭināʿ al-maʿrūf* [...] *wa-yakūnu bihim mamdūḥan* [...] *wa-kaifa yumkinu an yabqā wa-yaslama min ghair aṣdiqāʾihi* [...] *wa-aiḍan fī'l-faqr wa-sāʾir radāʾāt al-bakht lā yuẓannu anna [hunāka] maljaʾan ākhar mā khalā al-aṣdiqāʾ wa-hum maljaʾ al-aḥdāth li-allā yukhṭiʾū wa-maʿūnat al-mashāʾikh* [...] *wa-yuʿīnu ash-shabāb fī 'l-afʿāl al-jiyād fa-inna 'l-ithnain idhā 'jtamaʿā kānā aqwā ʿalā 'l-fiʿl wa'l-fahm.*

The text of al-ʿĀmirī shows a different arrangement from the translation of EN in the Fez manuscript, which follows the Greek. One notices especially the position of the words *fa-inna'l-ithnain idhā 'jtamaʿā* in al-ʿĀmirī, whose wording, throughout the passage, however, is much influenced by the Arabic EN.

In another passage, too long to quote here (ed. Minovi, pp. 254-255, corresponding to EN VIII, 10, 1-3 = 1160a 31 - 1160b 17), we find the same terms used for the three constitutions of Aristotle, monarchy, aristocracy and timocracy, and their perversions, thus:

monarchy (*al-mulk*)	passing into	tyranny (*at-taghallub* or *at-taghallubīyah*);

aristocracy (*riyāsat al-akhyār*)	oligarchy (*riyāsat qalīlīn*);
timocracy (*riyāsat al-karāmah*)	democracy (*riyāsat al-ʿāmmah*)[91]

The most significant of these terms in the present context is *riyāsat qalīlīn*—without the article—for oligarchy, the same in both texts. This alone should give the dependence of the one upon the other, and of course it is al-ʿĀmirī who is dependent. A common source is scarcely to be thought of. We thus have to allow that the version of the *Nicomachean Ethics* in the Fez manuscript was known to al-ʿĀmirī, and that he used it in his book.

Arberry thought that al-ʿĀmirī in writing the *Kitāb as-saʿādah wa'l-isʿād* used some kind of digest or epitome of the *Ethics* and with reference to the passage last quoted he wrote:

> The virtual identity of the technical vocabulary of the two translations, and the close correspondences of phrasing, suggest that the translator of the complete text and the translator of the epitome were one and the same.[92]

This, however, is not apparently quite correct, for there is little difficulty in allowing that al-ʿĀmirī had access to the complete translation of the *Ethics*, as now known from the Fez text. On the other hand, no epitome of EN in Arabic is known except the original, now lost, of the Latin *Summa Alexandrinorum*, which al-ʿĀmirī appears not to have used.[93] It would seem rather that al-ʿĀmirī knew

---

[91] *Riyāsat al-ʿawāmm* is the alternative rendering of 'democracy' at 1160a 36 (where it is in error for 'timocracy'), 1161a 6 and b 9-10.

[92] Arberry, "An Arabic Treatise on Politics", *loc. cit.*, p. 19.

[93] Evidence for this is to be found in a comparison of passages of al-ʿĀmirī with the existing fragments of the Arabic text behind the Latin of the *Summa Alexandrinorum*. These occur in the *Mukhtār al-ḥikam wa-maḥāsin al-kalim* of al-Mubashshir b. Fātik, and where they fail, the Latin version of the *Summa* may be adduced. Cf. al-ʿĀmirī, ed. Minovi, p. 139, already quoted, with al-Mubashshir b. Fātik, *Mukhtār al-ḥikam*, ed. ʿAbdarraḥmān Badawī, Madrid 1958, p. 213, and al-ʿĀmirī, ed. Minovi, pp. 70, 124, 138 and 225 with *Summa Alexandrinorum*, ed. Concetto Marchesi, in: *L'Etica Nicomachea nella tradizione latina medievale*, Messina 1904, pp. XLI-LXXXVI, here pp. XLV-XLVI, LIX, LXXVII and LXIII. To these may be added the passage discussed above, al-ʿĀmirī, ed. Minovi, pp. 254-255 (transcribed in Arberry, "An Arabic Treatise on Politics", *loc. cit.*, pp. 17-18): *qāla Arisṭūṭālīs: anwāʾ al-haiyah al-madanīyah thalāthah. qāla: wa-zawālātuhā ilā thalāthah. qāla: wa-aʿnī bi-zawālātihā fasādahā. qāla: fa-auwaluhā al-malik wa-*

the text of the version of the *Ethics* in the Fez manuscript, but used it quite freely, without troubling always to give the exact wording and perhaps relying on memory. His procedure will have been somewhat like that of Miskawaih, an author who concerns us later.[94] Miskawaih undoubtedly had a text of the *Ethics* before him, which he follows in sequence throughout his book (al-ʿĀmirī did not do this), his language sometimes suggesting the Arabic of the Fez manuscript, while sometimes he paraphrases. Miskawaih, however, knew the Arabic original of the *Summa Alexandrinorum*, differing again from al-ʿĀmirī, who, as in the case of al-Fārābī, must be judged not to have known it.

But al-ʿĀmirī's *Kitāb as-saʿādah wa'l-isʿād* also contains quotations from the Commentary of Porphyry on the *Nicomachean Ethics*, a work apparently unknown from the Greek sources, though mentioned in the *Fihrist* of Ibn an-Nadīm,[95] circa 377/987. These quotations are four in number:

1. Al-ʿĀmirī (ed. Minovi, p. 53) specifically mentions Porphyry's Commentary as follows:[96]

> And Porphyry said, commenting on what Aristotle said: Pleasure ranks as an end, because it supervenes last. He said: And it is not perfect, because we do not stop at it, but we seek something else (*wa-qāla Furfūriyūs mufassiran li-mā qālahu Arisṭūṭīlis: al-ladhdha ka'n-nihāya fī 'l-martabah li-annahā taḥduthu ākhiran. qāla:*[97] *wa-laisat bi-kāmilah li-annā lā naqifu ʿindahā wa-lakinnā naṭlubu shai'an ākhara*).

The text of Aristotle which Porphyry would here explain immediately precedes:

> Aristotle said, and I say: Pleasure is an end, not as a state which comes into existence in the person feeling the pleasure, but as a completion,

gharaḍuhu mā huwa khairun li-man yakūnu taḥta riyāsatihi [...]. We do not have the corresponding Arabic text, but the Latin translation thereof shows that it was different (ed. Marchesi, pp. LXXIII-LXXIV, ll. 29ff.), beginning: "Principatus ciuiles tres sunt, principatus regum et principatus bonorum et principatus comunitatum. Et omnium optimus est regum principatus, et omnis principatus contrarium habens corrumpet ipsum et tollet a forma sua [...]."

[94] Cf. below, pp. 28ff.

[95] See below, p. 26.

[96] For a slightly different translation see now Porphyry, *Porphyrii philosophi fragmenta*, ed. Andrew Smith, fragmenta arabica David Wasserstein interpretante, Stuttgart 1993, 165 F (ii).

[97] *Qālat*, MS., cf. Minovi's note in his edition of al-ʿĀmirī, *in loco*.

> like the perfection which occurs in sequence, not through the form, like the beauty which comes in youth (*qāla Arisṭūṭīlis wa-aqūlu: al-ladhdha nihāyah lā ka-hai'ah taṣīru fī 'l-multadhdh lākin ka-tamām ka'l-kamāl alladhī yakūnu bi'l-martabah lā bi'ṣ-ṣūrah wa-bi'l-jamāl* [corr. *wa-ka'l-jamāl*] *alladhī yaṣīru fī 'sh-shabāb*).

This of course is EN X, 4, 8 = 1174b 31-33, in the Fez manuscript: *tammamat al-ladhdhah al-fi'l lā ka-hai'ah hiya fīhi bal ka-tamām mā yaṣīru fīhi min baʿḍin ka'l-jamāl alladhī yaṣīru fī 'sh-shabāb.*

2. Al-ʿĀmirī (ed. Minovi, pp. 5-6; Smith/Wasserstein 165 F [i]), without mention of the Commentary of Porphyry but doubtless from the same source, has:

> Porphyry said: Happiness is simply a man's perfecting his form, and man's perfection, in so far as he is a man, is in voluntary actions, and his perfection, in so far as he is an angel and an intelligence, is in speculation, and each of the two perfections is complete in each of the two subjects, and if one be compared with the other, it is the human perfection which is defective (*qāla Furfūriyūs: as-saʿādah innamā hiya istikmāl al-insān ṣūratahu wa-kamāl al-insān bi-ḥasabi mā huwa insān fī 'l-afʿāl al-irādīyah wa-kamāluhu bi-ḥasabi mā huwa malak wa-ʿaql fī 'n-naẓar wa-kull wāḥidin min al-kamālain tāmm ʿinda kull wāḥidin min al-mauḍūʿain fa-in qīsa aḥaduhuma ilā 'l-ākhar kāna al-kamāl al-insī nāqiṣan*).

With this we may compare EN X, 7, 1 and 8-9. The sense of the notice, which comes under a heading 'On human and intellectual happiness, whether it is one subject or two, and whether each of them is complete or one of them is deficient' (*Fī's-saʿādah al-insīyah wa'l-ʿaqlīyah hal mauḍūʿ wāḥid au mauḍūʿain* [sic] *wa-kull wāḥidin minhumā tāmmah am iḥdāhumā nāqiṣah*), is not Aristotelian, cf. *malak*, 'angel', but as we should expect from Porphyry.

3. Al-ʿĀmirī (ed. Minovi, pp. 192-193, Smith/Wasserstein 165 F [iv]) has:

> And Porphyry said: The man who deserves leadership is he who has ruled himself rightly, and ruled his household rightly, and can rule the city rightly. He said: That is, the artist is he who can raise the perfections which are in his art to the most perfect perfection and has at the same time the perfection of command and interdiction (*wa-qāla Furfūriyūs: al-mustaḥiqq li'r-riyāsah huwa alladhī qad dabbara amr nafsihi ʿalā 'ṣ-ṣawāb wa-amr baitihi ʿalā 'ṣ-ṣawāb wa-yumkinuhu an yudabbira amr al-madīnah ʿalā 'ṣ-ṣawāb. qāla: wa-dhālika anna aṣ-*

> *ṣāniʿ huwa alladhī yumkinuhu an yuraqqiya al-kamālāt allati takūnu fī ṣināʿatihi ilā 'l-kamāl al-akmal wa-yakūnu lahu maʿa dhālika kamāl al-amr wa'n-nahy).*

This also is presumably from Porphyry's Commentary on the *Ethics*, and may refer to EN VIII, cc. 10-11 (discussion of kingship, etc.).

4. Al-ʿĀmirī (ed. Minovi, pp. 353-354) also has:

> And Porphyry said: Everyone who is expert in anything is a judge of that thing, and he who is expert in everything is the judge of everything. He said: And it is customary with these people to call the expert in the thing whoever possesses enough knowledge of that thing to make it possible for him to pass judgement about it *a posteriori* (*wa-qāla Furfūriyūs: kull adībin fī shaiʾin faʾinnahu yakūnu qāḍiyan fī dhālika 'sh-shaiʾ wa'l-adīb fī 'l-kull huwa al-qāḍī fī kull shaiʾin qāla: wa-min ʿādat hāʾulāʾi al-qaum an yusammā al-adab* [corr. *al-adīb*] *fī 'sh-shaiʾ man kāna ʿindahu min ʿilm dhālika 'sh-shaiʾ mā yumkinuhu al-ḥukm fīhi ʿalā mā baʿdahu*).[98]

The reference is to EN I, 3, 5 = 1094b 27 - 1095a 2, and again presumably to Porphyry's Commentary.

In view of these passages we may, I think, conclude that al-ʿĀmirī, whatever other Aristotelian material he may have had before him for his numerous quotations from Aristotle,[99] at least had a text of the *Nicomachean Ethics* and a Commentary of Porphyry thereon. On the other hand, there is no evidence, as already indicated, that al-ʿĀmirī knew the Arabic original of the *Summa Alexandrinorum*.

It is scarcely a mere coincidence that about this same time we have a notice of the work to which both al-ʿĀmirī and al-Fārābī appear to refer. In the *Fihrist* of Ibn an-Nadīm there is a programmatic heading which promises an account of the works of Aristotle on logic, natural science, theology (metaphysics) and ethics.[100]

---

[98] The second part only of this quotation seems properly to belong to Porphyry: *kull adībin* [...] *fī kull shaiʾin* is the lemma (different from the Arabic of the Fez MS.)

[99] Richard Walzer, *Al-Farabi on the Perfect State*, Oxford 1985, p. 429, thought of another work of Porphyry *On the Identical Philosophy of Plato and Aristotle* (Περὶ τοῦ μίαν εἶναι τὴν Πλάτωνος καὶ Ἀριστοτέλους αἵρεσιν) in seven books (not mentioned in the list of works of Porphyry given *ibid.*, p. 532) as the source of the material in al-ʿĀmirī's book. But it is not known for certain that this work was translated into Arabic, and Porphyry's Commentary on the *Ethics* is quoted by al-ʿĀmirī, as above noted.

[100] Ibn an-Nadīm, *Fihrist*, *op. cit.*, vol. I, p. 248.

The notice under the last of these is short and obscure, but has always been considered by investigators to be highly important, as in our discussion it undoubtedly is, for no other text in Arabic except this and its derivatives has anything to say about how an Arabic translation of the *Ethics* came into existence.

We here read, following the 19th century edition which is still standard:

> *wa-min kutub Arisṭālīs* [sic] *nusikha*[101] *min khaṭṭ Yaḥyā b. ʿAdī min fihrist kutubihi kitāb al-akhlāq fassarahu Furfūriyūs ithnatā ʿashrata maqālatan naqala*[102] *Isḥāq b. Ḥunain wa-kāna ʿinda Abī Zakariyāʾ bi-khaṭṭ Isḥāq b. Ḥunain ʿiddat maqālāt bi-tafsīr Thāmistiyūs wa-kharajat suryānī.*[103]

This may be translated as follows:

> And among the books of Aristotle—copy made from the handwriting of Yaḥyā b. ʿAdī, from the catalogue of his books—was the *Book of Ethics* explained by Porphyry, twelve discourses, translated by Isḥāq b. Ḥunain. And there was with Abū Zakariyāʾ [sc. Yaḥyā b. ʿAdī] in the handwriting of Isḥāq b. Ḥunain a number of discourses with the Commentary of Themistius.[104] They came out in Syriac.

This notice is repeated with minor changes and one major change by al-Qifṭī (568/1173-646/1248):

[101] For *nusakh* (August Müller in his edition of Ibn Abī ʿUṣaibiʿah, *ʿUyūn al-anbāʾ, op. cit.*) and *nasakha* (Steinschneider, *Die arabischen Übersetzungen aus dem Griechischen, op. cit.*, p. 107).

[102] Perhaps *naqalahu* should be read, cf. al-Qifṭī below, or *naqlu* in both places.

[103] Ibn an-Nadīm, *Fihrist, op. cit.*, vol. I, p. 252.

[104] Apart from Ibn an-Nadīm in the *Fihrist* and following him al-Qifṭī, there is little or nothing in the Arabic sources specifically about this Commentary. Al-Fārābī perhaps mentions it inclusively when he speaks about 'Porphyry and many others after him' (*Furfūriyūs wa-kathīr mimman baʿdahu*) as commentators on the *Nicomachean Ethics* (*Kitāb al-jamʿ baina raʾyai al-ḥakīmain*, in: al-Fārābī, *Philosophische Abhandlungen, op. cit.*, text p. 17; transl. p. 27, cf. Abū ʿAlī Aḥmad b. M. Miskawaih, *Tahdhīb al-akhlāq*, ed. Qusṭanṭīn Zuraiq, Beirut 1966, pp. 76 and 229). Al-ʿĀmirī cites Themistius a few times, but not for the *Ethics*. Some sayings attributed to him are given in Abū Sulaimān as-Sijistānī, *Muntakhab ṣiwan al-ḥikmah*, ed. Douglas M. Dunlop, The Hague 1979, p. 101, § 217, where the excellence of his commentaries on the works of Aristotle is mentioned in general terms. Details about his commentaries on Aristotle are to be found in Ibn Abī Uṣaibiʿah and al-Qifṭī, but there seems to be no further information about the Commentary on EN.

> The ethical works [sc. of Aristotle:] The *Book of Ethics* by him explained by Porphyry. It is twelve discourses, translated by Ḥunain b. Isḥāq. And there was with Abū Zakariyā' Yaḥyā b. ʿAdī in the handwriting of Isḥāq b. Ḥunain a number of discourses [with] the Commentary of Themistius. They came out in Syriac (*al-khulqīyāt: Kitāb al-akhlāq lahu fassarahu Furfūriyūs wa-huwa ithnā ʿashara maqālatan naqalahu Ḥunain b. Isḥāq wa-kāna ʿinda Abī Zakariyā' Yaḥyā b. ʿAdī bi-khaṭṭ Isḥāq b. Ḥunain ʿiddat maqālāt [bi-] tafsīr Thāmistiyūs wa-kharajat suryānī*).[105]

Al-Qifṭī adds the titles of some other 'ethical' books (*khulqiyāt*), including a *Kitāb ikhtiṣār al-akhlāq* (*Abbreviation of the Ethics*).

The notice has usually been taken to mean that Isḥāq b. Ḥunain, and not, as al-Qifṭī says, Ḥunain b. Isḥāq, translated the ten Books of the *Nicomachean Ethics* into Arabic, plus other two Books, which have been identified as the two Books of the *Magna Moralia*. Since the discovery of the Fez manuscript with the Arabic text of EN in 11 Books, it has become clear that the additional Book is quite different from the *Magna Moralia*, but it remains the most probable opinion that Ibn an-Nadīm's notice refers to the Fez text.[106]

The argument in favour of Isḥāq as the author of the translation rather than Ḥunain is two-fold: 1) Ibn an-Nadīm, who says so, is the earlier and better authority; 2) Isḥāq is more especially associated with the translation of philosophical works than his father Ḥunain, who was concerned chiefly with medical translation. We hear of no other translation of the *Nicomachean Ethics in extenso* into Arabic. We therefore assume, at least as a working hypothesis, that the text which we find in the Fez manuscript includes this translation, stated to have been mentioned in a list of books in the hand of Yaḥyā b. ʿAdī and actually seen by Ibn an-Nadīm, as he expressly records of another work of Aristotle (*ra'aituhā maktūbah bi-khaṭṭ Yaḥyā b. ʿAdī fī fihrist kutubihi*, 'I saw it written in the hand of Yaḥyā b. ʿAdī in the catalogue of his books').[107]

Thus while the identity of the translation attributed to Isḥāq b. Ḥunain, or to his father, and the Arabic version of EN in the Fez manuscript cannot be demonstrated by positive proof, it has been

---

105 Jamāl ad-Dīn al-Qifṭī, *Ta'rīkh al-ḥukamā'*, ed. Julius Lippert, Leipzig 1320/1903, p. 43.

106 For a further discussion of this see pp. 85f.

107 Ibn an-Nadīm, *Fihrist*, *op. cit.*, vol. I, p. 252.

generally regarded as 'evident'. Quotations in Arabic from EN or from the *Kitāb al-akhlāq* (*Book of Ethics*) usually appear to derive from the version or else to be paraphrased, i.e. most Arabic authors who cite the work seem to depend on this version, which, however, they often give in their own words. This will be further seen as we proceed. If it could be shown that authors agree in another wording, distinct from the version in the Fez text, the situation of course would be different, but this does not appear to be the case.[108]

Abū ʿAlī Aḥmad b. Muḥammad Miskawaih, who died at an advanced age in 421/1030, has left a well-known ethical work, the *Kitāb tahdhīb al-akhlāq* (*Book of the Rectification of Morals*), in which he makes use of the *Nicomachean Ethics*, mentioned once as '[Aristotle's] book known as *Nīqūmākhiyā*' (*kitābuhu al-maʿrūf bi-Nīqūmākhiyā*),[109] once as 'his book called the *Ethics*' (*kitābuhu al-musammā bi'l-Akhlāq*),[110] or simply as 'the *Book of Ethics*' (*Kitāb al-akhlāq*).[111]

It is evident that Miskawaih in composing his own book went through EN consecutively, so that his rather frequent references begin with Book I and end with Book X. Dr. Constantine Zuraiq in his admirable edition of the *Tahdhīb al-akhlāq* accounts for the absence of exact correspondence between the wording of the Aristotelian quotations in that work and the text of EN by suggesting that Miskawaih used the *Nicomachean Ethics* not directly but through commentaries.[112] It would be natural that he made use of the book mentioned by Ibn an-Nadīm (the *Book of Ethics* with Commentary by Porphyry), though Miskawaih refers to Porphyry by name once only, in the following passage:

> *al-khair ʿalā mā qasamahu Arisṭūṭālīs wa-ḥakāhu ʿanhu Furfūriyūs wa-ghairuhu hākadhā. qāla: al-khairāt minhā mā hiya sharīfah wa-minhā mā hiya mamdūḥah wa-minhā mā hiya bi'l-qūwah ka-dhālika*, i.e. the good according as Aristotle divided it, and Porphyry and others

---

[108] On the other hand, Walzer in al-Fārābī, *Al-Farabi on the Perfect State, op. cit.*, p. 413: "There seems to have been more than one translation of the Aristotelian text", and Gauthier and Jolif in Aristotle, *L'Éthique à Nicomaque, op. cit.*, vol. I/1, p. 108: "D'autres traductions de l'*Éthique* parurent sans doute par la suite."

[109] Miskawaih, *Tahdhīb al-akhlāq, op. cit.*, p. 116.

[110] *Ibid.*, p. 92.

[111] *Ibid.*, pp. 33 and 97.

[112] *Ibid.*, p. 234.

> reported it on his authority, is as follows. He said: Some good things are honourable, some are commendable, some are potentially so.[113]

The reference is apparently to Aristotle's *Magna Moralia* I, 2, 1 = 1183b 20-21, but the passage will have reached Miskawaih, in all probability, by way of Porphyry's Commentary.[114]

But Miskawaih will also have made use of the Arabic original of the *Summa Alexandrinorum*, traces of which we first find in his work. We may compare Miskawaih's text with the *Mukhtār al-ḥikam*, or where that fails, recourse may be had to the Latin version. Thus, *Tahdhīb al-akhlāq*, ed. Zuraiq, p. 79:

> *qāla* [sc. Aristotle]: *wa-li-hādhā qulnā in kāna shai' ʿaṭīyah min Allāh taʿālā wa-mauhibah li'n-nās fa-huwa as-saʿādah li-annahā ʿaṭīyah wa-mauhibah minhu ʿazza 'smuhu fī ashraf manāzil al-khairāt wa-fī aʿlā marātibihā.*

For this the Latin translation (ed. Marchesi, pp. XLIV, ll. 17-20) has:

> Et si aliqua rerum donata est hominibus a deo excelsa et gloriosa [leg. excelso et glorioso],[115] dignum est ut beatitudo sive felicitas donum sit divinum secundum quod ipsa est optima omnium rerum humanarum.

We note that one of the two ascriptions of praise in the Arabic has been retained in the Latin. The Latin also shows ("dignum est") a trace of dependence on the text of the EN in the Fez manuscript (cf. EN I, 9, 2 = 1099b 11: *in kāna hāhunā mauhibah min Allāh li'n-nās fa-khalīq an takūna as-saʿādah mauhiban minhu lahum*), but the presence of the ascription seems to determine dependence on the Arabic behind the *Summa Alexandrinorum*.

Another example is *Tahdhīb al-akhlāq*, ed. Zuraiq, p. 94:

> *fa-sīrat al-afāḍil as-suʿadā' sīrah ladhīdhah bi-nafsihā li'anna afʿāla-hum abadan mukhtārah wa-mamdūḥah wa-kull insānin yaltadhdhu bi-*

---

[113] *Ibid.*, p. 76. Cf. Porphyry, *Porphyrii philosophi fragmenta*, *op. cit.*, 166 F.

[114] It might readily have been cited there on EN I, 12, 1 = 1101b 10-12. Zuraiq compares *Magna Moralia* for other passages in the *Tahdhīb al-akhlāq*, *op. cit.*, pp. 77, 106, 108.

[115] This is the first of the ascriptions of praise in the *Summa Alexandrinorum*, not perhaps recognised as such by the copyist, who may have corrected the words to agree with *aliqua*. In George B. Fowler's text of the *Summa Alexandrinorum* ("Manuscript Admont 608 and Engelbert of Admont [c. 1250-1331]. Appendix 14: *Summa Alexandrinorum*", in: AHDLMA 49 [1983], pp. 195-252, here p. 200) "glorioso et excelso" is read.

> *mā huwa maḥbūb ʿindahu fa-yaltadhdhu bi'l-ʿadl al-ʿādil wa-yaltadh-dhu bi'l-ḥikmah al-ḥakīm,*

compared with the Latin (ed. Marchesi, pp. XLIV, ll. 7-10):

> et istorum [sc. bonorum et beatorum] vita est in se ipsa delectabilis. Unusquisque enim hominum delectatur in eo quod est amatum apud ipsum; delectetur [leg. delectatur][116] ergo iustus in iustitia et virtuosus in virtute et sapiens in sapientia.

EN I, 8, 10 = 1099a 7-11, the corresponding passage, in the Fez manuscript is quite different.

The case for the dependence of Miskawaih on the Arabic behind the *Summa Alexandrinorum* is put beyond doubt by two further examples. First, we have *Tahdhīb al-akhlāq*, ed. Zuraiq, p. 78:

> *wa-Arisṭūṭālīs yaqūlu innahu yaʿsuru ʿalā 'l-insān an yafʿala 'l-afʿāl ash-sharīfah bi-lā māddah mithl ittisāʿ al-yad wa-kathrat al-aṣdiqāʾ wa-jūdat al-bakht.*[117] *qāla: wa-li-hādha mā*[118] [sic] *iḥtājat al-ḥikmah ilā ṣināʿat al-mulk fī izhār sharafihā,*

to which the corresponding passage in the *Summa Alexandrinorum* (ed. Marchesi, p. XLIV, ll. 13-17) is:

> difficile est enim homini ut opera decora exerceat absque materia ut pote [sic] quod habeat [Oportet ergo haberi *Fowler*] partem competentem rerum bene vite pertinentium et copiam familie et parentum et prosperitatem fortune. Et hac quidem de causa indiget ars sapientie arte regnandi, ut apparere faciat honorificentiam sui atque valorem.

In Miskawaih the words *jūdat al-bakht* appear, not in the Greek EN, in the passage beginning I, 8, 15 = 1099a 31, nor in the Arabic of the Fez manuscript. The *Summa Alexandrinorum*, however, has them ("prosperitatem fortune"), and the same applies to the sentence *wa-li-hādha [mā] iḥtājat* [...], rendered in the *Summa* "Et hac quidem [...]".

Secondly, we find at Miskawaih, *Tahdhīb al-akhlāq*, ed. Zuraiq, p. 171, the words: *fa-inna 'l-insān wa-in kāna ṣaghīra 'l-juththan fa-innahu ʿaẓīm bi'l-ḥikmah*, and, agreeably to this, in the *Summa Alexandrinorum* (ed. Marchesi, p. LXXXIV, ll. 2-4): "et semper

---

[116] So Fowler, *ibid.*, p. 200 (IV, 17).

[117] Cf. *jūdat al-ʿaish* in al-Mubashshir b. Fātik, *Kitāb al-mukhtār al-ḥikam*, *op. cit.*, p. 210, evidently quoting the same passage, below, pp. 81f.

[118] The negative is here in error, cf. *Kitāb al-mukhtār al-ḥikam*'s *wa-li-hādhā 'l-maʿnā* (p. 210, l. 13), which may be the original text.

contendat ad vivendum vita nobiliore [sic] que est in ipso; licet enim homo parvus sit corpore, premio et honore superpositus est aliis." On the other hand, the Arabic of the Fez manuscript accords with the modern interpretation and renders the whole passage (EN X, 7, 8-9 = 1177b 33 - 1178a 3):

> do everything with a view to living life according to the best[119] that is in him, and if it is small in bulk (*wa-in kāna ṣaghīran bi'l-ʿiẓm*), yet in power and excellence it surpasses (*yafūqu*) all by far. It may be thought that every man is this, since it is the ruling and better part (*kāna al-musawwad al-ajwad*).

We have to conclude then that Miskawaih knew and used an Arabic text which corresponded closely to the Latin of the *Summa Alexandrinorum*, and that this text was in existence at least as early as A.D. 1030. Evidently he knew the complete Arabic translation of the *Nicomachean Ethics*, though he mentions it by this name only once. Also, as we saw, he mentions Porphyry, and this may indicate that he had the *Ethics* in 12 Books with Porphyry's Commentary, of which Ibn an-Nadīm and al-Qifṭī speak and which is usually taken to include the complete text of the *Ethics* as found in the Fez manuscript.

Ibn Sīnā (370/980-478/1037), who in general is sparing in reference to his sources,[120] does not appear to mention the *Nicomachean Ethics*, but at more than one point in the chapter *Fī 'l-bahjah wa's-saʿādah* (*On Joy and Happiness*) of his *Kitāb al-ishārāt wa't-tanbīhāt* there seems to be a trace of its influence, e.g. the magnanimous man is mentioned as *kabīr an-nafs*,[121] the expression regularly used in the Fez manuscript[122] (elsewhere we have *ʿaẓīm an-nafs*).[123] In another passage of the same work,[124] curiously enough, Ibn Sīnā's

---

[119] Literally 'strongest' (*aqwā*). Cf. 1177a 13 κατὰ τὴν κρατίστην rendered by *ʿalā 'l-faḍīlah al-qawīyah*.

[120] Cf. Minovi, p. V of his edition of al-ʿĀmirī's *Kitāb as-saʿādah wa'l-isʿād*, *op. cit.*: "Ibn Sīnā [...] who did not appreciate anybody but himself, and who did not think of any of the Moslem philosophers worth mentioning."

[121] Text: Ibn Sīnā, *Kitāb al-ishārāt wa't-tanbīhāt*, ed. Jacques Forget, Leiden 1892, p. 190. Transl.: Ibn Sīnā, *Livre des directives et remarques*, *op. cit.*, p. 468.

[122] EN IV, 3, 3 = 1123b 2 *et sqq.*

[123] al-Mubashshir b. Fātik, *Mukhtār al-ḥikam*, *op. cit.*, p. 212; 'Seventh Book' of the Fez MS. of EN, c. 5, §§ 11 and 12.

[124] Ibn Sīnā, text p. 20; transl. pp. 499-500. The correspondence was first noted

characterisation of the *ʿārif*[125] ('mature philosopher') coincides in various points with that of the magnanimous man of Aristotle, though without close verbal correspondence. He is courageous, courteous to those of humble station, does not bear a grudge, is fond of beautiful things, etc. (cf. EN IV, c. 3).

The Qāḍī Ṣāʿid (in full Abū 'l-Qāsim Ṣāʿid b. Aḥmad b. Ṣāʿid al-Andalusī) in his *Kitāb ṭabaqāt al-umam* (*Book of the Categories of the Nations*) written in or about 460/1068 has the following account of the ethical works of Aristotle:

> *wa-ammā al-kutub allatī fī aʿmāl al-falsafah fa-baʿḍuhā fī iṣlāḥ akhlāq an-nafs wa-baʿḍuhā fī 's-siyāsah fa-ammā allatī fī iṣlāḥ akhlāq an-nafs fa-kitābuhu al-kabīr alladhī kataba bihi ilā 'bnihi wa-kitābuhu aṣ-ṣaghīr alladhī kataba ilā 'bnihi aiḍan wa-kitābuhu al-musammā Udhīmiyā wa-ammā 'llatī fī 's-siyāsah fa-baʿḍuhā fī siyāsat al-mudun wa-baʿḍuhā fī siyāsat al-manzil*, i.e. as for the books which are on the actions of philosophy [= practical philosophy], some of them are on the improvement of morals and others on government. As for those which are on the improvement of morals, they are his large book which he wrote to his son, his small book which he wrote to his son also and his book called *Udhīmiyā* [= *Eudemian Ethics*]. As for those which are on government, some of them are on the government of cities and some of them on the government of the household.[126]

The longer statement in the *Ṭabaqāt al-umam*,[127] from which this is taken, also appears with some modifications in al-Fārābī's *Risālah fīmā yanbaghī an yuqaddama qabl taʿallum al-falsafah* (*Letter on the Necessary Preliminaries to the Study of Philosophy*).[128] There is no doubt that the Qāḍī depends upon al-Fārābī, unless we are to think of

---

by Clemens Vansteenkiste, "Études critiques", in: *Laval théolgique et philosophique* 7 (1951), pp. 202-217, here p. 215. See Gauthier and Jolif in Aristotle, *L'Éthique à Nicomaque*, *op. cit.*, vol. II/1, pp. 291-292.

[125] The word is hard to translate, literally 'he who knows'. Goichon distinguishes *ʿārif* from *ʿarīf*, 'gnostic', and explains the word to mean 'intellectualist mystic, more intellectualist than mystic, according to Ibn Sīnā' ("le *ʿārif* est donc le mystique intellectualiste, plus intellectualiste que mystique, d'après la doctrine avicennienne", *Livre des directives et remarques*, *op. cit.*, p. 475, n. 4).

[126] Ibn Ṣāʿid al-Andalusī, *Kitāb ṭabaqāt al-umam*, *op. cit.*, text pp. 25-26; transl. p. 66).

[127] *Ibid.*, text p. 24 (*wa-lahu fī jamīʿ al-ʿulūm*) - p. 26 (*balagha ʿudhrahu*); transl. pp. 63-67.

[128] al-Fārābī, *Philosophische Abhandlungen*, *op. cit.*, text p. 50; transl. pp. 84-87.

a common source. Al-Fārābī's account of the practical application of philosophy has already been given.[129]

Both these texts mention the particular (*juz'ī*) and general (*kullī*) works of Aristotle, the latter including 'notes[130] by reading which is remembered what has previously been learned of his philosophy'. The Qāḍī Ṣā'id adds to this 'and these are the seventy books[131] which he composed for Eupharus [?]' (*wa-hiya as-sab'ūna kitāban allatī waḍa'ahā li-Ufār.s*).[132] Blachère omitted the difficult words from his translation,[133] but in the table which he gives of the works of Aristotle according to Ṣā'id he admits "les 70 traités à Fuares [?]".[134] As regards the proper name, which is evidently corrupt in the Arabic text, the likeliest explanation is that it is for Thāwufrasṭus,[135] Theophrastus, who succeeded Aristotle as head of the Lyceum and inherited his books and manuscripts.[136]

Elsewhere the Qāḍī Ṣā'id in the *Ṭabaqāt al-umam* and al-Fārābī in the *Risālah* give the same account of seven schools of philosophy among the Greeks.[137] Ṣā'id here cites for his information 'al-Fārābī and other learned men', but he mentions in the first place the translator Ḥunain b. Isḥāq (*wa-dhakara Ḥunain ibn Isḥāq at-turjumān wa-Abū Naṣr Muḥammad ibn Naṣr* [sic] *al-Fārābī al-*

---

[129] Cf. above, p. 15f.

[130] Ibn Ṣā'id al-Andalusī, *Kitāb ṭabaqāt al-umam, op. cit.*, has *tadhākir*, plur. of *tadhkirah* (p. 24), which Blachère translates "livres mnémoniques" (p. 63). Al-Fārābī, *Philosophische Abhandlungen, op. cit.*, has *tadhakīr*, plur. of *tadhkīr*, and so also Ibn Abī Uṣaibi'ah, *'Uyūn al-anbā', op. cit.*, vol. I, p. 57, where the passage is quoted from Ṣā'id.

[131] The MS. readings vary between *as-sab'ūna* and *sab'ūna* (Ibn Ṣā'id al-Andalusī, *Kitāb ṭabaqāt al-umam, op. cit.*, p. 24, n. 9).

[132] *Ibid.*, p. 24. Cf. also Ibn Abī Uṣaibi'ah, *'Uyūn al-anbā', op. cit.*, vol. I, p. 57.

[133] Ibn Ṣā'id al-Andalusī, *Livre des catégories des nations, op. cit.*, p. 63.

[134] *Ibid.*, p. 65.

[135] So Moritz Steinschneider, *Al-Farabi (Alpharabius), des arabischen Philosophen Leben und Schriften, mit besonderer Rücksicht auf die Geschichte der griechischen Wissenschaft unter den Arabern* (Mémoires de l'Académie Impériale des Sciences de St.-Pétersbourg, VIIe série; XIII, 4), St. Petersburg 1869, p. 129, who reads *Thāfrasṭus*, by an oversight.

[136] Diogenes Laertius, V, 52, cf. Werner Jaeger, *Aristotle*, English translation by Richard Robinson, Oxford ²1967, p. 315. See now also Theophrastus of Eresus, *Sources for His Life, Writings, Thought and Influence*, ed. and transl. William W. Fortenbach *et al.*, 2 vols., Leiden 1992.

[137] Ibn Ṣā'id al-Andalusī, *Kitāb ṭabaqāt al-umam, op. cit.*, text pp. 31-32; transl. pp. 74-75, and al-Fārābī, *Philosophische Abhandlungen, op. cit.*, text pp. 49-50; transl. pp. 83-84.

manṭiqī), i.e. Ḥunain b. Isḥāq is his primary source. Not only so, but we have the same material on the schools of philosophy among the Greeks in the little work called *Ādāb al-falāsifah* attributed to Ḥunain b. Isḥāq.[138] It is fairly safe to conclude that all this material concerning Aristotle which is found practically *verbatim* in al-Fārābī and in the Qāḍī Ṣāʿid[139] goes back to Ḥunain b. Isḥāq,[140] and this would apply of course to the statement about the seventy books composed for the enigmatic Eupharus, since there is no ground for thinking that the Qāḍī here used another source or that it is an invention of his own.

We have already mentioned and made some use of the *Kitāb mukhtār al-ḥikam*, written in 440/1048-441/1049 or 445/1053-446/1054[141] by al-Mubashshir b. Fātik, an Egyptian *amīr*. Its principal importance for our purpose is that it contains a number of fragments of the Arabic behind the Latin of the *Summa Alexandrinorum*, and we shall have to return to this in a later section. The *Kitāb al-akhlāq* is mentioned once by al-Mubashshir b. Fātik in a listing of 'about twenty' (*naḥwa ʿishrīna*) works of Aristotle still extant in the author's time.[142]

---

[138] See Ḥunain b. Isḥāq, *Sittensprüche der Philosophen* (*Kitâb Âdâb al-Falâsifah*), transl. Karl Merkle, Leipzig 1921, pp. 37-38 and 40.

[139] The verbal correspondence between the texts was indicated by Moritz Steinschneider, *Al-Farabi*, *op. cit.*, pp. 188 and 192, but he mentioned as the work from which the Qāḍī Ṣāʿid 'highly probably' ("höchst wahrscheinlich") drew, not the *Risālah* (*Letter on Necessary Preliminaries to the Study of Philosophy*), but the *Fontes quaestionum* (*ʿUyun al-masā'il*) of al-Fārābī. This was evidently an oversight, perhaps due to confusing the two works which had earlier been published together by F. Augustus Schmölders (see Nicholas Rescher, *Al-Fārābī. An Annotated Bibliography*, Pittsburgh 1962, p. 34). The texts and translations of Dieterici were not, of course, available to Steinschneider, when he published his work in the Mémoires of the Academy of St. Petersburg, 1869, and also he had to compare MSS. of Ibn Abī Uṣaibiʿah with the printed text of Schmölders.

[140] Ḥunain b. Isḥāq's information goes back to a Greek Introduction to Aristotle used by Ammonius, Philoponus, Simplicius and others in Late Antiquity. See Leendert G. Westerink, *Anonymous Prolegomena to Platonic Philosophy*, Amsterdam 1962, pp. XXVff., who gives an analysis of the contents of this Introduction, corresponding closely to what we find in the above-mentioned Arabic texts.

[141] 445/1053 is sometimes given. Cf. Franz Rosenthal, "Al-Mubashshir Ibn Fâtik, Prolegomena to an Abortive Edition", in: *Oriens* 13-14 (1961), pp. 132-158, here p. 133.

[142] al-Mubashshir b. Fātik, *Mukhtār al-ḥikam*, *op. cit.*, pp. 183-184.

The Spanish philosopher Ibn Bājjah, who died comparatively young in 533/1138 or 1139, made rather extensive use of the *Nicomachean Ethics* in 11 Books, which he refers to variously as *Nīqūmākhiyā*, *Kitāb Nīqūmākhiyā* and *Kitāb al-akhlāq*, even in one instance, if the text is sound, simply 'Aristotle in the Sixth' (*Arisṭū fī 's-sādisah*, sc. *al-maqālah*).[143] The passages are as follows:

1. *Tadbīr al-mutawaḥḥid*, ed. Asín, p. 9 (transl. pp. 39-40);[144] ed. Fakhry, pp. 41-42:[145]

> *wa-baiyin anna 'l-madīnah al-fāḍilah al-kāmilah qad uʿṭiyah fīhā kullu insānin afḍal mā huwa muʿadd naḥwahu wa-anna arā'ahā kulluhā ṣādiqah* [...] *wa-anna aʿmālahā hiya fāḍilah bi'l-iṭlāq waḥduhā* [...] *wa-qad tulukhkhiṣat*[146] *hādhihi al-umūr fī Kitāb Nīqūmākhiyā*, i.e. it is clear that in the virtuous, perfect state every man is given the best that he is ready for [or 'adapted to'] and that all its opinions are true [...] and that its actions alone are the absolutely good [...]. These matters have been summarised in the *Nicomachean Ethics*.

Asín compared EN III, c. 1 *et passim*, and was followed by Majid Fakhry. An exact parallel to the first part of this, as far as the words 'and that its actions alone are the absolutely good', is hardly to be found, and this applies also to the following words:

> *wa-anna kulla ʿamalin ghairahu fa-in kāna fāḍilan fa-bi'l-iḍāfah ilā fasad maujūd*[147] *wa-anna qaṭʿa ʿudwin min al-jasad ḍārr bi-dhātihī illā annahu qad yakūnu nāfiʿan bi'l-ʿaraḍ ka-man nahashathu afʿan fa-yaṣiḥḥu bi-qaṭʿihi al-badan wa-ka-dhālika as-saqarūniyā ḍārrah bi-dhātihā illā annahā nāfiʿah li-man bihi ʿillah wa-qad tulukhkhiṣat hādhihi* [...], i.e. and that every other action, if it is good, is so in relation to an existent defect, and that the cutting off of a limb from the body is injurious essentially, but is sometimes useful accidentally, like a man bitten by a viper and healed by amputation. Similarly scammony is essentially injurious, but is useful to someone who is ill. These matters have been summarised [...]

---

143 See below, pp. 36 and 46f.

144 Ibn Bājjah, *Tadbīr al-mutawaḥḥid (El régimen del solitario)*, ed. and transl. Miguel Asín Palacios, Madrid/Granada 1946.

145 Ibn Bājjah, *Rasā'il Ibn Bājjah al-ilāhīya (Opera Metaphysica)*, ed. Majid Fakhry, Beirut 1968.

146 Ibn Bājjah uses 'summarise' (*lakhkhaṣa, talakhkhaṣa*) to describe the treatment of topics in EN, cf. below, p. 36, no. 2.

147 Or *wujūdihi*, 'a defect *of his existence*'.

The source then appears to be some commentary on EN, perhaps that of al-Fārābī, which Ibn Bājjah certainly knew.[148]

2. *Tadbīr al-mutawaḥḥid*, ed. Asín, pp. 13-14 (transl. p. 45); ed. Fakhry, pp. 45-46:

> *fa-talḥaquhu al-afʿāl aḍ-ḍarūrīyah allatī lā ikhtiyār lahu fīhā* [...] *mithl mā yafʿal al-insān ʿan al-khauf ash-shadīd mithl shatm aṣ-ṣadīq wa-qatl al-akh wa'l-ab ʿalā amr malikin* [...] *wa-qad lukhkhiṣat hādhihi kulluhā fī Nīqūmākhiyā*, i.e. and so there attach to him necessary actions in which he has no free choice [...] like what a man does from extreme fear, like abusing a friend, killing a brother or a father at the command of a king [...]. An account of all this is given in the *Nicomachean Ethics*.

Asín compared *Eudemian Ethics* II, cc. 7-10, and the same discussion comes in EN III, cc. 1-3, as noted by Fakhry, without very close correspondence in either case. There is scarcely enough here to validate Asín's statement (*in loco*) that Ibn Bājjah sometimes gives citations from the *Nicomachean Ethics* which belong to the *Eudemian Ethics*.[149]

3. In another place (*Tadbīr al-mutawaḥḥid*, ed. Asín, p. 29 [transl. p. 62]; ed. Fakhry, p. 57) we find:

> *wa-min aṣ-ṣuwar ar-rūḥānīyah al-kādhibah yakūnu 'r-ri'ā' wa'l-makr wa-quwā ukhar shabīhah bihi* [...] *wa-yarā al-jumhūr fīhā wa-kathīr min khawāṣṣ amthāl hādhihi 'l-mudun annahā at-taʿaqqul alladhī yadhkuruhu* [*tadhakkarahu*, Asín] *Arisṭū fī 's-sādisah*, i.e. of the false spiritual forms are hypocrisy and cunning and other faculties like it [...] and the common people and many of the upper class in states like these think of them as being the practical wisdom which Aristotle mentions in the Sixth [sc. Book VI of EN].

Practical wisdom, Greek φρόνησις, is discussed in EN VI, c. 5 *et sqq.*, lacking in the Fez manuscript of EN. Elsewhere φρόνησις is often rendered, as here, by *taʿaqqul*, e.g. 1145a 2, 5; 1146a 4; 1178a 17-19, but not always, for we have also φρόνιμος = *ʿaql*, e.g. 1152a 12, 1172b 30, with φρόνησις rendered *ʿāqil* at 1107a 1 and 1152a 11,

---

[148] See below, pp. 40f., no. 7.

[149] There is no evidence of the existence of an Arabic translation of the *Eudemian Ethics* or the *Magna Moralia*, though these works were known by name to the Arabs (pp. 7, 14, 32, 52, n. 215). Quotations or echoes of the *Eudemian Ethics* may have reached Ibn Bājjah by way of al-Fārābī's Commentary on EN.

and even repeatedly φρόνησις = *fahm* (1096b 24, 1098b 24). In view of this fluctuation of usage, there is again no indication that the Fez Arabic version was used.

4. Further, *Tadbīr al-mutawaḥḥid*, ed. Asín, p. 45 (transl. pp. 80-81); ed. Fakhry, p. 68:

> *wa-minhum man taghlibu ʿalaihi ar-ruḥānīyah al-laṭīfah jiddan* [...] *wa-fī hādha ʿṣ-ṣinf yuʿaddu Uwais al-Quranī wa-Ibrāhīm b. Adham wa-ammā* [*fa-ammā*, Fakhry] *Hirmis fa'innahu aṭ-ṭaraf al-aqṣā min hādha aṣ-ṣinf ʿalā mā yaqūluhu Arisṭū fī Kitāb Nīqūmākhiyā*, i.e. and among them are some over whom the most delicate spirituality predominates [...] and in this category are reckoned Uwais al-Quranī and Ibrāhīm b. Adham. As for Hirmis, he is the ultimate in this category, according to what Aristotle says in the *Nicomachean Ethics*.

Here we note the remarkable juxtaposition of Hirmis (= Hermes) and two early Muslim religious personalities. In the context Hirmis must indicate, not the legendary Hermes Trismegistus or one of his yet more shadowy successors bearing the same name, but Hermias of Atarneus, the friend and patron of Aristotle. Hermias was presumably unknown to Ibn Bājjah, who found the name in his sources. There is therefore no need to emend to Irmiyās, Hermias (cf. Ibn Abī Uṣaibiʿah, *ʿUyūn al-anbāʾ*, *op. cit.*, vol. I, p. 54: *Irmiyās al-khādim al-wālī kāna ʿalā Atarnūs*, i.e. 'Hermias the slave, the ruler of Atarneus'). Aristotle's *Hymn to Virtue*, which contains praise of Hermias, appearing to put him on a level with the greatest heroes of the Greek race, seems indicated as the ultimate source of Ibn Bājjah's reference. There is of course no mention of Hermias in the Greek text of the *Nicomachaen Ethics*, but perhaps the name occured as of one possessing all the virtues in the Commentary of Porphyry.

Ibn Bājjah speaks of him similarly in the *Risālat al-wadāʿ* (*Letter of Farewell*), ed. Asín, p. 28, § 14 (transl. p. 66);[150] ed. Fakhry, p. 128:

> *yaḥkī Arisṭū ʿan Hirmis annahu kāna fāḍilan bi-jamīʿ* [*fī jamīʿ*, Fakhry] *al-faḍāʾil ash-shaklīyah*, i.e. Aristotle relates of Hirmis [= Hermias] that he was virtuous in all the formal virtues.

---

[150] Ibn Bājjah, *Risālat al-wadāʿ (La Carta de adiós de Avempace)*, ed. and transl. Miguel Asín Palacios, in: *al-Andalus* 8 (1943), pp. 1-87.

This time Ibn Bājjah makes no mention of his source, presumably the same as for the other notice. He here uses the word *shaklī* for the ethical virtues,[151] and he has *fikrī* for the intellectual virtues (*Risālat al-wadāʿ*, ed. Asín, p. 34, § 23 [transl. p. 77]; ed. Fakhry, p. 136), quite as in the Cairo manuscript, p. 312:

> *al-faḍīlah nauʿān faḍīlah shaklīyah ʿillatuhā an-nafs al-ḥissīyah* [...] *wa-faḍīlah fikrīyah ʿillatuhā an-nafs an-nāṭiqah*, i.e. virtue is of two kinds, formal virtue, whose cause is the sensory soul [...], and intellectual virtue, whose cause is the rational soul.[152]

The *Summa Alexandrinorum* (ed. Marchesi, p. LXIV, ll. 25-26) contrasts "virtus figuralis" and "virtus intellectualis", i.e. the same terminology as here. The Arabic behind the *Summa Alexandrinorum* is not available for comparison (cf. pp. 62ff.) and the corresponding text, EN VI, 1, 4, is missing in the Fez manuscript.[153] The nomenclature for the distinction between ethical and intellectual virtues in fact varies considerably in the texts. The Fez version at II, 1, 1 has, for ethical and intellectual virtues, *faḍāʾil khulqīyah* and *faḍāʾil fikrīyah*, and in this is followed by al-Mubashshir b. Fātik, *Kitāb mukhtār al-ḥikam, op. cit.*, p. 210. The *Fuṣūl al-madanī* (*Fuṣūl muntazaʿah*) of al-Fārābī (*op. cit.*, pp. 31-32, §§ 7 and 10) has *khulqīyah* and *nuṭqīyah* ('rational'), and al-ʿĀmirī has *khulqīyah* and *naẓarīyah* (*Kitāb as-saʿādah wa'l-isʿād, op. cit.*, p. 70).

5. *Tadbīr al-mutawaḥḥid*, ed. Asín, p. 52 (transl. pp. 88-89); ed. Fakhry, p. 73:

> *yaqūlu Arisṭū fī 'l-maqālah al-ūlā min Nīqūmākhiyā: faʾinna 'n-naqṣ laisa min qibal as-sinn au bi-hā* [*auhā*, Asín] *bal min qibal al-ʿādah wa'l-khulq*, i.e. Aristotle says in the first treatise [= Book] of the *Nicomachean Ethics*: For the defect is not in consequence of age, or through it, but in consequence of habit and character.

This is quite different from EN in the Fez manuscript (I, 3, 7 = 1095a 7-8):

> *liʾanna 'n-naqṣ laisa innamā yalīqu bihi min qibal az-zamān lākinna min qibal anna ʿaishatahu wa-jamīʿ mā yaṭlubuhu fīhi innamā yaqṣidu*

151 So Asín, *in loco*, "virtudes morales".
152 For the Cairo MS. see below, pp. 79ff., and for the passage here quoted, p. 82.
153 Cf. above, p. 1, n. 3.

> *bihi qaṣda mā tadʿū ilaihi ash-shahwah,*

and different also from al-Mubashshir al-Fātik, *Mukhtār al-ḥikam*, *op. cit.*, p. 209:

> *li-ʾanna ʿn-nuqṣān laisa innamā utiya bihi min jihat az-zamān bal min jihat anna ʿaishahu wa-jamīʿ mā yaṭlubuhu fīhi innamā yaqṣidu bihi qaṣda mā yaʿdū ash-shahwah* [sic].

From the latter part of this the occasional similarity between the Arabic of the Fez manuscript and the language of the *Mukhtār* is readily seen.[154] Ibn Bājjah's quotation is not a literal transcript of the Fez text, and perhaps the intention was simply to give the sense, or, which comes to much the same thing, the quotation is from memory.

6. *Risālat al-wadāʿ*, ed. Asín, p. 15 (transl. pp. 42-43); ed. Fakhry, p. 114:

> *wa-aukadu min hādha wa-ashadduhu wujūban ʿalaiyā wa-aladhdhuhu wa-ashhāhu ilaiyā iʿlāmuka bi-ajalli ʿl-umūr allatī waqaftu ʿalaihā wa-hiya ṣifat al-ghaiyah allatī yantahī aṭ-ṭabʿ bi's-sulūk ilaihā fa-qad waṣafahā wa-aṭāla al-waṣf fīhā man taqaddamanī wa-aḥad man waṣafahā wa-karrara al-qaul fīhā Abū Naṣr wa-makānuhu min hādhā ʿl-ʿilm makānuhu lākin lā ajidu fī jamīʿ kutubihi allatī waṣalat al-Andalus hādhā ʿn-naḥw alladhī waqaftu ʿalaihi wa-sayubaiyanu laka dhālika min qaulī fīhā anna hādhā ʿn-naḥw min an-naẓar [laisa]*[155] *innamā tabaiyana lī faqaṭ fa'innī wajattu li-Arisṭū fī ʿl-ḥādiyah ʿashara min al-Akhlāq qad qāla*[156] *dhālika ghaira annahu mujmal jiddan lā yumkinu min al-iktifāʾ bihi faqaṭ an yūqafa minhu ʿalā hādhā ʿl-qadr*, i.e. more certain than this and the most essential, as well as the pleasantest and most desirable thing for me, is to inform you of the greatest matter that I have come to know, the description of the end to which nature, in its advance, attains. This has been described and described at length by my predecessors. One of those who have described it and done so repeatedly is Abū Naṣr [sc. al-Fārābī], whose expertise in the subject is recognised. However, I do not find in all his books which have reached al-Andalus the kind of thing that I have come to know. It will be clear to you from what I say of it that this kind of investigation has become clear [not] only to me. For I have found it in Aristotle in the Eleventh Book of the *Ethics*, only it is very much summarised, impossible to be understood if one is content with that alone, so small it is.

---

[154] Cf. below, pp. 65f.

[155] The negative *laisa* is supplied from the following parallel text; cf. below, p. 40.

[156] Fakhry's text omits the words *qad qāla*.

The reference in this passage is distinctly to EN X, c. 7. Evidently Ibn Bājjah has been deeply impressed by the last chapters of Book X in praise of the contemplative life (cf. no. 8 below).

The passage as it stands here is taken from the Berlin MS. of the works of Ibn Bājjah (used by Asín), which alone contains the first part of the *Risālat al-wadā'*, the Oxford manuscript here failing. On the other hand, the Oxford manuscript has at the end of the *Risālah*, after the termination of the Berlin manuscript (ed. Fakhry, p. 143), what is clearly a doublet:

> *wa-ākadu*[157] *min hādhā wa-ashaddu wujūban 'alaiyā i'lāmuka bi-ajalli 'l-umūr allatī waqa'tu 'alaihā wa-hiya al-ghaiyah allatī yantahī aṭ-ṭab' bi's-sulūk ilaihā wa-qad waṣafahā wa-aṭāla al-waṣf fīhā man taqaddama wa-aḥad man waṣafahā wa-karrara al-qaul fīhā Abū Naṣr wa-makānuhu min hādhā 'l-'ilm makānuhu lākin lā yūjadu fī jamī' kutubihi allatī waṣalat ilā 'l-Andalus hādhā 'n-naḥw min an-naẓar wa-sanubaiyinu dhālika bi'l-qaul fīhi 'alā anna hādhā 'n-naḥw min an-naẓar laisa innamā tabaiyana lī faqaṭ fa'innahu yujadu Arisṭū fī'l-ḥādiyah 'ashara min al-Akhlāq qad qāla dhālika ghaira annahu yujmalu jiddan jamlan lā yumkin min al-iktifā' bihi faqaṭ [an] yuqafu minhu 'alā hādhā 'l-qadr.*

This offers in several places the more intelligible text, e.g. *laisa* before *innamā tabaiyana lī faqaṭ* is evidently right. In the edition of Fakhry both passages appear to form integral parts of the text. But this cannot be right. Unless it is simply a case of dislocation, they may represent different recensions, or different recipients, though we know nothing of either elsewhere in the works of Ibn Bājjah.

7. Again, *Risālat al-wadā'*, ed. Asín, p. 17, § 2 (transl. p. 45); ed. Fakhry, p. 116:

> *fa-ammā al-muḥarrik fa-hunā 'khtalafa bi'n-nāẓirīn an-naẓar wa-min hunā yansha'u al-qaul bi't-tanāsukh alladhī yaṣifuhu Suqrāṭ fī Kitāb Fādūn wa-qad abṭala dhālika Arisṭū lākin laisa 'alā 'l-wajh alladhī yu'ṭīhi al-ifhām as-sābiq min al-qaul wa-huwa alladhī sha'n an-nās an yafhamūhu* [*yafhamūna*, Asín] *min kalām Abī Naṣr fī sharḥ Nīqūmākhiyā bal 'alā 'l-jihat allatī satubaiyanu min qaulī idhā waṣaltu ilaihā*, i.e. as to the Mover, there is a difference of opinion among the investigators, whence arises the doctrine of metempsychosis (*tanāsukh*), described by Socrates in the *Phaedo*. Aristotle has refuted that, not, however, in the sense which the previous under-

---

[157] Reading *ākadu* for *aukadu* with the Oxford MS. cited below.

> standing gives of the doctrine, namely what people usually understand from the words of Abū Naṣr [sc. al-Fārābī] in the Commentary of the *Nicomachean Ethics*, but under the aspect which will be made clear from what I say when I come to it.[158]

This is further evidence for the existence of a Commentary of al-Fārābī on EN and for use made of it by Ibn Bājjah. It remains unclear why al-Fārābī should there speak about metempsychosis, unless indeed the idea is derived from Porphyry's Commentary, already several times mentioned.

8. Also, *Risālat al-wadāʿ*, ed. Asín, pp. 21-22, § 8 (transl. pp. 53-55); ed. Fakhry, pp. 121-122; an important, relatively long passage:

> *wa-qad waṣala ilainā kitāb ar-rajul al-maʿrūf bi-Abī Ḥāmid al-Ghazālī wa-sammāhu al-Munqidh waṣafa fīhi ṭarafan min sīratihi wa-dhakara annahu shāhada ʿinda iʿtizālihi umūran ilāhīyatan wa-'ltadh-dha iltidhādhan ʿaẓīman wa-mimmā qālahu fīhi*[159] *fa-kāna mā kāna mimmā lastu adhkuruhu al-bait wa-hādhihi kulluhā ẓunūn wa-ashyā' yuqīmuhā mathālāt al-ḥaqq wa-hādhā 'r-rajul yubaiyanu min amrihi annahu lam yantaqil ʿan hādhā 'ṣ-ṣinf wa-lā ʿan ḥālihi* [*mā lahu*, Asín; *māa lahu*, Fakhry] *al-ūlā* [*al-aulā*, Asín] *wa-annahu ghāliṭ au mughāliṭ* [*mutaghāliṭ*, Asín] *bi-khayālāt al-ḥaqq* [...] *ilā sā'ir mā yaqūluhu mimmā yufhamu bihi anna 'l-ghāyat al-quṣwā min ʿilm al-ḥaqq al-iltidhādh wa-qad yumkin an yaḥtajja fī taswīb hādhā 'r-ra'y bi-mā qīla fī Nīqūmākhiyā ʿindamā yaqūlu anna 'l-ardiyā' yaṭlubūna*[160] *maʿa man yufnūna nahārahum fī'l-ḥadīth*[161] *wa'l-lahw fa'innahum matā khalau bi-anfusihim taʿallamū mimmā yajidūna fī anfusihim min ar-radā'ah wa-anna 'l-akhyār ʿalā khilāf dhālika li'annahum ya'nasūna bi-anfusihim wa-yaqūlu fī 'l-ḥādiyah ʿashara annahu matā kāna 's-saʿīd saʿīdan bi'l-ḥaqīqah wa-ʿamala bi-aʿmāl as-saʿādah kāna fī iltidhādh dā'im wa-tuḥaf wa-hadāyā ilāhīya ilā sā'ir mā yaqūluhu wa-kadhālika qāla al-Ghazālī ʿinda tafarrudihi rā'a wa-samiʿa martabāt ilāhīyah wa-samiʿa aṣwātan ilāhīyah wa-radda dhālika ilā 'l-iltidhādh ghaira annahu ghafala ʿan mā qālahu fī'l-ḥādiyah ʿashara* [*ʿashrata*, Fakhry] *bi-nafsihi ʿinda mā yaqūlu: wa-takūnu sakīnah, fa-lam yata'ammal min hādhā 'l-qaul aiya mā yuthbituhu bi'l-burhān fī sā'ir kutubihi*, i.e. there has reached us the book of the man known as Abū Ḥāmid al-Ghazālī, who called it *al-Munqidh* and described in it part of his life-story. He mentioned that

[158] Moritz Steinschneider gave a slightly different translation of the passage from a Hebrew MS. (cf. *Al-Farabi*, *op. cit.*, p. 60, n. 1).

[159] The last word (*fīhi*) omitted by Fakhry.

[160] Asín's text has *yuṭlabūna*, but it is a mistake followed by Fakhry (*yuṭl.būna*).

[161] Asín: *fī'l-ḥadīthah*.

> during his retreat he saw divine manifestations and experienced a great sense of pleasure. And among other things that he said of it was: *And there came to pass what came to pass, of what I do not mention.* All these are suppositions and things which he sets up as like the truth. It is clear that this man did not move on from this kind nor from his first condition and that he was either deceived or deceiving with illusions of the truth [...] with other remarks from which it is to be understood that the ultimate aim of knowledge of the truth is pleasure. It might be possible for him to adduce as proof of this opinion what is said in the *Nicomachean Ethics* where [Aristotle] says a) that the wicked seek people with whom to spend their day in talk and amusement, for when they are alone they are pained by the wickedness that they find in themselves, whereas b) good men are the opposite of that, because they are on good terms with themselves. And he says in the Eleventh [Book] c) that when the happy man is truly happy and does the works of happiness, he enjoys constant pleasure and divine gifts and bounties, and so on. Thus al-Ghazālī said that in his solitude he saw and heard divine degrees of existence and heard divine voices, and he referred that to pleasure. He disregarded, however, what [Aristotle] himself said in the Eleventh [Book] when he says d): *And there is a tranquility*, and did not consider in regard to this expression whatever [Aristotle] establishes with proof in the rest of his books.[162]

Al-Ghazālī, says Ibn Bājjah, might have derived support for his view from passages in the *Nicomachean Ethics*, which he proceeds to give. The first of these, a) above: *al-ardi'ā' yaṭlubūna maʿa man yufnūna nahārahum* [...], i.e. EN IX, 4, 9 = 1166b 13ff., shows some resemblance to the Fez version, which is as follows:

> *wa-dhawū 'r-rad'ah yaṭlubūna qauman yaqḍūna nahārahum maʿahum wa-yahrubūna min radā'atihim fa'innahum yatadhākarūna ashyā'a kathīrah ṣaʿbah wa-yatarjjauna ashyā'a ukhar mithl hādhihi idhā kānū waḥdahum* [...].

This is perhaps as near as we get to a quotation from the Fez version in Ibn Bājjah. Arberry considered it "a very fair paraphrase" of the version.[163] It is accompanied by b) above: *al-akhyār ʿalā khilāf dhālika li'annahum ya'nasūna bi-anfusihim*, an echo of EN IX, 4, 5 = 1166a 23-24, but unlike the Fez version, which runs: *wa-lā sīyamā in*

---

[162] Asín, who read *aiya mā yuthbituhu* [...] in his text, appears to have translated *annahu mā yuthbituhu* ("que es [...] lo mismo que [...] establece"). Arthur J. Arberry translated in the Introduction to his unpublished edition of the Arabic EN: "He did not consider in his saying whatever he might have established by way of demonstrative argument."

[163] Arberry, unpublished edition.

arāda mithl hādhā an yuʿāshira dhātahu faʾinnahu yafʿalu dhālika bi-ladhdhatin.

A third passage is c) above: *matā kāna as-saʿīd saʿīdan bi'l-ḥaqīqah* [...]. Asín was content to refer to the "general ideas of Aristotle on pleasure and virtue", without seeking a parallel in the Eleventh Book.

Further, though this is cited by Ibn Bājjah not as a possible support for al-Ghazālī but as a reminder of something else, we have d) *wa-takūnu sakīnah*, also from the Eleventh Book. Asín translated "y es un reposo" and compared EN VII, c. 14 (against the indication in the text), where at § 8 the Fez version has: *al-fiʿl laisa huwa li'l-ḥarakah faqaṭ bal li's-sukūn aiḍan wa'l-ladhdhah fī's-sukūn akthar minhā fī'l-ḥarakah* (1154b 26-28). Arberry, who took c) and d) together as both referring to the Eleventh Book of the Arabic EN, for Asín's parallel prefers EN X, 8, 13, which applies very well to c). As to the words *wa-takūnu sakīnah*, Arberry translated "and there is a tranquility" and reports simply that the phrase "does not occur anywhere in the *Nicomachean Ethics* so far as what remains of our translation goes".[164] But we have what Burnet called "Aristotle's theory of rest"[165] at EN 1176b 34 = X, 6, 6 to which Ibn Bājjah evidently refers, though he appears to have confused this with another passage, EN 1127b 33 = IV, 8, 1 beginng: Οὔσης δὲ καὶ ἀναπαύσεως ἐν τῷ βίῳ [...].

It seems, however, that *sakīnah* is here used in some special sense. Al-Ghazālī's view, according to Ibn Bājjah in the *Risālat al-wadāʿ*, is expressed in the words already quoted: *al-ghāyat al-quṣwā min ʿilm al-ḥaqq al-iltidhādh*, i.e. 'the ultimate aim of knowledge of the truth is pleasure',[166] more succinctly a little later in the same work: *[al-Ghazālī] naṣaba ghayātahu al-quṣwā al-ladhdhah*, i.e. '[al-Ghazālī] made pleasure his ultimate goal'.[167] But here al-Ghazālī, according to Ibn Bājjah, shows his limitations and is open to severe criticism. Pleasure, even spiritual pleasure,[168] is not the goal. It is only the first

---

[164] *Ibid.*

[165] Aristotle, *The Ethics of Aristotle*, ed. John Burnet, London 1900 (reprinted New York 1973), p. 197, n.

[166] Cf. pp. 41f.

[167] Ibn Bājjah, *Risālat al-wadāʿ*, ed. Asín, p. 24, § 11 (transl. p. 58); ed. Fakhry, p. 124.

[168] Ed. Asín, p. 58.

stage of the mystical experience, or rather pleasure is the accompaniment of the first stage, and al-Ghazālī did not realise this:

> *yubaiyanu min amrihi annahu lam yantaqil min hādhā 'ṣ-ṣinf wa-lā ʿan ḥālihi al-ūlā* [...] *ghafala ʿan mā qālahu fī'l-ḥādiyah ʿashara binafsihi ʿinda mā yaqūlu wa-takūnu sakīnah*, i.e. he evidently did not move on from this kind, nor from his first condition [...] he disregarded what [Aristotle] himself said in the Eleventh [Book], when he says: *And there is tranquillity.*

The sense of *sakīnah* here appears to be, as in Ibn Sīnā, the second stage of the mystic's progress, of which the first stage is *al-waqt*, 'the moment', and the third, final stage *al-ittiṣāl*, 'the union' (sc. with the Divine), also in Ibn Sīnā *al-wuṣūl*, 'the arrival'.[169]

In Ibn Sīnā *sakīnah* is not simply rest or calm but is more heavily charged, to retain at least something of the transcendental significance which it has in the Qur'ān.[170] Thus in his little work *Kitāb fī 's-saʿādah* he says:

> *wa-baiyin li-man taḥaqqaqa al-umūr anna 'l-ladhdhāt al-ʿājilah laisa shai' minhā bi-saʿadah idh kullu wāḥidin minhā lā yakhlū min naqā'iṣ jammatin* [...] *minhā anna kulla man yataʿāṭāhā wa-yanhamiku fīhā inqaṭaʿat as-sakīnāt al-ilāhīyah ʿan ṣadrihi wa 'mtanaʿa al-faiḍ ar-rabūbīyah ʿan al-ḥulūl fīhi*, i.e. it is clear to anyone who has a true knowledge of the facts that no transitory pleasures constitute happiness, since not one of them is exempt from numerous defects [...] among other things, whoever is addicted to them and sunk in them [finds that] the divine *sakīnāt* are shut off from his heart and the emanation of the Lord is prevented from descending upon him.[171]

Again we have an important, long passage in Ibn Sīnā's *Kitāb al-ishārāt wa't-tanbīhāt* (*op. cit.*, pp. 202-204), which was quoted in part by Ibn Ṭufail in the introduction to *Ḥaiy ibn Yaqẓān*.[172] The text was given earlier by August F. Mehren[173] and has been translated by

---

[169] See Goichon in Ibn Sīnā, *Livre des directives et remarques*, *op. cit.*, p. 493, n. 2.

[170] Cf. Arthur Jeffery, *The Foreign Vocabulary of the Qur'ān*, Baroda 1938, p. 174, and James Robson in Samuel G. F. Brandon (ed.), *A Dictionary of Comparative Religion*, London 1970, s.v. *sakīna*.

[171] Ibn Sīnā, *Majmūʿ rasā'il ash-Shaikh ar-Ra'īs*, Haidarabad 1354/1935, p. 3.

[172] Ibn Ṭufail, *Risālat Ḥaiy ibn Yaqẓān fī asrār al-ḥikmah al-mushriqīyah*, ed. and transl. Léon Gauthier, Beirut ²1936, text pp. 6-7; transl. pp. 5-6.

[173] Ibn Sīnā, *Rasā'il (Traités mystiques)*, ed. and transl. August F. Mehren, 4 fasc., Leiden 1889-1899, fasc. II, text pp. 15-18; transl. (partial or résumé in which Mehren finds eleven stages before the final arrival) pp. 13-14.

Amélie-Marie Goichon.[174] *Sakīnah* is here mentioned twice, first:

> *wa-laʿallahu ilā hādhā 'l-ḥadd tastaʿlī ʿalaihi ghawāshīhi wa-yazūlu huwa ʿan sakīnatihi*, i.e. and perchance [as he goes forward] towards this limit, feelings of weakness assail him and he ceases from his calm.[175]

There follows almost immediately in the next directive (*ishārah*):

> *thumma innahu la-tablughu bihi ar-riyāḍah mablaghan yanqalibu lahu waqtuhu sakīnatan*, i.e. then indeed the spiritual exercise brings him to a point at which his moment changes to quietude.[176]

This meaning gives to the expression *wa-takūnu sakīnah* a significance which is appropriate and cogent in the context *vis-à-vis* al-Ghazālī, whose account of his experiences as set down in *al-Munqidh* Ibn Bājjah is criticising. We might cite for *sakīnah* EN X, 7, 6 = 1177b 4 (a reminder of the pleasure of the rest) or compare EN VII, 14, 8 = 1154b 26-28 (the importance of leisure).[177] But Ibn Bājjah has said of al-Ghazālī that in his description of his spiritual experiences he has neglected something evidently of great importance, and the passages last cited lack relevance to the discussion. On the other hand, the words *wa-takūnu sakīnah* with *sakīnah* meaning quietude in the mystical sense are very relevant, as signifying a stage in the mystical experience which al-Ghazālī has failed to mention (*ghafala ʿan mā qālahu fī 'l-ḥādiya ʿashara*) and, it is implied, knows nothing about. What then becomes of his claims seems to be the further implication.

The words are certainly not Aristotle's, though attributed to the 'Eleventh Book' of the *Nicomachean Ethics*, i.e. to Book X of the Greek text, where they do not appear. In similar cases[178] we have referred the quotations to the commentaries on EN, of which we know at least two, those made by Porphyry and al-Fārābī, once available in Arabic, though now lost.[179] Here we can do no better than make the same reference in general terms.

---

[174] Ibn Sīnā, *Livre des directives et remarques*, *op. cit.*, pp. 493-497.

[175] It is plain from this expression that Ibn Sīnā here thinks of *sakīnah* as a subjective state of some kind, but at the same time it is evidently a stage in the spiritual progress, cf. above (p. 44, n. 169) and the next directive.

[176] Ibn Sīnā, *Rasāʾil*, *op. cit.*, text p. 203; transl. p. 494.

[177] Cf. above, p. 43.

[178] See above, pp. 36f.

[179] See above, pp. 12, 18f., 25.

9. *Risālat al-wadāʿ*, ed. Asín, p. 33, § 20 (transl. p. 74); ed. Fakhry, p. 134:

> *yaqūlu Abū Naṣr anzil*[180] *anna insānan ʿalima jamīʿ mā fī kutub Arisṭū*[181] *ghair annahu lam yaʿmal bi-shaiʾ mimmā fīhā wa-ākhar ʿamila illā annahu lam yaʿlam fa-yafḍulu al-ʿāmil al-jāhil ʿalā at-tārik al-ʿālim*,[182] i.e. Abū Naṣr [= al-Fārābī] says: Suppose that a man knows all there is in the books of Aristotle, but does nothing that is in them, and another does [what is in them] but without knowing, then the ignorant man who does [what is in them] is superior to the knowledgeable man who does not.

Asín mentions that he had not found this passage among the collected works of al-Fārābī.[183] A note of Steinschneider suggests that it may belong to al-Fārābī's Commentary on EN.[184] On the other hand, there is a very similar passage in the *Fuṣūl al-madanī* of al-Fārābī, beginning: *nunazzil*[185] *insānain aḥaduhumā qad ʿalima mā fī kutub Arisṭūṭālīs kullihā* [...], which is quite possibly the passage which Ibn Bājjah had in mind.

10. Finally, *Risālat al-wadāʿ*, ed. Asín, p. 35, § 23 (transl. pp. 77-78); ed. Fakhry, p. 137:

> *wa-ka-dhālika al-ʿaql alladhī yadhkuruhu Arisṭū fī ʾs-sādisah min Nīqūmākhiyā innamā huwa muʿadd li-an tufʿala ʿanhu al-afʿāl allatī tūjibuhā al-ḥikmah*,[186] i.e. and similarly the intelligence which Aris-

---

[180] Fakhry's text has *aqūlu [inna]*, which is the reading of the Bodleian MS. Pococke 206, but it is a mistake for *anzil [anna]*, read by Asín. An exact parallel is at § 19 of Ibn Bājjah's *Ittiṣāl al-ʿaql bi'l-insān* (*On the Union of the Intellect with Man*) in Asín's edition (in: *al-Andalus* 7 [1942], pp. 1-47, here p. 20 [transl. p. 43]): *fa-anzil anna tilka ar-rutbah maujūdah li-shakhṣin mā*, and *anzil* is confirmed by the Hebrew translation (see note 184), as well as by the similar passage in al-Fārābī's *Fuṣūl al-madanī* mentioned below.

[181] The Bodleian MS. followed by Fakhry has *jamīʿ mā kataba Arisṭū*, apparently by omission of *fī*, which the Hebrew translation (see note 184) retained.

[182] For *fa-yafḍulu al-ʿāmil al-jāhil* [...] Asín read from the Berlin MS.: *fa-tufaḍḍilu* [sic] *al-auwal ʿalā 'th-thānī*.

[183] Ibn Bājjah, *Risālat al-wadāʿ*, ed. Asín, p. 74, n. 1.

[184] Steinschneider, *Al-Farabi*, *op. cit.*, p. 60, n. 1, where Steinschneider translates from what he calls "der incorrecten und undeutlichen Leipziger [Hebrew] HS.", not further specified here: "Desshalb sagt Abu Nazar: Setzen wir den Fall, dass ein Mensch Alles wisse, was in den Büchern des Aristoteles steht [...]."

[185] *Nunazzil* corresponds to the Arabic verbal form II as in the printed text (al-Fārābī, *Fuṣūl al-madanī*, *op. cit.*, p. 169, § 93).

[186] *Al-ḥikmah* stands in the MS. and is printed by Fakhry in his text, omitted by Asín in both text and translation. It is not in the Greek at 1140b 4-6 and 1140b 20-21.

> totle mentions in the Sixth [Book] of the *Nicomachean Ethics* as only intended for there to be done through it the acts which wisdom necessitates.

Asín thought of EN VI, 5, 4 = 1140b 20-21, where a similar definition is given. The Arabic of these passages, missing in the Fez manuscript like most of Book VI,[187] is not available for comparison.

From these citations it is evident that Ibn Bājjah knew and used an Arabic translation of the *Nicomachean Ethics* in 11 Books. While it cannot be proved that this was the version found in the Fez manuscript, this would be a natural assumption. Hence Arberry thought that Ibn Bājjah (d. 533/1139) might have seen the archetype of the Fez manuscript (dated 619/1222). To this it may be added that, as we have seen, the surprising mention of Hermes/Hermias (no. 4, above) definitely stated to be in the *Nicomachean Ethics*, but certainly not in the Greek original nor in the Arabic translation, as we have it, is probably to be referred to Porphyry in the 12-Book work noted by Ibn an-Nadīm.[188] Similarly, a passage like *Tadbīr al-mutawaḥḥid*, ed. Asín, pp. 59-60 (transl. p. 98); ed. Fakhry, p. 78:

> *ka-aqwām yadhkuruhum fī kibār al-anfus Arisṭūṭālīs ḥarramū* [*kharamū*, Fakhry] *anfusahum wa-muddatahum ʿindamā aiqanū anna ʿaduwahum yaghlibuhum*, i.e. like people mentioned by Aristotle among the great-spirited, who devoted themselves and the term of their lives when they were certain that the enemy would overcome them,

may be traceable to Porphyry. Asín followed by Fakhry compared *Eudemian Ethics* III, c. 1 *ad finem* (1230a) (discussion of courage and states resembling courage), but in this case there is strictly no parallel.[189] We should rather look for a lead in the words *kibār al-anfus*, 'the great-spirited', which suggest EN IV, c. 3, where the great-spirited (magnanimous) man is discussed. It turns out, however, that there we have for *kibār al-anfus* a somewhat different expres-

[187] Cf. above, p. 1, n. 3.

[188] Cf. above, p. 26.

[189] Asín and other editors of Arabic philosophical texts occasionally adduce for comparison passages from the *Eudemian Ethics*, *Magna Moralia* and even the little work *On Virtues and Vices*. All such citations in the Arabic authors will have been at second hand, e.g. from Porphyry's Commentary. There seems to be no trace of an Arabic translation of any of the ethical works of Aristotle, except the *Nicomachean Ethics*.

sion, *al-kabīrī al-anfus* and *kabīrū al-anfus* (1124a 24, 28) and, apart from this, the passages are again not parallel. We are thus thrown back on the position that Ibn Bājjah's mention of Aristotle here looks like another reference to Porphyry's Commentary.[190]

Ibn Ṭufail (d. 561/1185-1186), like Ibn Bājjah a native of Spain, in the introduction to his celebrated *Ḥaiy ibn Yaqẓān* has an interesting passage in which he mentions al-Fārābī and al-Fārābī's Commentary on the *Nicomachean Ethics*, as follows:

> *wa-ammā mā waṣala ilainā min kutub Abī Naṣr fa-aktharuhā fī 'l-manṭiq wa-mā warada minhā fī 'l-falsafah fa-hiya kathīrat ash-shukūk. fa-qad athbata fī Kitāb al-millah al-fāḍilah baqā' an-nufūs ash-sharīrah ba'd al-mawt fī ālām lā nihāyata lahā baqā' lā nihāyata lahu. thumma ṣaraha fī 's-Siyāsa al-madanīyah bi-annaha munḥallah wa-ṣā'irah ilā 'l-'adam wa-annahu lā baqā'a illā li'n-nufūs al-fāḍilah al-kāmilah. thumma waṣafa fī sharḥ Kitāb al-akhlāq shai'an min amr as-sa'ādah al-insānīyah wa-annahā innamā takūnu fī hādhihi 'l-ḥaiyāt wa-fī hādhihi 'd-dār. thumma qāla bi-'aqbi dhālika kalāman hādhā ma'nāhu: wa-kullu mā yudhkaru ghair hādhā fa-huwa hadhayān wa-khurāfāt 'ajā'iz. fa-hādhā qad a'yasa an-nās jamī'an min raḥmat Allāh wa-ṣaiyara al-fāḍil wa'sh-sharīr fī rutbah wāḥidah*, i.e. as to what has reached us of the books of Abū Naṣr [= al-Fārābī], most of them are on logic, and those of them that have come dealing with philosophy contain many doubtful matters. In the *Book of the Excellent Community* (*Kitāb al-millah al-fāḍilah*) he affirmed the survival of the souls of the wicked after death for ever in everlasting pains.[191] Then he stated in the *Political Government* (*Siyāsah al-madanīyah*)[192] that they dissolve and pass away, and that there is no survival except for virtuous and perfect souls. Then he described in the Commentary of the *Book of Ethics* (*Kitāb al-akhlāq*)[193] something of the nature of

[190] Cf. some remarks of Fakhry in Ibn Bājjah, *Rasā'il*, *op. cit.*, p. 21.

[191] al-Fārābī, *Kitāb al-milla wa-nuṣūṣ ukhrā (Book of Religion and Related Texts)*, ed. Muḥsin Mahdī, Beirut 1968, p. 45. Al-Fārābī there speaks in general terms of the misery (*shaqā'*) of the wicked in the after-life and of retribution (*iqtiṣāṣ*) for their misdeeds; Ibn Ṭufail seems to have embroidered this. Cf. Mahdi in *ibid.*, pp. 13-14.

[192] al-Fārābī, *as-Siyāsāt* [sic] *al-madanīyah*, Haidarabad 1346/1927, p. 53, cf. also al-Fārābī, *Risālah fī arā' ahl al-madīnah al-fāḍilah*, ed. Friedrich Dieterici, Leiden 1895 (reprinted Frankfurt am Main 1999), p. 67; al-Fārābī, *Der Musterstaat*, transl. Friedrich Dieterici, Leiden 1900 (reprinted Frankfurt am Main 1999), p. 106.

[193] Ockley translated *fī Kitāb al-akhlāq*, a variant in some MSS. for *fī sharḥ Kitāb al-akhlāq*, cf. Ibn Ṭufail, *Philosophus Autodidactus or Ḥaiy ibn Yaqẓān*, transl. Simon Ockley, London 1708 (reprinted Cairo 1905), p. 12. For the variants see Léon

> man's happiness and that it is only in this life and in this abode. Then immediately after this he declared: *And everything that is mentioned apart from this is nonsense and old wives' tales.* This makes all men despair of the mercy of God and puts good and bad on one level.[194]

We do not have the text of al-Fārābī to which this refers. On the other hand, evidently the same text is the subject of an interesting discussion by Ibn Bājjah,[195] who denies that al-Fārābī in his Commentary on the *Ethics* (*fīmā sharaḥahu min Kitāb al-akhlāq*) said what is attributed to him (by whom Ibn Bājjah does not say, but he is not referring to Ibn Ṭufail),[196]

> that survival after death is separation, and there is no happiness except the happiness of the city and no existence except the existence perceived by the senses, and that what is said of there being another existence, different from the existence perceived by the senses, is old wives' tales (*khurāfāt ʿajāʾiz*).[197]

Such a view, says Ibn Bājjah, is not the view of al-Fārābī, and is wrongly attributed to him.[198]

Moses Maimonides (Mōše ben Maimon, Mūsā b. Maimūn), born Cordova 1135, died Fusṭāṭ 1204, is another author who used the Arabic version of the *Nicomachean Ethics* in 11 Books. In his well-known *Dalālat al-ḥāʾirīn* (*Guide of the Perplexed*) we have:

> *wa-qad dhakara Arisṭū fī tāsiʿat al-Akhlāq anna hākadhā kāna al-amr al-mashhūr fī al-milal qadīmah ʿindahum. qāla bi-hādhā 'n-naṣṣ: adh-dhabāʾiḥ al-qadīmah wa'l-ijtimāʿāt kānat takūnu baʿd jamʿ ath-thimār ka-annahā qarābīn min ajl al-faraghah* [sic]. *hādhā naṣṣuhu,* i.e. Aristotle mentioned in the Ninth of the *Ethics* that this was the well-known practice in the religions of old. He said, in the actual words of the text: *The ancient sacrifices and assemblies among them were after the*

Gauthier's edition of Ibn Ṭufail, *Ḥaiy ibn Yaqẓān*, *op. cit.*, p. 14.

194 *Ibid.*, text pp. 13-14; transl. p. 12; Ockley's English translation, p. 12.

195 From an extract without title in Bodleian MS. Pococke 206, fol. 125a *et sqq.* See below, pp. 88f.; for a more complete treatment of the passage, also Douglas M. Dunlop, "Remarks on a Text of Avempace", in: Renato Traini (ed.), *Studi in onore di Francesco Gabrieli nel suo ottantesimo compleanno*, vol. I, Rome 1984, pp. 291-300.

196 Ibn Ṭufail was Ibn Bājjah's junior, and his *Ḥaiy ibn Yaqẓān* was written towards 1169 or even later, long after Ibn Bājjah's death in 1139.

197 So apparently in the MS., *khurāfāt a-ʿajāʾiz* further down.

198 Cf. *ibid.*: *hādhā kulluhu bāṭil wa-makdhūb bihi ʿalā Abī Naṣr.*

> *gathering of the fruits, as if they were offerings for the holiday!* This is his actual text.[199]

The same passage will be found with a single unimportant change at EN VIII, 9, 5. The number of the Book of EN in the text is of course that of the Arabic version. Similarly at *Guide of the Perplexed* III, 49, 113a,[200] we have a reference to Aristotle in the Ninth Book of the *Ethics* for man's need of friends throughout his life, i.e. the passage 1155a 3ff., at the beginning of Book VIII of the Greek. One phrase of the *Ethics* is repeated three times by Maimonides, i.e. EN III, 10, 10 = 1118b 2: *hādhihi 'l-ḥāssah ʿār ʿalainā.*[201]

Maimonides refers also to al-Fārābī's Commentary on EN as follows:

> *qāla Abū Naṣr fī ṣadr sharḥihi li-kitāb Nīqūmākhiyā. qāla wa-ammā 'lladhīna lahum qudrah an yanqulū anfusahum min khulq ilā khulq fa-ulāʾika humu 'lladhīna qāla Aflāṭūn fīhim inna ʿināyat Allāh bihim akthar*, i.e. Abū Naṣr [= al-Fārābī] said in the first part of his Commentary on the *Nicomachean Ethics*: *As regards those who have the power to make their souls pass from ethical quality to ethical quality, they are those of whom Plato said that God's care for them is greater.*[202]

Elsewhere al-Fārābī speaks of passing from ethical quality to ethical quality (*at-tanaqqul min khulq ilā khulq*) as treated of in the 'little *Nīqūmākhiyā*' of Aristotle.[203] The idea is explained as passing from one ethical quality to another in order to attain supreme virtue.[204] If this is the meaning, the source may well be Porphyry, i.e. Porphyry's *tafsīr* (Commentary on the *Ethics*).[205]

A slightly older contemporary of Maimonides, Ibn Rushd (520/1126-595/1198), also used an Arabic translation of the *Nicomachean Ethics* basically the same as that contained in the Fez manuscript. Ibn

---

[199] Text: Moses Maimonides, *Dalālat al-ḥāʾirīn*, ed. and transl. Salomon Munk, 3 vols., Paris 1856-1866 (reprinted Osnabrück 1964), III, 43, 96a. Transl.: Moses Maimonides, *The Guide of the Perplexed (Dalālat al-ḥāʾirīn)*, transl. Shlomo Pines, Chicago 1963, pp. 571-572.

[200] Transl. p. 601.

[201] Text II, 36, 79b; III, 8, 12b; III, 49, 117a; transl. pp. 371, 432, 608.

[202] Text III, 18, 38b-39a; transl. p. 476.

[203] The passage has already been given above, pp. 12f. For the 'little *Nīqūmākhiyā*' see pp. 12ff.

[204] Maimonides, *Dalālat al-ḥāʾirīn*, transl. Munk, *op. cit.*, vol. III, p. 139.

[205] See also below, p. 87.

Rushd remarks in the epilogue of his *Middle Commentary* (*talkhīṣ*) on the *Ethics* that at first he had only the first four Books and later received the complete work through the good offices of a friend, called in the Latin translation "Omar, filius Martini".[206] Another version of the same incident calls the friend Abu ʿAmor (Abū ʿAmr) b. Martin and says that the complete copy was brought from Egypt. There seems to be enough evidence to allow us to say that this copy of the Arabic EN was in 11 Books.[207]

Ibn Rushd's Commentary on the *Ethics* is lost in Arabic, apart from a few fragments—short quotations in the margins of the Fez manuscript—, but survives in both a Hebrew and a Latin translation. The Latin version of the Commentary, available in the Juntine edition of the works of Aristotle, is in 10 Books, corresponding to the Greek. Similarly, of the thirty or so quotations from the original Arabic of the Commentary found in the margins of the Fez manuscript,[208] none is from the 'Seventh Book', which has simply been dropped. This calls for explanation, and since we have hitherto had no mention by an Arabic author of the *Nicomachean Ethics* in 10 Books, it is natural to think that Ibn Rushd himself has for the first time rejected the 'Seventh Book' of the Arabic *Nicomachean Ethics* as no integral part of it. On the other hand, the *Middle Commentary* on the *Ethics* is accompanied in some manuscripts by a preamble which, if acceptable as it stands, provides a very different solution. The preamble begins:

> Dixit Abunazrin Alfarabius in commento suo super hunc librum: Partes huius libri sunt X, quod declaratur per hoc quod auctor terminat quemlibet tractatum per principium sequentis. In tractatu primo declaratur res felicitatis secundum quod est felicitas ciuitatum. In secundo est summa collectionis uirtutum moralium secundum unamquamque uirtutem et rememoratio suarum descriptionum. In tertio mentio fit de rebus uoluntariis et distinctio inter eas et non uoluntarias,

---

[206] Amable Jourdain, *Recherches critiques sur l'âge et l'origine des traductions latines d'Aristote. Nouvelle édition revue et augmentée par Charles Jourdain*, Paris 1843, reprinted New York 1960 (Burt Franklin Bibliographical Series; 19) with a new title *Recherches sur les anciennes traductions latines d'Aristote*, or (on spine) *Recherches critiques sur les anciennes traductions d'Aristote*, p. 439.

[207] Cf. Lawrence V. Berman, "Ibn Rushd's *Middle Commentary* on the *Nicomachean Ethics* in Medieval Hebrew Literature", in: Jean Jolivet (ed.), *Multiple Averroès*, Paris 1978, pp. 287-321, here p. 291.

[208] These are discussed by Lawrence V. Berman in his paper "Excerpts from the Lost Arabic Original of Ibn Rushd's *Middle Commentary* on the *Nicomachean Ethics*", *loc. cit.*, pp. 31-59.

> et in ipso etiam est determinatio quarundam uirtutum ex illis quas in summa posuit in tractatu secundo. In quarto est determinatio residuarum uirtutum quarum mentio facta fuerat in tractatu secundo. In quinto loquitur de iusto et iusticia. In sexto est notificatio uirtutum intellectualium. In septimo loquitur de continente et incontinente, et dicitur aliquid de delectatione et tristicia. In VIII de modis dilectionis et modis amicicie. In IX de modis actionum prodeuntiuum a modis dilectionis et modis amicicie. In decimum [sic] est complementum dictionis in dilectationibus [sic] et complementum dictionis in felicitate et declaracio indigencie regiminis et gubernationis ad faciendum ciues bonos. Et principium cuiuslibet istorum tractatuum est postremum tractatus antecedentis ipsum. Ex hinc ergo declaratur quod tractatus qui ponitur inter tractatum sextum et septimum in abreuiata compilatione quorundam alexandrinorum huius libri non est de ipso libro.[209]

This notice clearly attributes to al-Fārābī the statement that EN, in Arabic, that is, is in 10 Books, and proceeds to give a short table of contents. What is more, the statement is said to come in al-Fārābī's Commentary on EN, a work which is quoted by and was apparently in the hands of the predecessors or contemporaries of Ibn Rushd (Ibn Bājjah, Ibn Ṭufail and Maimonides), as we have seen. Since theirs was evidently an 11-Book *Nicomachean Ethics*,[210] like the Fez manuscript in this as in other respects, it is very surprising. Having al-Fārābī's Commentary, which they clearly valued, since they used it, why did they not accept his (correct) idea of a 10-Book EN? Was the statement that Aristotle's *Ethics* is in 10 Books really before them in al-Fārābī's Commentary as mentioned? Is there not some mistake in the notice which appears to say so? If the attribution to al-Fārābī is right, of course, Ibn Rushd was not the first to reject the 'Seventh Book', but was simply following al-Fārābī. There is an element of paradox here. In attempting to clear it, we have to take account of two considerations. First, the reference in the last sentence of the notice is to the *Summa Alexandrinorum*, not to the complete version of EN. This points away from al-Fārābī, who made no use of the

---

[209] The beginning and end of the text are given by Lawrence V. Berman, "Ibn Rushd's *Middle Commentary*", *loc. cit.*, p. 308, n. 2, from Dominique Salman, "The Medieval Latin Translations of Alfarabi's Works", in: *The New Scholasticism* 13 (1939), pp. 245-261, here p. 250. I quote from José María Millás-Vallicrosa, *Las traducciones orientales en los manuscritos de la Biblioteca Catedral de Toledo*, Madrid 1942, pp. 67-68, who might have had a more correct MS.

[210] This is certain for Ibn Bājjah and Maimonides.

Summma and cannot have known it, since he died many years before its appearance in Arabic,[211] and towards Hermannus Alemannus, the translator of the *Middle Commentary* of Ibn Rushd on EN. This was in 1240.[212] Hermannus also knew the *Summa Alexandrinorum*, which he translated into Latin in 1243/44.[213] Hermannus could therefore have written, i.e. added, the last sentence of the notice ("Et hinc declaratur [...]"). But so also al-Fārābī could have written: "Et hinc declaratur quod tractatus qui ponitur inter tractatum sextum et septimum non est de ipso", i.e. the last sentence with omission of the words: "in abreuiata compilatione quorundam alexandrinorum huius libri." Clearly no comment would be necessary if the sentence stood, as it doubtless did originally, in the preamble to a work dealing with the Arabic EN, before and after this, in 11 Books, but it cannot have seemed clear to Hermannus, who did not have the 11-Book text and found 10 Books of Ibn Rushd's *Middle Commentary*, without reference to the *Summa Alexandrinorum*. It is not difficult to think that the words: "in abreuiata compilatione quorundam alexandrinorum huius libri", are an addition to the original text due to Hermannus, by way of explanation. The second consideration is that while Ibn Bājjah and Maimonides used the 11-Book version of the *Ethics*, i.e. one containing the 'Seventh Book', they do not quote from it. This indeed applies generally. The 'Seventh Book' is scarcely ever referred to.[214]

The case of al-Fārābī seems to be put beyond doubt by a long passage in a Hebrew manuscript, quoted by Berman,[215] the second part of which is the preamble just discussed, elsewhere attributed, as

---

211 Al-Fārābī died in 339/950. Ibn Zurʿah, author of the Arabic behind the *Summa Alexandrinorum*, was then a boy of seven or eight years (cf. pp. 69ff.).

212 René A. Gauthier in Aristotle, *Ethica Nicomachea* (Aristoteles Latinus; XXVI, 1-3), Leiden/Brussels 1972-1974, fasc. I, p. CXLIX; Berman, "Ibn Rushd's *Middle Commentary*", *loc. cit.*, pp. 293 and 308, n. 2.

213 Gauthier in Aristotle, *Ethica Nicomachea*, *op. cit.*, p. CL.

214 The Cairo MS. (for which see below) is exceptional in having one or two quotations from this source, cf. pp. 82f.

215 Paris, Bibliothèque Nationale, MS. Hébreu 956, for which see Berman, "Ibn Rushd's *Middle Commentary*", *loc. cit.*, pp. 298-299 and 302-311, including p. 306: "That which is well-known in this connection is that Aristotle composed books on ethics. The first is this book which is called *Nicomachean* and the second is that called *Eudemian* and the third is the book called *The Great Statements* (*Magna Moralia*)."

we have seen, to al-Fārābī,[216] but here anonymous. The first part of the Hebrew manuscript is also anonymous, but bears marks of the style of al-Fārābī at his most didactic which practically exclude another authorship. Berman is of opinion that what we have here is from the introduction to the Commentary of al-Fārābī on the *Nicomachean Ethics*. This must be right, since we cannot assume that in the Latin notice "Abunazrin Alfarabius" has been substituted for Averroes.[217] Nor can we assign a different authorship to the two parts of the Hebrew passage and, while admitting that the first part is by al-Fārābī, attempt to save the second part of the passage for Ibn Rushd. Both parts belong together, as seems proved by the recurrence in both of the same semi-technical expression 'Law and Custom' (once as an alternative title for the *Nicomachean Ethics*).[218]

It is al-Fārābī then who has written the preamble to the *Middle Commentary* on EN, and he there explains that the number of the Books is shown to be 10 by the fact that each Book ends with the beginning of the next Book. This evidently refers not to the formulae of closure *tammat al-maqālah* [...] and *ākhir al-maqālah* [...], and the formula of opening, the *bismillāh* followed by the number of the Book, but to the words repeated at the beginning of a Book from the end of the previous Book. In the Fez manuscript Book VI ends with some nearly indecipherable words, perhaps *wa-baʿd hādhā fal-naqul innā ṣanaʿnā 'btidā'an ākhar*, which are not in the Greek. Book VII (VIII of the Arabic) then begins, following the Greek, with very similar wording: *qāla Arisṭū fal-naṣir baʿd hādhihi 'l-aqāwīl ilā 'btidā' ākhar*. Another example[219] is at the end of Book IX of the Arabic text and the beginning of Book X, where the last (superfluous) words of Book IX are:

> *wa-ammā fī jamīʿ al-maḥabbāt allatī anwāʿuhā mukhtalifah fa'inna 'l-mulā'amah tusāwī al-maḥabbah kamā qad qīla*,

and Book X begins:

---

[216] Above, pp. 51f.

[217] This substitution has been pointed to by Dominique Salman, "The Medieval Latin Translations of Alfarabi's Works", *loc. cit.*, p. 251, but there is no reason to think that it has taken place here.

[218] Berman, "Ibn Rushd's *Middle Commentary*", *loc. cit.*, pp. 306 and 310.

[219] In the Fez MS. the connecting words between the Books of EN are mostly omitted.

> *qāla wa-ammā [fī] jamīʿ al-maḥabbāt allatī anwāʿuhā mukhtalifah fa'inna 'l-mulā'amah tusāwī wa-tusallimu al-maḥabbah kamā qad qīla.*

It was apparently the absence of such connecting words at the beginning and end of the 'Seventh Book'[220] and the presence of words connecting Book VI and Book VII (Book VIII of the Arabic) which suggested to al-Fārābī that the 'Seventh Book' belonged elsewhere and was no part of the *Nicomachean Ethics*.[221] Succeeding generations, however, made little of his finding, perhaps because, like the Fez text, their manuscripts of the Arabic EN did not always show the connecting words between the Books which al-Fārābī laid stress on. The 11-Book EN evidently continued to be used down to the time of Ibn Rushd and later.[222]

IV

The most striking feature of the Arabic version of the *Nicomachean Ethics* is its additional Book, i.e. it is in 11 Books as against the 10 Books of the original Greek. This is due not to a redistribution of the material but to the insertion of another Book between Books VI and VII,[223] so that Book VII and later Books are here numbered one in advance of the numeration of the Greek. The text of this intrusive 'Seventh Book' as it stands in the Fez manuscript is approximately of the same length as a Book of the Greek text (the Books there of course varying somewhat), but lacks the beginning which has not been preserved, or at least not in legible form.[224] It is also unfortunately defective at the end, though we have in the manuscript at the top of a page a closure, as follows: *ākhir* [or *tammat*] *al-maqālah as-sābiʿah min al-akhlāq wa'l-ḥamdu li'llāh wa-sallama ʿalā ʿibādihi*

---

220 The formula of closure *ākhir al-maqālah as-sābiʿah* [...] is, however, given, see below.

221 His attention may first have been drawn to the additional Book by finding 10 Books only mentioned in Porphyry's Commentary.

222 The Fez MS. itself was copied 1222 (cf. above, p. 1).

223 In the Cairo MS. the additional Book comes before Book VI, see pp. 79 and 83.

224 The beginning of the 'Seventh Book' has been so damaged as to remain practically illegible, in spite of the best efforts of the photography department at Cambridge University Library. It began with the *bismillāh*, like the other Books. In the next line only *al-maqālah* [...] can be made out.

'lladhīna 'ṣṭafā, i.e. there is a gap immediately preceding of at least one folio.

The subject-matter of this 'Seventh Book' is the ethical virtues and vices discussed in Books III-V of the Greek, the discussion dealing successively with courage, the five dispositions commonly called courage, temperance, good temper or calm, liberality, magnificence, magnanimity, other minor virtues, friendship and finally justice. The maximum extent of what has survived of the 'Seventh Book' is EN III, c. 6 - V, c. 7, i.e. nearly the whole of the section on the virtues and vices. This material is somewhat differently arranged in the 'Seventh Book' with a glance perhaps at some other listing, and most of the virtues are named differently, e.g. we have here for 'courage' and 'friendship' *najdah* and *ṣadāqah* respectively, but in the authentic Books of the Arabic EN *shajāʿah* and *maḥabbah*.[225]

The case here is evidently different from that of Aristotle's zoological works, several of which have been placed together in the Arabic *Kitāb al-ḥayawān* (*Book of Animals*) in 19 Books, i.e. Aristotle's *History of Animals* (10 Books), *Parts of Animals* (4 Books) and *Generation of Animals* (5 Books), for the 'Seventh Book' of the Arabic *Ethics*, though Aristotelian, is evidently not by Aristotle. The Greek background, however, is obvious from quotations from Homer (5, 10) and Theognis (4, 4), the latter unnamed, also from a general reference to the Greek poets (6, 1) or a reference like that of 5, 8 to sailors on a quadrireme (*mallāḥī dhāt al-arbaʿah ṣufūf*) or mention of Pythagoreans and Rhadamanthys (9, 10). Greek certainly is (9, 11) 'the father of Androtion, who wasted olive oil belonging to the city' (*abū Andrūṭyūn alladhī kāna yuqaṭṭiru min az-zait li'l-madīnah*), with the possibility that Androtion is Demosthenes' opponent of that name, and the Greek equivalents of some expressions occur once or twice, as at 5, 5 'money was called in Greek νόμισμα' (*yusammā ad-dīnār bi'l-yūnānīyah nāmūsī mā*), cf. 1, 3 'called in Greek' (*alladhī yuqālu lahu bi'l-yūnānīyah*). Aristotelian equally clearly is the scheme according to which the material of the 'Seventh Book' is arranged (see above); mention by name of Philoxenus, son of Eryxis at 3, 3 (unnamed in EN III, 10, 10, but cf. EE III, 2, 12); and especially at 8, 3 the

---

[225] Sometimes *ṣadāqah*, see further below, p. 59.

reference to *al-aqāwīl al-khārijah* which can only mean the 'exoteric teachings' (ἐξωτερικοὶ λόγοι) mentioned half-a-dozen times in the works of Aristotle. In the *Nicomachean Ethics* the exoteric teachings are mentioned twice, at I, 13, 9 = 1102a 26-27 (the soul consists of an irrational and a rational part) and again at VI, 4, 2 = 1140a 2-3 (making is different from doing). The passage in the 'Seventh Book', 8, 3, is as follows:

> *fa-ammā sā'ir al-faḍā'il fa-qad qulnā fīhā fī 'l-aqāwīl al-khārijah wa-qad qīla fīhā qaulan kāfiyan fa'innahu lammā kānat aqāwīl mushtarakah ta'ummu al-akhlāq faqad sullimat fīhā aqāwīl kathīrah jaiyidah wa-lākin rubbamā ṭalabnā al-ashyā' al-khāṣṣīyah akthar min al-ashyā' al-khafīyah wa-khalīq an yaqūla qā'ilun inna 'l-'illah fī dhālika min ajli annā maḥbūb li'l-karamah akthar min ḥubbinā li'l-falsafah*, i.e. as to the rest of the virtues, we have already spoken of them in the exoteric discourses, where sufficient has been said. For these being common doctrines applying to ethics in general, there are contained in them many excellent doctrines. But perhaps we seek special things more than concealed things. Someone may say that the reason for that is that we are loved because of honour more than because of philosophy.

This is evidently Aristotelian. For the last words we may compare EN I, 6, 1 and the parallels cited by the commentators.[226] The passage also affords confirmation of the view of Jacob Bernays and Werner Jaeger that the exoteric teachings "were definite writings, and in fact the literary works of Aristotle".[227] The source can only be guessed at. In any case, the 'Seventh Book' is not by Aristotle. It contains references to a mysterious Ibn 'Aus (1, 3), perhaps a corruption of some Greek name, and to a scarcely less mysterious Sā'ūs (6, 9), mentioned elsewhere as a pupil of the great Hippocrates.[228] It mentions also the Banū 'Udhra and the Arabic poets who sang of them (3, 5). These references are evidently no part of a Greek text and extraneous to EN.

Positive indications of a later date than Aristotle for the Greek original are not numerous, but we have the following at 8, 4-5:

---

[226] Especially Burnet, *in loco*.

[227] Jaeger, *Aristotle*, *op. cit.*, p. 249. See also Gauthier and Jolif in Aristotle, *L'Éthique à Nicomaque*, *op. cit.*, vol. I/1, p. 66, and more recently Enrico Berti, *La filosofia del "primo" Aristotele*, Milan ²1997.

[228] Cf. Abū Sulaimān as-Sijistānī, *Muntakhab ṣiwān al-ḥikmah*, *op. cit.*, p. 20, § 24.

> *wāḍiʿ an-nawāmīs fī jamīʿ hādhihi yurīdu at-taṣḥīḥ wa-an yusāwī bain al-muntaqiṣ wa-bain al-mutazaiyid bi-mā yazīdu wa-yanquṣu wa'l-Masīḥīya* [MS. *al-Masā'iḥah*] *fī hādhā khalīq an takūna lā tuḥsin wa-an yakūna laʿiban fa'innahum yazʿumūna anna 'l-maḍrūb bi's-siyāṭ lahu al-birr akthar wa-laisa yaẓhur dhālika li-wāḍiʿ an-nawāmīs min ajl anna lahu akthar ar-radīʾ wa-hādhā huwa an yakūna lahu aqall* [sc. *al-birr*], i.e. the legislator in all this wished to rectify and to equalise between the man who falls short and the man who has an excess by what the one exceeds and is defective [respectively]. It seems that the Christians in this do not do well and that it is ludicrous, for they assert that he who is beaten with whips has more good. It does not appear so to the legislator, because the man has more evil, which means that he has less [good].

Here the correction to *al-Masīḥīyah*, 'the Christians', is virtually certain[229] and gives an indication of the comparatively late date of the Greek text from which the writer of the 'Seventh Book' drew his material. Further, there appears to be some animus against the Christians, contrasted here with the impartial law-giver. Both indications are appropriate for Porphyry as author, the author of a work against the Christians now lost, like his Commentary on the *Nicomachean Ethics*. Since, however, we have the notice in the *Fihrist* of an Arabic translation of the *Ethics* with a Commentary by Porphyry in 12 Books, we probably need look no further for the Greek source of the 'Seventh Book' in the Fez manuscript. It would be consonant with its character to allow that the 'Seventh Book' is part of the *tafsīr* of Porphyry,[230] i.e. his Commentary in its Arabic form. We might thus obtain an explanation of the place of the 'Seventh Book' in the Arabic EN and the texts depending upon it, especially the *Summa Alexandrinorum* (see V below), i.e. that we have in the 'Seventh Book', in truncated and presumably otherwise modified form, the first part of Porphyry's Commentary (*tafsīr*) dealing with the first part of EN, inserted appropriately in the middle of the work.[231] The second part of the *tafsīr* will have disappeared as a 'Twelfth Book' at an early date. The quotations given by al-ʿĀmirī as from Porphyry (see above)[232] appear to have been taken from

---

[229] Due to Lyons, "A Greek Ethical Treatise", *loc. cit.*, p. 48.

[230] Cf. above, pp. 12, 23, 25f.

[231] The Cairo MS. is exceptional in apparently placing the 'Seventh Book' of the Arabic EN and the *Summa Alexandrinorum* before, not after, the authentic Book VI, as already mentioned (p. 55, n. 223, cf. also pp. 79 and 83).

[232] Cf. above, pp. 23ff.

Book I or from the latter part of the *Ethics*, and consequently cannot be expected in the existing 'Seventh Book' of EN.

In addition and in contrast to expressions such as 'exoteric teachings' (*aqāwīl khārijah*), already mentioned, or 'animate justice' (*ʿadl mutanaffis*) (EN V, 4, 7 = 1132a 22 and 'Seventh Book', 9, 8), which are found alike in the authentic books of the Arabic EN and in the 'Seventh Book', there are other expressions which are quite different. Thus in addition to the terms for 'courage' and 'friendship' given above as different in the two texts,[233] we have also the following:

	'Seventh Book'	EN
'intemperate'	3, 3 *lā ʿafīf*	III, 10, 11 *sharih*
		IV, 11,6
'intemperance'	3, 8 *lā ʿiffah*	III, 11, 5 *sharah*
		12,1
'crane's gullet'	3, 3 *mariʾ ghurnūq*	III, 10, 10 *ḥalq al-kārākī*
'good temper, calm'	4, 1 *daʿah*	IV, 5, 1 *ḥilm*
'liberality'	5, 1 *ḥurrīyah*	IV, 1, 1 *sakhāʾ*
'magnificence'	5, 1 *ʿiẓm al-istiʾhāl*	IV, 2,1 *karam*
'magnanimous'	5, 12 *ʿaẓīm an-nafs*	IV, 3, 1 *kabīr an-nafs*
'magnanimity'	5, 1 *ʿiẓm an-nafs*	IV, 3, 1 *kibr an-nafs*
'vain'	5, 12 *mustarkhin*	IV, 3, 13, 35 *mutafattiḥ*
'vanity'	5, 13 *istirkhaʾ*	IV, 3, 37 *tafattuḥ*
'irony'	–	II, 7, 12 *mazḥ*
	–	IV, 3, 28 *muzāḥ*
'ironical'	6, 5, 6 *mustahziʾ*	II, 7, 12 *mazzāḥ*

While there are some differences of usage,[234] in the main these distinctions are consistently retained as between the 'Seventh Book' and the rest of the Arabic EN. It seems impossible to disallow that here we have the hand of another translator. For the presence of a

[233] Cf. above, p. 56.

[234] In the 'Seventh Book', 5, 10 and 11, 'magnanimous' is rendered by *kabīr an-nafs*, as in EN; and EN which regularly has *shajāʿah* for 'courage', upon occasion has *najdah* (V, 1, 14 = 1129b 19-20). It is curious that again at 1178a 32, where the Greek signifies 'the brave man will need strength', as here where we have 'the acts of the brave man', the Arabic text has apparently *an-najdah* corrected by Arberry to *an-najid*. There is therefore some doubt as to the reading in both places, but certainly elsewhere in Books X and XI of the Arabic EN forms from NJD rather than SHJʿ are used, so IX, 5, 4 = 1167a 20; X, 7, 4 = 1177a 32; X, 8, 1 = 1178a 10.

second hand no elaborate argument is needed. A new set of terms for the virtues is introduced in the 'Seventh Book'. This is not by inadvertence or simply for stylistic reasons. With the change of the basic text[235] the technical vocabulary has altered and another hand is at work.

Hitherto the difficulty of reconciling the notice of al-Kindī concerning Aristotle's *Nicomachean Ethics* in 11 Books with the notice in the *Fihrist* and al-Qifṭī of Aristotle's *Ethics* in 12 Books commented on by Porphyry, though considerable, has not been stressed.[236] The author of the *Fihrist*, Ibn an-Nadīm, says that the translation of the *Ethics* in 12 Books was the work of Isḥāq b. Ḥunain (d. 299/911-912). Al-Qifṭī (568/1172-646/1248), writing much later, states that the translator was Ḥunain b. Isḥāq (d. 260/873). On the grounds which have already been mentioned,[237] it has been customary to accept Ibn an-Nadīm's account. Chronologically this is difficult since al-Kindī died, according to a reliable opinion, in 252/866.[238] It has accordingly been thought that al-Kindī knew of the *Nicomachean Ethics* in 11 Books before it was translated from some listing of the works of Aristotle or other data obtained from an informant, and it is consistent with this that al-Kindī, unlike al-Fārābī and later writers, seems never to cite the *Nicomachean Ethics* or indeed to mention it anywhere else in his available writings. On the other hand, it may be that al-Kindī actually knew the translation of the *Ethics* in Arabic, not simply as an item in a catalogue or from hearsay but as a work which could be studied. This would seem to be the implication of his words at the beginning of the *Risālah fī kammīyat kutub Arisṭūṭālīs*. Al-Kindī will speak of

> the books in which the Greek Aristotle expressed his philosophy, according to their number and their classes, which are indispensable for anyone who wants to attain to philosophy and acquire it and confirm it (*kutub Arisṭāṭālīs al-Yūnānī alladhī tafalsafa fīhā ʿalā ʿiddatihā wa-marātibihā allatī lā ghinān li-man arāda nail al-falsafah wa-iqtināʾahā wa-tathbītahā ʿanhā*).[239]

---

[235] I.e. the basis of the 'Seventh Book' is no longer the Greek EN.
[236] Cf. pp. 7 and 26f.
[237] Cf. p. 27.
[238] Abū Rīdah in al-Kindī, *Rasāʾil*, *op. cit.*, vol. I, p. 5.
[239] al-Kindī, *Rasāʾil*, *op. cit.*, vol. I, p. 363, cf. the passage already quoted pp. 7ff.

There is at all events no suggestion that the *Risālah* is not an authentic work of al-Kindī, and his citation carries the 11-Book *Nicomachean Ethics* back to a date in the 3rd/9th century. The 12-Book *Ethics* has a much more uncertain existence, and though it can be accounted for, it has to be allowed that it is nowhere mentioned as such except in the passage of the *Fihrist* and al-Qifṭī. The colophon of the Eleventh Book (= Book X) in the Fez manuscript of EN gives the date when the copying was completed. This is apparently final, and there is nothing about a Twelfth Book.

A feature of the 'Seventh Book' is the large number of proper names which it contains. These may be tabulated:

Achilles, 5, 10
Alcmaeon, 1, 5
Androtion, 9, 11
Atreus?, *see* Ibn ʿAus
Christians, *see* al-Masīḥīyah
Ghūras (Protagoras?), 8, 1
Greeks, *see* al-Yūnānīyūn
Homer, 1, 7; 2, 4; 5, 20
Ibn ʿAus (Atreus?), 1, 3
Laconians, 5, 2; 6, 6; 8, 2
al-Masīḥīyah,[240] 8, 5
Odysseus, 1, 11
Persians, 2, 3
Philoxenus, son of Eryxis, 3, 3
Plato, 8, 1; 10, 1
Polydamas, 1, 7
Protagoras (?), *see* Ghūras
Pythagoras, 9, 10
Rhadamanthys, 9, 10
Sāʾūs, 6, 9
Sicily, 7, 1
Socrates, 6, 6
(Theognis), quoted, 4, 4
Trojans, 1, 7
al-Yūnānīyūn, 1, 7

[240] Cf. above, p. 58.

al-ʿUdhrīyūn (Banū ʿUdhrah), 3, 5
Zeus, 5, 10

There is no evidence that the 'Seventh Book' was translated from Syriac, e.g. no Syriac plurals in *-ayā*, as in several places in other Books.

V

The *Summa Alexandrinorum* is the name usually given to a Latin summary of the *Nicomachean Ethics*, translated from the Arabic by Hermannus Alemannus and completed in 1243 or 1244.[241] Hermannus Alemannus had already completed a translation of Ibn Rushd's *Middle Commentary* on the *Ethics* a few years previously (in June, 1240).[242] The *Summa Alexandrinorum* appears to have been first made known in modern times by Amable Jourdain[243] and was later edited in a praiseworthy first effort by Concetto Marchesi, from a single manuscript.[244] The more recent work of Professor George B. Fowler should also be consulted.[245]

The Arabic original of the *Summa* has not come to light *in extenso*, but what are evidently excerpts from it exist, notably in the *Mukhtār al-ḥikam* of al-Mubashshir b. Fātik,[246] a work variously dated circa 1050 A.D.[247] This was adumbrated by Ezio Franceschini

---

[241] Georges Lacombe, *Aristoteles Latinus – Codices I*, Rome 1939, pp. 60-69 and 110.

[242] *Ibid.*

[243] Jourdain, *Recherches critiques, op. cit.*, p. 144, n. 1. Jourdain was mistaken in indicating that both MSS. Sorbonne 1771 and 1773 (now Paris, Bibliothèque Nationale 16581 and 16583) contain the *Summa Alexandrinorum* (*ibid.*, p. 438, n. 2), and I, alas, have followed him in error ("Divine Ascriptions in the *Summa Alexandrinorum*", in: *Hamdard Islamicus* 6/3 [1983], pp. 43-45, esp. p. 43). This was pointed out to me by Marie-Thérèse d'Alverny. Only MS. Sorbonne 1771 (formerly, now Paris, Bibliothèque Nationale 16581, as above) contains the *Summa Alexandrinorum*. For this and other MSS. containing the *Summa* see her article, "Remarques sur la tradition manuscrite de la *Summa Alexandrinorum*", in: AHDLMA 49 (1982), pp. 265-272.

[244] Marchesi, *L'Etica Nicomachea nella tradizione latina medievale, op. cit.*, pp. XLI-LXXXVI (uses MS. Gaddiano 89 inf. 41 of the Laurentian Library, Florence).

[245] Fowler, "Manuscript Admont 608", *loc. cit.*

[246] al-Mubashshir b. Fātik, *Mukhtār al-ḥikam*, *op. cit.*

[247] Cf. Rosenthal, "Al-Mubashshir ibn Fâtik", *loc. cit.*, p. 133.

who, using a Latin version of the *Mukhtār al-ḥikam*, was able to show that the *Summa Alexandrinorum* was utilised by al-Mubashshir b. Fātik extensively for the dicta of Aristotle.[248] This result is confirmed by direct comparison of the *Summa* with the Arabic text of the *Mukhtār al-ḥikam*. Here we have some 30 quotations, amounting to nearly 100 lines of print, the bulk of which can easily be identified in the *Summa Alexandrinorum* and in the *Nicomachean Ethics*. These passages are as follows:

Mukhtār al-ḥikam	EN	*Summa Alex.* (ed. Marchesi)
p. 209	I, 3, 5	p. XLII, ll. 14-16
209	I, 3, 7	XLII, 17-19
209	I, 3, 7	XLII, 20-22
209-210	I, 4, 6-7	XLII. 29-34
210	I, 6, 9, cf. 7, 4-5	XLIII, 3-5
210	I, 8, 2	XLIII, 34 - XLIV, 1
210	I, 8, 9	XLIV, 1-3
210	I, 8, 14-15	XLIV, 11-17
210	I, 13, 15	XLV, 33-34
210	II, 1, 1	XLVI, 6-9
211	II, 2, 6-7	XLVI, 29-35
211	II, 3, 1	XLVII, 1-5
211	II, 3, 10	XLVII, 18-21
211	II, 4, 6	XLVII, 29-35
211	II, 6, 14	XLVIII, 32-36
212	cf. III, 1, 8	LI, 15-17
212	III, 1, 14	LI, 17-20
212	cf. IV, 7, 1 end	LX, 2-6
212	cf. IV, 7, 4ff.	LX, 6-11
212	V, 8, 6-8	LXIII, 33-37[249]
213	–	LXIX, 7-14

[248] Ezio Franceschini, "Il *Liber philosophorum moralium antiquorum*", in: *Atti della Reale Accademia Nazionale dei Lincei. Memorie. Classe di Scienze Morali, Storiche e Filologiche*, Rome 1930, pp. 355-399, here pp. 364-369.

[249] "Non quedam", ed. Marchesi, p. LXIII, l. 35, leg. "nam quedam", ed. Fowler, p. 223 (V, 3).

213	–	LXIX, 15-20
213	VIII, 1, 1	LXXII, 4-8
213	VIII, 1, 2	LXXII, 13-14
213	VIII, 3, 4-6	LXXII, 33-37
213	IX, 4, 5	LXXVII, 16-17
213	cf. IX, 6, 3	LXXVIII, 8-10
214	IX, 9, 2, 3	LXXIX, 25-28
214	IX, 11, 1	LXXX, 2-4
214	X, 3, 10-12	LXXXI, 16-17

It will be noticed that all the excerpts from the *Mukhtār al-ḥikam* are found in the Latin of the *Summa*, though not everything in the *Mukhtār al-ḥikam* represents the original text of the *Nicomachean Ethics*. It is evident that these excerpts have been taken in sequence from a text similar to that used by Hermannus for his Latin rendering, the *Summa Alexandrinorum*. The similarity extends to small details. Thus the quotation from Hesiod at EN I, 4, 7 = 1095b 10ff. is attributed by Hermannus Alemannus in error to Homer (ed. Marchesi, p. XLII, l. 33). This is no doubt because he has simply followed the Arabic text which he had before him (*Mukhtār al-ḥikam*, *op. cit.*, p. 209, last line).

Like the Arabic version of the *Nicomachean Ethics* as found in the Fez manuscript, the *Summa Alexandrinorum* (though this does not appear in every manuscript containing the work) is in 11 Books and follows the version in the Fez manuscript in having the extra Book between Books VI and VII of the original Greek.[250] The dependence of this intrusive Book in the *Summa Alexandrinorum* upon the 'Seventh Book' of the Arabic version of EN in the Fez manuscript is readily shown from some examples, using the English translation of the 'Seventh Book' with its present pagination:

EN c. 3, § 4	'a three-fold great misfortune', cf. "tripliciter ignominiosior" (ed. Marchesi, p. LXVI, l. 27).
c. 4, § 2	'dull of feeling on whom pain makes no impression', cf. "cui intus [leg. nihil][251] imprimunt dolores" (ed.

[250] The 'Seventh Book' begins ed. Marchesi, p. LXVI, l. 6: "Fortitudo est habitus laudabilis", and ends p. LXVIII, l. 30: "singularibus corruptibilibus" = ed. Fowler, pp. 226 (V, 2) - 228 (XI, 18) with slightly different wording.

[251] = "nichil", ed. Fowler, p. 226 (VII, 7). Marchesi's "intus" is again a misreading.

Marchesi, p. LXVI, l. 35).

c. 5, § 1 'liberality, magnificence and magnanimity', cf. "liberalitas et magnificentia et magnanimitas" (ed. Marchesi, p. LXVI , ll. 35-36).

c. 5, § 3 'the getting and giving of goods [...] from where it is fitting and as much as is fitting', cf. "acceptio pecuniarum et datio earum unde oportet et quantum oportet" (ed. Marchesi, p. LXVI, ll. 37-38).

c. 5, § 3 'giving is more excellent than getting', cf. "datio pulcrior et decentior quam acceptio" (ed. Marchesi, p. LXVII, l. 1).

c. 9, § 1 '[the equal] is in two things at least', cf. "ad minus inter duos" (ed. Marchesi, p. LXVII, l. 30).

c. 9, § 8 'the judge in a transferred sense is animate justice', cf. "iudex enim per modum transumptionis est iustitia animata" (ed. Marchesi, p. LXVIII, ll. 5-6).

c. 10, § 3 'what is more excellent than the excellent is excellent in any case, and similarly what is more just than justice', cf. "qui ergo bono melior est bonus est modis omnibus; et qui plus est quam iustus iustus est modis omnibus" (ed. Marchesi, p. LXVIII, ll. 22-23).[252]

But also, in the other Books, while generally the Arabic is different in the passages from the *Mukhtār al-ḥikam* as compared with the version of EN in the Fez manuscript, in a number of cases the two texts tally word for word, thus:

Mukhtār al-ḥikam, p. 209:

> *lā farq baina 'l-ḥadath as-sinn wa-baina 'l-ḥadath al-khulq li'anna 'n-nuqṣān laisa innamā utiya bihi min jihat az-zamān bal min jihat anna ʿaishahu wa-jamīʿa mā yaṭlubuhu fīhi innamā yaqṣidu bihi qaṣda mā yadʿū* [sic] *ash-shahwah,*

cf. EN I, 3, 7:

> *lā farq baina an yakūna ḥadath as-sinn au ḥadath al-khulq li'anna 'n-naqṣ laisa innamā yalīqu bihi min qibal az-zamān lākinna min qibal*

[252] "Qui ergo bono melior est [...]"—These words are omitted in Fowler's text, but are evidently part of the original, as determined by the Arabic.

anna ʿaishatahu wa-jamīʿ mā yaṭlubuhu fīhi innamā yaqṣidu bihi qaṣda mā taʿdū ilaihi ash-shahwah;

Mukhtār al-ḥikam, p. 213:

al-maḥabbah faḍīlah min faḍāʾilinā wa-hiya min al-ashyāʾ al-muḍṭarrah fī ʾl-ḥaiyāt waʾl-ʿumr [...] *al-afʿāl al-jaiyidah liʾanna al-ithnain idhā ʾjtamaʿā kānā aqwāʾ ʿalā al-fahm waʾl-ʿaql waʾt-tabdīr*,

cf. EN VIII, 1, 1-2:

al-maḥabbah faʾinnahā faḍīlah mā min faḍāʾilnā wa-hiya min al-ashyāʾ al-muḍṭarrah jiddan fī ʾl-ʿumr [...] *al-afʿāl al-jiyād faʾinna al-ithnain idhā ʾjtamaʿā kānā aqwā ʿalā al-fiʿl waʾl-fahm*;

Mukhtār al-ḥikam, p. 213:

waʾl-maḥabbah at-tāmmah hiya ṣadāqah al-akhyār waʾl-mutashābihīna biʾl-faḍīlah,

cf. EN VIII, 3, 6:

waʾt-tāmmah hiya ṣadāqat al-akhyār al-mutashābihīna biʾl-faḍīlah.

The indications thus are that, while in general the excerpts from the *Mukhtār al-ḥikam* do not follow closely the Arabic version of EN in the Fez manuscript, the influence of the version seems to appear in them to a certain extent, this influence not being confined to the 'Seventh Book'. The *Summa Alexandrinorum*, as the rendering of a text similar to that from which the excerpts in the *Mukhtār al-ḥikam* were drawn, is not simply an abbreviation of the Arabic version of the *Nicomachean Ethics* but must stand in some relation to the latter.

To speak now of special characteristics of the *Summa Alexandrinorum*, one is very soon struck by the comparative infrequency of proper names. As compared with the 'Seventh Book' of EN, the proper names of which have been listed above,[253] this is a notable difference. The names in the *Summa Alexandrinorum* are as follows:

Anaxagoras, ed. Marchesi, p. LXXXIV, l. 37
Epicurus, ed. Marchesi, p. LXIX, l. 2
Ethiopes, ed. Marchesi, p. LXIX, l. 4
Getae, ed. Marchesi, p. LII, l. 9
[H]eraclitus, ed. Marchesi, p. XLVII, l. 17

[253] Cf. pp. 61f.

Homer, ed. Marchesi, p. XLII, l. 33
Lacedaemonians, ed. Marchesi, p. LII, l. 8
Pythagoras (Pictagoras), ed. Marchesi, p. LXXVI, l. 35
Plato, ed. Marchesi, p. LXXX, l. 28
Sclavi, ed. Marchesi, p. LXIX, l. 5
Socrates, ed. Marchesi, p. LX, l. 28
Venus, ed. Marchesi, p. LXX, l. 20

The difference is more notable since the *Summa Alexandrinorum* should evidently have a Greek origin. *All* the Greek names, 20 or more, in the 'Seventh Book' of the Arabic EN have disappeared in the corresponding 'Seventh Book'[254] of the *Summa Alexandrinorum* (ed. Marchesi, pp. LXVI-LXVIII; ed. Fowler, pp. 226-228). The remaining 10 Books of the *Summa* yield the dozen names listed above, i.e. little more than one name for each Book, in striking contrast with the 'Seventh Book' of the Arabic EN even taking into account that the latter represents several Books.[255]

Another characteristic of the *Summa* is its containing a number of divine ascriptions, a feature which is an extreme rarity in the other texts which we have been considering,[256] and which in the 'Seventh Book' of the Fez manuscript does not occur at all. The ascriptions are found at Marchesi, p. XLIV, l. 18: "deo excelsa et gloriosa [leg. deo excelso et glorioso]"; p. XLV, l. 6-7: "deus benedictus et excelsus"; p. LXIII, ll. 11-12: "deus sublimis et excelsus"; p. LXIV, l. 23 and p. LXXXIV, l. 22: "deo glorioso". As already mentioned, Marchesi used for his 1904 edition a single manuscript, Gaddiano 89 inf. 41 of the Laurentian Library in Florence. Fowler's modern text is based on MS. Admont 608, with variants from the Bodleian MS. Canon. Class. Lat. 271, and shows these ascriptions with slight variants in the same places. This applies also to the two Paris manuscripts of the *Summa Alexandrinorum*, Bibliothèque Nationale 12954 and 16581, i.e. the ascriptions are found with minor differences in these manuscripts. Since ascriptions of this kind are well known and usual in Arabic, the

---

[254] I.e. the part of the *Summa Alexandrinorum* which corresponds to the 'Seventh Book' of EN Fez but is sometimes numbered differently in the MSS., cf. p. 55, n. 223.

[255] See above, pp. 55ff.

[256] The Arabic version of the EN in the Fez MS. at I, 12, 5 has exceptionally *Allāh ʿazza wa-jalla*, 'God who is great and glorious'.

presumption was strong that the translator, Hermannus Alemannus, found those which have been mentioned in the Arabic text with which he worked. The Arabic behind the Latin of Hermannus, as we have seen, is available only in fragments.[257] One such fragment, already quoted from the *Tahdhīb al-akhlāq* (*Rectification of Morals*) of Miskawaih includes the expressions *Allāh taʿālā* and *ʿazza ʿsmuhu*, 'God who is exalted' and 'great is His name', rendered in the Latin, as above, "deo excelso et glorioso".[258] This passage seemed slender evidence for a firm conclusion, especially since the origin of the Arabic text behind the Latin was unknown. Was it a translation from Greek? This appeared to be very likely in view of the title *Summa Alexandrinorum*, in Arabic *Ikhtiṣār al-Iskandarānīyīn*.[259] Or was it translated into Arabic from Syriac? This also seemed not unlikely. The full text of the *Nicomachean Ethics* in Arabic appears to have been translated from Syriac,[260] as was the case with other Greek texts. The ascriptions which, as already indicated,[261] are not unknown in the full text, have been added at some point.

Fortunately we have an explicit statement as to the author of the Arabic behind the Latin of the *Summa Alexandrinorum* which makes speculation superfluous. This is to be found in a work entitled *Muntakhab* (*Selection*) from the *Ṣiwān al-ḥikmah* (*Casket of Wisdom*) of Abū Sulaimān as-Sijistānī (as-Sijazī) in the 4th/10th century, and is as follows:

> *Abū ʿAlī ʿĪsā ibn Zurʿah al-Baghdādī* [...] *wa-mimmā tarjamahu min kalām Arisṭūṭīlas qauluhu: al-insānīyah*[262] *ufuqun wa'l-insān mutaḥarrik ilā ufuqihi bi'ṭ-ṭabʿ wa-dā'ir ʿalā markazihi illā an yakūna ma'ūfan bi-ṭabīʿatihi makhlūṭan bi-akhlāq bahīmīyah wa-man rafaʿa ʿaṣāhu ʿan nafsihi wa-alqā ḥablahu ʿalā ghāribihi wa-saiyaba hawāhu fī marʿāhu wa-lam yaḍbiṭ nafsahu ʿammā yadʿu ilaihi bi-ṭabʿihi wa-kāna laiyin al-ʿarīkah li-'ttibāʿ ash-shahawāt ar-radī'ah fa-qad kharaja ʿan ufuqihi wa-ṣāra ardhal min al-bahīmah bi-sū' ikhtiyārihi*, i.e. Abū ʿAli ʿĪsā ibn Zurʿah al-Baghdādī [...] and of what he translated of the words of Aristotle is his saying: *Humanity is [or rather, has]*[263] *a limit. A man moves naturally to his limit and circles round his centre,*

[257] Cf. pp. 29ff. and 63f.
[258] Ed. Marchesi, p. XLIV, l. 18. See above, p. 29.
[259] Cf. below, pp. 77f.
[260] See below, p. 106.
[261] Cf. above, p. 67, n. 256.
[262] *Sic* MSS., but perhaps we should read *li'l-insānīyah*.
[263] See previous note.

> *unless he is marred in his nature [and] shares the characteristics of brute beasts. He who rejects discipline and abandons restraint, does what he pleases, refrains not from what his nature calls to and is ready to follow wicked desires, has passed beyond his limit and has become worse than the beasts through his bad choice.*[264]

This text of Abū Sulaimān as-Sijistānī was reproduced a little later in the *Kitāb al-muqābasāt* of Abū Ḥaiyān at-Tauḥīdī.[265] The last sentence, 'he who rejects discipline [...]' (*wa-man rafaʿa ʿaṣāhu* [...]), to the end is found word for word in the *Mukhtār al-ḥikam*, *op. cit.*, p. 213, with minimal changes (*fa-lam* for *wa-lam* and *ṭabʿuhu* for *bi-ṭabʿihi*). Further the whole passage occurs in the *Summa Alexandrinorum* positioned after EN VII, 1, 3, but not of course in the Greek (ed. Marchesi, p. LXIX, ll. 8-14 = Fowler, p. 229 [I, 22-28]):

> Homo habet metas suas ad quas mouetur naturaliter et contra quas reuoluitur circa ipsarum centrum nisi acciderit nature sue occasio ad mores bestiarum ipsum inclinans, que solutis habenis secundum morem proprii appetitus uagantur per pascua, neque continent se ab aliquo eorum ad que ducit eas natura sua. Et hoc modo transgreditur ambitum metarum suarum. Qui [leg. Quin][266] immo peior tunc efficitur bestiis propter sue eligentie prauitatem.

In view of the correspondence of these passages—the excerpt from the *Mukhtār al-ḥikam* corresponds as usual with the Latin of the *Summa Alexandrinorum* and both correspond with the passage quoted as from Ibn Zurʿah in the *Muntakhab ṣiwan al-ḥikmah* (also in the *Muqābasāt* of Abū Ḥaiyān at-Tauḥīdī)—there can be no doubt that the 'translation of the words of Aristotle' made by Ibn Zurʿah according to the last mentioned texts was the Arabic which Hermannus Alemannus rendered into Latin as the *Summa Alexandrinorum*.

If uncertainty remains, it is as to the correctness of the attribution to Ibn Zurʿah. The name is little known in the West, yet Ibn Zurʿah—in full Abū ʿAlī ʿĪsā b. Isḥāq b. Zurʿah b. Marqus b. Zurʿah b. Yuhannā—, a Jacobite Christian of 4th/10th century Baghdad, was

---

264 Abū Sulaimān as-Sijistānī, *Muntakhab ṣiwan al-ḥikmah*, *op. cit.*, p. 143, § 281.

265 Abū Ḥaiyān at-Tauḥīdī, *al-Muqābasāt*, ed. Ḥasan as-Sandūbī, Cairo 1374/1929, p. 197.

266 Correct in Fowler's text, where, however, the original Latin translation of the difficult Arabic has been altered. Thus we find "propter sue arrogantie prauitatem"; Marchesi's "propter sue eligentie (*īthārihi*) prauitatem" is clearly the better reading.

evidently in his lifetime (331/943-398/1008) a man of note as philosopher, Christian apologist and translator—the last acceptable translator of Aristotle, we are told—,[267] and he is mentioned in some of the principal Arabic bio-bibliographical compilations.[268] In addition, Ibn Zurʿah's contemporary Abū Ḥaiyān at-Tauḥīdī, who knew Ibn Zurʿah personally,[269] gives the following description of him in the *Kitāb al-imtāʿ wa'l-muʾānasah* (*Book of Gratification and Entertainment*) for the benefit of the *wazīr* Ibn Saʿdān, to whose circle Ibn Zurʿah belonged:

> *wa-ammā Ibn Zurʿah fa-huwa ḥasan at-tarjamah ṣaḥīḥ an-naql kathīr ar-rujūʿ ilā 'l-kutub maḥmūd an-naql ilā 'l-ʿarabīyah jaiyid al-wafāʾ bi-kull mā jalla min al-falsafah laisa lahu fī daqīqihā manfadh wa-lā lahu min lughzihā maʾkhadh wa-lau lā tawazzuʿ fikrihi fī't-tijārah wa-maḥabbatuhu fī'r-ribḥ wa-ḥirṣuhu ʿalā 'l-jamʿ wa-shiddatuhu ʿalā 'l-manʿ lā kānat qarīḥatuhu tastajību lahu wa-ghāʾimatuhu tadirru ʿalaihi*', i.e. as for Ibn Zurʿah, he is an excellent interpreter and a correct translator, constantly referring to books, and praised for his translation into Arabic. He is very reliable in all the great matters of philosophy, without entering into its subtleties and handling its obscurities, and were it not for his attention being distracted by mercantile affairs, his love of gain, eagerness for amassing and stress on withholding, his genius would answer him and his cloud would rain upon him. But he is divided and exposed to criticism. It is love of the present world that makes us blind and deaf![270]

Ibn Zurʿah's dates are right for his having been the author of the Arabic original of the *Summa Alexandrinorum*, the traces of which are first found in a work of Miskawaih, as already mentioned.[271] Miskawaih died old in 421/1030. In his younger days he had been, like Ibn Zurʿah, a member of the circle of Abū ʿAbd Allāh al-Ḥusain b. Aḥmad b. Saʿdān, *wazīr* of the Buwaihid Ṣamṣām ad-Daulah in Baghdad for a year or two from 372/983.[272] Miskawaih was therefore

---

[267] Abū Sulaimān as-Sijistānī, *Muntakhab ṣiwan al-ḥikmah*, *op. cit.*, p. 143, § 281.

[268] In addition to the passage from the *Muntakhab* already cited, Ibn an-Nadīm, *Fihrist*, *op. cit.*, vol. I, p. 264; Ibn Abī Uṣaibiʿah, *ʿUyūn al-anbāʾ*, *op. cit.*, pp. 235-236; al-Qifṭī, *Taʾrīkh al-ḥukamāʾ*, *op. cit.*, pp. 245-246.

[269] Abū Ḥaiyān at-Tauḥīdī mentions a question on the intellect (*ʿaql*) put by himself to Ibn Zurʿah (*Muqābasāt*, *op. cit.*, pp. 198-199) and answered by him.

[270] Abū Ḥaiyān at-Tauḥīdī, *Kitāb al-imtāʿ wa'l-muʾānasah*, *op. cit.*, vol. I, p. 33.

[271] See pp. 29ff.

[272] For this and what follows see the Introduction to Abū Ḥaiyān at-Tauḥīdī, *Kitāb al-imtāʿ wa'l-muʾānasah*, *op. cit.*, vol. I and pp. 32 and 35.

well placed to know about Ibn Zurʿah's work. At this time Abū Sulaimān as-Sijistānī was still alive, though he did not attend the *wazīr*'s circle, of which Abū Ḥaiyān at-Tauḥīdī was another member. Both men are reliable authorities for a matter of this kind. Abū Ḥaiyān, as already mentioned, knew Ibn Zurʿah personally. Abū Sulaimān probably knew him. Their statements attributing the translation to Ibn Zurʿah seems unassailable. With reference to the divine ascriptions in the Arabic behind the Latin of the *Summa Alexandrinorum*, notably in the *Summa Alexandrinorum* itself, it may be added that the insertion of such ascriptions was the regular practice of Ibn Zurʿah. This is plain from his works printed by Paul Sbath,[273] in which such expressions as *jalla 'smuhu*, *Allāh taʿāla*, *subḥānahu* [...], are frequent.[274]

The similarities which we have already noted[275] between the Arabic behind the *Summa Alexandrinorum* as preserved in the *Mukhtār al-ḥikam* and the text of EN in the Fez manuscript are insufficient to prove that Ibn Zurʿah simply abbreviated on the basis of the already existing Arabic text. That he should have done so is made difficult by the expression *tarjama*, indicating most naturally actual translation, in the *Muntakhab ṣiwan al-ḥikmah* where Ibn Zurʿah's work on Aristotle is mentioned and the crucial passage is quoted,[276] and seems impossible in view of the title of the translation *Summa Alexandrinorum* = *Ikhtiṣār al-Iskandarānīyīn*.[277] Some other explanation of the similarities must be sought, e.g. that Ibn Zurʿah had before him the existing Arabic translation of the EN in 11 Books when he was making his translation of what became the *Summa Alexandrinorum*, and that he sometimes adduced it.

Nor will the translation necessarily have been made directly from the Greek. We do not have explicit evidence that Ibn Zurʿah was a translator from Greek. If he actually translated the abbreviation of the *Ethics* from Greek, we should have to allow, as does not seem likely, that the intrusive 'Seventh Book', which is found in the *Summa* as well as in the Fez text of the *Ethics*, already existed in this form in

---

[273] Ibn Zurʿah, *Vingt traités philosophiques et apologétiques d'auteurs arabes chrétiens*, ed. Paul Sbath, Cairo 1929.

[274] See further on this above, pp. 67f.

[275] See above, pp. 62ff.

[276] Cf. above, pp. 68f.

[277] See below, pp. 77f.

Greek, or alternatively that Ibn Zurʿah abbreviated and added it from the existing Arabic text of the *Ethics*. Perhaps therefore it is preferable to think of Ibn Zurʿah as having made his translation directly from Syriac, as he did in other cases. Ibn an-Nadīm in the *Fihrist* states this distinctly,[278] giving a breakdown of 'what [Ibn Zurʿah] translated from Syriac' (*mā naqalahu min as-Suryānī*) and even mentioning a treatise on ethics (*maqālah fī 'l-akhlāq*) translated from Syriac by Ibn Zurʿah, which he tells us was anonymous (*majhūlah*).[279] If by this the Arabic abbreviation of the *Nicomachean Ethics* is meant, the description at first sight seems appropriate, for the identity of the original author as distinct from the Arabic translator as yet eludes us.

Gregorius Abū 'l-Faraj ibn al-ʿIbrī (Bar Hebraeus), born 623/1226, died 685/1286, in his *Ta'rīkh mukhtaṣar ad-duwal* has the following:

> *wa-min al-falāsifah al-qarībat al-ʿahd min hādhā 'z-zamān Nīqūlā'ūs qad taqaddama fī maʿrifah al-ḥikmah wa-lahu min at-taṣānīf: Kitāb min jumal*[280] *falsafat Arisṭūṭālīs wa-lanā nuskhatuhu bi's-Suryānī naqal Ḥunain b. Isḥāq*[281] *wa-Kitāb an-nabāt wa-Kitāb ar-radd ʿalā 'l-jāʿil al-ʿaql wa'l-maʿqūlāt shai'an wāḥidan. qāla Ibn Buṭlān: inna aṣlahu min al-Lādhiqīyah wa-biha wulida*, i.e. and of the philosophers of nearly the same time [i.e. the time of the Emperor Julian, 4th century A.D.][282] was Nicolaus, who made progress in knowledge of wisdom and was the author of several works: *Summaries*[283] *of the Philosophy of Aristotle*, of which we possess a copy in Syriac, trans-

---

[278] Ibn an-Nadīm, *Fihrist*, *op. cit.*, vol. I, p. 264.

[279] Bayard Dodge in Ibn an-Nadīm, *The Fihrist of al-Nadīm. A Tenth-Century Survey of Muslim Culture* (Records of Civilization: Sources and Studies; 83), 2 vols., New York/London 1970, vol. II, p. 632, translates "not extant", but it is a mistake.

[280] In the edition *ḥumal*.

[281] Cf. al-Qifṭī, *Ta'rīkh al-ḥukamā'*, *op. cit.*, p. 41: *wa-Kitāb al-ḥaiwān lahu* [sc. Aristotle] [...] *wa-li-Nīqūlā'ūs ikhtiṣār li-hādhā 'l-kitāb wa-naqalahu Abū ʿAlī ibn Zurʿah ilā 'l-Arabī wa-ṣaḥḥaḥahu wa-malaktu bihi nuskhatan wa'l-ḥamdu li'llāh*. A similar expression of gratitude for the possession of a book at al-Qifṭī, *ibid.*, p. 89.

[282] For the date of Nīqūlā'ūs see below, p. 76.

[283] *Jumal* has much the same sense as *jawāmiʿ*, cf. Masʿūdī, *Murūj adh-dhahab wa-maʿādin al-jauhar (Les prairies d'or)*, ed. and transl. Barbier de Meynard, 9 vols., Paris 1861-1876, vol. III, p. 365: *dhikr jumal min akhbār al-kuhhān*, where Pellat (Masʿūdī, *Les prairies d'or [Murūj adh-dhahab wa-maʿādin al-jauhar]*, transl. Barbier de Meynard and Pavet de Courteille, revised by Charles Pellat, 5 vols., Paris 1962-1997, vol. II, p. 473) translates: "Renseignements généraux sur les devins", and again, ed. Meynard, vol. III, p. 431: *jumal mimmā qīla fī dhālika*, transl. Pellat, vol. II, p. 505: "Résumé des opinions émises à cet égard." See below, pp. 73f., n. 290 and 76, n. 307.

> lated by Ḥunain b. Isḥāq; the *Book of Plants*; *Refutation of Him Who Makes the Intellect and the Intelligibles One Thing*. Ibn Buṭlān said that his origin was from Laodicea [= Latakia], and in it he was born.[284]

This passage occurs also in the *Ta'rīkh al-ḥukamā'* of al-Qifṭī (568/1172-646/1248) as follows:

> *Nīqūlā'ūs kāna failasūfan fī waqtihi*[285] *min falāsifah Yūnān wa-lahu taqaddum fī ma'rifat al-ḥikmah wa-sharaḥa shai'an min kutub Arisṭūṭālīs wa-lahu min at-taṣānīf ba'd dhālika: Kitāb fī jumal falsafat Arisṭūṭālīs;*[286] *Kitāb an-nabāt wa-kharaja minhu maqālāt; Kitāb ar-radd 'alā jā'il al-'aql wa'l-ma'qūlāt shai'an wāḥidan; Kitāb ikhtiṣār falsafat Arisṭūṭālīs. wa-kāna Nīqūlā'ūs hādhā min ahl al-Lādhiqīyah bihā wulida wa-bihā qaumuhu wa-minhā aṣluhu. dhakara dhālika Ibn Buṭlān wa-kāna kathīr al-iṭṭilā' 'āliman bimā yanquluhu*, i.e. Nicolaus was in his time [sc. the time of the Emperor Julian] one of the Greek philosophers. He made progress in knowledge of wisdom and commented on some of the books of Aristotle. He was in addition the author of several books: *Summaries of the Philosophy of Aristotle*; the *Book of Plants*, of which some discourses[287] came out; *Refutation of Him Who Makes the Intellect and the Intelligibles One Thing*; *Abridgement of the Philosophy of Aristotle*. This Nicolaus was of the people of Laodicea [= Latakia], where he was born, where his people were, and whence his origin was. This was mentioned by Ibn Buṭlān, who was a great student and knew what he transmitted.[288]

The *Fihrist* of Ibn an-Nadīm, dated to 377/987 also has the following:

> *Nīqūlā'ūs mufassir kutub Arisṭālīs* [sic] *wa-qad dhakarnā aiḍan mā fassaraḥu fī mauḍi'ihi.*[289] *wa-lahu min al-kutub ba'd dhālika Kitāb fī jumal*[290] *falsafat Arisṭālīs* [sic] *fī'n-nafs maqālah; Kitāb an-nabāt wa-*

---

[284] Gregorius Abū 'l-Faraj ibn al-'ibrī (Bar Hebraeus), *Ta'rīkh mukhtaṣar ad-duwal*, ed. Anṭūn Salḥānī, Beirut ^{2}1958, p. 82.

[285] It is well known that the text of al-Qifṭī's *Ta'rīkh al-ḥukamā'*, as we have it, is an epitome by az-Zauzanī written in 647/1249 (cf. Lippert in al-Qifṭī's *Ta'rīkh al-ḥukamā'*, *op. cit.*, pp. 11ff.; Albert Dietrich in EI^2, s.v. Ibn al-Qifṭī). The context is better given in the extract from Abū 'l-Faraj above.

[286] The epitome omits the words *wa-lanā nuskhatu* [...] found in Abū 'l-Faraj, but they must have been in the original, cf. p. 72 and n. 281.

[287] The same word as here (*maqālāt*) is used for the 10+1 Books of the Arabic *Nicomachean Ethics*.

[288] al-Qifṭī, *Ta'rīkh al-ḥukamā'*, *op. cit.*, p. 336.

[289] The last two words occur in C alone of Flügel's MSS. Ibn an-Nadīm uses this expression again on the same page.

[290] Bayard Dodge's translation *On the Beauty of Aristotle's Philosophy* [...] is

> *kharaja minhu maqālāt; Kitāb ar-radd ʿalā jāʿil al-fiʿl wa'l-mafʿūlāt shai'an wāḥidan; Kitāb ikhtiṣār falsafat Aristālīs* [sic], i.e. Nicolaus, interpreter of the books of Aristotle. We have already mentioned what he interpreted in its place.[291] He was in addition the author of several works: *Summaries of the Philosophy of Aristotle*, a *Treatise on the Soul*, the *Book of Plants*, of which some tractates came out; *Refutation of Him Who Makes the Action and the Effects One Thing*; *Abridgement of the Philosophy of Aristotle*.[292]

It has already been noted[293] that Abū 'l-Faraj in various places depends on al-Qifṭī, and so here. On the other hand, it is readily seen that the notice of Nicolaus in the *Fihrist* is the basis of the first part of al-Qifṭī's notice, or comes from the same source (perhaps from the list of books of Yaḥyā b. ʿAdī which Ibn an-Nadīm himself used). The second part of al-Qifṭī's notice comes from a different source. This is the account by Ibn Buṭlān of his journeying from Baghdad to Cairo,[294] in the course of which he visited al-Lādhiqīyah (Latakia), the ancient Laodicea. His interesting remarks on the Syrian city in the year 446/1054, according to Yāqūt, end with the mention of two of its famous sons:

> *wa-min hādhihi 'l-madīnah aʿnī al-Lādhiqīyah kharaja Nīqūlā'ūs ṣāḥib jawāmiʿ al-falsafah wa-Tūfls ṣāḥib al-Ḥujaj fī qidam al-ʿālam*, i.e. and from this city, I mean al-Lādhiqīyah, came forth Nicolaus, author of the summaries of philosophy, and Tūfls[295] [sic], author of *The Arguments for the Eternity of the World*.[296]

---

quite erroneous (Ibn an-Nadīm, *The Fihrist of al-Nadīm*, *op. cit.*, vol. II, p. 611).

[291] Ibn an-Nadīm has previously mentioned Nīqūlā'ūs in one place as follows: *wa-li-Nīqūlā'ūs ikhtiṣār li-hādhā 'l-kitāb* [...] *wa-qad ibtada' Abū ʿAlī ibn Zurʿah bi-naqlihi ilā 'l-ʿArabī wa-taṣḥīḥihi*, i.e. 'Nicolaus was the author of a compendium of this book and Abū ʿAlī ibn Zurʿah began to translate it into Arabic and correct it.'—The composite *Kitāb al-ḥaiwān, Book of Animals*, of Aristotle, in 19 Books in Arabic, is meant (Ibn an-Nadīm, *Fihrist*, *op. cit.*, vol. I, p. 251).

[292] Ibn an-Nadīm, *Fihrist*, *op. cit.*, vol. I, p. 254.

[293] Steinschneider, *Al-Fārābī*, *op. cit.*, p. 152, n. 1.

[294] See especially, Joseph Schacht, "Über den Hellenismus in Baghdad und Cairo im 11. Jahrhundert", in: ZDMG 90 (1936), pp. 526-545, here pp. 530-533; the same, "Ibn Buṭlān", in EI^2.

[295] *Tūfls* (توفلس) is for *Proclus* (برقلس), see below, p. 75, n. 298.

[296] Yāqūt, *Jacut's Geographisches Wörterbuch [Muʿjam al-buldān] aus den Handschriften zu Berlin, St. Petersburg, Paris, London und Oxford*, ed. Ferdinand Wüstenfeld, 6 vols., Leipzig 1866-1870, here vol. IV, p. 339, where Ibn Faḍlān is cited in error for Ibn Buṭlān. The parallel passage in al-Qifṭī, *Ta'rīkh al-ḥukamā'*, *op. cit.*, p. 336, does not contain the quotation concerning the famous sons of Latakia.

The Arabic notices of Nīqūlā'ūs speak of these summaries. We have already seen what was said by al-Qifṭī and Ibn an-Nadīm. Abū Sulaimān as-Sijistānī in his notice of Ibn Zur'ah in the *Muntakhab ṣiwān al-ḥikmah* is very explicit: *qad athāra al-wahaj fīmā naqalahu min jawāmiʿ Nīqūlā'ūs*, i.e. 'he [= Ibn Zur'ah] created a sensation [lit. 'stirred up a blaze'] with his translations of the summaries of Nīqūlā'ūs'.[297] In these notices, save where Ibn Buṭlān is cited as the authority, there is no mention of a Nicolaus of Laodicea. As to Tūfls, mentioned by Yāqūt along with Nicolaus as a native of Laodicea, there is no doubt that this name for an author of a work on arguments for the eternity of the world is an error and should be Proclus, the ductus in the Arabic script being nearly the same.[298] The work of Proclus on the eternity of the world, lost in the original Greek, is known from its refutation by John Philoponus. It is also known from a single Arabic manuscript,[299] where it bears the same title as in the words quoted above from Yāqūt, *Ḥujaj Burqls fī qidam al-ʿālam* (*Arguments of Proclus for the Eternity of the World*).[300] There is general agreement that Proclus was of Lycian origin, from Xanthus in Lycia. The Arabic sources make him a native of a place which appears as Aṭāṭrīyah[301] or Aṭāṭūlah[302] and may represent Attaleia, modern Antalya.[303] It is obviously out of the question that Proclus was from al-Lādhiqīyah, but, since we are not to think of Ibn Buṭlān speaking at random, possibly it is due to some confusion between Laodicea and Lycia, the latter name being hardly known to the

---

[297] Abū Sulaimān as-Sijistānī, *Muntakhab ṣiwān al-ḥikmah*, *op. cit.*, p. 143, § 281.

[298] See above, p. 74, n. 295.

[299] See Abdarrahman Badawi, *La transmission de la philosophie grecque au monde arabe* (Études de philosophie médiévale; 66), Paris 1968, p. 72: "Dans un très précieux manuscrit arabe du XIIe siècle (daté 558/1162), j'ai découvert la traduction arabe des neuf premiers arguments de Proclus; cette traduction remonte (elle est faite par Ishaq ibn Hunain, mort en 298/910) au IXe siècle [...]." A French translation of Proclus' first argument is given by Badawi in the same work, pp. 119-120. The Arabic text of nine arguments (amounting to one half of the work) had already appeared in his *Neoplatonici apud Arabes* (Islamica; 19), Cairo 1955, pp. 34-49. The provenance of the MS. is not stated.

[300] Nearly the same title is reported from the Proclus MS. ('Abdarraḥmān Badawī, *Neoplatonici apud Arabes*, *op. cit.*, Introd. p. 31, and the text p. 34 is so headed).

[301] Ibn an-Nadīm, *Fihrist*, *op. cit.*, vol. I, p. 252.

[302] al-Qifṭī, *Ta'rīkh al-ḥukamā'*, *op. cit.*, p. 89.

[303] The suggestion is made by Bayard Dodge in Ibn an-Nadīm, *The Fihrist of al-Nadīm*, *op. cit.*, vol. II, p. 607, n. 142.

Arabs, unless Laodicea ad Lycum is meant (with which there is nothing special to connect Proclus).

However this may be, the sole authority for Nicolaus of Laodicea appears to be Ibn Buṭlān, on whom al-Qifṭī and Abū 'l-Faraj depend.[304] Abū 'l-Faraj adds, apparently on his own authority, that Nicolaus was a philosopher nearly contemporary with the emperor Julian (4th century A.D.). It is evidently through Abū 'l-Faraj that the name Nicolaus of Laodicea has passed into use.[305] But this Nicolaus is an unreal figure and can have no independent existence apart from Nicolaus of Damascus (1st century B.C.), who is usually intended by the Arabic sources when Nicolaus is mentioned.[306] Nicolaus of Laodicea, who according to Ibn Buṭlān was the author of the summaries of philosophy (*ṣāḥib jawāmiʿ al-falsafah*), cannot be separated from the Nicolaus whose summaries (*jawāmiʿ jumal*)[307] of the philosophy of Aristotle are mentioned by the *Fihrist* and al-Qifṭī

---

[304] See the notices of these authors on Nicolaus quoted above.

[305] So Sir William Smith (ed.), *Dictionary of Greek and Roman Biography and Mythology* II (1844), pp. 1192-1193; Dodge in Ibn an-Nadīm, *The Fihrist of al-Nadīm, op. cit.*, vol. II, p. 1072. Malcolm C. Lyons refers to "that shadowy figure, Nicolaus of Laodicea" ("A Greek Ethical Treatise", *loc. cit.*, p. 48).

[306] E.g. ʿAbd al-Laṭīf al-Baghdadī, *Kitāb al-ifādah wa'l-iʿtibār (The Eastern Key)*, transl. Kamal Hafuth Zand, John A. and Ivy E. Videan, Cairo/London 1204/1964, pp. 35 and 45, also the heading of the anonymous *Maqālah fī 'l-madkhal ilā ʿilm al-akhlāq* at the end of the Fez MS. of the Arabic *Nicomachean Ethics*, which includes the words: *ghair mansūbah ilā waḍiʿ wa-ẓanantuhā li-Nīqūlā'ūs.*

[307] The word has caused difficulty. *Jumal* here, i.e. in the passages already quoted from Abū 'l-Faraj, al-Qifṭī and Yāqūt, is the plural of *jumlah*, 'a summing up', 'summary', a meaning not given apparently in the Arabic dictionaries, but cf. Lane, s.v. *ajmala*: "*He collected* a thing. [...] – *He reduced* a calculation *to its sum*; *summed it up*: [...] and in like manner, *he summed up* a speech or discourse, *and then analyzed and explained it*." A good example of its use is Ibn Abī Uṣaibiʿah, *ʿUyūn al-anbā', op. cit.*, vol. I, pp. 103-104. Certain medical men met regularly in Alexandria to study the works of Galen: *wa-kānū yaqra'ūnahā ʿalā 't-tartīb wa-yajtamiʿūna fī kulli yaumin ʿalā qirā'ati shai'in minhā thumma ṣarrafūhā ilā 'l-jumal wa'l-jawāmiʿ li-yashula ḥifẓuhum lahā wa-maʿrifatuhum īyāhā*, i.e. 'they were reading them in order, assembling every day to read a part of them. Then they made them into summaries and epitomes.' Cf. above, p. 72, n. 283. Moritz Steinschneider (*Die arabischen Übersetzungen aus dem Griechischen, op. cit.*, p. 139) is apparently in error when he makes the word singular "ein Summarium (*fī Djuml*)"—*sic*—and so Malcolm C. Lyons ("A Greek Ethical Treatise", *loc. cit.*, p. 48) "a compendium" and Hendrik J. Drossaart Lulofs (in Nicolaus Damascenus, *On the Philosophy of Aristotle*, Leiden 1965, p. 9) "a summary". The *jumal falsafat Arisṭ[ūṭ]ālīs* are evidently not to be identified with the *ikhtiṣār falsafat Arisṭ[ūṭ]ālīs* mentioned in the same notice (cf. the passages quoted above from Ibn an-Nadīm, *Fihrist*, and al-Qifṭī, *Ta'rīkh al-ḥukamā'*).

and when translated into Arabic created a sensation.[308] Ibn Buṭlān may perhaps have had information of a connexion of Nicolaus Damascenus with Laodicea. More probably there has been some mistake.

We have indeed other evidence for Nicolaus as a writer of summaries or abridgements of the works of Aristotle. This comes from several good authorities, once very distinctly in Ibn Abī Uṣaibiʿah, quoting a well-known letter of Isḥāq b. Ḥunain, where there is mention of 'Anqilaus, i.e. Nicolaus, the abbreviator of the books of Aristotle [*al-mukhtaṣir li-kutub Arisṭūṭālīs*]'.[309] The titles of some of these productions are known, e.g. an *Ikhtiṣār* (abbreviation) of Aristotle's *Book of Animals* (*Kitāb al-ḥayawān*).[310] Another was an *Ikhtiṣār* of the *Metaphysics* of Aristotle, referred to by Ibn Rushd: *najidu fī kitāb Nīqūlā'ūs al-mashshā' fī mukhtaṣarihi fī hādhā 'l-ʿilm*, i.e. 'we find in the book of Nicolaus the Peripatetic in what he abbreviated of this science'.[311] (The reference here to Nicolaus the Peripatetic, quite as in the Greek sources for Nicolaus Damascenus,[312] is to be remarked.) Again, the notice of Nicolaus in the *Fihrist* already cited[313] may refer to an abbreviation of Aristotle's *On the Soul*.[314]

All this brings us near to the solution of the problem of the origin of the *Summa Alexandrinorum*, which is now seen to fall into line with other abbreviations of the works of Aristotle made by Nicolaus of Damascus. We have also to consider the title, in Arabic *Ikhtiṣār al-Iskandarānīyīn*, *Abbreviation of the Alexandrians*, as restored with a high degree of certainty from a Cairo manuscript.[315] While the general population of Alexandria is regularly called in the Arabic

---

[308] As above, p. 75, from the *Muntakhab*.

[309] Ibn Abī Uṣaibiʿah, *'Uyūn al-anbā'*, *op. cit.*, vol. I, p. 36. For the letter see Franz Rosenthal, "Ishaq b. Hunayn's *Ta'rīkh al-aṭibbā'*", in: *Oriens* 7 (1954), pp. 55-80; Dunlop in Abū Sulaimān as-Sijstānī, *Muntakhab ṣiwan al-ḥikmah*, *op. cit.*, p. XVIII.

[310] Ibn an-Nadīm, *Fihrist*, *op. cit.*, vol. I, p. 251, quoted above, p. 74, n. 291.

[311] Ibn Rushd, *Tafsīr mā baʿd aṭ-ṭabīʿa*, ed. Maurice Bouyges (Bibliotheca Arabica Scholasticorum; 5-7), 4 vols., Beirut 1938-1952, vol. II, p. 843, l. 8.

[312] See Felix Jacoby, *Fragmente der griechischen Historiker* (*F. gr. Hist.*), vol. IIA, no. 90, pp. 324-430 *passim*.

[313] See above, pp. 73f.

[314] Cf. Steinschneider, *Die arabischen Übersetzungen aus dem Griechischen*, *op. cit.*, p. 139, § 52.

[315] See the following § VI, below p. 79.

sources *ahl al-Iskandarīyah*,[316] the term *al-Iskandarānīyūn* was used with reference to the school of Alexandria and more generally to the later Greek scholars before Islam.[317] Thus Ibn Abī Uṣaibiʿah mentions that Isḥāq b. Ḥunain produced a work *Iṣlāḥ jawāmiʿ al-Iskandarānīyīn li-sharḥ Jālīnūs li-Kitāb al-fuṣūl li-Abuqrāṭ*, i.e. *Correction of the Summary of the Alexandrians to the Commentary of Galen on the 'Aphorisms' of Hippocrates*.[318] Ibn an-Nadīm in his notice of Aristotle in the *Fihrist* states that the Alexandrians had a paraphrase[319] of the *De anima* in about 100 pages (*wa-li 'l-Iskandarānīyīn talkhīṣ hādhā 'l-kitāb naḥwa miʾat waraqah*).[320] According to Ibn Abī Uṣaibiʿah in another passage,[321] the *Kitāb al-ʿilal wa 'l-aʿrāḍ* (*De morborum causis*) of Galen was in 6 discourses (*maqālāt*), but the Alexandrians collected, i.e. summarised[322] them and made them a single volume (*al-Iskandarānīyūn jamaʿūhā wa-jaʿalūhā kitāban wāḥidan*). It is doubtless in the same sense that the Alexandrians are mentioned in the title of the *Summa*, and we need make no difficulty in regard to Nicolaus of Damascus, the Peripatetic philosopher,[323] as the author of the original Greek. The work, ren-

---

[316] al-Balādhurī, *Futūḥ al-buldān (Liber expugnationis regionum)*, ed. Michael J. de Goeje, Leiden 1866, pp. 220-222; ed. Ṣalāḥ ad-Dīn al-Munajjid, Cairo 1956, pp. 259 and 261; Abū Jaʿfar Muḥammad ibn Jarīr aṭ-Ṭabarī, *Taʾrīkh ar-rusul wa 'l-mulūk (Annales)*, ed. Michael J. de Goeje *et al.*, 15 vols., Leiden 1879-1901, here Prima Series V, p. 2587; Ibn al-Athīr, *al-Kāmil fī 'l-taʾrīkh*, ed. Carolus J. Tornberg, 13 vols., Leiden 1851-1876 (reprinted Beirut 1385/1965-1386/1966), sub annis 25 et 487, vol. III, p. 81, and vol. X, p. 238; Masʿūdī, *Murūj adh-dhahab, op. cit.*, vol. II, p. 436; Ibn Khaldūn, *Les Prolégomènes d'Ebn Khaldoun (Muqaddimah)*, ed. Étienne Marc Quatremère, 3 vols., Paris 1858, vol. I, p. 12.

[317] Ibn Abī Uṣaibiʿah, *ʿUyūn al-anbāʾ*, *op. cit.*, vol. I, p. 3, places the Alexandrians immediately before the physicians of early Islam.

[318] *Ibid.*, vol. I, p. 201.

[319] For *talkhīṣ*, the word here used, Steinschneider (*Arabische Übersetzungen aus dem Griechischen, op. cit.*, p. 329) gave "Paraphrasen oder Extracte"; elsewhere he mentions *talkhīṣ* as the name for the *Middle Commentaries* of Ibn Rushd and says it means "wörtlich: Extract, dem Sinne nach *Résumé*" (*Die hebraeischen Übersetzungen des Mittelalters und die Juden als Dolmetscher*, Berlin 1893 [reprinted Graz 1956], p. 52, § 16). Cf. also Alfred Ivry, "Averroes' Three Commentaries on *De anima*", in: Gerhard Endreß and Jan A. Aertsen (eds.), *Averroes and the Aristotelian Tradition, Sources, Constitution and Reception of the Philosophy of Ibn Rushd (1126-1198)*, Leiden 1999, pp. 199-216.

[320] Ibn an-Nadīm, *Fihrist, op. cit.*, vol. I, p. 251.

[321] Ibn Abī ʿUṣaibiʿah, *ʿUyūn al-anbāʾ*, *op. cit.*, vol. I, p. 92.

[322] Arabic *jamaʿa* as used here explains *jawāmiʿ*, plural of *jāmiʿ* = 'summary'.

[323] Cf. above, p. 77, n. 312. Nicolaus described himself as an enthusiast for Aristotle (Jacoby, *F. gr. Hist.*, *op. cit.*, vol. IIA, no. 90, frg. 132 [2], p. 421).

dered into Syriac by a good translator and then from Syriac into Arabic by Ibn Zurʿah, was eventually put into Latin with the title *Summa Alexandrinorum* by Hermannus Alemannus.

VI

There remains another document from which light on the *Nicomachean Ethics* may be expected. This consists of a few pages in a Cairo manuscript of miscellaneous contents, Taimur Pasha 290 Akhlāq, the existence of which was first signalised by Paul Kraus in 1937.[324] In the table of contents of the manuscript, which is dated to the 14th or 15th century A.D., the title appears as *Min kitāb al-ikhlāṣ ikhtiṣār* plus another word or words. This has already caused difficulty, but no doubt *kitāb al-ikhlāṣ* should be read *kitāb al-akhlāq* (*Book of Ethics*). The latter part of the notice reads *al-Iskandar ahmīn* (?) with the correction in a later hand *al-Iskandarānīn*, apparently for *al-Iskandarānīyīn*.[325] *Ikhtiṣār al-Iskandarānīyīn* (*Summary of the Alexandrians*) appears to have been read by Hermannus Alemannus in the Arabic text which he was translating, hence for the work discussed in part V of this Introduction the title *Summa Alexandrinorum*.

The Cairo manuscript adds to our knowledge of the Arabic behind the *Summa* by providing excerpts not in the *Mukhtār al-ḥikam* and offers quotations from Books I, VI, 'Seven' and VII of the *Ethics* which in general agree with the Latin. It also contains additional material of uncertain origin and differs from the other texts which contain the 'Seventh Book', i.e. the complete Arabic version of EN in the Fez manuscript and the *Summa Alexandrinorum*, in placing it apparently before, and not after, the authentic Book VI, here called Book VII.

The passages are as follows:

a) MS. Cairo, pp. 310-311:

min al-maqālah al-ūlā. kull ṣināʿah wa-madhhab wa-himmah wa-fiʿl

---

[324] *"Kitāb al-akhlāq li-Jālīnūs"*, in: *Majallat Kullīyat al-ādāb bi'l-Jāmiʿa al-miṣrīya (Bulletin of the Faculty of Arts of the University of Egypt)* 5 (1937), Arabic Section, pp. 1-51, here p. 7.

[325] For this name see pp. 77f.

> *wa-ikhtiyār fa'innahu yuẓannu bihi annahu yaqṣid ilā khair mā fa'l-khair huwa alladhī yatashauwaquhu al-kull. wa'l-maqṣūdāt aṣ-ṣinā'īyah kathīrah mukhtalifah minhā mā huwa fi'l wa-minhā mā huwa infi'āl wa'l-infi'āl fīhā afḍal min al-fi'l fa'inna gharaḍ aṭ-ṭibb aṣ-ṣiḥḥah wa-ba'ḍ aṣ-ṣinā'āt yadkhulu taḥta ba'ḍ ka'l-jins wa'n-nau' wa'sh-shaḥṣ. wa'l-muqauwimah ashraf. wa-kamā anna li'l-maṭbū'āt tamāman taqṣiduhu aṭ-ṭabī'ah bi-dhātihā wa-li'l-ma'qūlāt tamāman yaqṣiduhu al-'aql bi-dhātihi ka-dhālika li'l-maṣnū'āt tamāmun taqṣiduhu al-mihnah al-insānīyah bi-dhātihā wa-huwa al-khair al-maqṣūd.*

This represents EN 1, 1 - 2, 1, and gives in an abbreviated form what we find in the *Summa Alexandrinorum* (ed. Marchesi, p. XLI, ll. 1-5; ed. Fowler, pp. 195-196 [I, 2-7]):

> Omnis ars et omnis incessus (*madhhab*) et omnis sollicitudo uel propositum et quelibet actionum et omnis electio ad bonum aliquod tendere uidetur. Optime ergo diffinierunt bonum dicentes quod ipsum est quod intenditur ex modis omnibus. Sunt autem intenta per artes multas [leg. multa et *Fowler*] diuersa. Quedam enim sunt actio ipsamet (ipsamet] quid ipsarum artium *Fowler*) et quedam sunt ipsum actum [...].

This excerpt is not in the *Mukhtār al-ḥikam.*

b) MS. Cairo, p. 311:

> *al-aḥdāth ghair al-maqmū'īn wa'ṭ-ṭubbā' fī 'sh-shahawāt lā yuntafa'u bihim fī 'd-dunyā fī 's-siyāsah. wa-ammā alladhī yasta'milu ash-shahawāt 'alā qadr mā yanbaghī wa-fī 'l-waqt wa-bi'l-miqdār alladhī yanbaghī wa-ḥaithu yanbaghī fa-mā akthara 'l-intifā' bihi fīmā 'alima min sinā'at as-siyāsah.*

In the *Mukhtār al-ḥikam*, p. 209, the second part of this reads:

> *alladhī yasta'milu ash-shahawāt 'alā mā yanbaghī wa-fī 'l-waqt alladhī yanbaghī wa-bi'l-miqdār alladhī yanbaghī wa-ḥaithu yanbaghī fa-mā akthara 'l-intifā' bihi fī ṣinā'at as-siyāsah.*

The whole passage is rendered in the *Summa* (ed. Marchesi, p. XLII, ll. 19-22; ed. Fowler, p. 197 [IV, 7-11]):

> Pueri ergo dissoluti et desideriorum prosecutores [persecutores *Fowler*] non proficiunt penitus ex arte ciuili. Qui autem utitur desiderio secundum quod oportet et quando oportet et quantum oportet et ubi oportet, hic plurimum proficit [proficiet *Fowler*] ex scientia artis ciuilis.

The corresponding passage is EN I, 3, 5-7.

c) MS. Cairo, p. 311:

> *al-khair ḍarbān khair bi-dhātihi wa-khair min ajl ghairihi wa'l-maṭlūb li-dhātihi afḍal min al-maṭlūb li-ghairihi. fa-naḥnu nurīdu as-saʿādah al-quṣwā li-dhātihā idh hiya ghāyat gharaḍinā wa-nurīdu al-faḍā'il min ajl as-saʿādah.*

This appears to combine EN I, 6, 9 and 7, 4-5. *Mukhtār al-ḥikam*, p. 210, has the first part only: *al-khair ʿalā ḍarbain aḥaduhumā bi-dhātihi wa'l-ākhar khair min ajl ghairihi wa'l-maṭlūb li-ghairihi. Summa Alexandrinorum* has the passage (ed. Marchesi, p. XLIII, ll. 3-7; ed. Fowler, p. 198 [II, 11-15]):

> Est autem bonum secundum duos modos: bonum per se et bonum propter aliud; et quesitum quidem propter se melius est quesito propter aliud. Nos uero beatitudinem ultimam propter se uolumus, cum sit finis noster et intentum [intentus *Fowler*] a nobis; honores autem et uirtutes propter beatitudinem.

d) MS. Cairo, p. 311:

> *al-khair yanqasimu ʿalā thalāth jihāt khair fī 'n-nafs wa-khair fī 'l-badan wa-khair fī 'l-ashyā' al-khārijah wa-khair an-nafs afḍaluhā wa-hādhā lā taẓharu ṣūratuhu illā bi-afʿāl al-faḍīlah fa's-saʿādah fī iqtinā'ihā wa-istiʿmālihā maʿan wa's-saʿādah al-ḥaqīqah muḥtājah fī hādhā 'l-ʿālam ilā 'l-khairāt allatī min khārij li'annahu yaʿsuru ʿalā 'l-insān an yukmila al-aʿfāl al-jamīlah allatī hiya al-faḍā'il* [breaks off].

After *maʿan* (l. 4 here) Cairo omits a passage in both *Mukhtār al-ḥikam* (p. 210: *idhā kānat* [...]) and *Summa Alexandrinorum* (ed. Marchesi, p. XLIV, top = ed. Fowler, p. 200 [IV, 8ff.]: "Cumque fuerit beatitudo in homine [...]"). We have the following text in the *Mukhtār*, p. 210:

> *wa-qāla: al-khair yanqasimu ʿalā thalāth jihāt khair fī 'l-badan wa-khair fī 'n-nafs wa-khair min khārij al-badan fa'l-khair alladhī huwa aulā bi-maʿnā al-khair mā huwa minhā fī 'n-nafs wa-lā taẓhar ṣūrat hādhā 'l-khair illā bi'l-afʿāl allatī bi'l-faḍīlah wa's-saʿādah fī iqtinā' al-faḍīlah wa'stiʿmālihā maʿan. wa-qāla: idhā kānat as-saʿādah sa-jīyah maknūnah fī 'l-insān lā tafʿal fa-laʿallahu kāna ka'l-fāḍil an-nā'im alladhī lā yaẓhar faḍluhu. wa-qāla: as-saʿādah al-ilāhīyah hā hunā muḥtājah ilā 'l-khairāt al-khārijah ʿan al-insān li'annahu yaʿsuru ʿalā 'l-insān an yafʿala al-afʿāl al-jamīlah bi-lā māddah mithl ṣāliḥ al-aqsām fī jūdat al-ʿaish wa-kathrat al-ikhwān wa-li-hādhā 'l-maʿnā*

> *iḥtājat al-ḥikmah ilā ṣawāb al-mamlakah* [corr. *ṣināʿat al-mulk*][326] *fī iẓhār sharafihā wa-faḍlihā,*

and in the *Summa Alexandrinorum* (ed. Marchesi, pp. XLIII, l. 34 - XLIV, l. 17; ed. Fowler, p. 200 [IV, 2-26]):

> Bonum tripliciter diuiditur; est bonum anime et bonum corporis et bonum extra corpus. Bonum ergo quod dignissime bonum dicitur est bonum anime, neque apparet forma istius boni, nisi in actibus qui sunt a uirtute. Et beatitudo quidem est in acquisitione uirtutum et in usu earum simul. Cumque fuerit beatitudo in homine tamquam in possessione [dispositione *Fowler*] et habitu et non actu, tunc est tamquam uirtuosus dormiens cuius non apparet actio neque uirtus [...]. Beatitudo tamen que est hic [in parte *Fowler*][327] bonis exterioribus indiget; difficile est enim homini ut opera decora exerceat absque materia ut pote [Oportet *Fowler*] quod habeat partem competentem rerum bone uite pertinentium et copiam familie et parentum et prosperitatem fortune. Et hac quidem de causa indiget ars sapientie arte regnandi, ut apparere faciat honorificentiam sui atque ualorem.

The corresponding passages in the Greek are EN I, 8, 2, 9 and 15. One notes in the Arabic of the Cairo manuscript *as-saʿādah al-ḥaqīqah*, less original perhaps than *as-saʿādah al-ilāhīyah* in *Mukhtār al-ḥikam*. "Beatitudo" is left unqualified in the Latin translation.

The extent of the gap already referred to after *maʿan* in l. 4 of the quotation from Cairo above amounts to a dozen lines in *Summa Alexandrinorum* (ed. Marchesi, p. XLIV, ll. 1-12 = Fowler, p. 200 [IV, 8-21]), six or seven lines in *Mukhtār* (p. 210).

e) MS. Cairo, p. 312:

> *min al-maqālah as-sābiʿah. al-faḍīlah nauʿān faḍīlah shaklīyah ʿillatuhā an-nafs al-ḥissīyah allatī lā kalimah lahā wa-faḍīlah fikrīyah ʿillatuhā an-nafs an-nāṭiqah wa'n-nafs al-ḥissīyah taṭlubu wa-tahrubu bi-lā rawiyah wa-lā ikhtiyār wa'n-nafs an-nāṭiqah tūjibu wa-taslubu wa-tuṣaddiqu wa-tukadhdhibu bi'r-rawiyah wa'l-ikhtiyār fa-shahwah taṭlubu wa'l-ʿaql yujību an yamnaʿu. al-ikhtiyār shahwah ʿaqlīyah. al-ḥikmah saʿādah li-dhātihā taḥṣul bi'l-ikhtiyār.*

This passage (not among the excerpts in the *Mukhtār al-ḥikam*) represents EN VI, 1, 4ff., though said to be from the 'Seventh Book'.

---

[326] This reading is confirmed by the Latin translation "arte regnandi" in the texts of Marchesi and Fowler and is actually found in the parallel passage of Miskawaih quoted p. 30. Cf. also al-Fārābī, *Fuṣūl al-madanī*, *op. cit.*, p. 104, § 3.

[327] The other reading, "hic", is preferable in view of *hā hunā* in the Arabic.

This is because in the Cairo manuscript material from the intrusive Book, which in the other sources comes after Book VI of the Greek EN, comes before Book VI.[328] Since two passages from the 'Seventh Book' in the Arabic EN and in the *Summa Alexandrinorum* immediately precede the new heading in the Cairo manuscript *min al-maqālah as-sābiʿah*, we may suppose that the intrusive Book was here numbered the Sixth Book. To the Arabic of Cairo, p. 312, corresponds *Summa Alexandrinorum* (ed. Marchesi, pp. LXIV, l. 25 - LXV, l. 31; ed. Fowler, pp. 224-225 [I, 2 - IV, 2]):

> Virtutum duo [leg. due *Fowler*] sunt species, uirtus uidelicet figuralis pertinens anime sensibili que non habet rationem, et uirtus intellectualis que pertinet anime rationali que habet rationem et discretionem et intellectum. Anima igitur sensibilis agit et fugit et prosequitur absque preconsiliatione et electione. Anima uero rationalis agit et affirmat et negat et assentit et discernit ex consiliatione et electione.[329] Ideoque dictum est quod concupiscentia quidem appetit, intellectus autem affirmat, et non fit electio nisi ab intellectu: principium ergo electionis intellectus est. Et electio est desiderium intellectuale [...] Sapientia felicitas est eligibilis propter se ipsam.

After "desiderium intellectuale" there is an interval of 30-40 lines.

f) MS. Cairo, p. 312:

> *al-muḥākī al-muḍḥik yunaqqiṣu dhātahu wa-ahlahu wa-yaṣbiru ʿalā kull shaiʾ wa-yuqābiluhu al-fadm al-ghabī alladhī lā yaqūlu wa-lā yasmaʿu wa'l-mumāzih mutawassiṭ bainahumā haiyin at-tanaqqul min ḥāl ilā ḥāl.*

This is from the 'Seventh Book' of the Arabic EN, c. 6, §§ 8-9, and the original is EN IV, 8, 10. *Summa Alexandrinorum* is similar (ed. Marchesi, p. LXVII, ll. 19-22; ed. Fowler, p. 227 [IX, 12-16]):

> Histrio est ridiculose se habens in omnibus donec se ipsum et uxorem et filios derideat; et huic contrarius [add. est *Fowler*] qui semper seuerum uultum pretendit nec aliis colloquitur nec eos audit: horum uero medius est qui mediocriter se habet in hiis.

This passage is not in *Mukhtār al-ḥikam*.

g) MS. Cairo, p. 312:

> *ad-ʿadl fī 'l-madīnah tawassuṭ baina 'l-gharāmah wa'r-ribḥ fī'l-akhdh*

---

[328] Above, p. 79.

[329] This sentence is lacking in Fowler's text, *loc. cit.*, p. 224.

> *wa'l-iʿṭā' wa'l-muqāyaḍah ka'l-ḥā'ik yuqāyiḍu bi'l-athwār* [corr. *bi'l-athwāb*] *wa-lammā kānat al-muqāyaḍah li-sā'ir al-aṣnāf ʿasirah jiddan wuḍiʿa qadr wāḥid li-jamīʿihā wa-qābalūhā bihi wa-ṭuliba fīhi imkān baqā'ihi wa-ḥamlihi wa-min hā hunā ṣāra ad-dirham wa'd-dīnār yastaʿmiluhu al-bannā' wa'l-fallāḥ wa'l-ḥā'ik.*

This again is from the 'Seventh Book' of the Arabic EN, c. 10, § 1, cf. EN V, 5, 10-11. The *Summa Alexandrinorum* has (ed. Marchesi, p. LXVIII, ll. 13-18; ed. Fowler, p. 228 [XI, 2-7]):

> Iustitia in ciuitate est medium intra [leg. inter *Fowler*] perditionem et lucrum, et non est possibile ut fit [leg. sit] absque acceptione et datione et concambio; ut textor qui dat pannos pro rebus aliis et ferrarius qui dat ferramenta pro rebus aliis. Et quare [leg. quia *Fowler*] circa huiusmodi cambia [concambia *Fowler*] incidit difficultas, statuerunt in ciuitatibus rem unam mediante qua adequatio fiat inter connegotiantes: et hoc est nummisma.

In the Latin the 'coppersmith' (*naḥḥās*) of the Arabic 'Seventh Book' has become "ferrarius". The passage is not in *Mukhtār al-ḥikam.*

h) MS. Cairo, p. 312ff.:

> *min al-maqālah ath-thāminah. nabtadi' bi-dhikr ajnās al-amrāḍ al-ʿāliyah thumma bi-mudāwat al-aʿẓam fa'l-aʿẓam minhā nikāyatan. fa-naqūlu: al-ajnās al-ʿāliyah li'r-radhā'il allatī hiya al-amrāḍ an-nafsānīyah muqābilat li'l-faḍā'il al-arbaʿ wa-hiya al-ḥikmah wa'n-najdah wa'l-ʿiffah wa'l-ʿadālah.*

There follows in MS. Cairo, pp. 313-315, a long development on the main heads of the vices as excess and defect of the four virtues (wisdom, courage, temperance and justice), and thus eight in number. To wisdom (*ḥikmah*) are opposed foolishness (*balah*) and deceitfulness (*jarbazah*); to courage (*najdah* or *shajaʿah*), rashness (*tahauwur*) and cowardice (*jubn*); to temperance (*ʿiffah*), greed (*sharah*) and lack of feeling (*khumūd*); to justice (*ʿadālah*), injustice (*jaur*) and abjection (*mahānah*). One or two minor vices are next mentioned, and there follows (MS. Cairo, pp. 315-316) an account of the nature and causes of anger.

The starting point in all this is clearly EN VII, 1, 1, but the compiler of the Cairo text has gone his own way. In the *Summa Alexandrinorum* (ed. Marchesi, p. LXVIII, ll. 31-33; ed. Fowler, p. 229 [I, 2-4]) Book VII begins as follows: "Vitia moralia detestabilia a quibus fugiendum [est *Fowler*] tria sunt: malitia, ferocitas, incastitas. Et uirtutes hiis opposite tres sunt: benignitas, clementia, castitas." The passage is not in *Mukhtār al-ḥikam*, but the Arabic text of EN VII, 1, 1 in the Fez manuscript has: *al-anwāʿ allatī li'l-ashyā' al-khulqīyah allatī yuhrabu ʿanhā thalāthah ash-sharrīyah wa'l-lā ʿiffah wa's-sabʿīyah wa'l-aḍdād* [...]. The compiler of the Cairo text has, however, substituted for a threefold list of vices to be avoided and their corresponding virtues a fourfold list of the same. In this he may have made use of a *Risālah fī ḥudūd al-ashyā' wa-rusūmihā*[330] attributed to al-Kindī, where several of the same terms occur (*tahauwur, jubn, sharah, jarbazah*—the last specially noticeable) and each of the virtues has two opposing vices, i.e. of defect as well as excess. On the other hand, in the *Risālah* attributed to al-Kindī the definition of anger is given in a line.[331]

It is thus easily shown that the Cairo manuscript contains a substantial amount of material from the Arabic behind the Latin of the *Summa Alexandrinorum*, which is to be found among the fragments in the *Mukhtār al-ḥikam* and, where these fail, in the *Summa Alexandrinorum* itself. This material it tends to abbreviate, sometimes on a small scale,[332] sometimes on a much larger scale.[333] On the other hand, this text offers also quite extensive additional material, notably the account of the vices and their corresponding virtues, and the long development on anger, which can scarcely have belonged to the Arabic behind the Latin of the *Summa*. But this is little more than to say that the compiler of the Cairo text, like al-Mubashshir b. Fātik in the *Mukhtār al-ḥikam*, has made his own selection from the Arabic original of the *Summa Alexandrinorum* and, while evidently retaining the title *Ikhtiṣār al-Iskandarānīyīn*, has added substantially to what he found there either his own observations, or what he took from some other text or texts unknown.

VII

It has hitherto been assumed on all hands rather than proved that the Arabic version of EN in 11 Books as in the Fez manuscript is the

330 al-Kindī, *Rasā'il, op. cit.*, vol. I, pp. 163-179.
331 *Ibid.*, p. 176.
332 Cf. c) and e) above.
333 Cf. d) and e) above, where 12 and up to 40 lines respectively have been omitted.

same as the work in 12 Books mentioned by Ibn an-Nadīm as Aristotle's *Kitāb al-akhlāq* commented by Porphyry.[334] The ambiguity of Ibn an-Nadīm's statement was noted by Arberry, whose comment was that the wording leaves it uncertain as to whether it was the text of Aristotle or the Commentary of Porphyry that was composed in 12 Books. Fortunately it is not necessary to say more on this before proceeding.[335] In any case it is not evident that the two works are the same, though the work in 12 Books may include the other.

We may now consider that with most of the Arabic authors cited above for EN the text from which they quote can be determined with little difficulty. Thus al-ʿĀmirī, in addition to much unidentified ethical material from Aristotle,[336] quotes for the first time the Arabic text of EN as found in the Fez manuscript.[337] Miskawaih on the other hand in the *Kitāb tahdhīb al-akhlāq* and al-Mubashshir b. Fātik in the *Mukhtār al-ḥikam* quote the Arabic behind the Latin of the *Summa Alexandrinorum*, while later in Spain Ibn Bājjah and others evidently used the Fez text. In these cases the identification is usually clear though it cannot always be demonstrated.[338] Al-Fārābī is the exception, for though he refers a number of times in his extant works to the *Nīqūmākhiyā* and, what is the same thing, the *Kitāb al-akhlāq*, as we have seen,[339] and himself wrote a commentary on the first part of it (*sharḥ ṣadr Kitāb al-akhlāq li-Arisṭūṭālīs*),[340] he cannot be cited *verbatim* for either the Fez text or the *Summa Alexandrinorum*.

One's impression that al-Fārābī's information about the *Nicomachean Ethics* is derived from some other source is confirmed by what we know of his Commentary. This in its entirety must be judged lost. We have, however, a number of references to it in the Arabic texts, several of which have already been given above. In considering these references we find a somewhat striking lack of correspondence between the words, and even the subject-matter, of the Commentary as quoted and the Fez text, not to mention the

---

334 Cf. above, p. 26.
335 A solution of the question is attempted elsewhere (p. 27).
336 Cf. above, p. 25.
337 See above, pp. 19ff.
338 In line with all the evidence cf. pp. 47ff.
339 See above, pp. 11ff.
340 Ibn Abī Uṣaibiʿah, *ʿUyūn al-anbāʾ*, *op. cit.*, vol. II, p. 138.

Summa. Al-Fārābī's own citation of his Commentary[341] contrasts the subject of EN (*Kitāb Nīqūmākhiyā*) as 'the rules of the city' (*al-qawānīn al-madanīyah*) 'according to what we have explained in places of our Commentary on that book', rather than simply ethics or 'ethical rules' (*al-qawānīn al-khulqīyah*) 'according to what Porphyry and many of the commentators after him have said' (*ʿalā mā qālahu Furfūriyūs wa-kathīr mimman baʿdahu min al-mufassirīn*). This is tantalising[342]—too brief to make much of—but we can readily understand that al-Fārābī may have had before him the version of EN with Porphyry's Commentary mentioned by Ibn an-Nadīm.

Earlier in the same passage al-Fārābī had quoted the *Kitāb Nīqūmākhiyā* to the effect that all ethical qualities or dispositions alter and that none of them is by nature (EN II, 1, 1-2), adding that it is possible for a man to change from one to another through habituation and use.[343] At a later stage in the discussion he quotes Aristotle in the 'little *Nīqūmākhiyā*' as having 'enumerated the causes of the difficulty of changing from ethical quality to ethical quality and the causes of its being easy [...]'.[344] But what Aristotle is this? Granted that the 'little *Nīqūmākhiyā*' is a translation of Greek τὰ μικρὰ Νικομάχια, i.e. the *Nicomachean Ethics* itself,[345] the last quotation cannot be made to fit satisfactorily into the text of either the Arabic EN as found in the Fez manuscript or the *Summa Alexandrinorum*.[346] It is clear, however, that al-Fārābī treated the 'change from ethical quality to ethical quality' in his Commentary. We have this from Maimonides, already quoted: 'Abū Naṣr [= al-Fārābī] said in the first part of his Commentary on the *Nicomachean*

---

[341] al-Fārābī, *Kitāb al-jamʿ baina 'l-ḥakīmain*, in: the same, *Philosophische Abhandlungen aus Londoner, Leidener und Berliner Handschriften*, *op. cit.*, p. 17, quoted above, p. 12.

[342] It is not clear what commentators on EN al-Fārābī may have known apart from Porphyry and perhaps Themistius (cf. Ibn an-Nadīm, *Fihrist*, *op. cit.*, vol. I, p. 252, cited above, p. 26).

[343] al-Fārābī, *Kitāb al-jamʿ baina 'l-ḥakīmain*, in: the same, *Philosophische Abhandlungen aus Londoner, Leidener und Berliner Handschriften*, *op. cit.*, p. 16, quoted above, p. 11.

[344] *Ibid.*, p. 18, quoted p. 13.

[345] For the 'little Nīqūmākhiyā' see pp. 14f.

[346] Cf. Douglas M. Dunlop, "The Manuscript Taimur Pasha 290 Aḫlāq and the *Summa Alexandrinorum*", in: *Arabica* 21 (1974), pp. 252-263, esp. pp. 258-259, where, however, the wrong inference is drawn.

Ethics: *As regards those who have the power to make their souls pass from ethical quality to ethical quality* [...].'[347] Ibn Bājjah also in his *Risālat al-wadāʿ* (*Epistle of Farewell*) referring to the same or another passage of al-Fārābī's Commentary mentions that the doctrine of metempsychosis (*tanāsukh*) is to be found there.[348] There is of course no reference to metempsychosis in EN. This idea, belonging especially to the later development of Greek philosophy, is appropriate in the work attributed to Porphyry by the *Fihrist*.

There is an interesting notice of al-Fārābī's Commentary on EN in the *Ḥaiy b. Yaqẓān* of Ibn Ṭufail (d. 561/1185-1186).[349] The same passage as attracted the attention of Ibn Ṭufail was also discussed at some length by Ibn Bājjah. The Bodleian manuscript of the works of Ibn Bājjah, Pococke 206, contains the following, headed simply *Wa-min qaulihi aiḍan* (*And of his words also*), i.e. we do not certainly know from which of Ibn Bājjah's larger works, if from any, it may have been taken:

> *Ammā mā yuẓannu bi-Abī Naṣr fī kalāmihi fīmā sharaḥahu min Kitāb al-akhlāq anna 'l-baqā' baʿd al-maut al-mufāraqah wa-lā as-saʿādah*[350] *illā 's-saʿādah al-madanīyah wa-lā 'l-wujūd illā 'l-wujūd al-maḥsūs wa-anna mā yuqālu inna bihā wujūd ākhar ghair al-wujūd al-maḥsūs khurāfāt ʿajā'iz hādhā kulluhu bāṭil wa-makdhūb fīhi ʿalā Abī Naṣr. wa-dhakara dhālika Abū Naṣr fī qaulin qara'tuhu wa-laisa yushbihu qauluhu fī hādhā aqwālahu allatī hiya lawāzim burhānīyah wa-aqwāluhu fī hādhā 'l-kitāb aktharuhā mansūbah wa-tushūwifa ar-radd fīhā ʿalā jihat taubīkh at-taqbīḥ lā yalīqu bi-mithlihi mithlu mā yaqūluhu fī man yaqūlu inna bihā wujūd ākhar ghair al-wujūd al-maḥsūs anna qaulahu khurāfāt ʿajā'iz*, i.e. as to what is thought of Abū Naṣr [= al-Fārābī] regarding his words on what he commented on of the *Book of Ethics*, to the effect that survival after death is separation (*mufāraqah*), and there is no happiness except the happiness of the city,[351] and no existence except sensible existence, and that what is

---

[347] See above, p. 50.

[348] Cf. above, pp. 40f.

[349] Text and translation have already been given on pp. 48f.

[350] *Sic* MS.

[351] Cf. MS. Pococke 206, fol. 126b: *as-saʿādah innamā hiya an yakūna ash-shakhṣ juz' madīnatin yakhdimu bi-ḥasab martabatihi fī an yaḥṣula lahu wa-li-ahlihā al-khairāt al-mukthirah al-maḥsūsah al-madanīyah al-mulidhdhah ʿalā mā yalīqu bi-masālin al-jamīʿ ʿalā afḍal al-aḥwāl al-madanīyah wa-ablaghihā fī baqā' an-nauʿ ʿalā 's-salāmah bi-ṭūl al-baqā'*, i.e. 'happiness is simply that a person should be part of a city, serving in accordance with his rank, so that there accrues to him and to its people the abundant delightful tangible goods of the city, conformably

> said regarding there being another existence different from the existence perceived by the senses is old wives' tales—all this is untrue and a calumny forged against Abū Naṣr. Abū Naṣr mentioned[352] that in a statement which I have read.[353] What he says in it is unlike his statements which are consequences drawn from [or 'depending on'] proof (*lawāzim burhānīyah*). His words in this book are attributed,[354] and their rejection is to be expected on the ground of being censured and disapproved—unworthy of such a man is such a remark as he made of whoever affirms another existence, different from the sensible existence, that what he says is old wives' tales.[355]

There follows a long development here omitted (except for some lines in n. 351) which concludes:

> *wa-qad tabaiyana mimmā dhakartuhu anna wujūd ghair al-wujūd al-maḥsūs. wa-mā aʿẓama hādhā 'n-naẓar! kaif khurāfāt al-aʿjāʾiz?*, i.e. it has now become clear from what I have mentioned that there is an existence, other than sensible existence. What a glorious view is this! How is it *old wives' tales*?[356]

The position of al-Fārābī in his Commentary on EN, severely castigated by Ibn Ṭufail and defended by Ibn Bājjah, took the form of a 'denial of the union of the active intellect with man' (*ittiṣāl al-ʿaql al-faʿʿāl bi'l-insān*), a conception belonging to the emanationist thought of Alexander of Aphrodisias (late 2nd century A.D.). According to it, the active intellect, a 'separate intelligence' emanating from the First (God), might enter the 'material intelligence' of man—man, that is, who as coming into existence and passing away has no 'separate existence'. Here we may compare passages of Ibn Rushd, the first of which is from his Commentary on the *De intellectu et intellecto* of Alexander of Aphrodisias, which had been translated into Arabic by Isḥāq b. Ḥunain.[357] Ibn Rushd there

---

with the interests of all, in conditions best for the city and most conductive to the survival of the race in permanent security.'

352 MS. *wʾdhkr* for *wdhkr*.

353 Apparently in al-Fārābī's Commentary on EN.

354 Sc. to their author(s), Arabic *mansūbah*, cf. Lane, s.v.

355 MS., fol. 126b. Ibn Bājjah, *Rasāʾil falsafīyah li-Abī Bakr Ibn Bājjah*, ed. Jamāl ad-Dīn al-ʿAlawī, Beirut/Casablanca 1983, p. 197.

356 See also Dunlop, "Remarks on a Text of Avempace", *loc. cit.*, p. 299.

357 Steinschneider, *Die arabischen Übersetzungen aus dem Griechischen*, *op. cit.*, p. 134. A Latin translation with the title *Alexandri Aphrodisei de intellectu* was edited by Alessandro Achillinus in his *Opus Septisegmentatum*, Bologna 1501, and later editions, cf. Steinschneider, *Al-Farabi*, *op. cit.*, p. 93, and *Die hebraeischen Übersetzungen des Mittelalters*, *op. cit.*, p. 204. For a modern edition see Gabriel

mentions the objections of several philosophers to the possibility of the union of man's intellect with the 'separate intelligences', and says:

> This has led Abū Naṣr [= al-Fārābī] in his Commentary of EN to assume that man has no other perfection than that to be attained through the speculative sciences, and he remarks: *The view that man becomes a separate intelligence is old wives' tales, for that which comes into existence and passes away is not eternal.*[358]

Ibn Rushd expressed himself somewhat differently in a short work *De animae beatitudine*, which appears to represent his *Maqālah fī ittiṣāl al-ʿaql al-mufāraq bi'l-insān*:[359]

> Et cum Avennasar credidit in fine suorum dierum pervenire ad hanc perfectionem et non pervenit, posuit impossibile hoc et vanum et dixit esse fabulas vetularum, sed est solum ut nos diximus, non autem ut dixit vir iste.[360]

Al-Fārābī's phrase 'old wives' tales' for the possibility of the union echoes down through a series of expositors and commentators.[361] What place, we may ask, have such emanationist ideas in a commentary on Aristotle's *Ethics*? Al-Fārābī can have introduced them from the Commentary of Porphyry.[362]

Théry, *Autour du décret de 1210: II. Alexandre d'Aphrodise, Aperçu sur l'influence de sa noétique*, Kain 1926, pp. 69-83.

358 Steinschneider, *Al-Farabi*, *op. cit.*, p. 94.

359 Ibn Abi Usaibiʿah, *ʿUyūn al-anbāʾ*, *op. cit.*, vol. II, p. 78. Cf. Steinschneider, *Die hebraeischen Übersetzungen des Mittelalters*, *op. cit.*, p. 199.

360 Steinschneider, *Al-Farabi*, *op. cit.*, p. 99. Cf. also the new edition by Marc Geoffroy and Carlos Steel, Averroes, *La béatitude de l'âme*, Paris 2001, pp. 164 and 165.

361 Ibn Bājjah (pp. 88f.) and Ibn Ṭufail (pp. 48f.) quoted above. See also Steinschneider, *Al-Farabi*, *op. cit.*, pp. 102, 107 and 108.

362 Emanationist ideas were known in Arabic after the translation in the Caliphate of al-Muʿtaṣim (834-843) of the so-called *Theology of Aristotle*, actually based on a portion of the *Enneads* of Plotinus. The *Theology* is stated in the preface to have been translated by ʿAbd al-Masīḥ b. ʿAbd Allāh Nāʿimah al-Ḥimsī and to have been corrected (*aṣlaḥahu*) by al-Kindī. Here we find (Pseudo-Aristotle, *Die sogenannte Theologie des Aristoteles aus arabischen Handschriften*, *op. cit.*, p. 104) a statement of the emanationist view, cf. also *ibid.*, p. 137: *afaḍa ʿalaihi* [sc. *al-ʿaql*] *al-wāḥid al-ḥaqq quwān kathīrah ʿaẓīmah*, i.e. 'and the One, the Truth, pours forth upon [the intellect] many splendid faculties.' The *De intellecto et intellectu* of Alexander of Aphrodisias with explicit emanationist explanations of Aristotle's teaching on the soul was translated a little later by Isḥāq b. Ḥunain (d. 910), cf. p. 89. Al-Fārābī quotes the *Theology of Aristotle* repeatedly in the *Kitāb al-jamʿ baina raʾyai al-ḥakīmain Aflāṭūn wa-Arisṭū* (in: the same, *Philosophische Abhandlungen aus*

On the other hand, quite a different, favourable, view of the union is expressed by al-Fārābī in his work *Fī 'l-ʿaql*[363] (*On the Intellect*). At this point there is no question of rejecting the idea:

> *hādhihi hiya as-saʿādah al-quṣwā wa'l-ḥaiyāt al-ākhirah wa-hiya an yaḥṣula li'l-insān ākhiru shaiʾin yatajauharu bihi wa-an yataḥaṣala lahu kamāluhu al-akhīr*, i.e. this is the ultimate happiness and the After Life, that is, that a man sustains a last substantiation and that there results for him his final perfection.[364]

The Latin translation[365] speaks of the action of the 'active intellect' on man's intellect, i.e. the union, as affording 'the ultimate end and another [sic] life by which [...] man's ultimate perfection is acquired (*hic est finis ultimus et vita alia qua* [...] *acquiritur perfectio eius ultima*)'. This is what readers of al-Fārābī's Commentary on EN expected him to say, and what he evidently did not there say,[366] giving rise to a very long debate.[367]

Londoner, Leidener und Berliner Handschriften, *op. cit.*, pp. 23, 24, 28 and 31) and certainly knew of Alexander of Aphrodisias whom he occasionally cites (*ibid.*, p. 31). But the connexion with EN seems to be only here.

363 Dieterici has *Fī maʿānī al-ʿaql* (in: al-Fārābī, *Philosophische Abhandlungen aus Londoner, Leidener und Berliner Handschriften*, *op. cit.*) an unimportant difference. I have followed the edition of Maurice Bouyges (al-Fārābī, *Risālah fī 'l-ʿaql* [Bibliotheca Arabica Scholasticorum; 8/1], Beirut 1938).

364 al-Fārābī, *Risālah fī 'l-ʿaql*, *op. cit.*, p. 43, cf. also pp. 44-45 and 47-48.

365 Dieterici found the work incomplete in the two Arabic MSS. which he used, and completed it from Hebrew translations in a Breslau dissertation: Michael Rosenstein, *Abū-Nassr Alfarabii De intellectu intellectisque*, Sulzbach 1858. A Latin version, *De intellectu* (*De intelligentiis*), has been several times printed with the works of Ibn Sīnā, e.g. Venice 1508, and reprinted in *Avicenna* [sic] *Opera*, Frankfurt am Main 1961. Cf. also al-Fārābī, *De intellectu et intellecto*, ed. Étienne Gilson, in: AHDLMA 4 (1929), pp. 115-141.

366 Later writers continued to cite his Commentary on EN in the sense which Ibn Bājjah wished to avoid, cf. above, pp. 88f.

367 We may here mention a similar change of front in another context. Al-Fārābī is quoted by Maimonides in his *Dalālat al-ḥāʾirīn* (text II, 15 end; transl. p. 292) as 'holding it clear and manifest and proved by demonstration' (*yarā Abū Naṣr anna 'l-amr baiyin wāḍiḥ yadullu ʿalaihi al-burhān*) that the heavens are eternal, i.e. without beginning and without end, and what is within them is subject to coming into existence and passing away—this with reference to Aristotle, *Topics* I, 11, 3 = 104b 13, where the question is asked: Is the world eternal or not? Al-Fārābī even found it disgraceful, according to Maimonides in the same passage, that Aristotle should doubt the eternity of the world and thoroughly disapproved of Galen for saying that this was a difficult question for which no proof was known (*istashnaʿa an yakūna Aristū yashukku fī qidam al-ʿālam wa'stakhaffa bi-Ġālīnūs kulla istikhfāf fī qaulihi inna hādhihi 'l-masʾalah mushkilah lā yuʿlamu lahā burhān*). In another passage (transl. p. 222) Maimonides says that al-Fārābī refuted the createdness of the world

A passage from the *Tadbīr al-mutawaḥḥid* of Ibn Bājjah, as Erwin Rosenthal has suggested, may come from al-Fārābī's Commentary on EN:

> *wa-lammā kānat jamī' as-siyar allatī fī hādhā 'z-zamān wa-fīmā kāna qablahā min mu'ẓam mā balaghnanā khabruhu allāhuma illā mā yaḥkī Abū Naṣr 'an sīrat al-Furs al-ūlā fā-kulluhā murakkabah min as-siyar al-khams*, i.e. now since all the types of state at present and in the past the majority of those news of whose existence has reached us, unless indeed what Abū Naṣr tells of the life of the primitive Persians, are compounded of the five lives.[368]

Al-Fārābī seems to say that the ancient Persians lived under a system of aristocracy which he calls *al-madīnah al-imāmīyah*, 'the priestly state'.[369] We should say more naturally 'state with a priest-king'. The

---

in his *Kitāb al-maujūdāt al-mutaghaiyirah al-mausūm bi'l-Kalām aṭ-ṭabī'ī* (*Book of the Changing Beings entitled Physical Dispute*), cf. Ibn Abī Uṣaibi'ah, *'Uyūn al-anbā'*, *op. cit.*, vol. II, p. 139, also Steinschneider, *Al-Farabi*, *op. cit.*, pp. 119-122. But elsewhere he expresses in the strongest language the opposite view. That the world should be without beginning and without end is a vile and detestable opinion (*hādhā 'ẓ-ẓann al-qabīḥ al-mustankar*, *Kitāb al-jam' baina ra'yai al-ḥakīmain*, in: al-Fārābī, *Philosophische Abhandlungen*, *op. cit.*, text p. 22; transl. p. 36), and Aristotle cannot be thought to have held it. For in the passage of the *Topics* where Aristotle asks the question: Is the world eternal or not?, he is not concerned to explain about the world but is giving an example in logic, and so: *ẓāhir annahu lā yumkin an yunsaba ilaihi al-i'tiqād bi-anna 'l-'ālam qadīm bi-hādhā 'l-mithāl alladhī utīya bihifī hādhā 'l-kitāb*, i.e. 'plainly the belief that the world is eternal cannot be attributed to him by this example which is cited in the above-mentioned book' (*ibid.*, pp. 22-23; transl. p. 36). Al-Fārābī goes on to support his argument by quotations from authentic works of Aristotle in Arabic translation, as well as the non-authentic *Theology*, to show that Aristotle regarded the world as created (*ibid.*, text pp. 23-24; transl. pp. 36-39). The remark of Pines (in his translation of Maimonides, *The Guide of the Perplexed*, *op. cit.*, pp. lxxix and lxxxi) that al-Fārābī changed his views in different works is amply justified. On the other hand, that al-Fārābī expressed opposite views to accomodate different kinds of readers, the main reason for these changes, as estimated by Pines, seems more than doubtful. It would have to be allowed that al-Fārābī is still a pioneer in the study of Aristotle among the Arabs, and that he only gradually comes to terms with Aristotle's ideas, even that he appears not to have known Aristotle's *Ethics* till comparatively late (unmentioned in his *Falsafat Arisṭūṭālīs* and *Kitāb iḥṣā' al-'ulūm*, see pp. 16-19).

[368] Ibn Bājjah, *Tadbīr al-mutawaḥḥid*, ed. Asín, p. 12; transl. p. 42; ed. Fakhry, p. 43; Ibn Rushd, *Averroes' Commentary on Plato's 'Republic'*, ed. and transl. Erwin I. J. Rosenthal, Cambridge 1956 (reprinted Cambridge 1969), pp. 288-289.

[369] See the discussion by Erwin I. J. Rosenthal, *Averroes' Commentary on Plato's 'Republic'*, *op. cit.*, pp. 288-289, cf. also pp. 215 and 281, and the same, "The Place of Politics in the Philosophy of Ibn Bajja", in: *Islamic Culture* 25 (1951), pp. 187-211, here p. 208, n. 72. The expression *[al-madīnah] al-imāmīyah* comes in the *Tadbīr al-mutawaḥḥid*, where Asín read *al-iqāmīyah* (text p. 54; transl. p. 91,

passage has not been identified in the extant works of al-Fārābī, and it may well come from the lost Commentary on EN.

Two certain references to al-Fārābī's Commentary in the works of Albertus Magnus should also be taken into account. The first of these[370] is as follows: "Et Alpharabius in *Commento* Arabico dicit, quod impotentia et paupertas et infortunia pronepotis contristant beatitudinem, et ita impediunt optimum actum beati", cf. EN I, 8, 15-16 and 10, 3-5. This is evidently not an exact quotation, but for once there seems to be an observable relation between al-Fārābī's Commentary and the actual text of the *Ethics*. Most citations in the Commentary, as we have seen, tend to be a long way from the text. How is this to be explained? From what has already been said it would appear that al-Fārābī used the *Ethics* with the Commentary of Porphyrius in 12 Books mentioned by Ibn an-Nadīm. Again, secondly, Albertus has with reference to the Commentary: "Id autem quod dicit in X *Ethicae*, est quod fiducia philosophantis est non conjungi agenti intellectum ut efficienti, sed etiam sicut formae [...]."[371] This is certainly not the doctrine of Aristotle.

There is also the preamble to Ibn Rushd's *Middle Commentary* on the *Ethics* discussed above which begins: "Dixit Abunazrin Alfarabius in commento suo super hunc librum [sc. EN]",[372] and proceeds to mention a 10-Book *Nicomachean Ethics*, as in the Greek, but which meets us here in Arabic for the first time. This appears to point to Porphyry's Commentary, but, at first sight at least, away from the 11-Book version in the Fez manuscript.

It would seem, however, that al-Fārābī had his knowledge of a 10-Book EN from Porphyry's Commentary, which he knew[373] and must have used for his own works, as al-ʿĀmirī certainly did a little later. But al-ʿĀmirī, with passages from Porphyry's Commentary, gives

---

n. 112). The correction was first made by Rosenthal, "The Place of Politics", *loc. cit.*, and so Majid Fakhry in Ibn Bājjah, *Rasāʾil*, *op. cit.*, p. 74.

370 Quoted by Salman, "The Mediaeval Latin Translations of Alfarabi's Works", *loc. cit.*, p. 247, from Albertus, *Commentarii in Librum IV Sententiarum*, dist. XLIV, B, art. 6 (Ed. Borgnet, vol. XXX, p. 675).

371 Salman, "The Mediaeval Latin Translations of Alfarabi's Works", *loc. cit.*, p. 248, quoting Albertus, *De anima*, lib. III, tract. III, c. 11 (Ed. Borgnet, vol. V, p. 386; Ed. Colon., vol. VII/I, p. 221).

372 See above, pp. 51f.

373 al-Fārābī, *Kitāb al-jamʿ bain raʾyai al-ḥakīmain*, in: the same, *Philosophische Abhandlungen*, *op. cit.*, text p. 17; transl. p. 27.

also word for word citations of EN as found in the Fez manuscript, and apparently had Aristotle's *Ethics* in 12 Books with Porphyry's Commentary, as mentioned in the *Fihrist*. This would apply also to al-Fārābī, since there is no reason to suppose that he could have had the Commentary without the text. This result agrees with other facts. The *Ethics* with the Commentary of Porphyry was translated by Isḥāq b. Ḥunain (d. 299/911-912)[374] and is mentioned by al-Kindī[375] as being in 11 Books. The generally accepted opinion that the work mentioned as the *Ethics* in 12 Books with Porphyry's Commentary and the text of EN in the Fez manuscript are the same work is not invalidated by what has just been said, but remains paradox.

VIII

In view of the early date which has been assigned to the Arabic translation of the *Nicomachean Ethics* as found in the Fez text, the nature of the Greek text upon which it was based—whether or not through an intervening Syriac translation of the Greek original—[376] becomes a matter of considerable interest. The earliest Greek manuscripts available for establishing the text of the *Ethics* are dated to the 10th (K^b) and 12th (L^b) centuries. On the probable assumption that the Arabic version in the Fez MS. dates from the late 9th or early 10th century,[377] the version offers at least the theoretical possibility of getting back to a form of the *Ethics* earlier than the oldest Greek manuscripts.[378] The difficulties of recovering more than the general type of the Greek text lying behind the Arabic translation are, however, so great as to be nearly insuperable. Apart from the likelihood of a Syriac version having been used for the Arabic translation,[379] the Fez manuscript of 619/1222 was written, pre-

[374] See above, p. 27.

[375] See above, p. 8.

[376] For a Syriac version of EN as intermediary between the original Greek and the Arabic version of the Fez MS. see pp. 26, 62, 106.

[377] Cf. pp. 2, 27f.

[378] Cf. Gauthier and Jolif in Aristotle, *L'Éthique à Nicomaque*, *op. cit.*, vol. I/1, p. 302: "La découverte de la traduction arabe des livres VII-X devrait nous permettre de remonter pour ces livres à un état du texte antérieur à nos plus anciens manuscrits grecs." This applies also to Books I-VI (the last incomplete), see my article "The *Nicomachean Ethics* in Arabic", *loc. cit.*

[379] Cf. n. 376.

sumably, more than three hundred years later than the date when the translation was first made and represents at least a transference of the Arabic from the Oriental script in which it must be assumed to have been set down into the *Maghribī* or Western hand in which it is now found in the Fez manuscript. The comparatively late date of the manuscript and the incomplete state of the text, as well as the probable language change from Syriac to Arabic and the change from one form of Arabic script to another, are all circumstances unfavourable to the Fez manuscript's offering a text which can serve as representative in any complete sense of the Greek text of EN before the 10th century A.D.

But it is certainly possible to come to some findings about the Greek text behind the translation in the Fez manuscript. Among Greek manuscripts of EN those designated K^b (10th century) and L^b (12th century) hold a special interest because of their age. Readings of both are to be found in the Arabic translation. Thus for K^b we have EN I, 7, 6 = 1097b 8-10: *wa-lasnā nurīdu bi'l-kifāyah an takūna sīrat al-insān sīrat al-mutakhallī wa'l-munfarid waḥdahu lākinnahu yakūna maʿa abawain wa-aulādin wa-nisā'in wa-ahli madīnatin*, Greek: τὸ δ' αὔταρκες λέγομεν οὐκ αὐτῷ μόνῳ, τῷ ζῶντι βίον μονώτην, ἀλλὰ καὶ γονεῦσι καὶ τέκνοις καὶ γυναικὶ καὶ ὅλος τοῖς φίλοις καὶ πολίταις, where for γυναικί K^b has the plural γυναιξί = *nisā'in* of the Arabic. Again, EN 1168b 2 = IX, 8, 2: *wa-aḥrā an yakūna ṣadīqan alladhī yurīdu al-khairāt au alladhī yurīdu al-khairāt li-ṣadīqihi min ajlihi*, Greek: φίλος δὲ μάλιστα ὁ βουλόμενος ᾧ βούλεται τἀγαθὰ ἐκείνου ἕνεκα, where for ᾧ K^b has ἢ ὢ (ᾧ), cf. *au alladhī*. Similarly, EN VIII, 9, 3 = 1160a 7-8: *wa-yaẓharu anna al-ʿadl yatazaiyadu maʿa al-maḥabbah*, Greek: αὔξεσθαι δὲ πέφυκεν ἅμα τῇ φιλίᾳ καὶ τὸ δίκαιον, where for πέφυκεν K^b read φαίνεται = *yaẓharu* of the Arabic. Or we may consider EN III, 8, 12 = 1117a 2-3, where Greek: οὐ δή ἐστιν ἀνδρεῖα [...] πρὸς τὸν κίνδυνον, is omitted by K^b and also in the Arabic translation, or again, EN VIII, 13, 9 = 1163a 2, where Arabic omits καὶ ἑκόντι with K^b. But the Arabic version is not constant to K^b, as we can see from cases like EN I, 7, 12 = 1098a 2: *yaẓharu min amr hādhihi aiḍan*, where φαίνεται δὲ καὶ αὐτή—not αὕτη—was the reading of K^b, or EN II, 7, 11 = 1108a 15-16: τὰ δ' ἄκρα οὔτ' ἐπαινετὰ οὔτ' ὀρθὰ ἀλλὰ ψεκτά, rendered *wa'l-aṭrāf laisat bi-sawāb wa-lā maḥmūdah*, where ἐπαινετὰ οὔτ' ὀρθά was the reading of K^b, or again EN X, 5, 1 =

1175a 24, where Arabic reads *al-asnām*, plural, against ἄγαλμα of K^b^. A reading of K^b^ which has been widely discussed is at EN IX, 12, 2 = 1172a 8 where ὡς οἷόν τε appears for οἷς οἴονται in a text rendered in the Arabic *wa-yushārikūna 'lladhīna yarauna an yushārikū fī 'l-ḥayāt*. It is quite clear that *'lladhīna yarauna* represents οἷς [masc.] οἴονται, not K^b^.

But further in the Arabic version we have the readings also of L^b^. A good example of this is EN III, 5, 15 = 1114a 25: *laisa yūjadu aḥadun min an-nās ya'nufu man huwa samij bi't-ṭab'a bal innamā ya'nufu man huwa kadhālika li-tawānin wa-ihmāl wa-ka-dhālika al-ḥāl fī 'l-maraḍ wa'l-qubḥ wa'z-zamānah*, of which the last part in the Greek is: ὁμοίως δὲ καὶ περὶ ἀσθένειαν καὶ πήρωσιν. Arabic has added *wa'l-qubḥ*, but this is καὶ αἶσχος, the reading of L^b^, wanting in Bywater's other manuscripts and modern texts. Other examples of L^b^ readings are EN IV, 3, 23 = 1124b 7: *kathīr al-mukhāṭarah*, Greek: μικροκίνδυνος, where Arabic evidently read μυκνοκίνδυνος with L^b^; EN V, 2, 9 = 1130b 11: *wa'l-akthar*, Greek: καὶ τὸ παράνομον, where Arabic read καὶ τὸ πλέον of L^b^; EN V, 4, 2 = 1131b 31-32: *wa'l-jaur alladhī yuqābilu bi'l-waḍ' hādhā 'l-'adl fa-huwa 'alā ghair al-munāsabah*, Greek: καὶ τὸ ἄδικον τὸ ἀντικείμενον τῷ δικαίῳ τούτῳ τὸ παρὰ τὸ ἀνάλογόν ἐστιν. Bywater's note reads τό ante παρά, om. L^b^, M^b^, and so Arabic probably; EN VIII, 9, 3 = 1160a 3: *fa'inna 'l-'adl aiḍan ākhar li-kulli wāḥidin minhum*, Greek: ἕτερα δὴ καὶ τὰ ἄδικα πρὸς ἑκάστους τούτων, where Arabic evidently read τὰ δίκαια of L^b^.

A feature of the Arabic version of EN is the frequency with which it indicates the vulgate readings[380] rather than the corrections of the Greek introduced into the text by editors. Thus we find in EN II, 6, 12 = 1106b 25-26: *wa'l-faḍīlah tūjadu fī'l-'awāriḍ wa'l-af'āl allatī az-ziyādah fīhā khaṭa' wa'n-nuqṣān fīhā madhmūm*. This implies the reading ψέγεται, which was bracketed by Bywater, Burnet and Rackham, cf. Ross "passions and actions, in which excess is a form of failure, and so is defect."[381] EN III, 1, 17 = 1111a 14-15: *wa-*

---

[380] 'Vulgate' is here used in Bywater's sense for the readings of several Greek MSS. in agreement. It hardly needs to be said that the vulgate is not necessarily the best text. The prevalence of vulgate readings in the Arabic version of EN may simply show that the mistakes which conjectural emendation seeks to correct were quite old in the textual tradition.

[381] Cf. Gauthier and Jolif, *L'Éthique à Nicomaque*, *op. cit.*, vol. II/1, p. 142.

rubbamā ḍaraba insān insānan li-manfaʿatin fa-qatalahu, Greek: καὶ ἐπὶ σωτηρίᾳ πίσας ἀποκτεῖναι ἄν, where πίσας is the widely accepted emendation of Bernays for παίσας of the codices which was evidently read by the Arabic translator; EN VII, 2, 10 = 1146b 1-2: *wa-ammā al-ān fa-laisa qunūʿuhu bi-dūni mā kāna al-battata wa yafʿalu ashyāʾ ukhar*, where Greek is: νῦν δὲ πεπεισμένος οὐδὲν ἧττον ἄλλα πράττει, emended variously by the editors but evidently read by Arabic. EN VII, 13, 2 = 1153b 7: *wa-laisa yamnaʿu mānīʿ an takūna ladhdhah mā khairan*, Greek: τἄριστόν τ' οὐδὲν κωλύει ἡδονήν τινα εἶναι, where τἄριστον is Spengel's emendation, adopted by Bywater, and later by Burnet and Rackham, of the manuscripts' ἄριστον which is followed by the Arabic; Bywater remarks: "The article is wanting in the manuscripts of the *Magna Moralia* in the parallel statement in 1206a 31-35."[382] EN VII, 14, 1 = 1154a 8-9: *fa-yanbaghī an nabḥatha ʿan al-ladhdhāt al-jismīyah wa 'l-aqāwīl allatī tuqālu ʿalaihā fa-innahu yuqālu inna ladhdhāt mukhtārah*, Greek: περὶ δὲ δὴ τῶν σωματικῶν ἡδονῶν ἐπισκεπτέον τοῖς λέγουσιν ὅτι ἔνιαί γε ἡδοναὶ αἱρεταὶ σφόδρα, where for τοῖς Coraes followed by Rackham read πῶς, cf. Gauthier and Jolif,[383] unconfirmed by Arabic. Other examples will be found at EN II, 6, 18 = 1107a 12; VII, 9, 1 = 1151b 4; VII, 12, 1 = 1152b 31; VII, 14, 4 = 1154a 34; X, 2, 4 = 1173a 4; etc. Occasionally a modern conjecture is confirmed, thus EN IV, 1, 27 = 1121a 7: *mā yuwaṣṣī bihi Sīmūnīdīs*, 'the injunction of Simonides', corresponding to Bywater's conjecture τῷ Σιμωνίδου for τῷ Σιμωνίδῃ, the common reading, and Bekker's αὑτούς at EN IX, 1, 3 = 1164a 10: *min ajl annahumā lam yakūnā muḥibbaini dhātahumā*, Greek codices οὐ γὰρ αὐτοὺς ἔστεργον.

The question of possible improvements in the Greek text of EN to be deduced from the Arabic has to be approached with caution, and it may be sufficient here to cite a typical case. At EN VII, 14, 8 = 1154b 20-22 Greek is: οὐκ ἀεὶ δ' οὐθὲν ἡδὺ τὸ αὐτό, διὰ τὸ μὴ ἁπλῆν ἡμῶν εἶναι τὴν φύσιν, ἀλλ' ἐνεῖναί τι καὶ ἕτερον καθὸ φθαρτοί, where Arabic translates: *wa-laisa shaiʾun ladhīdhan bi-dhātihi* [...] *min ajl anna ṭabīʿatahā laisat bi-mabsūṭatin bal fīhā shaiʾ ākhar aiḍan alladhī bihi takhṭaʾ*. Arberry conjectured that for καθὸ φθαρτοί Arabic read καθ' ὃ ἁμάρτοι. But is this the correct reading in

[382] Ingram Bywater, *Contributions to the Textual Criticism of Aristotle's Nicomachean Ethics*, Oxford 1892, p. 57.

[383] Cf. Gauthier and Jolif, *L'Éthique à Nicomaque*, *op. cit.*, vol. II/2, p. 804.

the Greek text? The answer will depend in each individual case on various considerations, and no rules of procedure can easily be laid down. Here the answer is unclear, apparently: No, e.g. Arberry's conjecture corrects not the codices but the reading of Aspasius, and φθαρτά of the manuscripts remains unexplained.

The Fez text of the *Nicomachean Ethics* lacks the following portions:

1094a 18-25 (I, 2, 1-3): Εἰ δή τι τέλος [...] πειρατέον, 7 lines.

1099b 26 - 1101b 8 (I, 9, 7 - I, 11, 6): κατ' ἀρετὴν [...] ὥστε μήτε, 2 folios.

1102b 31-33 (I, 13, 18): οὕτω δὴ [...] τῶν μαθηματικῶν, 2 lines, i.e. Rackham's 'parenthetical note' is omitted.

1108b 1 - 1109a 25 (II, 7, 15 - II, 9, 2): εἰσὶ δὲ περὶ [...] κύκλου τὸ μέσον, 1 folio.

1109a 31-32 (II, 9, 3): καθάπερ καὶ ἡ Καλυψὼ παραινεῖ and the following quotation from Homer, *Odyssey*, XII, 219, are omitted (cf. below on ignorance of Greek history and literature).

1117a 6-16 (III, 8, 12-14): μὲν ἀλγοῦσι [...] ἀνδρείου δὲ, 1/2 page missing.

1117a 31 - 1118a 32 (III, 9, 1 - III, 10, 10): καὶ περὶ ταῦθ' [...] διὸ καὶ ηὔξατό, corresponding 1/2 page + 1 folio missing.

A line or two have dropped out at 1120b 7-9 = IV, 1, 19.

1127a 7-12 (IV, 6, 9): ὠνόμασται δέ [...] τὸ μέσον, 6 lines illegible.

1127a 23 - 1127b 9 (IV, 7, 4-9): αὐθέκαστός τις [...] ὑπερβολὰς εἶναι, 20 lines mostly illegible.

1127b 19-30 (IV, 7, 13-16): δόξης χάριν [...] τὰ μὴ λίαν ἐμποδών, 1/2 page nearly illegible.

1136a 25 - 1144b 29 (V, 9, 3 - VI, 13, 5): καὶ ἐπὶ τοῦ πάσχειν [...] λόγους τὰς ἀρετάς, missing are the last chapters of Book V and most of Book VI.

Books VII-X are better preserved, and while damage to the manuscript[384] has caused recurrent short lacunae, there are no long gaps.

[384] Qarawīyīn MS. L 3043/80 (pp. 2ff.)

The intrusive 'Seventh Book'[385] is illegible at the beginning and is incomplete.

An omission of a different kind is to be found at 1133a 14-16 = V, 5, 9 of the Greek text where the words ἔστι δὲ τοῦτο [...] καὶ τοσοῦτον are not rendered. The same three lines occur at 1132b 9-11 = V, 4, 12, where they are usually regarded as interpolated from 1133a 14-16. The Arabic text goes its own way, rendering the lines without comment at 1138b 9-11 and omitting them at 1133a 14-16, quite as if it here represented a different recension from our vulgate.

The Fez text has also additions which at least offer the possibility of belonging to the original Greek. Thus at 1095b 32-33 (I, 5, 6):

> *wa-qad yaẓharu anna 'l-faḍīlah aiḍan lā taktamilu li-hādha [li-anna 'l-amr lau kāna ka-dhālika la-mā 'khtāra aḥadun an yanāma] wa-dhālika annā naʿlamu annahu qad yumkinu an yanāma al-insān wa-maʿahu al-faḍīlah,*

the words within brackets are not in the Greek as we have it, but have been added to the text. We may render thus:

> It appears, however, that virtue also is incomplete for this [sc. to be the end of the political life], *because if the matter were so, no one would have chosen to sleep*. That is, we know that it is possible that a man should sleep and retain virtue.

A line or two further down in the same paragraph (1096a 2) Arabic has:

> *wa-man kāna bi-hādhihi 'l-ḥāl fa-laisa min aḥadin yaqūlu innahu saʿīd illā an yakūna yurīdu ḥafẓa aṣlin [qad waḍʿahu wa-iʿtiqādin yanṣuruhu]*, i.e. there is no one who would say that such a man is happy, unless he wanted to maintain a principle *which he had laid down and a conviction which he was defending.*

The addition here appears to be stylistic.

A somewhat remarkable addition is at 1095b 13 (end of I, 4) where Arabic has:

> *qāla al-mutarjim: hādhā mā dhakarahu Arisṭū min shiʿr Isyūdūs*[386] *wa-huwa ʿalā khilāf mā najiduhu fī kitāb ar-rajul. wa-laʿalla Arisṭū ikhtaṣara al-qaul wa-naḥnu nuthbituhu hunā kamā qālahu ash-shāʿir:*

---

[385] See above, pp. 4 and 55ff.

[386] I.e. Hesiod. Cf. Isuris, corrected Īsyūd.s, in Abū Sulaimān as-Sijistānī, *Muntakhab ṣiwan al-ḥikmah*, *op. cit.*, p. 96, § 186, where the same passage as here (*Works and Days*, 293-297) is evidently referred to.

> *ammā afḍal an-nās fī jamī' al-ḥālāt fa-huwa man fahima jamī' / mā yajibu 'alaihi min tilqā'i nafsihi / wa's-sadīdu man lam yablugh dhālika lākinnahu yaqbalu qaula ghairihi idhā kāna musīban / wa'r-rajul* [...] *alladhī lā yafham min tilqā' nafsihi mā yajibu 'alaihi wa-lā yaqbaluhu min ghairihi / wa* [...], i.e. the translator[387] said: This is what Aristotle mentioned of the poetry of Hesiod, and it is contrary to what we find in the man's book. Perhaps Aristotle abbreviated the wording. We set it down here as the poet spoke it:
>
> As for the most excellent of men in all circumstances, he is the one who understands all
>
> That is necessary for him, of himself;
>
> And well-guided is the man who has not attained that, but accepts the speech of another, when he is right;
>
> But the [...] man who understands not of himself what is necessary for him nor accepts it from another,
>
> And [...].

Hesiod was known to the Arabs at least for this quotation, which in the passage already cited (n. 386 above) from the *Muntakhab ṣiwān al-ḥikmah* of Abū Sulaimān as-Sijistānī appears as:

> *yuqālu inna 'l-insān khairun fī 't-ṭabaqah al-ūlā idhā kāna istikhrājuhu li'l-umūr al-jamīlah bi-ṭab'ihi min tilqā'i nafsihi wa-yuqāl innahu khairun fī 't-ṭabaqah ath-thāniyah idhā kāna qā'ilan li'l-umūr al-jamīlah idhā 'arafahā*, i.e. it is said that a man is good in the first category when his production of good things is by his own nature, of himself (*min tilqā'i nafsihi*), and it is said that he is good in the second category when he says good things when he has got to know them.

Similarly, in the *Mukhtār al-ḥikam* we have:

> *al-insān yaḥtāju fī 'l-iṭṭilā' 'alā ḥaqā'iq al-khairāt immā ilā ālah jaiyidah ya'lam bihā al-ḥaqq wa-immā ilā taṣauwur ya'khudha bihi awā'il al-ashyā' min ghairihi bi-sahulah. fa-man laisa fīhi wāḥidan min al-khallatain fal-yastami' qaul Ūmīrūs* [sic] *ash-shā'ir fīhi ḥaithu yaqūlu: ammā hādhā fa-fāḍil wa-ammā dhāka fa-ṣāliḥ fa-ammā 'lladhī lā yafqahu min nafsihi wa-lā yafqahu idhā faqqahu ghairuhu fa-huwa ghāyat ash-shaqā' wa'l-'aṭab*, i.e. a man needs to investigate the facts of the different goods either an excellent instrument by which he may know the truth, or the power of conception by which he may readily obtain from another the principles of things. Let the man who

[387] Is this perhaps the Syriac translator of the Greek (cf. pp. 26, 62, 106) whose version was then put into Arabic? Most naturally he should be the Arabic translator Isḥāq b. Ḥunain (pp. 27f.). The Commentary of Porphyry (pp. 23ff.) appears ruled out as the source. We may note that the disputed verse: Φρασσάμενος [...] (*Works and Days*, 294), does not appear to have been in the text of Hesiod which is here said to have been consulted.

> does not have either of these qualities listen to the word of Homer [corr. Hesiod] concerning him, where he says: The former is excellent, the latter good, but as for him who understands not of himself, and understands not when another instructs him, he is the extreme of wretchedness and ruin.

This group of references to Hesiod in Arabic, which does not seem to have been isolated previously, evidently depends on EN I, 4, 7.[388]

At 1096a 14 (I, 6, 1) we read:

> *al-baḥth ʿan dhālika mimmā yaṣʿubu ʿalainā li-anna qauman aṣdiqāʾa lanā adkhalū aṣ-ṣuwar [wa-ʿtaqadūhā]*, i.e. investigation of that is a difficult thing for us because friends of ours have introduced the forms *and have believed in them*.

Here we have a very common form of addition in the Arabic text of EN, the introduction of a synonymous phrase for a stylistic reason (balance), cf. 1109b 13 (II, 9, 7): *qadarnā an nuṣība at-tawassuṭ [wa-nanāluhu]*, i.e. 'we are enabled to strike the mean *and attain it*'; and 1110a 32-33 (III, 1, 9):

> *al-ashyāʾ allatī natawaqqʿu muʾlimah [muʾdhiyah] wa'l-ashyāʾ allatī yukallafuhā al-insān [wa-yuqharu ʿalaihā] qabīḥah*, i.e. the things whose pain *and painful effect* we fear and the things a man is constrained *and forced* to do are base.

As before, the phrases bracketed are not in the Greek. Similarly, 1110b 13 (III, 1, 11): *fa-mā yuḍḥaku minhu [wa-yuhzaʾu bihi]*, i.e. 'absurd *and ridiculous*', and 1164a 30 (IX, 1, 6): *lā yafʿalūna mā qad aqarrū bihi [wa-waʿadū min anfusihim]*, i.e. 'they do not do what they agreed to *and promised of themselves*'.

Another noticeable form of addition to the text is the insertion of the negative *lā*, which occurs in a number of places. We thus have 1110b 33-34 (III, 1, 15): *lā al-kullīyah li-anna adh-dhamm [lā] yakūn bi-sababi hādhihi*, i.e. 'not [ignorance of] the universal, because there is *no* blame on account of this'; 1130b 30 (V, 2, 12): *fa-ammā fī nauʿ al-ʿadālah al-juzʾīyah wa'l-ʿadl alladhī [lā] yakūnu bihā fa-wāḥid*, i.e. 'as regards the class of partial justice and the just which is *not* according to it, they are one'; 1149b 19-20 (VII, 6, 3): *wa-kadhālika yakūnu lā dabṭ bi-nauʿ mabsūṭ [lā] sharrīyah bi-nauʿ mā*, i.e. 'and thus lack of restraint absolutely is *not* vice in a sense';

---

[388] For a similar addition suggesting direct knowledge of the text of Homer see below, p. 104.

1162a 36 - 1162b 1 (VIII, 13, 1): *fa'inna al-akhyār yakūnūna aṣdiqā' bi's-sawiyah wa-[lā] yakūnu al-ajwad ṣadīqan li'l-ardā'*, i.e. 'for good men are friends equally, and the best man is *not* a friend to the worst.'

A few additions refer to the Greeks and their language. Thus 1107b 2 (II, 7, 2): *wa-kathīr minhā [ʿinda 'l-Yūnānīyīn] lā isma lahu*, i.e. 'many of the states have no name *among the Greeks*'; 1107b 7-8 (II, 7, 3):

> *an-nuqṣān fī 'l-ladhdhah laisa yakādu yakūnu wa-li-dhālika lam yuḍaʿ lahu [fī lisāninā] ismun*, i.e. defect in pleasure scarcely exists, and therefore no name is assigned to such a man *in our language*;[389]

1108b 1 (II, 7, 15): *ḥāl mutawassiṭah baina 'l-ḥasad wa 'sh-shamātah [yuqālu lahā bi'l-Yūnānīyah]* [...], i.e. 'an intermediate state between envy and spite, *called in Greek* [...]'; 1112a 15-16 (III, 2, 17): *ismu'l-ikhtiyār [fī lughatinā] yadallu ʿalā 'l-mu'thir shai'an ʿalā shai'in*, i.e. 'the word choice *in our language* signifies the agent who choses one thing in preference to another'; 1115b 24-25 (III, 7, 7):

> *fa-ammā az-zā'id fī 'sh-shajāʿah ammā fī ʿadam al-khauf fa-lā isma lahu [fī lughatinā]*, i.e. as for the man who exceeds courage, as regards absence of fear he has no name *in our language*;

1122a 22-23 (IV, 2, 1):

> *fa-innahu* [sc. *al-karam*] *yafḍulu al-ḥurrīyah fī 'l-infāq bi-kathrah mā yanfuqu wa-ʿuẓmihi kamā yadullu ismuhu [fī lughat al-Yūnānīyīn]*, i.e. it [sc. magnificence] exceeds openhandedness in spending by the extent and amount of what it spends, as its name *in the language of the Greeks* shows;

1133a 31 (V, 5, 11): *fa'inna isma 'd-dīnār [bi'l-Yūnānīyah] an-nāmūsmā*, 'for the name for money in Greek is *nomisma*'. We also have the following reference to the Arabs, at 1108a 30 (II, 7, 13): *huwa al-maqīt al-mustathqal ʿinda jamīʿ an-nās [wa'l-ʿArab taʿrifuhu bi'sh-shanā']*, i.e. 'he is hateful and unbearable to all men. *The Arabs know and loathe him*'.

---

[389] Arabic is not intended, as might appear at first sight. 'Aristotle' is the speaker, not the translator (*qāla*, 'he said', at the beginning of each Book of the text).

By far the largest addition to Aristotle's Greek is the so-called 'Seventh Book', placed between Books VI and VII of the Arabic in the Fez manuscript.[390] This has special features of its own and was discussed separately earlier in the Introduction.[391] For the most part, with one or two possible exceptions, the additions appear to be explanatory glosses (not always successful)[392] or stylistic improvements. A simple example of the former is at 1160a 34 (VIII, 10, 1): *būlūṭīyā [aiy sīrah]*, 'politeia, *i.e. way of life*', cf. 1160b 20 for *sīrah* = πολιτεία and rather frequently, and similarly 1130a 32 (V, 2, 5): *radā'ah lā 'adl [allatī hiya al-jaur]*, i.e. 'the vice of injustice *which is wrongdoing*.' Or we have 1151a 9 (VII, 8, 3): *ahl Mīlisūs laisa hum bi-juhhāl wa-hum yaf'alūna fa'l al-juhhāl [li-qillat at-tajribah]*, i.e. 'the Milesians are not fools, but they act like fools *through lack of experience*', and sometimes the addition is considerably longer, e.g. 1102a 18 (I, 13, 6):

> *fa-wājib 'alā ṣāḥib tadbīr al-mudun an yanẓura fī amr tadbīr an-nafs idh kunnā naqūlu inna 'l-fi'l lahā*, i.e. it is incumbent on the man who rules cities that he should consider the matter of the rule of the soul, since we said that the activity [sc. happiness] belongs to it.

The whole sentence is added at the end of § 6. Examples of stylistic improvement are at 1115a 26 (III, 6, 6): *wa-ahwalu al-ashyā' [allatī tutakhauwafu] al-maut*, i.e. 'the most terrifying of the things *which are feared* is death', and 1126a 34 (IV, 5, 13):

> *ilā aiy ḥadd min al-ghaḍab yanbaghī an yaghḍaba ḥattā yakūna qad aṣāba [fī ghaḍabihi] au akhṭa'*, i.e. to what limit of anger one should be angry, in order to have hit the mark *in one's anger* or missed.

In these latter cases the addition does not have the special function of making the meaning more intelligible, which belongs to the gloss, and seems to be introduced merely to modify the run of the sentence. But the distinction between the two kinds of addition is sometimes difficult to draw. Speaking generally, it would be hazardous, given the probable character of the Greek text from which the Arabic translation was made,[393] to point to such and such a passage in the

[390] But see above, pp. 79 and 83.
[391] § IV, pp. 55ff.
[392] Several instances in Book III are 1112b 23-24 (III, 3, 12); 1112b 33 - 1113a 1 (III, 3, 16); 1116b 8 (III, 8, 6).
[393] Cf. above, p. 96, n. 380.

Fez manuscript where something has been added to the text of our modern editions and claim that it represented the original Greek of Aristotle. But it is not theoretically impossible that the additions contain authentic ancient readings. One passage which has a reasonable chance of being of this kind is at 1116a 33-35 (III, 8, 4) the Homeric quotation (*Iliad*, II, 391-393) where Hector threatens the Trojans, and the Arabic reads:

> *fa-man kuntu arāhu yahrubu min al-ḥarb mā kuntu aqnaʿu illā an ajʿalahu ma'kalah li'l-kilāb [wa'ṭ-ṭuyūr]*, i.e. the man whom I see fleeing from the battle I shall not be sufficed except by making him food for dogs *and birds*.

The last words stand in our texts of Homer but are an addition to Aristotle's text here. How do they come in the Arabic? Aristotle uses the same quotation again at *Politics* 1285a 10-14 where the birds are mentioned (ἠδ' οἰωνούς), as perhaps they were originally mentioned in the Greek text of EN, the words being simply taken as they came by the Arabic translator. On the other hand, they may be the addition of the translator himself or another, who recollected the complete wording in Homer and made the addition to the text. Especially in view of the note on Hesiod's text, found in the Arabic at 1095b 14 and already discussed,[394] we should have to allow the latter possibility as an alternative explanation of the completion of a quotation from Homer in Aristotle's *Nicomachean Ethics* found in the Arabic translation. A probable indication of a knowledge of Homer on the part of the translator is the rendering of οἱ 'Αργεῖοι, 'the Argives', by *al-Yūnānīyīn*, 'the Greeks' (1117a 26 [III, 8, 16]). But again such modifications of our Greek text may come from a commentary, in particular that of Porphyry.

A group of transcriptions of Greek proper names in the Arabic manuscript consists of forms which seldom occur elsewhere. These throw light on the process of transmission of EN and may be briefly considered here. The Lacodaemonians are mentioned a few times: 1102a 10-11 (I, 13, 3): [...] *an-nawāmīs li-ahl Iqrīṭish wa-Laqādāmūnā* (τοὺς Κρητῶν καὶ Λακεδαιμονίων νομοθέτας); 1112a 29 (III, 3, 6): *laisa aḥad min ahl Lācādāmūnyā* (οὐδεὶς Λακεδαιμονίων); 1167a 31 (IX, 6, 2): *yushārika ahl Lāqādūmūnyā* (συμμαχεῖν Λακεδαιμονίοις); 1180a 25 (X, 9, 13): *madīnat*

[394] See above, pp. 100f.

Lāqādāmūnyā (τῇ Λακεδαιμονίων πόλει). The correct, i.e. the stereotyped form appears to be *Lāqādāmūnyā*, without the article, found also in the Arabic translation of Aristotle's *Poetics* 1461b 6 = XXV, 16 (XXXI, l, 7, p. 280 of Tkatsch's edition[395] and p. 149 of the Cairo edition, 1387/1967, of Shukrī Muḥammad ʿAiyād): *fī Lāqādāmūnyā*, and similarly: *bi-Laqadāmūniyah* in Aristotle's *Rhetoric* 67a 29 = I, 9, 26 (p. 45 in the edition of Malcolm C. Lyons). The long *u*-vowel represents long *o* in Λακεδαίμων which has disappeared in the word for Lacedaemonians in the *Rhetoric* 61a 11 = I, 5, 6 (ed. Lyons, p. 25): *al-Laqadamanīna*,[396] and 98b 13, 17 = II, 23, 11 (ed. Lyons, p. 152): *al-Laqadamanūna bis*. The *Rhetoric* thus has distinct expressions for 'Lacedaemon' and 'Lacedaemonians', and the *Poetics* has a word for Lacedaemon, while the *Ethics* uses the same word for both meanings, *Lāqādāmūnyā* standing alone at 1102a 11 and 1180a 25 for Lacedaemonians and at 1112a 29 and 1167a 31 for Lacedaemon (with *ahl*, 'people of Lacedaemon').[397]

We also have at EN 1112a 28-29 = III, 3, 6: *ahl Sqūthyā* for Σκύθαι, and again at 1150b 14-15 = VII, 7, 6: *mulūk al-Isqūthā* (Arberry) for τοῖς Σκυθῶν βασιλεῦσιν, cf. *Mukhtār al-ḥikam*, p. 35: *Anākhārsīs alladhī min Sqūthyā*, i.e. 'Anacharsis, who was from Scythia.'[398] Similarly we have EN 1117a 27 = III, 8, 16: *Sfūnywā* for the Sicyonians. As the context shows (*al-ummah allatī yuqālu lahā Sfūnywā*, i.e. 'the nation called Sicyonians', the name refers to the people.

The form *Athīnyā* occurs at EN IV, 3, 25 = 1124b 17 in the phrase *ahl Athīnyā* for the Athenians (τοὺς 'Αθηναίους), quite parallel to *ahl Lāqādūmūnyā* (Λακεδαιμονίοις) noted above. Elsewhere this form is rare, but it is found once in Ibn Abī Uṣaibiʿah (*ʿUyūn al-anbāʾ*, *op. cit.*, vol. I, p. 49, quoting Ibn Juljul):[399] *ahl madīnat Athīnyā* again

[395] Jaroslaus Tkatsch, *Die arabische Übersetzung der Poetik des Aristoteles und die Grundlage der Kritik des griechischen Textes* (Akademie der Wissenschaften in Wien. Philosophisch-historische Klasse; 1), Vienna/Leipzig 1928.

[396] Unpointed in the text.

[397] Editors have often gone wrong with this form, thus *Lāwqādamūnyā* Tkatsch, *Die arabische Übersetzung der Poetik des Aristoteles, op. cit.*, p. 280; Arthur J. Arberry *Lākhādāmūnyā* (EN I, 9, 13); Badawī, *Lāqādhāmūnā* (EN 1112a 29 = III, 3, 6).

[398] Cf. Manfred Ullmann, *Wörterbuch zu den griechisch-arabischen Übersetzungen des 9. Jahrhunderts*, Wiesbaden 2002, s.v. Σκύθης.

[399] Cf. Ibn Juljul, *Ṭabaqāt al-aṭibbāʾ wa 'l-ḥukamāʾ* (*Les générations des médecins et des sages*), ed. Fuʾād Saiyid, Cairo 1955, p. 23: *Athīnyā*, but *Athīnā* in the index.

parallel to *madīnat Lāqādāmūnyā* above. The usual word for Athens in the old Arabic is *Athīniyah*, as noted by Flügel for the *Fihrist*, though there is a great diversity of other forms: *Athīnās* (Abū Sulaimān as-Sijistānī, *Ṣiwan al-ḥikmah*, *op. cit.*, pp. 49, § 65; 51, § 66), *Athīnūs* (*Rhetoric* 98b1 = II, 23, 11 and Ibn Khaldūn, *Ta'rīkh al-ʿallāmah*, ed. Beirut 1956-1959, 7 vols., vol. II, p. 418); *Athīnā*, the modern name[400] (already Ibn Abī Uṣaibiʿah, *ʿUyūn al-anbā'*, *op. cit.*, vol. I, p. 54 and Ibn Khaldūn, *Ta'rīkh al-ʿallāmah*, *op. cit.*, vol. II, p. 334 and p. 382). Al-Fārābī has *Athīnah* in the expression *haikal Athīnah* (*Fī 'l-ashya' allatī yuḥtāju an tuʿlama qabla 'l-falsafah*, in: al-Fārābī, *Philosophische Abhandlungen*, *op. cit.*, text p. 50; transl. p. 83), but this is 'the temple of Athene', not "die Tempel von Athen", cf. *Ṣiwān al-ḥikmah*, *op. cit.*, p. 90, § 162.[401] The Qāḍī Ṣāʿid, here expanding[402] al-Fārābī's text to *haikal madīnat Athīnah*, made the same mistake (*Ṭabaqāt al-umam*, *op. cit.*, text p. 32; transl. p. 74). Evidently, these forms are of varying origin: *Athīnās* must be the accusative case of 'Αθῆναί which has become isolated as the city's name, while some of the forms, especially those in EN, have the ductus, if not the vocalisation, of Syriac (of emphatic plural masculine of nouns in Syriac). We may also adduce the form feminine singular *Īṭālyā*, which though not occuring in EN occurs notably in Ibn Abī Uṣaibiʿah's account of Pythagoras (*ʿUyūn al-anbā'*, *op. cit.*, vol. I, pp. 38ff.), for which he used extensively the *History of the Philosophers*[403] of Porphyry. Elsewhere we find the form *Īṭāliyah* (*Rhetoric* 98b 14 = II, 23, 11, ed. Lyons, p. 152); *Ṣiwan al-ḥikmah*, p. 5, §2; Ibn al-Athīr, *al-Kāmil*, *op. cit.*, *sub anno* 92 *bis*. The form *Īṭālyā* may well come from Porphyry's *History of the Philosophers*, which we know was in Syriac.[404] The proposition that the Arabic *Nicomachean Ethics* was a translation from Syriac is difficult to demonstrate but may, I think, be regarded as evident. It is certainly no paradox that at the time when this translation was made a

---

400 Common also in Abū Sulaimān as-Sijistānī, *Muntakhab ṣiwan al-ḥikmah*; al-Mubashshir b. Fātik, *Mukhtār al-ḥikam* and Ibn Abī Uṣaibiʿah, *ʿUyūn al-anbā'*.

401 The form in the *Ṣiwan* ends with *yā'*, i.e. *Athīnī* or *Athīnā*.

402 So apparently. Otherwise he is quoting al-Fārābī's source, probably Ḥunain ibn Isḥāq, cf. pp. 33f.

403 I.e. the Φιλοσόφων 'Ιστορία now lost in Greek.

404 Ibn an-Nadīm, *Fihrist*, *op. cit.*, vol. I, p. 245.

Greek text should be translated into Syriac and the Syriac made the basis of a subsequent Arabic translation.

A good deal of importance has usually been attached to the readings of Aspasius (second century A.D.),[405] whose Commentary on a substantial amount of EN, i.e. Books I-IV, part of Book VII, and Book VIII, has come down to us, and was edited a century ago by G. Heylbut.[406] Readings in the Commentary indicate differences between the text used by Aspasius and the later Greek text, and because of their early date, centuries before any of the existing Greek manuscripts,[407] the presence or absence of Aspasius readings in the Arabic text of EN might even afford an indication of the date of the Greek original from which it was made. But again the evidence of the text is ambiguous.[408] At 1152b 30-31 = VII, 12, 1 we read: *wa-baʿḍūha fa-lā li-hādhā aiḍan illā fī waqtin mā wa-fī zamānin qalīlin wa-ammā ikhtiyārun*[409] *fa-lā*, i.e. 'and some [pleasures] are not [chosen] even for this [neuter];[410] except at a particular time and for a short time, and as for choice, there is none.' The last words represent αἱρεταὶ [or αἱρετὰ] δ' οὔ. Bywater followed by Burnet on the other hand construed αἱρεταί with the forgoing words and supplied ἁπλῶς from Aspasius, reading ἔνιαι δ' οὐδὲ τῷδε ἀλλὰ ποτὲ καὶ ὀλίγον χρόνον αἱρεταί, <ἁπλῶς> δ' οὔ. The Arabic has no trace of ἁπλῶς, which had been rendered two lines and again four lines above *bi-nauʿin mabsūṭin*. Again at 1154a 34 Arabic differs from Aspasius, reading *wa-baʿḍuhā min ajl anna lahum naqṣan*, which represents ὅτι ἐνδεοῦς of the Greek. But ὅτι bracketed by Bywater and omitted by Burnet was not read by Aspasius. Yet at 1154b 7 = VII, 14, 5 we have an Aspasius reading φυσιολόγοι which has been generally preferred to φυσικοί of K^b and φυσικοὶ λόγοι of the vulgate, and appears in the Arabic version as *aṣḥāb al-aqāwīl aṭ-ṭabīʿīyah*, cf. 1147b 8-9: *aṣḥāb al-kalām aṭ-ṭabīʿī* for the φυσιολόγοι.

Turning now to the Arabic translation, we find a number of peculiarities, some of which are doubtless due to the transmission

---

405 Cf. Burnet in Aristotle, *The Ethics of Aristotle*, *op. cit.*, p. xix; Gauthier and Jolif in Aristotle, *L'Éthique à Nicomaque*, *op. cit.*, vol. I/1, p. 100.

406 In the series *Commentaria in Aristotelem Graeca* of the Berlin Academy, 19/1, 1889.

407 See above, pp. 94f.

408 As for K^b and L^b, see pp. 94ff.

409 Or *bi'khtiyārin*.

410 Greek τῷδε is masculine.

rather than the original translator, a difference not always easy to determine. Among these peculiarities is the rendering of ἤ by *wa*, 'and' (1111a 13 = III, 1, 17; 1133b 24 = V, 5, 15; 1177b 7 = X, 7, 6); difficulty with Greek proper names (Milo, 1106b 3 = II, 6, 7; Calypso, 1109a 31 = II, 9, 3; temple of Hermes, 1116b 19 = III, 8, 9; people of Megara, 1123a 24 = IV, 2, 20; 'Kestus', 1149b 16 = VII, 6, 3; Epicharmus, 1167b 25 = IX, 7, 1; Anacharsis, 1176b 33 = X, 6, 6); difficulty also with facts of Greek life and institutions (actors, 1147a 23 = VII, 3, 8, cf. 1111b 24 = III, 2, 8, 1148b 8 = VII, 4, 6, 1136a 21 = V, 9, 2; parades, 1123a 33 = IV, 2, 20; decrees, 1151b 16 = VII, 9, 3; members of a demo, 1160a 18 = VIII, 9, 5; voting for a general, 1164b 24 = IX, 2, 1; fluting a pillar, 1174a 24 = X, 4, 2); translation of single words (ἀγαθῷ for ἀλόγῳ, 1168b 20 = IX, 8, 4; τὴν ψυχήν rendered *al-bakht*, 1147a 28 = VII, 3, 9, and the opposite of this, τῆς τύχης rendered *li'n-nafs*, 1153b 18 = VII, 13, 2); some confusion between two terms of importance in Aristotle's system, self-indulgence (ἀκολασία) and lack of self-control (ἀκρασία), thus ἀκρατής, 1145b 11-12 = VII, 1, 6, is rendered *lā 'afīf*, usual for ἀκόλαστος, and *lā 'iffah*, usual for ἀκολασία, is frequently (1145a 16-17, etc.) for ἀκρασία.

The extraordinary diversity of forms sometimes available to the Arabic translator for the same Greek can be illustrated from his rendering of λόγος, κατ' ἀξίαν, διά with the accusative, etc., for some of which the Graeco-Arabic Glossary may be consulted. A striking example of this variety is afforded by renderings of the Greek particle ἄν for which there is no equivalent in Arabic. Sometimes it is rendered by *khalīq an* (1136a 21 = V, 9, 2; 1155b 17 and 19 = VIII, 2, 1; 1166a 34 = IX, 4, 6; 1181b 10 and 13 = X, 9, 2), but it is very often omitted (1096a 1 = I, 5, 6; 1159b 2 = VIII, 8, 5). Or it may be rendered by *aḥrā an* (1159b 1 = VIII, 8, 5) or by *yanbaghī an* (1179a 15 = X, 8, 11).

Another feature of the Arabic translation is the insertion of the negative *lā* where the Greek text shows no negative. A few examples of this have already been given above where additions to the text were discussed. Occasionally the opposite phenomenon, omitted, occurs (1119b33 = IV, 1, 4; 1120a16 = IV, 1, 8; 1121a 5 = IV, 1, 27). The translation also shows various affections of the elative, thus positive for comparative (1151a 2 = VII, 8, 2), positive for superlative (1154b 25 = VII, 14, 8; 1177a 13 = X, 7, 1; 1177a 19 = X, 7, 2), comparative for positive (1147a 6 = VII, 3, 6), comparative for superlative (1119b 32 = IV, 1, 4; 1162b 6 = VIII, 13, 2), superlative for comparative (1162b 32 = VIII, 13, 7). A somewhat similar peculiarity is the substitution of neuter for masculine (1130a 2 *et sqq.* = V, 1, 16, 17, 20; 1162a 15 = VIII, 12, 7), sometimes masculine for neuter (1172a 6 = IX, 12, 2).

The demonstrative which has no exact equivalent in Arabic is expressed in various ways, again illustrating the flexibility of Arabic. Frequently for τοιοῦτος we find *hādhā, hādhihi, hā'ulā'i*, as at 1158a 7 = VIII, 6, 1; 1158a 34 = VIII, 6, 6; 1164b 22 = IX, 2, 1; 1172b 7 = X, 1, 4; 1176b 15-16 = X, 6, 3; 1177a 30 = X, 7, 4. Otherwise for τοιοῦτος we have *mithl hādhā, mithl hādhihi, mithl hā'ulā'i*, which forms also render exceptionally τηλίκος (1156a 25 = VIII, 3, 4) and τοιόσδε (1180b 15). Again, τοιοῦτος may be rendered by a relative clause (*alladhī mithl hādhā*, 1177b 26 = X, 7, 8), or with the verb expressed *allatī tushbih hādhihi* (1168b 12 = IX, 8, 3).

A feature of this Arabic is the presence of *faʿil* forms of the adjective to a remarkable extent. We note a few examples: *khabir* (1095a 3 = I, 3, 5; cf. Lane, 696a); *ʿaṭib* (1095b 13 = I, 4, 7, cf. Lane, 2077a); *ṭamiʿ* (1117a 23 = III, 8, 16, cf. Lane, 1881c); *badhikh* (1123a 19 = IV, 2, 20).

TEXT AND TRANSLATION

BOOK I

In the name of God, the Merciful, the Compassionate
God bless Muhammad and his family and give them peace abundantly

The First Discourse of the Book of Aristotle on Ethics

1094a 1. He said: By every art and every system, and similarly every action and choice, it is known that there is desired a certain good, and therefore he did well who judged of the good that it is the thing which all desire. (2) Now it appears that between the ends aimed at there is a difference, i.e. some of them are the actions themselves, and others are the effects resulting from those actions. In the things which have certain ends apart from the actions, the effects are superior to the actions. (3) Since the actions and arts and sciences are many, the ends become many, i.e. the end of the art of medicine is health, the end of the art of shipbuilding is the ship, the end of military strategy is victory, the end of household management is wealth. (4) There are found, among these arts and their like, arts subordinate to a single art,[1] as the art of making bridles and the rest of the arts which make the equipment of horsemanship are subordinate to the art of horsemanship and the art of horsemanship and all military actions subordinate to military strategy, and[2] in this way there are found arts subordinate to other, different arts. In all of them the ends of the principal arts are preferable for us to all the ends of the arts which are subordinate to them, because the ends of the latter are pursued for the ends of the former. (5) There is no difference between the ends[3] being the actions themselves or other, different things, as in the case of the sciences which we have mentioned [...]

---

[1] Arabic *ṣināʿah* naturally enough for Greek δύναμις, which would usually be rendered by *qūwah*.

[2] I.e. δέ rather than δή, cf. Gauthier *in loco*.

[3] The words τῶν πράξεων are omitted, for which the Arabic would have had to use *al-afʿāl* (as well as for τὰς ἐνεργείας).

المقالة الأولى

[١/٢] بسم الله الرحمن الرحيم
صلّى الله على محمّد وعلى آله وسلّم تسليماً

المقالة الأولى من كتاب أرسطو في الأخلاق

١. قل إنّ كلّ صناعة وكلّ مذهب وكذلك كلّ فعل واختيار فقد يعلم أنّه إنّما يتشوّق به خيراً ما ولذلك أجاد من حكم على الخير أنّه الشيء الذي يتشوّقه الكلّ (٢) فقد يظهر أنّ بين الغايات المقصودة اختلافاً وذلك أنّ منها ما هي الأفعل أنفسها ومنها ما هي المفعولات الحادثة عن تلك الأفعل والأشياء التي لها غايات ما سوى الأفعل فالمفعولات فيها أفضل من الأفعل (٣) ولمّا كانت الأفعل والصناعات والعلوم كثيرة صارت الغايات كثيرة وذلك أنّ غاية صناعة الطبّ الصحّة وغاية صناعة عمل السفن السفينة وغاية تدبير الحرب الغلبة وغاية تدبير المنزل الثروة (٤) وقد توجد في هذه الصناعات وأمثالها صناعات تحت صناعة واحدة بمنزلة ما أنّ صناعة عمل اللجم وسائر الصناعات التي تعمل آلات الفروسية تحت صناعة الفروسية وصناعة الفروسية وكلّ فعل من أفعل الحرب تحت تدبير الحرب وعلى هذا النحو قد توجد صناعات تحت صناعات أخر غيرها وفي جميعها فإنّ غايات الصناعات الرئيسية آثر عندنا من غايات الصناعات التي تحتها كلّها [...] الغايات هذه (٥) ولا فرق بين أن [...] الأفعل أنفسها أو أخر غيرها [...] الحل [...] العلوم التي ذكرناها [...]

---

5 فقد : F وقد Bad || 8 ولما : F وإذا Bad || 8 second الأفعل Bad, Dun : illegible F || 15 first [...] : illegible F, *because the ends of the latter are pursued for* Dun || 15 second [...] : illegible F, *the ends being* Dun || 15 أو Dun : illegible F || 15 third [...] : illegible F, *as in* Dun || 16 [...] : illegible F, *of* Dun

2. (3) [...] the end by way of outline and pattern, and the description of what it [i.e. the supreme good] is, and to which of the sciences or arts[4] it belongs. (4) It is thought to belong to the most authoritative and noblest of the arts and the one of them most entitled to primacy. (5) It appears that the art which is such is the art of ruling cities.
1094b (6) For this art is that which determines which of the arts and the sciences[5] must be in the cities, and which of the arts and sciences it is necessary for every [...] and what point the learner must reach in them. We see also the most perfect and noblest arts[6] placed under this, e.g. the art of war, household management and the art of rhetoric. (7) Since this art employs the practical sciences and lays down clearly what must be done and what must be avoided, its end comes to include the ends of the rest of[7] the other arts, and for that reason its end should be the good which is proper to man. (8) That is, even if the good for one man and for the city is one and the same, it appears that the good for the city is greater and more perfect, and that its acquisition and preservation[8] for a single individual only may be deemed desirable, but for the nation and for cities it is more excellent and nobler. These are things aimed at by this method with which we are concerned.[9] It is the method of ruling cities.[10]

3. It may suffice for what we are speaking about if we explain it according to what is possible in the subject matter, for it is not necessary that we should seek completeness[11] in all discussions in the same manner, just as it is not necessary either that we seek it in all the objects that are actually made. (2) Noble deeds and those related to justice, which the art of politics investigates, contain an amount of difference and error [...], so that it is thought that we have them only by law and not by nature. (3) A similar error occurs also

---

[4] Arabic *aṣ-ṣināʿāt* for Greek δυνάμεων, as above § 4.

[5] Arabic *aṣ-ṣināʿāt wa 'l-ʿulūm*, Greek has similarly τῶν ἐπιστημῶν.

[6] As in Arabic *aṣ-ṣināʿāt*, Greek τῶν δυνάμεων.

[7] Arabic *sāʾir*, representing Greek λοιπαῖς misplaced from 1094b 4.

[8] The Arabic translator construes καὶ λαβεῖν καὶ σῴζειν with what follows in the Greek (ἀγαπητὸν [...]).

[9] The Arabic translator now uses different words, *ṭarīq* and *yuqṣadu*, for Greek μέθοδος and ἐφίεται, repeated here from c. 1, § 1 (there *madhhab* and *yutashawwaqu*).

[10] Or 'of politics', not 'for ruling cities' (*li-tadbīr al-mudun*).

[11] Arabic *istiqṣāʾ*, lit. for 'going far' into a subject, treating it exhaustively, which is not quite the same as Greek τὸ ἀκριβές but is used elsewhere as a synonym by the Arabic translator, cf. 1094b 24 and 1159a 3 (*mustaqṣan*).

٢. (٣) [...] [١/١٣] الغاية على طريق الرسم والتمثيل ووصف ما هي ولأيّ العلوم أو الصناعات هي (٤) وقد يظنّ أنّها لأحقّ وأشرف الصناعات وأولاها بالرياسة (٥) وقد يظهر أنّ الصناعة التي هي بهذه الحال هي صناعة تدبير المدن (٦) فإنّ هذه الصناعة هي التي تقدّر أيّ الصناعات والعلوم ينبغي أن يكون في المدن وأيّ الصناعات والعلوم ينبغي لكلّ [...] وإلى أيّ غاية ينبغي أن يبلغ المتعلّم منها وقد نرى أيضاً أسمى الصناعات وأشرفها موضوعة تحت هذه مثل صناعة الحرب وتدبير المنزل وصناعة الخطابة (٧) فإذ كانت هذه الصناعة تستعمل العلوم العملية وتضع تبيين ما ينبغي أن يعمل وما ينبغي أن يجتنب صارت غايتها تحتوي على غايات سائر الصناعات الأخر فيجب لذلك أن تكون غايتها هي الخير الذي يخصّ الإنسان (٨) وذلك أنّه وإن كان الخير لإنسان واحد وللمدينة واحداً بعينه فقد يظهر أنّ الخير للمدينة أعظم وأكمل وأنّ تناوله وحفظه ألاّ يزول قد يستحبّ للواحد فقط إلاّ أنّه للأمّة والمدن أفضل وأشرف. فإلى هذه الأشياء يقصد بهذا الطريق الذي نحن عليه وهو طريق تدبير المدن.

٣. وقد يكتفي بما نقوله فيه إن نحن شرحناه بحسب ما يمكن في المادّة الموضوعة له فإنّه ليس ينبغي أن نطلب الاستقصاء في جميع الأقاويل على مثل واحد كما أنّه لا ينبغي أيضاً أن نقدّمه في جميع الأشياء التي تعمل عملاً (٢) والأمور الجميلة والتي تنسب إلى العدل التي تبحث عنها صناعة تدبير المدن قد بلغ ما فيها من الاختلاف والغلط [...] حتى إنّها إنّما هي بالشريعة فقط وليست بالطبع (٣) وقد وقع مثل هذا الغلط أيضاً في الخيرات من

3 second الصناعة corr. Bad*, Dun* (αὕτη) : الصناعات F || 5 أيضا أسمى Bad, Dun : illegible F || 6 فإذ : F وإذ Bad || 7 العملية F*, Dun* (πρακτικαῖς) : العلمية Bad || 11 والمدن Bad, Dun : illegible F || 15 نقدمه في Bad, Dun : illegible F || 16 التي F*, Dun* : والتي Bad || 16 [...] : illegible F, *so that it is thought* Dun || 17 الغلط أيضا F*, Dun* (πλάνην) : الاختلاف Bad

in the case of good things, as a result of which harm accrues to many people from them. Many people have been destroyed by reason of wealth and others by reason of courage. (4) So we are content, when we speak of things like these and from such data, that we should make the truth clear by way of summary[12] and pattern and when we speak of the things which are only for the most part and from such data, that what we conclude in regard to them should be such. In this same way should everything we speak of be received. For it is characteristic of the educated man that the extent of his search for completeness[13] in each class of the things sought for should be in accordance with what the nature of that thing which is sought for admits, because it is the same if one accepts from a mathematician probable words [...] from a rhetorician demonstrative proof. (5) Each man judges well only [...] and in these things is found a skilful judge. The skilful judge in each matter is the man educated in that
1095a matter, and the skilful judge absolutely is the man educated in everything. Therefore to study politics is not suitable for a young man, because a young man is inexperienced in the actions which occur in the course of life, and our discussion here derives from and is concerned with these actions only. (6) And because also he follows the desires which his soul calls him to, his listening to our discussion becomes vain and without profit, because our end in what we speak of here is not knowledge but action. (7) There is no difference between his being young in years or young in character, because the defect does not simply attach to him as a result of time, but as a result of his life, and all he seeks in it, aiming simply at what desire calls him to, i.e. people like these do not profit by knowledge, just as those who do not restrain themselves from pleasures do not profit by it. But as for those who desire and act according to what reflection and prudence enjoin, knowledge of these things is exceedingly useful to them. (8) This is the extent of what it was necessary for us to preface to our discussion, in regard to how the learner of this art must be[14] and what the aim is which we pursue in it.

---

[12] Arabic *ʿalā ṭarīq al-ijmāl* for Greek παχυλῶς, a rare word which has not been understood.

[13] See note 11 above.

[14] The Arabic translator has apparently construed ἀκροατοῦ with ἀποδεκτέον, but the text as it stands in the MS. is sound. Otherwise we may read *wa-kaifa yanbaghī an yakūna*. Either way, Greek ἀποδεκτέον fails to be rendered adequately.

قبل أنّه قد يعرض لكثير من الناس منها ضرر. فقد تلف كثير من الناس بسبب الغنى وآخرون بسبب الشجاعة (٤) فبودّنا إذا تكلّمنا في أمثل هذه الأشياء وممّا هذه حاله أن نبيّن الحقّ على طريق الإجمل والتمثيل وإذا تكلّمنا في الأشياء [١/١٤] التي إنّما تكون في أكثر الأمر وفيما هذه حاله أن يكون ما ننتجه فيها على هذه الحل. وعلى هذا المثل بعينه ينبغي أن يقبل كلّ شئ ممّا كلامنا فيه فإنّ من شأن الأديب أن يكون مبلغ طلبه للاستقصاء في كلّ واحد من أجناس الأمور المطلوبة بحسب ما تحتمله طبيعة ذلك الأمر المطلوب لأنّه سواء إن قبلت من صاحب التعاليم كلاماً محتملاً [...] الخطيب برهاناً (٥) وكلّ واحد من الناس إنّما يجيد الحكم على [...] وفي هذه الأشياء يوجد حاكم حاذق فالحاكم الحاذق في كلّ واحد من الأشياء هو الأديب في ذلك الشئ والحاكم الحاذق على الإطلاق هو الأديب في كلّ شئ. ولذلك لا يليق تعلّم تدبير المدن بالحدث لأنّ الحدث غير خبير بالأفعل التي تجري في السيرة وكلامنا ها هنا إنّما هو من هذه الأفعل وفي هذه الأفعل (٦) ولأنّه أيضاً تابع لما تدعوه نفسه إليه من الشهوات صار استماعه لكلامنا باطلاً لا منفعة فيه لأنّ غايتنا فيما نتكلّم فيه ها هنا ليست علماً بل فعلاً (٧) ولا فرق بين أن يكون حدث السنّ أو حدث الخلق لأنّ النقص ليس إنّما يليق به من قبل الزمان لكن من قبل أنّ عيشته وجميع ما يطلبه فيه إنّما يقصد به قصد ما تدعو إليه الشهوة وذلك أنّ أمثل هؤلاء لا ينتفعون بالمعرفة كما لا ينتفع بها الذين لا يغبطون أنفسهم عن اللذّات فأمّا الذين يشتهون ويفعلون على حسب ما يوجبه الفكر والرأي فإنّ العلم بهذه الأشياء نافع لهم جدّاً (٨) فهذا مبلغ ما كان ينبغي أن نصوّر به كلامنا في المتعلّم لهذه الصناعة كيف ينبغي أن يكون وما الغرض الذي قصدنا فيها.

---

1 فقد F : وقد Bad || 1 الغنى Bad*, Dun* (πλοῦτον) : عبى F || 2 وآخرون F*, Dun* (ἕτεροι) : والآخرون Bad || 2 ومما F*, Dun* (ἐκ) : وما Bad || 4 ما ننتجه F*, Dun* (συμπεραίνεσθαι) : مقدماته prop. Bad || 5 مما كلامنا F*, Dun* : مما مثل كلامنا Bad || 7 كلاما محتملا Bad* (πιθανολογοῦντος) : illegible F, صحيح prop. Dun || 8 حاكم حاذق F, Dun : حاكما عادلا Bad || 12 غايتنا F : غايته Bad || 13 بين above line

4. We return to where we were. We say: Since all knowledge and every choice desires a certain good, what is the good which we say that politics desires and makes its aim, viz. the good which is highest and most elevated of all the things that are done? (2) We say that most men would be likely to agree on it in name, i.e. the majority of men and the sophisticated among them call it happiness and think that living well and doing well are happiness. They differ in regard to what the definition of happiness is, and the majority of men do not define it as do the wise. (3) That is, some people say that it is one of the visible, obvious things, like pleasure or wealth or honour. Different people describe it differently, and often the same man describes it by different things, since when he is ill [...] when he is in want, he says that it is wealth, and when they realize their ignorance of it, they admire those who speak of its benefits in words greater than what they understand of it. Some have thought there is another good, existing by itself besides these many goods, which is the cause of all these being goods. (4) The investigation of all these opinions respecting it is liable to be labour in vain, because it may suffice to investigate the most current of them or those that are thought to contain proof. (5) We should not forget that there is a difference between arguments that proceed from principles and those which lead to principles. Plato was right to doubt in regard to this and sought to know whether the method which proceeds to principles is like the
1095b course in the race-ground from the masters of the games[15] to the end of the race-ground, or the reverse. That is, a beginning must be made from obvious things, and these are of two kinds, some which are obvious to us, others which are obvious in the absolute sense. It may be that we should begin from the things obvious to us. (6) Therefore, if someone wants to learn adequately what is good and just and in general political affairs, his habits must have been on right lines. (7) For the beginning of knowledge of anything is knowledge of the fact. If this is sufficient, he does not need knowledge of the why of it. He who is such possesses the principles, or else acquires them easily. As for him who does not have either of these characteristics, let him hear the words of Hesiod the poet, where he says:

[15] Arabic *baʿlī ar-riyāḍah* for Greek τῶν ἀθλοθετῶν.

٤. ونحن راجعون إلى ما كنّا فيه فنقول إذا كان كلّ معرفة وكلّ اختيار إنّما يتشوّق خيراً ما فما الخير الذي نقول إنّ تدبير المدن يتشوّقه ويقصد قصده وهذا الخير الذي هو أعلى وأرفع من جميع الأشياء التي تفعل (٢) فنقول إنّه يكاد أن يكون أكثر الناس قد أجمعوا عليه بالاسم وذلك أنّ الكثير من الناس والحذّاق منهم يسمّونه السعادة ويرون أنّ [٣/٣] حسن العيش وحسن السيرة هي السعادة واختلفوا في حدّ السعادة ما هو وليس يحدّها كثير من الناس بمثل ما يحدّها بها الحكماء (٣) وذلك أنّ بعض الناس قال إنّها شيء من الأمور الظاهرة البيّنة مثل اللذّة أو الغنى أو الكرامة وقوم دون قوم وصفوها بشيء دون شيء وكثيراً ما يصفها الواحد من الناس بعينه بأشياء مختلفة فإذا مرض [...] إذا أفقر قال إنّها الغنى وإذا وقفوا على جهلهم بها تعجّبوا من قول من [...] قولاً أعظم ممّا فهموه منها. وقد ظنّ قوم أنّ ها هنا خيراً ما آخر موجوداً بذاته سوى هذه الخيرات الكثيرة وهو سبب لهذه كلّها في أن تكون خيرات (٤) وخليق أن يكون البحث عن جميع هذه الآراء فيها عناء وباطلاً لأنّه قد يكتفي بالبحث عن أشهرها أو ما يظهر منها أنّ فيه حجّة (٥) ولا ينبغي أن يذهب علينا أنّ بين الأقاويل التي تجري من المبادئ وبين الأقاويل التي تؤدي إلى المبادئ فرقاً. ونعم ما شكّ أفلاطون في هذا وطلب أن يعلم هل الطريق الذي يجري إلى المبادئ كالطريق في الميدان من بعلي الرياضة إلى آخر الميدان أم بعكس ذلك. وذلك أنّه ينبغي أن يبتدئ من الأشياء البيّنة وهذه الأشياء صنفان فمنهما ما هي بيّنة عندنا ومنها ما هي بيّنة على الإطلاق وخليق أن يكون إنّما ينبغي أن نبتدئ من الأشياء البيّنة عندنا (٦) ولذلك ينبغي لمن أراد أن يتعلّم الأمور الجميلة والعادلة وبالجملة أمور تدبير المدن تعلّماً كافياً أن تكون أخلاقه قد جرت على ما ينبغي (٧) فإنّ ابتداء العلم بالشيء هو العلم بأنّه. فإن اكتفى بهذا لم يحتج إلى العلم بلِمَ هو. ومن كان بهذه الحل فمعه المبادئ أو يتناولها بسهولة ومن لم تكن معه واحدة من هاتين الخصلتين فلينصت إلى قول إسيودوس الشاعر حيث يقول:

1 ونحن [...] ما كنا فيه F, Dun : om. Bad || 8 أفقر F : اقتصد Bad || 9 second من Dun : illegible F || 9 [...] : illegible F, *of its benefits* Dun || 11 فيها corr. Bad : فيه F || 13 first بين الأقاويل F, Dun : من بين الاقاويل Bad || 14 وطلب F : فطلب Bad || 14-15 كالطريق في الميدان من بعلى الرياضة F, Dun : كالطريق من المبادئ مثل الافاضة Bad || 16 وهذه الاشياء صنفان فمنها F : وذلك أن الاشياء منها Bad || 17 أو corr. Bad*, Dun* (ἤ) : و F || 20 ولذلك F : ولذا Bad

As for this one, he is the best of men on all
circumstances;
As for that one, he is rightly guided;
But as for him who understands not of himself
and accepts not from another what is necessary,
And his heart heeds it not, he is the perishing man[16].[17]

5. We return to the argument where we broke it off.

The translator said: This is what Aristotle mentioned of the poetry of Hesiod, and it is contrary to what we find in the man's book. Perhaps Aristotle abbreviated the wording. We set it down here as the poet spoke it:

As for the most excellent of men in all circumstances,
he is the one who understands all
That is necessary for him, of himself;
And well-guided is the man who has not attained that, but
accepts the speech of another, when he is right;
But the [...] man who understands not of himself what is
necessary for him, nor accepts it from another
And [...].[18]

We say: It seems that men in their thinking that the good and happiness depend on the lives[19] have not erred from the truth. (2) As for the generality of them and the roughs, they say that the good and happiness are pleasure, and therefore they prefer the life of the enjoyment of pleasures. That is, the outstanding, predominant lives are three, viz. the life which we have just mentioned;[20] the life of the political man; and the third, the life of the speculative man. (3) Now you see that the generality are very near to slaves and have chosen the life of the brutes. They gain a mention only because many of those who are invested with the affairs of government resemble the life of Sardanapalus in the enjoyment of pleasures. (4) As for the well-conducted and the men of noble actions, they say that the good and happiness are honour—thinking that honour is almost an end

---

[16] Arabic *ar-rajul al-ʿaṭib*, which is far from the Greek ἀχρήϊος ἀνήρ.

[17] Hesiod, *Works and Days*, 293-297.

[18] The translator has apparently consulted the original in Hesiod, but has not rendered it at all accurately. We may note that the text of Hesiod apparently consulted did not contain the disputed line 294: φρασσάμενος [...].

[19] Sc. which they live, but Greek ἐκ τῶν βίων is wrongly construed and should be taken with ἐοίκασιν.

[20] I.e. the life of pleasure.

أمّا هذا فأفضل الناس في جميع الحالات
وأمّا ذاك فعلى السداد
فأمّا من لم يفهم من تلقاء نفسه ما يجب ولم يقبل من غيره
وبعد قلبه فهو الرجل العطب

٥. ونحن نعود إلى القول من حيث تركناه.

[٣/٤] قل المترجم هذا ما ذكره أرسطو من شعر إسيودوس وهو على خلاف ما نجده في كتاب الرجل ولعلّ أرسطو اختصر القول ونحن نثبته هنا كما قاله الشاعر:

أمّا أفضل الناس في جميع الحالات فهو من فهم جميع
ما يجب عليه من تلقاء نفسه
والسديد من لم يبلغ ذلك لكنّه يقبل قول غيره إذا كان مصيباً
والرجل [...] الذي لا يفهم من تلقاء نفسه
ما يجب عليه ولا يقبله من غيره
و [...]

فنقول يشبه أن يكون الناس في ظنّهم بأنّ الخير والسعادة إنّما هما من السير لم يخرجوا عن الصواب (٢) أمّا العامّة منهم والجفلة فقالوا إنّ الخير والسعادة هما اللذّة ولذلك يؤثرون سيرة المتمتّع باللذّات. وذلك أنّ السير المستولية الغالبة ثلاث: السيرة التي ذكرنا الآن وسيرة صاحب تدبير المدن والثالثة سيرة صاحب النظر (٣) فالعامّة تراهم قد قربوا جدّاً من العبيد واختاروا سيرة البهائم وإنّما صاروا يذكرون من قبل أنّ كثيراً ممّن تقلّد أمور السلطان يتشبهون بسيرة سردانابلس في التمتّع باللذّات (٤) فأمّا الحسنوا المذاهب وأصحاب الأفعل الجميلة فيقولون إنّ الخير والسعادة هما الكرامة يرون أنّ الكرامة تكاد

2 فعلى السداد F*, Dun* (ὃς εὖ εἰπόντι πίθηται) : فمن الشرار Bad || 5 نعود إلى القول F, Dun : نغدو إلى الأول Bad || 6 أسيودوس read. Bad : استودوس F || 11 الذي Bad, Dun : illegible F || 16 السيرة corr. Bad*, Dun* (ὁ) : السير F || 17 المدن F*, Dun* (ὁ πολιτικός) : المنزل Bad || 18 جدا F*, Dun* (παντελῶς) : جزءا Bad || 18 العبيد F*, Dun* (ἀνδραποδώδεις) : السير Bad || 19 سردانابلس Bad*, Dun* (Σαρδαναπάλλῳ) : دانابلس w.p. F || 19 المذاهب corr. Bad : المذهب F || 20 تكاد F*, Dun* (σχεδόν) : تكان Bad ||

and that honour is almost the end of the life of the political man. We may think that this end is too mean[21] to be the object of our search. That is, it may be thought that honour depends on being in the bestower of honour rather than in the person honoured, while as to the good, it seems[22] to be proper to the possessor and is difficult to detach from him, (5) because[23] they seek[24] for honour only in order that it may be established in their minds that they are good. That is,[25] they seek honour from the intelligent and from those who know them for virtue. It is clear according to the view of these that virtue is better. (6) Perhaps someone might think that virtue is more suitable to be the end of political life. It appears, however, that virtue also is incomplete for this, because if the matter were so, no one would have chosen to sleep. That is, we know that it is possible that a man should sleep and retain virtue, and it is possible that he should
1096a be idle all his life long and possible that he should be miserable and unsuccessful in the most important of his affairs. There is no one who would say that such a man is happy, unless he wanted to maintain a principle which he had laid down and a conviction which he was defending.

Of these matters there is enough in what we have already said, and we have spoken of them sufficiently[26] in the discussions that are current. (7) The third life is the life of the people of speculation, and we shall investigate it in what follows of the discourse.[27] (8) As for [...] it is a kind of life.[28] It is plain that wealth is not the good which is sought, because, though a very useful thing, it is sought only for something else. Therefore the things which have been spoken of previously are more entitled to be thought of as ends, because they are preferred and sought for themselves. Yet we may think that these too are not ends. We have spoken much about them, and have refuted[29] the argument of those who claim that they are ends. We must now leave this matter.

---

[21] Arabic *akhassu*; Greek ἐπιπολαιότερον has hardly been understood.

[22] Arabic *yurā*, elsewhere (1155a 28) the rendering of Greek δοκεῖ, disregarding the special force of μαντευόμεθα.

[23] Arabic *li'annahum*, which looks like Greek ὅτι, misread for ἔτι.

[24] Greek ἐοίκασι, i.e. 'they *seem* to seek', is disregarded.

[25] Arabic *dhālika anna* here renders Greek γοῦν, not γάρ—a slip?

[26] Aristotle does not exactly say this. The 'current discussions' (τὰ ἐγκύκλια) are not necessarily his.

[27] I.e. in Book X.

[28] Arabic *sīrah mā* , i.e. Greek βίος for βίαιος.

[29] Again (cf. n. 26) the translator makes the subject personal where Aristotle has

أن تكون غاية وتكاد أن تكون الكرامة هي غاية سيرة صاحب تدبير المدن. وقد يرى أنّ هذه الغاية أخسّ من المطلوب وذلك أنّه قد يظنّ أنّ الكرامة بأن تكون في المكرِم أولى بأن تكون في المكرَم فأمّا الخير فيرى أنّه خاصّ للذي هو له ويعسر انتزاعه منه (٥) لأنّهم إنّما يطلبون الكرامة ليتقرّر عندهم أنّهم خيار وذلك أنّهم يطلبون الكرامة من العقلاء ومن يعرفهم بالفضيلة وبيّن على مذهب هؤلاء أنّ الفضيلة أجود (٦) ولعلّ ظانّاً يظنّ أنّ الفضيلة أولى بأن تكون غاية السيرة المدنية وقد يظهر أنّ الفضيلة أيضاً لا تكتمل لهذا لأنّ الأمر لو كان كذلك لما اختار أحد أن ينام. وذلك أنّا نعلم أنّه قد [٣/٥] يمكن أن ينام الإنسان ومعه الفضيلة ويمكن أن يبطل دهره كلّه ويمكن أن يشقى ويخيب في أعظم أموره ومن كان بهذه الحال فليس من أحد يقول إنّه سعيد إلاّ إن يكون يريد حفظ أصل قد وضعه واعتقاد ينصره.

ففيما قلناه من هذه الاشياء كفاية فقد تكلّمنا فيها كلاماً كافياً في الأقاويل الذائعة (٧) والسيرة الثالثة هي سيرة أهل النظر وسنبحث عنها فيما يأتي بعد من الكلام (٨) وأمّا [...] فسيرة ما. والغنى فبيّن أنّه ليس هو الخير المطلوب لأنّه شئ نافع جدّاً وإنّما يطلب لغيره ولذلك صارت الأشياء التي قيلت قبل أولى يظنّ أنّها غايات لأنّها إنّما تستحبّ وتطلب لنفسها وقد نرى أنّ تلك أيضاً ليست غايات وقد تكلّمنا فيها كلاماً كثيراً وفسخنا قول من ادّعى فيها أنّها غايات فينبغي لنا أن ندع هذا.

---

2 مكرم [...] مكرَم Dun* : مكرَم [...] مكرم Bad || 2 second بأن F : من ان Bad || 5 يعرفهم F, Dun* (παρ’ οἷς γιγνώσκονται) : نعرفهم read. Bad || 5 على منهب F*, Dun* (κατά γε τούτους) : أن منهب corr. Bad || 6 لهذا F, Dun : لهؤلاء Bad || 11 فقد F : وقد Bad || 12 الثالثة هي Bad, Dun : illegible F || 12 عنها F : فيها corr. Bad || 12 [...] : illegible F, *money-making* Dun || 13 فبين F : فتبين Bad || 14 اولى يظن F : اولى بأن يظن add. Bad || 14-16 انها غايات [...] لانها F, Dun : om. Bad

6. As for the universal good, it seems to be best to investigate it and consider what is meant by it, although the investigation of that is a difficult thing for us because friends of ours have introduced the forms and have believed in them. But we think that it is best to maintain the truth and in its defence give up a special theory of ours, if we need to. This would be so if we were not inclined to philosophy. How much more when we choose it and put it first?[30] That is, when we have two friends who differ,[31] one of them the truth, it is our duty to choose the truth. (2) Those who brought us this doctrine did not posit forms in the things in which they spoke of prior and posterior, and therefore they did not posit a form for the numbers. The good is spoken of as in the categories of substance, quality and relation, and the substance and essence are prior by nature to the relative, for the relative is like the offshoot and accident of substance. These then have no common form. (3) Also, since the good is spoken of according to the ways in which the existent is spoken of, i.e. it may be spoken of in the category of substance as when we say 'God' and 'intellect', in the category of quality, like the virtues, in the category of quantity, like the moderate, in the category of relation, like the useful, in the category of time, like the fitting time, and in the category of place, like one's native land, and other similar things, it is plain that there is not for them one common, universal good, because if it were one,[32] it would not be spoken of in all the categories but would be spoken of in one of them only. (4) Also for knowledge of what is in one form[33] is one knowledge, if all the goods were in one form, there would be one knowledge for all the goods. The fact is not so, for[34] under one category of goods there are many knowledges, e.g. opportunity, knowledge of which in war belongs to military strategy, and knowledge of which in sickness belongs to medicine, while knowledge of the moderate with reference to nourishment belongs to medicine, and with reference to exertion to athletics.[35] (5) It is open to a doubter to doubt and say: Why do

---

the passive (καταβέβληνται), and he has taken καταβάλλω in the sense of 'overthrow, refute', rather than 'waste' or 'disseminate' (Burnet, Gauthier). We may note that there is no trace of καίτοι (the reading of K^b and M^b is καί), cf. Gauthier *in loco*.

[30] The translator expands the text here.

[31] Or 'two different friends'.

[32] The addition "if it were one" is natural, cf. Rackham's translation.

[33] Arabic *fī ṣūrah wāḥidah* for Greek κατὰ μίαν ἰδέαν, as again at § 11, end.

[34] Or 'but'.

[35] Arabic *li-tadbīr al-ḥarb, li'ṭ-ṭibb* [...], apparently for στρατηγικῇ [...] (datives).

٦. فأمّا الخير الكلّي فيشبه أن يكون الأجود أن نبحث عنه وننظر كيف يقل وإن كان البحث عن ذلك ممّا يصعب علينا لأنّ قوماً أصدقاء لنا أدخلوا الصور واعتقدوها إلاّ أنّا نرى أنّ من الأجود أن نتحفّظ بالحقّ وأن نبذل في نصرته خاصّ أشيائنا إذا احتجنا إلى ذلك. هذا لو لم نكن نميل إلى الفلسفة فكيف ونحن نؤثرها ونقرّبها وذلك أنّا إذا كان لنا صديقان قد اختلفا أحدهما الحقّ فالواجب إيثار الحقّ (٢) والذين أتونا بهذا الرأي لم يجعلوا في الأمور التي قالوا إنّ منها المتقدّم والمتأخّر صوراً ولذلك لم يجعلوا للأعداد صوراً والخير قد يقل على أنّه في الذات وفي الكيف وفي المضاف والذات والجوهر أقدم بالطبع من المضاف فإنّ المضاف يشبه الفرع والشيء العارض للذات فليس لهذه إذاً صورة ما عامّية (٣) وأيضاً لمّا كان الخير يقل على حسب الأنحاء التي يقل بها الموجود وذلك أنّه قد يقل في الذات كما يقل الله والعقل ويقل في الكيف مثل الفضائل ويقل في الكمّ مثل المعتدل ويقل في المضاف مثل النافع ويقل في الزمان مثل [٦/٣] الوقت الموافق ويقل في المكان مثل الوطن وأشياء أخر شبيهة بها فبيّن أنّها ليس لها خير واحد مشتركاً كلّياً لأنّه لو كان واحداً لما كان يقل في جميع المقولات لكن كان يقل في واحدة منها فقط (٤) وأيضاً فإنّ علم ما في صورة واحدة علم واحد فلو كانت الخيرات كلّها في صورة واحدة لكان لجميع الخيرات علم واحد وليس الأمر كذلك بل تحت مقولة واحدة من الخيرات علوماً كثيرة مثل ذلك الوقت [...] العلم به في الحرب لتدبير الحرب والعلم به في المرض للطبّ والعلم بالمعتدل أمّا للغذاء فللطبّ وأمّا للتعب فلعلم الرياضة (٥) ولشاكّ أن يشكّ فيقول: لِمَ يقولون في الخير إنّه جزئي إذ كان حدّ صورة الإنسان وحدّ

---

1 الاجود أن نبحث عنه وننظر F : اجود إن بحث عنه ونظر Bad || 2 عن corr. Bad : على F || 2 الصور Bad, Dun : illegible F || 3 أشيائنا Bad, Dun : illegible F || 5 الذين corr. Bad, Dun : التي F || 9 لما corr. Bad, Dun : ما F || 11 المعتدل F*, Dun* (τὸ μέτριον) : العدل Bad || 11 الزمان مثل Bad, Dun : partly illegible F || 14 second في F, Dun : لها Bad || 15 كذلك بل Dun : partly illegible F || 16 [...] : illegible F, *opportunity* Dun || 18 لشاك أن يشك F, Dun : لسائل أن يسأل Bad

they say of the good that it is partial[36] when the definition of the
1096b form of man and the definition of partial man[37] are one and the same, because there is no difference between them in so far as they both are man? If this is so, there is no difference between good and good in so far as they are both good. (6) And good is not more than good[38] on account of its being eternal, since a long-lasting white object is not more white than one of short duration. (7) It seems that what the Pythagoreans said concerning this is more convincing because of their placing the One in the sphere of goods,[39] and it seems that Speusippus followed them therein. (8) But the investigation into these things is treated elsewhere. As to what we have mentioned, it may be supposed that it contains a certain doubt, from the fact that our words did [not] refer to every good, and that the goods which are sought and loved for themselves are spoken of under one species,[40] and that the things which produce these and preserve them somehow, or repel their opposites, are called goods on account of these and in a different way from them. (9) It is thus plain that the goods are spoken of in two ways, some being goods in themselves and others being goods on account of these. When then we have separated the goods in themselves from the useful goods, let us investigate whether they are spoken of in one form[41] or not. (10) We say that no one believes[42] that there are goods in themselves except those which are sought separately when isolated, like understanding, and sight, and some of the pleasures and honours. That is, these things, even if we seek them for something else, a man would in any case range among the goods which are goods in themselves, or would he not posit anything else as good except the form, so that the species[43] would thus become useless? (11) If these goods are among the goods in themselves, we must see the definition of the good in them all as one and the same, like the definition of whiteness, which is one in snow and white lead. As for honour and understanding and pleasure, their definitions are unlike and different in respect of their

[36] Arabic *juz'ī*, maybe rendering αὐτοέκαστον.

[37] I.e. Greek αὐτοάνθρωπος.

[38] Arabic *wa-lā yakūn khair akthar min khair*, implying Greek μᾶλλον ἢ ἀγαθόν.

[39] I.e. with reference to the double column of goods and bads of the Pythagoreans, cf. *Met*. 986a 22 *sqq*.

[40] The translator here and at 1096b 29 renders εἶδος by *nau'*.

[41] Cf. n. 33 on § 4.

[42] The translator here disregards the questions, and the sentence goes wrong.

[43] Arabic *nau'* (for εἶδος) as in 1096b 10.

الإنسان الجزئي واحداً بعينه لأنّه لا فرق بينهما في أنّهما إنسان وإذا كان هذا هكذا فلا فرق بين خير وخير في أنّهما خير (٦) ولا يكون خير أكثر من خير من جهة ما هو أزلي إذ كان البياض الطويل المدّة ليس بأشدّ بياضاً من القصير المدّة (٧) ويشبه أن يكون ما قاله فوثاغورشيون في هذا أكثر إقناعاً لوضعهم الواحد في حيز الخيرات وأرى أنّ أسفوسفس قد أتبعهم في ذلك (٨) ولكن النظر في هذه الأشياء يجري في كلام آخر. فأمّا ما ذكرناه فقد يخيّل أنّ فيه شكّاً ما من قبل أنّ كلامنا [لا] كان في كلّ خير وأنّ الخيرات المطلوبة والمحبوبة لذاتها تقال تحت نوع واحد وأنّ الفاعلة لهذه والحافظة لها بضرب من الضروب أو الرافعة لأضدادها يقال لها خيرات من أجل هذه وعلى جهة أخرى غيرها (٩) فبيّن أنّ الخيرات تقال على ضربين: فمنها ما هي خيرات بذاتها ومنها ما هي خيرات من أجل هذه فإنّه قد لخّصنا الخيرات بذاتها من الخيرات النافعة فلنبحث عنها هل تقال في صورة واحدة أم لا (١٠) فنقول إنّه ليس يعتقد أحد أنّ خيرات بذاتها إلاّ التي تطلب على حدتها إذا انفردت بمنزلة الفهم والبصر وبعض اللذّات والكرامات. وذلك أنّ هذه الأشياء وإن كنّا إنّما نطلبها لشيء آخر غيرها فإنّ [٣/٧] الإنسان على حل قد يضعها على أنّها من الخيرات التي هي خيرات بذاتها أو يكون لا يضع شيئاً آخر خيراً سوى الصورة فيصير النوع لذلك باطلاً (١١) فإن كانت هذه الخيرات من الخيرات بذاتها فيجب أن نرى حدّ الخير فيها كلّها واحداً بعينه كحدّ البياض الذي هو واحد في الثلج والإسفيداج فأمّا الكرامة والفهم واللذّة فحدودها متغايرة [...] هي خيرات فليس إذاً الخير شيئاً مشتركاً في

4 فوثاغورشيون Dun* (Πυθαγόρειοι) : فوثاغورش F, Bad || 5 ولكن F : لكن Bad || 8 لأضدادها F*, Dun* (ἐναντίων) : لاضرارها Bad || 6 لا suppl. Dun || 10 قد لخصنا الخيرات F : قد فصلنا الخيرات mrg. || 12 third و Bad, Dun : illegible F || 13 يضعها F*, Dun* (θείη) : يصفها Bad || 14 لا Bad || 14 أو لا يكون F : أو يكون Bad || 14 الصورة F*, Dun* (τῆς ἰδέας) : الصور Bad || 15 من F*, Dun* (τῶν) : هي Bad || 17 [...] : illegible F, *and different in respect of* Dun || 17 الخير F*, Dun* (τὸ ἀγαθόν) : الخيرات Bad || 17 في F, Dun : ذا Bad

being goods. The good therefore is not something common in one form. (12) How then do we speak of them as having a common name, since they are not like the things which have a common name by chance? But they are rather[44] among the things which have a common name through being derived from one thing or through bringing all[45] that they do to one thing, and the most fitting is that they are so by way of analogy, just as reason in the soul is like sight in the body, and other things in other cases. (13) But we must dispense with mention of these things in this place, for the detailed investigation of them is more proper and more fitting for another kind of philosophy than this. Similarly the argument about the form, i.e. if the universal predicated good is a single thing, distinct and separate, it is clear that it is not something that any man can do or acquire, and we are in this place seeking such a good—I mean one which is practicable and acquirable. (14) Perhaps it may be thought
1097a that the best thing would be to get to know that good with reference to the goods which are practicable and acquirable, and it would be like an example which if we had, we should be more knowledgeable in regard to the goods for us, and if we knew it, we should obtain these goods [...]. (15) In this argument is some plausibility, but it seems to be in opposition to the procedure of the sciences. That is, they all desire and aim at a good [...] the completion of what is lacking to them, then knowledge of it fails to result.[46] Besides there is no excuse[47] for all the technicians being ignorant of what is helpful to them in their craft to this extent and not seeking it. (16) Nor is it known in what respect the weaver and the joiner will benefit in their craft when he knows the good itself, or how the doctor will be more skilled in medicine, and the general further advanced in strategy, when he has contemplated the form of the art.[48] That is, we know that the doctor is not investigating health in this way, but investigates only the health of man, or rather investigates only the health of a particular man, because he treats only individuals. This is the extent of what we have to say on these matters.

---

[44] Arabic *lākin akhlaq bihā an*, lit. 'it is more appropriate for them that [...]'. The question has disappeared (ἄρα read for ἆρα).

[45] Arabic *min ṭarīq annahā ta'tī bi-kull*, i.e. Greek ἅπαντα.

[46] MS. *yaqaʿu*. The sense seems to demand insertion of the negative *lā*.

[47] *lā ʿudhra*, a misreading of οὐκ εὔλογον.

[48] Arabic *ṣūrat aṣ-ṣināʿa* for Greek τὴν ἰδέαν αὐτήν, the idea itself, i.e. the form of the good.

صورة واحدة (١٢) فكيف [...] أنها مشتركة في الاسم إذ ليست تشبه المشتركة في الاسم من جهة الاتّفاق لكن أخلق بها أن تكون من المشتركة في الاسم من طريق أنّها من شئ واحد أو من طريق أنّها تأتي بكلّ ما تفعله إلى شئ واحد والأولى بها أن تكون على طريق المشاكلة بمنزلة ما أنّ العقل في النفس كقياس البصر في البدن وبمنزلة أشياء أخر في أشياء غيرها (١٣) ولكنّه ينبغي لنا أن نلقي ذكر هذه الأشياء في هذا الموضع فإنّ استقصاء البحث عنها بصنف آخر غير هذا الصنف من الفلسفة أخصّ وأولى وكذلك الكلام في الصورة وذلك أنّه إن كان الخير العامّ المشترك شيئاً واحداً مفارقاً على حدته فمن البيّن أنّه ليس شيئاً يمكن أن يفعله أو يقتنيه إنسان من الناس ونحن فإنّما نطلب في هذا الموضع الخير الذي بهذه الحل أعني الذي يفعل ويقتنى (١٤) ولعلّ ظانّاً يظنّ أنّ الأجود يكون تعرّف ذلك الخير فيما كان من الخيرات [التي] تفعل وتقتنى ويكون بمنزلة المثل الذي إذا كان معنا كانت الخيرات التي لنا أكثر معرفة وإذا علمناه أصبنا هذه الخيرات [...] (١٥) إنّ في هذا الكلام بعض الإقناع ولكن يشبه أن يكون بخلاف ما عليه العلوم. وذلك أنّها بأجمعها تشتاق وتقصد قصد خير [...] استتمام ما ينقصها ثم [لا] يقع العلم به. هذا و لا عذر لجميع الصنّاع أن يجهلوا ما لهم من المعونة في صناعتهم هذا المقدار ولا يطلبونه (١٦) ولا يعلم أيضاً بماذا ينتفع الحائك والنجّار في صناعته إذا علم الخير نفسه ولا كيف يكون الطبيب لطبّ ويدبّر [٣/٨] الجيش أقوم تدبير إذا نظر إلى صورة الصناعة. وذلك أنّنا نعلم أنّ الطبيب ليس ينظر في الصحّة من هذا الوجه لكنّه إنّما ينظر في صحّة الإنسان بل إنّما ينظر في صحّة إنسان ما لأنّه إنّما يعالج الأشخاص فهذا مبلغ ما ينبغي أن نقوله في هذه الأشياء.

---

1 [...] : illegible F, *do we speak* Dun || 4 العقل F*, Dun* (νοῦς) : الفعل Bad || 5 أن F*, Dun* : الا Bad || 10 التي appar. suppl. Dun || 10 تفعل وتقتنى appar. read. Dun : يفعل ويقتنى F, Dun || 11 كانت corr. Bad, Dun : كنا F || 13 لا suppl. Bad, Dun || 14 لهم corr. Dun : له F, Bad || 15 يعلم F, Dun : يسلم Bad || 16 لطب F : يطب Bad || 16 الجيش F*, Dun* (στρατηγικώτερος) : لبشر Bad || 16 وذلك اننا F, Dun : ولكننا Bad

7. We must resume from the beginning[49] the discussion of the sought-for good and investigate what it is. We say: The good in each of the actions and arts is different from what it is in the other. That is, the good in the art of medicine is different from what it is in military strategy, and similarly in all the remaining arts. What, think you, is the good in each of the arts? I say that it is the thing on account of which the art does all that it does. In medicine it is health, in military strategy it is victory and in the art of building a house. In each it is something different from what it is in another, and it is the end aimed at in every action and choice, for all men do everything they do on account of the end aimed at. It necessarily follows that if there is something which is the end for all the things which are done, it is the good which must be done,[50] and if the ends are many, it is these. (2) The discussion then has shifted and returned to one meaning, and we must also[51] seek to explain that. (3) We say: Since it appeared that the ends are many, and we were choosing some of them for the sake of something else, as wealth, the flute, and in general all instruments, it is clear that not all ends are perfect, and it appears that the best is something perfect. It follows necessarily that, if there is one thing only perfect, it is the thing sought, and if the perfect things are many, it is the most perfect and most complete of them. (4) We say: The thing sought for itself is more perfect than what is sought for something else, and that which is not preferred at any time for anything else is more perfect than those which are preferred for something else, not for themselves. The perfect in general is that which is preferred always for itself and is not preferred at any time for anything else. (5) The thing most entitled to
1097b this description is happiness. That is, happiness is that which we prefer for itself, not seeking it at any time for something else. As for honour, pleasure, intelligence and every virtue, we prefer them also[52] for themselves, because we choose each one of them and we do not thereby aim at anything else,[53] and we prefer them also for happiness, since we think that we attain happiness by means of them. As for happiness, no one prefers it on account of these nor on account of [...] else at all. (6) It is clear that that is a necessary con-

[49] Arabic *min ar-ra's*, apparently rendering Greek πάλιν.

[50] Arabic *al-khair alladhī yanbaghī an yufʿal* for Greek τὸ πρακτὸν ἀγαθόν. It is inconsistent with the translation of τῶν πρακτῶν ἁπάντων immediately preceding.

[51] Arabic *aiḍan* for Greek ἔτι μᾶλλον.

[52] Arabic *aiḍan* for Greek μέν.

[53] This clause renders μηθενὸς γὰρ ἀποβαίνοντος.

٧. فينبغي أن نعود من الرأس إلى الكلام في الخير المطلوب وننظر ما هو فنقول [...] من الأفعال والصناعات غيره في الآخر وذلك أنّ الخير [...] الطبّ غيره في تدبير الحرب وكذلك الأمر في سائر الصناعات الباقية فما ترى الخير في كلّ واحد من الصناعات أقول إنّه الشئ الذي من أجله تفعل الصناعة سائر ما تفعله. وهو في الطبّ الصحّة وفي تدبير الحرب الظفر وفي صناعة البناء البيت وهو في كلّ واحد من الأشياء شئ غيره في آخر وهو الغاية المقصودة في كلّ فعل واختيار فإنّ جميع الناس إنّما يفعلون كلّ ما يفعلونه بسبب الغاية المقصودة. فيجب من ذلك إن كان ها هنا شئ هو غاية لجميع الأشياء التي تفعل فهو الخير الذي ينبغي أن يفعل وإن كانت الغايات كثيرة فهي هذه (٢) فالكلام إذاً قد انتقل ورجع إلى معنى واحد فينبغي أيضاً أن نلتمس إيضاح ذلك (٣) فنقول إنّه إذا كان يظهر أنّ الغايات كثيرة وكنّا إنّما نؤثر بعضها بسبب شئ آخر مثل الثروة والمزمار وبالجملة الآلات كلّها فبيّن أنّ ليس جميع الغايات كاملة وقد يظهر أنّ الأفضل هو شئ كامل. فيجب من ذلك إن كان ها هنا شئ واحد فقط كاملاً فهو الشئ المطلوب وإن كانت الأشياء الكاملة كثيرة فهو أكملها وأتمّها (٤) ونحن نقول إنّ الشئ المطلوب لذاته أكمل من المطلوب لغيره والذي لا يؤثر في وقت من الأوقات من أجل غيره أكمل من التي تؤثر لغيرها لا لنفسها. فالكامل بالجملة هو الذي يؤثر لذاته أبداً ولا يؤثر في وقت من الأوقات لغيره (٥) وأولى الأشياء بهذه الصفة السعادة وذلك أنّ السعادة هي التي [٣/٩] نؤثرها لنفسها ولا نطلبها في وقت من الأوقات لغيرها فأمّا الكرامة واللذّة والعقل وكلّ فضيلة فقد نؤثرها أيضاً لنفسها لأنّا قد نختار كلّ واحد منها ونحن لا نقصد بها غيرها وقد نؤثرها أيضاً للسعادة إذا ظنّنا أنّا إنّما نصل إلى السعادة بتوسّطها فأمّا السعادة فليس من أحد يؤثرها من أجل هذه ولا من [...] غيرها أصلاً (٦) وبيّن أنّ ذلك إنّما لزم فيها من قبل أنّها مكتفية

1 ننظر F, Dun : ذكر Bad || 1 [...] : illegible F, *The good in each* Dun || 2 [...] : illegible F, *in the art of* Dun || 3 second الصناعات F : الصناعات به add. Bad || 5 شئ F, Dun : om. Bad || 8 فهي Bad, Dun : illegible F || 13 أكمل من F*, Dun* (τελειότερον) : ولكنه ليس Bad

sequence of its being sufficient [...]. That is, we think that the perfect good is self-sufficient. We do not mean by sufficiency[54] that the life of man is to be the life of a solitary, living by himself, but he is to be with his parents and children and women[55] and fellow citizens, because man is political by nature. (7) We must set a limit to these things, because if we attend to[56] ancestors and sons and sons' sons and friends of friends, we shall reach infinity. But we shall investigate this hereafter. We lay down that sufficiency is the thing which, when a man possesses it alone, makes his life preferable, not needing anything, and we think that that is happiness. (8) We think also that it is preferable to all things and is not reckoned along with the other things. If it is reckoned with them, then it is plain that it is reckoned with what is below it of the goods,[57] being preferable to it. That is, the goods vary in superiority,[58] and that of them which is more excessive in good is preferable to anything else. The greatest good is always the most preferable of them. It would appear that happiness is a perfect thing, self-sufficient, an end for the things which are done. (9) But it is likely to be generally admitted that happiness is the best thing, and what we wish to elucidate about it is to know what it is. (10) Perhaps that would be authenticated for us if we ascertained what the function of man is. For as we think that the good and the excellence for a flute player and a sculptor and any other of all the artists, and in general everyone who has a certain function or work, is simply in his function, so we think that if man has a particular function, the good for him is simply in that function. (11) Do you really think that the joiner and the shoemaker have functions and works, and man is fashioned to be idle? Or, as we see a definite function for eye and hand and foot and in general for every member of the body, may it similarly be laid down that for man there is a definite function, besides all these? (12) If this function exists, what then is it? We say that if his function is that he should grow, then we see that growth[59] is common to man and plants, but the thing here sought is
1098a the special function of man. We must then [...] the nutritive

[54] *Sic*, but the Arabic translator should say 'self-sufficiency'.
[55] Arabic *nisā'*, not 'wife' (γυναικί) as in the original.
[56] *Am'annā* rendering ἐπεκτείνοντι.
[57] The sense is misunderstood: Greek μετὰ τοῦ ἐλαχίστου τῶν ἀγαθῶν, 'with the least of goods', is mistranslated, and this phrase should not be construed with συναριθμουμένηύ but with αἱρετώτερον.
[58] This sentence is also misunderstood, τὸ προστιθέμενον being left untranslated.
[59] Arabic *namā'* for Greek ζῆν, not quite accurately.

[...] وذلك أنّ الخير الكامل نظنّ أنّه مكتفٍ بنفسه ولسنا نريد بالكفاية أن تكون سيرة الإنسان سيرة المتخلّي والمنفرد وحده لكنّه يكون مع أبوين وأولاد ونساء وأهل مدينة لأنّ الإنسان مدني بالطبع (٧) وينبغي أن نجعل لهذه الأشياء حدّاً لأنّا إذا أمعنّا في الأجداد والأولاد وأولاد الأولاد وأصدقاء الأصدقاء صرنا إلى ما لا نهاية له ولكنّا سنبحث عن هذا فيما بعد ونضع أنّ الكفاية هي الشيء الذي إذا انفرد به الإنسان جعل سيرته مؤثرة غير محتاجة إلى شيء ونحن نرى أنّ ذلك هو السعادة (٨) ونرى أيضاً أنّها آثر من جميع الأشياء وليست تعدّ مع الأشياء إن عدّها معها فمن البيّن أنّها تعدّ مع ما هو دونها من الخيرات على أنّها آثر منه. وذلك أنّ الخيرات تتفاضل وأزيدها في الخير آثر من غيره وأعظم الخيرات آثرها أبداً. فقد يظهر أنّ السعادة شيء كامل مكتفٍ بنفسه غاية للأشياء التي تفعل (٩) ولكن خليق أن يكون ممّا اتّفق عليه القول بأنّ السعادة هي الشيء الأفضل والشيء الذي نريد أن نوضحه من أمرها أن نعلم ما هي (١٠) ولعلّ ذلك يصحّ لنا إن نحن حصلنا فعل الإنسان ما هو وذلك أنّه كما يظنّ أنّ الخير والجودة للزامر ولصانع التماثيل ولغيرهم من جميع الصنّاع وبالجملة كلّ من له فعل ما أو عمل إنّما هو في فعله كذلك نظنّ أنّ الإنسان إن كان له فعل من الأفعال فالخير إنّما هو له في ذلك الفعل (١١) أفترى للنجّار والإسكاف أفعالاً وأعمالاً والإنسان مطبوع [٣/١٠] على البطالة أو كما أنّا نرى للعين ولليد وللرجل وبالجملة لكلّ عضو من الأعضاء فعلاً ما كذلك لواضع أن يضع أنّ للإنسان فعلاً ما سوى هذه كلّها (١٢) فإن كان هذا الفعل موجوداً فما هو فنقول إنّه إن كان فعله هو أن ينمي فقد نرى أنّ النماء عامّ للإنسان والنبات والشيء المطلوب ها هنا إنّما هو الفعل

1 وذلك Bad, Dun : partly illegible F || 1 نظن F, Dun : يظن Bad || 7 ليست F : ليس Bad || 7 عدها F, Dun : نعدها Bad || 7 مع ما F, Dun : مما Bad || 9 يظهر F : ظهر Bad || 10 مما F : ما Bad || 12 لغيرهم corr. : لغيرها F || 13 عمل F : يفعل Bad || 13 نظن F, Dun : يظن Bad || 16 لواضع F : واضع Bad || 16 يضع F, Dun : نضع Bad

and growing faculty.[60] There follows this faculty a perceptive faculty [...] to belong to this also that it is common to man and horse and ox and every animal. (13) It remains that there is an active faculty of the rational part. Some of this part is amenable to reason, and some of it is reflective. Since this faculty is spoken of in two ways, our discussion must be of that which is in act, since it is more fitting and proper to speak about. (14) If the function of a man is the function of the soul according to what reason necessitates, or not divested of reason, and we said that the function of the average performer in an art and the function of the expert in it are generically one, e.g. the function of the average lute-player and the function of the expert, and this is the case in general in all the arts adding the mention of excellence along with the function, so that we say of the average performer that he plays the lute and of the excellent performer that he plays the lute well, we lay down[61] that the function of man is a certain life, and this life is a function belonging to the soul and an action with intellectual discrimination, and the function of the good man is with this function according to the necessary excellence, (15) and the function of every single thing is excellent according to its virtue. If the matter is so, then the good which specially characterises man is a function belonging to the soul according to what virtue necessitates, and if the virtues are many, it is a certain function which the best or most perfect of them necessitates. (16) And this function is in a perfect life, because one swallow does not announce spring, nor does one day of temperate weather announce that. Similarly also one day of his life does not make a man [either] happy [or miserable], nor does a short time of it. (17) In this way then must the good be summarised. Presumably we must outline it first, then acquire knowledge of it afterwards. It is thought that it belongs to anyone to take care to summarise the beautiful things and to acquire knowledge of them,[62] and that time is either the originator of things like these or is a real helper thereto. Therefore the arts have increased. That is, it is necessary for everybody [...] that he should increase in his art, when what is lacking of the art is at his disposal,

---

[60] Arabic *qūwah* for Greek ζωή, 'life', and the word is retained in what follows.

[61] Arabic *fa-innā naḍaʿu*. The Arabic translator omits Greek εἰ δ' οὕτως and evidently makes this the apodeixis of the next sentence, cf. 1118b 14: *fa-innā naqūlu*.

[62] This is far from the Greek original.

الخاصّ بالإنسان فينبغي إذاً [...] القوّة الغاذية والنامية ويتبع هذه القوّة قوّة حسا[...] من أمر هذه أيضاً أنّها مشتركة للإنسان والفرس والثور ولكلّ حيوان (١٣) فقد بقي أن يكون ها هنا للجزء الناطق قوّة فعّالة وهذا الجزء منه ما هو منقاد للنطق ومنه ما هو مفكّر وإذا كانت هذه القوّة تقال على ضربين فينبغي أن يكون كلامنا في التي هي منها بالفعل إذ كانت أحقّ وأولى بالكلام فيها (١٤) فإن كان فعل الإنسان إنّما هو فعل للنفس على ما يوجبه النطق أو غير معرّى من النطق وكنّا نقول إنّ فعل المقارب في الصناعة وفعل الفاضل فيها واحد بالجنس بمنزلة فعل المقارب في ضرب العود وفعل الفاضل فيه وكان الأمر بالجملة في جميع الصناعات يجري هذا المجرى بز[...]تها ذكر الفضيلة مع الفعل فنقول في الضارب المقارب إنّه يضرب بالعود وفي الضارب الفاضل إنّه يضرب ضرباً جيّداً فإنّا نضع أنّ فعل الإنسان سيرة ما وهذه السيرة فعل للنفس وعمل بتمييز نطقي وفعل الإنسان الفاضل هو مع هذا الفعل على ما يجب من الجودة (١٥) وكلّ واحد من الأشياء إنّما يجود فعله بحسب فضيلته. وإذا كان الأمر هكذا فالخير الذي يخصّ الإنسان هو فعل للنفس على ما توجبه الفضيلة فإن كانت الفضائل كثيرة فهو فعل ما يوجبها أفضلها أو أكملها (١٦) وإنّما يكون هذا الفعل في السيرة الكاملة لأنّ خطّافاً واحداً لا ينذر بالربيع ولا يوماً واحداً معتدل الهواء ينذر بذلك. كذلك أيضاً لا يجعل الإنسان سعيداً يوم واحد من حياته ولا زمان يسير منها (١٧) فعلى هذا [١/١١] الوجه ينبغي أن نلخّص الخير وخليق أن يكون ينبغي أن نرسمه أوّلاً ثمّ نحصّله بعد ذلك وقد يظنّ أنّه واجب على كلّ أحد أن يقدّم العناية بتلخيص الأمور الجميلة وتحصيلها والزمان إمّا أن يكون هو المستنبط لأمثال هذه الأشياء وإمّا أن يكون عوناً صالحاً على ذلك ولذلك صارت الصناعات تتزيّد وذلك أنّه واجب على كلّ [...] أن

2 فقد F : وقد Bad || 4 إذ corr. Bad : إذا F || 8 ذكر F, Dun : فركبنا Bad || 10 second فعل F, Dun : نرسمه : F نرسمها 16 || F والوجه : corr. Dun الوجه 16 || add. Bad خطافا ما : F خطافا 14 || Bad إن Bad || 17 العناية F, Dun : الصناعة Bad

and maintain [...] (18) his principles in regard to it.[63] Completeness is not to be sought in everything that one does in the same way, but our search for it is according to the subject matter and to the extent to which it resembles the art in question. (19) That is, the carpenter and the geometrician are different in their search for the right angle. For the carpenter seeks it only to the extent that he profits by it in his work, whereas the geometrician seeks to know what it is and what kind of thing it is, because he is the one who regards its truth. In this manner we must act in all cases, lest what is superfluous to the function of the art not being incumbent upon us to do should be too much
1098b for us. (20) Nor must we seek the cause in everything in the same way, but in some things it is sufficient to know that it exists, as is the case with principles, for our saying that a thing exists is a first principle.[64] (21) Principles are known partly by induction, partly by perception, partly by habituation and repetition,[65] partly in other ways. (22) We must seek to employ each principle according to what its nature necessitates, and make an effort to acquire knowledge of them and define them in the right way, (23) for their usefulness in what follows them is great. It is thought that the beginning of a thing is more than half of the whole of it, and that many of the things sought are made plain and apparent by the appearance of the principle.

8. We must investigate it[66] and not restrict ourselves to investigating it as regards the conclusion and the premises only but also how it is described. For everything agrees with the truth and attests it, but quickly opposes and differs from falsehood.[67] (2) Since the goods have been divided into three kinds, some spoken of as external, others as in the soul and others again as in the body, we say that the most worthy and the most entitled of them to be goods are those which are in the soul, and we lay down that the functions and actions

---

[63] The short sentence in Greek παντὸς γὰρ προσθεῖναι τὸ ἐλλεῖπον is much expanded.

[64] Arabic *mabda' auwal* for Greek πρῶτον καὶ ἀρχή (ἀρχή is usually rendered by *mabda'* alone).

[65] Arabic *wa-ilā auwalihi*, not in the Greek.

[66] If Susemihl and Gauthier are right, the good (τἀγαθόν), reading here περὶ αὐτοῦ for περὶ αὐτῆς. Otherwise the reference is to the principle (ἀρχή), i.e. the definition is man's good which has been given in the foregoing (happiness), and the Arabic translator evidently took the passage so, with the common reading.

[67] Omitting Greek τὰ ὑπάρχοντα and notably τἀληθές.

يزيد في صناعته إذا تهيّأ له ما ينقص من الصناعة وأن يحفظ [...] (١٨) أصوله منها. ولا ينبغي أن نطلب الاستقصاء في كلّ شيء نفعله على مثل واحد لكن يكون طلبنا له بحسب المادّة الموضوعة له وبالمقدار الذي يشاكل تلك الصناعة (١٩) وذلك أنّ النجّار والمهندس مختلفان في طلب الزاوية القائمة فإنّ النجّار إنّما يطلبها بمقدار ما ينتفع بها في عمله وأمّا المهندس فيطلب أن يعلم ما هي وأيّ الأشياء هي لأنّه الناظر في حقيقتها وعلى هذا المعنى ينبغي أن يعمل في سائر الأشياء لئلا يكثر علينا ما يفضل عن فعل الصناعة ممّا لا يجب أن نفعله (٢٠) ولا ينبغي لنا أيضاً أن نطلب السبب في كلّ شيء على مثل واحد لكن قد يكتفي في بعض الأشياء أن يعلم أنّه موجود كالحال في المبادئ فإنّ قولنا في الشيء إنّه موجود هو مبدأ أوّل في المبادئ (٢١) فمنها ما يعلم بالاستقراء ومنها ما يعلم بالحسّ ومنها ما يعلم بالاعتبار وإلى أوّله ومنها ما يعرف بطرق أخر (٢٢) وينبغي أن نلتمس استعمل كلّ واحد من المبادئ بحسب ما توجبه طبيعته ونجدّ في تحصيلها وتحديدها على ما يجب (٢٣) فإنّ منفعتها فيما يتلوها عظيمة. فقد يظنّ بمبدأ الشيء أنّه أكثر من نصف جملته وأنّ كثيراً من الأشياء المطلوبة تبيّن وتظهر بظهور المبدأ.

٨. فينبغي أن نبحث عنه ولا نقتصر على أن يكون بحثنا عنه من النتيجة والمقدّمات فقط لكن ما يوصف به فإنّ الحقّ كلّ شيء يوافقه ويشهد له وأمّا الكذب فسريع ما يخالفه ويباينه (٢) فإذا كانت الخيرات قد انقسمت على ثلاثة أضرب فمنها ما يقل من خارج ومنها ما يقل [١/١٢] في النفس ومنها ما يقل في البدن فإنّا نقول إنّ [...] وأولاها بأن تكون خيرات ما هو منها في النفس ونضع أنّ الأعمل والأفعال في النفس فنعم ما وصف به الخير على

---

1 أصوله Dun : وصوله Bad; F illegible || 2 نفعله read. Bad : يفعله F || 6 يعمل F, Dun : يجعل Bad || 6 فعل F*, Dun* (ἔργων) : المزاولة Bad; بعض Bad || 10 إلى أوله Dun : partly illegible F; ... وقد Bad || 12 فقد F : وقد Bad || 17 [...] illegible F, *most worthy* Dun

[of the soul] are concerned with the soul. Thus the good is excellently described according to this old opinion, with which the philosophers[68] agree. (3) And it is said with truth that the end which is aimed at is certain actions and functions, for in this way the end aimed at is the end of the goods of the soul, not the end of the external goods. (4) As confirmation of this statement and in agreement with it [...] right living and good deeds. That is, happiness will almost have been described as right living and good deeds. (5) It would appear that all the things sought for in happiness exist for the happy man.[69] (6) For some think that happiness is virtue and understanding,[70] and others that it is a certain wisdom. Yet others think that it is all of these things, or at least one of them,[71] either with pleasure or not deprived of pleasure. (7) Other people add to it, together with these things, prosperity. Some of these opinions are given by a number of the ancients, others by a few famous people. None of them went wrong[72] in all that he believed in the matter, but they were right either in one thing of what they said, or in most of it. (8) The account of those of them who said that happiness is virtue and those who said that it is a particular virtue is in agreement,[73] for the action which is in accordance with what virtue necessitates is virtue. (9) Presumably the difference is not slight between the belief that the chief good is in acquisition and possession[74] and the belief that it is in use and act,[75] because possession[76] may exist in a man
1099a without his doing any good at all, as in the case of the sleeper or some other who is precluded from action in some way. But when the thing exists for the man in act, that is quite impossible, because in

[68] Arabic *al-mutafalsifah* (for Greek τῶν φιλοσοφούντων), strictly 'those who affect philosophy', cf. Arthur J. Arberry, "An Arabic Treatise on Politics", in: *The Islamic Quarterly* 2 (1955), pp. 9-22, here p. 15.

[69] I.e. understanding τῷ λεχθέντι not as 'our definition', but as 'the man defined'.

[70] He should say 'and others understanding'.

[71] Arabic *baʿḍahā*, Greek τούτων τι.

[72] Greek εὔλογον is omitted.

[73] Greek ὁ λόγος is wrongly construed by the Arabic translator with τοῖς λέγουσι and the force of ἤ is disregarded

[74] Arabic *malkah*, Greek ἕξις.

[75] The Greek offers two pairs of contrasting terms. In the Arabic, probably owing to misunderstanding of the meaning of ἕξις here, these have been rearranged and are no longer alternatives: 'acquisition', *qunyah*, κτῆσις and (*wa-* for *au* = ἤ) 'possession', *malkah*, ἕξις – 'use', *istiʿmāl*, χρῆσις and (again *wa-* for *au*) act, *fiʿl*, ἐνέργεια.

[76] See note 74.

حسب هذا الرأي القديم الذي أجمع عليه المتفلسفة (٣) وبالصواب قيل إنّ الغاية المقصودة أفعل ما وأعمل فإنّ بهذه الجهة تكون الغاية المقصودة إنّما هي غاية خيرات النفس لا غاية الخيرات التي من خارج (٤) وممّا يشهد لهذا القول ويوافقه [...] من حسن السيرة وجميل الأفعل وذلك أنّ السعادة تكاد أن تكون قد وضعت بأنّها حسن سيرة وجميل أفعل (٥) وقد يظهر أنّ جميع الأشياء المطلوبة في السعادة هي موجودة للسعيد (٦) فإنّ قوماً رأوا أنّ السعادة فضيلة وفهم وقوم رأوا أنّها حكمة ما وغيرهم رأوا أنّها جميع هذه الأشياء أو بعضها إمّا مع لذّة وإمّا غير معرّاة من اللذّة (٧) وقوم آخرون ضمّوا إليها مع هذه الأشياء الإقبال وبعض هذه الأشياء قد يقول به خلق من القدماء وبعضها يقول به قليل من المشهورين من الناس. ولم يخطئ أحد منهم في جميع ما اعتقد من ذلك لكنّهم أصابوا إمّا في شئ واحد ممّا قالوه وإمّا في أكثره (٨) فمَن قل منهم إنّ السعادة هي الفضيلة ومَن قل إنّها فضيلة ما فقولهم متّفق فإنّ الفعل الذي يكون على ما توجبه الفضيلة هو الفضيلة (٩) وخليق ألاّ يكون الفرق يسيراً بين الاعتقاد بأنّ الشئ الأفضل في القنية والملكة وبين الاعتقاد بأنّه في الاستعمل والفعل لأنّ الملكة قد يمكن أن تكون موجودة في الإنسان وهو لا يفعل خيراً أصلاً بمنزلة حل النائم أو غيره ممّن لا يتهيّأ له الفعل بضرب من الضروب فأمّا إذا وجد الشئ للإنسان بالفعل فليس يمكن ذلك له أصلاً لأنّه في تلك الحل يفعل

2 فإن F : وإن Bad || 2-3 خيرات النفس Dun : illegible F || 4 وضعت F : وصفت Bad

that case he will act of necessity and will act well. Just as the rewards in the games[77] are not won by the skilful[78] and strong of the competitors, but by those who contend and struggle and who conquer,[79] so the virtuous and good among men in their life[80] are those who perform their actions according to what is right and fair. (10) The life of these is pleasant in itself, because pleasure is of the things related to the soul, and every man takes pleasure in the thing which is related to his love, e.g. the lover of horses takes pleasure in horses, and he who loves to contemplate things takes pleasure in contemplating them. Similarly the lover of justice takes pleasure in matters related to justice, and in general the lover of the virtues takes pleasure in virtuous matters. (11) Things pleasant in the opinion of most people are opposed to noble things,[81] since they are not naturally pleasant. Things naturally pleasant are pleasant in the opinion of lovers of the noble and noble things,[82] viz. actions which are done in accord with what virtue necessitates, must be pleasant in the opinion of lovers of the noble and in themselves. (12) Therefore they have no need in their life for increase of this pleasure,[83] since they have it in their life itself. For, in addition to what we have mentioned, there is no good man who does not delight in noble actions, and no one says of a man that he is just unless of one who loves the things related to justice, and we do not say of a man that he is generous unless of one who loves the actions related to generosity. Things are similar in the case of the other virtues. (13) Since this is so, the actions which are done in accordance with what virtue necessitates are pleasant in themselves. They are also at the same time good and noble, and every one of these actions is specially characterised by this description, since the good man judges of them truly, and his judgement of them is as we have described. (14) Happiness then is the best and most excellent of things, and in it

---

[77] Arabic *maidān*, lit. 'the race ground', 'Olympic' has disappeared in the translation.

[78] Arabic *al-maharah* rendering οἱ κάλλιστοι. It did not occur to the translator to take the words in simplest meaning: 'handsomest', which is no doubt here intended.

[79] The nuance τούτων γάρ [...] is missed.

[80] I.e. τῶν ἐν τῷ βίῳ καλῶν κἀγαθῶν is made the subject of the sentence with the omission of ἐπήβολοι γίνονται.

[81] This is not in the Greek (τοῖς μὲν οὖν πολλοῖς τὰ ἡδέα μάχεται).

[82] Apparently renders τοιαῦται, 'such', i.e. pleasant, and the construction is wrong (τοιαῦται is predicate).

[83] The words ὥσπερ περιάπτου τινός are omitted.

ضرورةً ويجيد الفعل وكما أنّ الجوائز ليس ينالها في الميدان المهرة والجياد من المناضلين لكن المجاهدين منهم والباطشين والذين يغلبون كذلك الأفاضل والخيار من الناس في سيرتهم إنّما هم الذين يفعلون أفعالهم [١/١٥] على الصواب والاستواء (١٠) وسيرة هؤلاء لذيذة بنفسها لأنّ الاستلذاذ من الأمور المنسوبة إلى النفس وكلّ واحد من الناس إنّما يستلذّ بالشيء الذي ينسب إلى محبّته. مثل ذلك أنّ محبّ الخيل يلتذّ بالخيل ومحبّ النظر إلى الأشياء يلتذّ بالنظر وكذلك محبّ العدل يلتذّ بالأمور المنسوبة إلى العدل وبالجملة محبّ الفضائل يلتذّ بالأمور الفاضلة (١١) الأشياء اللذيذة عند أكثر الناس تنافي الأشياء الجميلة من قبل أنّها ليست لذيذة بالطبع والأشياء اللذيذة بالطبع هي لذيذة عند محبّي الجميل والأشياء الجميلة هي الأفعال التي تفعل بحسب ما توجبه الفضيلة يجب أن تكون هذه الأفعال لذيذة عند محبّي الجميل بنفسها (١٢) فلذلك ليست بهم حاجة في سيرتهم إلى زيادة على هذه اللذّة إذ كانت لهم في نفس سيرتهم. فإنّه ليس يوجد مع ما ذكرنا إنسان خير إلاّ وهو يسرّ بالأفعال الجميلة ولا يقول أحد في إنسان إنّه عدل إلاّ فيمن يحبّ الأمور المنسوبة إلى العدل ولا يقول في إنسان إنّه سخي إلاّ فيمن يحبّ الأفعال المنسوبة إلى السخاء وكذلك تجري الأمور في سائر الفضائل (١٣) وإذا كان هذا هكذا فالأفعال التي تتمّ بحسب ما توجبه الفضيلة لذيذة بنفسها وهي أيضاً مع ذلك حسنة وجميلة وكلّ واحد من هذه الأفعال يكون بهذه الصفة خاصّة إذا حكم عليها الفاضل حكماً صواباً

5 ينسب : F يتتسب Bad || 6 محب العدل يلتذ Dun : illegible F || 7 بالأمور corr. Bad : الامور F || 7 الأشياء Dun : illegible F || 13 المنسوبة Bad, Dun : illegible F || 14 السخاء Bad, Dun : illegible F || 15 تتم بحسب Bad, Dun : illegible F

is absolute pleasure. These are not distinguished and separated as they are distinguished and separated[84] in the tablet at Delos, for it is written thus:

> Best of things is the justest, most excellent the healthiest
> Pleasantest the most desired.[85]

That is, all these things exist for the actions of virtue. We say that happiness is either all these, or one of them and that the best. (15) Yet it appears that happiness needs the external goods as we have said. That is, it is impossible, or not easy, to do noble actions so
1099b long as there is no assistance from outside. For many noble deeds are done with the help of things which are like tools, I mean money, friends and auxiliaries in war.[86] (16) Some things when they are lacking to the happy man trouble his happiness, such as honourable descent, fine children and good looks. For a man is not happy who is extremely ill-favoured and ugly, or of low birth, or who is alone or childless. Presumably he is less [...] he has bad sons or bad friends, or had good sons, or good friends, and they died. (17) It seems that the matter is as we have said, that the happy man lacks assistance from outside,[87] and therefore people put happiness and good fortune on one level, and others make happiness and virtue equivalent.

9. For this reason the doubt is raised in regard to happiness whether it is a thing that can be learned or acquired by practice or obtained in another way, or that it comes to a man by special favour from God, or by luck and chance. (2) But if there is a gift from God[88] to men, presumably happiness is a gift from Him to them, especially since it is the best thing which [...] to men. (3) But consideration of this is more liable to be [...] in another art. Yet it is clear that if it is not a gift from God, but has come through virtue and learning or acquirement,[89] it is one of the things which are extremely noble and important,[90] because the end of virtue and what is acquired from it[91]

[84] Text *wa-fusirat*. Or *wa-fussirat*, i.e. 'and explained' or 'commented on'.
[85] The Greek verses are rendered only very approximately in the Arabic translation.
[86] Concrete *al-aʿwān ʿalā ʾl-ḥarb* for abstract πολιτικῆς δυνάμεως.
[87] Arabic *madad min khārij*, but Greek is τῆς τοιαύτης εὐημερίας, "this sort of prosperity" (Ross).
[88] Greek θεῶν.
[89] Arabic *iktisāb*, Greek ἄσκησιν.
[90] Direct translation of Greek τῶν θειοτάτων seems to be avoided intentionally.
[91] I.e. Greek τὸ ἆθλον.

وحكمه عليها يكون على ما وصفنا (١٤) فبالسعادة إذاً أفضل الأشياء وأجودها واللذائة بالإطلاق فيها ولم تميّز هذه الأشياء وتفصّل كما ميّزت وفسرت في اللوح في ديلوس فإنّه كتب هكذا:

أجود الأشياء أعدلها وأفضلها أصحّها
وألذّها أشهاها

وذلك أنّ هذه الأشياء كلّها قد توجد لأفعل الفضيلة ونحن نقول إنّ السعادة إمّا أن تكون هذه كلّها وإمّا واحدة منها وهي أفضلها (١٥) على أنّه قد يظهر أنّ السعادة محتاجة إلى الخيرات التي من خارج كما قلنا وذلك أنّه من الممتنع أو ممّا لا يسهل أن يفعل الأمور الجميلة ما لم يكن له مدد من [١/١٦] خارج فإنّ كثيراً من الأمور الجميلة قد يستعان على فعلها بأشياء هي كآلات أعني المل والأصدقاء والأعوان على الحرب (١٦) وبعض الأشياء إذا أعوزت السعيد كدّرت سعادته مثل جودة الحسب وإنجاب الأولاد والجمل فإنّه ليس سعيداً من كان في غاية القبح والسماجة أو [...] الحسب أو من كان وحيداً أو لا ولد له وخليق أن يكون أقلّ [...] كان له أولاد شرار أو أصدقاء شرار أو كان له أولاد خيار أو أصدقاء خيار فماتوا (١٧) فيشبه أن يكون الأمر كما قلنا إنّ السعيد يحتاج إلى مدد من خارج ولذلك صار قوم يجعلون السعادة وجودة البخت في مرتبة واحدة وآخرون يجعلون السعادة والفضيلة سواء.

٩. ولهذا وقع الشكّ في أمر السعادة هل هي شئ يتعلّم أم يعتاد أم يستفاد بجهة أخرى أم إنّما تأتي الإنسان بحظّ من اللّه أم بالبخت والاتّفاق (٢) إلاّ أنّه إن كان ها هنا موهبة من اللّه للناس فخليق أن تكون السعادة موهبة منه لهم [...] إذ كانت أفضل الأمور [...] إلى الناس (٣) ولكن النظر في هذا أخلق [...] أشبه بصناعة أخرى فقد تبيّن أنّه إن لم تكن

1 بالإطلاق appar. corr. Dun : بالإملاك F || 2 ولم F : ولا Bad || 2 وفسرت F, Dun : om. Bad* || 2 أيضا في : (ἐνεργείαις) F*, Dun* لافعل 6 || F دجلوس : (Δηλιακόν) corr. Bad*, Dun* ديلوس Bad || 8 يفعل F, Dun : نفعل Bad || 9 خارج فإن F, Dun : خارج ذلك أن Bad || 10 كآلات F*, Dun* (ὀργάνων) : هذه Bad || 10 المل F*, Dun* (πλούτου) : الحل Bad || 11 والجمل Bad, Dun : illegible F || 12 first أو Dun : illegible F || 12 [...] : illegible F, *low* Dun || 17 بجهة Bad, Dun : illegible F || 17 third أم Dun : illegible F; أو Bad || 19 فخليق Bad, Dun : illegible F || 19 first [...] : illegible F, *especially* Dun || 19 إذ F : إن Bad

is thought to be the chief good and the thing which a man is happy for.[92] (4) And it is given to many people, because anyone who is not blind to virtue can acquire it by instruction and care. (5) If the existence of happiness with this condition is better than its existence by chance and luck, then it is necessary that it should be with this condition, since things which run the natural course are such that they are the best possible. (6) Similar is the case with the things of art and every cause, and particularly the best of arts.[93] It would be the greatest error to assign the most important and most splendid thing to chance and the result of luck. (7) What we are looking for is plain also from the preceding statement, for we have said that it is an action (...)

1101b 8 11. (6) (...)[94] happy those who are not happy, and conversely.

12. Now that we have summarised these questions, let us investigate whether happiness is among the things that are praised or[95] the things of great account, for indeed it is clear that it is not a potentiality. (2) It appears that everything [is praised] because it has a particular quality and a relation to something. For we praise the just man and the brave man, and generally the good and virtue, on account of the actions and what results from them. As for the [...] running and all the rest like that, we praise them because they have a particular quality and are so[96] in relation to a particular good and a particular virtue. (3) That is plain from the praise of those who are deified,[97] for when it is applied to us, it is ridiculous. That occurs only because praise is relative, as we said. (4) If praise is for things like these, then it is plain that the things which are the ultimate in excellence do not have praise, but are too exalted and excellent to be praised, as is plain from what they are. That is, we relate those who are deified[98]

---

[92] Again θεῖόν τι is not directly translated. Arabic *yughbaṭu bihi*, not *yughbaṭu ʿalaihi*, which would mean 'envied for'.

[93] Arabic *afḍal aṣ-ṣanāʿāt* but the Greek is κατὰ τὴν ἀρίστην [sc. αἰτίαν], 'the best of causes'.

[94] A folio seems to be missing.

[95] Arabic omits μᾶλλον, 'rather'.

[96] Arabic *ka-dhālika* for Greek πώς.

[97] Or 'those who deify themselves', cf. R. Dozy, *Supplément aux Dictionnaires arabes*, vol. I, p. 34. The translator avoids directly translating Greek τούς θεούς, cf. above, c. 9, §§ 2 and 3.

[98] See previous note.

موهبة من اللّه بل كانت بالفضيلة وبعلم أو اكتساب فهي من الأمور التي في غاية الشرف والجلالة لأنّ غاية الفضيلة وما يستفاد منها يرى أنّه أفضل الأمور والشئ الذي يغبط الإنسان به (٤) وهو مبذول لكثير من الناس لأنّه قد يمكن أن يقتنيه بتعلّم وعناية كلّ من ليس عيّاً عن الفضيلة (٥) فإن كان كون السعادة بهذه الحل أفضل من كونها بالاتّفاق والبخت فمن الواجب أن تكون بهذه الحل إذ كانت الأمور التي تجري على الحل الطبيعية من شأنها أن تكون على أجود ما يمكن (٦) وكذلك تجري أمور الصناعة وكلّ سبب وخاصّةً أفضل الصناعات ومن أعظم الخطأ أن يسلم أعظم الأمور وأسراها للاتّفاق وما يقع بالبخت (٧) وقد تبيّن أيضاً الأمر المطلوب من القول الذي تقدّم كما قد قلناه إنّها فعل ما (...)

١١. (٦) (...) [١/١٧] السعداء غير السعداء وبضدّ ذلك.

١٢. فإذ قد لخّصنا هذه الأشياء فلنبحث عن السعادة هل هي من الأمور الممدوحة أم من الأمور الخطيرة وذلك أنّه من البيّن أنّها ليست من القوى (٢) فقد يظهر أنّ كل ممدوح [هو الممدوح] لأنّه بكيف ما وبالإضافة إلى شئ فإنّا إنّما نمدح العادل و[...] وبالجملة الخير والفضيلة بسبب الأفعل وما يحدث عنها فأمّا [...] العدو وكلّ واحد ممّا أشبه ذلك فإنّا إنّما نمدحهم لأنّهم بكيفية ما وأنّهم كذلك بالإضافة إلى خير ما وفضيلة ما (٣) وذلك بيّن من مديح المتألّهين فإنّه إذا نسب إلينا كان ممّا يضحك منه وإنّما عرض ذلك لأنّ المديح إنّما يكون بالإضافة كما قلنا (٤) وإذا كان المديح إنّما هو لأمثل هذه الأشياء فبيّن أنّ الأشياء التي هي في غاية الفضل ليس لها مديح لكنّها أجلّ وأفضل من أن تمدح كما

2 الذي F, Dun : الهي Bad || 3 يغبط F, Dun : يغتبط Bad || 3 بتعلم perh. corr. Dun : بتعليم F, Bad || 4 كون F, Dun : تحصيل Bad || 5 إذ corr. Bad : إذا F || 7 وأسراها F, Dun : واشرفها Bad || 10 om. Bad || 12-13 [هو ممدوح] كل ممدوح suppl. Bad : كل ممدوح F, كلا ممدوح Dun || 13 و نمدح العادل Dun : illegible F || 13 [...] : illegible F, *the brave man* Dun || 14 فأما Dun : illegible F || 15 first ما F, Dun : om. Bad

and the best of men[99] to happiness. There is no one who praises happiness as he praises justice, but he exalts and honours it as something divine and excellent. (5) Eudoxos is thought to have introduced pleasure among the things which are the ultimate in excellence.[100] That is, since it is part of what is not praised, he made it of the excellent things[101] which he thought indicate that they are superior to the things that are praised, and the things which are superior to being praised are God, who is great and glorious,[102] and the good. That is, all other excellent things are related to God and the good. (6) For praise is for virtue, since we do noble deeds through virtue, while elegies[103] are for actions of the soul and of the body in the same way. (7) But it is more suitable that a complete investigation into these matters should be the special concern of those
1102a whose attention has been directed to composing elegies.[104] To us it is clear from what has been said that happiness is among the things of great account and perfect. (8) It is likely that it has become so [...] a principle, and because all of us do all the other things on account of it, and we assume, in what is the principle and cause of goods, something divine and glorious.

13. Since happiness is a certain activity of the soul in accordance to perfect virtue, we must investigate perfect virtue, and perhaps our inquiry into happiness, if we proceed in this way, will be better and more excellent. (2) It is thought with truth[105] of him who is ruler of a city that his concern is with virtue particularly, because his purpose and intention are to render the people of the city good and subject to the laws. (3) For example, [...] of laws to the people of Crete and Lacedaemon[106] and others besides like them. (4) If this investigation

---

[99] Arabic omits several words, perhaps to avoid the expression τῶν ἀνδρῶν τοὺς θειοτάτους (cf. above c. 9, § 3) or simply owing to homoioteleuton (μακαρίζομεν), (Arabic *al-khiyār min an-nās* evidently renders τῶν ἀγαθῶν, read as accusative plural masculine).

[100] Arabic *al-ashyā' allatī fī ghāyat al-faḍl*, here for Greek τῶν ἀριστείων as for τῶν ἀρίστων, § 4 above, and συνηγορῆσαι, means 'to advocate the claims of', not 'to introduce'.

[101] The words τῶν ἀγαθῶν οὖσαν, which go closely with τὸ γὰρ μή, are wrongly construed, and Arabic *jaʿalahā* is not in the Greek.

[102] A Muslim formula is needed.

[103] Arabic *marāthin*, 'dirges, elegies', is not the best rendering of Greek ἐγκώμια.

[104] See previous note.

[105] Arabic *ʿalā 'l-ḥaqīqah*, Greek κατ' ἀλήθειαν, faultily construed with δοκεῖ.

[106] Arabic *L.qādāmūnā* [sic], cf. 1112a 29.

يتبيّن من أمرها وذلك أنّه قد ينسب المتألّهون والخيار من الناس إلى السعادة وليس يوجد واحد من الناس يمدح السعادة كما يمدح العدل لكنّه يجلّها ويكرمها على أنّها أمر إلهي فاضل (٥) وقد يظنّ بأودقسس أنّه قد أدخل اللذّة في الأشياء التي في غاية الفضل وذلك أنّها لمّا كانت ممّا لا يمدح جعلها من الأمور الجيّدة التي كان يرى أنّها تنذر بأنّها أفضل من الأشياء الممدوحة والأشياء التي هي أفضل من أن تمدح الله عزّ وجلّ والخير وذلك أنّ سائر الأشياء الفاضلة إنّما تنسب إلى الله والخير (٦) فإنّ المديح إنّما هو للفضيلة إذ كنّا إنّما نفعل الأمور الجميلة بالفضيلة وكانت المراثي إنّما هي للأفعل النفسانية والجسمانية على مثل واحد (٧) ولكن أخلق بهذه الأمور أن يكون استقصاء البحث عنها أخصّ الأشياء [...] مصروفة إلى وضع المراثي فأمّا نحن فقد تبيّن لنا ممّا قيل أنّ السعادة من الأمور الجليلة الخطر الكاملة (٨) ويشبه أن يكون إنّما صارت [...] مبدأ ولأنّا جميعاً إنّما نفعل سائر الأشياء كلّها من أجلها ونحن نعتقد فيما كان مبدأ الأمور الخيرة وسببها أمراً إلهياً جليلاً.

١٣. وإذا كانت السعادة [١/١٨] فعلاً للنفس تكون بحسب الفضيلة الكاملة فينبغي أن نبحث عن الفضيلة الكاملة فلعلّ نظرنا في السعادة إذا سلكنا فيه هذا الطريق كان أجود وأفضل (٢) وقد يظنّ على الحقيقة بمن هو مدبّر مدينة أنّ عنايته إنّما هي بالفضيلة خاصّةً لأنّ وكده وإرادته أن يصيّر أهل المدينة خياراً ومنقادين للنواميس (٣) ومثل ذلك [...] لأهل إقريطش ولقلادامونا وغير هؤلاء ممّن يجري مجراهم (٤) وإذا كان هذا البحث إنّما هو

3 فاضل F, Dun : تام Bad || 3 بأودقسس corr. Bad* (Εὔδοξος) : باودقسين F, ق w.p. || 6 إذ كنا F, Dun : لأننا Bad || 7 المراثي F, Dun : المدائح corr. Bad* (ἐγκώμια) || 9 [...] : illegible F, *of those whose attention* Dun || 9 المراثي F, Dun : المدائح corr. Bad* (ἐγκώμια) || 10 من F*, Dun* (τῶν) : هي Bad || 13 فينبغي F : فيجب Bad || 15 يظن F, Dun : نظن Bad || 15 هي corr. Bad : هو F || 16 أن يصير أهل Dun : illegible F || 16 third و corr. Dun* (καί) : أو F || 16 [...] : partly illegible F, *of laws* Dun

is of the rule of cities,[107] it is clear that the search and inquiry are in accordance with our intention from the first. (5) We must then investigate human virtue—that is clear—because we were seeking simply human good and human happiness. (6) By human virtue I do not mean virtue of the body but virtue of the soul, and we say that happiness is an activity of the soul. It is incumbent on the man who rules cities[108] that he should consider the matter of the rule of the soul, since we said that the activity belongs to it.[109] (7) If this is so, then it is clear that it is incumbent on the man who rules cities[110] that he should know how[111] are the conditions of the soul, as it is incumbent on him who treats the eyes and treats the body as a whole that he should know the conditions of the eyes and of the body as a whole, taking into account that the rule of cities[112] is nobler and more excellent than the art of medicine, and the skilful among those who profess medicine do their utmost to investigate the conditions of the body. (8) It is incumbent then on the man who rules cities[113] to consider the conditions of the soul, and incumbent upon him to consider them for the sake of these things.[114] This is what suffices[115] in what we are here concerned with of the things sought for, because a complete investigation on a larger scale is more liable to be a trouble and extend beyond what we intended in this book. (9) Enough has been said about it[116] in the exoteric discussions,[117] and we must use some of them.[118] (10) Do you not see that part of the soul is irrational and part rational? There is no difference in the investigation which we are engaged whether these two are separate, like the parts of the body and everything divisible, or are verbally two things which are

[107] Or 'politics', Arabic *tadbīr al-mudun*, Greek τῆς πολιτικῆς.

[108] Or 'political man', Arabic *ṣāḥib tadbīr al-mudun* as at 1095b 2.

[109] This sentence is a somewhat redundant addition to the Greek with regard to what follows.

[110] Or 'political man', see note 111.

[111] I.e. πῶς for πώς.

[112] Or 'politics', as above, § 4.

[113] See note 111.

[114] Arabic *min ajl hādhihi 'l-ashyā'*. The Greek is here equally vague: τούτων χάριν, and the translators expand the words differently. The political interests of the 'man who rules cities', as indicated earlier in the chapter, are meant.

[115] The words ἐφ' ὅσον ἱκανῶς ἔχει should be closely construed with θεωρητέον not as here, where the Arabic translator reads as if ἐπὶ τοσοῦτον stood in the Greek (demonstrative for relative).

[116] I.e. the soul.

[117] The parallel passage (VI, 4, 2) is not in the ms.

[118] Arabic *baʿḍahā*, Greek ἔνια, construed here with χρηστέον.

لتدبير المدن فمن البيّن أنّ الطلب والفحص إنّما يكونان على حسب غرضنا من أوّل الأمر (٥) فينبغي إذاً أن نبحث عن الفضيلة الإنسانية وذلك بيّن لأنّا إنّما كنّا نطلب الخير الإنساني والسعادة الإنسية (٦) ولست أعني بالفضيلة الإنسية فضيلة الجسد بل فضيلة النفس ونحن نقول إنّ السعادة فعل للنفس. فواجب على صاحب تدبير المدن أن ينظر في أمر تدبير النفس إذ كنّا نقول إنّ الفعل لها (٧) وإذا كان هذا هكذا فمن البيّن أنّه واجب على صاحب تدبير المدن أن يعلم أحوال النفس كيف هي كما يجب على من يعالج العيون ويعالج البدن كلّه أن يعلم أحوال العيون وأحوال البدن كلّه هذا على أنّ تدبير المدن أشرف وأفضل من صناعة الطبّ والمهرة من المتطبّبين يبالغون في الفحص عن أحوال الجسم (٨) فيجب إذاً على صاحب تدبير المدن أن ينظر في أحوال النفس ويجب عليه أن ينظر فيها من أجل هذه الأشياء وهذا ما يكتفي به فيما نحن بسبيله من الأمور المطلوبة لأنّ استقصاء البحث بأكثر من هذا المقدار أخلق به أن يكون عناءً وخارجاً عمّا قصدنا له في هذه الكتاب (٩) وقد قيل فيها من الأقاويل الخارجة ما فيه كفاية وينبغي أن نستعمل بعضها (١٠) ألا ترى أنّ من النفس ما هو غير ناطق ومنها ما هو ناطق ولا فرق بتّةً فيما نحن بسبيله من البحث هل هذان هما منفصلان مثل أعضاء البدن وكلّ شئ ينقسم أو هما بالقول شيئان وهما غير منفصلين بالطبع بمنزلة المحدّب [١٨٩] والمقعّر في قوس

2 إذا F : إذن Bad || 4 فعل corr. Dun* (ἐνέργειαν) : افضل F, Bad || 10 يكتفي F, Dun : نكتفي Bad || 11 عما F : مما Bad || 13 الا ترى Dun : illegible F || 13 بتة F : om. Bad || 14 هذان corr. Bad : هذين F || 15 والمقعر Bad, Dun : illegible F || 15 قوس F, Dun : محيط Bad

indivisible by nature, like convexity and concavity in an arc of the circle and elsewhere. (11) Of the irrational element part is general, viz. the vegetative. I mean by the vegetative the cause of nourishment and growth. It is necessary to assign this faculty of the
1102b soul to all things which take nourishment and to embryos. Exactly the same exists in the fully grown of [...] be in these things than another. (12) It appears that this faculty has a common, shared virtue which is not specifically human. It is thought of this part especially and this faculty especially that they are active in time of sleep, while as to the good and the bad man, it is scarcely evident in time of sleep that they are so. It is therefore said that there is no difference between the happy and the wretched [during] half of their lives. (13) This is bound to follow, because sleep is inactivity of the soul, in respect of which it is said to be good and bad, unless indeed some of its movements penetrate to the body[119] in time of sleep little by little, so that thereby the imagination of the good is better than the imagination of the wicked.[120] (14) We have spoken sufficiently of these things and must omit mention of the nutritive part, because it is devoid of human excellence. (15) It is likely that the soul possesses another, irrational nature, except that it shares in reason in a certain way. That is, we praise the man who restrains himself from pleasures and the man who restrains his reason[121] and the rational part of his soul. That is, it is in the right way[122] and calls to the excellent things. It appears that in it[123] is another, irrational thing which opposes and contends with reason. And just as paralysed limbs when we wish to move them to the right incline to the left, so is the condition in the soul. For the movements of those who do not restrain themselves from pleasure are towards disorder, (16) except that we may see with our eyes the limb which moves confusedly in the body, but in the soul we do not see it. Presumably we must think that in the soul there is something contrary and opposed to reason and resistant no less than what we see in the body thwarts the natural move-

---

[119] Evidently in error.

[120] Arabic *ash-sharār* for Greek τῶν τυχόντων = 'ordinary men', cf. Burnet's note.

[121] I.e. τὸν λόγον read as τοῦ λόγου apparently with ἐγκρατοῦς. The passage has gone completely wrong, and in the next sentence ὀρθῶς is taken as if it were with ὀρθός with reference to the 'rational part' (*juz' nafsihi an-nāṭiq*).

[122] Arabic *mustaqīm al-amr* representing ὀρθῶς, vid. previous note.

[123] I.e. the soul (Arabic *fīhā*).

الدائرة وغيره (١١) وغير الناطق منه ما هو عامّ وهو النباتي وأعني بالنباتي سبب التغذية والنمو ولواضع أن يضع هذه القوّة من قوى النفس في جميع الأشياء التي تتغذّى وفي الأجنّة وهي أيضاً بعينها موجودة في الكامل من [...] تكون في هذه الأشياء من غيرها (١٢) وقد يظهر أنّ لهذه القوّة فضيلة عامّية مشتركة وليست إنسانية وقد يظنّ بهذا العضو خاصّةً وهذه القوّة خاصّةً أنّهما يفعلان في وقت النوم فأمّا الخير والشرّ فليس يكاد يبيّن في وقت النوم أنّهما كذلك ولذلك يقل إنّه لا فرق بين السعداء والأشقياء [طوال] نصف أعمارهم (١٣) وبالواجب يلزم هذا لأنّ النوم إنّما هو بطالة من النفس التي يقل فيها إنّها فاضلة وخسيسة اللهم إلاّ أن يكون بعض حركاتها تنفذ في البدن في وقت النوم قليلاً قليلاً فيكون بها تخيّل الخيار من الناس أفضل من تخيّل الشرار (١٤) وقد تكلّمنا في هذه الأشياء ما فيه كفاية وينبغي أن نلغي ذكر الجزء الغذي لأنّه معرّى من الفضيلة الإنسية (١٥) ويشبه أن تكون ها هنا للنفس طبيعة أخرى غير ناطقة إلاّ أنّها مشاركة للنطق بجهة من الجهات وذلك أنّا إنّما نمدح من يضبط نفسه عن اللذّات ومن يضبط نطقه وجزء نفسه الناطق وذلك أنّه مستقيم الأمر ويدعو إلى الأمور الفاضلة وقد يظهر أنّ فيها شيئاً آخر غير النطق يضادّ النطق ويجاذبه وكما أنّ أعضاء البدن إذا نالها استرخاء فأردنا أن نحرّكها إلى جانب اليمين مالت إلى الجانب الأيسر كذلك الحل في النفس فإنّ حركات الذين لا يضبطون أنفسهم عن اللذّة تكون إلى ضدّ الاستواء (١٦) إلاّ أنّ العضو الذي يتحرّك في البدن حركة مضطربة قد نراه عياناً فأمّا في النفس فلسنا نراه وخليق أنّه ينبغي أن نرى أنّ في النفس

---

2 وفي corr. Dun* (καί) : أو في F, Bad || 3 second في F : فيه corr. Bad || 4 يظهر F*, Dun* (φαίνεται) : يقصد Bad || 4 فضيلة عامية Bad, Dun : partly illegible F || 4 خاصة F : بخاصة Bad || 6 طوال add. Bad || 7 بطالة F*, Dun* (ἀργία) : حاله Bad || 9 ما F : بما Bad || 17 نرى F : ندرك Bad

ment.[124] (17) It appears that this part shares in reason, as we said. This part in the man who restrains himself is amenable to reason and presumably also in the temperate and brave man it is more easily amenable to reason, because all its conditions are in agreement with reason. (18) It appears that the part which is not rational is of two kinds, one vegetative, not sharing in reason in any way, and one concupiscent, which shares in reason in so far as [...] therefore it is amenable to it and obeys.[125] One thing that shows us that the part which is not rational is amenable to reason is the effect upon us of
1103a admonition, reprehension and reproof, blame and warning. (19) If we must say of this part that it has reason, that is of two kinds, one which has it truly and in itself, the other like what happens to the child from listening to and obeying the father. (20) Virtue is differentiated and classified in this way, that is, we say that the virtues are partly intellectual, partly ethical. Wisdom and understanding and discernment are intellectual, while generosity and temperance are ethical. For when we describe a man's character, we do not say that he is wise or understanding, but we say that he is gentle or temperate. We praise the wise man for his disposition, and praiseworthy dispositions we call virtues.

The First Discourse of the Ethics is complete, and praise be to God and peace upon His servants whom He has chosen.

[124] The words "than what we [...] natural movement" are not in the Greek and are due to failure to construe οὐδὲν ἧττον correctly. The translator then omits the sentence πῶς δ' ἕτερον, οὐδὲν διαφέρει.

[125] Two lines of Greek are here omitted in the MS. (οὕτω δὴ καὶ [...] τῶν μαθηματικῶν). These words are called a "parenthetical note" by Rackham, and their authenticity has been doubted, though they apparently are found in all the Greek manuscripts. It cannot of course be claimed that they were omitted in the original text as known to the Arabic translator.

شيئاً غالباً للنطق مضاداً له معانداً ليس بدون ما نراه في البدن يضاد الحركة الطبيعية (١٧) ويظهر أنّ هذا الجزء مشارك للنطق كما قلنا [١/٢٠] فهذا الجزء من يضبط نفسه منقاد للنطق وخليق أيضاً أن يكون في العفيف والشجاع أسهل انقياداً للنطق لأنّ أحوالها كلّها موافقة للنطق (١٨) ويظهر أنّ الجزء الذي ليس بناطق صنفان منه نباتي ليس يشارك النطق بوجه من الوجوه ومنه شهواني وهو يشارك النطق [...] ولذلك يناقد له ويطيع وممّا يدلّنا على أنّ الجزء الذي ليس بناطق منقاد للناطق ما يؤثره فينا العظة والتأنيب والعقاب والعذل والتفنيد (١٩) وإن كان ينبغي أن نقول في هذا الجزء إنّ له نطقاً فذلك على ضربين أحدهما له بالحقيقة وبذاته والآخر بمنزلة ما يحدث للولد من الاستماع والانقياد للأب (٢٠) والفضيلة تتميّز وتتصنّف هذا التصنيف وذلك أنّا نقول إنّ الفضائل منها ما هي فكرية ومنها ما هي خلقية فالحكمة والفهم والذهن فكرية والحرّية والعفّة خلقية فإنّا إذا وصفنا خلق الإنسان لم نقل إنّه حكيم أو فهم لكنّا نقول إنّه حليم أو عفيف وقد يمدح الحكيم بالهيئة التي له وما كان من الهيئات ممدوحاً سميناه فضائل.

تمّت المقالة الأولى من الأخلاق والحمد للّه وسلّم على عباده الذين اصطفى

---

1 بدون F : دون B || 2 يضبط F*, Dun* (ἐγκρατοῦς) : om. Bad || 4 موافقة F*, Dun* (ὁμοφωνεῖ) : تنقاد Bad || 4 يشارك F*, Dun* (κοινωνεῖ) : يشبه Bad || 6 بناطق منقاد Dun : illegible F || 10 الذهن F : العقل Bad || 13 سلم F : سلام corr. Bad

BOOK II

In the name of God, the Merciful, the Compassionate
God bless Muhammad and his family and give them peace

The Second Discourse of the Book of Aristotle on Ethics

1. Virtue is of two kinds, one intellectual, one ethical. The existence and increase of intellectual virtue is mostly through teaching, and therefore it needs long experience and length of time. Ethical virtue is acquired through habit, therefore the Greeks derived the name of character [*êthos*] from habit [*ethos*] by changing it slightly. (2) From this it is evident that none of the ethical virtues is in us by nature in any case,[1] and is accustomed[2] to be its opposite. For example, the stone falls down naturally even if someone has thrown it up innumerable times, intending by that to accustom it to the movement upwards when it becomes accustomed to that.[3] Similarly fire is not accustomed to move downwards, nor is anything naturally in any case [...] a different case. (3) The virtues then are not ours by nature,[4] but we are naturally formed to receive them, and they are perfected[5] and completed in us by habit. (4) Also of everything that is in us naturally we first have the potentiality, then its actuality comes to us[6] lastly. That is plain in the case of the senses. That is, the senses did not come to us from our seeing many times or hearing many times. But the fact is rather the exact opposite, I mean, we had them and used them, and they became ours.[7] As for the virtues, we acquire

---

[1] Arabic *ʿalā ḥāl min al-aḥwāl*. These words are not exactly additional, but rather represent an attempt to render Greek οὐθὲν γὰρ τῶν φύσει ὄντων (construed with οὐδεμία τῶν ἠθικῶν ἀρετῶν).

[2] The real subject 'nothing in nature' has not been recognized, vid. previous note.

[3] The Arabic translator goes his own way in rendering this sentence.

[4] The words οὔτε παρὰ φύσιν ('nor contrary by nature') are omitted.

[5] But according to Aristotle here, it is we who are perfected by habit, not the virtues, i.e. Greek τελειουμένοις is wrongly construed.

[6] Greek ἀποδίδομεν, "we exhibit" (Ross), is not rendered in the Arabic.

[7] The point of the antithesis ἔχοντες ἐχρησάμεθα, οὐ χρησάμενοι ἔσχομεν ('having them, we used them, not having used them, we had them') is missed.

المقالة الثانية

بسم الله الرحمن الرحيم
صلّى الله على محمّد وعلى آله وسلّم

المقالة الثانية من كتاب أرسطو في الأخلاق

١. والفضيلة صنفان منها فكرية ومنها خلقية فالفكرية كونها وتزيّدها في أكثر الأمر يكون بالتعليم ولذلك تحتاج إلى دربة طويلة ومدّة من الزمان والخلقية تكتسب من العادة ولذلك اشتقّ اليونانيون اسم الخلق من العادة بأن يحرّفوه تحريفاً يسيراً (٢) ومن هذا يتبيّن أنّه ليس شيئاً من الفضائل الخلقية يكون فينا بالطبع على حل من الأحوال ويعوّد أن يكون [١/٢١] على خلافها مثال ذلك أنّ الحجر يهبط إلى أسفل بالطبع فلو أنّ رامياً رمى به إلى فوق مراراً لا تحصى كثيرة يريد بذلك أن يعوّده الحركة إلى فوق لمّا اعتاد عليه وكذلك النار لا تعتاد أن تحرّك إلى أسفل ولا شئ من الأشياء المطبوعة على حل من الأحوال [...] حالاً غيرها (٣) فالفضائل إذن ليست تكون لنا بالطبع ولكنّا مطبوعون على قبولها وتكمل فينا وتتمّ بالعادة (٤) وأيضاً فإنّ كلّ ما لنا بالطبع فقوّته لنا أوّلاً ثمّ يصير لنا فعله بأخرة ذلك بيّن في الحواسّ وذلك أنّ الحواسّ ليست تصير لنا من قبل أنّا نرى مراراً كثيرة أو نسمع مراراً كثيرة لكن الأمر فيها بالعكس إذ أنّها إنّما كانت لنا فاستعملناها فصارت لنا أمّا الفضائل فإنّا نكتسبها إذا عملناها أوّلاً كالحل في سائر الصناعات لأنّ الأشياء التي ينبغي

---

7 يتبين F : يبين Bad || 11-12 تكمل فينا F, Dun : نكمل بها corr. Bad* (τελειουμένοις) || 12 first ما لنا F*, Dun* : مالنا Bad || 13 ليست corr. Bad : ليس F || 14 فصارت F : وصارت Bad || 15 عملناها perh. Dun : استعملناها Bad

them when we first practise them, as is the case in all the arts, because the things which we must do when we have learned them, we learn when we do them. For example, when we build, we become
1103b builders, and when we play the lute, we become lute-players. Similarly when we do just deeds, we become just; when we do temperate deeds, we become temperate; and when we do brave deeds, we become brave. (5) What we see happening in cities bears witness to that, i.e. the legislators by accustoming the people of the city to do good, make them good. Every legislator wishes and intends this, except that the man who does it badly, fails, and in this the excellent polity differs from the bad. (6) Also, every virtue comes into existence and is spoiled through exactly the same things, and similarly every art, for the man who plays the lute well and the man who plays it badly both become so from playing the lute, and the case of builders and all other craftsmen is analogous. That is, from excellent building the builder becomes an excellent builder and from bad building he becomes a bad builder, (7) because if the fact were not so, there would be no need in anything for a teacher, but all men would be either skilled in the art or unskilled, and similarly in the case of the virtues. That is, people in transacting business with each other become, some of them just, others unjust, when they do terrible things[8] and are habituated to fear and confidence, become, some of them brave, others cowardly, and similarly in regard to desire and anger. For when people do the actions, they become, some of them temperate, restrained and forbearing, and others self-indulgent and irascible, and they become such according as each of them conducts himself in those [...]. For states of character result from actions. (8) Therefore the actions must proceed according to a certain state,[9] for in accordance with the difference of the acts are the states that follow them. The difference then between a man's being accustomed from his youth to be good or accustomed to be bad is no small difference. It is a great difference, or rather all the difference.

2. Since this book[10] does not aim at speculation and knowledge, like the other books, our investigation here not being in order to know what virtue is, but in order that we should become good, otherwise

---

[8] Arabic *al-ashyā' al-muhauwilah* for Greek τὰ ἐν τοῖς δεινοῖς.

[9] Arabic *'alā ḥāl mā* for Greek ποιάς. Greek ἀποδιδόναι is again not rendered, cf. above 1103a 27-28 (= II, 1, 4).

[10] For Greek πραγματεία, cf. 1105a 6 and 11, where Arabic *kitāb* again renders the Greek word.

أن نعملها إذا تعلّمناها نحن إذا فعلناها تعلّمناها مثل ذلك إذا بنينا صرنا بنائين وإذا ضربنا العود صرنا ضرابين للعود وكذلك إذا فعلنا أمور العدل صرنا عادلين وإذا فعلنا أمور العفّة صرنا أعفّاء وإذا فعلنا أمور الشجاعة صرنا شجعاء (٥) وقد يشهد على ذلك ما نراه يحدث في المدن وذلك أنّ واضعي النواميس إنّما يعوّدون أهل المدينة على فعل الخير ليجعلوهم خياراً وكلّ واضع ناموس فهذه إرادته وقصده إلا أنّ من لم يحسن ذلك منهم قد يخطئ وبهذا تخالف السياسة الجيّدة والسياسة الرديئة (٦) وأيضاً كلّ فضيلة إنّما تكون وتفسد من أشياء واحدة فيها وكذلك كلّ صناعة فإنّ المحسن في ضرب العود والمسئ إنّما يصيران كذلك من ضرب العود وعلى هذا القياس يجري أمر البنائين وسائر الصنّاع الباقين وذلك أنّ من البناء الجيّد يصير البنّاء مجيداً ومن البناء الردئ يصير البنّاء بنّاءً رديئاً (٧) لأنّ الأمر ولم يكن كذلك لما احتيج في ذلك إلى معلّم ولكان جميع الناس إمّا حذّاقاً بالصناعة وإمّا غير حذّاق كذلك الحل في الفضائل وذلك أنّ الناس إذا عامل بعضهم بعضاً صار بعضهم عادلين بعضهم ظلوماً وإذا [١/٢٢] فعلوا الأشياء المهوّلة وتعوّدوا التهيّب والجرأة صار بعضهم شجاعاً وبعضهم جباناً وكذلك يجري الأمر في أمور الشهوة وأمور الغضب فإنّ الناس إذا ما فعلوها صار بعضهم عفيفاً وادعاً حليماً وبعضهم فاجراً غضوباً وإنّما يصيرون كذلك بحسب تصرّف كلّ واحد منهم في تلك [...] فإنّ الحالات إنّما تكون من الأفاعيل (٨) ولذلك ينبغي أن تجري الأفاعيل على حل ما فإنّه على حسب اختلاف الأفعل يكون ما يتبعها من الحالات فليس الخلاف إذاً بين أن يعوّد الإنسان منذ صباه أن يكون خيراً أو يعوّد أن يكون شريراً صغيراً لكنّه عظيم لا بل الخلاف كلّه.

٢. وإذا كان هذا الكتاب ليس فيه قصد النظر والعلم مثل الكتب الأخر وذلك أنّ بحثنا فيه ليس هو ليعلم ما الفضيلة لكن لنصير خياراً ولو لا ذلك لما كان فيه لنا درك قصد يجب

---

1 نحن F*, Dun* : هنا Bad || 2 كذلك F : om. Bad || 5-6 تخالف [...] إلا أن F, Dun : ما يميز بين فيها Bad || 6 كل فضيلة F*, Dun* (πᾶσα ἀρετή) : أصل Bad || 7 فإن قصر في عمل ذلك فسد عمله وهذا F : om. Bad || 8 يجري F : om. Bad || 10 جميع F*, Dun* (πάντες) : في طبع Bad || 11 بالصناعة F, Dun : أبدا Bad || 14 الغضب F*, Dun* (τὰς ὀργάς) : العفة Bad || 17 الحالات F*, Dun* (αἱ ἕξεις) : الملكات Bad || 20 ليعلم F, Dun : لنعلم Bad || 20 يجب F : فيجب Bad

there would be no utility in it for us, it is indispensable that we should investigate how we are to do the actions. For the main thing in regard to the states[11] being different are the actions, as we have said. (2) Let us lay down as an agreed principle that to say that actions must be done with right discrimination is held in common.[12] We shall speak of it later, and say what right discrimination is, and
1104a how it is related to the other virtues. (3) What we must agree on first is that everything said about the things which must be done or not done is only said[13] by way of illustration, not by way of exhaustive treatment, as we said at the beginning of our discussion that the argument must be pursued according to its subject matter.[14] In matters connected with useful actions[15] nothing is fixed and permanent, as also matters productive of health[16] are not fixed and permanent. (4) Since the argument about the general matter is of this kind, how much more does the argument about the particular matters not admit of complete treatment, because it is not included under a single art nor a single prescription, and the agent must always consider what is appropriate to the time in which he is, as is the case in medicine and in the art of seamanship. (5) Yet even if our present argument is of this kind, we must wish to say how it is to be strong. (6) First we must consider that the thing in itself is such that it is spoiled by excess and defect, and we must use as evidence for that which is hidden those things which are evident, as we see in the case of strength and health, for exercises [...] spoil the strength, and similarly foods and drinks, when they are in excess of what is necessary, or defective, spoil the health. As for moderate amounts, they produce health, and increase and preserve it. (7) Similar is the case with temperance and courage and all the other virtues. For the man who runs from and fears everything and endures nothing becomes a coward. As for him who does not fear anything at all, but goes to meet everything boldly, he becomes courageous.[17] Similarly the man who takes part in every pleasure and does not avoid any pleasure becomes greedy. The man who shuns every pleasure, like the rustic

---

[11] Arabic *al-ḥāl* for Greek τὰς ἕξεις, but above (c. 1, §§ 7-8) αἱ ἕξεις has been translated by Arabic *al-ḥāl* and *al-ḥālāt*.

[12] The sentence has gone wrong: Greek κοινόν is wrongly construed and καί (l. 32) is neglected.

[13] The original has 'is bound to be said' (ὀφείλει λέγεσθαι).

[14] Cf. 1094b 12 = I, 3, 1 and 1098a 28 = I, 7, 18.

[15] I.e. running together two ideas (τὰ δ' ἐν ταῖς πράξεσι and τὰ συμφέροντα).

[16] Arabic *al-umūr al-fāʿilah li'ṣ-ṣiḥḥah* for Greek τὰ ὑγιεινά.

[17] Arabic *shujāʿ* for Greek θρασύς, 'rash', i.e. the point is missed.

ضرورةً أن نبحث عن الأفعال كيف ينبغي أن نفعلها فإنّ ملاك الأمر في أن تكون الحال مختلفة إنّما هو من الأفعال كما قلنا (٢) ولنضع أصلاً موطأً أنّ القول بأنّه ينبغي أن تفعل الأفعال بتمييز صواب مشترك ونتكلّم فيه بأُخرة ونقول ما هو التمييز الصواب وكيف حالة غيرها من الفضائل (٣) والذي ينبغي أن نتّفق عليه أوّلاً وهو أنّ جميع الكلام في الأشياء التي ينبغي أن تفعل أو لا تفعل إنّما يقال على طريق الرسم لا على طريق الاستقصاء كما قلنا في ابتداء قولنا إنّ الكلام إنّما ينبغي أن يطلب بحسب مادّته والأمور في الأفعال النافعة ليس منها شيء ثابت قائماً كما أنّ ليست الأمور الفاعلة للصحّة أيضاً ثابتة قائمة (٤) وإذا كان الكلام في الأمر الكلّي يجري هذا المجرى فبالحري أن يكون الكلام في الأمور الجزئية لا يحتمل الاستقصاء لأنّه ليس بمحصور تحت صناعة واحدة ولا وصية واحدة وإنّما ينبغي للفاعل دائماً أن ينظر فيما ينفع للوقت الذي يكون فيه كالحال في الطبّ وفي صناعة الملاحة (٥) إلاّ أنّه وإن كان كلامنا هذا الذي نحن بسبيله يجري هذا المجرى فينبغي [٣٣/١] لنا أن نروم أن نقول كيف ينبغي أن يقوى (٦) وأوّل ما ينبغي أن ننظر فيه أنّ الشيء الواحد بعينه من شأنه أن يفسد من الزيادة والنقصان وقد ينبغي أن نستشهد على ما خفي بالأشياء الظاهرة كما قد نرى في القوّة وفي الصحّة فإنّ الرياضة [...] مفسدة القوّة وكذلك الأطعمة والأشربة إذا كانت زائدة على ما ينبغي أو ناقصة أضرّت الصحّة وأمّا المعتدلة فإنّها تفعلها وتزيد فيها وتحفظها (٧) وكذلك الحال في العفّة والشجاعة وسائر الفضائل الأخر فإنّ من تهرّب من كلّ شيء وخافه ولم يحتمل شيئاً صار جباناً وأمّا من لم يخف من شيء أصلاً لكن يلقى على كلّ شيء مقداماً فإنّه يصير شجاعاً وكذلك من تناول كلّ لذّة ولم يتجنّب لذّة من اللذّات صار شرهاً والذي يفرّ من كلّ لذّة كالقروي فلا حسّ

3 صواب : عام above line || 7 قائما F*, Dun* (ἑστηκός) : تماما Bad || 7 أن F : أنه Bad || 7 ليست F : ليس corr Bad || 10 يكون F, Dun : ينظر Bad || 11 وإن F : ان Bad || 13 يفسد من F*, Dun* (φθείρεσθαι) : يصير إلى Bad || 15 وأما F : فأما Bad || 17 ولم يحتمل F*, Dun* (μηδὲν ὑπομένων) : فلا يفعل Bad

is insensible because,[18] temperance and courage are spoiled by excess and defect, while the mean preserves them. (8) Not only do the virtues and their increase and corruption result from identical things,[19] but the actions also are in identical things. We see that taking place in all the other things which are more apparent than these, as in the case of strength, for it comes from our taking much food and enduring much toil, and the most able to apply[20] these things is the strong man. (9) Similarly in the case of the virtues, for we become temperate by our refraining from pleasures, and when we have become temperate we are more able to refrain from pleasures.
1104b It is similar with courage, for if we accustom ourselves to make light of dreadful, frightening things, we come to be able to endure them,[21] and when we have come to be able to endure them we have more power to make light of them.[22]

3. We must make the pleasure and pain which follow the actions our proof of the dispositions. For the man who refrains from all bodily pleasures happily is temperate, and he who is pained by refraining from them is self-indulgent. The man who endures hardships[23] gladly, or without being pained by them is brave, and the man who is pained by them is a coward. That is, ethical virtue is concerned with pleasure and pain, because we do bad deeds on account of pleasure, and we refrain from good deeds on account of pain. (2) Therefore we must lead a man [from his youth] by a certain way, as Plato said, which will bring him to take pleasure in what he ought to take pleasure in, and be pained by what he ought to be pained by, for this is right, sound education. (3) Also the virtues[24] are only concerned with actions and passions, and every passion and every action has connected with it pleasure and pain, and for that reason virtue must be concerned with pleasure and pain. (4) A proof of that is that restraining of the passions[25] only takes place by means of these, be-

---

[18] Greek δή.

[19] The Arabic translation is loose until αἱ γενέσεις and καὶ ὑπὸ τῶν αὐτῶν. Cf. Rackham's "not only are the virtues both generated and fostered [...]".

[20] Arabic *isti'māl* for Greek ποιεῖν.

[21] The construction of καὶ ὑπομένειν αὐτά is wrong, and ἀνδρεῖοι is omitted.

[22] Arabic *al-istikhfāf bihā*. But the Greek is ὑπομένειν τὰ φοβερά.

[23] Or 'misfortunes' (*shadā'id*). Neither meaning renders τὰ δεινά well (= 'terrible things', 'dangers').

[24] Arabic *wa-aiḍan fa'inna 'l-faḍā'il* [...], i.e. Greek ἔτι δὲ αἱ ἀρεταί, the reading of K[b] (witout εἰ).

[25] The translator has gone wrong with Greek κολάσεις, 'punishments'.

له لأنّ العفّة والشجاعة يفسدان من الزيادة والنقصان ويحفظهما المتوسّط (٨) وليس تكون الفضائل وتزيّدها وفسادها إنّما تكون من أشياء واحدة فقط بل الأفعال أيضاً تكون في أشياء واحدة بعينها فقد نرى ذلك يكون في سائر الأشياء الأخر التي هي أبين من هذه كالحال في القوّة فإنّها تكون من تناولنا طعاماً كثيراً واحتمالنا أيضاً كثيراً وأقوى الناس على استعمل هذه الأشياء من كان قوياً (٩) وكذلك الحال في الفضائل لأنّا إنّما نصير أعفّاء من امتناعنا من اللذّات وإذا صرنا أعفّاء نكون أقوى على الامتناع من اللذّات وكذلك الحال في الشجاعة فإنّا إذا اعتدنا أن نستخفّ بالأمور الهائلة المفزعة صرنا محتملين لها وإذا صرنا محتملين لها كنّا أقدر على الاستخفاف بها.

٣. وينبغي أن نجعل دلالتنا على الحالات ما يتبع الأفعال من اللذّة والأذى فإنّ الممتنع من اللذّات الجسدانية وهو مسرور بذلك هو عفيف والذي يتأذّى بالامتناع منها هو شره والذي يحتمل الشدائد وهو مسرور بها أو غير متأذٍّ بها هو شجاع والذي يتأذّى بها هو جبان وذلك أنّ الفضيلة [١/٢٤] الخلقية إنّما هي في اللذّة والأذى لأنّنا إنّما نفعل الأشياء الشريرة بسبب اللذّة وإنّما نمتنع من الأشياء الجميلة بسبب الأذى (٢) ولذلك ينبغي أن نسلك بالإنسان مذهباً وطريقاً ما كما قل أفلاطون يؤدّي به إلى أن يسرّ بما ينبغي أن يسرّ ويتأذّى بما ينبغي أن يتأذّى به فإنّ ذلك هو السلوك المستوى الصحيح (٣) وأيضاً فإنّ الفضائل إنّما هي في الأفعل والانفعالات وكلّ انفعل وكلّ فعل تلحقه لذّة وأذى ولذلك يجب أن تكون الفضيلة في اللذّة والأذى (٤) وممّا يدلّ على ذلك أنّ منع العوارض إنّما يكون بهذا

16-17 ولذلك [...] والأذى repeated in F

cause the restraining is simply a remedy, and it is characteristic of a remedy to be by opposites. (5) Also we say, as we said previously,[26] that every state of the soul[27] is a nature concerned with or related to those things which are such that from them it is worse and better, and people become worse only on account of pleasure and pain, by seeking of them what they ought not and by running away from what they ought not, or they do that at a time they ought not or in a manner they ought not or [they go wrong] in some other way of those like of which sound thought[28] determines. Therefore they define the virtues as the death and cessation of the passions. But they are not right in expressing in an absolute way what they say about that,[29] without making exceptions and saying: 'as one ought' and 'at the time that one ought', and the other exceptions that are made in the matter. (6) We have posited then that this virtue[30] is found in pleasure and pain, and that it is productive of the best matters, whereas baseness is the opposite of that. (7) The things which we have mentioned become clear to us also from what I shall describe,[31] viz. that the things which we choose are three:[32] the beautiful, the useful and the pleasant, and their opposites are three: the ugly, the useless and the unpleasant, so that the good man is he who goes right in all of them, the bad man he who goes wrong in all of them, especially in regard to pleasure. That is, pleasure is common to all the
1105a animals, and follows upon everything which depends on choice, because the beautiful and the useful are found pleasant. (8) Also pleasure has grown up with us since we were infants, and therefore it is difficult for us to get rid of these passions, owing to our having them engrained[33] in our life, and we measure actions by pain and pleasure, some of us more, some less. (9) Therefore it is quite necessary in all this book[34] to attend to pleasure and pain, for it is not the thing [...] actions as one ought or as one ought not is no trifling

---

[26] Arabic *qablu*, i.e. Greek πρότερον, rather than πρώην, the reading of K^b.

[27] τὴν φύσιν is wrongly construed, and ἔχει accordingly has disappeared.

[28] Arabic *al-fikr aṣ-ṣaḥīḥ*, cf. the familiar phrase ὁ ὀρθὸς λόγος (rendered variously, i.e. *al-qaul aṣ-ṣaḥīḥ*, 1147b 3; *al-qaul al- 'adl*, 1147b 31 mrg.; *al-qiyās aṣ-ṣaḥīḥ*, 1151a 12, 21 and 22), but the text here is simply τοῦ λόγου.

[29] The construction here seems faulty, and ὅτι is taken as the relative ὅ τι.

[30] Arabic *hādhihi 'l-faḍīlah*, i.e. rendering Greek αὕτη for τοιαύτη.

[31] The force of Greek περὶ τῶν αὐτῶν is disregarded. With *aiḍan*, ἔτι rather than ὅτι appears to have been read.

[32] Arabic omits καὶ τριῶν τῶν εἰς τὰς φυγάς.

[33] Lit. 'our being dyed by them'.

[34] Greek πραγματεία, cf. 1103b 26.

السبيل لأنّ القمع إنّما هو مداواة والمداواة فَمِن شأنها أن تكون بالأشياء المضادّة (٥) وأيضاً نقول كما قلنا قبل إنّ كلّ حال من حالات النفس فإنّها طبيعة في تلك الأشياء أو نحو تلك الأشياء التي من شأنها أن تكون عنها أردأ وأجود وإنّما يصير الناس أردياء بسبب اللذّة والأذى عندما يطلبون منهما ما لا ينبغي وفرّ بذلك ممّا لا ينبغي أو يفعلون ذلك في وقت لا ينبغي أو على وجه لا ينبغي أو على نحو آخر من الأنحاء التي يحدّد الفكر الصحيح أمثالها ولذلك يحدّون الفضائل بأنّها موت العوارض وسكونها ولم يصيبوا في إطلاقهم القول في ذلك من غير أن يستثنوا فيقولوا كما ينبغي وفي الوقت الذي ينبغي وسائر ما يستثنى في ذلك (٦) فقد وضعنا إذاً أنّ هذه الفضيلة توجد في اللذّة والأذى وأنّها فعّالة لأفضل الأمور فأمّا الخساسة فضدّ ذلك (٧) وقد تبيّن أيضاً لنا الأشياء التي ذكرناها ممّا أنا واصفه وهو أنّ الأشياء التي نختارها ثلاثة الجميل والنافع واللذيذ وأضدادها ثلاثة القبيح وما لا ينفع والمكروه فالخير من الناس هو المصيب في جميعها والخسيس هو المخطئ في جميعها وخاصّةً في اللذّة وذلك أنّ اللذّة مشتركة لجميع الحيوان وتابعة لكلّ ما وقع عليه الاختيار لأنّ الجميل والنافع يوجد لذيذاً (٨) وأيضاً فإنّ اللذّة قد تربّت معنا منذ [١/٢٥] نحن أطفل ولذلك يصعب علينا نفي هذه العوارض عنّا لاصطناعها في عيشتنا ونحن نقدّر الأفعل بالأذى واللذّة وبعضنا يفضل في ذلك على بعض (٩) فلهذه وجب ضرورةً أن يكون قصدنا في هذا الكتاب كلّه نحو اللذّة والأذى فإنّه ليس الشئ [...] الأفعل على ما ينبغي أو على

---

4 فر F*, Dun* (φεύγειν) : هو Bad || 14 عيشتنا Bad : عيشتنا به F

thing. (10) Also, to resist pleasure is more difficult than to resist anger, as Heraclitus says, and art and virtue are always concerned with what is more difficult, because in it what is fine is better. So in accordance with this the aim of the possessor of virtue and statecraft in this book[35] is towards pleasure and pain, because he who uses these as he ought becomes good, and he who uses them as he ought not becomes bad. (11) We have already said that virtue is found only in pleasure and pain, and that through the very things from which it comes into existence it increases and through them also is spoiled, when those are not the same, and that it acts only in the things from which it originated.

4. Perhaps one would be at a loss and say: Whence do we say that a man must do the deeds of justice in order to become just, and the deeds of temperance in order to become temperate? Because, he says, the man who does the deeds of justice and the deeds of temperance *is* just and temperate, like as the man who performs the actions of writing *is* a scribe and the man who performs the actions of singing *is* a singer. (2) I say that the case in the arts, to say nothing of the virtues,[36] is different. That is, it is possible for a man to perform one of the matters of writing by chance and by a pattern which someone else shows to him. A man only becomes a scribe when he has done something of the matters of writing according to the method of writing, I mean that he does what he does by the writing which is in him. (3) And I say also that the case is not equal in the arts and in the virtues. That is, the excellence of the products of the arts is only in themselves, and the artist is satisfied with the thing which he creates being excellent.[37] As for the things which come into existence through the virtues, they are not done according to the method of temperance[38] if they are excellent absolutely,[39] but are only so if the man does them under the following conditions, first, if he knows what it is that he is doing; next, if he chooses it and his choice of it is for itself; third, if he does it, being in a fixed and
1105b unchangeable state [...] none of them is taken into account in what the arts require except that [...] artist knows what he does. As to what the virtues require, either the need for knowledge of what he does

[35] The Arabic translation (with *kitāb* again = πραγματεία) is not accurate.
[36] The reference to the virtues is an addition to the Greek.
[37] *Jaiyidan*, but the Greek merely πώς, 'a certain kind'.
[38] Greek δικαίως ἢ has been omitted, or dropped out, before σωφρόνως.
[39] *Jaiyidah ʿalā ʾl-iṭlāq*. Again the Greek has simply πώς (cf. n. 37).

غير ما ينبغي فسمو (١٠) وأيضاً فإنّ مقاومة اللذّة أصعب من مقاومة الغضب كما يقول إيراقليطس والصناعة والفضيلة إنّما تكونان دائماً في الأمر الأصعب لأنّ فيه يكون الأمر الجليل أجود فبحسب هذا يكون قصد صاحب الفضيلة والسياسة في هذا الكتاب نحو اللذّة والأذى لأنّ مَن استعمل هذين على ما ينبغي صار جيّداً ومَن استعملها على غير ما ينبغي صار رديئاً (١١) فقد قلنا إنّ الفضيلة إنّما توجد في اللذّة والأذى وإنّ الأشياء التي تكون منها بعينها تتزيّد ومنها بعينها تفسد إذا لم تكن تلك الأشياء على حال واحدة بعينها وإنّها إنّما تفعل في الأشياء التي عنها كانت.

٤. ولعلّ متحيّراً يتحيّر فيقول من أين قلنا إنّه ينبغي للإنسان أن يفعل أمور العدل حتّى يصير عادلاً وأمور العفّة حتّى يصير عفيفاً لأنّه يقول إنّ مَن فعل أمور العدل وأمور العفّة فهو عادل وعفيف كما أنّ من يفعل أمور الكتابة فهو كاتب ومن يفعل أمور الغناء فهو مغنٍ (٢) فأقول إنّ الأمر في الصناعة فضلاً عن الفضائل ليس يجري هذا المجرى وذلك أنّه قد يمكن للإنسان أن يفعل أمراً من أمور الكتابة بالاتّفاق وبرسم يرسمه له غيره وإنّما يصير الإنسان كاتباً إذا عمل شيئاً من أمور الكتابة على طريق الكتابة أعني أن يفعل ما يفعله بالكتابة التي فيه (٣) وأقول أيضاً إنّ الأمر في الصناعة والأمر في الفضائل ليس بمتساوٍ وذلك أنّ الأمور التي تحدث عن الصناعات جودتها إنّما توجد فيها فقد يكتفي الصانع بأن يكون الشيء الذي يصنعه جيّداً فأمّا الأشياء التي تكون بالفضائل فليس إنّما تفعل على [١/٢٦] طريق العفّة إذا كانت جيّدة على الإطلاق لكنّها إنّما تكون كذلك إذا فعلها الإنسان وهو بهذه الأحوال أمّا أوّلاً فإذا كان يدري أيّ شيء يفعل ثمّ إذا كان مختاراً له وكان اختياره إيّاه لنفسه والثالث إذا كان يفعل ذلك وهو بحال ثابتة غير منتقلة [...] ليس منها شيء يعدّ فيها تحتاج إليه الصناعات خلا أن [...] صانع يدري ما يفعل فأمّا ما تحتاج إليه الفضائل فإنّ

10 الغناء corr. Bad : الغنى F || 11 وذلك : ذلك F || 20 فأما Bad : أما F

is slight, or it is not needed. As for the other two conditions, their utility is not slight, rather they are all important, and this is simply from the doing of the deeds of justice and the deeds of temperance many times. (4) So deeds are called deeds of justice and of temperance when they are like the things which the just or temperate doer would do, and the just man and the temperate man are not those who do the deeds of justice and the deeds of temperance, but those who do this as the just and temperate man does. (5) And if[40] it is said that from the doing of the deeds of justice a man becomes just, and from the doing of the deeds of temperance he becomes temperate, no one becomes [good][41] without doing the deeds of justice and the deeds of temperance. (6) Yet the multitude do not do these deeds, but they have recourse to the knowledge[42] of them, and they think on that account that they will in this case become excellent people. This proceeding of theirs resembles what the sick do, who listen to what the doctors order them with eagerness and attention, but do nothing of it. Just as the bodies of those people will not be cured by such treatment, so the souls of the others will not be cured by this philosophising.

5. After this we must investigate and consider what virtue is. We say: Since the things which arise in the soul are three: feelings,[43] faculties and states, would that I knew which of these is virtue![44] (2) I mean by the feelings desire, anger, fear, confidence, envy, joy, love, hate, longing, jealousy, pity and in general everything that is followed by pleasure and pain, I mean by the faculties the capacities[45] by which we are said to be liable to the feelings[46] by which we are able to be angry, or sad, or feel pity, and I mean by the states the things [...] at the occurrence of the feelings either good or otherwise. For example, at the occurrence of anger [...] we become violently angry, or deficiently angry, our state is then a bad state, but if we are moderately angry our state is a good state, and similarly as regards the rest of them. (3) The virtues and vices are not feelings, because it

---

[40] I.e. Greek εἰ for εὖ.

[41] Arabic *yaṣīru*, but *khairan* should be supplied, the word ἀγαθός being omitted by the Arabic translator, or perhaps rather having fallen out of the text.

[42] Arabic *al-ʿilm* exceptionally for Greek τὸν λόγον.

[43] Or 'passions' (Arabic *ʿawāriḍ*).

[44] I.e. rendering τούτων ἄν τι εἴη ἡ ἀρετή.

[45] Arabic *al-umūr* (lit. 'things', 'matters').

[46] Lit. 'the things' (Arabic *al-ashyāʾ*).

الدراية بما يفعل إمّا أن تكون الحاجة إليها يسيرة وإمّا أن لا يحتاج إليها فأمّا الشريطتان الأخريان فليست منفعتهما يسيرة بل تنفعان كلّ المنفعة وهذا إنّما يكون من فعل أمور العدل وأمور العفّة مراراً كثيرة (٤) والأمور إنّما يقل فيها إنّها من أمور العدل وأمور العفّة إذا كانت على مثل الأشياء التي يفعلها العادل أو العفيف وليس العادل والعفيف هما اللذان يفعلان أمور العدل وأمور العفّة لكنّهما اللذان يفعلان ذلك كما يفعل العادل والعفيف (٥) فإن كان يقل إنّ من فعل أمور العدل يصير الإنسان عادلاً ومن فعل أمور العفّة يصير عفيفاً فليس يصير [خيراً] أحد من الناس من غير فعل أمور العدل وأمور العفّة (٦) إلاّ أنّ الجمهور لا يفعلون هذه الأمور لكنّهم يلتجئون إلى العلم بها فيظنّون بذلك أنّهم يصيرون بهذه الحل من أهل الفضل وفعلهم هذا يشبه ما يفعله المرضى الذين يسمعون ما يأمرهم به الأطبّاء بحرص وعناية ولا يفعلون شيئاً منه فكما أنّ أولئك ليست تصحّ أبدانهم بهذا التدبير كذلك هؤلاء ليست تصحّ أنفسهم بهذا التفلسف.

٥. وينبغي أن نبحث وننظر بعد هذه الأشياء في الفضيلة ما هي فنقول إذا كانت الأشياء التي تحدث في النفس ثلاثة عوارض وقوى وحالات فليت شعري أيّما من هذه هي الفضيلة (٢) وأعني بالعوارض الشهوة والغضب والخوف والجرأة والحسد [١/٢٧] والسرور والمحبّة والبغضاء والشوق والغيرة والرحمة وبالجملة كلّ ما كان يتبعه لذّة أو أذى وأعني بالقوى الأمور التي بها يقل فينا إنّا معترضون بهذه الأشياء التي بها نحن قادرون على أن نغضب أو نحزن أو نرحم وأعني بالحالات الأمور [...] عند العوارض إمّا جيّداً وإمّا غير جيد مثل ذلك عند الغضب [...] غضبنا غضباً شديداً أو غضبنا غضباً ضعيفاً كانت حالتنا عنده حالة رديئة وإن غضبنا غضباً متوسّطاً كانت حالتنا حالاً جيّدة وكذلك يجري الأمر في سائرها (٣) فليست الفضائل والخسائس عوارض لأنّنا ليس يقل فينا بالعوارض إنّا من

1 first إليها, corr. Bad : إليه F || 2 فليست corr. : فليس F || 3 الأمور F : الأفعل Bad, الأمر mrg. || 3 third و Bad*, Dun* (καί) : أو F || 7 خيرا suppl. Dun* (ἀγαθός) || 9 أنهم corr. Bad, Dun : وانهم F || 15 يتبعه F : يتلوه Bad || 16 بهذه F, Bad : لهذه perh. Dun

is not said of us on account of the feelings that we are virtuous or vicious people. That is said of us on account of the virtues and vices. Also we are neither praised nor blamed for the feelings, because he who fears or is angry is not praised, nor is he blamed who is angry
1106a simply, but only when he is angry in a certain way. But for the virtues and vices we are praised or blamed. (4) Also, we are angry and afraid against our will, and the virtues are either acts of will or are not without will. In addition to this also it is said of us that we are moved by the feelings. It is not said of us that we are moved by the virtues and vices, but that on account of them we are in a certain condition. (5) Therefore they are not faculties, i.e. it is neither said of us that we are good nor that we are not good, from the fact that we are susceptible to the feelings, and we are neither praised nor blamed from this point of view. Also we are able by nature to become good or bad,[47] but we are not by nature good or bad. We have described that previously. (6) If then the virtues are not feelings and are not faculties, it remains that they are states. We have thus described what virtue is generically.

6. We must not restrict ourselves to saying that it is states of character only, but should describe what states they are. (2) So we say that every virtue makes the thing of which it is the virtue, excellent, and makes its action similar. For example, the virtue of the eye makes the eye excellent and its action excellent, because by the virtue of the eye we see well. Similarly the virtue of the horse makes the horse excellent—you see him running obedient to his rider and enduring wars.[48] (3) If this meaning is analogous in everything, then the virtue of man is a condition by which a man becomes excellent, and by which thereby his work is made [...] how the way to that is.[49] (4) It has already become clear[50] to us also, if we [...] which nature its nature is. We say that it is possible for us, in everything which is continuous and divisible, to take something that is more, something that is less, and something that is equal. These things are so either in

[47] The words 'to become good and bad' are added by the Arabic translator.

[48] I.e. πολέμους read for πολεμίους.

[49] Greek πῶς δὲ τοῦτ' ἔσται. In the Arabic these words are construed with what goes before.

[50] Arabic *wa-qad tabaiyana*, where the tense is wrong (Greek ἔσται φανερόν, perhaps read ἔστι φανερόν). The words ἤδη μὲν εἰρήκαμεν appear to have fallen out.

أهل الفضيلة أو من أهل الخسائس وقد يقل ذلك فينا بالفضائل والخسائس وأيضاً فإنّا لا نحمد ولا نذمّ بالعوارض لأنّ الذي يخاف أو يغضب ليس يحمد ولا يذمّ أيضاً الذي يغضب على الإطلاق بل إنّما يذمّ إذا غضب نوعاً ما من الغضب فأمّا بالفضائل والخسائس فقد نحمد أو نذمّ (٤) وأيضاً فإنّا نغضب ونفزع بغير إرادتنا والفضائل فإمّا أن تكون إرادات أو ليس تكون بغير إرادة ومع هذه الأشياء أيضاً فقد يقل فينا إنّا نتحرّك بالعوارض فأمّا بالفضائل والخسائس فليس يقل فينا إنّا نتحرّك بل يقل بشأنها إنّا بحل من الأحوال (٥) وكذلك ليست قوى وذلك أنّه ليس يقل فينا إنّا خيار ولا أنّا غير خيار من قبل أنّنا نقوى على تحمّل العوارض ولا نحمد ولا نذمّ من هذه الجهة وأيضاً فإنّا قادرون بالطبع على أن نصير خيراً أو أشراراً ولسنا بالطبع خياراً أو شراراً وقد وصفنا ذلك من قبل (٦) فإن كانت الفضائل ليست عوارض ولا قوى فقد بقي أن تكون حالات فقد وصفنا الفضيلة بما هي الجنس.

٦. وليس ينبغي أن نقتصر على القول بأنّها حالة فقط بل نصف أيّ الحالات هي (٢) فنقول إنّ كلّ فضيلة تجعل الشيء الذي هي له فضيلة جيّداً وتجعل فعله كذلك مثل ذلك أنّ فضيلة العين تجعل [١/٢٨] العين جيّدة وفعلها جيّداً لأنّ فضيلة العين الإبصار وكذلك فضيلة الفرس تجعل الفرس جيّداً وحسناً للركوب ومعيناً راكبه على الحرب (٣) فإذا كان هذا المعنى في كلّ شيء فعلى هذا تكون فضيلة الإنسان هي حل يصير بها الإنسان جيّداً ويفعل بها فعلاً [...] أمّا السبيل إلى ذلك كيف يكون (٤) وقد تبيّن لنا إذا [...] طبيعتها أيّ الطبائع هي فنقول إنّه قد يمكننا أن نأخذ في كلّ شيء متّصل ومنفصل شيئاً هو أكثر وشيئاً هو أقلّ وشيئاً هو مساوٍ وهذه الأشياء إمّا أن تكون كذلك في المعنى أو عندنا والمساوي

1 الخسائس : F الخساسة Bad || 4 نفزع F*, Dun* (φοβούμεθα) : نفرح Bad || 9 ولسنا خيارا أو اشرارا
F, Dun : إما اشرارا وإما Bad || 17 وقد F : فقد Bad || 18 first and second شيئا F : شيئا ما Bad

the strict sense[51] or for us. The equal is an intermediate between excess and defect. (5) I mean by the intermediate in the strict sense[52] what is equidistant from each of the two extremities. It is one and the same in everything.[53] But the intermediate for us is neither excessive nor defective, and it is not one and the same in everything.[54] (6) For example, if ten be posited as a large number and two as a small number then six is a mean between them in the strict sense[55] because its excess over two is equal to the excess of ten over it. (7) This is the mean in the numerical relationship.[56] As for the mean for us we
1106b must not take it in this way. That is, if taking ten *minae*[57] of food for a particular man is much and taking two *minae* is little, the trainer does not advise taking six *minae*, for this amount is perhaps much or little for the one who takes it. That is, it is little for the experienced man,[58] but much for the beginner in athletics. The case is similar in running and wrestling. (8) Thus every expert in an art avoids excess [and defect], and seeks and chooses the mean, I mean the mean for us, not the mean in the strict sense. (9) And because every art does its action well by aiming at the mean and directing its action towards it, therefore[59] people are accustomed to say of good actions[60] that excess and defect are impossible in them, in the sense that excess and defect in their opinion spoil excellence, while the mean preserves it, and because skilled artists [...], as we said, do their works, aiming at the mean, and virtue is more excellent than all the arts and more exact, as is the case with nature, virtue turns out to aim at the mean. (10) I mean ethical virtue, for this is concerned with emotions and actions, and in emotions and actions are excess and defect and the mean. For example, we are afraid, desire, become angry, feel pity, and in general feel pleasure and pain either more than we

---

[51] *Fī al-maʿnā*, i.e. in the strict meaning of the term, rendering κατ' αὐτὸ τὸ πρᾶγμα.

[52] See previous note.

[53] I.e. πᾶσιν taken as neuter rather than masculine ('for all').

[54] See previous note.

[55] *Fī al-maʿnā*, again rendering κατὰ τὸ πρᾶγμα , see n. 51.

[56] I.e. the arithmetical proportion, cf. 1132a 1-2.

[57] The Greek plural of μνᾶ (Latin *mina*, about 1 lb.) is rendered by *amnā'* in the Arabic.

[58] So (*li 'l-muḥtanik*) for Μίλωνι of the Greek. The proper name is not significant, and is not rendered.

[59] Greek ὅθεν.

[60] *Fiʿl, afʿāl*, but 'work, works of art' seems to be what is intended by the Greek (ἔργον, ἔργα).

هو توسّط ما بين الزيادة والنقصان (٥) وأعني بالتوسّط في المعنى البعد عن كلّ واحد من الطرفين بعداً متساوياً وهو واحد بعينه في كلّ شيء وأمّا التوسّط عندنا فهو الذي لا يزيد ولا ينقص وليس واحداً بعينه في كلّ شيء (٦) ومثل لذلك أنّ العشرة إذا فرضت عدداً كبيراً والاثنين عدداً قليلاً فإنّ الستّة متوسّطة بينهما في المعنى لأنّ فضلها على الاثنين مساوٍ لفضل العشرة عليها (٧) وهذا هو المتوسّط في النسبة العددية فأمّا المتوسّط عندنا فليس ينبغي أن نأخذه على هذه الجهة وذلك أنّه ليس إذا كان تناول عشرة أمناء من الطعام لإنسان ما كثيراً وتناول مناوين قليلاً فلن يشير معلّم الرياضة بتناول ستّة أمناء فإنّ هذا المقدار إمّا أن يكون كثيراً أو قليلاً للمتناول له وذلك أنّه قليل للمحتنك كثير للمبتدئ في الرياضة وكذلك يجري الأمر في العدو والصراع (٨) فعلى هذا الوجه يهرب كلّ حاذق في صناعته من الزيادة [والنقصان] ويلتمس المتوسّط ويختاره أعني المتوسّط عندنا لا المتوسّط في المعنى (٩) فلأنّ كلّ صناعة إنّما تجيد فعلها بأن تقصد قصد المتوسّط وتسوق فعلها نحوه لذلك اعتاد الناس أن يقولوا في الأفعل الجيّدة إنّها لا يمكن فيها زيادة ولا نقصان من طريق أنّ الزيادة والنقصان عندهم تفسدان الجودة والتوسّط يحفظها [١/٢٩] فإذا كان حذاق [...] كما قلنا إنّما يفعلون أفعالهم وهم يقصدون قصد المتوسّط كانت الفضيلة أفضل من جميع الصنائع وأشدّ تحقيقاً كالحل في الطبيعة صارت الفضيلة تقصد قصد المتوسّط (١٠) أعني الفضيلة الخلقية فإنّ هذه تكون في عوارض وأفعل وفي العوارض والأفعل تكون الزيادة والنقصان والمتوسّط وذلك إذا نفزع ونشتهي ونغضب

---

7 فلن F*, Dun* (οὐ) : فإن Bad || 8 للمحتنك F, Dun : بالنسبة إلى ميلون corr. Bad* (Μίλωνι) || 10 والنقصان suppl. Dun || 11 تجيد F*, Dun* : نجيد Bad || 11 تقصد F*, Dun* : نقصد Bad || 12 تسوق F*, Dun* : نسوق Bad || 12 الأفعل F : الأعمل Bad || 14 قصد المتوسط Dun : illegible F || 16-17 في عوارض Dun : illegible F || 17 والمتوسط Dun : illegible F

ought, or less, and both of these ways are not as they ought. (11) But that these feelings should be ours at the right time, with reference to the objects which should be ours, and in the matters[61] which we ought to be concerned with, this is the excellent mean,[62] which is the accepted sense of virtue. (12) Similarly we find in the actions excess and defect and a mean. Virtue is found in the emotions and actions, in which excess is a fault and defect is blamed,[63] while the mean is praised and right, and praise and rightness both belong to virtue. (13) Virtue then is a mean, since it aims at the intermediate. (14) Further, error exists in many kinds, because evil is of the realm of the unlimited, as the followers of Pythagoras represented it, while good is of the realm of the limited. As for rightness, it is of one kind. For that reason error is simple and easy, and rightness is difficult and hard, for it is the easiest of things for a man to mistake his mark and the most difficult of things to hit it. Therefore excess and defect are of the realm of vice, and the mean is of the realm of virtue. That is:

> The good become good in one way,
> The wicked become wicked in all ways.

(15) Virtue then is a condition having free choice,[64] existing in the
1107a mean which is for us, a mean defined in word[65] as the intelligent man defines it. It is intermediate in between two vices, one of them by excess and the other by defect. (16) Further, while the vices occur by coming short of what is necessary in the emotions and actions, and some of them exceed it, virtue brings out and chooses the intermediate. (17) Therefore virtue becomes, according to its substance and its definition which shows what it is in itself, a mean and, according to what is most excellent and best, an extreme and an end. (18) No doubt not every action nor every emotion admits of the mean. That is, some emotions are specially called bad because evil includes[66] them, like malice, shamelessness and envy, and among

---

[61] Arabic *ʿinda ʾl-umūr*. We expect a rendering of Greek πρὸς οὕς. The Arabic phrase is perhaps intended to cover οὗ ἕνεκα and ὡς δεῖ as well, as for which of course it will not stand.

[62] So apparently (Arabic *at-tawassuṭ al-fāḍil*).

[63] There is no evidence here (Arabic *wa-ʾn-nuqṣān fīhā madhmūm*) that ψέγεται is to be bracketed, as Bywater and the English school.

[64] Arabic *mukhtārah* for Greek προαιρετική.

[65] So probably (Arabic *biʾl-qaul*) rather than 'by reason', cf. 1109b 2.

[66] Arabic *liʾḥtiwāʾ ash-sharr ʿalaihi* with change of subject, for Greek συνειλημμένα μετὰ τῆς φαυλότητος.

ونرحم وبالجملة تلتذّ ونتأذّى إمّا أكثر ممّا ينبغي وإمّا أقلّ فكلاها [...] ليس تجريان على ما ينبغي (١١) فأمّا إن يكون منّا هذه الأشياء في الوقت الذي ينبغي وفي الأشياء التي يجب أن تكون منّا وعند الأمور التي ينبغي أن نكون عليها فهو التوسّط الفاضل هو معنى الفضيلة (١٢) وكذلك نجد في الأفعل زيادة ونقصاناً وتوسّطاً والفضيلة توجد في العوارض والأفعل التي الزيادة فيها خطأ والنقصان منها مذموم والتوسط محمود صواب والحمد والصواب هما للفضيلة (١٣) فالفضيلة إذاً توسّط ما إذ كانت تقصد قصد المتوسّط (١٤) وأيضاً فإنّ الخطأ يكون على ضروب كثيرة لأنّ الشرّ من حيّز ما لا نهاية له كما مثله شيعة الفيثاغوريين والخير من حيّز التناهى وأمّا الصواب فضرب واحد ولذلك صار الخطأ هيناً سهلاً والصواب صعباً عسراً فإنّه من أسهل الأمور أن يخطأ الإنسان الغرض ومن أصعبها أن يصيبه فلذلك صارت الزيادة والنقصان من حيّز الخساسة والتوسّط من حيّز الفضيلة وذلك

الخيار يصيرون خياراً بجهة واحدة
والشرار يصيرون شراراً بكلّ جهة

(١٥) فالفضيلة إذاً حل مختارة موجودة في التوسّط الذي هو عندنا متوسّط محدود بالقول كما يحدّها العاقل وهي متوسّطة فيما بين خسيستين أحدهما بالزيادة والآخر بالنقصان (١٦) وأيضاً يعرض ذلك لبعض الخسائس بنقص عن الواجب في العوارض والأفعل وبعضها بالزيادة فأمّا الفضيلة فإنّها تستخرج المتوسّط وتختاره (١٧) فلذلك كانت الفضيلة [١/٣٠] بحسب جوهرها وقولها الدالّ على ما هيئتها توسّطاً وبحسب ما الأفضل والأجود طرف وغاية (١٨) وليس كلّ فعل وكلّ عارض يقبل التوسّط لا محالة وذلك أنّ بعض العوارض يسمّى بالشرّ خاصّاً لاحتواء الشرّ عليه مثل الشماتة والقحة والحسد فأمّا في الأفعل

1 [...] : illegible F, *of these ways* Dun || 5 والحمد Dun : illegible F || 8 الفيثاغوريين corr. Dun* (Πυθαγόρειοι) : فوثاغورش F; الفيثاغوريين Bad* || 14 مختارة F*, Dun* (προαιρετική) : معتادة Bad || 18 second ما Dun : illegible F || 18-19 طرف و corr. Dun : طرق Bad; uncertain F || 19 وكل عارض F*, Dun* (πᾶν πάθος) : om. Bad

actions adultery and murder. For all these and their like are described[67] [...] in the way they are as being in themselves evil, not because they are an excess or defect of things, because at all times they are wrong and there is no right in them whatsoever. There is no excellence and non-excellence in them, e.g. adultery is not good at one time and at another not good, and in one situation good and in another not good, but the doing of anything whatever of these is wrong absolutely. (19) Similarly it is not likely that there should be excess and a mean and defect in injustice, cowardice and greed, otherwise there would be a mean of excess and defect and an excess of excess and a defect of defect. (20) Just as temperance and bravery have neither excess nor defect, since the mean is in a sense an extreme and end, so the extremes and ends[68] do not have a mean nor excess nor defect, but however they are done, they are wrong. For, in general, there is no excess nor defect of a mean, nor a mean of excess and defect.[69]

7. We must not confine ourselves to giving this summary statement, but the particular cases must correspond with it, because general summary statements about actions are not very correct.[70] Particular statements are nearer to the truth, because actions are in particular things, and we must make our words correspond with them. Let us take these things from the forms which represent them.[71] (2) We
1107b say[72] that courage is intermediate between fear and rashness. As for him who exceeds in lack of fear, there is no name for him—many of the states have no name among the Greeks[73]—the man who exceeds in boldness is called rash, and the man who exceeds in fear and is defective in bravery is called cowardly. (3) As for pleasure and pain, the mean does not exist in all of them, and less so in regard to pain,[74] except that the mean existing in them is temperance, and the

---

[67] Arabic *tūṣafu*, i.e. λέγεται, not ψέγεται.

[68] Arabic *al-aṭrāf wa'l-ghāyāt* expands Greek ἐκείνων, but the sense is wrong. The vices just mentioned, injustice, etc. appear to be intended.

[69] Arabic reverses the order of the clauses.

[70] I.e. Arabic read κενώτεροι (*laisat fī ghāyat aṣ-ṣiḥḥah*).

[71] The significance of Greek διαγραφή for the table of virtues and their opposites as in the *Eudemian Ethics*, 1220b 38ff. (there ὑπογραφή) was not understood by the Arabic translator.

[72] Greek οὖν, omitted by K^b, is doubtfully represented in Arabic *fa-naqūlu*.

[73] Arabic *ʿinda 'l-Yūnānīyīn*, not in the Greek text.

[74] Arabic *wa-aqallu mā yūjadu fī 'l-adhā* which perhaps represents ἧττον δὲ περὶ τὰς λύπας (i.e. with omission of καί).

الفجور وقتل النفس فإنّ هذه كلّها وأشباهها إنّما توصف [...] على أنّها في أنفسها شرور لا لأنّها زيادة أشياء أو نقصانها لأنّها في كلّ وقت من الأوقات خطأ وليس فيها صواب أصلاً ولا يوجد فيها الجودة وغير الجودة مثل الفجور فإنّه ليس يكون في وقت جيّداً وفي وقت غير جيّد وفي حل جيّداً وفي حال غير جيّد لكن فعل أيّ شيء كان من هذه هو خطأ على الإطلاق (١٩) وكذلك لا يجب أن يكون في الظلم والجبن والشره زيادة وتوسّط ونقصان وإلاّ صار للزيادة والنقصان توسّط وللزيادة زيادة وللنقصان نقصان (٢٠) وكما أنّ العفّة والشجاعة ليس لهما زيادة ولا نقصان من قبل أنّ التوسّط هو طرف وغاية من جهة كذلك الأطراف والغايات ليس لها توسّط ولا زيادة ولا نقصان لكن كيف ما فعلت فهي خطأ فإنّ بالجملة ليس للتوسّط زيادة ولا نقصان ولا للزيادة والنقصان توسّط.

٧. وليس ينبغي أن نقتصر على أن نقول هذا قولاً مجملاً لكن ينبغي أن نطابق به الأمور الجزئية لأنّ الأقاويل الكلّية المجملة في الأفعل ليست في غاية الصحّة فأمّا الجزئية فهي أقرب إلى الحقّ لأنّ الأفعل إنّما هي في الأمور الجزئية فينبغي أن نوفّي القول فيها ونأخذ هذه الأشياء من الصور الممثّلة بها (٢) فنقول إنّ الشجاعة متوسّطة فيما بين الخوف والتقحّم فأمّا الزائد في عدم الفزع فلا اسم له وكثير منها عند اليونانيين لا اسم له والزائد في الجرأة يقل له متقحّم والزائد في الفزع الناقص في الجرأة يقل له جبان (٣) فأمّا اللذّة والأذى فليس يوجد التوسّط في جميعها وأقلّ ما يوجد في الأذى إلاّ أنّ [١/٣٦] التوسّط

1 الفجور Dun : illegible F || 3 second وقت F, Dun : قت Bad || 8-9 لكن [...] زيادة F, Dun : om. Bad

excess is greed.[75] Defect in pleasure scarcely exists, and therefore no name is assigned to such a man[76] in our language. He may be called insensible.[77] (4) As to giving and taking, the mean between them is liberality. The excess and defect are prodigality and stinginess, and those who show these traits of character are mutually opposed to one another in excess and defect, for the prodigal is excessive in giving and defective in taking, and the stingy man is excessive in taking and defective in giving. (5) Let us be satisfied with this amount of discussion, since we are simply mentioning what we mention of these things summarily by way of an outline. We shall give a complete differentiation and definition afterwards. (6) Now there exist other states in giving and taking, as for the mean, magnificence,[78] as to the excess, ostentation,[79] as to the defect, meanness. These extremes differ from the extremes of liberality, and we shall describe the thing in which they differ afterwards. (7) As to honour and lack of honour, the mean in them is magnanimity, the excess is inflated pride and the defect small-mindedness. (8) As we say that liberality has a relation to magnificence, since they differ[80] in small things, so there exists a certain state concerned with honour which has a relation to magnanimity, for that state requires little honour while magnanimity requires great honour. That is, it is possible for us to desire honour rightly, and more than rightly, and less. He who exceeds in love of it is called ambitious, he who is defective is called unambitious while the intermediate in love of it has no name. Of the states of these also none has a name, except the state of the ambitious men, for its name is ambition. Therefore the two extremes[81] come to contend with each other for the mean,[82] and we some-
1108a times praise the ambitious man, and sometimes we praise the

[75] Arabic *sharah* for Greek ἀκολασία as for ἀκολασταινεῖν above (1107a 19).

[76] Arabic *lahu*, lit. 'to him'.

[77] Arabic *lā ḥiss lahu*, cf. 1104a 24.

[78] Nearly two lines have dropped out.

[79] Arabic *al-badhakh*, which renders Greek βαναυσία at 1122a 31, misunderstood there and here; ἀπειροκαλία is disregarded or with following καί has dropped out.

[80] But Greek is διαφέρουσαν, i.e. liberality differs from magnificence by being concerned with small things.

[81] Arabic *aṭ-ṭarafān*, but the Greek (οἱ ἄκροι) is explicit: "the people who are at the extremes" (Ross).

[82] Arabic *at-tawassuṭ* for Greek τῆς μέσης χώρας.

الموجود فيها هو العفّة والزيادة الشره والنقصان في اللذّة ليس يكاد يكون ولذلك لم يوضع له في لساننا اسم فاسمه لا حسّ له (٤) فأمّا الإعطاء والأخذ فالتوسّط فيما بينهما السخاء والزيادة والنقصان التبذير والتقتير وأصحاب هذا الأخلاق متضادّون في الزيادة والنقصان فإنّ المبذّر يزيد في الإعطاء وينقص في الأخذ والمقتّر يزيد في الأخذ وينقص في الإعطاء (٥) ولنكتفِ بهذا المقدار من القول إذ كنّا إنّما نذكره ما نذكره من هذه الأشياء مجملاً على جهة الرسم وسنستقصي تمييزها وتحديدها فيما بعد (٦) وقد توجد أحوال أخر في الإعطاء والأخذ وهي أمّا التوسّط فالكرم وأمّا الزيادة فالبذخ وأمّا النقصان فالنذالة وقد يخالف هذان الطرفان لطرفي السخاء وسنصف الشيء الذي يختلف فيما بعد (٧) فأمّا الكرامة وعدم الكرامة فالتوسّط فيهما كبر النفس والزيادة هي التنفّج والنقصان صغر النفس (٨) وكما أنّا نقول إنّ للسخاء نسبة إلى الكرم إذا كانا يختلفان في أشياء يسيرة كذلك توجد حال ما في الكرامة لها نسبة إلى كبر النفس فإنّ تلك الحال تقتضي كرامة يسيرة وكبر النفس يقتضي كرامة كثيرة وذلك أنّه قد يمكننا أن نشتهي الكرامة كما ينبغي وأكثر ممّا ينبغي وأقلّ ويقل للزائد في محبّتها محبّ للكرامة والناقص غير محبّ للكرامة والمتوسّط في حبّها لا اسم له وأحوال هؤلاء أيضاً فليس منها شيء له اسم إلاّ حال محبّ الكرامة فإنّ اسمه محبّة الكرامة ولذلك صار الطرفان يتجاذبان على التوسّط ونحن فربّما حمدنا محبّ الكرامة وربّما حمدنا الذي لا يحبّ الكرامة وربّما سمّينا المتوسّط محبّ الكرامة وربّما سمّيناه

2 فاسمه F, Dun : فلنسمه Bad || 3 هذا Dun : illegible F || 7 وهي F : om. Bad || 9 فيهما corr. Bad : فيها F || 9 هي suppl. mrg. || 10 إذا F : إذ Bad || 12 يمكننا F, Dun : يمكن Bad* || 12 نشتهي F, Dun : تشتهي Bad* || 14 محبة corr. Dun : محب F, Bad

unambitious,[83] and sometimes we call the intermediate man ambitious, and sometimes we call him unambitious. (9) We afterwards describe the cause for which we do that. Meanwhile we give an account of the states of the remainder along the same lines. (10) We say that in anger there exist excess and defect and a mean. The two extremes[84] are practically nameless. As for the intermediate man, he is called[85] mild, and the mean is mildness. As for the two extremes,[86] let the excessive be called irascible and the vice anger, and let the defective be called non-irascible. (11) There are three [other] means which have something in common and resemble each other, and yet are at the same time different. That is, they all take part in words and actions, [...] in that they are partly concerned with the truth therein and partly concerned with[87] this pleasant which exists in pleasure,[88] some of it in jesting and some of it in all in which people engage. We must now describe them in order that it may be clear to us that in all of them the mean is right and praiseworthy, and the extremes neither right nor praiseworthy but worthy of blame. Most of these do not have names, and we have to assign them names as we did in other cases, so that they may be clearer and that it may be easy to understand them. (12) So we say: In regard to truth, the name of the intermediate man is the truthful, and the mean is truth. As to pretence to truth, the excess in it is called boastfulness, and the man who employs it [a boaster]. The defect of it is called irony and the man who employs it ironical. (13) As to what pleasure there is in jesting, the intermediate is the witty man and the state is wit, while the excess in that is called buffoonery, and its possessor buffoon, and the defect is boorishness, and its possessor the boor. As for the remaining type of pleasure which is in social relations, the intermediate in it, the man who is generally likeable in the right way, is

---

[83] '[...] and we sometimes praise the ambitious man [...].' This reverses the order of the Greek of our editions where 'and sometimes we call the intermediate man [...]' precedes. But the Greek text is doubtful, vid. Gauthier *in loco*, and perhaps the Arabic represents another recension.

[84] Arabic *aṭ-ṭarafān* for αὐτῶν, in error.

[85] Suggesting *yusammā* (καλέσωμεν, K^b) which appears necessary for the sense.

[86] Arabic *aṭ-ṭarafān* for Greek τῶν ἄκρων, cf. n. 81.

[87] We translate 'concerned with' for the sake of English, but strictly 'are found in', 'exist in' (Arabic *yūjadu*).

[88] Arabic *al-ladhīdh hādhā alladhī*. The Arabic translator apparently read τοῦτο for τούτου and added some words.

غير محبّ الكرامة (٩) ونحن نصف فيما بعد السبب الذي له نفعل ذلك فأمّا الآن فإنّا نجد أحوال الأمور الباقية على ذلك النسق (١٠) فنقول إنّه قد يوجد في الغضب زيادة ونقصان وتوسّط ويكاد أن يكون الطرفان لا اسم لهما فأمّا [١/٣٢] المتوسّط فيسمّى حليماً والتوسّط حلماً وأمّا الطرفان فليسمّ الزائد منهما غضوباً والخساسة غضباً فأمّا الناقص فليسمّ غير غضوب (١١) وهنا ثلاثة توسّطات فيما بينهما مشاركة ما وتشابه وهي مع ذلك مختلفة وذلك أنّها بأجمعها تشترك في الأقاويل والأفعال [...] في أنّ بعضها يوجد في الحقّ الموجود فيها وبعضها يوجد في اللذيذ وهذا الذي يوجد في اللذّة فبعضه يوجد في الهزل وبعضه يوجد في كلّ ما يتصرّف فيه الناس فينبغي لنا الآن أن نصفها ليبيّن لنا أنّ التوسّط في جميعها صواب محمود والأطراف ليست بصواب ولا محمودة بل مذمومة وأكثر هذه ليس لها أسماء وينبغي أن نضع لها أسماء كما فعلنا في غيرها ليكون أمرها أوضح ويسهل فهمها (١٢) فنقول أمّا في الحقّ فلنسمّ المتوسّط الصادق والتوسّط الصدق فأمّا الزيادة بالصدق فإنّ الزائد فيها يسمّى [...] ومستعمله والنقصان منها المزح ومستعمله المزّاح (١٣) وأمّا ما هو من اللذّة في الهزل فالمتوسّط منه هو الظريف والحال هي الظرف والزيادة في ذلك تسمّى المجون وصاحبها الماجن والنقصان هو الغرامة وصاحبها الغرم فأمّا صنف اللذّة الباقي الذي يكون في المعاشرة فإنّ التوسّط فيه المستحلى بين الناس على ما ينبغي

1 نصف F, Dun : نضيف Bad || 8 الآن F*, Dun* (οὖν) : om. Bad || 12 [...] : illegible F, *boastfulness* Dun || 12 first ومستعمله F, *who employs it [a boaster]* suppl. Dun

the accepted and loved,[89] and the mean is acceptance.[90] The man who exceeds, if he does what he does without a cause, is ingratiating, if he does it to gain an advantage, a flatterer. As for the man who is defective, who is disagreeable to all men, he is hateful and unbearable to all men. The Arabs know and loathe him.[91] (14) There are means in the emotions,[92] for shyness is not a virtue, yet it is praised, and so the shy man.[93] The man who exceeds in it, who feels shy about everything, is the awkward man,[94] and the man who is defective is not shy about anything[95] and shameless. The intermediate is
1108b modest. (15) There is also an intermediate state between envy and spite, called in Greek[96] (...)

1109a 25 9. (2) (...)[97] for not everyone can take it, but only the man who knows it. Similarly being angry and giving and spending money are easy, anyone is capable of them. But as for doing it to the right person, to the right extent, at the right time, and in the right way,[98] not everyone can, nor is it an easy matter, and this is the excellent, rare, praised, and noble action.[99] (3) Therefore the man who has the intermediate as his aim must depart from the extreme more opposed to the mean.[100] That is, the extremes are some more wrong, some less. (4) And since striking the mean truly[101] is hard and difficult, we must seek the second best,[102] viz. that the evil which we do, if it has recurred and it is unavoidable should be the least possible.[103] It will

---

[89] The Greek of this sentence is somewhat expanded by the Arabic translator.

[90] Arabic *qabūl*, rendering Greek φιλία.

[91] Not of course in the Greek.

[92] Some words of Greek are omitted.

[93] Greek καὶ γὰρ [...] μέσος has dropped out, and the Arabic translation of the next sentence goes wrong; see the following notes.

[94] *al-khariq*, i.e. ὁ καταπλήξ construed as a predicate, ὡς being disregarded.

[95] The Arabic translator disregards ἤ.

[96] The last three words are not in the Greek.

[97] A folio is missing (1108b 1 - 1109a 25).

[98] Or 'in the right place' (Arabic *ḥaithu yanbaghī*), but the phrase should render ὥς (the preceding οὗ ἕνεκα has been omitted in the Arabic translation, or has dropped out).

[99] The Arabic translation again construes wrongly.

[100] The reference to Calypso and the quotation from Homer (*Odyssey*, XII, 219-220) are omitted.

[101] Arabic *ʿalā 'l-ḥaqīqah* for Greek ἄκρως, construed with τυχεῖν (so Burnet and Gauthier) rather than with χαλεπόν (Ross).

[102] Arabic *al-martabah ath-thāniyah*, lit. 'the second grade'. The metaphor in κατὰ τὸν δεύτερον πλοῦν is lost.

[103] Arabic 'viz. that the evil [...] the least possible' expands and paraphrases. But

هو المقبول المحبوب والتوسّط هو القبول فأمّا الزائد فإن كان ما يفعل ما يفعله لغير سبب فهو المتودّد وإن كان يفعله لاكتساب منفعة فهو الملاّق فأمّا الناقص المستكره عند جميع الناس فهو المقيت المستثقل عند جميع الناس والعرب تعرفه بالشناه (١٤) وقد توجد في العوارض توسّطات فإنّ الحياء ليس بفضيلة إلاّ أنّه محمود وكذلك المستحي والزائد فيه وهو الذي يستحي من كلّ شئ هو الخرق والناقص هو الذي لا يستحي من شئ وهو الخليع والمتوسّط هو الحيي (١٥) وها هنا حل متوسّطة بين الحسد والشماتة يقل لها باليونانية (...)

٩. (٢) (...) [١/٣٣] فإنّه ليس كلّ أحد يقدر على أخذه بل إنّما يقدر على ذلك العالم به وكذلك الغضب وإعطاء المل وإنفاقه سهل يقدر عليه كلّ أحد فأمّا فعل ذلك بمن ينبغي وبمقدار ما ينبغي وفي الوقت الذي ينبغي وحيث ينبغي فليس يقدر عليه كلّ أحد ولا هو بأمر سهل وهذا هو الفعل الجيّد النادر المحمود الجميل (٣) فلذلك ينبغي لمن قصد قصد المتوسّط أن يتباعد من أكثر الطرفين مضادّة للمتوسّط وذلك أنّ الأطراف منها ما هي أكثر خطأ ومنها ما هي أقلّ خطأ (٤) فلمّا كانت إصابة المتوسّط على الحقيقة عسرة صعبة وجب أن نلتمس المرتبة الثانية وهي أن يكون ما نعمله من الشرّ إن كان ولا بدّ أقلّ ما

3 بالشناه corr. Dun : بالشنة F

1109b be most feasible for us to do that in this way. I say that we must consider the vices towards which we are more inclined, for different people are more inclined to different vices, and we know the thing towards which we are more inclined from the pleasure and pain which accrue to us. (5) When we have become aware of that, we must pull ourselves to its opposite, for whenever we depart from error, we draw near to the mean, like man straightening a crooked stick. (6) In everything we must caution ourselves against the pleasant and pleasure, since we cannot pass judgement on pleasure while we see the inclination towards it.[104] We must have a feeling towards pleasure like what the old men felt towards Helen, and in all these things employ their words,[105] which they spoke to Helen. For when we drive pleasure from us in this way, our error is small. (7) In general I say, if we do this, we are enabled to strike the mean and attain it. But it is more apt to be difficult and hard, and especially in the particular cases. For it is not easy for us to define the case, so as to know how we should be angry, and with whom, and at what things and for how long, because sometimes we praise the man whose anger is slight and call him forbearing, and sometimes we praise the man whose anger is severe and call him manly. (8) But the man who diverges a little from excellence either towards excess or towards defect is not blamed. The man who diverges much in one direction is blamed, because his divergence to this extent is not concealed. It is not easy for us verbally[106] to define the matter or the amount which when a man has reached, he is blameworthy, since in neither this nor anything else of the sense perceptions is that attainable, because judgement upon things like these is only in the particular cases and by sense. (9) By the amount of what we have said on these things it is shown that the intermediate state is praiseworthy in everything, and that we must incline sometimes to excess and sometimes to defect, for in this way we shall attain the mean and excellence.[107]

End of the Second Discourse of the Ethics, and praise be to God and peace upon His servants whom He has chosen.

Greek is simply 'and we must take the least of the evils'.

[104] '[...] while we see [...]' apparently for Greek ἀδέκαστοι.

[105] Cf. Homer, *Iliad*, III, 156ff.

[106] So apparently (Arabic *bi'l-qaul*), cf. II, VI, 15 (1107a 1).

[107] Arabic *al-jamīl* for Greek τοῦ εὖ, which is very variously translated in this book.

يمكن وأكثر ما يتهيّأ لنا فعل ذلك بهذا الوجه أقول إنّه ينبغي لنا أن ننظر الشرور التي نحن إليها أميل فإنّ بعض الناس إلى بعض الشرور أميل وإنّما نعرف الشئ الذي نحن إليه أميل من اللذّة والأذى اللذان يعرضان لنا (٥) فإذا وقفنا على ذلك وجب لنا أن نجذب أنفسنا إلى ضدّه فإنّا كلّما تباعدنا من الخطأ قربنا من التوسّط بمنزلة الذين يقوّمون الخشب المعوجّ (٦) وفي كلّ شئ ينبغي أن نتحفّظ من الشئ اللذيذ واللذّة إذ كان لا يمكننا أن نحكم على اللذّة ونحن نرى الميل إليها فينبغي أن يكون ما ينالنا عند اللذّة مثل الذي ينل المشائخ عند ألاني وأن نستعمل كلامهم الذي قالوه لألاني في جميع هذه الأشياء فإنّا إذا صرفنا اللذّة عنّا بهذا الطريق قلّ فسلدنا (٧) وبالجملة أقول إن فعلنا ذلك قدرنا أن نصيب المتوسّط ونناله وأخلق به أن يكون صعباً عسراً وخاصّةً في الأمور الجزئية فإنّه ليس يسهل علينا أن نحدّد الأمر حتّى نعلم كيف ينبغي أن نغضب وعلى من نغضب وفي أيّ الأشياء وبأيّ مقدار من الزمان لأنّا ربّما حمدنا من قلّ غضبه وسمّينه حليماً وربّما حمدنا من استصعب غضبه وسمّينه فحلاً (٨) ولكن من يجاوز الأمر الحدّ قليلاً إمّا إلى الزيادة وإمّا إلى النقصان لم يذمّ ومن يجاوزه إلى أحد الجهات [١/٣٤] كثيراً فهو بذمّ لأنّ تجاوزه إيّاه بهذا المقدار لا يخفى وليس يسهل أن نحدّ بالقول الأمر أو المقدار الذي إذا صار إليه الإنسان من ذلك كان مذموماً إذ كان هذا ولا غيره من المحسوسات يتهيّأ ذلك فيه لأنّ الحكم على مثل هذه الأشياء إنّما يكون في الأشياء الجزئية وبالحسّ (٩) وبمقدار ما قلناه في هذه الأشياء يدلّ على أنّ الحل المتوسّطة محمودة في كلّ شئ وإنّه ينبغي لنا أن نميل مرّةً إلى الزيادة ومرّةً إلى النقصان فإنّا بهذا الطريق نظفر بالمتوسّط والجميل.

آخر المقالة الثانية من الأخلاق والحمد للّه وسلّم على عباده الذين مصطفى

7 الانى corr. Dun* (Ἑλένην) : الانى F, Bad

BOOK III

In the name of God, the Merciful, the Compassionate
God bless Muhammad and his family and [give them peace]

The Third Discourse of the Book of Ethics of Aristotle[1]

1. Since virtue is concerned with passions and actions, and praise and blame are concerned with what proceeds from us voluntarily, and pardon with what proceeds from us involuntarily, and sometimes pity also, it is likely that he who investigates virtue must necessarily give a short statement on what voluntary and involuntary are. (2) This meaning is also useful to legislators, for laying down reward and punishment in its place. (3) It is thought that things
1110a which are done by their agents perforce or in ignorance are involuntary, and the thing which is done involuntarily is that of which the principle which does it is from without, there being no help in it towards the action on the part of the agent or the man to whom it is done, as, for example, the wind carries a man from one place to another, he meanwhile being out of control of himself.[2] (4) As to what is done through apprehension of great evils or for a noble motive, e.g. that some tyrant orders people to do a shameful act to their parents while in full control of themselves,[3] and if they do it, they are safe, and if they do not, they are to be killed, there is a doubt whether it is among the deeds done voluntarily or something done involuntarily. (5) A similar case occurs when seafarers jettison their cargoes to escape a sea raging from the violence of the winds. For, in general, to jettison one's cargo is not voluntary, yet all reasonable men do so for their own safety and the safety [of their companions]. (6) Actions like these are mixed, but it is likely that they are voluntary. And such actions at the time when they

---

[1] Note the slightly different title of this 'Third Discourse' (Book III), retained in the following Books.

[2] Arabic *wa-huwa fī dhālika ghair mālik li-nafsihi*, i.e. a mistranslation of ἢ ἄνθρωποι κύριοι ὄντες where ἢ has evidently been taken as = '(other) than'.

[3] The construction is wrong (Arabic *bi-ābā'ihim* [...] *wa-hum mālikū anfusihim* for κύριος ὢν γονέων καὶ τέκνων).

المقالة الثالثة

بسم الله الرحمن الرحيم
صلّى الله على محمّد وعلى آله [وسلّم]

المقالة الثالثة من كتاب الأخلاق لأرسطو

١. لمّا كانت الفضيلة إنّما هي في الانفعالات والأفعال وكان الحمد والذمّ إنّما يكونان فيما يكون منّا طوعاً والعذر فيما يكون منّا كرهاً وربّما كانت الرحمة أيضاً فالخلق بمن يبحث عن الفضيلة أن يكون واجباً عليه ضرورةً أن يلخّص القول فيما يكون طوعاً وكرهاً (٢) وهذا المعنى أيضاً نافع لواضعي النواميس لوضع الثواب والعقاب في موضعه (٣) وقد يظنّ بالأشياء التي إنّما تكون قسراً أو جهلاً من فاعليها أنّها تكون كرهاً والشئ الذي يكون كرهاً هو الذي مبدؤه الذي يفعله يكون من خارج وليس فيه للفاعل وللمنفعل معونة عليه مثل أن تحمل الريح إنساناً من مكان إلى مكان وهو في ذلك غير مالك لنفسه (٤) فأمّا ما يفعل للجزع من شرور عظيمة أو لأمر جميل مثل أن يأمر بعض المتغلّبين قوماً أن يفعلوا بآبائهم أمراً قبيحاً وهم مالكو أنفسهم فإن فعلوا سلموا منهم وإن لم يفعلوا قتلوا ففيه شكّ [١/٣٥] هل هو من الأمور التي تكون طوعاً أو من الشئ الذي يكون كرهاً (٥) وقد يعرض مثل هذا عند طرح ركاب البحر أحمالهم عند اضطراب البحر من عصوف الرياح فإنّ بالجملة ليس يطرح أحماله طوعاً وجميع من له عقل يفعل ذلك لسلامته وسلامة [رفاقه] (٦) وأمثال هذه الأفعال مختلطة إلاّ أنّها أشبه بأن تكون طوعاً وما يجري هذا

---

2 وسلم suppl. Bad, Dun || 5 منا طوعا F*, Dun* (ἑκουσίοις) : مناظرهما Bad || 5 منا كرها F*, Dun* (ἀκουσίοις) : مناكرهما Bad || 11 قوما F, Dun : قدما Bad || 14 second عند corr. Bad : عن F || 16 رفاقه suppl. Bad*, Dun* (τῶν λοιπῶν)

are[4] done are by the choice of the agent, and the end and completion of the action are according to the time. It should be said of a thing that it is voluntary or involuntary at the time when it is done. As for the agent, he does it voluntarily,[5] i.e., the principle of movement of his instrumental members in these actions belongs to him, and to whom the principle of anything belongs, the doing of that thing[6] belongs. So cases like these are voluntary, though it is likely that they are involuntary in the absolute sense, for no man chooses anything of this kind for itself. (7) In such actions a man is often praised when he endures something disgraceful or painful for the sake of great and noble objects, and if he does the opposite, he is blamed, because to bear disgraceful things patiently[7] for other than an altogether noble end[8] is the action of a base man. Some things a man is not praised for doing, but he is pardoned, when he has done them for causes which exceed[9] human nature, and no one can endure them. (8) It is likely that there are things which a man is not forced to, but it is preferable that he should die in them enduring hardships. That is, the causes which forced Alcmaeon, whom the poet Euripides mentioned, to kill his mother are ridiculous. (9) Sometimes it is difficult for us to give a short account[10] of what ever it is that we must bear[11] and endure in exchange for what, and more difficult than this even is to persevere in the things which we have come to know,[12] because mostly the things whose pain we fear and the things a man is constrained and forced to do are base. Therefore praise and blame
1110b occur in what a man is or is not forced to do. (10) We must describe what the things are which are perforce: What kind of things are they? We say generally,[13] they are whenever their cause lies in something which is external, and the agent was not helping towards them. As for the things which are in themselves involuntary, yet at

---

[4] A word or words have been omitted in the Arabic text corresponding to τῶν λοιπῶν.

[5] This is apparently the reading of the vulg. (δέ) against Susemihl and Gauthier (δή).

[6] Greek καὶ μή is not rendered.

[7] The Greek superlative (αἴσχιστα) is not rendered.

[8] Arabic omits ἢ μετρίῳ.

[9] Arabic *tafūqu* for Greek ὑπερτείνει is inaccurate.

[10] I.e. *nulakhkhiṣa*, for Greek διακρῖναι, 'distinguish, decide'.

[11] Arabic *naḥtamilahu* for αἱρετέον, apparently misread αἰρετέον.

[12] Arabic *al-ashyā' allatī qad 'arafnāhā* for Greek τοῖς γνωσθεῖσιν.

[13] Arabic *'alā 'l-iṭlāq*, cf. 1148a 4, 1149a 24, 1155b 24. The question with ἤ is disregarded.

المجرى من الأفعل فهو في وقت ما يفعل يكون بلختيار من فاعله وغاية الفعل وتمامه إنّما هو بحسب الوقت وإنّما أن يقل في الشئ إنّه كان طوعاً أو كرهاً في وقت ما يفعل فأمّا فاعله فيفعله طائعاً وذلك أنّ مبدأ تحريك أعضائه الآلية في هذه الأفعل هو إليه ومن كان مبدأ شئ إليه ففعل ذلك الشئ إليه فأمثل هذه الأشياء تكون طوعاً وخليق أن تكون كرهاً على الإطلاق إذ ليس أحد من الناس يختار شيئاً من هذه الأشيله لذاته (٧) وفي مثل هذه الأفعل ربّما أُحمِدَ الإنسان إذا ما احتمل أمراً قبيحاً أو مؤذياً بسبب أمور جميلة عظيمة وإن فعل ضدّ ذلك يذمّ لأنّ الصبر على الأشياء القبيحة بغير أمر جميل أصلاً من فعل إنسان خسيس وبعض الأشياء لا يحمد الإنسان على فعلها إلاّ أنّه يُعذر إذا فعلها لأسباب تفوق طبيعة الإنسان ولا يقدر أحد على احتمالها (٨) وخليق أن تكون ها هنا أشياء ليس يُقهر الإنسان عليها ولكن الأولى أن يموت فيها بصبرهم على الأمور الصعبة وذلك أنّ الأسباب التي اضطرّت ألقماون الذي ذكره أرويفيدس الشاعر إلى أن يقتل أمّه هي من الأمور التي يُضحك منها (٩) وربّما صعب علينا أن نلخّص أيّ شئ ينبغي أن نحتمله ونصمد عليه بدل أيّ شئ وأصعب من هذا أيضاً الثبات على الأشياء التي قد عرفناها لأنّ في أكثر الأمر الأشياء التي نتوقّع مؤلمة مؤذية والأشياء التي يكلّفها الإنسان ويقهر عليها قبيحة فلذلك صار الحمد والذمّ فيما يقهر الإنسان عليه أو لا يقهر (١٠) فينبغي أن نصف الأشياء التي تكون قسراً أيّ الأشياء [٣٦/١] هي فنقول على الإطلاق فهي إذا كان سببها في الشئ الذي من خارج ولم يكن الفاعل معيناً عليها فأمّا الأشياء التي تكون في نفسها كرهاً إلاّ أنّها في

5 إذ corr. Bad : فإن F || 11 يقتل corr. Bad : قتل F

the time when they are done their being brought into existence[14] is preferred to other things, they are voluntary. They are like the matters which are voluntary, because actions are among particular things, and particular things are done voluntarily. It is not easy for us to describe what actions we must choose in preference to others. That is because there is much difference in individual things. (11) If someone says that noble and pleasant things are perforce, because they, he asserts, compel us, being outside us, in this way[15] everything is perforce, because all men do all that they do because of these. He who does anything perforce and by constraint is pained thereby, and he who does a thing for something noble or pleasant takes delight in it. It is absurd and ridiculous for a man to refer the cause here to external actions, and not to himself, since he easily falls into things like these[16] and makes himself the cause of noble deeds and pleasant things the cause of disgraceful deeds. (12) So it is likely that what is perforce is that of which the principle is external, without any help on the part of the self towards it. (13) What is done without knowledge on the part of the agent is not all voluntary: what is painful and its doing repented of, is involuntary. That is, he who has done something, whatever it is, not knowing and not vexed by his action, has not done it voluntarily, because he did not know it, nor has he done it involuntarily, because he is not pained by it. So then as regards for the man who has done something [not] being aware of it, if he repents of his action it is thought of him that he has done it involuntarily, and if he does not repent of his action but is content with what he has done,[17] it must be thought of him that what he has done, he has done '[not] voluntarily'. For there is a difference between them, and it is better that each of the two should have a special name. (14) It is likely that what a man does 'not knowing' is different from what he does being ignorant of it. That is, the drunk or the man in a rage are not thought to do what they do at the time of drunkenness and the time of rage 'without knowledge',[18] but they do it in ignorance of it.

---

[14] I.e. reading *taṣyīruhā*.

[15] Arabic *'alā hādhihi 'l-jihah* i.e. reading οὕτω—rather than αὐτῷ (Bywater)—with the old Latin translation (Bywater) and most of the moderns (Burnet, Rackham, Gauthier: "à ce compte").

[16] I.e. pleasures.

[17] Arabic *bal ightabaṭa* apparently explains Greek ἐπεὶ ἕτερος.

[18] It would have been better if the Arabic translator had retained the same rendering of the Greek (δι' ἄγνοιαν) in both cases where it occurred, but 'without knowledge' is at least as good as 'not knowing' above. The words ἀλλὰ διά τι [...] εἰδὼς δέ have dropped out here.

وقت ما تفعل يؤثر على غيرها تصييرها تكون طوعاً وهي أشبه بالأمور التي تكون طوعاً لأنّ الأفعال إنّما تكون في الأمور الجزئية والأمور الجزئية إنّما تفعل طوعاً وليس يسهل علينا أن نصف أيّ الأفعال ينبغي أن نؤثرها على غيرها وذلك لأنّ الاختلاف في الأمور الجزئية كثير (١١) فإن قال قائل إنّ الأمور الجميلة واللذيذة ممّا تكون قسراً لأنّها زعم تضطرّنا إذ كانت من خارج صار على هذه الجهة كلّ شيء إنّما يكون قسراً لأنّ جميع الناس إنّما يفعلون جميع ما يفعلونه بسبب هذه ومَن فعل شيئاً بالقسر والقهر تأذّى به ومَن فعل شيئاً للأمر الجميل أو اللذيذ التذّ فما يضحك منه ويهزأ به تصيير الإنسان السبب في الأفعال الخارجة وألاّ يُصَيّر السبب في ذلك نفسه إذ كان سهل الوقوع في أمثال هذه الأشياء ويجعل سبب الأمور الجميلة نفسه وسبب الأمور القبيحة الأشياء اللذيذة (١٢) فيشبه أن يكون الشيء الذي يكون قسراً هو الذي مبدؤه من خارج من غير أن يكون للنفس معونة عليه (١٣) وما يكون بغير علم من فاعله فليس كلّه يكون طوعاً فأمّا الشيء المؤذي وما يندم على فعله فإنّما يكون كرهاً وذلك أنّ مَن فعل شيئاً من الأشياء أيّ شيء كان وهو لا يعلم ولم يمتعض من فعله فلم يفعله طوعاً لأنّه لم يعلمه ولا فعله كرهاً لأنّه لم يتأذّ به فأمّا مَن فعل شيئاً وهو [لا] يعلم فإن هو ندم على فعله فقد يظنّ به أنّه فعله كرهاً وإن لم يندم على فعله بل اغتبط بما فعل فينبغي أن يظنّ به أنّه فعل ما فعله [لا] طوعاً فإنّ بينهما فصلاً والأجود أن يكون لكلّ واحد منهما اسم يخصّه (١٤) ويشبه أن يكون ما يفعله الإنسان وهو لا يعلم غير ما يفعله وهو جاهل به وذلك أنّ السكران أو المغتاظ لا يظنّ بهما أنّهما [١/٣٧] يفعلان ما يفعلانه وقت السكر ووقت الغيظ بغير معرفة لكنهما يفعلانه وهما

1 تصييرها F, Dun : فقصدها Bad || 2 لأن (...) طوعا F, Dun : om. Bad || 3 لأن corr. : أن F, Bad || 5 إذ F : إذا Bad || 7 فما F : مما Bad || 8 هذه F : هذا Bad || 14 لا suppl. Dun* (ἄγνοιαν) || 15 لا suppl. Dun* (οὐχ) || 17 يفعله corr. Bad : يفعل F

For every wicked man is ignorant of the things which it is necessary for him to do and the things which it is necessary for him to avoid, and because of this error they become unjust and in general bad. (15) It is not characteristic of an action that it should be said to have been done involuntarily if the agent was ignorant of the advantages, because it is not ignorance of the choice that is the cause of the act being involuntary, but it is the cause of vice, and not the universal,[19] because there is blame on account of this, but ignorance of the par-
1111a ticulars, since the action only exists in them. That is, in these are pity and the extension of pardon,[20] because the man who is ignorant of any of these does what he does involuntarily. (16) There is no harm in our distinguishing these things[21] and knowing what they are, and how many they are,[22] what the agent is doing,[23] and in what[24] he is acting, and sometimes we need to know with what, I mean the instrument, for what purpose, e.g. he does the thing for safety, and how, as that he does the thing gently or violently. (17) All these things no one is ignorant of except a madman, and it is plain also that he is not ignorant of the agent, because it is not possible that anyone should be ignorant of himself when he is acting,[25] e.g. it is said that they are out of their minds,[26] or that they do not know that what they say must not be uttered, as Aeschylus said of the mysteries, or someone who wishes to show something and lets it go from his hand, like the man who let go the instrument[27] which he was throwing. Someone might suppose that his son was his enemy, as Merope supposed; that the end of a spear-shaft, on which a head had been fitted, was round, since it was in appearance round, and that the stone with which he struck a man was pumice. Sometimes a man strikes[28] a man for his advantage and kills him, and sometimes one

---

[19] This should be 'ignorance of the universal' (ἡ καθόλου, sc. ἄγνοια), unless we are to read *bi 'l-kullīyah*.

[20] I.e. pity and pardon depend on "the circumstances of the action and the objects with which it is concerned" (Ross).

[21] I.e. the circumstances of the act.

[22] Here words corresponding to the Greek τίς τε δή (= who the agent is) have fallen out.

[23] Greek καὶ περὶ τί is here omitted.

[24] Arabic *fī aiyi shai'in*, i.e. Greek τίνι is taken as neuter. Cf. Gauthier *in loco*.

[25] These words are wrongly construed.

[26] This represents an old translation of the difficult passage, vid. Burnet *in loco*.

[27] Greek τὸν καταπέλτην is not understood.

[28] I.e. reading παίσας (vulg.) in the Greek text.

جاهلان به فإنّ كلّ ردئ يجهل الأشياء التي ينبغي له أن يفعلها والأشياء التي ينبغي له أن يهرب منها ولهذا الخطأ يصيرون ظلمة وبالجملة شراراً (١٥) وليس من شأن الفعل أن يقل فيه إنّه فعل كرهاً إذا كان فاعله يجهل الأمور النافعة لأنّه ليس الجهل بالاختيار سبباً لأن يكون الفعل كرهاً لكنّه سبب للرداءة ولا الكلّية لأنّ الذمّ يكون بسبب هذه لكن الذي في الجزئيات إذ كان الفعل إنّما يوجد فيها وذلك أنّه قد يوجد في هذه الرحمة وبسط العذر لأنّ من يجهل شيئاً من هذه فإنّما يفعل ما يفعله كرهاً (١٦) ولا بأس أن نفصّل هذه الأشياء ونعلم ما هي وكم هي وما الذي يفعل وفي أيّ شئ يفعل وربّما احتجنا أن نعلم بأيّ شئ أعني الآلة ولأيّ شئ مثلما يفعل الشئ للسلامة وكيف بمنزلة ما يفعل الشئ برفق أو بشدّة (١٧) فهذه الأشياء كلّها ليس من أحد يجهلها إلاّ مجنون ومن البيّن أيضاً أنّه لا يجهل الفاعل إمّا لأنّه لا يمكن أن يكون أحد جاهلاً بنفسه إذ كان يفعل مثلما يقل إنّهم يهترون أو إنّهم لا يعلمون أنّ ما يقولونه ممّا لا يجب أن ينطق به بمنزلة ما يقوله أسخولس في الأسرار أو من يريد أن يري شيئاً ويخليه من يده مثل الذي خلى الآلة التي يرمي بها وقد يتوهّم متوهّم أنّ ابنه عدوه كما توهّمت ماربي وأنّ رأس الرمح الذي ركب عليه السنان كري إذ كان يتراءى كرياً وأنّ الحجر الذي يرمي به إنساناً قشور وربّما ضرب إنسان إنساناً

---

4 الذم Dun*: لا الذم F, Bad || 10 إذ F: إن Bad || 12 مثل F*, Dun* (ىمں): فحل Bad || 18 ماربي F: مارفى Bad || 18 عليه F: om. Bad || 19 قشور Dun: لسود F; om. Bad

wishes to show[29] another something and touches him with the tips of his fingers and kills[30] him. (18) Since ignorance exists in regard to all these things in which the action consists,[31] the man who is ignorant of any one of them is thought to do it[32] involuntarily, and especially when he is ignorant of the most important in it, and the most important in it is thought to be the thing in which the action consisted,[33] and on account of which it was. (19) What is said to be involuntary[34] according to this sense of ignorance must also be painful to the agent, and he must repent of it. (20) Since what is done perforce and without knowledge is said to be done involuntarily, what is done voluntarily is thought to be the thing whose principle is in the agent and its agent knows its particulars in which the action consists, (21) because likely enough to say that what is done through desire and anger is not done voluntarily is not rightly said. (22) In the first place, none of the animals except man does anything voluntarily, nor do infants. (23) Also, we cannot avoid either[35] that we do voluntarily nothing at all of what is done through desire and anger, or that we do good deeds voluntarily, and evil deeds involuntarily. Or is this absurd, since the cause is the same? (24) It is likely to be unacceptable[36] for us to say that our desire for the thing that we ought to desire or our anger at the person whom we must be angered at is involuntary—for we must be angry at some things and desire something,[37] e.g. health and learning. (25) It is maybe thought of the things which are involuntary that they are painful and the things which are with desire pleasant. (26) Also how does one say that what is involuntary differs from what is erroneous of reflection
1111b and anger[38] since both are avoided? (27) It is maybe thought that the

---

[29] I.e. Greek δεῖξαι, again vulg.

[30] Correctly 'strikes' (πατάξειεν).

[31] The Greek phrase ἐν οἷς ἡ πρᾶξις is rendered differently below (n. 33).

[32] Arabic *yafʿaluhu* (Greek πεπραχέναι).

[33] Arabic *ash-shaiʾ alladhī fīhi kāna al-fiʿl* here, but immediately above *al-ashyāʾ allatī fīhā yakūn al-fiʿl*, which is more correct. Cf. also § 20.

[34] But we need '[The doing of] which is said to be involuntary [...]' rather than the *constructio ad sensum*.

[35] The question has in the Greek disappeared (πότερον apparently taken as indefinite).

[36] Arabic *min al-munkar* for Greek ἄτοπον.

[37] Arabic *shaiʾan* for Greek τινῶν.

[38] The sentence has been misunderstood by the translator, who evidently read τὰ ἀκούσια for τῷ ἀκούσια, disregarding the following εἶναι.

لمنفعة فقتله وربّما أراد مريد أن يري آخر شيئاً فنخسه بأطراف أصابعه فقتله (١٨) فلمّا كان الجهل موجوداً في هذه الأشياء كلّها التي فيها يكون الفعل كان من جهل منها شيئاً ظنّ به أنّه يفعله كرهاً وخاصّةً إذا جهل أقوى ما فيه ويظنّ أقوى ما فيه الشئ الذي فيه كان الفعل ومن أجله كان (١٩) وما يقل إنّه يكون كرهاً على هذا الوجه من [١/٣٨] الجهل يحتاج أيضاً أن يكون الفاعل له يتأذّى به ويندم عليه (٢٠) وإذ كان ما يُفعَل قسراً وبغير معرفة يقل إنّه يُفعل كرهاً فما يُفعَل طوعاً يظنّ به أنّه الشئ الذي مبدؤه فيه وفاعله يعلم جزئياته التي فيها يكون الفعل (٢١) لأنّه خليق ألاّ يكون القول بأنّ ما يُفعل بالشهوة والغضب ليس إنّما يفعل طوعاً يقل على قياس (٢٢) أمّا أوّلاً فإنّه لا يكون شئ من الحيوان غير الإنس يفعل شيئاً طوعاً ولا الأطفل (٢٣) وأيضاً فلسنا نخلو من أن نكون إمّا إلاّ نفعل شيئاً أصلاً ممّا يكون بالشهوة والغضب طوعاً وإمّا أن نكون نفعل الأمور الجيّدة طوعاً والرديئة كرهاً أو يكون هذا ممّا يُضحك منه إذ كان السبب واحداً (٢٤) وخليق أن يكون من المنكر أن نقول إنّ شهوتنا للشئ الذي ينبغي أن نشتهيه أو غضبنا على من يجب أن نغضب عليه يكون كرهاً لأنّه قد يجب أن نغضب في بعض الأشياء وأن نشتهي شيئاً مثل الصحّة والتعلّم (٢٥) وقد يظنّ بالأشياء التي تكون كرهاً أنّها مؤذية والأشياء التي تكون بالشهوة لذيذة (٢٦) وأيضاً بماذا يقول إنّ ما يكون كرهاً يخالف ما يكون بخطأ من الفكر والغضب إذ كان

3 second و corr. Dun : أو F, Bad || 4 وما F : فما Bad || 13 شيئا F*, Dun* (τινῶν) : om Bad || 15 يقول F, Bad : نقول Bad ||

animal[39] passions belong to mankind no less than to others,[40] and a man's actions are from aversion and anger.[41] It is unacceptable then to make these part of what is involuntary.

2. Since we have distinguished what is voluntary and what is involuntary, we must follow that up by the description of choice, for choice is thought to be most intimately connected with virtue. In particular, it judges character from actions.[42] (2) We say: Choice is plainly voluntary. Yet the meaning of choice and the meaning of what is voluntary are not the same, but what is voluntary is more extensive than what is by choice. That is, infants and dumb animals share in what is voluntary but do not share in choice. Things done on the spur of the moment we say are voluntary. We do not say that they are by choice. (3) Those who maintain that choice is desire or anger or wish or a certain opinion are not likely to be right in what they say, because choice is not common.[43] What is common is desire and anger. (4) He who does not restrain his desire acts when he desires, not when he chooses. The situation of the man of restraint and the situation of the man who follows his appetite is the opposite: when he chooses he acts, not when he desires. (5) Desire is the opposite of choice; desire does not oppose desire. Desire is with reference only to the pleasant and the painful: choice is not with reference to anything painful or pleasant. (6) Still less is it anger, because it is thought that the thing which is done because of anger is rarely[44] done by choice. (7) Nor again is choice wish, even though it is thought to be close to it, because choice is not of impossibilities. If any one maintains that impossibilities are chosen[45] he is thought to be foolish. (8) Wish is sometimes for impossibilities, e.g. one wishes for immortality. Wish also is sometimes in respect of things the doing of which does not belong to us, e.g. the excellent man[46] and the

---

[39] Arabic *bahīmīyah*, but Greek is ἄλογα, 'irrational', for which the Arabic EN offers a number of renderings.

[40] I.e. apparently the lower animals, but the Greek means 'no less human', sc. than reason.

[41] I.e. taking τοῦ ἀνθρώπου as dependent on αἱ πράξεις rather than as predicate.

[42] 'In particular', i.e. Arabic *khāṣṣatan* for Greek μᾶλλον. The rest of the sentence follows as if τὰ ἤθη κρίνει ἐκ τῶν πράξεων were read.

[43] I.e. to man and the irrational creatures (the Arabic translation omits καὶ τῶν ἀλόγων).

[44] Arabic *qallamā*, but the meaning of Greek ἥκιστα, 'least of all', is lost.

[45] The Arabic translator takes Greek προαιρεῖσθαι as passive.

[46] Arabic *al-fāḍil* for Greek ἀθλητήν. Cf. below 1116b 13.

يُهرَب من كليهما (٢٧) وقد يظنّ بالعوارض البهيمية أنّها للناس ليس بدون غيرهم وأفعل الإنسان إنّما هي من النفرة والغضب فمن المنكر أن يجعل هذه الأشياء ممّا يكون كرهاً.

٢. فإذ قد ميّزنا ما يكون طوعاً وما يكون كرهاً فينبغي أن نتبع ذلك بصفة الاختيار فإنّ الاختيار يظنّ به أنّه أخصّ الأشياء بالفضيلة وهو خاصّةً يحكم على الأخلاق من الأفعل (٢) فنقول إنّ الاختيار تبيّن من أمره أنّه يكون طوعاً وليس معنى الاختيار هو معنى ما يكون طوعاً لكن ما يكون طوعاً أكثر ممّا يكون بالاختيار وذلك أنّ ما يكون طوعاً قد يشترك فيه الصبيان والحيوان غير الناطق وليس يشتركون في الاختيار والأشياء التي تكون بغتة نقول إنّها تكون طوعاً ولا نقول إنّها تكون باختيار (٣) والذين يزعمون أنّ الاختيار شهوة أو غضب أو الهوى [٣٩/١] أو رأي ما فيشبه ألاّ يكون قولهم ذلك صواباً لأنّ الاختيار ليس بعامّ بل الشئ العامّ هو الشهوة والغضب (٤) والذي لا يضبط شهوته إذا اشتهى فعل ليس إذا اختيار وحل الضابط وحل الذي يطلب نفسه بعكس ذلك إذا اختار فعل ليس إذا اشتهى (٥) والشهوة مضادّة للاختيار وشهوة لا تضادّ شهوة والشهوة إنّما هي للّذيذ والمؤذي فأمّا الاختيار فليس هو لشئ مؤذ ولا لذيذ (٦) والغضب أيضاً أقلّ منه لأنّه يظنّ أنّ الشئ الذي يكون بسبب الغضب قلّما يكون باختيار (٧) وليس الاختيار أيضاً هوى وإن كان يرى أنّه قريب منه لأنّ الاختيار لا يكون للأشياء الممتنعة فإن زعم زاعم أنّ الأشياء الممتنعة تختار ظنّ به أنّه غبي (٨) والهوى قد يكون للأشياء الممتنعة بمنزلة ما يهوى البقاء والهوى أيضاً قد يكون في الأشياء التي ليس فعلها إلينا مثل أن يهوى الفاضل والحاكي وليس أحد

---

6 مما F*, Dun* (πλέον) : ما Bad || 11 الضابط F*, Dun* (ὁ ἐγκρατής) : انضبط Bad || 17 فعلها
ليس : F فعلها ليس Bad || 17 الفاضل F*, Dun* (ἀθλητήν) : المناضل Bad

actor wish,[47] but no one chooses things like these. Rather a man chooses what he sees that he can do. (9) Also, wish is mostly for the end of something, while choice is for what leads to the end. For example, we wish to be healthy, and we choose the things by which we are healthy. We wish to be happy and rejoice.[48] We must not say that we choose to be happy, because, in general, it is likely that choice is concerned simply with the things which are in our power to do. (10) Nor is choice opinion either, because opinion is thought to be concerned with everything, nor is it less in respect of eternal and impossible things than what it is in what is in our power. And it is divided into truth and falsehood, not into good and bad, whereas choice is divided into good and bad. (11) In general, it is not likely
1112a that anyone would say that choice and opinion are one in anything.[49] That is, it is sometimes said of us that by our choosing good and bad we are in a particular condition, but that is not said of us when we opine. (12) We choose to take something, and to flee from something, and[50] to do something like that. As for opinion, by it we believe what the thing is, or for whom it is good, or how it is good. As for taking the thing or fleeing from the thing, it scarcely involves our opining. (13) Choice is not praised for anything more than it is praised for being right and opinion for being true. And we choose the things which are known particularly as being good, while we opine the things which we scarcely do. (14) We think of those who choose what is best, they are not those who opine best, but some have the best opinion, and because of their wickedness choose what they ought not. (15) As to opinion preceding choice or following it, it makes no difference, because this is not the matter which we were investigating. Rather what we were investigating is to know if choice and opinion agree in anything.[51] (16) Since then choice is not one of the things which we have mentioned, let us consider what it is, and what sort of thing. We say: It is likely to be what is done voluntarily, except that not all that is voluntary is chosen,

---

[47] Greek νικᾶν has dropped out of the translation.

[48] Apparently rendering φαμέν (taken to represent εὐφραινόμεθα).

[49] Construction and translation are alike wrong (the meaning is that choice is not simply not identical with opinion in general but not even with any opinion, vid. Burnet, Gauthier).

[50] *wa-* [...] *wa-* apparently for ἦ [...] ἤ, the latter the reading of the vulg. But the correction Arabic *an* [...] *an* is easy.

[51] The point that the choice does not agree with any opinion is again missed, cf. above, n. 49.

من الناس يختار أمثل هذه الأشياء بل إنّما يختار الإنسان ما يرى أنّ فعله إليه (٩) وأيضاً فإنّ الهوى أكثر ما يكون لغاية الشيء فأمّا الاختيار فإنّما يكون لما يؤدّي إلى الغاية ومثل ذلك أن نهوى أن نصحّ ونختار الأشياء التي بها نصحّ ونهوى أن نسعد ونفرح وليس ينبغي أن نقول إنّا نختار أن نسعد لأنّ بالجملة يشبه أن يكون الاختيار إنّما هو في الأشياء التي فعلها إلينا (١٠) وليس الاختيار أيضاً رأياً لأنّ الرأي يظنّ به أنّه يكون في كلّ شيء وليس هو من الأمور الدائمة البقاء والممتنعة بدون ما هو فيما كان إلينا وإنّما ينقسم بالصدق والكذب لا بالخير والشرّ فأمّا الاختيار فبالخير والشرّ ينقسم (١١) وبالجملة فخليق ألاّ يكون أحد يقول إنّ الاختيار والرأي شيء واحد بشيء من الأشياء وذلك أنّه قد يقل فينا باختيارنا للخير والشرّ أنّا بكيف ما ولا يقل ذلك فينا إذا رأينا رأياً (١٢) وقد نختار أن نأخذ شيئاً وأن نهرب من شيء وأن نفعل شيئاً ممّا يشبه ذلك وأمّا الرأي فبسببه نعتقد ما الشيء أو لمن يصلح أو كيف يصلح فأمّا أخذ الشيء أو الهرب من [١/٤٠] الشيء فليس يكاد يكون منّا بالرأي (١٣) والاختيار فليس يحمد بشيء أكثر من أن يحمد بأنّه صواب والرأي بأنّه صادق وإنّما نختار الأشياء التي يعلم خاصّةً أنّها خير ونرى الأشياء التي لا يكاد نعملها (١٤) ونظنّ بالذين يختارون ما هو أفضل ليس هم الذين يرون رأياً أفضل لكن قوماً يرون الشيء الأفضل وبسبب شرّهم يختارون ما لا ينبغي (١٥) فأمّا أنّ الرأي يتقدّم الاختيار أو يتبعه فليس في ذلك اختلاف لأنّ ليس هذا الشيء الذي كنّا نبحث عنه بل الذي كنّا نبحث عنه هو أن نعلم إن كان الاختيار والرأي متّفقين في شيء من الأشياء (١٦) فإذا كان الاختيار ليس هو واحد من الأشياء التي ذكرنا فلننظر ما هو وأيّ الأشياء فنقول يشبه أن يكون ما يفعل طوعاً إلاّ أنّ ليس كلّما يكون طوعاً فهو مختار (١٧) لكن المختار ما أوجبته الروية

2 الهوى F*, Dun* (ἡ βούλησις) : القوى Bad || 4 التي F, Dun : التي صار suppl. Bad || 8 بشيء F :
19 || Bad .read نكاد نفعلها : F يكاد نعملها 13 || repeated من 11 || Bad أما : F وأما 10 || Bad لشيء
إلا أن F : إلا أنه Bad || 19 كلما F : كل ما Bad

(17) but what is chosen is what deliberation necessitates,[52] because choice is with discrimination and intelligence. It is likely that the word 'choice' in our language signifies the agent who chooses[53] one thing in preference to another.

3. We must know whether deliberation is necessary in all things, so that each thing is deliberated on, or are some things not deliberated on? (2) It is likely that we must say that the object of deliberation is not what the fool and the madman deliberate on, but what the intelligent man deliberates on. (3) We find no one employing deliberation in eternal things, I mean the world, and the incommensurability of the diagonal and the side of a square. (4) Nor does anyone deliberate either on the things which are in movement when they take place in one and the same way, whether that is of necessity or by nature, or for some other cause,[54] (5) like draught and abundance of rain, nor on the things which are by chance, such as the finding of a treasure. (6) One does not deliberate either on the affairs of all mankind, for no one of the Lacedaimonians deliberates on the condition in which the Scyths[55] have come to have an excellent constitution, because none of these things is in our power. (7) We deliberate only on that the doing of which is within our power and happens through our agency.[56] That is, it is thought that the causes of these things are nature, necessity and chance, also reason, and everything which is by human means. Every individual of mankind deliberates only on the things which are possible for him to do and happen through his
1112b agency. (8) There is no deliberation on the accurate, self-sufficient sciences, such as orthography, i.e. we have no doubt so as to deliberate how we must write the letters. We only deliberate on that the doing of which is within our power and is not also[57] in the same way, as is the case in the art of medicine and in all the faculties.[58] There is more deliberation on navigation than on gymnastics, according to the defect of the one compared with the other in giving a complete account of the action. (9) The case is similar in all the remaining arts, and the employment of deliberation in the arts is

---

[52] The question with ἆρα is not noticed.
[53] But the Greek is 'something chosen' (ὡς ὂν [...] αἱρετόν).
[54] A line of the original Greek is omitted here by homoioteleuton.
[55] Arabic *ahl Suqūthyā*. Cf. 1150b 14 = VII, 7, 6: *mālik al-Isqūthī*.
[56] Several words of Greek are here omitted.
[57] *Sic* (Arabic *aiḍan*) for Greek ἀεί.
[58] Arabic *wa-fī jamī' al-quwā* but this does not render Greek χρηματιστικήν.

لأنّ الاختيار إنّما يكون بالتمييز والعقل ويشبه أن يكون اسم الاختيار في لغتنا يدلّ على المؤثر شيئاً على شيء.

٣. فينبغي أن نعلم هل الروية تجب في جميع الأشياء حتّى يكون كلّ أمر من الأمور يُرَوّى فيه أو بعض الأشياء لا يروّى فيه (٢) وخليق أنّه ينبغي أن نقول إنّ الأمر الذي تقع عليه الروية ليس هو الذي يروّي فيه الغبي والمجنون لكن الذي يروّي فيه العاقل (٣) وليس نجد أحداً يستعمل الروية في الأمور الدائمة البقاء أعني في العالم والقطر والضلع أنّهما متباينان (٤) ولا يروّي أحد أيضاً في الأشياء التي في الحركة إذا كانت تكون على حل واحدة بعينها كان ذلك من الضرورة أو بالطبع أو بسبب ما آخر (٥) مثل عدم المطر وكثرته ولا في الأشياء التي بالاتّفاق بمنزلة وجود كنز (٦) ولا يروّى أيضاً في أمور الناس كلّهم فإنّه ليس أحد من أهل لاقدامونيا يروّي في الحل التي بها صار أهل سقوثيا يسيرون سيرة فاضلة لأنّ ليس شيء من هذه الأمور إلينا (٧) وإنّما نروّي فيما كان فعله إلينا ويجري على أيدينا وذلك أنّه يظنّ أنّ أسباب هذه هي الطبيعة والضرورة والاتّفاق والعقل أيضاً [٤١/١] وكلّ ما يكون بتوسّط الإنسان فكلّ واحد من الناس إنّما يروّي في الأشياء التي يمكنه أن يفعلها ويجري على يديه (٨) وليس تكون الروية في العلوم الحقيقية المكتفية بنفسها بمنزلة علم الكتابة وذلك أنّا لا نشكّ حتّى نروّي كيف ينبغي أن نكتب الحروف وإنّما نروّي فيما كان فعله إلينا ولا يكون أيضاً على حال واحدة بعينها كالحل في صناعة الطبّ وفي جميع القوى والروية في الملاحة أكثر منها في الرياضة بحسب نقصان هذه عن تلك في استقصاء الفعل (٩) وكذلك يجري الأمر في سائر الصنائع الباقية واستعمل الروية في

10 لاقدامونيا F, Dun : لاقذامونيا Bad || 11 نروي F, Dun : يروى Bad || 13 يمكنه corr. Bad : يمكن F || 14 first و F*, Dun* : أو Bad

more extensive than in the sciences, and especially where doubt occurs to us.[59] (10) Deliberation is only on what exists for the most part and it is not clear to what it tends, and on the things of which the result is not determined and defined. We seek for someone to deliberate with us on great matters, and we consult him when we are not sufficiently confident in ourselves of performing them.[60] (11) We do not deliberate on the ends of affairs but only on what leads to the ends. That is, the doctor does not deliberate as to healing nor the operator as to persuading, nor the ruler of a city as to making the laws[61] excellent, nor does any one of mankind[62] deliberate on the ends of affairs, but they posit a certain end and investigate how it may come into existence, and by what means. When it is clear that the end comes into existence by many things, they investigate that by which it comes into existence most easily and best. When the end is completed by one thing, they investigate how it comes into existence by that thing, and by what it in turn comes into existence, till they reach the first cause, which is last to be discovered, because he who deliberates is likely to investigate and analyse contrariwise[63] in the manner we have described. (12) And it is clear that not every [investigation is] deliberation, e.g. investigation of mathematics, but every deliberation is investigation. The last thing in analysis on the contrary is first in investigation, last in existence,[64] and it is the thing for the sake of which are all the remaining things. (13) If in the course of investigation they encounter something impossible, they desist from it, e.g. if there is need for money, and it is not possible to obtain it except by earning.[65] But if earning[66] is possible, they seek it. The possible things are those which are in our power to do. That is, what is in the power of our friends to do, is in our power to do in a sense, because its principle is in us. (14) The things which we investigate are sometimes the instruments by which the thing is

[59] The sense is wrong here.

[60] Arabic *fī ʿamalihā*, but Greek is διαγνῶμαι, 'distinguish' or 'decide'.

[61] *al-farāʾiḍ*, a characteristic Islamic term for 'divine precepts', 'ordinances of God'.

[62] Arabic *min an-nās* for Greek τῶν λοιπῶν does not fit quite the nuance.

[63] Arabic *bi 'l-ʿaks*, apparently for ὥσπερ διάγραμμα.

[64] 'Discovery', Arabic *al-wujūd*, which above (§§ 5, 11) and at VII, 2, 12 renders εὕρεσις. The regular word for γένεσις is *kaun* (1103a 16, 1173a 30, 1173b 4, 1174b 10, 12).

[65] The words 'except by earning' are not in the Greek.

[66] 'Earning' (*iktisāb*) is not in the Greek.

الصناعات أكثر منها في العلوم وخاصّةً فيما كان منها يقع لنا فيه الشكّ (١٠) والروية إنّما تكون فيما يوجد في أكثر الأمر وليس يبين إلى ماذا يؤول أمره وفي الأشياء التي لا تكون عاقبة أمرها محصّلة محدودة وقد نلتمس مَن يُروَى معنا في الأمور العظام ونشاوره إذا لم نثق من أنفسنا بكفاية في عملها (١١) وليس نروّي في غايات الأمور بل إنّما يروّى فيما يؤدّي إلى الغايات وذلك أنّ الطبيب ليس يروّي في أن يبرئ ولا الخطيب يروّي في أن يقنع ولا سائس المدينة يروّي في تجويد الفرائض ولا واحد من الناس يروّي في غايات الأمور لكنّهم يصنعون غاية ما ويبحثون عنها كيف تكون وبأيّ شئ وإذا تبيّن أنّ الغاية تكون بأشياء كثيرة بحثوا عن الشئ الذي به تكون أسهل وأجود وإذا كانت الغاية تتمّ بشئ واحد بحثوا عن ذلك الشئ كيف يكون وبأيّ شئ يكون هو أيضاً إلى أن ينتهوا إلى السبب الأوّل الذي هو أخير في الوجود لأنّ الذي يروّي يشبه أن يكون يبحث ويحلّل بالعكس على الجهة التي وصفنا (١٢) وقد تبيّن أنّ ليس كلّ [بحث] روية مثل البحث في التعاليم وكلّ روية بحث والشئ الأخير في التحليل بالعكس هو أوّل في البحث أخير في الوجود وهو الشئ الذي من أجله سائر الأشياء الباقية (١٣) فإن صادفوا وهم في البحث شيئاً ممتنعاً تنحّوا عنه مثل ذلك أنّه إذا أحتيج إلى المال فليس [١/٤٢] يمكن الوصول إليه إلاّ بالاكتساب فإن كان الاكتساب ممكناً التمسوه والأشياء الممكنة التي فعلها إلينا وذلك أنّ ما فعله إلى أصدقائنا ففعله إلينا بجهة من الجهات لأنّ مبدأه فينا (١٤) والأشياء التي نبحث عنها ربّما كانت الآلات التي يعمل بها الشئ وربّما كانت الحاجة إلى الآلات وكذلك

4 إنما F*, Dun* (ἀλλά) : أيضا Bad || 8 بحثوا F, Dun : بحثنا Bad || 11 بحث suppl. Dun

done, and sometimes the need[67] for the instruments. The case is similar in the remaining things, for sometimes the investigation is of the things which produced the action, and sometimes of the way in which it comes into existence.[68] (15) It is likely that man, as we have said, is a principle for his actions. Deliberation is on the things which we do, and some actions are for the sake of others.[69] (16) The end then is not included in what is deliberated on, but deliberation is merely on what leads to the end. We do not deliberate either on the
1113a particular things, e.g. on whether this thing is best[70] and whether this thing is in good condition or has been made[71] as it should. For these things are perceived by sense, and if they are deliberated on, pass to infinity. (17) The things which we deliberate on and the things chosen are one meaning, except that what is chosen is determined. That is, the thing chosen is preceded by a resolution[72] resulting from deliberation, because every man refrains from investigating how to act when he has brought back the principle to himself and what he thinks,[73] and this is the thing which chooses. (18) This is clear from the ancient constitutions which Homer imitated, i.e. he says that the kings revealed to the people the matters which they chose. (19) Since the thing chosen is that which is deliberated on with a kind of desire, being in our power to do,[74] i.e. when we have resolved on something in deliberation, we desire it by wishing.[75] (20) We have now described choice by way of outline, and we have said with what sort of thing it is concerned, and that it is among the things which lead to ends.

4. As for wish, we have already said that it is concerned with the end. Some people think that it is concerned with the good, others

[67] Arabic *al-ḥājah*, but Greek χρεία here has its other meaning, 'use'.

[68] Greek ἢ διὰ τίνος has been dropped.

[69] The Greek is simply 'actions are for the sake of other things' (ἄλλων ἕνεκα).

[70] Greek ἄρτος, 'bread', 'loaf', read as ἄριστος.

[71] Arabic *'umila* for Greek πέπεπται.

[72] This must render προκριθέν, the reading of vulg., but the construction is faulty (προκριθέν separated from τὸ γὰρ ἐκ τῆς βουλῆς and made predicate).

[73] I.e. for τὸ ἡγούμενον, "the commanding part" (Burnet), "partie dirigeante" (Gauthier).

[74] The sentence is incomplete, the important definition of choice being omitted owing to homoioteleuton (τῶν ἐφ' ἡμῖν).

[75] I.e. Greek βούλησιν, the reading of M^b. This is preferred by Gauthier as the reading of Averroes, i.e. in his Commentary on EN. We should expect that Averroes would follow the Arabic translation here and elsewhere. Vid. Introduction pp. 50ff.

يجري الأمر في الأشياء الباقية فإنّه ربّما بحث فيها عن الشئ الذي به يكون الفعل وربّما بحث فيها عن الوجه الذي به يكون (١٥) ويشبه أن يكون الإنسان كما قلنا مبدءً لأفعاله والروية تكون في الأشياء التي نفعلها والأفعال فبعضها تكون من أجل بعض (١٦) فليست الغاية إذاً ممّا يروّى فيه لكن الروية إنّما تكون فيما يؤدّي إلى الغاية ولا نروّي أيضاً في الأمور الجزئية مثل أن نروّي في أنّ هذا الشئ خير وأنّ هذا الشئ قد يصحّ أو قد عمل على ما ينبغي فإنّ هذه الأشياء إنّما تدرك بالحسّ فإن روّي فيها مرّت إلى لا نهاية (١٧) والشئ الذي نروّي فيه والشئ المختار معنى واحد إلاّ أنّ المختار محصّل وذلك أنّ الشئ المختار هو الذي تتقدّم العزيمة عليه من الروية لأنّ كلّ واحد من الناس يمسك عن أن يبحث كيف يعمل إذا ردّ المبدأ إلى نفسه وإلى ما يراه وهذا هو الشئ الذي يختار (١٨) ويتبيّن هذا من السياسات القديمة التي اقتدى بها أوميرس وذلك أنّه زعم أنّ الملوك كانوا يبوحون للعامّة بالأمور التي كانوا يختارونها (١٩) وإذا كان الشئ المختار وهو المروّى فيه مع تشوّق ما إلينا فعله وذلك أنّا إذا عزمنا على الشئ عند الروية تشوّقناه بالهوى (٢٠) فقد وصفنا الاختيار على طريق الرسم وقلنا في أيّ شئ يكون وأنّه في الأشياء التي تؤدّي إلى الغايات.

٤. فأمّا الهوى فقد قلنا إنّه يكون في الغاية وبعض الناس يظنّ أنّه في الخير وبعض يظنّ

1 الذي corr. : والذي F, Bad || 5 قد يصح F, Dun : قديم Bad || 9 يختار F, Dun : نختار Bad || 12 تشوقناه F*, Dun* (ὀρεγόμεθα) : تشوفناه Bad

that it is concerned with what is imagined to be good. (2) It necessarily follows, for those who say that the object of wish is good, that the object of wish[76] is not what the man who does not choose the right [wishes for], because if what is wished for comes to pass,[77] it is good. For it sometimes happens that what is wished for is bad. (3) As for those who say that the thing which is imagined to be good is the object of wish, it necessarily follows for them that it is not wished for naturally, but is for every man according to his opinion, and it happens that opposite things are imagined by different people at different times. (4) If these things are not convincing, we must say[78] that the good is wished for absolutely and in truth, and every man wishes for it according to his imagination, so that the good man wishes for the good which is good in truth and the bad man wishes for what he happens to, as is the case in bodies, for those who are in a condition of health distinguish the things which are truly healthy, and those who are sickly distinguish them contrarily. Thus it is also in their distinguishing things bitter and sweet, heavy and hot, and each of all the other things. For the good man judges soundly of each of these things, and the truth is imagined by him in each of them, (5) because in each of the states are noble things and pleasant things which are special to them, and the good man is apt to possess much[79] superiority over others from his seeing the truth in each of the things, of which he is as it were the standard and measure. It is likely that error in regard to that enters most people[80] on account of pleasure,
1113b because it is imagined as a good, and is not so. (6) They choose the pleasant as being good, and flee from the thing which is painful as being bad.

5. Since the end is desired and everything which leads to the end is deliberated on and chosen, the actions in that case which are concerned with the latter are with choice and are voluntary. The actions of virtue are concerned with the latter.[81] (2) Virtue is one of the things which are within our power, and similarly vice. That is, the

---

[76] Arabic *ash-shai' alladhī yuhwā*, i.e. τὸ βουλητόν in both places.

[77] Greek βουλητόν is wrongly construed as subject of ἔσται.

[78] The question (ἆρα) is apparently disregarded.

[79] Arabic *kathīr* for Greek πλεῖστον.

[80] Arabic *akthar an-nās*, i.e. Greek τοῖς πολλοῖς taken as masculine with Rackham, Gauthier and most, not as neuter (Ross). K[b] has ἐν τοῖς πολλοῖς wich was perhaps read here.

[81] I.e. the means to an end.

أنّه فيما يتخيّل أنّه خير (٢) ويلزم الذين يقولون إنّ الشيء الذي يهوى هو خير ألاّ يكون الشيء الذي يهوى الذي من لا يختار الصواب [يهويه] لأنّه إذا صار ما يهوى فهو خير فإنّه ربّما اتّفق [١/٤٣] أن يكون ما يهوى شرّاً (٣) فأمّا الذين يقولون إنّ الشيء الذي يتخيّل أنّه خير هو الشيء الذي يهوى فيلزمهم ألاّ يكون يهوى بالطبع لكنّه يكون لكلّ أحد بحسب رأيه ويتّفق أن تتخيّل الأشياء المضادّة لواحد دون واحد في وقت دون وقت (٤) فإن كانت هذه الأشياء ليست مقنعة فينبغي أن نقول إنّ الخير يهوى على الإطلاق وبالحقيقة وكلّ واحد من الناس يهواه على حسب تخيّله فالفاضل يهوى الخير الذي هو خير بالحقيقة والشرير يهوى ما يتّفق له كالحال في الأجسام فإنّ الذين هم بحال صحّة يميّزون الأشياء الصحيحة بالحقيقة والذين هم ممراضون يميّزونها بخلاف ذلك وكذلك يجري الأمر في تمييزهم للأشياء المرّة والحلوة والثقيلة والحارّة وكلّ واحد من سائر الأشياء الأخر فإنّ الفاضل يحكم على كلّ واحد من هذه الأشياء حكماً صحيحاً ويتخيّل له الحقّ في كلّ واحد منها (٥) لأنّ في كلّ واحد من الأحوال أشياء جميلة وأشياء لذيذة تخصّها وخليق أن يكون للفاضل فضل كثير على غيره ممّا يراه من الحقّ في كلّ واحد من الأشياء التي هو لها بمنزلة الدستور والقدر ويشبه أن يكون الغلط في ذلك إنّما يدخل على أكثر الناس من أجل اللذّة لأنّها تتخيّل خيراً وليست كذلك (٦) وهم يختارون اللذيذ على أنّه خير ويهربون من الشيء المؤذي على أنّه شرّ.

٥. فإذا كانت الغاية تهوى وكلّ ما يؤدّي إلى الغاية يروّى فيه ومختاراً فالأفعال إذاً التي في هذه تكون باختيار وتكون طوعاً وأفعال الفضيلة في هذه تكون (٢) والفضيلة من الأشياء

1 الذين corr. Bad : الذي F || 2 من F*, Dun* (ὁ) : قول Bad || 2 يهويه suppl. Dun || 3 الذين corr. Bad : الذي F || 7 تخيله F*, Dun* (τὸ φαινόμενον) : تحمله Bad || 10 الحارة F*, Dun* (θερμά) : الحادة Bad

things which are in our power to do are in our power not to do, and we may also say No in regard to the things in regard to which we may say Yes. (3) If the doing of good is in our power, the doing of evil is also in our power, and when the doing of good and evil deeds is in our power, similarly not to do them is within our power. This is the meaning of our being good or bad, so that it is within our power to be good or bad. (4) As for the saying that no one is wicked voluntarily, and no one is happy against his will, it seems that it is partly false, partly true. That it, no one is happy against his will, but as for wickedness, it is voluntary. (5) Otherwise we must doubt what we said just now, and not say that man is a principle or begetter of actions as he is a begetter of children. (6) Yet if these matters are clear, and we do not have the possibility of relating the actions to other principles than the things which are in our power, then anything of which the principles are in our power is in that case in our power, and is voluntary. (7) It is likely that all men individually[82] and the lawgivers themselves bear witness to these things, since they punish whoever does evil unless he has done the action perforce or through ignorance of it, not being its cause,[83] and they honour whoever does noble deeds, in order to incite these to the one and deter from the other.[84] No one encourages the doing of anything which is not in our power and is not voluntary, since there is no gain in our wishing to prevent a man's body from being hot or his feeling pain, being hungry, and being affected by something of this kind, for these things no doubt do affect us. (8) They sometimes also punish for ignorance itself whoever is thought to be the cause of it,[85] as they do with drunkards, for they double their punishment. That is, the principle of this action is in the drunkard, since it was in his power not to be
1114a drunk, and this is the cause of the ignorance. They punish also whoever is ignorant of anything in the laws which he ought to have knowledge of and is not difficult for him to understand. (9) Similarly they punish for the doing of the things the doers of which are thought to be ignorant of by their own negligence, as it was in their power not to be ignorant of them, since it was in their power to attend to them. (10) It is likely that they do not attend to them. But

[82] Arabic *khuṣūṣan*, i.e. 'in particular', but we need 'privately', 'in private life' (ἰδίᾳ).

[83] I.e. apparently of the action, but it is the cause of the ignorance which is intended by the Greek.

[84] The construction is here confused.

[85] I.e. reponsible for his ignorance.

التي هي إلينا وكذلك الخساسة وذلك أنّ الأشياء التي إلينا أن نفعلها فإلينا ألاّ نفعلها والأشياء التي فيها نقول لا فيها نقول نعم (٣) وإن كان فعل الجميل إلينا ففعل القبيح أيضاً إلينا وإذا كان فعل الأمور الجميلة والقبيحة إلينا كذلك إلينا ألاّ نفعلها وكان هذا هو معنى أن نكون خياراً أو شراراً فإلينا إذاً أن نكون خياراً أو شراراً (٤) فأمّا القول بأنّه لا يكون أحد رديئاً طوعاً ولا سعيداً كرهاً فيشبه [١/٤٤] أن يكون بعضه باطلاً وبعضه حقّاً وذلك أنّه لا يكون أحد سعيداً كرهاً فأمّا الرداءة فتكون طوعاً (٥) أو ينبغي أن نكون نشكّك فيما قلناه الآن وألاّ نقول إنّ الإنسان مبدئ ولا مولّد للأفعال كما هو مولّد للأولاد (٦) إلاّ أنّه إن تبيّنت هذه الأشياء ولم يكن لنا أن ننسبها إلى مبادئ أخر غير الأمور التي هي إلينا فما كان من الأمور مبادؤه إلينا فهو إذاً إلينا وهو ممّا يكون طوعاً (٧) ويشبه أن يكون كلّ واحد من الناس خصوصاً وواضعو النواميس أنفسهم يشهدون بهذه الأشياء إذ كانوا يعاقبون من يفعل الرداءة من لم يكن أتى ذلك الفعل قسراً أو جهل به لم يكن هو سببه ويجلّون من يفعل الأمور الجميلة ليحثّوا هؤلاء على هذا الفعل ويردعوا عن ذلك الفعل وليس أحد من الناس يحضّ على فعل شئ ممّا ليس هو إلينا ولا يكون طوعاً إذ كان لا درك في التماسنا أن نمنع إنساناً أن يسخن بدنه أو ألاّ يألم وألاّ يجوع وألاّ يناله شئ ممّا يجري هذا المجرى فإنّ هذه الأشياء تنالنا لا محالة (٨) وقد يعاقبون أيضاً على الجهل نفسه من يظنّ به أنّه سببه مثلما يفعلون بالسكارى فإنّهم يضعفون عليهم العقوبة وذلك أنّ مبدأ هذا الفعل في السكران إذ كان إليه ألاّ يسكر وهذا هو سبب الجهل ويعاقبون أيضاً من يجهل شيئاً ممّا في النواميس قد يلزمه علمه ولا يعسر عليه فهمه (٩) وكذلك يعاقبون على فعل الأشياء التي يظنّ بفاعليها أنّهم جهلوها لتوانيهم من قبل أنّ الأمر إليهم في ألاّ يجهلوها إذ كان الأمر إليهم في أن يعنوا بها (١٠) وخليق أن يكون إليهم ألاّ يعنوا بها لكنّهم إذا كانوا

6 نكون نشكك read. Bad, Dun : تكون تشكك F || 7 مبدئ ولا مولد corr. Bad : مبدءا ولا مولدا F || 10 وواضعو corr. Bad : وواضعوا F || 11 first ومن Bad : من F || 11 يجلون : ويمدحون لخصه القاضي mrg. || 14 يجوع F*, Dun* (πεινῆν) : يجزع Bad || 16 مثلما corr. Bad : مثل F || 16 يضعفون corr. appar. Dun* (διπλᾶ) : يضعون F, Bad || 18 علمه corr. Bad*, Dun* (ἐπίστασθαι) : عمله F || 19 يجهلوها F*, Dun* (ἀγνοεῖν) : يختاروها Bad || 20 يكون لانهم : يكون suppl. mrg.

when they were living[86] they were responsible for being so, as the man who does evil is for being wicked, and the man who is addicted to drinking wine and the like is responsible for being self-indulgent, because the actions in everything make the agents such as they are. (11) That is clear from practice and application in any direction or action, because they addict themselves to the action. (12) As for ignorance that states of character come to a man in consequence of his action in each individual thing, it is the mark of a senseless person. (13) Also it is unreasonable that the wicked man should not wish to be wicked, and the self-indulgent should not wish to be self-indulgent. If not, a man becomes wicked in ignorance of the actions which he does, and becomes wicked by them.[87] (14) Also he does not cease from wickedness when he wishes to become just,[88] nor does the sick man either become healthy if he wishes it. If this turns out to be so, then he who is not attentive to a regimen and does not accept advice from the doctors when ill, is ill only voluntarily, because it was possible for him at that time not to be ill, only he did not choose[89] that, just as the man who throws a stone cannot recall it, although it was in his power to take it and throw it, because the principle of that was in his power. Similarly in the case of the wicked man and the self-indulgent man, for it was in their power originally not to be so. Therefore the wicked man becomes wicked voluntarily and the self-indulgent man self-indulgent, but when they have become so, it is not possible for them not to be. (15) It is not only the vices of the soul that are voluntary, but in some people the vices of the body are also voluntary. They are those whom we rebuke and blame, for there is no one who blames a man ugly by nature, but he only is blamed who is so through negligence[90] and neglect. Similarly in the case of disease and ugliness[91] and being crippled. For no one reproaches a man blind by nature or because of disease or a blow—rather one pities him—but as for the man who has been overtaken by blindness through excessive drinking of wine or some other form of self-indulgence, all censure him. (16) Thus the possessor of those

---

[86] A word corresponding to the Greek ἀνειμένως, 'carelessly', has dropped out.

[87] The Arabic, separating μή and ἀγνοῶν, which go closely together, and disregarding ἑκών, fails to render the Greek.

[88] I.e. Greek καὶ ἔσται δίκαιος is made dependent on βούληται.

[89] Greek προεμένῳ is rendered badly, οὐκέτι as a simple negative.

[90] Arabic *tawānin*, hardly with the force of ἀγυμνασίαν, "lack of exercise" (Ross).

[91] Arabic *wal-qabḥ*. This is the reading of L^b and Γ (καὶ αἶσχος), wanting in the other MSS. and mondern texts.

أحياءً كانوا أسباباً ليكونوا كذلك كما قد يكون من يفعل الشرّ ليكون ظالماً ومن يدمن شرب الخمر وما أشبهه سبباً ليكون شرهاً لأنّ الأفعل في كلّ واحد من الأشياء تجعل الفاعلين بهذه الحل (١١) وذلك بيّن من التدرّب والمواظبة على أيّ جهات كان أو فعل لأنّهم يدمنون الفعل (١٢) فأمّا الجهل بأنّ الحالات إنّما تصير للإنسان من قبل فعله في واحد واحد من الأشياء فإنّه من شأن من لا [١/٤٥] حسّ له (١٣) وأيضاً ممّا هو خارج عن القياس أن يكون الظالم لا يهوى أن يكون ظالماً والشره لا يهوى أن يكون شرهاً وإلاّ صار الإنسان ظالماً وهو جاهل بالأفعل التي يفعلها فيصير بها ظالماً (١٤) ولا يكفّ أيضاً عن الظلم إذا هوى أن يصير عدلاً ولا العليل أيضاً يصير صحيحاً إن هوى ذلك وإن اتّفق أن يكون هذا هكذا فالذي لا يتحفّظ في تدبير ولا يقبل من الأطبّاء إذا اعتلّ فإنّما يعتلّ طوعاً لأنّه قد كان يمكنه في ذلك الوقت ألاّ يعتلّ إلاّ أنّه لم يختر ذلك كما أنّ من رمى حجراً لم يمكنه أن يردّه إليه وإن كان إليه أن يأخذه ويرمي به لأنّ مبدأ ذلك إليه وكذلك الحل في الظالم والشره فإنّ الأمر إليهما بدءً في أن لا يكونا كذلك فكذلك يصير الظالم ظالماً طوعاً والشره شرهاً فأمّا إذا صارا كذلك فليس يمكنهما ألاّ يكونا (١٥) وليس شرور النفس فقط تكون طوعاً لكن في بعض الناس قد تكون شرور البدن أيضاً طوعاً وهم الذين نزجرهم ونعنّفهم فإنّه ليس يوجد أحد من الناس يعنّف من هو قبيح بالطبع بل إنّما يعنّف من هو كذلك لتوان وإهمل وكذلك الحل في المرض والقبح والزمانة فإنّ أحداً ليس يعيّر أعمى بالطبع أو بسبب مرض أو ضربة بل يرحمه فأمّا من ناله العمى من كثرة شرب الشراب أو غيره من أصناف الشره فكلّ أحد يعذله (١٦) فشرور البدن إذاً ما كان منها إلينا

---

12 يكونا F : يكون Bad || 15 قبيح F*, Dun* (αἰσχροῖς) : سمح Bad || 18 أصناف F, Dun : أسباب Bad

vices of the body which are in our power, is blamed, while the possessor of those which are not in our power is not blamed. If the matter is so, then in all other cases, to practise the vices for which the possessor is blamed, is in our power. (17) If anyone says that all men strive towards what is imagined by them as good, as regards the
1114b imagination it is not in their power, but each of them imagines the end in accordance with his condition. Now if every man is in a certain sense cause of his condition, he also is in a certain sense cause of his imagination, and if no man[92] is cause of the doing of evil deeds, but only does them through his ignorance of the end, and therefore[93] thinks that the best thing is therein,[94] the striving towards the end is not voluntary, but he must have it by nature, as he has sight by which he distinguishes well, and he may choose the authentic good. The man in whom this quality exists as it ought is the excellent, the clear-sighted by nature, and the greatest[95] thing which a man cannot take from another or learn, but which exists for him according as it was imprinted in him to the highest degree of excellence, is the excellence of the perfect, authentic nature. But if this is true, virtue is no more voluntary than vice. (18) That is, the end exists for the good and the bad man alike, either by nature or as it is laid down and appears, and all the remaining things which they do in whatever way are related to these. (19) Whether the end is not a certain existent which belongs to every man by nature, but something else,[96] or the end is by nature, and the good man does all the things voluntarily, virtue is voluntary, and vice also is voluntary no less, since the possibility exists for the bad man to be concerned with actions and with the end himself.[97] (20) If the virtues, as is said, are voluntary because we are in a certain way causes of states, and because we make the end by the state in which we are, the vices then are voluntary just as are the virtues. (21) We have now described the question of the virtues generally, and have mentioned their genus by way of outline. We have said that they are means, that they are states, that they are productive of the things from which they come into existence by themselves, that they are in our power to do, and

---

[92] I.e. εἰ δὲ μηδείς of L^b, M^b, Γ, rather than εἰ δὲ μή, οὐθείς of vulg.
[93] Arabic *li-dhālika* for Greek διὰ τούτων.
[94] Apparently for Greek ἑαυτῷ (αὑτῷ) read as ἐν ἀυτῷ.
[95] Arabic omits καὶ κάλλιστον.
[96] Rendering παρ' αὑτόν.
[97] Arabic *fī 'l-ghāyah bi-nafsihi*. This is evidently for ἐν τῷ τέλει (καὶ εἰ μή is omitted) together with τὸ δι' αὑτόν [*sic*].

فقد يعذل صاحبها وما كان منها ليس إلينا فليس يعذل صاحبه وإن كان الأمر كذلك ففي سائر الأشياء الأخر للشرور التي يعذل صاحبها عليها فعلها إلينا (١٧) فإن قال قائل إنّ الناس كلّهم يتوقون إلى ما يتخيّل لهم أنّه خير فأمّا التخيّل فليس هو إليهم لكن كلّ واحد منهم يتخيّل له الغاية على حسب حاله فإن كان كلّ واحد من الناس هو بجهة من الجهات سبباً لحاله فهو أيضاً يكون بجهة من الجهات سبباً لتخيّله وإن لم يكن أحد من الناس سبباً لفعل الشرور لكنّه إنّما يفعله لجهله بالغاية ولذلك يظنّ أنّ الأمر الأفضل في ذلك كان التوقان إلى الغاية ليس هو بإرادة [١/٤٦] لكنّه يحتاج إلى أن يكون له بالطبع مثل ما له البصر الذي به يميّز تمييزاً جيّداً فقد يختار الخير الحقيقي والذي يوجد هذا المعنى فيه على ما ينبغي هو الجيّد الذكي بالطبع والشيء الأعظم الذي لا يمكن أن يأخذه الإنسان من غيره ولا يتعلّمه لكنّه يوجد له بحسب ما طبع عليه بالغاً في الجودة هو جودة الطبع التامّ الحقيقي فإذا كان هذا حقّاً فليس تكون الفضيلة طوعاً أكثر من الرذيلة (١٨) وذلك أنّ الغاية توجد للخير والشرّ جميعاً على مثال واحد إمّا بالطبع أو كيف وضعت وظهرت وسائر الأشياء الباقية التي يفعلونها على أيّ وجه كان إلى هذه ينسب (١٩) فإن لم تكن الغاية كائناً ما كانت لكلّ واحد من الناس بالطبع بل بشيء غيره أو إن كانت الغاية بالطبع وكان الفاضل يفعل سائر الأشياء الأخر طوعاً فالفضيلة تكون طوعاً والرذيلة أيضاً تكون طوعاً ليس بدونها إذ كان قد يوجد للشرّ أيضاً أنّه في الأفعال وفي الغاية بنفسه (٢٠) فإن كانت الفضائل كما يقال تكون طوعاً لأنّا أسباب للحالات بجهة من الجهات ولأنّا نجعل الغاية بالحال التي نحن عليها فالرذائل إذاً تكون طوعاً مثلما تكون الفضائل (٢١) فقد وصفنا أمر الفضائل وصفاً عامّياً وذكرنا جنسها على طريق الرسم فقلنا إنّها توسّطات وإنّها حالات وإنّها فعّالة للأشياء التي عنها تكون بذاتها وإنّ فعلها إلينا وإنّها تكون طوعاً وكما يجب

6 بالغاية F : الغاية Bad || 9 هو corr. Bad, Dun : و F || 13 ينسب corr. : تسب F, Bad || 14 أو Bad*, Dun* (εἴτε) : و F || 15 first طوعا F*, Dun* (ἑκουσίως) : طبعا Bad || 19 علميا : عاميا corr. mrg.* (κοινῇ)

that they are voluntary and as right discrimination[98] necessitates. (22) Actions are not voluntary in the same way as states. That is, we are masters of and have power over actions from first to last through our knowing the particulars. But as for states, we have power over
1115a the beginning of them, but the addition of their particulars is not known, as is the case with diseases, but since the matter is within our power as to our not employing them in this state,[99] it is therefore voluntary. (23) So let us resume and describe each one, saying what it is and with what kind of things it deals and how, and at the same time it should become plain how many they are. Let us speak first of courage.

6. We say: We have already described courage in what has preceded, and have said that it is a mean between fear and rashness.[100] It is plain that we fear alarming things, and these in general are evils. (2) For that reason they have defined fear and said that it is anticipation of evil. (3) Thus all evils are feared, e.g. disgrace, poverty, disease, lack of friends and death, but it is not thought that in respect of all these a man is courageous. That is, he should fear some of them, the fear of which is noble while not fear them is base, e.g. disgrace. For the man who fears it and is on his guard against it is modest, and the man who does not fear it and guard against it is shameless. People call him courageous by way of homonymy,[101] because there is something in him which resembles what is in the courageous man, i.e. the courageous man does not fear. (4) As for poverty, it is likely that we should not fear it, nor disease, nor anything at all which does not result from evil and is not through the fault of the possessor. But he who does not fear these is not courageous, yet we call him courageous by way of similitude. That is, some people are cowardly in wars and at the same time are related to boldness, bold in spending their money.[102] (5) No one who fears disgrace for his children or his

---

[98] Arabic *at-tamyīz aṣ-ṣaḥīḥ*, Greek ὁ ὀρθὸς λόγος. This is 'right reason' or "the right rule" (Ross), not regarded by the translator, however, as practically a technical term, cf. 1103b 32 where he renders it differently: [*at-*] *tamyīz* [*aṣ-*] *ṣawāb*, also *al-qaul aṣ-ṣaḥīḥ*, 1147b3 (*al-qaul al-ʿadl*, 1147b 31); *al-qiyās aṣ-ṣaḥīḥ*, 1151a 12.

[99] 'Them' referring to the particulars (*juzʾīyāt*). Greek οὕτως ἤ is unaccounted for in the Arabic.

[100] But Greek is περὶ φόβους καὶ θάρρη.

[101] Arabic *al-ishtirāk fī 'l-ism*, rendering Greek κατὰ μεταφοράν.

[102] This renders χρημάτων ἀποβολήν, 'loss of money', inexactly.

التمييز الصحيح (٢٢) وليس تكون الأفعل طوعاً على مثل كون الحالات وذلك أنّا مستولون قادرون على الأفعل من أوّل الأمر إلى آخره لعلمنا بالجزئيات فأمّا الحالات فنحن قادرون على أوائلها فأمّا جزئياتها فتزيّدها غير معروف كالحل في الأمراض ولكنّه لمّا كان الأمر إلينا في ألاّ نستعملها على هذه الحل صار لذلك يكون طوعاً (٢٣) فلنعد ونصف كلّ واحدة ما هي وفي أيّ الأشياء هي وكيف هي وقد نبيّن مع ذلك كم هي فنتكلّم أوّلاً في الشجاعة.

٦. فنقول قد وصفنا الشجاعة فيما تقدّم وقلنا إنّها توسّط فيما [١/٤٧] بين الخوف والتقحّم ومن البيّن أنّا نخاف من الأمور المفزعة وهذه بالجملة هي الشرور (٢) ولذلك حدّوا الخوف فقالوا إنّه توقّع شرّ (٣) فقد نتخوّف إذاً جميع الشرور مثل الدناءة والفقر والمرض وعدم الأصدقاء والموت ولكنّه ليس يظنّ أنّ في هذه كلّها يكون الإنسان شجاعاً وذلك أنّه قد ينبغي أن يخاف من بعضها والخوف منه جميل وترك الخوف منه قبيح مثل الدناءة فإنّ من يخافها ويتّقيها حيي ومن لا يخافها ويتّقيها وقح وقد يسمّيه قوم شجاعاً على طريق الاشتراك في الاسم لأنّ فيه شيئاً يشبه ما في الشجاع وذلك أنّ الشجاع لا يخاف (٤) فأمّا الفقر فخليق أن يكون لا ينبغي أن يخاف منه ولا من مرض ولا من شئ أصلاً ممّا لا يحدث عن الشرّ ولا يعيّنه صاحبه ولكنّه ليس من لا يخاف من هذه هو شجاع ولكنّا نسمّيه شجاعاً على طريق التشبيه وذلك أنّ بعض الناس يكون جباناً في الحروب وهو مع ذلك ينسب إلى الجرأة جرئ على إخراج ماله عن يده (٥) وليس من خاف من العار في ولده أو

11 يخاف F, Dun : نخاف Bad || 14 يخاف F : نخاف Bad || 15 يعينه corr. mrg., Bad : يعيبه F || 17 الجرأة F, Dun : الجرأة لأنه suppl. Bad || 17 ماله F*, Dun* (χρημάτων) : ما له Bad

friends[103] or anything of this kind is a coward, nor is he who stands up to flogging courageous. (6) In which of the alarming things then must we say that man is courageous? In the greatest of them,[104] for there is no one more enduring than he of terrifying things. The most terrifying of the things which are feared is death, because it is a termination, and the dead man is not thought to be affected afterwards by either good or evil. (7) It would be thought that the courageous man is not he who does not fear every death, like death at sea or in sicknesses, (8) but he does not fear death[105] in the noblest circumstances, which is death in battle. That is, this death is in the greatest and most excellent contest.[106] (9) People have agreed[107] that death with kings[108] brings honour and glory to him who endures it. (10) The man is truly called courageous who does not dread a noble death nor the circumstances which do not avoid death[109] when they
1115b are near him.[110] These specially occur in war. (11) The courageous man is not he who does not fear this death only, but he who does not dread death on the sea and in diseases, except that his state is not like that of sailors in this regard. That is, the courageous man may despair of safety and find this kind of death painful, while the sailors estimate safety by their long experience. (12) A man is also at the same time courageous who has firmness, or neither of the two kinds of this death in such destruction is noble.[111]

7. The alarming circumstance is not the same for every man, because[112] there is something which is above human nature. This kind is what every intelligent man is afraid of. As for the things which are

---

[103] The Arabic translator substitutes 'friends' for 'wife' (γυναῖκα), and omits ἢ φθόνον.

[104] The question with ἤ is apparently disregarded here and below, § 8 (ἢ ἐν τοῖς καλλίστοις).

[105] Greek ἐν τίσιν οὖν is not rendered, and the further question with ἤ is disregarded, as apparently also in § 6 above.

[106] The Arabic is *jihād*, a remarkable translation of Greek κινδύνῳ, 'danger'.

[107] Greek ὁμόλογοι δὲ τούτοις is wrongly translated. The whole sentence then goes awry, and several words are omitted (ἐν ταῖς πόλεσι καί).

[108] This phrase (*al-maut maʿa al-mulūk*) is not in the Greek.

[109] Or 'which involve death', reading *taḥtamilu* for *lā tajtanibu* of the MS., cf. Greek ἐπιφέρει.

[110] Arabic *idhā qaribat minhu*, a defensible rendering of ὑπόγυια ὄντα, cf. Burnet *in loco*.

[111] The last clause is badly misunderstood (by construing καλὸν τὸ ἀποθανεῖν with ὑπάρχει).

[112] Arabic *li'anna*, apparently a slip.

أصدقائه أو في شيء ممّا أشبه هذه هو جبان ولا من أقام على ضرب السياط بجرأة هو شجاع (٦) ففي أيّ شيء من المفزعات ينبغي أن نقول إنّ الإنسان يكون شجاعاً في أعظمها لأنّه لا يوجد أحد أصبر منه على الأمور الهائلة وأهول الأشياء التي تخوّف الموت لأنّه نهاية وليس يظنّ أنّ الميّت يناله فيما بعد شيء من الخير أو من الشرّ (٧) وقد يظنّ أنّ الشجاع ليس هو الذي لا يخاف من كلّ موت بمنزلة الموت في البحر أو في الأمراض (٨) لكنّه لا يخاف من الموت الذي يكون في الأمور الجميلة جدّاً وهو الموت في الحرب وذلك أنّ هذا الموت إنّما يكون في أعظم الجهاد وأجوده (٩) وقد أجمع الناس في أنّ الموت مع الملوك على تعظيم وإجلال مَن صبر عليه (١٠) وإنّما يقال بالحقيقة شجاع للإنسان الذي لا يتهيّب الموت الجميل ولا الأمور التي لا تجتنب الموت إذا قربت منه وهذه خاصّةً هي تكون في الحرب (١١) وليس الشجاع [١/٤٨] هو الذي لا يتهيّب هذا الموت فقط لكن الذي لا يتهيّب الموت في البحر وفي الأمراض إلاّ أنّ حاله في ذلك ليس كحال البحريين وذلك أنّ الشجاع يكون قد يئس من السلامة ويصعب عليه مثل هذا الموت والبحريون يقدّرون السلامة بطول التجربة (١٢) وقد يشجع مع ذلك أيضاً من له جلد أو يكون ولا واحد من صنفي هذا الموت في مثل هذا الفساد جميلاً.

٧. والأمر المفزع ليس هو عند كلّ إنسان أمراً واحداً بعينه لأنّ ها هنا شيئاً فوق طبيعة الإنسان فهذا الصنف قد يفزع منه كلّ عاقل فأمّا الأشياء التي لا تفوق طبيعة الإنسان فقد

11 الذي corr. Bad : والتي F || 13 مع ذلك F, Dun : om. Bad

not above human nature, they differ in magnitude and in more and less, and similarly the circumstances in which rashness is displayed.[113] (2) The heart of the courageous man does not faint so that he is not dismayed like others, except that he is afraid of terrifying things as he ought to be, and as intelligence necessitates, and he endures[114] for the sake of what is noble, for this is the end and aim of virtue. (3) We sometimes are afraid of these things more or less, and sometimes also we are afraid of things which are not alarming, like the man who is afraid of these,[115] (4) except that error therein occurs either when the fear is of what he should not be afraid of, or[116] when it is as it should not be, or when it is where it should not be, or the like, and the case is similar in regard to the things in which rashness is displayed.[117] (5) He who endures the things which he ought to endure and for the sake of the thing for which he ought to endure them, and fears them as he ought,[118] and at the time when he ought, and likewise plunges into them,[119] is the courageous man. That is, the courageous man is he who acts and is acted upon as situation[120] and discrimination necessitate. (6) The end of every action is that which is according to the situation, and courage is to the courageous man a noble thing, and similarly also his end. That is, each is defined by his end. The courageous man then endures for the sake of the noble, and does what courage necessitates. (7) As for the man who exceeds courage, as regards absence of fear he has no name in our language—we have already said in what preceded that many things have no names—, except that the man who fears nothing at all, not earthquake nor waves, is a madman, feeling no pain, as is related of the people called Celts. As for the man who exceeds in bravery in face of alarming things, he is rash. (8) It is thought of the rash man that he is a boaster and simulator of courage, because he wishes it to appear that he is brave in face of alarming things, like

---

[113] This does not well translate Greek τὰ θαρραλέα; we need a reference to confidence here, not rashness (cf. § 9).

[114] Arabic *yaṣbiru*, perhaps for Greek ὑπομενεῖ <τε>, the reading of Susemihl and Gauthier.

[115] Evidently a mistranslation, with τοιαῦτα taken = ταῦτα, as elsewhere.

[116] I.e. emending Arabic *wa-idhā* to *wa-immā idhā*. The Arabic translator may have read ἤ for ἥ (ἡ) in 1115b 15-16, but Rackham translated: "Error arises either from fearing [...] or [...] or [...]", with ἥ (ἡ) in his text in each case.

[117] As above, § 1, lit. 'which are entered upon rashly'.

[118] I.e. construing φοβούμενος separately from ὑπομένων.

[119] For Greek ὁμοίως δὲ καὶ θαρρῶν.

[120] Arabic *al-ḥāl*, i.e. κατ' ἀξίαν was read as καθ' ἕξιν.

تختلف بالعظم والكثرة والقلّة وكذلك الأمور التي يتقحّم عليها (٢) والشجاع لا يخيب قلبه فيتحيّر مثل غيره من الناس إلاّ أنّه يفزع من الأشياء الهائلة كما ينبغي وكما يوجبه العقل ويصبر من أجل الجميل فإنّ هذا هو غاية الفضيلة وقصدها (٣) وقد نفزع من هذه الأشياء أكثر وأقلّ وقد نفزع أيضاً من أشياء ليست بمفزعة كمن يفزع من هذه (٤) إلاّ أنّ الخطأ في ذلك يكون إمّا إذا كان الفزع ممّا لا ينبغي أن يفزع منه و [إمّا] إذا كان كما لا ينبغي أو إذا كان حيث لا ينبغي أو ما جرى هذا المجرى وكذلك الأمر في الأشياء التي يتقحّم عليها (٥) فالذي يصبر على الأشياء التي ينبغي أن يصبر عليها ومن أجل الشئ الذي ينبغي أن يصبر عليها له ويفزع منها كما ينبغي وفي الوقت الذي ينبغي وكذلك يتقحّم عليها هو الشجاع وذلك أنّ الشجاع هو الذي يفعل وينفعل على ما تؤدّيه الحال والتمييز (٦) وغاية كلّ فعل هي التي تكون بحسب الحال والشجاعة للشجاع أمر جميل وكذلك غايته أيضاً وذلك أنّ كلّ واحد إنّما يحدّ بغايته فالشجاع إذاً إنّما يصبر من أمر الجميل وإنّما يفعل ما توجبه الشجاعة (٧) فأمّا الزائد في الشجاعة أمّا في عدم الخوف فلا اسم له في لغتنا وقد قلنا فيما تقدّم إنّ أشياء كثيرة لا أسماء لها إلاّ أنّ من لا يخاف شيئاً بتّةً لا زلزلة ولا أمواجاً فهو مجنون لا يحسّ بألم كما [١/٤٩] يحكى عن القوم الذين يسمّون الكلتيين فأمّا الذي يزيد في الحرب على الأشياء المفزعة فمتقحّم (٨) وقد يظنّ بالمتقحّم [أنّه] مطرمذ مراء بالشجاعة لأنّه يريد أن يظهر أنّه جرئ على الأمور المفزعة مثل الشجاع

1 يخيب F, Dun : ينخب Bad || 4 إلا أن corr. mrg., Bad, Dun : الان F || 5 إما suppl. Dun || 8 يصبر read. Bad*, Dun* (ὑπομένων) : يصير F || 11 بغايته F, Dun : بغاية Bad || 11 يصبر F*, Dun* (ὑπομένει) : يصير Bad || 12 first في F : على Bad || 15 الكلتيين above line || 16 أنه suppl. Bad

the courageous man, and he resembles him in whatever he can. (9) Therefore most of them are found 'cowardly-foolhardy'.[121] That is, he embarks rashly upon matters and does not endure the alarming of them. (10) As for the man whose fear is exaggerated, he is a coward. It is characteristic of him[122] that he is afraid of what he ought not to be afraid of, and as he ought not to be, and everything like this.
1116a He is defective also in bravery, and when he is excessively distressed, his case therein is more apparent. (11) The coward then has little confidence and is not readily confident, because he fears everything. The courageous man is his opposite, because rashness is found only in the man who abounds in confidence and is readily confident. (12) The coward, the rash man and the courageous man are concerned with these things, but they are different in regard to them. The rash man is excessive in regard to them, the coward is defective, while the courageous man is intermediate in regard to them, doing them as he ought. The rash man is impetuous, purposing to enter into alarming affairs, but when he is in the middle of them, he turns away from them. When the courageous man is involved in actions he is assiduous and quick in regard to them, and before that he is calm. (13) Thus courage, as we said above, is a mean in regard to what is between[123] terrifying things and things in which bravery is displayed. They are the things among which we said[124] that the courageous man chooses the noble, and which he endures and thinks that the contrary is base. As for the choice of death to escape poverty or love or some affliction or other, it is not the part of the courageous man but rather the part of the coward. That is, to fly from the things which are painful and injurious is base.[125] The courageous man does not endure them because they are a noble matter, but he flies from evils.

8. What is like this is courage. Now courage is the name given to other kinds, five in number.

(a) The first is civic courage, because it is likely that it is the kind which is most characteristic of man.[126] That is, the people of the cities are thought to endure dangers because of what the laws enjoin in

[121] Arabic *jabānan mutahawwiran*, Greek θρασύδειλοι.
[122] Arabic *yalzamuhu*, i.e. Greek ἀκολουθεῖ αὐτῷ construed with ἃ μὴ δεῖ.
[123] Or simply 'a mean between', which is not quite what the Greek says.
[124] I.e. Greek ἐν οἷς εἴρηται construed with what follows.
[125] Arabic *yaqbuḥu*, rendering μαλακία.
[126] But Greek μάλιστα γὰρ ἔοικεν, 'for it is most like', sc. true courage. On the other hand, the Latin Averroes has "videtur nam magis proprius homini", as here.

فيشبه به في أيّ شئ أمكنه (٩) ولذلك يوجد أكثرهم جباناً متهوّراً وذلك أنّه يتقحّم على الأمور ولا يصبر على الهائلة منها (١٠) فأمّا المفرط في الخوف فجبان ويلزمه أن يكون يفزع ممّا لا ينبغي أن يفزع منه وكما لا ينبغي وجميع الأشياء التي تجري هذا المجرى وهو ناقص أيضاً في الجرأة ولمّا كان زائداً في الغموم صار أمره فيها أبين (١١) فالجبان إذاً قليل الثقة عسرها لأنّه يخاف من كلّ شئ والشجاع ضدّه لأنّ التقحّم إنّما يوجد لمن هو كثير الثقة سهلها (١٢) الجبان والمتقحّم والشجاع في هذه الأشياء يوجدون وهم فيها مختلفون فالمتقحّم زائد فيها والجبان ناقص والشجاع متوسّط فيها يفعلها كما ينبغي والمتقحّم مقدام يهمّ بالدخول في الأمور الهائلة فإذا كاد يتورّطها تنحّى عنها والشجاع إذا تورّط الأفعل كان جلداً سريعاً فيها وقبل ذلك يكون ساكناً (١٣) فالشجاعة كما قلنا إنّما توسّط فيما بين الأمور المفزعة والأمور التي يتجرّأ عليها وهي التي قلنا إنّ الشجاع يختار فيها الجميل ويصبر عليها ويرى أنّ خلاف ذلك قبيح فأمّا اختيار الموت هرباً من الفقر أو من العشق أو من إثم ما فليس هو من شأن الشجاعة بل الأولى أن يكون من شأن الجبان وذلك أنّ الهرب من الأشياء التي تؤلم وتؤذي يقبح وليس يصبر الشجاع عليها لأنّها أمر جميل لكنّه يهرب من الشرور.

٨. فما جرى هذا المجرى هو الشجاعة وقد تقل الشجاعة على أصناف أخر غير هذه وهي خمسة:

الأولى المدنية لأنّه يشبه أن تكون أخصّها وذلك أنّ أهل المدن يرون أن يصبروا على الشدائد من أجل ما تأمر به النواميس من العقوبات والهوان والكرامات ولذلك يظنّ بهم

1 فيشبه : F فيتشبه Bad || 4 ناقص أيضا في الجرأة corr. Bad* (δειλός) : ناقص أيضا في الحية F || 4 الغموم F, Dun : الفزع Bad* (φοβεῖσθαι) || 7 Second فيها Bad, Dun : illegible F || 8 تنحى F, Dun : تخلى Bad || 9 إنما Bad, Dun : illegible F || 9 توسط F, Dun : متوسط Bad || 10 يتجرأ F, Dun : نتجرأ Bad || 17 أخصها : بالانسان أظنه ينقص وكذا لخصه القاضي mrg. || 18 الشدائد Bad, Dun : illegible F

way of penalties and disgrace and honours. Therefore they seem to be the most courageous people, since[127] cowards obtain disgrace and the courageous obtain honour, (2) as Homer represented Diomede and Hector, and said:

> Polydamas will be the first to speak and blame me,[128]

then Diomede:

> For Hector will declare that among the Trojans.[129]

(3) This courage is like the courage which we described first, because it is for the sake of virtue, since it is on account of shame and desire for the noble, which together are honour, and the avoiding of disgrace, since it is base. (4) At the same time, one might place in this class those whom the chiefs force and compel to do something. The basest of them[130] is the man who[131] does what he does, when forced to, through fear, not shame, or to avoid something hurtful, not what is base. That is, the lords compel their followers, as Hector did when he said:

> The man whom I see fleeing from the battle
> I shall not be sufficed[132] except by making him food for dogs and birds.[133]

1116b (5) Those who order the striking of the man who flees from the battle do the same, and those who do what they do before the tombs[134] and the like, for all these compel people to act. The brave man must do what he does, not because he is forced to, but because he sees that the action in question is noble.

(6) (b) It is thought also that experience in everything is courage, and therefore Socrates thought that courage is knowledge. Different

---

[127] The sense has been missed.

[128] Cf. Homer, *Iliad*, XXII, 100.

[129] Cf. Homer, *Iliad*, VIII, 148. The following half-line of poetry has been left out.

[130] I.e. superlative for comparative (χείρους).

[131] Apparently for Greek ὅσοι, the reading of K^b (singular for plural, as often).

[132] Rendering ἄρκιον.

[133] 'And birds', the translator's addition, but it may have stood in his text, cf. Homer, *Iliad* II, 393. It is also in the Latin Averroes.

[134] An obvious mistake: τάφρων, 'ditches, trenches', being read as τάφων, 'tombs'. The translator has also failed to give any significant meaning for παρατάττοντες.

أنّهم أشجع الناس من قبل أنّ أهل الجبن ذوو هوان وأهل الشجاعة ذوو كرامة (٢) كما جعل [١/٥٠] أميروش ديوميدس وأقطر فقل:

بولودامس أوّل من يبكّتني ويعذلني

ثم ديوميدس:

وذلك أنّ أقطر يخطب بذلك في الأطروس

(٣) وهذه الشجاعة تشبه الشجاعة التي وصفناها أوّلاً لأنّها إنّما تكون من أجل الفضيلة إذ كانت إنّما هي بسبب الحياء والشهوة للجميل اللذان هما الكرامة والهرب من العار إذ كان قبيحاً (٤) ولجاعل أن يجعل الذين يضطرّهم الرؤساء ويجبرونهم على أن يفعلوا شيئاً في هذه المرتبة وأخسّهم من يفعل ما يفعله إذ أجبر خوفاً لا حياء أو هرباً من الشئ المؤذي لا القبيح وذلك أنّ السلاة قد يجبرون أتباعهم كما فعل أقطر حين قل:

فمن كنت أراه يهرب من الحرب
ما كنت أقنع إلاّ أن أجعله مأكلة للكلاب والطيور

(٥) والذين يأمرون بضرب من يهرب من الحرب يفعلون هذا الفعل بعينه والذين يفعلون ما يفعلونه أمام القبور وما أشبه ذلك فإنّ هؤلاء كلّهم يجبرون الناس على الفعل وينبغي أن يكون الشجاع يفعل ما يفعله لا لأنّه يضطرّ ولكن لأنّه يرى أنّ ذلك الفعل جميل.

(٦) وقد يظنّ أيضاً بالحنكة في كلّ واحد من الأشياء أنّها شجاعة ولذلك ظنّ سقراط أنّ

2 أميروش : F اميروس Bad || 2 ديوميدس read. Bad : w.p. F || 2 أقطر corr. Bad* ("Εκτορα) : اقطن F || 3 يبكتني corr. Bad*, Dun* (μοι ἐλεγχείην ἀναθήσει) : يبكى F || 3 بولودامس read. Bad : w.p. F || 4 ديوميدس read. Bad : w.p. F || 7 الذان corr. : الذين F || 8 قبيحا : الصحيح وليس على هذا النحو لخصه القاضي ويظهر أنه mrg. || 8 لجاعل corr. Bad : لجاعلي F || 9 أخسهم corr. mrg.*, Bad* (χείρους) : اخصهم F || 10 اتباعهم corr. Bad : تباعهم F || 10 أقطر corr. Bad* ("Εκτωρ) : اقطن F || 14 القبور : أي أمام الموت فمن تشجع خوفا من أن يموت إذا لم يشجع فليس بشجاع كذا لخصه القاضي ويعني أمام القبور أي أمام الحالة التي تؤدي إلى القبور mrg.

people are found in this state in different things. The army[135] is found so in wars, because it is thought that in war are many strange[136] happenings which these understand specially, so that they are seen to be[137] courageous people, by reason of what it is possible for them to do in war, so that they are confident that there will not affect them what others do not know. (7) It is possible for them specially by their abundant skill to guard against anything befalling them, and they [...] their enemies by their power to employ arms, since they are in a position in which it is possible for them to cause an effect without being affected themselves. (8) They are like armed men fighting people without arms, and champions[138] fighting inexperienced people. That is, in contests like this the champion in war is not the most courageous,[139] but the strongest and the man the form of whose body is an excellent form. (9) As for the army, they act cowardly when the contest is long and overwhelms them,[140] and their numbers and equipment are defective, because they are the first to fly, while the people of the cities[141] endure death.[142] That is, they think that flight is base, and that death is preferable to salvation from it. As for men experienced in wars, they at first contend on account of their superiority. But when they know the incidence of death, they fly, since they fear death more than they fear dishonour. (10) The courageous man is not so.

(c) People sometimes relate anger to courage. That is, they think that anyone doing a thing through anger is courageous, like wild animals which leap at whoever angers[143] them, because the courageous man is also angry. That is, anger wells up naturally in time of conflict,[144] and for that reason Homer said that 'he made strong his

---

[135] Arabic *al-jund* renders οἱ στρατιῶται.

[136] Arabic *badīʿah*, which renders καινά (K^b, M^b) not κενά. Cf. κενώτεροι for κοινότεροι, at 1107a 30 = II, 7, 1.

[137] Or 'seem to be', Arabic *yurauna*.

[138] Arabic *qaum mubarrizīn*, Greek ἀθληταί.

[139] The sense is again missed.

[140] Arabic *ṭāla al-jihād wa-ghamarahum*.

[141] Arabic *ahl al-mudun* for Greek τὰ πολιτικά, here 'citizen troops'.

[142] The words 'as happened at the temple of Hermes' are omitted.

[143] Arabic *yughḍibuhā*, but Greek τοὺς τρώσαντας is 'those who have wounded (them)'.

[144] Arabic *al-ghaḍab yahīju bi'ṭ-ṭabʿ fī waqt al-mujāhadah*. This fails to render the Greek ἰτητικώτατον γὰρ [...].

الشجاعة علم وقد يوجد إنسان دون إنسان في شئ دون شئ بهذه الحال فالجند يوجدون كذلك في الحروب لأنه قد يظنّ أنّ في الحرب أشياء كثيرة بديعة يقف عليها هؤلاء خاصّةً فيرون أنّهم من أهل الشجاعة لمّا يمكنهم أن يفعلوه في الحرب فيتوقّفوا ألاّ يصيبهم ما لا يعلمه غيرهم (٧) وقد يمكنهم بكثرة الحيلة خاصّةً أن يتحفّظوا من أن يصيبهم شئ وهم [...] في أعدائهم بقدرتهم على استعمل السلاح لأنّهم بحل يتهيّأ لهم بها أن يؤثروا ولا يؤثّر فيهم (٨) فهم بمنزلة قوم متسلّحين يقاتلون قوماً بدون سلاح وقوم مبرّزين يقاتلون قوماً أغماراً وذلك أنّ في أمثل هذا الجهد ليس المبرّز في الحرب هو الأشجع لكن الأقوى والذي هيئة بدنه هيئة فاضلة (٩) فأمّا الجند فقد يخيسون إذا طل الجهد وغمرهم ونقص مددهم وعدتهم لأنّهم أوّل من يهرب فأمّا أهل المدن فيثبتون على الموت وذلك أنّهم يرون أنّ الهرب قبيح وأنّ [١/٥١] الموت آثر من السلامة منه فأمّا المحنكون من الحروب فإنّهم في أوّل الأمر يجاهدون لما فيهم من الفضل فإذا علموا بوقوع الموت هربوا إذ كانوا يخافون الموت أكثر ممّا يخافون الأمر القبيح (١٠) والشجاع فليس كذلك وقد ينسبون الغضب إلى الشجاعة وذلك أنّهم يظنّون أنّ الذي يفعل شيئاً للغضب هو شجاع بمنزلة السباع التي تثب على من يغضبها ولأنّ الشجاع أيضاً غضوب وذلك أنّ الغضب يهيج بالطبع في وقت المجاهدة ولذلك قل أوميروش إنّه قوّى غضبه وإنّه هيج منه

2 لأنه Bad, Dun : illegible F || 3 فيتوقفوا F, Bad, Dun : فيتوثقوا corr. mrg. || 4 وهم Dun : illegible F || 5 لأنهم Bad, Dun : partly illegible F || 6 بدون سلاح corr. Dun* (ἀνόπλοις) : بالسلاح F || 6 مبرزين F : مبرزون corr. mrg. || 7 وذلك : على ما في النص ويشبه أن يكون في النص نقص كما قد يكون المبرز في الحرب الأقوى والذي هيئة بدنه هيئة فاضلة كذا لخص القاضي هذا الفصل وفيه زيادة وذلك أن في أمثال هذا ليس المبرز في الحرب هو الأشجع لكن الذي هو أعلم بصناعة الحرب بدنه mrg. || 8 Bad, Dun : illegible F || 8 يخيسون corr. mrg. : يجبنون F || 13 للغضب F*, Dun* (θυμόν) : للمغضب Bad || 15 منه F, Dun : من Bad

anger',[145] that 'the strength of his anger welled up'[146] and that 'his blood boiled',[147] for all these things point to the welling up and raging of anger. (11) The courageous man then does what he does for the sake of the noble, and anger helps him towards his action. Wild animals act on account of pain, I mean, on account of a blow or fear, because if they are in a forest or thicket[148] they do not come forth. Thus they are not courageous, since it is simply pain and anger that stir them up to fight,[149] without their having come forward and seen anything alarming. Were it not for that, when hungry they[150] would
1117a be like courageous people, when struck not turning aside from prey.[151] And lovers dare alarming deeds because of desire.[152] (12) It[153] is more likely to be natural than due to anger, and when there is added to it [...] and when men are angry [...]

(14) (d) [...] endurance of the things which frighten people and appear to them so, is characteristic of the courageous man, because it is noble, or because to leave it is base. (15) Therefore the courageous man is thought to be unafraid and calm at the occurrence of sudden fear, rather he is more courageous[154] than at the occurrence of what is clear and apparent to him before he falls into it. That is, this belongs to the courageous man more and less[155] in consequence of his state of character, not in consequence of preparation. For a man thinks of the things which are clear and apparent, and he distinguishes them and chooses them, but the things which occur suddenly are according to the state of character.

---

[145] Homer, *Iliad*, XIV, 151 or XVI, 529.

[146] Homer, *Iliad*, V, 470. Greek 'δριμὺ δ' ἀνὰ ῥῖνας μένος' (Homer, *Odyssey*, XXIV, 318) has not been rendered, or has fallen out.

[147] Theocritus, XX, 15.

[148] Arabic *au ajamah*, i.e. Greek ἢ ἐν ἕλει, the vulg. reading. Modern edd. bracket.

[149] Arabic *jihād* for Greek κίνδυνον.

[150] Omitting the subject, οἱ ὄνοι, 'asses'.

[151] The translator is still thinking of wild beasts and mistranslates νομῆς (= pasture).

[152] Here the words οὐ δή ἐστιν ἀνδρεῖα [...] πρὸς τὸν κίνδυνον are omitted in the Arabic translation (with K^b).

[153] I.e. this kind of courage, but the translator spoils the sense by rendering ἢ διὰ τὸν θυμόν for ἡ διὰ τὸν θυμόν.

[154] The Arabic translation contrasts two states of the courageous man, not two men, one of whom is more courageous.

[155] The construction is wrong, and the contrast is not fully brought out. See previous note.

قوّة الغضب وإنّ دمه غلى فإنّ هذه الأشياء كلّها تدلّ على هيجان الغضب وثورانه (١١) فالشجاع يفعل ما يفعله للجميل والغضب يعينه على فعله والسباع تفعل من أجل الأذى أعني من أجل ضرب أو خوف لأنّها إن كانت في غيضة أو أجمة لم تخرج فليست إذاً شجاعة إذ كان إنّما يثيرها إلى الجهاد الوجع والغضب من غير أن تكون تقدّمت فرأت شيئاً من الأمور الهائلة ولو لا ذلك لكانت ستكون إذا جاعت بمنزلة أهل الشجاعة إذا ضربت لا تنتحي عن الفريسة والعشّاق قد يجسرون على الأمور الهائلة بسبب الشهوة (١٢) وهي بأن تكون طبيعية أشبه من أن تكون بسبب الغضب وإذا انضاف إليها [...] والناس إذا غضبوا [...]

(١٤) [...] [١/٥٢] الصبر على الأمور التي تفزع الناس وتظهر لهم كذلك فمن شأن الشجاع لأنّه جميل أو لأنّ تركه قبيح (١٥) ولذلك يظنّ بالشجاع أنّه يكون عند الفزع الذي يفاجئه غير فزع ولا قلق بل يكون أشجع منه عند الذي يتبيّنه ويظهر له قبل وقوعه فيه وذلك أنّ هذا إنّما يكون في الشجاع أكثر وأقلّ من قبل الهيئة لا من قبل الاستعداد فإنّ الأشياء التي تتبيّن وتظهر قد يفكّر الإنسان فيها ويميّزها فيختارها فأمّا الأشياء المفاجئة فإنّما تكون على قدر الهيئة.

12 الاستعداد F*, Dun* (παρασκευῆς) : الاستعداء Bad || 13 تتبين F : تبين Bad

(16) (e) One imagines in regard to the man who is ignorant of the frightening thing that he is courageous, and he is not far from the eager man but is inferior to the latter, since the eager man has an established principle according to which he works,[156] and the other has not. Therefore he abides for a time. As for those who go out to war through deception, when they know or suspect that those against whom they are making war are different from those whom they intended to make war against, they fly, as did the Greeks[157] when they got into a battle with the nation called Laconians under the impression that they were the nation called Sicyonians.[158] (17) We have now described the nature of true courage, and those to whom courage is imputed, showing who they are.

9. Courage is found in frightening matters and where confidence is shown, except that it is not concerned with both in the same way [...] is in frightening things [...] confused in these [...]

10. (10) [...][159] the gourmand that his neck might be as long as a
1118b crane's, since he delighted in its touch. The commonest of the senses is the sense which is in greediness. And it is thought truly that this sense is a disgrace to us, since it is not ours in respect of our being men but in respect of our being animals. (11) The inclination of things of this kind and violent love for them are indeed characteristic of the brutes. Of the pleasures which are by touch we must allow[160] those which are most worthy of free men, and they are those which are produced in gymnastic exercises through rubbing and heating. That is, the touch in which the greedy man delights is not in all his body, but is only in some of its members.

11. It is thought of the desires that some are general and others particular.[161] For example, the desire for food is natural, because everyone whose body needs it desires food, wet or dry, and sometimes desires them both. The young and vigorous, as Homer said, desire

---

[156] Rendering Greek ἀξίωμα, 'self-confidence'.

[157] Arabic *al-Yūnānīyūn*. It is remarkable that the translator so renders Greek οἱ Ἀργεῖοι. Does this point to a knowledge of Homer (as of Hesiod above, I, 4, 7) with whom Ἀργεῖοι is a common name for the Greeks?

[158] Arabic *Sfūnywā*, suggesting a Syriac original for the form.

[159] More than two folios illegible.

[160] Arabic *nasūghu*, or reading *tasūghu*, 'permissible should be, will be those [...]'.

[161] Greek καὶ ἐπίθετοι, 'and adventitious', is omitted in the translation.

(١٦) وقد يتخيّل من أمر الجاهل بالشيء المفزع أنّه شجاع وليس هو ببعيد من الطمع إلاّ أنّه أخسّ منه من قبل أنّ الطمع له أصل موضوع يعمل عليه وذلك ليس له ولذلك يلبث زماناً فأمّا الذين يخرجون إلى الحرب بالخديعة فإنّهم إذا علموا أو توهّموا أنّ الذين يحاربونهم غير الذين قصدوا لمحاربتهم هربوا كما فعل اليونانيون لمّا وقعوا في حرب الأمّة التي يقل لها اللاقونس على أنّها الأمّة التي يقل لها سفونيوا (١٧) فقد وصفنا أمر الشجاعة الحقيقية والذين يظنّ بهم الشجاعة أيّ الناس هم.

٩. والشجاعة توجد في الأمور المفزعة وفيما يتجرّأ عليه إلاّ أنّها ليست فيهما على مثل واحد [...] يكون في الأمور المفزعة [...] لا يضطرب في هذه [...]

١٠. [...] [١/٥٥] الطبيخ أن يكون حلقه بطول حلق الكركي من قبل أنّه يلتذّ بلمسه وأعمّ الحواسّ هي الحاسّة التي بها يكون الشره ونحن ما نظنّ أنّ هذه الحاسّة عار علينا من قبل أنّها ليست لنا من جهة ما نحن ناس لكنّها من جهة ما نحن حيوان (١١) فالميل إلى مثل هذه الأشياء وشدّة المحبّة لها إنّما هو من شأن السباع وينبغي أن نسوغ من اللذّات التي تكون باللمس أليقها بالأحرار وهي التي تحدث في الرياضات من الدلك والتسخين وذلك أنّ مسّ الذي يستلذّه الشره ليس يكون في جميع بدنه لكن إنّما يكون في بعض أعضائه.

١١. وقد يظنّ بالشهوات أنّ منها ما هو عامّ ومنها ما هو خاصّ مثل شهوة الغذاء فإنّها طبيعية لأنّ كلّ من بدنه محتاج يشتهي غذاء رطباً أو يابساً وربّما اشتهاهما جميعاً والحدث والشابّ كما قل أوميروش يشتهي معهما المضجع فأمّا الشهوة لغذاء دون غذاء أو لأغذية

2 يلبث Bad, Dun : illegible F || 3 زمانا : ولذلك لا يلبث زمانا ما أعني لجهله كذا لخصه القاضي mrg. || 5 سقونيوا read. Bad || 5 سفونيوا Dun : partly w.p. F, سقونيوا read. Bad || 5 اللاقونس F, Dun : اللاقونيين Bad || 9 بلمسه corr. Bad : لامسه F || 9 أعم F*, Dun* (κοινοτάτη) : اهم Bad || 12 نسوغ Dun : ننوع F; ننزع Bad || 13 تحدث Bad, Dun : illegible F

love in addition. As for the desire for one food rather than another, or for the same foods, it is not present to everyone whose body requires food. (2) Therefore the desire for these things turns out to be within our power. They are not merely within our power simply, but in them is something natural. That is, men differ in respect of what they delight in, and some delight in one thing, some in another, and there are people who delight in one thing more than others.[162] (3) In the natural desires it is seldom that anyone makes an error, and when an error occurs in regard to them, it is mostly[163] in a single thing. That is, he who eats and drinks whatever he happens to[164] till he is surfeited passes the natural amount in quantity. Natural desire is simply a filling up of what is contrary to[165] defect. Therefore these men are called 'possessors of bellies',[166] because they fill their bellies more than they need to, and in this condition slaves[167] are found. (4) As for the special pleasures, many people go wrong in regard to them, in many ways of error. That is, the greedy ones, of those[168] who love the like of the things which we have mentioned, either because they enjoy what they ought not to enjoy, or through their making use of that more than they ought, or[169] through their making use of these pleasures as do the multitude, or as they ought not, go to excess in all these things. That is, some people[170] enjoy things they ought not to enjoy because they are such as ought to be hated, and if there are any of these things that they ought to enjoy, they employ that in what is more than due measure and as the common people employ them. (5) It is clear that greed is an excess in regard to pleasures and that it is blamed. As for pain, a man is not called temperate in regard to it on account of his enduring it and bearing it, as is said in the case of courage, nor is he called greedy because he does not endure it. But a man is called greedy from his being pained more than he ought if he has not got something that he delights in,

---

[162] Here the translator has failed to understand the sense of τῶν τυχόντων, which he translates correctly below, cf. n. 164.

[163] Arabic *akthar dhālika*, but the corresponding Greek (ἐπὶ τὸ πλεῖον) means 'towards, in the direction of, excess'.

[164] Greek τὰ τυχόντα is now translated quite correctly.

[165] The addition (*mā yukhālif*) does not help the sense.

[166] Arabic *aṣḥāb al-buṭūn*, a weak translation of Greek γαστρίμαργοι.

[167] Greek 'extremely slavish people' (οἱ λίαν ἀνδραποδώδεις).

[168] The construction of οἱ ἀκόλαστοι with τῶν φιλοτοιούτων λεγομένων as subject is quite wrong.

[169] But ἤ here is 'than' (μᾶλλον ἤ).

[170] Apparently ἐνίοι for ἐνίοις of the Greek text.

واحدة بعينها فليست تكون لكلّ من احتاج بدنه إلى غذاء (٢) ولذلك صارت الشهوة لهذه الأشياء إلينا وليس إنّما هي إلينا فقط بل فيها شئ طبيعي وذلك أنّ الناس يختلفون فيما يلتذّونه فبعضهم يلتذّ شيئاً وبعضهم يلتذّ غيره وقوم يلتذّون شيئاً أكثر ممّا يلتذّه غيرهم (٣) وفي الشهوات الطبيعية قلّ من يخطئ وإذا وقع الخطأ فيها فإنّما يقع في شئ واحد أكثر ذلك وذلك أنّ الذي يأكل ويشرب ما اتّفق به حتّى أن يفرط في التحلّي فإنّما يتجاوز الأمر الطبيعي بالكثرة والشهوة الطبيعية إنّما هي تملّؤ ما ممّا يخالف النقصان ولذلك يقل لهؤلاء أصحاب بطون لأنّهم يملأون بطونهم أكثر ممّا يحتاجون إليه وبهذه الحل يوجد العبيد (٤) فأمّا اللذّات الخاصّية فإنّ الكثير من الناس يخطئون فيها بأنحاء كثيرة من الخطأ وذلك أنّ الشرهين ممّن يحبّ أمثال هذه التي ذكرنا إمّا لأنّهم يسرّون بما لا يجب أن يسرّوا به وإمّا لاستعمالهم ذلك بأكثر ممّا ينبغي وإمّا لاستعمالهم إيّاها كاستعمل العامّة أو على غير ما ينبغي يفرطون في جميع هذه الأشياء وذلك أنّ بعض الناس يسرّ بأشياء لا يجب أن يسرّ بها لأنّها ممّا يجب أن يبغض فإن [١/٥٦] كانت أشياء من هذه ينبغي أن يسرّ بها استعمل ذلك فيها أكثر من المقدار وكما تستعملها العامّة (٥) فقد بان أنّ الشره إفراط في اللذّات وأنّه مذموم وأمّا الأذى فليس يقل للإنسان فيه عفيفاً لصبره عليه واحتماله له كما يقل في الشجاعة ولا شرهاً لأنّه لا يصبر عليه لكن الإنسان يسمّى شرهاً من قبل أنّه يتأذّى

---

1 فليست corr. : فليس F, Bad || 12 يسر بها F*, Dun* (χαίρειν) : تستعمل Bad || 14 عفيفا F, Dun : عفيف Bad

and the pleasure causes him pain. He is called temperate through his
1119a not being grieved at the loss of the pleasant thing. (6) The greedy man desires all pleasant things and the best of them. His subjection to desire goes so far that he chooses pleasant things above everything else, and for that reason is grieved if he does not get them when he desires them.[171] That is, desire is accompanied by pain, but to suffer pain for the sake of what is pleasant seems absurd. (7) Scarcely any man would be defective in respect of pleasures to the point that he would enjoy them less than he ought, because this kind of insensibility is not characteristic of mankind. That is, all the other animals distinguish the kinds of food and take pleasure in some and in some not. If any one existed who found nothing whatever pleasant, and pleasant things in his opinion did not differ, he would be far from being a man, and for this reason he has not received a name, since he scarcely exists. (8) As for the temperate man, he is intermediate in these things. That is, he does not take pleasure in what the greedy man takes pleasure in particularly,[172] but is annoyed. He by no means takes pleasure in what he ought not to take pleasure in, nor is his pleasure intense in anything of this. He is not grieved when he loses pleasant things, nor does he desire, except in a moderate degree. He does not desire more than he ought, nor at a time when he ought not, nor, in general, does he desire any such thing. As for the things which bring health and a temperate condition, being pleasant, he desires them in a moderate degree and as he ought, and all the other pleasant things when they do not interfere with these, either because they are outside what is noble, or because[173] they are above our nature.[174] That is, the man who is in this state loves these pleasures more than they deserve. As for the temperate man, this is not his state, but he desires in accordance with what right reason necessitates.

12. Greed is liker to what is voluntary than cowardice, because the former exists because of pleasure, the latter because of pain, and

---

[171] Arabic *wa-huwa yashtahīhā*, i.e. Greek καὶ ἐπιθυμῶν, but the somewhat artificial paradox has been missed. (He suffers pain καὶ ἀποτυγχάνων καὶ ἐπιθυμῶν, i.e. both when he fails to obtain pleasures and when he desires them.)

[172] Arabic *khāṣṣatan* for Greek μάλιστα. So for μᾶλλον at 1111b 6.

[173] 'Either because [...] or because [...].' These clauses should not be made subordinate to 'interfere with these', and we should have 'or are outside [...] or above [...]'.

[174] Arabic *jauhar* for Greek οὐσίαν.

أكثر ممّا ينبغي إن لم ينل ما يلتذّه واللذّة تحدث له أذى ويسمّى عفيفاً من طريق أنّه لا يغتمّ لفقد الشئ اللذيذ (٦) فالشره يشتهي جميع الأشياء اللذيذة وأفضلها ويبلغ من انقياده للشهوة أنّه يختار الأشياء اللذيذة على كلّ شئ ولذلك يغتمّ إذا لم ينلها وهو يشتهيها وذلك أنّ الشهوة تكون مع الأذى والتأذّى بسبب اللذيذ كأنّه محل (٧) وليس يكاد أن يكون إنسان ناقصاً في اللذّات حتّى يسرّ بها أقلّ ممّا ينبغي لأنّ هذا الصنف من عدم الحسّ ليس هو من شأن الناس وذلك أنّ سائر الحيوانات الباقية قد تميّز أنواع الطعم فتسرّ ببعضها وببعضها لا فإن وجد أحد ليس شئ من الأشياء عنده لذيذاً ولا تختلف الأشياء اللذيذة عنده فهو بعيد من أن يكون إنساناً ولم نصب لهذا اسماً من قبل أنّه لا يكاد يكون (٨) فأمّا العفيف فمتوسّط في هذه الأشياء وذلك أنّه ليس يلتذّ بما يلتذّ به الشره خاصّةً لكنّه يمتعض ولا يلتذّ البتّةَ بما لا ينبغي أن يلتذّ به ولا تشتدّ لذّته بشئ من هذا ولا يغتمّ إذا فقد الأشياء اللذيذة ولا يشتهي إلاّ بمقدار معتدل ولا يشتهي أكثر ممّا ينبغي ولا في الوقت الذي لا ينبغي ولا يشتهي بالجملة شيئاً من هذه فأمّا الأشياء التي تجلب الصحّة واعتدال الهيئة وهي لذيذة فإنّه يشتهيها بمقدار معتدل وكما ينبغي وسائر الأمور اللذيذة الأخر إذا لم تعتّم هذه إمّا لأنّها خارجة عن الجميل أو لأنّها تفوق جوهرنا وذلك أنّه من كان بهذه الحل فإنّه يحبّ هذه اللذّات أكثر من استحقاقها فأمّا العفيف فليست هذه حاله لكنّه يشتهي على حسب ما يوجب التمييز الصحيح.

١٢. والشره أشبه بما يكون طوعاً من الجبن لأنّ ذلك يكون بسبب اللذّة [١/٥٧] وهذا

1 يسمى Bad, Dun : illegible F || 4 مع F : من corr. above line || 7 وجد F, Dun : واجد Bad || 14 هذه : المعنى يفهم بنحوه أو وبه القاضي لخصه كذا صح فيتركها الأخر اللذات سائر وأما mrg.

pleasure is preferred while pain is avoided. (2) Pain alters and spoils the nature of its subject while pleasure does nothing of the kind, and thus it[175] should rather be voluntary. For that reason disgrace attaches to the man more in consequence of it.[176] That is, our becoming accustomed to it[177] is easy because the pleasurable things in the world are many, and in becoming accustomed to them there is no difficulty.[178] In regard to frightening things the situation is the reverse. (3) It is sometimes thought that cowardice is not to be avoided[179] in the way that the individual frightening things are, because cowardice is without pain, and frightening things oblige the man to whom they occur, on account of the pain, even to throw away his arms involuntarily, and to commit other disgraceful acts. It is thought of them that they are involuntary. (4) What occurs to the greedy man is the reverse of that, I mean that the individual cases of the things which he takes pleasure in are voluntary, because he desires and longs for them, but their totality is less so. That is, there is no one who desires to be greedy. (5) We also apply the term greed to the fault in chil-
1119b dren, because there is some similarity between them. As for considering which took the name from the other, we have no need[180] for it here, yet it is evident that the last took its name from the first.[181] (6) It seems to be not a bad thing that it should be transferred from this, for whoever longs for disgraceful things and desires them increasingly must be curbed, and what is of this type especially is desire and childhood. That is, children especially simply live by desire, for the longing for what is pleasant is in them especially. If the child is not submissive to what disciplines him, he goes to extremes in pursuit of pleasures. (7) That is, the longing of those without intelligence for what is pleasant is not to be satisfied in any way, and the action of desire enhances what is akin to it. If the desires are great and violent, they alter thinking.[182] Therefore they should be with measure and few, and should not oppose reason. (8) The man who is in this state is called disciplined and chastened, and just as the child's desire should be according to what the instructor directs, so

---

175 As the feminine forms show, the references are (incorrectly) to pleasure (*ladhdhah*, feminine) rather than to greed (*sharah*, masculine).

176 The reference is still to pleasure (but Greek αὐτά).

177 See previous note.

178 Arabic *laisa fīhi ṣuʿūbah* for Greek ἀκίνδυνοι.

179 I.e. reading φευκτόν (K^b, L^b, M^b) instead of ἑκούσιον.

180 Arabic *laisa binā ilaihi ḥājah* for Greek οὐθὲν [...] διαφέρει.

181 I.e. the word was first applied to spoiled children.

182 Arabic *ghaiyarat al-fikr* for Greek τὸν λογισμὸν ἐκκρούουσιν, cf. 1154a 27.

بسبب الأذى واللذّة مأثورة والأذى يهرب منه (٢) والأذى يغيّر ويفسد طبيعة صاحبه واللذّة ليست تفعل شيئاً من هذا فهي أحرى أن تكون طوعاً ولذلك صار العار يلزمه من قبلها أكثر وذلك أنّ اعتيادنا إيّاها سهل لأنّ الأمور الملتذّة في العالم كثيرة واعتيادها فليس فيه صعوبة فأمّا الأمور المفزعة فالحال فيها بالعكس (٣) وقد يظنّ أنّ الجبن ليس يهرب منه على مثل ما يهرب من الأشياء الجزئية المفزعة لأنّ الجبن لا أذى فيه والأشياء المفزعة تجبر من تعرض له بسبب الأذى حتّى إنّه يلقي سلاحه قسراً ويرتكب سائر الأمور القبيحة ويظنّ بها أنّها تكون قسراً (٤) والذي يعرض للشره عكس ذلك أعني أنّ الجزئيات من الأشياء التي يلتذّها تكون طوعاً لأنّه يشتهيها ويشتاقها وأمّا جملتها فدونها في ذلك وذلك أنّه ليس يوجد أحد يشتهي أن يكون شرهاً (٥) ونحن نحمل اسم الشره على الخطأ الذي يكون من الصبيان لأنّ بينهم تشابهاً ما فأمّا الوقوف على أيّهما أخذ له الاسم من الآخر فليس بنا إليه حاجة فيما نحن بسبيله إلاّ أنّه من البيّن أنّ الأخير أخذ له الاسم من الأوّل (٦) ويشبه أن يكون ليس برديء أن ينتقل عن هذا فإنّه قد ينبغي أن نقنع من يتوق إلى الأمور القبيحة ويشتهيها ويتزيّد في ذلك والذي يجري هذا المجرى خاصّةً الشهوة والصبا وذلك أنّ الصبيان إنّما يعيشون بالشهوة خاصّةً فإنّ التوقان إلى الشيء اللذيذ في هؤلاء يكون خاصّةً فإن لم يكن الصبي منقاداً لما يؤدبه أمعن في طلب اللذّات (٧) وذلك أنّ التوقان إلى الشيء اللذيذ لا يشبع منه من كلّ جهة من لا عقل له وفعل الشهوة ينمي ما جانسها وإن كانت الشهوات عظيمة شديدة غيّرت الفكر فلذلك ينبغي أن تكون بقدر وتكون قليلة وألاّ تضادّ التمييز (٨) فإنّ من كان بهذا الحال سمّي منقاداً مقوّماً وكما أنّ الصبي ينبغي أن تكون شهوته بحسب ما يأمره المؤدّب كذلك الجزء الشهواني ينبغي أن يكون بحسب ما يوجبه

4 الجبن F, Dun : om. Bad || 5 الجبن F, Dun : الخير Bad || 16 منه F, Dun : به Bad || 18 مقوما : كذا لخصه القاضي متأدبا mrg.

the appetitive part should be according to what reason necessitates. Therefore the appetitive part of the temperate man must be in agreement with reason, for the aim of both is what is noble, and the temperate man desires what he should desire, as he should, and at the time that he should, and so also reason orders these things. This is what we needed to say about temperance.

End of the Third Discourse of the Ethics of Aristotle, and praise be to God and peace upon His servants whom He has chosen.

التمييز ولذلك ينبغي أن يكون الجزء الشهواني [١/٥٨] من العفيف موافقاً للتمييز فإنّ غرض كليهما الجميل فالعفيف يشتهي ما ينبغي أن يشتهي وكما ينبغي وفي الوقت الذي ينبغي وكذلك أيضاً يرتّب التمييز هذه الأشياء فهذا ما كان ينبغي لنا أن نقوله في العفّة.

آخر المقالة الثالثة من الأخلاق لأرسطو والحمد لله وسلّم على عباده الذين اصطفى.

1 من F, (Dun) : في Bad || 2 يشتهي F : يطلب Bad

BOOK IV

In the name of God, the Merciful, the Compassionate
God bless Muhammad and his family and give them peace

The Fourth Discourse of the Book of Ethics of Aristotle

1. He said: We must follow what we have said with a description of liberality. We say: It is thought to be a mean in regard to wealth. That is, liberality is not praised in matters of war, nor in the matters in regard to which a man is temperate, nor in juridical decisions, but in giving and taking with respect to wealth, and preferably in giving. (2) I mean by wealth everything which is estimated by *dīnārs* and *dirhams*. (3) Prodigality and meanness are[1] an excess over the mean and a defect of it, in respect of wealth. We constantly connect meanness with those who give attention to amassing wealth more than they ought. Sometimes we connect prodigality with them,[2] because we call people absorbed in desires and those who spend their wealth in pleasures prodigal. (4) Therefore we think of them as worse than others,[3] because they have many vices at one time. (5) Therefore this name is [not][4] suitable for them, because it is characteristic of the
1120a prodigal that he has a single vice, I mean, wasting his substance. That is, the prodigal is he who destroys himself by his own hand, because it may be thought that wasting one's substance is self-destruction, since one's life is fulfilled by means of one's substance. This is the sense of prodigality. (6) The things which are needed are those which we employ[5] for good and bad uses, and riches are one of the useful things. He who has virtue in respect of each one of the things is he who employs each of them in the best way. He who has virtue in respect of wealth is he who employs riches in the best way. This is the liberal man. (7) It is known that the use of wealth is spending and giving. As for amassing wealth and saving it, it is its

[1] I.e. respectively.
[2] 'With them'. This apparently represents the Greek word συμπλέκοντες, which is otherwise untranslated.
[3] Arabic *ardā* [sic] *min ghairihim* for Greek superlative φαυλότατοι.
[4] 'Not' has to be supplied, Greek οὐ has apparently been read as οὗ.
[5] The sense of ἔστι here ('it is possible') is disregarded.

المقالة الرابعة

بسم الله الرحمن الرحيم

صلّى الله على محمّد وعلى آله وسلّم

المقالة الرابعة من كتاب الأخلاق لأرسطو

١. قل ينبغي أن نتبع ما قلناه بصفة السخاء فنقول إنّه قد يظنّ به أنّه توسّط في الأموال وذلك أنّ السخاء ليس يحمد في أمور الحرب ولا في الأمور التي فيها يكون الإنسان عفيفاً ولا في الأحكام لكن في الإعطاء والأخذ في الأموال والأولى أن يكون في الإعطاء (٢) وأعني بالأموال كلّ ما يقوم بالدينار والدرهم (٣) والتبذير والتقتير زيادة على التوسّط ونقصان عنه في الأموال ونحن نلزم أبداً التقتير الذين يعنون بجمع الأموال أكثر ممّا ينبغي وربّما ألزمناهم التبذير لأنّا نسمّي المنهمكين في الشهوات والذين ينفقون أموالهم في اللذّات مبذورين (٤) ولذلك يظنّ بهم أنّهم أردأ من غيرهم لأنّ معهم شروراً كثيرة معاً (٥) فلذلك [لا] يليق بهم هذا الاسم لأنّ من شأن المبذّر أن يكون معه شرّ واحد أعني إتلاف ماله وذلك أنّ المبذّر هو الذي يهلك نفسه بيده لأنّه قد يظنّ أنّ تلف ماله هلاك نفسه من قبل أنّ عيشه إنّما يتمّ بماله فعلى هذه الجهة يكون التبذير (٦) والأشياء التي يحتاج إليها هي التي نستعملها استعمالاً جيّداً واستعمالاً رديئاً والغنى من الأمور النافعة والذي معه فضيلة في كلّ واحد من الأشياء هو الذي يستعمل كلّ واحد من الأشياء على أفضل ما يكون والذي معه فضيلة في الأموال هو الذي يستعمل الغنى على أفضل ما [٥٩/١] يكون وهذا هو السخي (٧) وقد يعلم أنّ استعمل المل هو النفقة والإعطاء فأمّا جمع

9 التبذير mrg. : وأما التبذير فإنما ننسبه إلى المنهمكين في الشهوات والذين ينفقون أموالهم في اللذات لأن أمثال هؤلاء هم الذين يسمون مبذرين كذا لخصه القاضي وهو خلاف ما ثبت في هذه النسخة والمعنى الصحيح هو الذي يثبت في التلخيص || 9 والذين F*, Dun* (καί) : الذين Bad || 11 لا suppl. Dun || 11 [لا] mrg. : لا كذا لخصه القاضي || 14 النافعة F*, Dun* (χρῆσθαι) : الناجعة Bad

acquisition. Therefore it becomes characteristic of the liberal man that he gives to those to whom he ought to give rather than takes from where he ought to and does not take from where he ought not to. For it is characteristic of virtue that by it a man does good to others rather than has not good done to him,[6] and that by it he does the noble action rather than avoids doing the base. (8) It is obvious that doing good and kindness follow giving, and that a man's accepting good from another and not acting basely follow acceptance of the favour.[7] And gratitude is for the giver, not [for] him who does [not] take, and praise also is more for him. (9) To abstain from taking is easier than giving, because men's giving what is theirs is more difficult than their omitting[8] to take what is not theirs. (10) The liberal are those who give. As for those who do [not][9] take, they are not praised for their being liberal, yet they are not below the liberal in employing justice. As for those who take, they are not much praised. (11) The liberal are much loved, because they are very useful through their giving. (12) The actions of virtue are noble and are done on account of the noble,[10] and to do them is right, because they are done to the person to whom they should be done, and in the right measure, at the right time and with all the things which follow right giving, (13) while he[11] does them with pleasure and without pain, because the pleasant with virtue[12] is either painless or its pain is slight.[13] (14) As for him who gives to whom he ought not and not for the sake of the noble but for another cause, he is not liberal, but is called by another name, nor is he who gives with pain liberal either. That is, he prefers wealth to noble action, and this is not characteristic of the liberal man. (15) Neither does the liberal man take from where he ought not, i.e. taking is not characteristic of the man who does not honour wealth, (16) nor does he ask from anyone, because it is not easy for the generous man who confers benefits to accept a kindness from anyone. (17) He will take from where he should take,

[6] But the Greek means 'rather than has good done to him'.

[7] Lit. 'the taking and the favour'.

[8] Arabic *tarkihim*, apparently rendering Greek οὐ.

[9] 'Not' has to be supplied (Greek οἱ δὲ μὴ λαμβάνοντες).

[10] Eight words are omitted by homoioteleuton (καὶ ὁ ἐλευθέριος οὖν δώσει τοῦ καλοῦ ἕνεκα).

[11] I.e. the liberal man, who has been mentioned in the words omitted (see previous note).

[12] The translator has misconstructed the words τὸ [...] κατ' ἀρετὴν ἡδύ as a single phrase.

[13] 'Or its pain is slight'. These words do not translate ἥκιστα δὲ λυπηρόν.

المل وحفظه فهو اقتناؤه ولذلك صار من شأن السخي أن يعطي لمن ينبغي أن يعطي أكثر من أن يأخذ من حيث ينبغي وألاّ يأخذ من حيث لا ينبغي فإنّ من شأن الفضيلة أن يكون الإنسان بها يحسن إلى غيره أكثر من أن يكون لا يحسن إليه وأن يكون بها يفعل الجميل أكثر من أن يكون لا يفعل القبيح (٨) وممّا لا يخفى أنّ الإحسان والمعروف يتبعان الإعطاء وأنّ قبول الإنسان الإحسان من غيره وألاّ يفعل القبيح يتبعان الأخذ والمنّة والشكر إنّما هو للمعطي لا للذي [لا] يأخذ والحمد أيضاً له أكثر (٩) والامتناع من الأخذ أسهل من الإعطاء لأنّ إعطاءهم ما لهم أصعب من تركهم أخذ ما ليس لهم (١٠) والأسخياء إنّما هم الذين يعطون فأمّا الذين [لا] يأخذون فليس يحمدون على أنّهم أسخياء إلاّ أنّهم ليسوا بدون الأسخياء في استعمل العدل فأمّا الذين يأخذون فليس يحمدون جدّاً (١١) والاسخياء يحبّون جدّاً لأنّهم نفّاعون في بذلهم (١٢) وأفعل الفضيلة جميلة وبسبب الجميل تفعل وفعلها صواب لأنّها إنّما تفعل لمن ينبغي أن تفعل به وبالمقدار الذي ينبغي وفي الوقت الذي ينبغي وفي جميع الأشياء التي تتبع البذل الصحيح (١٣) وعلى أن يفعلها باستلذاذ وغير تأذٍ لأنّ اللذيذ بالفضيلة هو إمّا ألاّ يكون معه أذى أو يكون أذاه يسيراً (١٤) فأمّا الذي يعطي لمن لا ينبغي ولغير الجميل بل لسبب آخر فليس هو سخياً لكنّه يسمّى باسم آخر ولا الذي يعطي بتأذٍ أيضاً سخي وذلك أنّه يختار الأموال على الفعل الجميل وليس هذا من شأن السخي (١٥) ولا يأخذ السخي أيضاً من حيث لا ينبغي وذلك أنّ الأخذ ليس هو من شأن من لا يكرم الأموال (١٦) ولا يسأل أيضاً أحداً لأنّه ليس يسهل على الجواد المحسن أن يقبل إحساناً من أحد (١٧) وقد يأخذ من حيث ينبغي الأخذ أعني من أملاكه

---

2 first حيث لا : حيث F, Bad; لا del. Dun || 6 للذي corr. Dun : الذي F, Bad || 6 second لا suppl. Dun* (μή) || 8 لا suppl. Dun* (μή) || 8 ليسوا corr. Bad : ليس F || 10 يحبون F*, Dun*
(φιλοῦνται) : يحمدون Bad || 12 البذل mrg. لائق بالكلام في السخاء وإنما تقدم القول في الفضيلة بالجملة
وبالجملة فيفعل جميع الشياء التي تتبع القول الصحيح صح كذا لخصه القاضي وهو الظاهر لأن البذل الصحيح ||
17 أحدا F, Dun : om. Bad || 18 ينبغي F : يجب Bad

1120b I mean, from his possessions, not that this is noble, but that he is obliged to in order to have wherewithal to give. Neither will he waste his substance, since he wishes by means of wealth to give sufficient provision to people, nor will he give to every chance person, in order to have ready what he may give to whoever he ought to give to, at the time that he ought, and where it is a noble gift. (18) It is very characteristic of the liberal man that he exceeds in giving till he only leaves himself a little,[14] since his aim is not self-regard. (19) Liberality then is spoken of only according to wealth, because a man who gives much[15] is not more liberal than[16] another who gives little, if his means from which he gives are small. (20) We know that those who have not earned money themselves but have acquired it without earning are more liberal than others, because they have not felt the pinch of necessity, and all men have the habit of loving their own works, like parents who love their children and poets who love their poetry. It is difficult for the liberal man to become rich, since he does not accept anything and does not save anything, but he spends money and does not value it for itself, but values it simply in order to give it away. (21) Therefore people blame luck and say: The man who deserves riches scarcely ever becomes rich. This is not something which happens unreasonably or by chance, because it is impossible that anyone should have wealth without paying attention to amassing it, just as in the case of everything else. (22) The liberal man also does not give to whom he should not give, and how he should not, and so on for the other conditions which are not allowable, because if he does that, his action is not according to what virtue[17] necessitates, and if he spends his money on these things, his spending is not on what he ought to spend it. (23) For the matter is as we have said, in respect that the liberal man is he who spends in accordance with what he possesses, and spends on the things which ought to be spent on. He who exceeds this is the prodigal. Therefore tyrants are not called prodigal, because their expenses and gifts are not excessive in comparison with the amount of their possessions. (24) If liberality is a mean in giving and taking in respect of possessions, then the liberal man gives and spends on what he should, and

[14] Greek ἐλάττω.

[15] A line and some words have been omitted here with reference to the state of character (ἕξις) of the liberal man, apparently by homoioteleuton.

[16] Greek τόν read as τοῦ, followed by διδόντος for διδόντα.

[17] Arabic *al-faḍīlah*, but he should have said 'liberality' (Greek κατὰ τὴν ἐλευθεριότητα).

ليس على أنّ ذلك جميل لكن على أنّه مضطرّ إليه ليكون عنده ما يعطي ولا يضيع أيضاً ماله إذ كان يريد بالمل أن يكفي قوماً وليس يعطي لكلّ من اتّفق له لكي يكون معه ما يعطي لمن ينبغي أن يعطيه وفي الوقت الذي ينبغي وحيث تكون [١/٦٠] عطيته جميلة (١٨) ومن شأن السخي جدّاً أن يزيد في العطية حتّى لا يترك لنفسه إلاّ القليل إذ كان ليس غرضه النظر لنفسه (١٩) فالسخاء إذاً إنّما يقل بحسب المل لأنّه ليس إنّما يكون إنسان يعطي كثيراً أسخى من آخر يعطي قليلاً إذ كان ملكه الذي يعطي منه قليلاً (٢٠) وقد نعلم أنّ الذين لم يكسبوا المل بأنفسهم لكنّهم ظفروا به عن غير اكتساب أسخى من غيرهم لأنّهم لم ينلهم مضض الحاجة والناس كلّهم جروا بأن يحبّوا أفعالهم كالوالدين اللذين يحبّان أولادهما والشعراء الذين يحبّون أشعارهم ويعسر على السخي أن يستغني إذ كان لا يقبل شيئاً ولا يحفظ شيئاً بل يبذل المل ولا يكرمه لنفسه بل إنّما يكرمه ليعطيه (٢١) ولذلك يعذل الناس البخت فيقولون ليس يكاد يستغني من كان للغنى مستحقّاً وليس هذا بشئ يعرض على غير قياس ولا بالاتّفاق لأنّه ليس يمكن أحداً أن تكون عنده أموال من غير أن يعنى بجمعها كما لا يكون في شئ من سائر الأمور الأخر (٢٢) وليس يعطي السخي أيضاً لمن لا ينبغي أن يعطي وكما لا ينبغي وغير ذلك من الأحوال التي لا تجب لأنّه إن فعل ذلك لم يكن فعله على ما توجبه الفضيلة وإن أنفق ماله في هذه الأشياء لم يكن إنفاقه فيما يجب أن ينفقه (٢٣) فإنّ الأمر على ما قلنا في أنّ السخي هو الذي ينفق على قدر ملكه وينفق في الأشياء التي يجب أن ينفق فيها والذي يزيد على هذا هو المبذّر ولذلك لا يسمّى المتغلّبون مبذّرين لأنّ نفقاتهم وعطاياهم ليست زائدة عند كثرة أموالهم (٢٤) فإذا كان السخاء توسّطاً في الإعطاء والأخذ في الأموال فالسخي إذاً يعطي وينفق فيما ينبغي وبمقدار

---

2 لكي appar. corr. Dun* (ἵνα) : لكن F, Bad || 3 جميلة F : حسنة Bad || 5 يقل F*, Dun* (λέγεται) : ينل Bad || 9 أولادهما corr. Bad : أولادهم F || 12 احدا corr. Bad : أحد F || 14 second ينبغي F, Dun : ينبغي أن يعطي suppl. Bad || 18 فإذا F : فإن Bad || 19 إذا F : إذن Bad

in the measure that he should, and he does that in much and little in the same manner and with pleasure to himself, and he takes from where he ought and the amount that he ought. That is, since virtue is a mean between[18] both things [he will do both,][19] as is proper, I mean, he gives and takes. That is, the excellent giving is followed by similar taking, and what is not similar taking is its opposite, because the giving and taking which follow one another are together in the
1121a same thing,[20] but the opposites are not. (25) That is, if it happens to him to spend his money contrary to what he ought and wrongly, he is grieved and pained, and if he spends it with due measure and as he should, he is happy and takes pleasure in that.[21] For it belongs to virtue that a man takes pleasure or is pained and grieved at the things which necessitate that in regard to them.[22] (26) The liberal man also is excellent to associate with in respect of money, (27) because he cannot be wronged[23] since he does not value money, and his vexation is great when he has not spent on something he ought to spend on.[24] He is opposed to the injunction of Simonides.[25] (28) As for the prodigal, he goes wrong in these things because he is not pleased with the things which he ought to be pleased with, nor as he should be, and he is not pained thereby similarly. When we have gone forward in the discussion, this meaning will be clearer. (29) We have said that prodigality and meanness are excess and defect, and they are in two things, in giving and in taking. That is, we have described expenditure under giving. Prodigality exceeds the mean in giving and not taking,[26] falls short of it in taking. Meanness falls short of it in giving, and exceeds it in taking, except in small matters. (30) The

---

[18] The Greek rather 'a mean in respect of (περί) both things', i.e. giving and taking.

[19] The words 'he will do both' (Greek ποιήσει ἀμφότερα) are omitted in Arabic.

[20] Greek is rather 'in the same person'.

[21] 'And if he spends it [...] in that'. This expands the Greek (μετρίως δὲ καὶ ὡς δεῖ), but the sense is wrong. These words go with what precedes: the liberal man, if he spends his money wrongly is grieved, 'but in due measure and as he ought'.

[22] Greek καὶ ὡς δεῖ (1121a 3-4) appears not to be translated.

[23] Arabic *yaqdur an yuẓlama*. But this is the opposite of the Greek, "he can be cheated" (Rackham). The negative *lā* has been wrongly inserted.

[24] Some words are omitted here, and the comparative (μᾶλλον) has been disregarded.

[25] *Mā yuwaṣṣī bihi Sīmūnīdīs*. This agrees better with Greek τῷ Σιμωνίδου tentatively suggested by Bywater, followed by Burnet, Ross and Rackham (rejected by Gauthier), than with τῷ Σιμωνίδῃ of the vulg.

[26] 'And not taking', Greek καὶ μὴ λαμβάνειν. These words are said by Rackham and Gauthier to be lacking in L[b], but this is not indicated in Bywater's apparatus.

ما ينبغي ويفعل ذلك في الكثير والقليل على مثل واحد وباستلذاذه ويأخذ من حيث يجب وبالمقدار الذي يجب وذلك أنّ الفضيلة لمّا كانت توسّطاً فيما بين الأمرين [يفعلهما] جميعاً كما ينبغي أعني يعطي ويأخذ وذلك أنّ العطية الفاضلة يتبعها مثل هذا الأخذ وما لم يكن مثل هذا الأخذ فهو ضدّها لأنّ الإعطاء والأخذ اللذين يتبع أحدهما الآخر قد يكونان في شيء واحد معاً فأمّا [١/٦١] المتضادّان فلا (٢٥) وذلك أنّه إن عرض له أن ينفق ماله على خلاف ما يجب وعلى غير الصواب اغتمّ وتأذّى وإن أنفقه بمقدار وعلى ما ينبغي سرّ والتذّ بذلك فإنّ من الفضيلة أن يلتذّ الإنسان أو يتأذّى ويغتمّ في الأشياء التي يوجب ذلك فيها (٢٦) والسخي أيضاً جيّد الشركة في المال (٢٧) لأنّه لا يقدر أن يظلم إذ كان لا يكرم المال يشتدّ غمّه إذا لم ينفق في شيء يجب أن ينفق فيه وكان على خلاف ما يوصي به سيمونيديس (٢٨) فأمّا المبذّر فقد يخطئ في هذه الأشياء لأنّه ليس يلتذّ بالأشياء التي يجب أن يلتذّ بها ولا كما ينبغي ولا يتأذّى به كذلك وإذا أمعنّا في الكلام يتبيّن هذا المعنى أكثر (٢٩) وقد قلنا إنّ التبذير والتقتير زيادة ونقصان وهما في شيئين في الإعطاء وفي الأخذ وذلك أنّا وصفنا النفقة في الإعطاء والتبذير يزيد على التوسّط بالإعطاء وبترك الأخذ وينقص عنه بالأخذ والتقتير ينقص عنه بالإعطاء ويزيد عليه بالأخذ إلاّ في أشياء يسيرة (٣٠) فأمور

---

2 يفعلهما suppl. Dun || 6 وإن F : فإن Bad || 9 غمه F*, Bad*, Dun* (ἀχθόμενος) : عمله corr. mrg. || 13 third و suppl. Dun || 14 فأمور mrg. التبذير لا تكاد تجتمع ولا تدوم صح كذا لخصه القاضي فحالتا

traits of prodigality are scarcely combined, because it is not easy for a man to give to everyone and not take anything from anyone, because the man who does not practise a profession[27] consumes his money quickly, and those who do not practise a profession are the people of whom it is thought that they are prodigal. (31) The prodigal is thought to be much better than the mean man, i.e. his case is easily cured through age and through want, and it is possible for him to approach the mean, since he possesses what the liberal man has, because he gives and does not take, except that he does neither of them as he should.[28] If he took heed[29] and submitted to change his ways, he would be liberal, because he would give to whom he ought and not take from where he ought not. Therefore he is thought not to be of bad character, because it is not typical of the bad and vile man to exceed in giving and not take, but that is typical of the foolish man. (32) He who is prodigal in this sense we know to be far better than the mean man, for the reasons which we have mentioned, and because the prodigal is useful to many people, and the mean man is useful to no one, not even himself. (33) But many of the prodigals, as we have said, take something from where they ought not, and they are in this sense mean. (34) They take because they wish to spend, and they wish spending to be easy for them.[30] That is, their money is
1121b quickly spent, and the situation obliges them to acquire from another quarter. And because at the same time they do not care for what is noble they are vexed,[31] so that they take from any quarter that occurs to them. That is, they desire to give and do not ask from where or how they take. (35) For that reason their gifts are not related to liberality or noble,[32] nor do they do them for the sake of the noble, nor in the proper way, but they sometimes enrich one for whom poverty is fitting and give nothing to men of acceptable morals. Sometimes they give much money to one who asks them with flattery or something else which they take pleasure in. Therefore most of them come to be absorbed in their pleasures.[33] That is, since spending is easy for

[27] Arabic *lā yaḥtarifu*, i.e. Greek ἰδιώτας.

[28] 'Nor well', Greek οὐδ' εὖ is omitted.

[29] Arabic *tanabbaha*, Greek ἐθισθείη, 'became habituated'.

[30] Construes the Greek ποιεῖν with βούλεσθαι, omitting the words μὴ δύνασθαι with K^b (which has μὴ τοῦτο ποιεῖν).

[31] Lit., 'their breasts are contracted'. This stands for Greek ὀλιγώρως, 'neglectfully, carelessly, recklessly', apparently taken as a verb.

[32] Greek γάρ has been omitted.

[33] Arabic *munhamikīna fī 'l-ladhdhah* for Greek ἀκόλαστοι. Cf. IV, 1, 3, 1119b 31, where *munhamikīna fī 'sh-shahawāt* renders Greek ἀκρατεῖς.

التبذير لا تكاد تقترن لأنّه ليس يسهل على الإنسان أن يعطي كلّ واحد ولا يأخذ من أحد شيئاً لأنّ من لا يحترف قد يفني ماله وشيكاً والذين لا يحترفون هم الذين يظنّ بهم أنّهم مبذّرون (٣١) والمبذّر قد يظنّ به أنّه أفضل من المقتّر كثيراً وذلك أنّه قد يسهل تلافي أمره من قبل السنّ ومن قبل العوز ويمكنه أن يقرب من التوسّط إذ كان معه ما للسخي لأنّه قد يعطي ولا يأخذ إلاّ أنّه لا يفعل واحداً منهما على ما ينبغي فإن هو تنبّه وانقاد إلى أن ينتقل عن هذا صار سخياً لأنّه يصير يعطي من يجب ولا يأخذ من حيث لا يجب ولذلك يظنّ به أنّه ليس أردأ في الخلق لأنّه ليس من شأن الردئ والخسيس أن يفرط في الإعطاء ولا يأخذ بل إنّما ذلك من شأن الغبي (٣٢) والذي هو مبذّر على هذه الجهة فنحن نعلم أنّه أفضل كثيراً من المقتّر للأسباب التي ذكرنا ولأنّ المبذّر ينفع كثيراً من الناس والمقتّر لا ينفع أحداً ولا ينفع أيضاً نفسه (٣٣) ولكن كثيراً من المبذّرين كما قلنا قد يأخذون شيئاً من حيث لا يجب فهم بهذه الجهة [١/٦٢] مقتّرون (٣٤) وإنّما يأخذون لأنّهم يريدون أن ينفقوا ويريدون أن تسهل عليهم النفقة وذلك أنّ مالهم ينفذ بسرعة فيضطرّهم الأمر إلى أن يكتسبوا من موضع آخر ولأنّهم مع ذلك لا يهتمّون بالأمر الجميل وقد تضيق صدورهم فيأخذون من كلّ موضع يسنح لهم وذلك أنّهم يشتهون أن يعطوا ولا يسألون من أين أو كيف يأخذون (٣٥) ولذلك صارت عطاياهم لا تنتسب إلى السخاء ولا هي جميلة ولا يفعلونها للجميل ولا كما يجب لكنّهم ربّما أغنوا من يصلح له الفقر ولم يعطوا ذوي الأخلاق الرضية شيئاً وربّما أعطوا الملـ الكثير لمن يسألهم بالملق أو بشئ آخر ممّا

---

8 الغبي read. Dun* (ἠλιθίου) : الغني F, Bad || 13 الجميل mrg. وعليه يبين المعنى وعلى إثباتها أيضا باسقاط الواو لخصه القاضي || 17 يسألهم corr. Bad : يسلهم F

them, they come to squander in their desires, and because their way of life is ignoble, they become inclined to pleasures. (36) The prodigal, if he does not submit to instruction, is brought to this, but if he is concerned about himself and examines his condition he is brought to the mean and attains the necessary condition. (37) As for meanness, it is a disease for which there is no cure, that is, it is thought that old age and any weakness render a man mean, and men are more naturally disposed to it than to prodigality, because most people love accumulating money more than they love disbursing it. (38) Meanness is applied to many things and is of many kinds. It is thought that its conditions[34] are many. That is, since it exists in two things, in defective giving and excessive taking, its two parts do not come together entirely for everybody, but sometimes its two kinds are separated, so that some people exceed in taking, and others fall short in giving. (39) It has been mentioned that any called stingy and grasping and miserly are defective in giving, but do not desire the wealth of others, nor do they wish to take anything from anyone. Some of them do that to be respectable and to guard against base deeds. For they say[35] that they are careful of their money for fear that they may be forced to a base action. Among these is the man whom the common people call 'counter of the lentils' and the like. They are called by names of this kind for their excessive refusal to give anyone anything. Others of them refuse to take anything from another, out of fear, for they think that it is not easy for a man to take another's money without an other taking his, so they are content neither to take nor to give. (40) Others are excessive in taking so far as to take from every quarter, and they take everything they can, like what disgraced persons[36] do, I mean, procurers and the rest, effeminate persons,[37]
1122a and those who take a little[38] at a high rate. For all these take from where they ought not and an amount which they ought not. (41) Their common feature is sordid gain, for they all endure disgrace and shame for a slight gain. (42) That is, those who take large gifts from where[39] they ought not,[40] we do not call mean, e.g. tyrants,

---

[34] Arabic *aḥwāl* for Greek τρόποι; γάρ is disregarded.

[35] Greek δοκοῦσι, then ἤ, are omitted.

[36] The idea of illiberal, 'banausic' occupations (τὰς ἀνελευθέρους ἐργασίας) is not brought out.

[37] Arabic *al-mu'annathīna*, not in the Greek.

[38] Arabic *alladhīna ya'khudhūna al-yasīr* does not well render the Greek τοκισταί ('those who lend on interest').

[39] I.e. Arabic omits δέ.

[40] Greek μηδὲ ἃ δεῖ.

يلتذّونه ولذلك صار أكثرهم منهمكين في لذّاتهم وذلك أنّ النفقة لمّا كانت تسهل عليهم صاروا ينهبون في شهواتهم ولأنّ سيرتهم ليست جميلة صاروا يميلون إلى اللذّات (٣٦) فالمبذّر إذا لم يكن منقاداً للأدب انتقل إلى هذه الأشياء وإذا عني بنفسه وتفقّد أمره انتقل إلى التوسّط وصار إلى الأمر الواجب (٣٧) فأمّا التقتير فداء لا برء له وذلك أنّه قد يظنّ بالشيخوخة وبكلّ ضعف أنّه يجعل صاحبه مقتّراً والناس أشدّ إلفاً له بالطبع من التبذير لأنّ أكثر الناس يحبّون جمع المل أكثر من محبّتهم لبذله (٣٨) والتقدير يقل على أشياء كثيرة وهو كثير الأنواع ويظنّ أنّ أحواله كثيرة وذلك أنّه لمّا كان يوجد في شيئين في نقصان الإعطاء وزيادة الأخذ صار لا يجمع جزآه بالكلّية لكلّ أحد لكن ربّما افترق نوعاه حتّى يكون بعض الناس يزيدون في الأخذ وبعضهم ينقصون في الإعطاء (٣٩) وذلك أنّ الذي يسمّى شحيحاً ولئيماً وبخيلاً ينقصون في العطية ولا يشتهون مل غيرهم ولا يريدون أن يأخذوا من أحد شيئاً فقوم منهم يفعلون ذلك للنزاهة توقّى الأمور القبيحة فإنّهم يقولون إنّهم إنّما يحفظون أموالهم خوفاً من أن يصيروا إلى فعل قبيح ومن هؤلاء الذي تسمّيه العامّة معلّد العدس وما أشبه ذلك وإنّما يسمّون بأمثل هذه الأشياء لإفراطهم في الامتناع من أن يعطوا أحداً شيئاً وقوم منهم يمتنعون من أن يأخذوا من [١/٦٣] غيرهم شيئاً فرقاً لأنّهم يرون أنّه لا يسهل أن يكون الإنسان يأخذ مل غيره ولا يأخذ غيره ماله فهم بذلك يكتفون بألاّ يأخذوا ولا يعطوا (٤٠) وقوم يفرطون في الأخذ حتّى يأخذوا من كلّ جهة ويأخذون كلّ شئ يقدرون عليه مثلما يفعلون المعيّرون أعني القوادين وأمثالهم والمأنّثين والذين يأخذون اليسير على الكثير فإنّ هؤلاء كلّهم يأخذون من حيث لا يجب والمقدار الذي لا يجب (٤١) والأمر العامّ لهم الربح القبيح فإنّهم كلّهم يحتملون العار والفضيحة بسبب الربح اليسير (٤٢) وذلك أنّ الذين يأخذون الرغائب من حيث لا يجب لا نسمّيهم مقتّرين مثل

8 يجمع read. Bad : تجمع F || 12-13 معلد العدس F, Dun: مقدد العدس Bad (κυμινοπρίστης) || 17 يفعلون F : يفعل corr. Bad || 17 المأنثين F, Dun : المرابين Bad || 17 third و F, Dun: om. Bad || 17-18 اليسير على الكثير F, Dun : الكثير على اليسير corr. Bad || 19 العام F*, Dun* (κοινόν) : العائد Bad

when they take property by force[41] and plunder temples, but rather we call them wicked and irreligious and unjust. (43) As for the gambler and the thief,[42] they are among the mean, because they both seek sordid gain, and both do what they do on account of gain, and they endure disgrace. Thieves endure great trials for the sake of getting, and gamblers gain at the expense of their friends, whom they ought to give to. Both groups seek gain from where they ought not. They therefore belong to the kinds of sordid gain, voluntarily,[43] and all these kinds of taking are characteristic of mean persons. (44) And it is necessarily said that meanness is the opposite of liberality. That is, meanness is a greater evil than prodigality, and people go wrong in regard to them more than they go wrong in regard to prodigality. (45) This is the extent of what we need to say about liberality and the contrary vices.

2. We must follow that up with the description of magnificence, for it is thought to be a certain virtue in regard to wealth. It does not, like liberality, cover all the actions which occur in regard to possessions but is restricted to spending only. It exceeds open-handedness in spending by the extent and amount of what it spends, as its name in the language of the Greeks shows, for it points to[44] proper expenditure in a great matter. (2) What is great is relative to the thing. That is, the expenditure on a great caravan[45] and the expenditure on a packsaddle[46] are not the same. What is proper in expenditure is according to the spender[47] and the thing on which he spends. (3) As for him who spends on small and[48] moderate things, according to what is proper expenditure thereon, he is not called magnificent,[49] but only the man who spends on great matters is so

[41] This hardly conveys Greek πόλεις πορθοῦντας.

[42] 'And the robber' (Greek καὶ ὁ λῃστής) is omitted.

[43] Arabic *bi-irādatihim*, i.e. Greek βουλόμενοι wrongly construed.

[44] Arabic *fa'innahu yadullu*. The sentence has been wrongly construed (γάρ out of place and ὑποσημαίνει taken twice).

[45] The translator did not know the meaning of τριήραρχος, cf. 1122b 23 = IV, 2, 11.

[46] I.e. Arabic *al-ukāfah*, cf. *ikāf*, *ukāf*. If this is what the translator wrote, there is at least a contrast, as intended by Aristotle. Not knowing the meaning of the Greek words, cf. τριηραρχεῖν below n. 63, the translator has given the general sense of the passage as best he could, using very different examples.

[47] Greek καὶ ἐν ᾧ is omitted here.

[48] Arabic *wa* for Greek ἤ.

[49] The quotation from Homer (πολλάκι δόσκον ἀλήτῃ, *Odyssey*, XVII, 420) is here omitted.

المتغلّبين إذا نهبوا المدن وسلبوا الهياكل لكن الأولى أن نسمّيهم شراراً وكفّاراً أو ظلمة (٤٣) فأمّا المقامر واللصّ فهما من المقتّرين لأنّهما يطلبان الربح القبيح ويفعلان ما يفعلانه بسبب الربح ويحتملون العار فاللصوص يحتملون البلايا العظيمة بسبب الأخذ والمقامرون يربحون على أصدقائهم الذين ينبغي لهم أن يعطوهم والفريقان كلاهما يطلبان الربح من حيث لا يجب فهم لذلك من أصناف الربح القبيح بإرادتهم وهذه الأصناف كلّها من أصناف الأخذ من شأن المقتّرين (٤٤) وبالواجب يقال إنّ التقتير يضادّ السخاء وذلك أنّ التقتير أعظم شرّاً من التبذير وخطأ الناس فيهما أكثر من خطئهم في التبذير (٤٥) فهذا مقدار ما ينبغي أن نقوله في السخاء والرذائل المضادّة له.

٢. وينبغي أن نتبع ذلك بصفة الكرم فإنّه قد يظنّ به أنّه فضيلة ما في المال وليست تشتمل مثل السخاء على جميع الأفعال التي تكون في الأموال لكنّه إنّما يكون في الإنفاق فقط فإنّه يفضل الحرّية في الإنفاق بكثرة ما ينفق وعظمه كما يدلّ اسمه في لغة اليونانيين فإنّه يدلّ على نفقة واجبة في أمر عظيم (٢) والعظيم من المضاف إلى الشيء وذلك أنّه ليس النفقة على الركب الكبير والنفقة على الأكافة واحدة بعينها والواجب في النفقة يكون بحسب المنفق والشيء الذي ينفق فيه (٣) فأمّا الذي ينفق في الأمور الصغار والمقتصرة على ما يجب من النفقة فيها [١/٦٤] فلا يقال له كريم بل إنّما يقال كريم لمن ينفق على الأمور

---

5 أصناف F, Dun : أصحاب Bad || 11 يفضل mrg. القاضي السخاء لخصه || 13 first على mrg. القاضي perh. F, الاكافة 13 || ولذلك كانت النفقة على الركب الكثير عظيمة بالإضافة إلى النفقة على الواجب كذا لخصه Dun : الاكانة Bad || 14 المقتصرة F : المقتصر Bad

called. That is, the magnificent man is liberal, and the liberal man is not necessarily magnificent. (4) The defect in this state is called meanness and the excess ostentation and boastfulness.[50] The haughty man does not exceed the magnificent man in regard to the importance of what he does in regard to the things which are right, but in regard to what is not right, and he does not abstain from what is not right.[51] We shall describe his state afterwards. (5) As for the magnificent man, he resembles the connoisseur, because he possesses knowledge of what is right and expands great sums with care.
1122b (6) That is, the matter stands as we said at first, that the state comes into existence and is defined by the actions and by him who does them.[52] The expenses then of the magnificent man are great and proper expenses, and so too are his works. That is, his expenditure in its extent and suitability to his works reaches a point where the work is equal[53] to the expenditure, and the expenditure is equal[54] to the work, or the work surpasses the expenditure.[55] (7) If the actions of the magnificent man are of this kind, he does them for the sake of what is noble, because this is something common to the virtues. (8) He does them also gladly and compliantly, because close inquiry and exact consideration in bargaining are meanness. (9) His consideration is directed towards what he does being for an end which is excellent and lofty, rather than[56] towards the amount of what he spends on it being small. (10) The magnificent man must of necessity be liberal, because the liberal man spends what he ought to spend, and as he should, and on account of the greatness of the ambition of the magnificent man he does what the liberal man does[57] and, from like expenditure to what he spends, with the most splendid[58] result. That is, the virtue of property and the virtue of a work are not the same, because the virtue of property is that there should be a share of greater amount, or it should be excellent, like gold,

---

[50] Arabic goes wrong here, rendering *al-badhakh wa'ṭ-ṭimidhal*.

[51] Greek λαμπρύνομαι is rendered here and below (1123a 22) by Arabic *lā yatanāhā*.

[52] 'And by him who does them'. The Greek is different: καὶ ὧν ἐστίν ("and by its objects", Ross).

[53] Arabic omits δεῖ.

[54] See previous note.

[55] But Greek says the opposite: 'the expenditure should (δεῖ) exceed the work'.

[56] Arabic omits Greek πόσου καί.

[57] This attempt to render the difficult Greek is unsuccessful. Perhaps περὶ ταὐτά was read.

[58] Superlative for comparative (Greek μεγαλοπρεπέστερον).

العظام وذلك أنّ الكريم سخي والسخي المنسوب ليس هو لا محالة كريماً (٤) والنقصان في هذه الحال يسمّى النذالة والزيادة تسمّى بالبذخ والطمنل وليس يزيد البذخ على الكريم بعظم ما يفعله في الأشياء التي تجب لكن فيما لا يجب ولا يتناهى ممّا لا يجب وسنصف حاله بأخرة (٥) فأمّا الكريم فيشبه العالم لأنّه يقدر على معرفة الواجب وينفق النفقات الجليلة بعناية (٦) وذلك أنّ الأمر على ما قلنا أوّلاً أنّ الحال تحصل وتحدّد بالأفعال وبمن يفعلها فنفقات الكريم نفقات جليلة واجبة وكذلك عماله أيضاً وذلك أنّ نفقته تبلغ من عظمتها ووجوبها لعمله ما يكون العمل يساوي النفقة والنفقة تساوي العمل أو يكون العمل يفوق النفقة (٧) وإذا كانت أفعال الكريم تجري هذا المجرى فإنّما يفعلها من أجل الجميل لأنّ هذا أمر عامّ للفضائل (٨) ويفعلها أيضاً بلذّة ومسامحة لأنّ الاستقصاء في المكاس وتدقيق النظر نذالة (٩) ونظره في أن يكون ما يعمله على غاية الجودة والسرد أكثر من نظره في أن يكون مقدار ما ينفق عليه يسيراً (١٠) فواجب ضرورةً أن يكون الكريم سخياً لأنّ السخي ينفق ما يجب أن ينفقه وكما ينبغي ولكبر همّة الكريم يعمل ما يعمله السخي ومن مثل النفقة التي ينفقها على أجلّ ما يكون من العمل وذلك أنّ ليس فضيلة القنية وفضيلة العمل واحدة بعينها لأنّ فضيلة القنية أن يكون قسط ذو مقدار أكبر أو يكون

---

2 الطمنل Dun : الطرمذة Bad || 3 لا first F*, Dun* (οὐ) : om. Bad || 5 بعناية F*, Bad*, Dun* (ἐμμελῶς) : بغناية read. mrg. || 5 تحدد F*, Dun* (ὁρίζεται) : تجود Bad

while the virtue of a work is that it should be great and beautiful. For whoever looks at a work like this wonders at it, and magnificence is something which is wondered at. The action of the magnificent man is a virtue in regard to the magnitude of the expenses.[59] (11) It is connected with expenses which we say are costly and magnificent, like expenses on the things of God, I mean, sacrifices and votive offerings and the construction of vessels,[60] and all that with which deified people are adorned[61], and what is bestowed on the common people,[62] such as entertaining guests and free donations[63] and bestowing food on the people of the city.[64] (12) These things, as we have said, are related to the agent, when it is known who he is and from what resources he spends, for the money should be appropriate[65] not only to the work but to its producer. (13) Therefore the poor man is not magnificent, because he does not have money from which to spend extensive sums as he ought. Any poor man who aspires to this is a fool, because he aspires to what surpasses both his scale and what is requisite, because a thing is according to what virtue requires only when it is on the right lines. (14) Magnificence is appropriate to the man who has precedence[66] in things like these, either in himself or through his ancestors,[67] or to the man who possesses high birth, reputation and the like. For all such things have the same greatness and importance, (15) even if[68] the magnificent man is of this description, and even if[69] the magnificent man is involved in expenses like these, as we have described, because they are the
1123a greatest and most magnificent expenses. As for private expenses,

---

[59] The Arabic translator apparently did not read μεγαλοπρέπεια. Cf. Gauthier *in loco*.

[60] Arabic *ʿamal al-awānī* for Greek κατασκευαί, 'buildings', i.e. temples (Burnet).

[61] Arabic *wa-kull mā yataḥallā bihi al-muta'allihūn*, apparently rendering Greek καὶ ὅσα περὶ πᾶν τὸ δαιμόνιον, i.e. the vulg. reading, but the sense has been missed.

[62] A serious misconception and mistranslation, connected with ignorance of Greek institutions. See next note.

[63] Arabic *aḍ-ḍiyāfah wa'ṣ-ṣilāt* for χορηγεῖν, 'to equip a chorus', and τριηραρχεῖν, 'to fit out a trireme'.

[64] For ἑστιᾶν τὴν πόλιν, 'giving a banquet to the whole city', as Conon and Cleisthenes did at Athens.

[65] The Arabic translator appears to have read ἄξια γὰρ δεῖ ταῦτα εἶναι.

[66] Arabic *sābiqah*, but the sense of the Greek is 'previously existing resources'.

[67] Greek ἢ ὧν αὐτοῖς μέτεστιν is not translated.

[68] Arabic *wa-'in* somehow comes to render Greek μάλιστα μὲν οὖν, and the sense goes wrong.

[69] See previous note.

جيّداً بمنزلة الذهب وفضيلة العمل أن يكون عظيماً حسناً فإنّ من نظر إلى مثل هذا العمل حتّى يعجب منه من يراه تعجّب منه والكرم شئ يعجب منه وفعل الكريم فضيلة في عظم النفقات (١١) وهي من النفقات التي نقول إنّها نفيسة كريمة مثل النفقات في أمور اللّه أعني القرابين والنذور وعمل الأواني وكلّ ما يتحلّى به المتألّهون وما يبذل للعامّة مثل الضيافة والصلات وبذل الطعام لأهل المدينة (١٢) وهذه الأشياء كما قلنا إنّما تنسب إلى فاعلها إذا علم من هو ومن أيّ مل ينفق فإنّ الأموال ليس إنّما ينبغي [١/٦٥] أن تكون تليق بالعمل فقط بل وبالذي يعمله (١٣) ولذلك لا يكون المسكين كريماً لأنّ ليس له أموال ينفق منها نفقات كثيرة على ما يجب ومن رام ذلك من المساكين فهو مائق لأنّه رام ما هو مجاوز لمقداره وللواجب لأنّ الشئ إنّما يكون على ما توجبه الفضيلة إذ كان يجري على الصواب (١٤) والكرم يليق بمن له في أمثل هذه الأشياء سابقة إمّا بنفسه وإمّا بأسلافه أو من له شرف وحسب وما أشبه ذلك فإنّ أمثل هذه الأشياء كلّها لها عظم وقدر واحد (١٥) وإن يكون الكريم بهذه الصفة وإن يكون الكريم في أمثل هذه النفقات كما وصفنا لأنّها أعظم النفقات وأكرمها فأمّا النفقات الخاصّية فكلّ ما ينفق في مرّة واحدة مثل ما ينفق في

11 واحد F*, Dun* : واجدر Bad || 12 وإن ... وإن F, Dun : وان ... وان Bad

they are everything which is spent on a single occasion, like what is spent on a wedding and the like, or on something in which all the people of the city and the persons of importance among them are concerned, or on entertaining strangers and sending out envoys[70] and presents.[71] That is, the magnificent man does not spend on his own but on public affairs, and there is a certain resemblance between gifts and sacrifices. (16) The magnificent man builds a house worthy of his riches, for in that there is *éclat* for him, and most of what he spends is on things which last for a long time, since they are the best there is. (17) He spends on each of his works what befits it, i.e. the matters which are appropriate for God[72] and for men are not the same, and what is appropriate for an oratory[73] is not so for a tomb. There is among the expenditures taking singly a great one in its kind, and the most magnificent of expenditures is great expenditure on a great matter.[74] (18) Between greatness in work and greatness in expenditure [there is a difference],[75] for a splendid ball and spinning-top[76] are among the finest things that can be given to a child, but their cost is small and paltry. (19) Therefore the work of the magnificent man, in whatever kind he works, is with great care.[77] That is, the likes of this action[78] do not come short of the amount of what has been spent[79] upon it. (20) This then is the description of the magnificent man. As for him who exceeds the latter, the ostentatious man, he exceeds him by going beyond what is proper in expenditure, as we said, because he consumes much in what requires small expenditures, and he does [not] restrain himself[80] in things. For example, he prepares a wedding banquet for people who pretend poverty and gives to singers[81] when they pass by him, and he hangs purple

[70] I.e. Greek ἀποστολάς taken alone, not construed with ξένων as it should be.
[71] Greek καὶ ἀντιδωρεάς is omitted in the Arabic translation.
[72] The translator avoids the polytheism of the Greek.
[73] Arabic *muṣallā*, avoiding mention of a pagan temple.
[74] The next few words of the Greek have fallen out (homoioteleuton).
[75] 'There is a difference'. Something to this effect has fallen out.
[76] Arabic *duwwāmah*. The Greek is λήκυθος, an oil-flask or bottle.
[77] Arabic *bi-kibr himmah* for Greek μεγαλοπρεπῶς.
[78] Greek οὐκ εὐυπέρβλητον does not appear to have been translated.
[79] Or 'he has spent'.
[80] Arabic *lā yatanāhā* rendering Greek λαμπρύνεται, cf. 1122a 33 = IV, 2, 4.
[81] Apparently attempts to render ἐπανιστάς and κωμῳδοῖς. The whole passage is misunderstood, cf. Douglas M. Dunlop, "The *Nicomachean Ethics* in Arabic, Books I-VI", in: *Oriens* 15 (1962), pp. 18-34, here pp. 31-32.

عرس وما أشبهه أو في شئ يعنى به أهل المدينة أجمعهم وذوو الأقدار منهم أو في ضيافة الغرباء وإنفاذ الرسل والهدايا وذلك أنّ الكريم ليس هو منفاقاً في أمور نفسه بل في الأمور العامّية والهدايا بينها وبين القرابين تشابه ما (١٦) والكريم قد يبني مسكناً يليق بغنائه فإنّ له في ذلك جمالاً وأكثر ما ينفق في الأشياء التي تبقى زماناً طويلاً إذ كانت أجود ما يكون (١٧) وينفق في كلّ واحد من أعماله ما يليق به وذلك أنّ ليس الأمور التي تصلح للّه والأمور التي تصلح للناس أموراً واحدة بعينها ولا ما يصلح للمصلّى يصلح للقبر وقد تكون في النفقات واحدةً واحدةً عظيمة في جنسها فأكرم النفقات النفقة العظيمة في الأمر العظيم (١٨) وبين العظيم في العمل والعظيم في النفقة [خلاف] فإنّ الكرة والدوّامة السريتين من أجلّ ما يتحف الصبي به وثمنهما قليل وتح (١٩) فلذلك صار الكريم في أيّ جنس عمل عمله بكبر همّة وذلك أنّ أمثل هذا الفعل لا ينقص عن مقدار ما أنفق عليه (٢٠) فهذه صفة الكريم فأمّا الزائد على هذا وهو البذخ فإنّما يزيد عليه بأنّه يتجاوز في النفقة والواجب كما قلنا لأنه يغني فيما يحتاج إلى اليسير من النفقات شيئاً كثيراً و[لا] يتناهى في أشياء [١/٦٦] مثل أن يعد طعام العرس للمتباهين ويهب للمغنين إذا اجتازوا به

1 أشبهه corr. Bad : أشبهها F || 3 بغنائه F : بغنه Bad || 8 خلاف suppl. Bad*, Dun* (διαφέρει) || 9 وتح read. Dun : وتخ F || 12 لا suppl. Dun*

curtains upon the outside doors as the arrogant and proud[82] do. He does not do what he does from love of the beautiful but in order that the people may see his wealth, and because he thinks that people admire this action of his. When he ought to spend much, he spends little, and when he should spend little, he spends much. (21) As for the mean man, he falls short of the magnificent man in everything. He wastes great sums on small matters,[83] and spoils and destroys the beautiful. His aim in all he seeks to do[84] is that his expenditure should be small.[85] Thus his giving and everything he does are, he thinks, above what is necessary. (22) These states then are vices, except that they do not bring disgrace on their possessors, because they do no harm to those who are neighbours of the possessors of the vices, and are not very bad.

3. As for greatness of soul,[86] it seems that it is concerned with great matters, as its name indicates. Let us then describe first the matters
1123b in regard to which it exists. (2) There is no difference whether[87] our investigation is of greatness of soul or of the great-souled individual. (3) It is thought that the great-souled man is he who believes himself worthy of great matters, being worthy of that; for the man who does so undeservingly is foolish, and none of the virtuous is foolish or ignorant. (4) He who is of this description is the great-souled man.[88] As for the man who is worthy of small matters, believing himself worthy of the same, he is sound in opinion. (5) But he is not great-souled, because greatness of soul is concerned with great matters, just as beauty is in large bodies and prettiness in small and well-proportioned bodies. (6) As for him who believes himself worthy of great things, not being worthy of them, he is the showy man, and not everyone who believes himself worthy of more than he deserves is showy. (7) As for him who believes himself worthy of less than he deserves, he is small-souled,[89] whether he deserves great things, or

---

[82] Arabic *ahl aṣ-ṣalaf wa'n-nakhwah*. But the Greek has 'the people at or of Megara' (οἱ Μεγαροῖ Bywater; οἱ μεγαρεῖς vulg.).

[83] I.e. ἐν μικρῷ construed with ἀναλώσας instead of with ἀπολεῖ.

[84] Greek μέλλων does not appear to be rendered.

[85] Greek καὶ ταῦτ' ὀδυρόμενος is omitted, or has fallen out.

[86] Or 'magnanimity' (Arabic *kibr an-nafs*). Burnet and Ross render "pride", Joachim has "dignity".

[87] Lit. 'between our investigation being [...]'.

[88] The Arabic translation is correct: Greek μεγαλόψυχος (without the article) is clearly the complement.

[89] Or 'pusillanimous'.

ويعلق ستور الفرقين على الأبواب الخارجة كما يفعل أهل الصلف والنخوة وليس يفعل ما يفعله محبّة للجميل لكن ليري الناس يساره ولظنّه أنّ الناس يعجبون بهذا من فعله وحيث ينبغي له أن ينفق كثيراً ينفق قليلاً وحيث ينبغي أن ينفق قليلاً ينفق كثيراً (٢١) فأمّا النذل فقد ينقص عن الكريم في كلّ شيء ويتلف الأشياء العظيمة فيما صغر من الأمور فيفسد الجميل ويهلكه وإنّما قصده في كلّ ما يريد أن يفعله أن تكون نفقته يسيرة وكذلك عطيته وكلّ ما يفعله يرى أنّه فوق الواجب (٢٢) فهذه الحالات رذائل إلاّ أنّها لا تكسب أصحابها عاراً لأنّها ليست تضرّ من يقرب من صاحبها ولا هي قبيحة جدّاً.

٣. فأمّا كبر النفس فيشبه أن يكون في أمور عظيمة كما يدلّ اسمه فلنصف أوّلاً الأمور التي يوجد فيها (٢) ولا فرق بين أن يكون نظرنا في كبر النفس أو في الكبير النفس (٣) وقد يظنّ أنّ الكبير النفس هو الذي يؤهّل نفسه للأمور العظيمة وهو لذلك أهل فإنّ من فعل ذلك على غير استحقاق فهو مائق وليس أحد من أهل الفضيلة مائقاً ولا جاهلاً (٤) فالذي بهذه الصفة هو الكبير النفس وأمّا من هو أهل لأمور يسيرة وهو يؤهّل نفسه لذلك فهو صحيح الرأي (٥) وليس هو كبير النفس لأنّ كبر النفس في الأمور العظام كما أنّ الجمل في الأبدان العظام والملاحة في الأبدان الصغار والمقتدرة (٦) وأمّا الذي يؤهّل نفسه للأمور الكبار وليس هو أهلاً لها فهو المتفنّج وليس كلّ من أهّل نفسه لأكثر ممّا يستحقّ هو متفنّجاً (٧) فأمّا من أهّل نفسه لدون ما يستحقّ فهو الصغير النفس كان مستحقّاً لأمور

1 first و F, Dun : om. Bad || 1 الخارجة F, Dun : المفتوحة Bad || 15 يستحق F : تستحق Bad

moderate, or small.[90] He believes himself worthy of less than his deserving, and it is thought of him that he is small-souled especially.[91] As for him who deserves great things, and believes himself worthy of small things, he, when he deserves great things, believes himself worthy of what is less. What do you think he would do if he did not deserve that? (8) The great-souled man then is an extreme in regard to the size of the things which he does and a mean in his doing them as he ought, because he believes himself worthy of his deserving,[92] and the small-souled man comes short of him therein, while the showy man exceeds him. (9) If the great-souled man believes himself worthy of great things deservedly and particularly of things which are in an extreme of size, then no doubt he is so in regard to one thing. (10) Desert is spoken of with reference to external goods, and we posit this one thing as the greatest there is, when it is that by which God is served,[93] that which the powerful desire, and the struggle[94] for the things which are most noble. Honour is of this kind, for it is the greatest of external goods. The great-souled man then is in the necessary state in regard to honours and their absence. (11) It is plain without any need for argument,[95] as regards great-souled men, that they seek honour, because great men[96] especially believe themselves worthy of honour, and they do so in accordance with their deserving. (12) As for the small-souled man, he falls short of himself and of the deserving of the great-souled man. (13) The showy man exceeds[97] himself and does not exceed[98] the great-souled man. (14) The great-souled man, if he is deserving of the greatest of things,[99] is the most excellent of men. That is, the excellent man always deserves things that are great,[100] and the most excellent of men deserves the greatest things. The great-souled

[90] Greek ἐάν τε καὶ μικρῶν has apparently been construed with the preceding words and the sense is lost for several lines.

[91] Arabic *khāṣṣatan* for Greek μάλιστα.

[92] I.e. Greek τοῦ [...] κατ' ἀξίαν.

[93] Avoids the polytheistic reference of τοῖς θεοῖς.

[94] Arabic *al-jihād* for Greek τὸ [...] ἆθλον.

[95] Arabic *qiyās*, analogical reasoning.

[96] I.e. the Arabic translation read οἱ μεγάλοι, which Bywater and others regarded as an addition to the text.

[97] This should be 'is excessive [sc. in his claims] with reference to (πρός) [...]', and the point is missed.

[98] See previous note.

[99] Arabic *aʿẓm al-umūr*, Greek τῶν μεγίστων.

[100] The Greek comparatives (βελτίων and μείζονος) are disregarded.

عظام أو متوسّطة أو صغار فأهّل نفسه لدون استحقاقه ويظنّ به أنّه صغير النفس خاصّةً فأمّا من كان يستحقّ الأمور العظام فأهّل نفسه للأمور الصغار فإنّه إذا كان يستحقّ الأمور العظام فأهّل نفسه لما دونها فما تراه كان يعمل لو لم يكن مستحقّاً لذلك (٨) فالكبير النفس نهاية في عظم الأشياء التي يعملها ومتوسّط في عمله إيّاها [١/٦٧] كما ينبغي لأنّه يؤهّل نفسه لاستحقاقه والصغير النفس ينقص عنه في ذلك والمتفنّج يزيد عليه (٩) وإذا كان الكبير النفس يؤهّل نفسه للأمور العظام وهو مستحقّ لذلك وخاصّةً للأمور التي في غاية العظم فلا محالة أنّه يكون كذلك في شيء واحد (١٠) والاستحقاق إنّما يقل بحسب الخيرات التي من خارج وإنّما نضع هذا الشيء الواحد أعظم ما يكون إذا كان يخدم به اللّه وما يشتهيه ذوو الأقدار والجهاد في الأمور التي في غاية الجمل والذي يجري هذا المجرى هو الكرامة فإنّها أجلّ الخيرات التي من خارج فالكبير النفس إذاً إنّما يوجد في الكرمات وعدمها على الحل الواجبة (١١) ويتبيّن من أمر كبيري الأنفس من غير أن يحتاج في ذلك إلى قياس أنّهم يلتمسون الكرامة لأنّ العظماء من الناس خاصّةً يؤهّلون أنفسهم للكرامة ويفعلون ذلك على قدر الاستحقاق (١٢) فأمّا الصغير النفس فهو ينقص عن نفسه وعن استحقاق الكبير النفس (١٣) والمتفنّج يزيد على نفسه ولا يزيد على الكبير النفس (١٤) والكبير النفس إن كان مستحقّاً لأعظم الأمور فهو أفضل الناس وذلك أنّ الفاضل يستحقّ أبداً ما عظم من الأمور وأفضل الناس يستحقّ أعظم الأمور فيجب إذاً أن يكون الكبير

---

7 أنه يكون corr. Dun* : أنها تكون F, Bad || 8 يخدم read. Bad : تخدم F || 9 يشتهيه F : تشتهيه Bad || 12 من F*, Dun* (οἱ μεγάλοι) : دين Bad

man[101] must then be good. It is thought of the great-souled man that he has what is great in each of the virtues. (15) It is not at all appropriate for the great-souled man that he should run away when the least thing moves him,[102] nor that he should act unjustly. That is, he whom nothing impresses has no cause inducing him to do a base action. To anyone who follows the particular instances, it is clear that the great-souled man, if he is not good, is laughed at by everyone. Neither is he deserving of honour if he is bad, since honour is
1124a the reward of virtue, and good people receive it. (16) So it is likely that greatness of soul is an embellishment to the virtues, because it enhances them, and the great-souled man does not exist except through the virtues. Therefore it is difficult for there to be a truly great-souled man, because he can only be good and excellent. (17) The great-souled man then is specially concerned with honours and their absence. When he is honoured for great deeds and by the best of mankind, he rejoices a little, since he only gets from them thereby what is his, or less than what is his, for no honour exists worthy of complete virtue. Yet often he may accept honour from them, since it is not possible for them to honour him more than that. But when he is honoured for little things and by ordinary people he takes no account of that and makes light of it, because it is not what he deserves. His case is the same in regard to dishonour, otherwise he would not be just in regard to himself.[103] (18) The great-souled man, as we have described, aspires to honours more than anything,[104] and he aspires also[105] to wealth and power, and in all happiness or trouble which attaches to him, whichever it is that has come to him,[106] he is with due measure. Neither when he has good fortune does he rejoice,[107] nor when he is in misfortune is he grieved,[108] because honour is not for him among the greatest of things.[109] Power and wealth are only preferred because of honour, and the man who has power

---

[101] Greek ὡς ἀληθῶς is not rendered.

[102] Arabic *idhā ḥarrakahu adnā shai'in* [*adhā shai'in*, mrg.] is meant to render the difficult word παρασείσαντι, "swinging his arms by his sides" (Ross), i.e. "at full speed" (Rackham, Gauthier).

[103] The Arabic translator evidently read δίκαιος περὶ αὐτόν.

[104] Arabic *akthar min kull shai'*, a serious mistranslation of Greek οὐ μὴν ἀλλά.

[105] The construction is wrong.

[106] The translation of ὅπως ἂν γίνηται is not exact.

[107] The force of περι- is disregarded in the adjectives περιχαρής, περίλυπος.

[108] See previous note.

[109] This translation desregards the difficulty of the Greek, giving a general sense only.

النفس خيراً. يظنّ بالكبير النفس أنّ له في كلّ واحدة من الفضائل ما عظم (١٥) وليس يليق بالكبير النفس أصلاً أن يهرب إذا حرّكه أدنى شئ ولا أن يظلم وذلك أنّ من لا يتعاظمه شئ ليس سبب يدعوه إلى فعل القبيح ومن يتبع الأمور الجزئية يستبين له أنّ الكبير النفس إذا لم يكن خيراً ضحك به كلّ أحد ولا يكون أيضاً مستحقّاً للكرامة إذا كان رديئاً إذ كانت الكرامة إنّما هي جائزة الفضيلة وإنّما يتناولها الخيار من الناس (١٦) ويشبه أن يكون كبر النفس زينة ما للفضائل لأنّه يجعلها عظيمة ولا يكون كبير النفس إلاّ بالفضائل ولذلك عسيراً ما يوجد كبير النفس على الحقيقة لأنّه ليس يمكن أن يوجد إلاّ خيراً جواداً (١٧) فالكبير النفس إذاً إنّما يوجد خاصّةً في الكرامات وعدمها وإذا أكرم [١/٦٨] على الأمور العظيم ومن الأفاضل من الناس سرّ سروراً يسيراً من قبل أنّه إنّما نل ذلك منهم ما هو له أو دون ما له فإنّ الفضيلة التامّة لا توجد لها كرامة تستأهلها ولكنّه كثيراً ما قد يقبل منهم الكرامة من قبل أنّه ليس يمكنهم أن يكرموه أكثر من ذلك فأمّا إذا أكرم على أمور صغار ومن أبناء الناس فإنّه يتهاون بذلك ويستخفّ به لأنّه على غير استحقاقه وكذلك يجري أمره في عدم الكرامة وإلاّ لم يكن عدلاً في نفسه (١٨) فالكبير النفس كما وصفنا يبتغي الكرامات أكثر من كلّ شئ ويبتغي أيضاً اليسار والمقدرة وكلّ سعادة أو مشقة تكون فيه إنّما يكون في أيّهما حصل له بمقدار فلا إذا أسعد فرح ولا إذا شقي اغتمّ لأنّه ليس الكرامة عنده من أعظم الأمور والمقدرة والغنى إنّما يؤثران بسبب

1 يظن F : ويظن Bad || 2 ادنى F, Dun : انى mrg., Bad || 3 يستبين F : يستبن Bad || 5 يشبه F*, Dun* (ἔοικε) : يجب Bad || 9 العظيمة corr. : العظيم appar. F || 10 ما له F, Dun : ماله Bad

and wealth likes to be honoured on account of them, so that for the man to whom honour is paltry all other things are paltry likewise. Therefore it is thought of them that they are haughty. (19) It is sometimes thought of happy states that they help greatness of soul, because the well-born deserve honour, and similarly the powerful and rich, because they possess a superiority, and the best of excellent things and every excellent man[110] deserves honour more. Therefore these things render the great-souled in whom they exist more great-souled, i.e. people honour other people.[111] (20) As for the man who is truly honourable,[112] he alone is the good man. As for him who unites both things, he deserves honour more. As for those who have these goods without having virtue, they do not justly think themselves worthy of great things, nor is it rightly said of them that they are great-souled. (21) That is, these things do not exist at all without virtue, because if they are without virtue,[113] they are haughty and sharp-tongued. That is, it is not easy to bear happy states fittingly
1124b without virtue, and if they are unable to bear them and think that they are superior to others, they despise them, while they do whatever it chanced them to do. That is, they imitate the great-souled man without being like him. They imitate him in what they can, but they do not do what virtue necessitates, and they hold others in contempt. (22) As for the great-souled man, he rightly holds others in contempt, because he believes the truth. As for the common people, they believe whatever it chanced them to believe. (23) He is not constantly in danger,[114] but he risks great danger. When he falls into danger he disdains his life, because he thinks that undoubtedly[115] he does not deserve to live in danger.[116] (24) He does good to people, and when good is done to him he is ashamed, because that is characteristic[117] of the inferior. When good is done to him, he requites it

[110] So apparently (Arabic *kull fāḍil* for Greek πᾶν), but something has gone wrong.

[111] The sense is again defective here.

[112] The construction of κατ' ἀλήθειαν with τιμητός violates the word-order, and τιμητός is the complement, not the subject.

[113] Apparently rendering Greek οἱ τὰ τοιαῦτα ἔχοντες as 'those who are such', disregarding ἀγαθά.

[114] Arabic *kathīr al-mukhāṭarah*, i.e. πυκνοκίνδυνος (L^b, M^b) rather than μικροκίνδυνος (vulg.). The words following (οὐδὲ φιλοκίνδυνος [...] τιμᾶν) have dropped out.

[115] Arabic *lā maḥālah* rendering Greek πάντως.

[116] Arabic *'alā khaṭar*, evidently added. But the sense has been missed.

[117] Greek ὑπερέχοντος, τὸ δέ has been omitted or has fallen out.

الكرامة فمن كان له مقدرة وغني فهو يحبّ أن يكرم بهما فمن كانت الكرامة عنده قليلة فسائر الأشياء الأخر أيضاً يقلّ عنده ولذلك يظنّ بهم أنّهم أصحاب النخوة (١٩) وقد يظنّ بالسعادات أنّها تعين على كبر النفس لأنّ ذوي الحسب يستحقّون الكرامة وكذلك ذوو المقدرة والأغنياء لأنّهم ذوو فضل والخير من الأمور الفاضلة وكلّ فاضل فاستحقاقه للكرامة أكثر فلذلك تصير هذه الأشياء من توجد له من الكبيري الأنفس أكبر نفوساً وذلك أنّ قوماً قد يكبرون قوماً (٢٠) فأمّا المكرم على الحقيقة فهو الخير وحده فأمّا الذي يجمع الأمرين جميعاً فهو يستحقّ الكرامة أكثر فأمّا الذين توجد لهم هذه الخيرات من غير أن توجد لهم فضيلة فليس يؤمّلون أنفسهم للأمور العظام على طريق العدل ولا يقال فيهم إنّهم كبيرو الأنفس بالصحّة (٢١) وذلك أنّ هذه الأمور ليس توجد خلواً من فضيلة البتّة لأنّهم إذا كانوا خلواً من الفضيلة كانوا ممتهنين حتّي الألسن وذلك أنّه ليس يسهل احتمل السعادات على ما يجب من غير فضيلة وإذا لم يقدروا أن يحتملوها وظنّوا أنّهم يفضلون غيرهم حقروهم وعملوا أيّ شيء اتّفق لهم وذلك أنّهم يقتدون بالكبير النفس وليس يشبهونه وإنّما يقتدون به فيما يمكنهم [١/٦٩] وما توجبه الفضيلة ليس يفعلونه ويزدرون بغيرهم (٢٢) فأمّا الكبير النفس فبالحقّ يزدر بغيره لأنّه يعتقد الحقّ فأمّا عامّة الناس فيعتقدون أيّ شيء اتّفق لهم (٢٣) وليس هو كثير المخاطرة لكنّه عظيم المخاطرة وإذا وقع في خطر تهاون بحياته لأنّه يرى أنّه ليس يستحقّ لا محالة أن يحيا على خطر (٢٤) وهو يحسن إلى الناس وإذا أحسن إليه يستحيي لأنّ ذلك من شأن المفضل عليه وإذا

5 له : F لهم Bad || 8 العدل Bad*, Dun* (ὀρθῶς) : القول F || 9 إنهم corr. Bad : إنه F || 10 لأنهم corr. Bad : لأنه F || 10 ممتهنين corr. Bad* (ὑπερόπται) : ممتحنين F

largely,[118] and he does that according to what he who began the kindness likes,[119] and is quick to be conciliated.[120] (25) It is thought of them that they remember their own good deeds but do not remember the good deeds of others towards them, because the beneficiary is below the benefactor, and he[121] likes to excel. He delights in hearing of virtue and hates hearing of what has been conferred upon him.[122] For the same reason Thetis did not mention to Zeus her services to him,[123] nor did the nation called Laconians[124] mention to the people of Athens[125] their services to them, but mentioned only the kindness they had met with from them. (26) It is characteristic of the great-souled man that he lacks nothing or scarcely anything, characteristic of him also that he does services with alacrity, and that he is haughty with the powerful and fortunate and modest with the middle people, because to be superior to the former is difficult and prestigious but to the latter is easy. To be haughty in the case of the former is not base, while in the case of the humble it is odious, and if a man does so, he is like one who advances bold as a lion against[126] the weak. (27) He does not vie with a greater than himself.[127] It is characteristic of him also that he is slow in movement[128] and inclined to put off, except on the occasion of a great honour or a great action. His actions are few, but great and notable. (28) He must necessarily hate openly and love openly, because concealment is [bad], and that is characteristic of the fearful, and his concern[129] for the truth is more

---

[118] The comparative (πλειόνων) is disregarded.

[119] This is apparently πρὸς ὅ φιλήσει for προσοφλήσει, and the Arabic translator scarcely read οἱ of K^b.

[120] Arabic *wa-yakūn maʿa sarīʿ al-inʿiṭāf*, representing Greek καὶ ἔσται εὖ πεπονθώς.

[121] I.e. the vulg. βούλεται.

[122] Arabic *al-faḍīlah* [...] *mā ufḍila bihi*. The parallelism seems intended to render Greek μὲν [...] δέ , but the sense is missed.

[123] This is the corrected text. The MS. has: *lam yakun* [sic] *Thāṭis yadhkuru* [sic] *li-Rūs* [leg. *li-Zaūs* or *li-Zāūs*] *iḥsānahu ilaihā*, which gives the required sense, but makes Thetis masculine and Zeus feminine.

[124] Or Spartans (Arabic *Lāqūns*).

[125] The form used here, apparently *Athīnayā*, is perhaps due to Syriac influence, cf. above 1112a 29 = III, 3, 6.

[126] Arabic *lā yaqdama ʿalā an yastaʾsida ʿalā*, i.e. 'does not venture to be bold as a lion against', which evidently gives the wrong sense. Perhaps *illā* should be added before *ʿalā*, or *lā* should be omitted.

[127] Paraphrasing the words καὶ εἰς τὰ ἔντιμα [...] ἄλλοι.

[128] Greek ἀργόν rendered by Arabic *baṭīʾ al-ḥaraka*.

[129] I.e. Greek μέλειν (vulg., Rackham and Gauthier) not ἀμελεῖν (Bywater, Burnet and Ross).

أحسن إليه كافأه بمكافأة كثيرة ويفعل ذلك بحسب الشيء الذي يحبّه الذي ابتدأه بالإحسان ويكون مع سريع الانعطاف (٢٥) ويظنّ بهم أنّهم يذكرون إحسانهم ولا يذكرون إحسان من أحسن إليهم لأنّ المحسن إليه دون المحسن ويحبّ أن يفضل وهو يستلذّ سماع الفضيلة ويستبشع سماع ما أفضل به عليه ولذلك لم يكن ثاطس يذكر لزوس إحسانه إليها ولا الأمّة التي يقال لها لاقونس كانت تذكر لأهل أثينيا إحسانهم إليهم لكنّهم إنّما كانوا يذكرون ما نالهم منهم من الإحسان (٢٦) ومن شأن الكبير النفس ألاّ ينقصه شيء إذ بكدّ ما ينقصه ومن شأنه أيضاً أن يخدم بنشاط وأن يتجالل عند ذوي الأقدار والسعادات ويتطأطأ عند أوساط الناس لأنّ الترفّع على أولئك صعب ذو فخر وعلى هؤلاء سهل والتجالل في أولئك ليس بالخسيس وفي الوضعاء مستثقل فهو في ذلك مثل من لا يقدم على أن يستأسد على الضعفاء (٢٧) ولا يباري أكبر منه ومن شأنه أيضاً أن يكون بطيء الحركة ذا مطل إلاّ في موضع كرامة جليلة أو فعل جليل وتكون أفعاله يسيرة إلاّ أنّها عظيمة مشهورة (٢٨) ومن الواجب ضرورةً أن يكون يبغض علانيةً ويحبّ علانيةً لأنّ المساترة [رديئة] فذلك من شأن

3 يحب read. Dun* (βούλεται) : يجب F, Bad || 4 تكن ... تذكر : F يكن ... يذكر read. Bad || 4 ثاطس read. Bad : w.p. F || 4 لزوس read. Bad, Dun : w.p. F || 5 لاقونس F, Dun : لاقونين Bad || 5 أثينيا read. Dun : w.p. F, اثينا Bad || 9 لا perh. om. Dun || 9 على : إلا على perh. Dun || 12 المساترة Bad*, Dun* (λανθάνειν) : المكاشرة appar. F || 12 رديئة suppl. Dun

than for opinion. He is open in word and deed, since he makes light of things, and for that reason is self-confident and truth-telling,[130] except in the things where jesting[131] is required, but he jests with many people[132] (29) and with the man[133] for whom there is no life
1125a possible except in friendship. For this is slavish, and therefore all flatterers are like hired servants who work for pay, and the humble use flattery. (30) Also he is [...] not one who admires anything, since nothing is great for him, nor does he bear grudges, since it is not characteristic of the great-souled man to call to mind wrongs in any fashion—rather it is characteristic of him to disregard them. (31) It is not characteristic of him to speak to people either about himself or about another. That is, his concern is not that he should be praised or another blamed. Neither is he inclined to praise, and for the same reason he is not a slanderer, even of his enemies, except in case of the need for sharpness[134] and in necessary things and small matters.[135] (32) He is not apt to be vexed or to make entreaty, for that is characteristic of the man who is serious in seeking these things.[136] (33) He is able[137] to choose beautiful things which have no profit rather than profitable, useful things, for this character belongs specially[138] to him who is satisfied with himself. (34) It is thought also of the great-souled man that he is slow in movement,[139] deep-voiced, deliberate in his speech, because the man whose endeavour is for few things is not in haste, and he who finds nothing important does

[130] This does not correspond exactly to any of the Greek MSS. as given by Bywater, and appears to render διὰ τὸ καταφρονητικὸς εἶναι· διὸ παρρησιαστικὸς (Arabic *mudillan*) καὶ ἀληθευτικός.

[131] Arabic *muzāḥ* for Greek εἰρωνείαν.

[132] Arabic *wa-qad yakūn mazzāḥan ʿinda kathīr min an-nās*, i.e. Greek εἰρωνεία δὲ πρὸς τοὺς πολλούς.

[133] Greek καὶ πρὸς ἄλλον is wrongly construed with πρὸς τοὺς πολλούς instead of with μὴ δύνασθαι ζῆν.

[134] Reading *at-taḥaddud*, cf. 1124a 29 = IV, 3, 21 (ὑβρισταί, rendered *ḥaddī al-alsun*, 'sharp-tongued').

[135] The construction appears wrong here: Arabic *wa-fī* [...] *aṣ-ṣighār* should go with what follows. But if *laisa* is read for *wa-laisa* the sense can perhaps be saved.

[136] I.e. Greek ἔχειν is apparently construed with σπουδάζοντος as a dependent infinitive.

[137] I.e. Greek οἷος read as οἷός τε.

[138] Arabic *khāṣṣatan* for Greek μᾶλλον, also frequently for μάλιστα (1119b 5, 6; 1176a 26; 1176b 25)

[139] Arabic *baṭīʾ al-ḥarakah* corresponds to Greek κίνησις βραδεῖα, but at 1124b 28 = IV, 3, 27 the same Arabic expression is used for ἀργός, "sluggish" (Ross), "idle" (Rackham).

الخائف واهتمامه بالحقّ أكثر منه بالظنّ وهو ظاهر القول والفعل إذ كان مستخفّاً بالأمور ولذلك يكون مدلاّ صدوقاً إلاّ في الأشياء التي يحتاج فيها إلى مزاح وقد يكون مزّاحاً عند كثير من الناس (٢٩) وعند من لا يتهيّأ له العيش إلاّ بالتحبّب فإنّ هذا الفعل من فعل العبيد ولذلك صار جميع أهل الملق بمنزلة الأجراء المكترين [١/٧٠] وأهل الضعة يملقون (٣٠) وليس [...] ممّن يعجب من شئ إذ كان لا يتعاظمه شئ ولا هو [...] إذ كان ليس من شأن الكبير النفس ذكر الشرور بوجه من الوجوه بل من شأنه التغافل عنها (٣١) وليس من شأنه أن يحدث الناس لا عن نفسه ولا عن غيره وذلك أنّ ليس اهتمامه بأن يمدح هو ولا أن يذمّ غيره وليس هو أيضاً مدّاحاً ولذلك ليس هو ثلاّباً ولا لأعدائه إلاّ عند الحاجة إلى التحدّد وفي الأشياء الضرورية والأمور الصغار (٣٢) وليس هو ذا تفجّع ولا ذا تضرّع لأنّ ذلك إنّما هو من شأن من يجدّ في طلب هذه الأشياء (٣٣) ويقدر على اتّخاذ الأمور الجميلة التي لا ثمرة لها أكثر من اتّخاذه الأمور المثمرة النافعة وهذا الخلق إنّما هو لمن كان مكتفياً بنفسه خاصّةً (٣٤) ويظنّ أيضاً بالكبير النفس أنّه بطئ الحركة ثقيل الصوت متوقّف في قوله لأنّ من كان وكده إنّما هو في أشياء قليلة فليس يكون عجولاً ومن ليس لشئ عنده خطر فليس يكون مجتهداً وحدّة الصوت وسرعة الحركة إنّما يوجدان

---

4 المكترين F, Dun : والمكترين Bad || 5 يملقون Bad, Dun : illegible F || 5 second [...] illegible F, *bear grudges* Dun || 9 التحدد F*, Dun* (ὕβριν) : التقدد Bad || 9 وليس F : فليس Bad

not exert himself.[140] Shrillness of voice and speed of movement are only found in him who is in haste and who exerts himself. (35) Such is the description of the great-souled man.[141] As for the man who exceeds him, he is the showy man. People of this character also are not thought to be wicked, because they are not evildoers, but they are in error. That is, the small-souled man is deserving of things[142] and he deprives himself of them. It is likely that there is some badness in him, since he does not believe himself worthy of good things. He also is ignorant of himself, otherwise he would desire the things which he is worthy of, since they are goods. Men like these are not foolish but rather they are stupid,[143] and this opinion of theirs is thought to make them worse than others, since every man desires what he is worthy of. That is, they run away from excellent actions and arts, as not being worthy of them, and similarly in regard to external goods. (36) As for showy people, they are foolish and ignorant of themselves at the same time. That is evident in their case, for they take up valued charges as if[144] they were worthy of them, and are exposed thereby. They adorn themselves in dress and outward form and the like, and want their good qualities to be apparent. They describe themselves[145] that people may honour them for that. (37) Smallness of soul is opposed to greatness of soul more than showiness is, for smallness of soul is more prevalent than is showiness, and it is worse than the other. (38) The great-souled man then requires the honour which is noble,[146] as we said at first.

1125b 4.[147] Or it is thought of this virtue[148] that in comparison with the great-souled man it is like generosity in comparison with magnificence. For both these virtues[149] stand apart from what is great, and their action is in inferior[150] and small matters, in the condition which

---

[140] Arabic *mujtahidan* for Greek σύντονος.

[141] Some words of the Greek are here omitted.

[142] Arabic *ashyā'*. Greek has 'good things' (ἀγαθῶν).

[143] Arabic *aghbiyā'*, but this does not render Greek ὀκνηροί, "timid", "retiring" (Ross, Rackham).

[144] Arabic *ka-annahum*, i.e. ὡς γάρ of the vulg. as opposed to οὐ γάρ of K^b.

[145] I.e. Greek αὗτων for αὐτῶν (line 32).

[146] Arabic *jamīlah*, as if καλήν stood in the Greek.

[147] Some words of the Greek have have dropped out.

[148] I.e. legitimate ambition, as appears from the context: it is not expressly named.

[149] I.e. the unnamed virtue (honour) and generosity.

[150] Arabic *al-umūr ad-dūn*, not exact for Greek τὰ μέτρια.

للعجول والمجتهد (٣٥) فهذه صفة الكبير النفس فأمّا الذي يزيد عليه فهو المتفنّج ولا أصحاب هذا الخلق أيضاً يظنّ بهم أنّهم شرار لأنّهم ليسوا بفاعلي شرّ لكنّهم يخطئون وذلك أنّ الصغير النفس يكون مستحقّاً لأشياء فيبخس نفسه إيّاها ويشبه أن يكون فيه شرّ ما من قبل أنّه لا يؤهّل نفسه للخيرات وهو أيضاً يجهل نفسه ولو لا ذلك لكان يشتاق الأشياء التي هو لها أهل إذ كانت خيرات وأمثل هؤلاء ليس هم حمقاء بل الأولى أن يكونوا أغبياء وهذا الرأي منهم يظنّ أنّه يجعلهم شرّاً من غيرهم إذ كلّ واحد من الناس قد يشتاق إلى ما هو له أهل وذلك أنّهم يهربون من الأعمال والصناعات الجيّدة على أنّهم لا يستأهلونها وكذلك يجري أمرهم في الخيرات التي من خارج (٣٦) فأمّا المتفنّجون فحمقى وجاهلون بأنفسهم معاً وذلك من أمرهم ظاهر فإنّهم يتناولون الأمور النفيسة كأنّهم أهل لها ويفتضحون بذلك ويتزيّنون باللباس والشكل وما أشبه [٢/١٥] ذلك ويحبّون أن تكون محاسنهم ظاهرة ويصفون أنفسهم ليكرمهم الناس لذلك (٣٧) وقد يقابل كبر النفس صغر النفس أكثر ممّا يقابله التنفّج فإنّ صغر النفس يكون أكثر ممّا يكون التنفّج وهو شرّ منه فكبير النفس يلتمس الكرامة الجميلة له كما قلنا آنفاً.

٤. أو يظنّ بها أنّ قياسها في التشابه عند كبير النفس كقياس السخاء عند الكرم فإنّ هاتين الفضيلتين كلتيهما قد تباعدتا من الأمر العظيم وفعلها في الأمور الدون والصغار بالحل

3 فيبخس read. Bad*, Dun* (ἀποστερεῖ) : فيجس F || 12 first and second التنفج corr. Bad*, Dun* (χαυνότητος) : التفنج F || 15 كلتيهما corr. Bad : كلتاهما F || 15 فعلها F, Dun : نجعلها Bad

is right. (2) And as in giving and taking in regard to money there are a mean and excess and defect, so it is that there are in the desire for honour more than there ought to be, or less than there ought to be, and whence and as there ought to be. (3) That is, we call 'lover of honour' the man who covets honour more than he ought and whence he ought not.[151] As for the man who does not love honour, he is one who does not wish to be honoured even in noble things. (4) Sometimes we praise the lover of honour for being manly and a lover of what is noble, and sometimes we praise the man who does not love honour as being modest and temperate, as we said in what has preceded. It is plain that since the lover of honour[152] is spoken of in many different ways, we do not always praise the lover of honour for the same thing,[153] but we praise him more than the mass of mankind praises him,[154] and we blame him because he exceeds what is proper. There being no name for the mean between the two, it is likely that doubt should occur in regard to the two extremes.[155] In things in which are excess and defect there is also a mean. (5) Since there is a man who desires honour more than is right and a man who desires it less than he ought, there is one who desires it as he ought. This condition is praised, because it is a mean in regard to love of honour[156] though without a name. It is clear regarding it that in comparison with love of honour[157] it is unambitiousness, and in comparison with unambitiousness it is love of honour, while in comparison with both it is in some sense both. (6) It is likely that this idea applies also in the other virtues. It is clear in regard to the two extremes here that they are opposites, because the mean has no name.

5. Good temper is a mean with respect to anger, and as this intermediate has no name and the extremes are nearly anonymous also, we apply the term good temper to the midmost, since[158] it inclines in

[151] The force of Greek φέγομεν is disregarded, and this and the following sentence are rendered inaccurately.

[152] But Greek is 'lover of such and such' (φιλοτοιούτου).

[153] Greek is οὐκ ἐπὶ τὸ αὐτὸ φέρομεν ἀεὶ τὸ φιλότιμον, i.e. 'we do not apply the term «love of honour» always to the same thing'.

[154] Again the Greek is misunderstood. In praising, we apply the term to loving honour more than most people do (ἐπὶ τὸ μᾶλλον ἢ οἱ πολλοί).

[155] Greek ὡς ἐρήμης is left untranslated.

[156] Arabic *maḥabbat al-karāma*, i.e. φιλοτιμίαν for τιμήν.

[157] I.e. ambition.

[158] Arabic *idh*, but apparently 'although' is wanted.

التي تجب (٢) وكما أنّ في الإعطاء والأخذ في الأموال قد يوجد توسّط وزيادة ونقصان كذلك قد يوجد في الشوق إلى الكرامة أن تكون أكثر ممّا ينبغي أو أقلّ ممّا ينبغي ومن حيث ينبغي وكما ينبغي (٣) وذلك أنّا نسمّي محبّ الكرامة الذي يشتهي الكرامة أكثر ممّا ينبغي ومن حيث لا ينبغي فأمّا الذي لا يحبّ الكرامة فهو الذي ولا في الأمور الجميلة يحبّ أن يكرم (٤) وربّما حمدنا محبّ الكرامة على أنّه ذو رجلة ومحبّ للجميل وربّما حمدنا الذي لا يحبّ الكرامة على أنّه متواضع عفيف على ما قلنا فيما تقدّم وتبيّن أنّ محبّ الكرامة لمّا كان يقل على أنحاء كثيرة وأنّا لا نحمد محبّ الكرامة على شئ واحد بعينه أبداً لكنّا نحمده أكثر ممّا يحمده جمهور الناس ونذمّه لأنّه يخرج عن الواجب وإذا كان التوسّط فيما بين هذين لا اسم له فيشبه أن يكون الشكّ يقع في الطرفين والأشياء التي فيها زيادة ونقصان فيها أيضاً توسّط (٥) وإذا كان ها هنا من يشتهي الكرامة أكثر ممّا ينبغي وها هنا من يشتهيها أقلّ ممّا ينبغي فها هنا من يشتهيها على ما ينبغي وقد تحمد هذه الحل لأنّها توسّط في محبّة الكرامة ليس لها اسم فقد تبيّن من أمرها أنّها بالقياس إلى محبّة الكرامة غير محبّة للكرامة وبالقياس إلى غير محبّة للكرامة محبّة للكرامة وبالقياس إلى كلتيهما كلتاهما بجهة من الجهات (٦) ويشبه أن يكون هذا المعنى يوجد أيضاً في سائر الفضائل الأخر وقد تبيّن من أمر الطرفين ها هنا أنّهما متقابلان لأنّ الأوسط لا اسم له.

٥. [٢/١٦] والحلم توسّط في الغضب ولمّا كان هذا المتوسّط لا اسم له ويكاد أن يكون الطرفان كذلك حملنا الحلم على الأوسط إذ كان مائلاً في النقصان إلى الذي لا اسم له

8 أبدا لكنا : F, Dun أبدا لكنا فإنا لا نحمد محب الكرامة على شئ واحد بعينه أبدا لكنا لما كان يقل على أنحاء كثيرة فإنا لا نحمد محب الكرامة على شئ واحد بعينه أبدا وتبين أن محب الكرامة suppl. Bad || 17 يكون F*, Dun* : يقترن Bad

respect of deficiency to what has no name. (2) The excess is called rage, i.e. the passion is called anger and the things which it causes[159] are many and various. (3) We praise him who is angry at the man with whom it is requisite that he should be angry, for the things which necessitate anger, as he ought, at the right time and in the right measure,[160] and this man should also be the good-tempered man, since good-temper is praised. That is, it is characteristic of the good-tempered man that he is calm, not subject to anger, but is
1126a therein as reason lays down, and his access of anger[161] is according to the time which reason determines. (4) It is thought that the error is more in the case of defect, because the good-tempered man does not love retaliation but extends pardon. (5) As for the defect, it is absence of anger or whatever it is, and it is blamed. That is, those who are not angry with those whom[162] they should be angry with,[163] (6) are thought to possess no feeling and not to suffer pain, and not being angry, a man does not retaliate, but patience under the hearing of abuse and not being angry on behalf of relations and friends is the behaviour of slaves. (7) The excess is in all these things, I mean that the man is angry with someone against whom there should be no anger, and for things which do not necessitate anger, and more than he ought[164] and for a long time.[165] Yet all these things are not the same in a single individual, because that cannot be, since evil destroys itself when its parts are all brought together or it would be unendurable.[166] (8) The hot-tempered man is overcome by sudden anger at what and against whom he ought not, and more than he ought. But their anger quickly calms down, and this is the best thing about them. It happens to them that they are so, because they do not restrain the anger. But they retaliate, and because of their shortness of temper they let anger appear, then they calm down. (9) These are surpassed by the quick-tempered and irascible, who become angry at

---

[159] Arabic *allatī yuḥdithuhā*, perhaps merely a copyist's error.

[160] Arabic *bi'l-miqdār alladhī yanbaghī*. Greek χρόνον appears to have been omitted, perhaps to avoid repetition of Arabic *waqt*, which has already been used to render ὅτε.

[161] Arabic *maujidatuhu*. Greek καὶ ἐπὶ τούτοις is not rendered.

[162] Arabic *'alā man yanbaghī*, i.e. οἷς δεῖ.

[163] More than a line of Greek has dropped out here (ἐφ' οἷς [...] μηδ' ὅτε μηδέ).

[164] Greek καὶ θᾶττον is omitted.

[165] The comparative (πλείω χρόνον) is disregarded.

[166] The construction of ὁλόκληρον with the foregoing is wrong, and ᾗ has evidently been read as ἤ.

(٢) والزيادة تسمّى غيظاً وذلك أنّ الانفعل يسمّى غضباً والأشياء التي يحدثها كثيرة مختلفة (٣) فالذي يغضب على من يجب أن يغضب عليه ومن الأشياء التي توجب الغضب وكما ينبغي وفي الوقت الذي ينبغي وبالمقدار الذي ينبغي قد نحمده وخليق أيضاً أن يكون هذا هو الحليم إذ كان الحلم يحمد وذلك أنّ من شأن الحليم أن يكون ركيناً غير منقاد للغضب لكن يكون في ذلك على ما رتّبه العقل وتكون موجدته بقدر الوقت الذي يقدّره العقل (٤) ويظنّ أنّ الخطأ إنّما يكون أكثر في النقصان لأنّ الحليم ليس هو محبّ للانتقام لكنّه باسط للعذر (٥) فأمّا النقصان كان عدم الغضب أو أيّ شئ كان فهو يذمّ وذلك أنّ الذين لا يغضبون على من ينبغي أن يغضب عليه (٦) قد يظنّ بهم أنّهم لا يحسّون ولا يتأذّون وإذا لم يغضب لم يكن منتقماً والصبر على سماع الشتيمة وترك الغضب للقرابات والأولياء من أخلاق العبيد (٧) والزيادة قد تكون في هذه الأشياء كلّها أعني أن يغضب الإنسان على من لا يجب الغضب عليه ومن الأمور التي لا توجب الغضب وأكثر ممّا ينبغي وزماناً طويلاً إلاّ أنّ هذه كلّها لا تكون في واحد بعينها لأنّ ذلك لا يمكن أن يكون إذ كان الشرّ يفسد نفسه إذا اجتمعت أجزاؤه كلّها أو كان غير محتمل (٨) فالغضوب قد يسرع إليه الغضب ممّا لا ينبغي على من لا ينبغي وأكثر ممّا ينبغي وقد يسكن غضبهم بسرعة وهذا أجود ما فيهم وإنّما عرض لهم أن يكونوا كذا لأنّهم لا يمسكون الغضب لكنّهم ينتقمون ولحدّتهم يظهرون الغضب ثمّ يسكنون (٩) والذين يزيدون على هؤلاء هم السريعو الغضب المحتدّون الذين يغضبون من كلّ شئ وفي كلّ

---

8 او F, Dun : om. Bad || 12 بعينها corr. mrg. : بعينه F || 12 كلها لا F*, Dun* (οὐ ἅπαντα ὑπάρχει) : كلها لا يمكن أن Bad || 13 محتمل corr. mrg. كان ذلك غير محتمل كذا لخصه القاضي || 17 السريعو Bad : السريعوا F

everything and for everything.[167] (10) As for the bitter-tempered man, he is without remission of his anger, and it remains a long time, because he restrains his anger. He calms down when he is appeased, because appeasement[168] calms the anger, because it causes pleasure in place of pain to the subject. But when they are not appeased, their rage is continuous. That is, since they do not allow their anger to appear, it is not possible for anyone to calm them, and therefore their rage remains for a long time. Whoever is in this condition troubles himself and his friends in particular.[169] (11) Those who are angry at what they should not be angry at, and more than they should be, and whose anger lasts a long time and who are not content till they are appeased or retaliate.[170] (12) It is preferable that we should oppose the excess to good temper because it is more frequent. Retaliation is manly,[171] and those whose temper is harsh are ill to live with.[172] (13) What we have said in what has preceded is clear also from what we say now. That is, it is not easy to define how anger should be, against whom, on what ground, for how long time and up to what limit of anger one should be angry, in order to have hit the mark in one's anger or missed. For to have passed the limit in anger by a
1126b little towards excess or towards defect is blamed.[173] That is, we sometimes praise those who are defective and call them good-tempered and those whose temper is harsh are brought into relation with manliness[174] through their being good for leadership. How far he goes in anger to pass the limit and measure for which he is blamed, is not easy for us to define in words because they are partial things, whose distinguishing is by sense. (14) But this amount of explanation is possible for us to reach, viz.: The middle condition, in which anger occurs against the right person,[175] in the right amount[176] and so

[167] I.e. apparently 'for every reason', which gives the necessary differentiation of meaning. But ἐπὶ παντί means "on every occasion" (Ross). The Greek words which follow (ὅθεν καὶ τοὔνομα) are omitted.

[168] Arabic *at-tashaffī* for τιμωρία: τιμωρεῖσθαι (§ 12) is differently rendered.

[169] Arabic *khāṣṣatan* for Greek μάλιστα.

[170] The words "we call harsh-tempered" (Rackham) (χαλεποὺς δὲ λέγομεν) have dropped out, and the sentence remains incomplete.

[171] This seems to be the meaning (Arabic *al-intiqām min ar-rujlah*), but the Greek is 'more human', ἀνθρωπικώτερον (the comparative is disregarded).

[172] The comparative (χείρους) is again disregarded.

[173] But the Greek says the opposite (οὐ ψέγεται, 'is not blamed').

[174] Here Greek ἀνδρώδεις is correctly rendered. Cf. above 1126a 30.

[175] The Arabic equivalent of Greek καὶ ἐφ' οἷς δεῖ is missing.

[176] Arabic *wa-kam miqdār mā yanbaghī an yakūna* for Greek ὡς δεῖ, perhaps misread.

شيء (١٠) فأمّا الحرّ النفس فيعسر سكون غضبه ويبقى زماناً طويلاً لأنّه يمسك غضبه ويسكن عن [٢/٨٧] الغضب إذا اشتفى لأنّ التشفّي يسكّن الغضب لأنّه يحدث لصاحبه لذّة موضع الأذى وإذا لم يشتفوا اتّصل غيظهم وذلك أنّهم لمّا كانوا لا يظهرون غضبهم لم يتهيّأ لأحد تسكينهم ولذلك يبقى غيظهم زماناً طويلاً ومن كان بهذه الحال فهو مؤذٍ لنفسه ولأصدقائه خاصّةً (١١) والذين يغضبون ممّا لا يجب أن يغضب منه وبأكثر ممّا يجب ويبقى غضبهم زماناً طويلاً ولا يرضون حتّى يشتفوا وينتقموا (١٢) فالأولى أن تجعل الزيادة مقابلة للحلم لأنّها تكون أكثر والانتقام من الرجلة والذين يصعب غضبهم سيئو العشرة (١٣) وقد تبيّن أيضاً ما قلناه فيما تقدّم ممّا نقوله الآن وذلك أنّه ليس يسهل تحديد الغضب كيف ينبغي أن يكون وعلى من ولأيّ شيء وكم يكون مقدار زمانه وإلى أيّ حدّ من الغضب ينبغي أن يغضب حتّى يكون قد أصاب في غضبه أو أخطأ فإنّ تجاوز الحدّ في الغضب قليلاً إلى الزيادة أو إلى النقصان قد يذمّ وذلك أنّا ربّما حمدنا أصحاب النقصان وسمّيناهم حلماء والذين يصعب غضبهم ينسبون إلى الرجلة من طريق أنّهم يصلحون للرياسة والذي يبلغ من تجاوزه الغضب الحال والمقدار اللذين يكونان بهما مذموماً فليس يسهل علينا تحديده بالقول لأنّها أمور جزئية نميّزها بالحسّ (١٤) ولكن قد يمكننا أن نبلغ من تبيين ذلك هذا المقدار فنقول إنّ الحال المتوسّطة التي بها يحدث الغضب على من يجب وكم مقدار ما ينبغي أن يكون وسائر ما أشبه ذلك محمود والزيادات والنقصانات مذمومة فإذا تجاوزت التوسّط قليلاً ذمّت ذمّاً يسيراً وإذا تجاوزت أكثر من ذلك ذمّت أكثر من ذلك وإذا

---

8 يسهل F : بسهل Bad || 9 مقدار زمانه F, Dun : هذا وزمانه Bad || 10 فإن F : فإن من suppl. mrg.

on, is praised, while the excesses and defects are blamed. When they exceed the mean by a little, they are blamed a little, when they exceed it more, they are blamed more, and when they exceed it by very much, they are blamed very much. So that it is plain that we must hold fast to the middle condition. (15) We have now described the conditions which exist in anger.

6. As for the conditions which apply in social contacts, conversations and associations, those who aim therein at people's favour[177] exhaust their devices that others may take pleasure in their company, and they do not contend with any[178] of those with whom they are in contact about anything. But they think not to cause pain to those with whom they are in contact. (2) The opposite to these, those who are different from them in all their conditions and do not heed anything which pains others, are called churlish, ill-natured and harsh. (3) It is plain that these conditions described are blameworthy, and that the middle condition here is praiseworthy, because in it we accept what we should accept, and as we should accept it, and similarly there sometimes is churlishness in its possessor.[179] (4) The middle condition has no name, but it resembles friendship particularly.[180] That is, he who is in this middle state is like what we are inclined to say of the agreeable man, that he is our friend, because of the quickness of his accepting affection.[181] (5) This disposition in fact differs from friendship because it is free from emotion and its possessor is not concerned for the affection of him with whom he is friendly.[182] That is, he does not accept everything that he accepts in the right way as liking the man and not[183] treating him as an enemy, but he accepts it because he is this kind of person. He is friendly with those whom he does not know, those whom he does know,[184] and those with whom he is not familiar in the same way, except that he does that in everything as is proper for it. That is, it is not proper that his concern for strangers and for intimates should be the same and not

[177] This renders Greek ἄρεσκοι, but the construction is not right in what follows, and ἐπαινοῦντες is not expressed.

[178] I.e. Greek οὐθέν taken as masculine.

[179] Arabic *wa-ʿalā hādha 'l-mithāl qad yakūnu fī ṣāḥibihā sharāsah*. The translator seems to have had difficulty with δυσχερανεῖ here and below in § 7 (*bis*).

[180] Arabic *khāṣṣatan* for Greek μάλιστα as at 1126a 26.

[181] This is not the meaning of the Greek (προσλαβόντα read as προλαβόντα).

[182] Arabic *man yuḥibbuhu*, but Greek is 'with whom he associates' (οἷς ὁμιλεῖ).

[183] Arabic *wa-lā* for Greek ἤ, 'or'.

[184] Greek καὶ συνήθεις is omitted in the Arabic translation.

جاوزت جدّاً ذمّت جدّاً فمن البيّن أنّه ينبغي لنا أن نتمسّك بالحال الوسطى (١٥) وقد وصفنا الأحوال الموجودة في الغضب.

٦. فأمّا الأحوال التي تكون في المعاشرات والمخاطبات والمشاركات فالذين يقصدون بها مرضاة الناس فإنّهم يستنفدون حيلهم في أن يلتذّ بمعاشرتهم غيرهم ولا يجاذبون أحداً بمن يعاشرونه على شيء ولكنّهم يرون ألاّ يغمّوا [٢/١٨] من يعاشرونه (٢) والمضادّون لهؤلاء والذين يخالفونهم في جميع أحوالهم ولا يبالون بشيء يغمّ غيرهم يسمّون شرسين شكسين وعرين (٣) ومن البيّن أنّ هذه الأحوال الموصوفة مذمومة وأنّ الحال المتوسّطة لها محدودة لأنّا نقبل بها ما ينبغي أن نقبله وكما ينبغي وعلى هذا المثل قد يكون في صاحبها شراسة (٤) وليس لها اسم وقد تشبه المحبّة خاصّةً وذلك أنّ الذي يكون بالحال المتوسّطة هذه صفتها مثل ما نميل إلى أن نقول في الليّن الجانب إنّه لنا محبّ لسرعة قبوله للمودّة (٥) وقد يخالف هذا الخلق المحبّة لأنّه يكون خلواً من الانفعال ولا يهتمّ صاحبه بمودّة من يحبّه وذلك أنّه ليس يقبل كلّ واحد ممّا يقبله على ما ينبغي بأن يحبّه ولا يعاديه لكنّه إنّما يقبل ذلك لأنّه بهذه الصفة ويحبّ من لا يعرفه ومن يعرفه ومن لم يألفه على مثل واحد غير أنّه يفعل ذلك في كلّ واحد من الأشياء كما يجب لها وذلك أنّه ليس يجب أن

---

5 الا يغموا F*, Dun* (ἄλυποι) : الا يعموا Bad || 5 يعاشرونه Dun : illegible F || 8 ما repeated in F

cause pain either to anyone. (6) We have then described how social life should be,[185] and if you relate his conditions to the noble and to the useful, you will see him aiming at not causing pain to anyone,[186] or at giving pleasure. (7) That is, it is likely that the conditions of social life[187] exist only in pleasures and pain. Whatever there is of these in which nothing noble exists[188] or in which something harmful does exist, it is difficult for its possessor to make anyone happy[189] and he may choose to give pain. This produces discredit[190] for the agent, and this discredit is either not small or its opposite.[191] As for the opposite of the condition, it produces no little pain,[192] but its possessor finds that difficult.[193] (8) He associates differently with
1127a the powerful and ordinary people,[194] with those whom he knows outright and those whom he knows less, and in all the other different conditions he gives each man his due. He is ashamed to rejoice alone[195] and dislikes to pain anyone. If the things in which his conditions result are great matters, I mean what is noble and useful, he accepts that and is content therewith, and he causes a little pain, for the sake of the future pleasure.[196] (9) Such is the man of the modest state, and he has not (...)[197]

1127a 13 7. And in regard to these people [...][198]
1127b 31 (16) [...] and apparent in it, it is clear in regard to them that they are acceptable. (17) It is plain that the boastful man is opposed to the truthful man, for he is below him.

---

[185] This apparently renders ὅτι ὡς δεῖ ὁμιλήσει, i.e. δεῖ construed with ὁμιλήσει read as ὁμιλῆται.

[186] The Arabic translation is here quite wrong, but evidently μή of the vulgate, not ἤ was read.

[187] Arabic *aḥwāl al-muʿāsharah* for Greek τὰς ἐν ταῖς ὁμιλίαις γινομένας, which is made the subject of an accusative and infinitive construction depending on Greek ἔοικε.

[188] Greek αὐτῷ is omitted.

[189] I.e. Greek συνηδύνειν construed with δυσχερανεῖ, which is wrongly rendered.

[190] Greek ἄν and the subjunctive (φέρῃ) are disregarded.

[191] The construction is wrong here.

[192] Arabic introduces an unnecessary negative: *laisat tumīlu ghamman yasīran*.

[193] The Arabic sentence is far wrong.

[194] Arabic *abnā' an-nās*, cf. 1124a 10.

[195] Arabic *yastaḥyī min an yusarra waḥdahu*, but this is to translate καθ' αὑτὸν [...] αἰδούμενος instead of the Greek text (καθ' αὑτὸ [...] αἱρούμενος).

[196] Greek μεγάλης omitted with K^b.

[197] The rest of c. 6 is missing from the manuscript.

[198] Most of c. 7 is fragmentary and is here omitted, down to § 16.

يكون الاهتمام بالغرباء وبالمألوفين على مثل واحد ألاّ يغمّ أيضاً أحداً (٦) فقد وصفنا كيف ينبغي أن تكون المعاشرة وإذا نسبت أحواله إلى الجميل وإلى النافع رأيته يقصد إلى ألاّ يغمّ أحداً أو إلى أن يسرّه (٧) وذلك أنّه يشبه أن تكون أحوال المعاشرة إنّما توجد في اللذّات والأذى وما كان من هذه لا يوجد فيه أمر جميل أو كان فيه أمر ضارّ فقد يصعب على صاحبه أن يسرّ أحداً وقد يختار أن يؤذي وهذا يكسب فاعله قبحاً وهذا القبح إمّا أن يكون ليس بالصغير وإمّا أن يكون ضدّه فأمّا ضدّ الحال فليست تميل غمّاً يسيراً لكن صاحبها يعسر عليه ذلك (٨) وقد يعاشر ذوي الأقدار وأبناء الناس ومن يعرفه معرفة صحيحة ومن يعرفه دون ذلك معاشرات مختلفة وفي سائر الأحوال المختلفة الأخر قد يعطي كلّ واحد ما يجب له وقد يستحيي من أن يسرّ وحده ويكره أن يغمّ أحداً والأشياء التي تؤول أحواله إليها إن كانت من الأمور العظام أعني الجميل والنافع استرسل إلى ذلك وانبسط فيه وقد يغمّ غمّاً يسيراً بسبب اللذّة التي تكون فيما بعد (٩) فهذه صفة المتوسّط ولم (...) [١/٥٣]

٧. أمّا الذين [...] (١٦) [١/٧٥] وظاهرة فيه فبيّن من أمرهم أنّهم مقبولون (١٧) وتبيّن أن يقابل الضدّ و[...] دونه.

---

1 بالمألوفين corr. Bad : بالمولوفين F || 1 ألا corr. Dun : لا F, Bad || 6 ضد corr. Bad, Dun : ضده F || 7 أبناء F, Dun : أفياء Bad || 14 يقابل الضد و [...] دونه partly illegible F, *the boastful man is opposed to the truthful man, for he is below him* Dun

8. Since a man in his life has rest, and his conduct, during the time of
1128a this rest, includes play, it is thought that here also is a certain pleasant association in which one speaks of what one should and as one should, and similarly listens. The moderate things like these which are heard and said in it[199] differ. (2) It is clear that in these things also there is the mean and excess and defect. (3) That is, those who exceed in what is laughable are thought to be amusing[200] because they inevitably swallow[201] anything that is laughable. The most of their aim is to be laughed at and that their speech should be amusing,[202] and that they should not pain those with whom they are joking. As for those who say nothing laughable at all and disapprove of anyone who does, they are thought to be wild[203] and rude. As for those who employ pleasant quips, they are called witty,[204] because all these states are thought to belong to the character [...][205] and just as bodies are judged by their movement, so also are characters. (4) Since the ludicrous is well-known and most of those present[206] enjoy jesting and raillery more than they should, mimics[207] are called [...].[208] The fact of their being very different is clear from what we have said. (5) Pleasantness belongs specially to the middle state also, and it is characteristic of the pleasant man that he says and hears what is appropriate for the well-mannered, free man to say and to hear. For there are things which it is appropriate for the man whose state this is to say and to hear by way of amusement. The amusement of a free man is different from the amusement of a slave, and the amusement of an educated man is different from the amusement of one who has no education. (6) That is known from the poems which

---

[199] Arabic *fīhā* again refers to *muʿāsharah*, but τοιούτοις and τοιούτων are taken as neuter, and the sentence goes wrong.

[200] Arabic *mustamlaḥūn*, but perhaps *mustathqalūn*, 'hateful', should be read, Greek φορτικοί, as at 1124b 22.

[201] Arabic *yusīghūna* for Greek γλιχόμενοι is of course not right.

[202] Greek ἢ τοῦ λέγειν εὐσχήμονα is badly translated, the sense of the preceding μᾶλλον, 'rather (than)', being disregarded.

[203] Arabic *waḥshīyūn*, i.e. reading ἄγριοι of the vulg. as against K^b's ἄγροικοι. Cf. also 1128b 2.

[204] Greek οἷον εὔτροποι is not translated.

[205] After Arabic *li l-khulq* a word or two is illegible.

[206] Arabic *al-ḥuḍūr* not in the Greek.

[207] Arabic *al-muḥākūn*, but perhaps *al-mājinūn* should be read, cf. § 3.

[208] After Arabic *al-muḥākūn* a word is illegible.

٨. ولمّا كان الإنسان في عيشته راحة وكانت سيرته في وقت هذه الراحة تكون بمداعبة يظنّ أنّ ها هنا أيضاً معاشرة ما مستطابة يتكلّم فيها فيما يجب وكما يجب وكذلك يسمع فيه وقد يختلف ما يقل فيها من أمثل هذه الأشياء المتوسّطة وما يسمع (٢) ومن البيّن أنّ في هذه الأشياء أيضاً التوسّط وزيادة ونقصاناً (٣) وذلك أنّ الذين يفرطون فيما يضحك منه يظنّ بهم أنّهم مستملحون لأنّهم يسيغون الأمر الذي يضحك منه لا محالة وأكثر قصدهم أن يضحك منهم وأن يكون كلامهم مستملحاً وألاّ يغمّوا من يتلهّونه وأمّا الذين لا يقولون شيئاً يضحك أصلاً وينكرون على من يقوله فيظنّ بهم أنّهم وحشيون جفلة فأمّا من يستعمل المداعبة الطيّبة فيسمّون ظرفاء لأنّ هذه الحالات كلّها يظنّ بها أنّها لخلق [...] وكما أنّ الأبدان يحكم عليها من حركتها كذلك الأخلاق (٤) وإذا انتشر الشئ المضحك فسرّ أكثر الحضور بالمداعبة والمهاترة أكثر ممّا ينبغي سمّي المحاكون [...] والأمر في أنّهم يختلفون اختلافاً ليس باليسير قد تبيّن ممّا قلنا (٥) والطلاقة خاصّةً بالحال الوسطى أيضاً ومن شأن الطلق أن يقول ويسمع ما يليق بالرجل الليّن الحرّ أن يقوله ويسمعه فإنّ ها هنا أشياء تليق بمن كانت هذه حالته أن يقولها ويسمعها على جهة المداعبة ومداعبة الحرّ تخالف مداعبة العبد ومداعبة الأديب تخالف مداعبة من لا أدب له (٦) ويعلم ذلك من

1 first و F : om. Bad || 2 كذلك Dun : partly illegible F || 8 الحالات F, Bad, Dun : الحركات perh. corr. Dun* (κινήσεις) || 8 لخلق Bad, Dun : للخلق appar. F || 9 انتشر corr. mrg. : انتشى F || 10 المحاكون F, Bad, Dun : الماجنون perh. corr. Dun

the ancients and the moderns have composed in satire.[209] That is, in respect of approval.[210] (7) Would that I knew whether it is right to define raillery and recrimination[211] as what is not speech such as is not appropriate for a free man, or as not paining the hearer, or as delighting him, or something like this not defined! Since what is hateful and pleasant for each individual man is different for the other. (8) Such things the hearer will listen to, for the thing which he will tolerate listening to, it is thought he will do, (9) because it is not everything that he will do. That is, amusement is abuse, and certain legislators[212] prohibit abuse, and it is more appropriate for some of them also to prohibit raillery. (10) The acceptable[213] free man has this state of character, since he is as it were the law for himself. The moderate man—and it is he who is found with this state of character—is called cheerful[214] or [...]. As for the mimic, he cannot resist what causes laughter,[215] and he does not accept[216] from himself or another anything save the things which cause laughter. He also
1128b says things which the acceptable man does not approve of saying and things which he does not approve of hearing. As for the wild[217] man, he is of no use for social intercourse like this, since nothing of it suits him[218] and he is vexed by all of it. (11) Yet it is thought that rest and play are necessities in a man's life. (12) Thus the mean states which have been described are three. All of them share in certain words and actions. They differ in that one of them is concerned with truth and the others with what is pleasant. As for the latter they

---

[209] Arabic *al-ash'ār allatī waḍa'ahā al-qudamā' wa 'l-ḥadath bi 'l-hijā'*. The translator's circumlocution for 'the old and new comedies' (τῶν κωμῳδιῶν τῶν παλαιῶν καὶ τῶν καινῶν) is not accurate, but natural enough, given that satire (*al-hijā'*) was a recognized genre of classical Arabic poetry. The term would convey something of the meaning of comedy to his readers. For the translator's apparent ignorance of the Greek theatre, cf. above 1123a 23 (= IV, 2, 20).

[210] Arabic *istiḥsān*, which is hardly Greek εὐσχημοσύνην.

[211] Arabic *at-tahātur wa 't-tafāḥush* does not of course render τὸν εὖ σκώπτοντα, and the sentence goes awry.

[212] Arabic *qaum min wāḍi'ī an-nawāmīs*. But this is to read ἔνιοι for ἔνια and construe it with νομοθέται.

[213] Arabic *maqbūl* for Greek χαρίεις, as at 1127b 31.

[214] Arabic *ṭalq*, then a word or two are illegible.

[215] Arabic *al-muḍḥik*, cf. § 4 *ash-shai' al-muḍḥik*.

[216] Arabic *yaqbalu*, translating apparently ἀνεχόμενος for ἀπεχόμενος.

[217] Arabic *al-waḥshī*, i.e. again the reading of the vulg. ἄγριος, cf. 1128a 9.

[218] Arabic *lā yuwāfiquhu shai' minhā*, but Greek οὐθὲν [...] συμβαλλόμενος is quite different ('he contributes nothing').

الأشعار التي وضعها القدماء والحدث في الهجاء وذلك أنّ قوماً منهم كان يضحكهم قبح القول وقوماً كانت تضحكهم التهمة وبين هذين الشيئين في الاستحسان فرق ليس باليسير (٧) ويا ليت شعري أينبغي أن يحدّ التهاتر والتفاحش بأنّه ما لا يكون القول ممّا لا يليق بالرجل الحرّ أو ما لا يكون يغمّ سامعه أو بأن يكون يطربه مثل هذا غير محدود إذ كان البغيض واللذيذ عند كلّ واحد من الناس غيره مثل الآخر (٨) ومثل هذه الأشياء [١/٨٦] يسمع السامع فإنّ الشئ الذي يحتمل سماعه قد يظنّ به أنّه يفعله (٩) لأنّه ليس كلّ شئ يفعله وذلك أنّ المداعبة مشاتمة وقوم من واضعي النواميس يمنعون المشاتمة وأخلق بقوم منهم أيضاً يمنعون التهاتر (١٠) والرجل الحرّ المقبول فهذه حاله إذ كان لنفسه بمنزلة الناموس فالمتوسّط وهو الموجود بهذه الحل يسمّى طلقاً أو [...] وأمّا المحاكي فدون المضحك لا يقبل من نفسه ولا من غيره إلاّ الأشياء التي تضحك ويقول أيضاً أشياء لا يستحسن الرجل المقبول أن يقولها وأشياء لا يستحسن أن يسمعها فأمّا الوحشي فلا يصلح لأمثل هذه المعاشرات إذ كان لا يوافقه شئ منها ويمتعض من جميعها (١١) وقد يظنّ أنّ الراحة والمداعبة في سيرة الإنسان ضروريتان (١٢) فالمتوسّطات الموصوفة ثلاث وجميعهن يشتركن في أقاويل وأفعل ويختلفون في أنّ إحداهن توجد في الصدق والأخرى

3 القول F, Dun : om. Bad || 4 يغم F*, Dun* (λυπεῖν) : يهم Bad || 6 يسمع Dun : partly illegible F || 10 المضحك F, Dun : الضحك Bad || 11 فأما F : وأما Bad

are partly concerned with amusements and partly with social associations in lives other than this life.[219]

9. As for shame, we must not speak of it as a virtue, because it is more like a passion than a condition. (2) Therefore it is defined as fear of disgrace. Its coming into existence[220] is similar to the coming into existence of the fear of frightening things. That is, those who are bashful blush, and those who fear death turn pale. Both effects appear to belong in some way to the states of the body, and this is something due to passion rather than to a condition. (3) This passion is not appropriate to every age, but is appropriate only to youth, since we think that the like of these should be ashamed because, their way of life being dependent on passion, they frequently make mistakes, and shame prevents them from this. Hence we tend to praise the shamefaced man,[221] but there is no one who praises an older man for being shamefaced, because we do not think that he should do anything of which he is ashamed. (4) The excellent man also is not ashamed, since shame comes from bad things, and[222] these[223] should not be done. (5) If disgraceful things are partly what are so in truth, partly what are so in opinion, there is no difference between them, because both sorts ought not to be done, so that one should not be ashamed of either.[224] (6) The bad man is he of whom it is characteristic that he is in a condition in which he does something disgraceful. When he has done anything like this, he is ashamed, and therefore to think of him[225] as good is absurd. That is, shame is for the things which exist voluntarily.[226] (7) It is good by agreement,[227] because if the bashful man[228] has done a thing, he is ashamed. This characteristic does not exist in regard to the virtues, except[229] that

---

[219] Arabic *siyar ghair hādhihi 's-sīrah*. This is a bad mistranslation of κατὰ τὸν ἄλλον βίον = 'in the rest of life'.

[220] Apparently Greek ἀποτελεῖται of both K^b and L^b was read, but taken as passive.

[221] The important qualification 'when young' (τῶν μὲν νέων) has dropped out.

[222] A slip for Greek γάρ.

[223] Arabic *hādhihi* for Greek τὰ τοιαῦτα.

[224] The Arabic translation is against the punctuation of Rackham and Gauthier.

[225] Arabic *aẓ-ẓann bihi*, but the sense requires 'for him to think of himself'.

[226] A line has been omitted through homoioteleuton with ἡ αἰδώς (or its Arabic equivalent).

[227] Conventionally (Arabic *iṣṭilāḥan*).

[228] Arabic *al-ḥaiyī*. But we want rather 'the excellent man' (*al-fāḍil*).

[229] Arabic *illā an*. But this is Greek εἰ μή rather than εἰ δ' ἡ.

في الأمر اللذيذ فأمّا الموجودة في اللذّة فمنها ما يكون في المداعبات ومنها ما يكون في معاشرات من سير غير هذه السيرة.

٩. فأمّا الحياء فليس ينبغي أن نتكلّم فيه على أنّه فضيلة ما لأنّه أشبه بالانفعل منه بالحل (٢) ولذلك يحدّ بأنّه الخوف من الدناءة وتكوّنه شبيه بتكوّن الفزع من الأمور الهائلة وذلك أنّ الذين يخجلون يحمرّون والذين يخافون الموت يصفرّون فالأمران كلاهما يظهر أنّهما من أحوال الجسم بضرب من الضروب وهذا شيء هو بالانفعل أولى منه بالحل (٣) وهذا الانفعل ليس يليق بكلّ سنّ بل إنّما يليق بالحداثة إذ كنّا نرى أنّه يجب أن يكون أمثال هؤلاء مستحيين لأنّ سيرتهم لمّا كانت تكون بالانفعل صاروا يكثرون الخطاء والحياء يمنعهم من ذلك فمن ذلك صرنا نحمد المستحيي وليس من أحد يحمد شيخاً على أنّه مستحيي لأنّا لا نرى أنّه ينبغي أن يفعل شيئاً يستحيي منه (٤) ولا الفاضل أيضاً يستحيي إذ كان الحياء إنّما يكون من الأشياء الرديئة وكانت هذه لا ينبغي أن تفعل (٥) وإذا كانت الأشياء القبيحة [١/٧٧] منها ما هي كذلك بالحقيقة ومنها ما هي بالظنّ ولا فرق بينهما لأنّ القسمين جميعاً ينبغي ألاّ تفعل لهذا لا يستحيى منها (٦) والرديء هو الذي من شأنه أن يكون بحال يفعل بها شيئاً من الأمور القبيحة ويكون إذا فعل شيئاً من هذه استحيا ولذلك صار الظنّ به أنّه سليم محالاً وذلك أنّ الحياء في الأمور التي تكون طوعاً (٧) هو حسن اصطلاحاً لأنّ الحيي إن فعل شيئاً استحيا وليس هذا الخلق في الفضائل إلاّ أنّ

4 بتكون F : بتكوين Bad || 11 لا F*, Dun* (οὐ) : om. Bad || 13 القسمين F*, Dun* (οὐδέτερα) : القبائح Bad || 14 استحيا corr. Bad : استحيى F || 15 محالا F*, Dun* (ἄτοπον) : بحل Bad || 16 الحيي F, Dun : المسى Bad || 16 استحيا corr. Bad : استحيي F

shamelessness is bad, and similarly that a man should not be ashamed to do evil, and strictly it is not right either[230] that a man should do things of this kind and be ashamed. (8) Nor is self-restraint either a virtue, but is a mixed thing. We shall speak about it later. We now speak about justice.

End of the Fourth Discourse of the Ethics of Aristotle, and praise be to God and peace upon His servants whom He has chosen.

[230] This translation is somewhat far from the Greek.

القحة شرّ وكذلك ألاّ يستحيي الإنسان أن يعمل القبيح وأجدر ألاّ يكون أيضاً من الصواب أن يفعل الإنسان مثل هذه الأشياء ويستحيي (٨) ولا ضبط النفس أيضاً فضيلة ولكنّه شيء مختلط وسنتكلّم فيه فيما بعد ونحن الآن نتكلّم في العدل.

آخر المقالة الرابعة من الأخلاق لأرسطو والحمد للّه وسلّم على عباده الذين اصطفى

4 وسلم F, Dun : om. Bad

BOOK V

In the name of God, the Merciful, the Compassionate
God bless Muhammad and his family and give them peace

The Fifth Discourse of the Book of Ethics of Aristotle

1129a 1. He said: As for justice and injustice, let us investigate what they are and in respect of what sort of thing they are, since they are actions,[1] and what sort of mean justice is, and for what sort of things the just is a mean. (2) But our investigation is exactly in accordance with what we have defined in the preceding part of our treatise. (3) For we see that all intend by justice this[2] state in consequence of which they are the doers of just things, and in consequence of which they are just and wish for just things, similarly also injustice is that in consequence of which they are unjust and wish for what is unjust. For this cause let these be your[3] subjects, or as it were a pattern, (4) seeing that the sciences and the faculties and states are of different kinds.[4] As regards the faculty and the science, it is thought that the faculty of opposite things[5] is one and the same and their science[6] one and the same, but as for the states of opposites, they are opposites,[7] e.g. health, for the opposites do not come from it, but only healthy things. For we say 'he walks in a healthy manner', when someone walks as a healthy person does. (5) Often the opposite state is known from its opposite, and often the states are known from their subjects. For if the good state is apparent, the bad state is apparent also. The good state appears from the things which possess a good state, and from the other than good state there appear the things

---

[1] Arabic *idh kānat afʿālan*, i.e. οὖσαι πράξεις is construed separately, not with τυγχάνουσιν.

[2] Arabic *hādhihi* for Greek τὴν τοιαύτην, cf. 1128b 23 = IV, 9, 4.

[3] Greek is ἡμῖν.

[4] Arabic *hai'āt* for Greek τρόπος (differently at 1129a 9).

[5] Greek τῶν ἐναντίων is wrongly construed with δύναμις, then with ἐπιστήμη and ἡ αὐτή is made the complement.

[6] See previous note.

[7] Arabic *fa-ammā hai'āt al-aḍdād fa-aḍdād*. This gives the general sense of the difficult Greek ἕξις δ' ἡ ἐναντία τῶν ἐναντίων οὔ.

المقالة الخامسة

بسم الله الرحمن الرحيم

صلّى الله على محمّد وعلى آله وسلم

المقالة الخامسة من كتاب الأخلاق لأرسطو

١. قل فأمّا العدالة ولا عدالة فلنفحص ما هي وفي أيّ شئ هي إذ كانت أفعالاً وأيّ توسّط هي العدالة والعدل وسط لأيّ أشياء (٢) ولكن بحثنا على ما حدّدنا بعينه فيما تقدّم من قولنا (٣) فإنّا نرى الجميع يريدون أن يقولوا العدالة هي هذه الهيئة التي منها يكون فاعلو الأشياء العادلة والتي منها يعدلون ويريدون الأشياء العادلة وكذلك أيضاً لا عدل التي منها لا يعدلون ويريدون ما ليس بعدل ولهذا السبب فلتكن لكم هذه مقدّمات أو كالرسم (٤) من أجل أنّه ليس النوع واحداً في العلوم والقوّات والهيئات فإنّه أمّا القوّة والعلم فإنّه يظنّ أنّ قوّة الأضداد واحدة بعينها وعلمها واحد بعينه فأمّا هيئات الأضداد فأضداد مثل البرء فإنّه لا تكون منه الأضداد بل تكون منه الأشياء [١/٧٨] البريئة فقط فإنّما نقول إنّه مشى بنوع برئ إذا كان يمشي كما يمشي ذو البرء (٥) وربّما عرفت الهيئة الضدّية من ضدّها وربّما عرفت الهيئات من موضوعاتها فإنّه إن كانت الهيئة الجيّدة ظاهرة تكون الهيئة الرديئة ظاهرة أيضاً وتظهر الهيئة الجيّدة في الأشياء التي هي ذوات هيئة جيّدة ومن الهيئة الغير جيّدة تظهر ذوات الهيئة الغير جيّدة فإنّه إن كانت الهيئة الجيّدة كثافة الجسم فمضطرّ أن

---

5 لأي F, Dun : في أي corr. Bad || 5 لكن F*, Dun* (δέ) : ليكن corr. Bad || 6 يكون فاعلو corr. Bad : يكونون فاعل F || 11 البريئة Dun : illegible F

which possess the other than good state.[8] For if the good state is thickness of body, inevitably then the bad state is thinness of body.[9] (6) It mostly follows as a consequence, if one of the two is spoken of in a general sense that the other is spoken of in a general sense, for example,[10] justice and injustice.[11] (7) But this is concealed because of the nearness of the equivocation, and is not very plain, as it is in the case of things which are far apart. For the difference in things which are far apart is greater than in the property,[12] e.g. 'key',[13] which is used equivocally for the collar-bone which is close to the neck of animals and that with which they lock doors. (8) Let it be considered in how many ways 'unjust' can be said. For it is thought of the man who contravenes the law that he is unjust, and similarly of the man of extensive property—he who takes by force—,[14] and the man who acts unfairly.[15] It is plain then that the just man[16] will be the man who keeps the law and who acts fairly. So
1129b then what is just is the law and the fair. And as for the unjust, it is not law and not fair. (9) Since the man of extensive property is unjust,[17] he is not concerned with all good things, but with those on which happiness and unhappiness depend, for among good things there are some which are so absolutely and at all times, but not always for a particular person. People ask for these things for themselves in their prayers and pursue them, but not always.[18] Rather they

[8] The sentence is misunderstood and mistranslated; 'other than good' is not in the Greek (καὶ ἐκ ταύτης τὰ εὐεκτικά).

[9] Eight words of Greek omitted through homoioteleuton.

[10] A line is again omitted (εἰ τὸ δίκαιον, καὶ τὸ ἄδικον. ἔοικε δὲ πλεοναχῶς λέγεσθαι).

[11] The Arabic text does not support Ramsauer, followed by Gauthier, in suppressing ἡ δικαιοσύνη καί in 1129a 26.

[12] Arabic *aktharu minhu fī 'l-khāṣṣah*. This must render ἡ γὰρ διαφορὰ πολλὴ ἡ κατὰ τὴν ἰδέαν misreading ἡ as ἤ, taking πολλή equivalent to a comparative, and rendering Greek ἰδέαν, misread as ἰδίαν, by Arabic *khāṣṣah*.

[13] Arabic *ghalaq*, lit. 'lock', for Greek κλείς.

[14] Arabic *man ghaṣuba*, evidently a gloss, cf. 1130a 17 and 20.

[15] I.e. the Greek original was ὁ ἄνισος of the vulg.

[16] Again the vulg. against [ὁ] δίκαιος of Bywater, Burnet, Ross and Rackham.

[17] This is the natural meaning of the Arabic (*wa-idh kāna lā ʿādil dhū qunyah kathīrah*), but the Greek is ἐπεὶ δὲ πλεονέκτης ὁ ἄδικος, i.e. ὁ ἄδικος is subject. Perhaps therefore read *dhā qunya kathīrah* for πλεονέκτης, but the sense of having or claiming to much, 'grasping', is lost, cf. above 1129a 32: πλεονεκτεῖν is rendered by *ghaṣuba*, 'take by force'.

[18] Arabic *wa-laisa abadan*, but this is to translate ἀεὶ δ' οὐ in error for δεῖ δ' οὐ, 'but they should not', continuing 'rather they should pray [...]', which depends on δεῖ.

تكون الهيئة الرديئة سخافة الجسم (٦) ويلزم أكثر ذلك إذا كان يقال أحدهما بنوع كلّي أن يقال الآخر بنوع كلّي مثل العدالة ولا عدالة (٧) ولكن يخفى ذلك لمقاربة اشتراك اسمها وليس هو بيّن جدّاً كما هو في الأشياء البعيدة فإنّ الاختلاف في الأشياء البعيدة أكثر منه في الخاصّة مثل الغلق فإنّه يسمّى على نوع اشتراك الاسم الترقوة التي تلي عنق الحيوان والذي يغلقون به الأبواب (٨) فليؤخذ على كم نوع يقال الذي ليس بعادل فإنّه يظنّ بالذي خالف الناموس أنّه ليس بعادل وكذلك لذي القنية الكثيرة من غصب والذي لا يساوي فبيّن إذاً أنّ العادل سيكون المتمسّك بالناموس والذي يساوي فإذاً فالشيء العادل فهو الناموس والمساوي وأمّا الشيء الذي ليس بعادل فهو الشيء الذي ليس بناموس ولا مساو (٩) وإذ كان لا عادل ذو قنية كثيرة فليس هو في جميع الخيرات بل في ما كان منها سعادة ولا سعادة فإنّ في الخيرات ما هو بنوع مبسوط أبداً وهو لبعض الناس ليس بأبد وأمّا

1 احدهما F : أحدها Bad || 2 اسمها F : اسمهما Bad || 3 وليس F : فليس Bad || 9 عادل corr. Dun : عدل F, Bad || 9 ما كان F : مكان corr. mrg. || 10 ولا Dun : ولا بلا F, Bad

pray[19] for themselves that those things which are goods absolutely should be goods for them also, and that they should choose what is good for them [...]. (10) As for the unjust man, he does [not] always choose the more, but chooses the less also in things absolutely bad, except that he thinks that that which is not bad[20] is also good in a way, and extensive property in his opinion is among the goods.[21] In consequence it is thought that he is a man of extensive property.[22] (11) And he is unfair, for this characterises him[23] and is a common term.[24] (12) Since it has been said that the man who contravenes the law is unjust and that the law[25] is just, it is clear that all lawful things are just in a way, for the things which are defined by legislation are lawful, and we say that each one of these is just. (13) As for the laws, all that they say is directed either towards what is good and is common to all, or towards what is good for the best men or for the chiefs[26] or in some other similar way, so that in one way it commands[27] what produces happiness and what preserves it, and what produces and preserves its parts from harm.[28] (14) The law commands that one should do the actions of courage, as that one should not leave one's post and should not take to flight nor throw away one's arms. It commands what belongs to the temperate man, e.g. that he should not commit adultery and outrage.[29] It commands what belongs to the humble[30] man, e.g. that he should not strike nor speak evil, and similarly in the rest of the virtues and wicked actions it

---

[19] See previous note.

[20] Arabic *alladhī laisa bi-radī'*, i.e. τὸ μὴ κακόν read by K^b and L^b rather than τὸ μεῖον κακόν of the vulg.

[21] Arabic *wa-kathrat al-qunyah*. This is to mistranslate Greek τοῦ δ' ἀγαθοῦ ἐστὶν ἡ πλεονεξία which is "taking more than one's due" (Rackham) or "graspingness" (Ross); ἡ πλεονεξία shoud be construed with τοῦ ἀγαθοῦ.

[22] Greek πλεονέκτης is 'grasping', cf. n. 17, end.

[23] Arabic *yakhuṣṣuhu* which renders περιέχει badly.

[24] I.e. for taking both too much and too little.

[25] Arabic *an-nāmūs*. The Greek, however, is ὁ νόμιμος, for which we have *al-mutamassik bi'n-nāmūs* above (1129a 33 = V, 1, 8).

[26] The Greek κατ' ἀρετήν, 'in virtue', is omitted, as in K^b.

[27] Arabic *fa-'innahu ya'muru*. The subject is *kull mā taqūlu an-nawāmīs* at the beginning of the paragraph, but how does this stand for δίκαια λέγομεν?

[28] Greek τῇ πολιτικῇ κοινωνίᾳ is omitted.

[29] Arabic *wa-allā yaftariya*, strictly 'and that he should not calumniate'. The Arabic translator elsewhere has the same rendering of ὑβρίζω (1149b 21), and *firyah* for ὕβρις (1149a 32 and b 23).

[30] Arabic *wadī'* for Greek πρᾶος, elsewhere rendered by Arabic *ḥalīm* (1103a 8, 1108a 6, 1126a 2, b 1, etc.).

الناس فإنّهم يدعون لأنفسهم في صلاتهم بهذه الأشياء ويطلبونها وليس أبداً بل يدعون لأنفسهم أن تكون التي خيرات بنوع مبسوط لهم خيرات أيضاً وأن يختاروا ما كان لهم [...] (١٠) وأمّا اللا عادل فإنّه [لا] يختار أبداً الأكثر ويختار الأقلّ أيضاً في الأشياء الرديئة بنوع مبسوط إلاّ أنّه يرى أنّ الذي ليس بردئ جيّد أيضاً بنوع ما وكثرة القنية عنده من الخيرات ومن أجل ذلك يرى أن يكون ذا قنية كثيرة [١/٧٩] (١١) وهو لا مساو فإنّ هذا يخصّه وهو مشترك (١٢) وإذ قد قيل إنّ مخالف الناموس ليس بعادل وإنّ الناموس عادل فبيّن أنّ جميع الأشياء الناموسية عادلة بنوع ما فإنّ الأشياء المحدودة بوضع الناموس ناموسية ويقال إنّ كلّ واحد من هذه عادل (١٣) وأمّا النواميس فإنّ كلّ ما تقوله إنّما يقصد به إمّا إلى ما هو خير وهو مشترك للجميع وإمّا إلى ما هو خير للأفاضل أو للسادة أو بنوع ما آخر مثل هذا حتّى إنّه أمّا بنوع واحد فإنّه يأمر بالتي تفعل السعادة والتي تحفظها والتي تفعل وتحفظ أجزاءها من الرداءة (١٤) ويأمر الناموس أن نفعل أفعل النجدة مثل ألاّ يترك الترتيب وألاّ يهرب ولا يرمي بالسلاح ويأمر بما للعفيف مثل ألاّ يفسق وألاّ يفتري ويأمر بما للوديع مثل ألاّ يضرب وألاّ يقول قولاً رديئاً وكذلك في سائر الفضائل والرداءات يأمر

---

3 [...] : illegible F, *good* Dun (partly) || 3 لا suppl. Dun* (οὐκ) || 4 إلا أنه F*, Dun* (ἀλλά) : لأنه Bad || 8 النواميس : F الناموس Bad

commands some things and forbids others, in a right way if rightly laid down and in a worse way when it has been perverted.[31] (15) This justice then is a perfect virtue but not simply, but related to something else. On this account it is often thought of justice, since it is related to something else, that it is the strongest of the virtues and is a marvel more marvellous than the star shining in the mornings and evenings which is proverbial.[32] As for all justice in general, it is a virtue, and perfect virtue mostly, because it is the employment that is perfect virtue.[33] It is only perfect because its possessor is able to employ virtue, and towards others also, not merely towards himself. Many a one employs virtue in the things which are special to him, and they are unable to employ it in the things which belong to an-
1130a other. (16) Because of this, we think that the saying of Bias[34] is right when he said: 'Rule shows the man', because the ruler is he who he is related [to them and to] the things in which there is sharing. (17) For this same reason it is thought that justice alone of the virtues is a stranger's good because it is related to another's affair. For it does what is good for another, either for ruler or for partner. (18) The wicked man[35] is he who practises wickedness towards himself and towards his friends. As for the virtuous man,[36] he is not one who practises virtue towards himself, but one who practises it towards others. For this action is difficult. (19) As for this justice, it is not a part of virtue but is the whole of virtue, nor is its opposite, which is injustice, a part of vice but the whole of vice. (20) As regards there being a distinction[37] between virtue and this justice, it is plain from what has been said, for even if they are the same in kind, in essence it is not so, but that which[38] is related to something else[39] is justice, and the state of character which[40] is like this is virtue in the absolute sense.[41]

---

[31] Arabic *ḥurrifa* for Greek ἀπεσχεδιασμένος, the meaning of which was not known.

[32] I.e. Greek καὶ παροιμιαζόμενοί φαμεν is construed with the foregoing words.

[33] The Arabic translation of the sentence goes far wrong.

[34] Arabic *qaul Biyānṭus* (= τὸ τοῦ Βίαντος).

[35] The Greek superlatives κάκιστος and ἄριστος are disregarded.

[36] See previous note.

[37] I.e. Greek τι not τί.

[38] I.e. Greek ἥ not ᾗ.

[39] But 'to someone else' is wanted (πρὸς ἕτερον).

[40] See n. 38.

[41] Greek ἁπλῶς is wrongly construed with ἀρετή.

ببعض وينهى عن بعض أمّا بنوع صحيح فالموضوع على الصحّة وبنوع أردأ الذي قد حُرّف (١٥) فأمّا هذه العادلة فإنّها فضيلة تامّة ولكن ليس بنوع مبسوط ولكن يضاف إلى شئ آخر ومن أجل هذا مراراً كثيرة يظنّ بالعادلة إذا أضيفت إلى شئ آخر أنّها أقوى الفضائل وتكون أشدّ إعجاباً من الكوكب المشرق بالعشيات والغدوات والذي يتمثّل به وأمّا جميع العدالة بالجملة ففضيلة وفضيلة تامّة أكثر ذلك من أجل أنّ الاستعمل إنّما هو الفضيلة التامّة وإنّما هي تامّة من أجل أنّ الذي هي له يقدر أن يستعمل الفضيلة وفي غيره أيضاً ليس في ذاته فقط وكثير من يستعمل الفضيلة في التي هي له خاصّةً ولا يقدرون يستعملونها في التي هي لآخر (١٦) ومن أجل هذا يظنّ أن قول بيانطس صواب حين قل إنّ الرياسة تظهر الرجل لأنّ الرئيس [من] يضاف [إليهم وإلى] الأشياء التي فيها شركة (١٧) ومن أجل هذا بعينه يظنّ بالعدالة أنّها وحدها من الفضائل خير غريب لأنّها تضاف إلى شئ آخر فإنّها تفعل ما هو خير لآخر إمّا لرئيس وإمّا لشريك (١٨) فذو الرداءة هو الذي يستعمل الرداءة في ذاته وفي الأصدقاء [١/٨٠] وأمّا الفاضل فليس الذي يستعمل الفضيلة في ذاته بل الذي يستعملها في غيره فإنّ هذا الفعل عسير (١٩) فأمّا هذه العدالة فليست جزء فضيلة بل هي الفضيلة كلّها ولا ضدّها الذي هو لا عدالة جزء رداءة بل كلّ الرداءة (٢٠) وأمّا أنّ فيما بين الفضيلة ومثل هذه العدالة فصلاً فبيّن ممّا قيل فإنّه وإن كانت هي بنوع ولكن بالإنّية ليس كذلك بل أيّها الذي يضاف إلى شئ آخر فهي عدالة وأمّا الهيئة التي هي مثل هذه ففضيلة بنوع مبسوط.

---

2 second ولكن corr. Dun* (ἀλλά) : ولا F, Bad || 4 أشد إعجابا corr. Bad : أشدا عجيبة F || 8 إليهم وإلى 9 suppl. Dun || 9 من corr. Bad || 9 بيافطس F, بنانطس : (Βίαντος) read. Dun* بيانطس suppl. Dun || 10 لأنها corr. Dun* (ὅτι) : لا F || 14 الذي هو corr. Bad : التي هي F || 15 العدالة F*, Dun* (δικαιοσύνη) : الحالة Bad || 17 هي F : om. Bad

2. We are looking for the justice which is in the part of virtue, for it is of a certain kind as we say. Similarly we are looking for the injustice which is partial. (2) The indication of that[42] is that in the rest of the vices there is an agent who does not act justly, and does not take by force from anyone,[43] e.g. he who throws away his shield through cowardice, or uses bad language by necessity,[44] or who does not spend money through meanness, or he who acquires great wealth from wrongdoing on account of meanness.[45] On account of that[46] he often takes by force from anyone in this, and whoever is bad, is so in one of all these ways. Accordingly as we take by force so we are bad and unjust, (3) because it is a part of the whole and an unjust part of the universally unjust which is contrary to the law. (4) Also, if one man commits adultery for the sake of gain and to obtain something, and another gives and loses through desire, it should be thought of the latter that he is intemperate more than that he has extensive property[47] and of the other that he is unjust, not intemperate. That is plain, since[48] he was acting for the sake of gain. (5) Also, as to the other kinds of wrong, they are always related to a certain vice, e.g. adultery to intemperance, flight from the ranks of war to cowardice, and murder[49] to anger. As for seeking gain, it is not related to any other vice at all, apart from the vice of injustice which is wrongdoing. (6) So it is clear that another kind of wrongdoing, different from the universal, is particular, which shares the name and the defini-
1130b tion,[50] because the definition is in the same genus. For both have a potentiality of being both of them connected with the other,[51] except that one of them is connected with honour or with wealth or with safety, or if it is possible for us to include all this under a single name, and on account of the pleasure which accrues from gain, while

[42] The substantive force of ἔστιν is disregarded in the Arabic translation.

[43] Arabic *wa-laisa yaghṣibu aḥadan*, i.e. Greek πλεονεκτεῖ δ' οὐδένα for πλεονεκτεῖ δ' οὐδέν.

[44] Arabic *li'ḍ-ḍarūrah* for Greek διὰ χαλεπότητα, 'from harsh temper'.

[45] The additional words 'or he who acquires [...] meanness' are perhaps an alternative translation of Greek ἢ οὐ βοηθήσας.

[46] Arabic *min ajl dhālika*, which should render διὰ τοῦτο (cf. 1129b 9), but Greek is ὅταν δέ. But this sentence and the next hardly represent the Greek and afford only a verbal sense.

[47] Arabic *dhā qunyah kathīrah*. The phrase is intended to translate πλεονέκτης as elsewhere (1129a 32 and b 1, 10).

[48] Arabic *idh*, but Greek ὅτι is here simply 'that'.

[49] Arabic *al-qatl*, Greek is ἐπάταξεν, 'struck'.

[50] Cf. Ross, "shares the name and nature" for Greek συνώνυμος.

[51] This mistranslates Greek πρὸς ἕτερον, for which cf. c. 1, §§ 15, 16, 17, etc.

٢. وإنّما نطلب العدالة التي هي في جزء الفضيلة فإنّها بنوع ما كما نقول وكذلك نطلب لا عدالة التي هي جزئية (٢) وعلامة ذلك أنّ في سائر الرداءات فاعلاً لا يعدل وليس يغصب أحداً مثل الذي طرح الترس لمكان الجبن أو أساء القول للضرورة أو الذي لم ينفق الأموال لمكان لا حرّية أو الذي اقتنى كثرة الأموال من ظلم من أجل لا حرّية ومن أجل ذلك كثيراً ما يغصب واحداً من هذا ومن كان رديئاً فبنوع واحد من هذه الأنواع كلّها فإنّا كما نغصب فذو الرداءة كذلك وذو لا عدل (٣) لأنّه جزء الكلّ وجزء ما لا عادل من اللا عادل الكلّ الذي هو على خلاف الناموس (٤) وأيضاً إن كان أحد يفسق من أجل أن يربح ويأخذ شيئاً وآخر يعطي ويخسر لمكان الشهوة فخليق أن يظنّ أمّا بهذا أنّه لا عفيف أكثر من أن يكون ذا قنية كثيرة وأمّا الآخر أنّه لا عادل وأمّا أنّه لا عفيف فلا وذلك بيّن إذ كان يفعل من أجل أن يربح (٥) وأيضاً أمّا سائر أنواع الجور فإنّها تنسب أبداً إلى رداءة ما مثل الفسق إلى لا عفّة والهرب من صفوف الحرب إلى الجبن والقتل إلى الغضب فأمّا التربّح فلا ينسب إلى رداءة أخرى البتّةَ خلا رداءة لا عدل التي هي الجور (٦) فبيّن أنّ جوراً ما آخر غير الكلّي جزئي يشترك بالاسم والحدّ من أجل أنّ الحدّ في الجنس الواحد فإنّ لكليهما قوّةً أن يضاف كلّ واحد منهما إلى الآخر إلاّ أنّ أحدهما مضاف إلى الكرامة أو إلى الأموال أو إلى السلامة أو إن أمكننا أن نحصر جميع هذا باسم [١/٨١] واحد ومن

3 ينفق F : يقتن corr. mrg. || 5 فبنوع appar. corr. Dun : بنوع F, Bad || 8 بهذا F : لهذا Bad || 14 أو corr. Bad*, Dun* (ἤ) : و F

the other is related to all the things which belong to the virtuous man. (7) That there are several justices and that one of them is different from the universal virtue [is plain]. Let mention then be made of what it is and what sort of thing it is. (8) What is not just has been distinguished as that which is contrary to the law and that which is not fair, and what is just also is distinguished as being the law and is fair. What is contrary to the law[52] is the wrongdoing which was first spoken of. (9) The unequal and the more[53] are not the same but different, and different as the part to the whole, for every more[54] is unequal, but not every unequal [is more]. The unjust and injustice are not the same thing but are different from the former,[55] as parts on the one hand and as universal parts[56] on the other hand. For this wrongdoing is part of universal wrongdoing, and similarly justice with reference to justice. Let us speak of partial justice and of partial injustice, and of the just and unjust likewise. (10) As for the justice which is classed with the totality of virtue and the corresponding injustice, since one of them employs the totality of virtue towards something else,[57] and the other is the employment of vice, let them be left aside.[58] The just man also and the unjust[59] who is related to these have plainly been distinguished.[60] Broadly speaking,[61] most of the things connected with the law are those which arise from the totality of virtue, for the law enjoins that life should be according to every kind of virtue and forbids every vice. (11) As for the factors which produce the totality of virtue, they belong to the things of the law which are set down in the laws for the general instruction. As for the partial instruction by which a man is good absolutely, let us distinguish afterwards whether it belongs to the device for aiding the city[62] or to another. It should not be the same [for] the good man and

---

[52] Arabic *'alā khilāf an-nāmūs*, Greek κατά rendered by *'alā*.

[53] Arabic has *wa 'l-akthar*, which is the reading of L^b and M^b (Greek τὸ πλέον).

[54] I.e. Greek πλέον (K^b and M^b).

[55] As in the Greek, the Arabic is not explicit, sc. the particular sense of the unjust and injustice is different from the general sense.

[56] Arabic *ajzā' kullīyah*, Greek ὅλα, i.e. wholes.

[57] But Greek πρὸς ἄλλον is 'towards another person', cf. above on V, 1, 16.

[58] Arabic *faltutrak*, Greek ἀφείσθω.

[59] Apparently masculine for neuter (Arabic *al-'ādil* [...] *al-jā'ir*).

[60] Arabic *qad fuṣila*, i.e. the force of Greek διοριστέον is disregarded (= 'must be distinguished').

[61] Greek σχεδόν, Arabic *kāda an*.

[62] Arabic *li'l-ḥīlah li'l-nijād al-madīnah*. This is an odd circumlocution for Greek τῆς πολιτικῆς.

أجل السرور الذي يكون من الربح والأخر ينسب إلى جميع الأشياء التي هي للفاضل (٧) وأمّا أنّ العدالات كثيرة وأنّ إحداها غير الفضيلة الكلّية [فبيّن] فليؤخذ في ذكر ما هي وأيّ هي (٨) وقد فُصل الذي ليس بعدل أنّه الذي على خلاف الناموس والذي ليس بمساو وفُصل العدل أيضاً أنّه الناموس والمساوي وما على خلاف الناموس فهو الجور الذي قيل أوّلاً (٩) فليس اللامساوي والأكثر شيئاً واحداً بل آخر وآخر كالجزء إلى الكلّ فإنّ كلّ أكثر لا مساو وليس كلّ لا مساو [أكثر] فالشئ الذي هو لا عادل ولا عدالة ليس هما شيئاً واحداً بل هما غير تلك وبعضها كالأجزاء وبعضها كأجزاء كلّية فإنّ هذا الجور جزء للجور الكلّي وكذلك العدالة للعدالة فلنقل في العدالة الجزئية وفي لا عدالة الجزئية وفي العادل ولا عادل مثل ذلك (١٠) فأمّا العدالة المرتَّبة بنوع كلّية الفضيلة ولا عدالة إذ كان أحدهما استعمل كلّية الفضيلة إلى شئ آخر وكانت الأخرى استعمل الشرّية فلتترك والعادل أيضاً والجائر الذي ينسب إلى هذه بيّن أنّه قد فُصل وكاد أن يكون أكثر الأشياء الناموسية التي تكون من كلّية الفضيلة فإنّ الناموس يأمر أن يكون المعاش بكلّ نوع فضيلة ويمنع من كلّ رداءة (١١) وأمّا الفاعلة لكلّية الفضيلة فمن الأشياء الناموسية التي وضعت في النواميس للأدب العامّ وأمّا الجزئي الذي به يكون الرجل خيراً بنوع مبسوط فلنفصل أخيراً هل هو للحيلة للنجاد المدينة أو لأخرى فخليق ألاّ يكون شيئاً واحداً للرجل الخير وللذي في

1 السرور read. Bad* (ἡδονήν) : الشرور appar. F || 1 والأخر Dun : والأخذ F || 2 فبين suppl. Dun || 3 الناموس F, Dun : الناموسي Bad || 5 أولا F*, Dun* (πρότερον) : إذا Bad || 5 اللا مساوى corr. Bad : اللامساو F || 5 والأكثر F*, Dun* (πλέον, L^b, M^b) : اللاناموسي corr. Bad* (παράνομον) || 5-6 فالشئ [...] فإن F : فإنه ليس كل لا ناموسي لا مساويا وان كان كل لا مساو هو لا ناموسي فكذلك الشئ Bad || 6 أكثر suppl. Dun || 7 تلك F : ذلك corr. Bad || 7 فإن corr. Dun* (γάρ) : فبين أن appar. F, أن غير Bad || 9 فأما F : أما Bad || 13 فمن corr. Dun : من F, Bad || 15 للحيلة للنجاد F, Dun : السياسة لصناعة (!) corr. Bad* (τῆς πολιτικῆς) || 15 للذي ... للرجل appar. corr. Dun : الرجل ... الذي F, Bad

the [citizen] in all things.[63] (12) As regards the class of partial justice and the just which is not[64] according to it, they are one. It is that which is concerned with the division of honour, or wealth, or anything else, which are divided among those who have the city in common. For it is in these things that there is also[65] an unequal and
1131a an equal different for different men. There is also one class which rectifies transactions. Of the latter there are two parts. (13) For some kinds of wrongdoing[66] are voluntary and others involuntary. As for the voluntary, they are like these—like selling, lending at interest, giving security, or loan, or deposit, and letting. [...] the term 'voluntary' is applied because the beginning of these transactions is voluntary. As for the [in]voluntary, some is clandestine,[67] like theft, adultery, witchcraft, procuring, enticing of slaves, assassination, and false witness, and some is perforce, like disabling, imprisonment, murder, robbery, oppression,[68] bad language and calumny.[69]

3. Since the unjust is unfair, it is what is fair.[70] (2) For in whatever action there are more and less, there is in it equality also. (3) If the unjust is unfair, the just is fair, and this all men see without argument also. When[71] the just is a mean, it will be a mean with reference to things.[72] (4) And equality involves at least two things. Thus it is necessary that the just is a mean and fair, and in a relation.[73] In so far as it is a mean, it is a mean of things, and those are either much or little. In so far as it is fair, it is in respect of two, and in so far as it is just, it is in respect of four.[74] (5) Necessarily then the just involves at least four things. For the things[75] in which the just subsists are two and

---

[63] I.e. apparently ἐν παντί was read.

[64] The negative (*lā*) is an unwarrented addition (maybe τοῦ οὐ for τοῦ), and the sentence is completely misunderstood.

[65] 'Also' (Arabic *aiḍan* for Greek καί) is not right here.

[66] Arabic *aẓ-ẓulm*, apparently for συνάλλαγμα, which has been correctly translated in the previous line.

[67] I.e. reading *fa-baʿḍuhā sirrīyah mithla* for *min ajl ann'ibtidā'* apparently repeated in error after *lā irādīyah*.

[68] Arabic *irhāq* for Greek πήρωσις.

[69] Arabic *firyah* for Greek προπηλακισμός.

[70] A line is omitted in Arabic giving an impossible sense.

[71] Arabic *idhā* for Greek ἐπεί. The following words are omitted (τὸ ἴσον μέσον).

[72] τι of the Greek text has been read as τισίν.

[73] Arabic omits καὶ τισίν with L^b.

[74] I.e. τισίν read in error as τέτταρσιν.

[75] Arabic *al-ashyā'*, but this is neuter for masculine, and the sentence becomes unintelligible.

جميع الأشياء (١٢) فأمّا في نوع العدالة الجزئية والعدل الذي لا يكون بها فواحد وهو الذي يكون في قسمة الكرامة أو الأموال أو شئ آخر التي هي مقسومة للذين تعمّهم المدينة فإنّ في هذه أن يكون أيضاً لا مساوٍ ومساوٍ آخر لآخر وأيضاً بنوع واحد الذي يصحّ المعاملات ولهذا جزءان (١٣) فإنّ بعض أنواع الظلم إرادية وبعضها ليست إرادية أمّا الإرادية فمثل هذه مثل البيع أو القرض أو الكفالة أو العارية أو الاستيداع والاكتراء [١/٨٢] [...] يقل إرادية من أجل أنّ ابتداء المعاملات إرادي وأمّا اللا إرادية فبعضها سرّية كالسرقة والفجور والسحر والقيادة وخداع الصعاليك والاغتيل وشهادة الزور وبعضها غشوية مثل الوهن والرباط والقتل والنهب والإرهاق ورداءة القول والفرية.

٣. وإذا كان لا عادل لا مساو فهو المساوي (٢) فإنّ في أيّ فعل كان الأكثر والأقلّ تكون فيه المساواة أيضاً (٣) فإذا كان لا عادل لا مساو فالعادل مساو وذلك يراه جميع الناس من غير قياس أيضاً وإذا كان العدل متوسّطاً فسيكون متوسّطاً لأشياء (٤) والمساواة أقلّ ما تكون لاثنين ويضطرّ أن يكون العادل متوسّطاً ومساوياً ومضافاً وبأنّه متوسّط فهو متوسّط أشياء وهذه إمّا أن تكون كثيرة أو قليلة وبأنّه مساو فهو في اثنين وبأنّه عادل ففي أربعة (٥) فإذاً مضطرّ أن يكون العادل أقلّ ما يكون في أربعة فإنّ الأشياء التي فيها العادل اثنان والتي فيها

3 المدينة F, Bad : الهيئة المدنية or السيرة المدنية prop. Dun || 6 اللا إرادية corr. Dun : إرادية F, Bad || 6 فبعضها سرية ܣ corr. Dun* (τὰ μὲν λαθραῖα) : من أجل أن ابتداء F, Bad || 8 الإرهاق F, Dun* (πήρωσις) : الازهاق read. Bad || 8 الفرية F : الشتيمة Bad || 9 في أي فعل كان F, Dun : om. Bad

those in which the things subsist are two. (6) Equality is the same for the many and those who are among them,[76] for like as those are related to the things[77] in which they subsist, so these are also, for if they are not equal, there will not be equal shares in them. But hence are opposed to each other mutual reproaches, when there are unequal shares in what is equal or equal in what is unequal, and there is an allotment. (7) That is also plain from the principle of merit, for all men admit that justice is in gifts,[78] and they do not say that merit is the same, but the supporters of democracy say that it is freedom, while supporters of oligarchy say that it is wealth. Some say that it is nobility of race, whereas the supporters of aristocracy have asserted that it is virtue. (8) Justice then is something proportional, for what is proportional is not special to a special number[79] but, in a general way, to number, because proportion is equality of word and involves at least four terms. As for discrete proportion, that it involves four terms is plain. (9) Continuous proportion also is the same, since it
1131b employs one term twice and repeats, e.g. as *alif* [the letter a] is to *bā'* [b], so *bā'* is to *jīm* [g]. Thus *bā'* is mentioned twice, and if *bā'* is posited twice, the proportionals are four. (10) Justice also involves at least four terms, and the word[80] is one and the same because it has been divided in that kind of way,[81] (11) so that as the term *alif* is to *bā'*, so *jīm* is to *dāl* [d], and contrariwise as *alif* is to *jīm*, so is *bā'* to *dāl*, and so then the whole also to the whole,[82] which the giving brings together, and if it is combined in this way, it is brought together justly. (12) So then the *alif* and the *jīm* together with the *dāl* and the *bā'* make up the justice which depends on giving.[83] Justice is intermediate also, I mean that it is related to proportion,[84] for proportion is intermediate, and justice is proportionate. (13) They call[85] the proportion which is of this kind geometrical, for it happens that

---

[76] Arabic *li 'l-kathīrīn wa 'lladhīna fīhim* for Greek οἷς καὶ ἐν οἷς.

[77] Arabic *ilā 'llatī*, i.e. Greek τὰ ἐν οἷς read as τούτοις ἐν οἷς.

[78] Greek κατ' ἀξίαν τινὰ δεῖν εἶναι is omitted to the detriment of the sense.

[79] Arabic *'adad khāṣṣ* for Greek μοναδικοῦ ἀριθμοῦ, 'abstract number'.

[80] Arabic *kalimah*, but Greek λόγος here again is *ratio*.

[81] Arabic *qad fuṣṣila mithl dhālika 't-tafṣīl*. This translation disregards Greek οἷς τε καὶ ἅ.

[82] I.e. the persons and things involved. But the translator does not distinguish clearly between these throughout the passage.

[83] I.e. distributive justice.

[84] The Arabic translator has construed τοῦτο with ἐστί ('I mean that') instead of with τὸ δίκαιον, and his *yuḍāfu ilā* renders περί not παρά.

[85] The subject in the Greek is οἱ μαθηματικοί, here omitted.

الأشياء اثنان (٦) وتكون المساواة واحدة للكثيرين والذين فيهم فإنّه كهيئة تلك إلى التي هي فيها كذلك كهيئة هذه أيضاً فإنّه إن لم تكن متساوية لا تكون فيها متساوية بل ها هنا تضادّ الملامات إذ كان في المساوي لا مساوية أو في لا متساوية متساوية وكانت قسمة (٧) وأيضاً ذلك بيّن من الاستئهل فإنّ جميع الناس يقرّون أنّ العدل في العطايا ولا يقولون إنّ الاستئهل واحد بل أمّا أصحاب رياسة العامّة فإنّهم يقولون إنّه الحرّية وأصحاب رياسة قلّة الرؤساء إنّه الغنى ومنهم من قل إنّه الشرف في الجنس وأمّا أصحاب رياسة الأشراف فقد قالوا إنّه الفضيلة (٨) فالعدل إذاً شئ مناسب فإنّ الشئ المتناسب ليس هو خاصّاً لعدد خاصّ بل بنوع كلّي لعدد لأنّ المناسبة مساواة كلمة وتكون في أربعة أقلّ ما تكون فأمّا المنفصلة أنّها تكون في أربعة فبيّن (٩) والمتّصلة أيضاً كذلك من أجل أنّها تستعمل الواحد مرّتين وبقول مرتين كما أنّ الألف إلى الباء كذلك الباء إلى الجيم [١/٨٣] فقد قيلت الباء مرّتين وإذا قد وضعت الباء مرّتين تكون المناسبات أربعاً (١٠) والعدل أيضاً في أربعة أقلّ ما يكون والكلمة واحدة هي فهي لأنّه قد فصّل مثل ذلك التفصيل (١١) حتّى إنّه كمناسبة حتّي الألف إلى الباء كذلك الجيم إلى الدال وعلى خلاف ذلك كما أنّ الألف إلى الجيم كذلك الباء إلى الدال فإذاً والكلّ أيضاً إلى الكلّ ما تجمعه العطية فإن هو ركّب بهذا النوع فبحقّ يجتمع (١٢) فإذاً الألف به الجيم بالذي يجتمع الدال مع الباء به العدل الذي في العطية والعدل متوسّط أيضاً أعني أنّه يضاف إلى المناسبة فإنّ المناسبة متوسّطة والعدل مناسب (١٣) ويسمّون المناسبة التي تكون على مثل هذه الحل مساحية

---

2 إن لم تكن متساوية Dun* (εἰ γὰρ μὴ ἴσοι) : إن لم تكن لا متساوية F, Bad || 2 ها هنا F : من mrg. || 4 الاستئهل corr. Dun* (ἀξίαν) : الاشياء F, Bad || 8 كلمة corr. Dun* (λόγων) : كلية F, Bad || 11 أربعا Bad, Dun : illegible F || 13 حتي corr. Dun* (ὅρος) : جزئي appar. F || 14 ما F : فما Bad || 14 فإن F : إن Bad || 16 والعدل F : والعدل هو Bad

whole is to whole as each is to each. (14) This proportion is not continuous, for there is not one single term which is for the person and is the thing.[86] As for justice,[87] it is that which is proportionate.[88] So then some of it[89] is more and some of it less. That occurs in actions also, for he who does wrong has more good, and he who is wronged has less good. (15) As regards evil, the opposite is the case, for the lesser evil compared with the greater evil is relatively the good. (16) For the lesser evil is chosen rather than the greater evil, and what is chosen is good, and the more so the more.[90] (17) As regards the class[91] of justice, it is this.

4. The remaining one is in the class of[92] the corrective in social relations and in things voluntary and involuntary.[93] (2) This is justice, but in it is a kind of what was previously,[94] for the division of the things held in common[95] is always according to the proportion which has been mentioned. For if the division is of property held in common,[96] it would be according to this analogy and to the relationship to one another of the things contributed. The injustice which is opposed by hypothesis to this justice is in accordance with the proportion.[97] (3) As for the justice which is in transactions,[98] it is something
1132a equal, and injustice is unequal, but not in accordance with the pre-

[86] Rendering ᾧ καὶ ὅ, assuming that the translator took ᾧ as masculine. But cf. above n. 82.

[87] Again the sense 'this justice' is missed, cf. n. 84.

[88] The sentence 'the unjust is that which violates proportion' has here fallen out, evidently owing to homoioteleuton.

[89] I.e. of what is unjust. See previous note.

[90] I.e. the more chosen (desirable) it is, the more it is good, but the Greek is the greater (μεῖζον) the good is.

[91] Greek ἕν is omitted.

[92] Arabic *wa 'l-bāqī fa-fī* implies the misreading of ἕν as ἐν (which is then construed with the accusative διορθωτικόν). This suggests an original Greek MS. in uncials.

[93] The Greek adjectives are construed as independent of Greek τοῖς συναλλάγμασι.

[94] Arabic *hādhā huwa al-ʿadl walākin fīhi nauʿ mina 'lladhī huwa qabl*, i.e. the translator read ἀλλά for ἄλλο and apparently πρότερον (K^b).

[95] I.e. Greek δίκαιον omitted with K^b.

[96] Three lines of the Greek have dropped out.

[97] Arabic *ʿalā qadr al-munāsabah*, but the Greek is 'contrary to the proportion'.

[98] Arabic *fī 'l-muʿāmalāt* for Greek ἐν τοῖς συναλλάγμασι translated above (§ 1) as *fī 'l-muʿāsharāt*.

فإنّه يعرض أن يكون لكلّ ككلّ واحد إلى كلّ واحد (١٤) وهذه المناسبة ليست بمتّصلة فإنّه لا يكون حدّ واحد بالعدد الذي هو له والذي هو وأمّا العدل فهو الذي يناسب فإذاً يكون أمّا بعضه فأكثر وبعضه أقلّ وذلك يعرض في الأفعال أيضاً فإنّ الذي يجور فله أكثر من الخير والذي يجار عليه فخيره أقلّ (١٥) فأمّا في الردئ فإنّه يكون على خلاف ذلك فإنّه على قدر قياس الخير يكون قياس الردئ الأقلّ إلى الردئ الأكثر (١٦) فإنّ الردئ الأقلّ مختار أكثر من الردئ الأكثر والمختار خير والأكثر أكثر (١٧) فأمّا نوع العدل فهو هذا.

٤. والباقي ففي نوع الصحيح الذي يكون في المعاشرات وفي الأشياء الإرادية ولا إرادية (٢) وهذا هو العدل ولكن فيه نوع من الذي هو قبل فإنّ قسمة الأشياء المشتركة هي أبداً على المناسبة التي قيلت فإنّ القسمة إن كانت من أموال مشتركة فإنّها تكون على هذا القياس والنسبة للأشياء المجموعة بعضها إلى بعض والجور الذي يقابل بالوضع هذا العدل فهو على قدر المناسبة (٣) وأمّا العدل الذي في المعاملات فإنّه شئ مساوٍ والجور لا مساو ولكن ليس على قدر تلك المناسبة بل على قدر المناسبة العددية فإنّه ليس بينها

2 بالعدد F*, Dun* (ἀριθμῷ) : بالعدل Bad || 3 الأفعل corr. mrg., Dun* (τῶν ἔργων) : الاعدل F, اللاعدل Bad || 6 العدل corr. Dun : العادل F, Bad

vious proportion, rather in accordance with numerical proportion.[99] For there is no difference at all whether it is the good man who has deprived the bad man or the bad man has deprived the good man, nor if the good or the bad man has committed adultery. But the law regards the difference before the wrong[100] and employs it as one employs the things which are equal,[101] even if one of them does wrong and the other is wronged. And one of them injures and the other is injured. (4) So then, as the wrong is inequality, for this reason the dispenser of justice desires to equalise it, for when this man has received a wound and that other has struck the blow, or has killed and the other has died, the effect and the action are divided unequally, and he desires to diminish the gain and equalise it by the loss. (5) For gain in a simple sense[102] is applied to cases like these, even if for some of them there is no suitable name, e.g. the striker of the blow, and loss is applied to the person who suffers. (6) For when the effect becomes clear and is measured, some of it is called loss and some of it gain. So then the equal is intermediate for the more and the less, while as for gain and loss, one of them is more and the other less in the opposite way, more good and less evil being gain and the opposite being loss, and the equal which we say is justice is between them. For corrective justice is between loss and gain. (7) Hence when there is dispute in regard to this, they go to the dispenser of justice, who is the just man,[103] for 'dispenser [of justice]' means animate justice, and they seek the dispenser [of justice] as intermediary. Some people call them 'intermediaries', since when they find what is intermediate, they have obtained justice. So then justice is something intermediate, since the dispenser of justice also is so. (8) The dispenser of justice equalises, as though we had a line divided into two unequal parts, and he takes away the part which is in excess of half and adds it to the first part.[104] When the whole has been divided into two equal halves, it is then said that a man has his own, having received what is equal. (9) What is equal is intermediate between the greater and the less in accordance with numerical[105]

---

[99] Arabic *al-munāsabah al-ʿadadīyah*, i.e. arithmetical proportion 1132a 30, cf. 1106a 35.

[100] Arabic *qabl aḍ-ḍarar* = Greek πρὸ τοῦ βλάβους (for προς̀ τοῦ βλάβους). The translator has then taken τὴν διαφοράν as object of βλέπει.

[101] Arabic *al-mutasāwiyah*, but the Greek word ἴσοις refers to the person.

[102] Arabic *bi-qaul mabsūṭ* for Greek ὡς ἁπλῶς εἰπεῖν, cf. 1151b 2.

[103] Arabic *alladhī huwa al-ʿādil*, apparently rendering τὸ δ' ἐπὶ τὸν [...] δίκαιον.

[104] Arabic *al-qism al-awwal* for Greek τῷ ἐλάττονι τμήματι.

[105] I.e. arithmetical, as above § 3.

اختلاف البتّةَ [إن] كان الفاضل [١/٨٤] [هو الذي] أعدم الشرير أو الشرير أعدم الفاضل إن فسق الفاضل أو الشرير ولكن الناموس يرى الاختلاف قبل الضرر ويستعمله كاستعمل المتساوية وإن كان أحدهما يجور والآخر يجار عليه وكان أحدهما يضُرّ والآخر يُضارّ به (٤) فإذاً لمّا كان الجور لا مساواة لهذا يروم صاحب العدل أن يصيّره على المساواة فإنّه إذا جرح هذا وضرب ذاك أو قتل ومات هذا فهذا يفصل الانفعل والفعل فهو لا متساوية ويروم أن ينقص من الربح ويساويه بالخسران (٥) فإنّ الربح بقول مبسوط يقل في مثل هذه الأشياء وإن كان لبعض الأشياء ليس باسم لائق مثل الذي ضرب ويقل للمنفعل خسارة (٦) فإنّ الانفعل إذا تبيّن وقدّر سُمّي بعضه خسراناً وبعضه ربحاً فإذاً أمّا الأكثر والأقلّ فالمساوي وسط وأمّا الربح والخسران فأحدهما أكثر والآخر أقلّ بنوع التضادّ أمّا للخير فأكثر ربحاً وأمّا للشرّ فأقلّ وأمّا الضدّ فخسران وكان بينهما المساوي الذي يقول إنّه العدل فإنّ العدل الصحيح هو يكون بين الخسران والربح (٧) من أجل ذلك إذا تشوجر في هذا يصيرون إلى صاحب العدل الذي هو العادل فإنّ صاحب [العدل] يراد أن [يكون] عدلاً متنفّساً ويطلبون صاحب [العدل] متوسّطاً ويسمّيهم بعض الناس متوسّطين إذ كانوا إذا صادفوا الوسط فقد قالوا العدل فإذاً العدل شيء متوسّط إذ كان صاحب العدل كذلك (٨) وصاحب العدل يساوي كخطّ إذا قسم بقسمين لا متساويين وينقص القسم الذي يزيد على النصف الزيادة ويزيدها على القسم الأوّل فإذا قسم الكلّ بنصفين متساويين حينئذ يقل إنّ فيه ما له عند قبوله المساوي (٩) والمساوي متوسّط فيما بين الأكبر والأصغر على قدر

1 إن suppl. Bad || 2 ويستعمله Dun : illegible F || 3 وإن F : إن Bad || 3 وكان F*, Dun* : وكأن Bad || 3 به F : om. Bad || 5 مات F*, Dun* (ἀποθάνῃ) : ما أشبه Bad || 5 فهو لا متساوية Bad*, Dun* (ἄνισα) : فصولا متساوية F || 8 فإذا F : وإذا Bad || 12 second العدل suppl. Bad || 12-13 يكون عدلا متنفسا corr. and suppl. Bad || 13 صاحب العدل متوسطا corr. and suppl. Dun : متوسط صاحب F, صاحبا متوسطا corr. Bad || 16-17 إن فيه ما له F : إن لكل ماله corr. Bad || 17 first المساوي corr. Dun : المساواة F || 17 متوسط F, Dun : يتوسط Bad

proportion. Justice is so called since the derivation of the name of justice in Greek is from what is divided into two parts, because justice is, so to say, that which is divided into two equal parts, and the dispenser of justice, that is the judge, is he who divides into two equal parts. (10) For when two things are equal and he subtracts from one of them two parts[106] and the other is increased, that which is increased is more than the other by these two parts. But if he sub-
1132b tracts[107] one and does not increase,[108] it exceeds the mean[109] by one. So then that from which subtraction was made is less than[110] the mean by one, which was subtracted from it. (11) We must then know what must be lessened from that which is more and what must be added to that which is less, for there must be added to that which is less than the mean the amount by which the mean exceeds it, and there must be lessened from that which is more what exceeds the mean. (12) Let there be equal lines AA', BB', GG'. Let AH be lessened from AA', and let GD[111] be added to GG'. Then the whole line DGG' exceeds HA' by GD plus GZ,[112] and BB' by GD.[113] This also applies in the rest of the arts, otherwise they would have been lost unless the agent and the patient had done and suffered the same thing and in the same amount and kind.[114] (13) These names, i.e. loss and gain, come from voluntary association,[115] because it is said that a man gains when he has more than he had, and it is said that he loses when he has less than he had at first, as in buying and selling and in the other matters which the law has made free. (14) On the other

---

[106] *Sic*, or taking the verb as passive and altering Arabic *juz'ain* to *juz'ān* and 'two parts are substracted [...]', but the expression is not in the Greek.

[107] Again there is doubt as to whether the verbs should not be read as passive (as in the Greek), emending *wāḥidan* to nominative *wāḥidun* as subject.

[108] See previous note.

[109] Arabic *yazīdu ʿalā*, awkward after *yazīd*, is equivalent to *yakūn akthar*, 'is more than', in the previous sentence, but should not be followed by *al-mutawassiṭ*, which is Greek ἑνὶ [...] μόνον wrongly construed.

[110] But we want rather 'is greater than, exceeds' and a different subject. The sentence has gone awry (omission of καὶ τὸ μέσον and of the second ἑνί).

[111] I.e. equal to AH.

[112] I.e. also equal to AH.

[113] The following diagram will explain the text:

A H A'
B B'
D G Z G'

[114] This sentence is found in the Greek text here, where since the time of Muretus it is usually deleted, and at 1133a 14-16. It is in the Arabic text only here.

[115] Arabic *muʿāmalah* for Greek ἀλλαγῆς.

المناسبة العددية وإنّما يسمّى عدلاً من أجل اشتقاق اسم العدل باليونانية ممّا يقسم بقسمين لأنّ العدل كقول القائل إنّما هو الذي قسم بقسمين متساويين وصاحب العدل أيّ القاضي الذي يقسم بقسمين متساويين (١٠) فإنّه إذا كان اثنان متساويين وانتزع من أحدهما جزئين وزيد على الآخر فإنّ الذي زيد عليه [١/٨٥] يكون أكثر بهذين الجزئين من الآخر وإن انتزع واحداً ولم يزد فإنّما يزيد على المتوسّط بواحد فإذاً الذي انتزع منه ينقص من المتوسّط واحداً الذي انتزع منه (١١) فينبغي إذاً أن نعلم ما ينبغي أن ينقص من الأكثر وما ينبغي أن يزاد على الأقلّ فإنّه ينبغي أن يزاد على الذي هو ينقص من المتوسّط الزيادة التي يزيد عليه المتوسّط وأن ينقص من الأكثر الذي يزيد على المتوسّط (١٢) مساوياً بعضها بعضاً التي عليها أا ب ب ح ح وينقص من أا أه ويزاد على ح ح الذي عليه ح د فإذاً كلّ د ح ح زائد على ه أ ح د و ح ز فإنّ ح د ب ب وهذا أيضاً في سائر الصناعات وإلاّ فقد كانت تبعد لو لم يكن يفعل وبالكمّية والكيفية ولم يكن المنفعل ينفعل بهذا وبالكمّية والكيفية (١٣) وإنّما جاءت هذه الأسماء أيّ الخسران والربح من المعاملة الإرادية من أجل أنّه إذا كان للإنسان أكثر ممّا هو له يقل إنّه ربح وإذا كان أقلّ ممّا كان له أوّلاً يقل إنّه يخسر مثلما يكون في الشراء والبيع وفي سائر الأشياء التي أطلقها الناموس (١٤) وأمّا إذا

4 جزئين F, Dun: جزءان perh. Dun, جزء Bad || 5 الأخر Dun : illegible F || 5 يزد Dun : illegible F || 5 على Dun : illegible F || 5 انتزع Dun : illegible F || 8 ينقص : F نقص Bad || 10 بب Bad, Dun : illegible F || 10-11 فقد كانت تبعد : F لكانت تنفد Bad || 11 first وبالكمية F, Dun : الكمية Bad || 12 الأسماء corr. Dun* (τὰ ὀνόματα) : الأشياء F, Bad

hand, when there is neither more nor less but things are as before,[116] it is said that he has what was his, and it is not said either that he loses or that he gains. So then justice is a mean between gain and loss in regard to the things which are voluntary,[117] and belongs to[118] what is equal before and after.

5. Some people think that justice simply is reciprocity.[119] (2) It does not correspond either with the justice which is distributive or with that which is corrective, (3) although they want to say that this is the justice of Rhadamanthys,[120] who takes vengeance for the doing of evil deeds.[121] (4) Often his words[122] are contradictory in many things, as when he says: If a man who holds rule has wounded,[123] it is right not merely that a wound should be inflicted in return, but the culprit should be beaten also. (5) As for the voluntary and involuntary, there is a difference between them in some things. (6) But in association for business transactions this justice particularises[124] the justice which is reciprocity[125] according to analogy, not according to equality. For it is analogous to counter-action,[126] because the inhabitants
1133a of the city in their transactions either seek what is of a bad kind or it is thought to be slavery[127] unless a man acts aggressively[128] or the excellent is chosen, otherwise there is no mutual giving, and their dwelling together depends on giving and taking. (7) On this account

---

[116] The Arabic translation *kānat al-ashyā'u ʿalā ḥālihā* possibly represents Greek αὐτὰ δι' αὐτῶν γένηται.

[117] Arabic *irādīyah*. The Arabic translator has apparently misunderstood παρά + accusative = 'contrary to', as at 1131b 32 (= V, 4, 2), but cf. Gauthier's note *in loco* (in view of the ambiguity of παρά, 'voluntary' is a possible translation of the Greek, though rejected by most commentators).

[118] Reading *wa-li'l-musāwī* in the Arabic text, i.e. τὸ ἴσον ἔχειν, but the construction is wrong.

[119] Arabic *muḍādd al-alam*, lit. 'counter-suffering'. After these words a reference to the Pythagoreans is omitted (1,5 lines).

[120] Arabic *Fāy Dhāsnn*. For a very different transliteration of this name, cf. 'Seventh Book', c. 9, § 10.

[121] 'Who takes vengeance [...]' is substituted for the verse of poetry in the Greek.

[122] In the Greek the subject is not Rhadamanthys or what he says.

[123] Greek οὐ δεῖ ἀντιπληγῆναι, καὶ εἰ ἄρχοντα ἐπάταξεν has been omitted.

[124] Arabic *yakhuṣṣu*, mistranslation of Greek συνέχει, also below § 11.

[125] 'Counter-suffering' (Greek ἀνάλογον is the object of τῷ ἀντιποιεῖν), and συμμένει is not translated. Cf. § 1 above.

[126] The construction is wrong here. The rest of the sentence is very far from being an accurate rendering of the Greek.

[127] Arabic *al-jarīr*, lit. 'the halter', for Greek δουλεία.

[128] I.e. in return (Greek εἰ μὴ ἀντιποιήσει).

لم يكن لا أكثر ولا أقلّ بل كانت الأشياء على حالها فيقل إنّ له ما كان له ولا يقل لا إنّه يخسر ولا إنّه يربح فإذاً العدل متوسّط فيما بين ربح وخسران من الأشياء التي تكون إرادية وللمساوي قبل وبعد

٥. وبعض الناس يرى أنّ العدل بنوع مبسوط هو مضادّة الألم (٢) وهو لا يقع لا على العدل الذي هو ذو القسمة ولا على الذي هو ذو تصحيح (٣) وإن كانوا يريدون أن يقولوا إنّ هذا هو عدل فلي ذاسنن الذي ينتقم من فعل الآفات (٤) وكثيراً ما يضادّ قوله في أشياء كثيرة مثل قوله إن جرح وله رياسة فلا ينبغي أن يجرح بدل ذلك أيضاً فقط بل وأن يعذّب أيضاً (٥) وأمّا الإرادي واللا إرادي فبينهما اختلاف في بعض الأشياء (٦) ولكن في اشتراكات المعاملات فإنّ هذا العدل يخصّ العدل الذي هو مضادّة الألم على المناسبة لا على المساواة فإنّه ناسب بمضادّة الفعل لأنّ سكّان المدينة معاملاتهم إمّا أن يكونوا يطلبون الذي هو بنوع ردئ أو كان يظنّ به أنّه الجرير [٨٦/١] [...] بعض ببعض وإنّما يكون سكناهم [...] والأخذ (٧) ومن أجل ذا يتحفّظون [...] يتمسّكون [...] تمسّكاً جيّداً

4 مبسوط mrg.*, Bad*, Dun* (ἁπλῶς) : متوسط F || 6 فلي ذا سنن F*, Dun* (Ῥαδαμάνθυος) : فإن ذا سنن Bad || 11 ردئ corr. Dun* (κακῶς) : إرادي F || 11 أو appar. corr. Dun : إن F, Dun || 11 الجرير F*, Dun* (δουλεία) : الجدير Bad || 11 [...] : illegible F, *unless a man acts aggressively or the excellent is chosen, otherwise there is no [...] giving* Dun || 12 first [...] : illegible F, *depends on giving* Dun || 12 second [...] : illegible F, *tradition* Dun || 12 third [...] : illegible F, *it* Dun

they maintain tradition[129] and hold fast to it well, so that there may be requital. For this is characteristic of tradition,[130] because it is right to serve the one who has given a gift, in order that he may begin again to give a gift and there is requital.[131] (8) The requital which is according to proportion comes into existence through the combination which is according to the correspondence like diametrical[132] correspondence. Let A be a builder, B a shoemaker, G a house and D shoes. Then the builder must take from the shoemaker the shoemaker's work and give him his work. If at first there is what is proportionately equal, and then reciprocity[133] takes place, there will result what has already been mentioned. Otherwise it is not equal and not living together,[134] for nothing prevents the work of one of the two being better than the work of the other, and these must be equal.[135] (9)[136] For association does not arise from two medical practitioners but from a doctor and a farmer, and, in general, from different people, not people who are equal, but an equation must be made between these. (10) Hence all the things which the transactor transacts and in which business is transacted must be those[137] in which money occurs, and money becomes in a way a mean, for it equalises[138] all things in a way, in regard to excess and defect, and equalises between shoes and a house and food. Thus there must be a proportionate relation of the shoes to the house or to the food like that of the builder to the shoemaker, for if that does not exist there is no society and no taking and giving. Nor does this exist either if the things are not in a way equal. (11) There must be a single measure

[129] Arabic *yataḥaffaẓūna as-sunna*. The mention at this point of Χαρίτων ἱερόν (the temple of the Graces) has entirely disappeared.

[130] Again Arabic *sunna* translates χάρις.

[131] The Arabic translation is of course incorrect.

[132] Or 'diagonal'.

[133] Cf. n. 125.

[134] Arabic *bi-sākin maʿan* for Greek συμμένει, cf. Gauthier: "la communauté ne subsistera pas", but others disagree.

[135] I.e. the reading of the mrg. (Text has *wa-yanbaghī an takūna hādhihi ghair mutaṣāwiyah.*)

[136] It is remarkable that the words at the beginning of § 9: ἔστι δὲ τοῦτο [...] (1133a 14-16), are here omitted, though apparently found in the other *testimonia*, including the Greek MSS. This looks like a real variant in the original, and confirms the idea that these words in both places where they occur (cf. 1132b 9-11) are an insertion, cf. Gauthier's commentary *in loco*.

[137] The construction here is wrong.

[138] Arabic *yusawī* for Greek μετρεῖ.

لتكون المكافأة فإنّ هذا خاصّ للسنّة من أجل أنّه ينبغي أن يخدم التي وهب هبة لكي يبتدئ أيضاً [...] وإنّما تصير المكافأة (٨) وإنّما تصيّر المكافأة التي على المناسبة بالاجتماع الذي يكون على المقابلة كمقابلة القطر فليكن البناء الذي عليه أ والإسكاف الذي عليه ب والبيت الذي عليه ح وخفاف الذي عليه د فينبغي أن يأخذ البناء من عمل الإسكاف وأن يعطيه عمله فإن كان أوّلاً الذي هو على النسبة متساوٍ ثمّ صار الذي يضاد الألم فسيكون الذي قد قيل وإلاّ فليس بمتساوٍ ولا بساكن معاً فإنّه ليس شئ يمنع أن يكون عمل أحدهما خيراً من عمل الآخر وينبغي أن تكون هذه متساوية (٩) فإنّ الاشتراك لا يكون من متطبّبين بل من طبيب وفلاح وبالجملة من آخر وآخر لا من متساويين ولكن ينبغي أن يساوي ما بين هؤلاء (١٠) ومن أجل ذلك ينبغي أن تكون جميع الأشياء التي تعامل ذو معاملات وتكون بها المعاملة التي يجنى فيها الدينار ويصير متوسّطاً بنوع ما فإنّه يساوي زيادة ونقصان جميع الأشياء بنوع ما ويساوي بين الخفاف والبيت والغذاء فقد ينبغي أن تكون كمناسبة البناء إلى الإسكاف أن تكون مناسبة الخفاف إلى البيت أو الغذاء فإنّه إن لم يكن ذلك لا تكون معاشرة ولا أخذ ولا عطاء ولا يكون هذا أيضاً إذا لم تكن الأشياء متساوية بنوع ما (١١) فقد ينبغي أن يكون لجميع الأشياء قدر واحد يعدّها كما قيل أوّلاً

2 [...] : illegible F, *to give a gift* Dun || 2 second المكافأة Bad, Dun : illegible F || 3 الذي Bad, Dun : illegible F || 4 فليكن البناء F*, Dun* (ἔργου) : om. Bad || 5 عمل F : بأن Bad || 5 وأن F*, Dun* (ἴσον) : شيئا Bad || 6 متساو Dun : بمساو Bad, F || 7 بمتساو corr. هذه متساوية mrg.*, Bad*, Dun* (ἰσασθῆναι) : هذه غير متساوية F || 9 يساوي corr. Dun : يسوي F, Bad || 9 ذو F, Dun : ذات Bad || 10 يساوي corr. Dun : يسوي F, Bad || 11 يساوي corr. Dun : يسوي F, Bad

which enumerates[139] them for all the things, as was said at first. This is in reality the need which characterises[140] all. For if there were no need for a thing, or if it were not of a similar kind, either there would be no taking and giving, or it would not be this. Money has come to be the equivalent of what is given,[141] the equivalent of the need by a kind of agreement.[142] On that account it has this name 'money', since it is not by nature but simply by *nomos*, for the name for money in Greek is *nomisma*,[143] and it is for us to alter that and make it useless. (12) There is reciprocal good[144] when it is equal, and when the relation of the farmer to the shoemaker is as the relation of the work of
1133b the farmer to the work of the shoemaker, if there has been a form of service in the exchange.[145] If not, one of the extremes will have both excesses. When they have what is theirs,[146] in this way they are equal and share in taking and giving, because this equality can be in them: farmer A, food G, shoemaker B, and the same work equalised D. If there were not reciprocity[147] in this way, there would be no sharing in taking and giving. (13) That it is the need which is characteristic for the connection is clear, for if one of the two did not need the other party, or neither of them did, they would not cooperate in giving and taking, as he who lacks what he needs does, like the man who needs wine and gives wheat[148] in exchange for it, and that has to be equal. (14) If there is now no need of a thing, when there will be need of it there is money, which is as it were a guarantee for us. This must be a recognised means for taking, for this too is affected in the same way, because it cannot always be equal, and thus[149] it tends to be more constant. Therefore all things should have a fixed price, so that in this way there is always giving and taking. As for the associa-

---

[139] Arabic *yaʿudduhā* now for Greek μετρεῖσθαι.

[140] Arabic *takhuṣṣu*, which does not render Greek συνέχει at all exactly, here and at § 6.

[141] The last six words are apparently a gloss.

[142] Arabic *bi-nauʿ al-ittifāq*, Greek κατὰ συνθήκην, for which at 1134b 35 (= V, 7, 5) the Arabic translation has simply *bi-'ttifāq*.

[143] Arabic *an-nāmūmsī* (leg. *an-nāmūsmā*). This explanation is not in the Greek.

[144] Arabic *muḍāddat al-khair* (so apparently) for Greek ἀντιπεπονθός (elsewhere rendered by *muḍāddat al-alam*).

[145] Arabic *in ṣāra tashakkul khidmah fī'l-muqābalah*. The Greek εἰς σχῆμα δ' ἀναλογίας οὐ δεῖ ἄγειν has been modified to give εἰ for εἰς, with omission of οὐ.

[146] 'When they [...].' These words are similarly construed by Rackham, but with the previous sentence by Bywater, Burnet and Gauthier.

[147] Cf. above §§ 1 and 6 and note 144 of this §.

[148] Greek ἐξαγογήν, 'permission for exportation', is left untranslated.

[149] Arabic *kadhālika*, i.e. οὕτως for ὅμως of the Greek text ('though').

وهذا هو أمّا بالحقيقة فالحاجة التي تخصّ الجميع فإنّه إن لم تكن حاجة إلى شئ أو إن لم تكن بنوع متشابه إمّا ألاّ يكون أخذ وعطاء وإمّا ألاّ يكون هذا وصار الدينار بدل الذي يعطى بدل الحاجة بنوع الاتّفاق ومن أجل ذلك له هذا الاسم دينار من أجل أنّه ليس بالطبع بل إنّما هو بالناموس فإنّ اسم الدينار باليونانية الناموسمى وإلينا أن [١/٨١] نبدّله ونصيّر لا يستعمل (١٢) فها هنا مضادّة الخير إذا ما صار مساوياً بأن كانت نسبة الفلاح إلى الإسكاف مثل نسبة عمل الفلاح إلى عمل الإسكاف إن صار تشكّل خدمة في المقابلة وإلاّ فسيكون لأحد الطرفين كلّ الزيادات فإذا كانت لها ما هي لها بهذا النوع تكون متساوية ومتشاركة في الأخذ والعطاء لأنّ هذه المساواة يمكن أن يكون فيها الفلاح أ والغذاء ح والإسكاف ب والعمل بعينه المساوي د وأمّا إن لم تكن على هذا النوع مضادّة الألم فلا يكون اشتراك بأخذ وعطاء (١٣) وأمّا أنّ الحاجة التي تخصّ كالصلة فبيّن فإنّه إذا لم يحتج أحد الاثنين إلى صاحبه أو كلّ واحد منهما إلى صاحبه لا يتعاملان بالعطاء والأخذ كما يفعل الذي ليس له ما يحتاج إليه كالذي يحتاج إلى النبيذ فيعطي بدله حنطة فقد ينبغي إذاً أن يكون ذلك متساوياً (١٤) فأمّا إن كان الآن لا يحتاج إلى شئ فلمّا كان سيحتاج إليه فيكون الدينار كأنّه كفيل لنا فقد ينبغي أن يكون هذا سبباً ظاهراً للأخذ فإنّ هذا أيضاً يلقى مثل هذا اللقاء ومن أجل أنّه لا يقوى على أن يكون أبداً متساوياً وكذلك يزيد ويبقى أكثر ومن أجل ذلك ينبغي أن تقوّم جميع الأشياء بثمن فبهذا النوع يكون العطاء والأخذ أبداً

1 أو إن Bad*, Dun* (ἤ) : وإن F || 2 first إما : F فإما Bad || 2 وصار : F فصار Bad || 4 الناموسمى
corr. Dun : الناموسي F || 4-5 نبذله ونصير لا يستعمل فها هنا مضادة Bad, Dun : illegible F || 5 إذا ما
الخير Bad, Dun : illegible F || 6 الإسكاف مثل نسبة عمل الفلاح Bad, Dun : illegible F || 8 والغذاء
Bad, Dun : illegible F || 9 والإسكاف ب والعمل corr. Dun* (σκυτοτόμος B, τὸ ἔργον) :
F; الاسكاف بالعمل والاسكاف ب وعمل الاسكاف corr. and suppl. Bad || 9 الألم : F للألم Bad || 11
يتعاملان corr. Bad : يتعاملون F || 13 الآن لا يحتاج : F لا يحتاج الآن Bad

tion of these things[150] which is money,[151] as it were an intermediary,[152] it measures and equates them. For if there were no cooperation, there would be no sharing, and if there were no equating, there would be no cooperation.[153] And though in truth it is impossible that things so different should be equal, yet when the need exists it is possible sufficiently. (15) [The standard] must be a single thing by agreement, and therefore it is called money,[154] for it is this which equates the values of all things, since everything is measured by money. Let there be a house A, ten *minae* B, a bed G. Then if the house is equal to five *minae*, it is the half of B, and[155] if it is equal to ten *minae*, it is equal to B. The bed is a tenth, then G is a tenth of B. (16) In that case it is clear how many beds B[156] is. If[157] the transaction of business were in this way before the existence of money, there is no difference at all whether [...] a house [...] five beds for a house, or the money for five beds. (17) It has now been stated what injustice and justice are. From what we have described it is plain that just action is midway between doing injustice and being unjustly treated, for the one has too much and the other too little. And justice is intermediate not in the same way as the previous virtues, but be-
1134a cause it is concerned with the mean, while injustice is of the extremes. As for justice[158] and he gives justice both to himself as regards another man and to another man as regards another, and not so as to give to himself more of what is desirable and to another less, and of what is harmful the opposite. Rather he gives what is proportionately equal, and therefore[159] gives to one man as against another. (18) Injustice is the reverse of that,[160] for the unjust man gives what

---

[150] Arabic *wa-ammā ishtirāk hādhihi 'l-ashyā'*, i.e. for Greek εἰ δὲ τοῦτο, κοινωνία misread.

[151] The construction here is wrong.

[152] Arabic *shai' wasaṭ*, which evidently translates Greek μέσον, not μέτρον of the text.

[153] Greek οὔτ' ἰσότης μὴ οὔσης συμμετρίας, which forms the third step in Aristotle's argument here, is omitted by the translator, or has fallen out of the MS.

[154] Arabic *dīnār* for Greek νόμισμα connected with νόμος, 'law, custom'.

[155] Apparently for Greek ἢ ἴσον.

[156] But in the Greek text we have A, the house. Hence, probably, Arabic omits Greek ὅτι πέντε.

[157] Arabic *lau*, but Greek ὅτι δέ.

[158] More than a line of the Greek is omitted.

[159] Arabic *fa-lidhālika* (corr. *wa-kadhālika*) for ὁμοίως, cf. above § 14, οὗτος for ὅμως.

[160] This does not render the Greek, where τοὐναντιόν is adverbial, 'on the contrary'.

وأمّا اشتراك هذه الأشياء الذي هو الدينار كأنّه شيء وسط فإنّه يقدّرها ويساويها فإنّه لو لم تكن معاملة لم تكن شركة ولو لم تكن مساواة لم تكن معاملة فأمّا بالحقيقة فلا يمكن ما كان على قدر هذا الاختلاف أن تكون متساوية وأمّا عند الحاجة فيمكن بنوع كافٍ (١٥) وينبغي أن يكون ذلك شيئاً واحداً بنوع الوضع ومن أجل ذلك يسمّى ديناراً فإنّ هذا الذي يساوي بين أفراد جميع الأشياء من أجل أنّ كلّ شيء يكل بالدينار. بيت أ عشرة أمناء ب سرير ح فإن كان البيت يساوي خمسة أمناء فهو نصف ب وإن كان يساوي عشرة أمناء فهو مساوٍ لب والسرير عشر فح عُشر ب (١٦) إذاً بيّن كم سرير ب لو كانت المعاملة على هذا النوع قبل أن يكون الدينار [١/٧٢] فبيّن لأنّه لا فارق [...] بيت أو [...] خمسة أسرة [...] (١٧) فقد حددنا طبيعة العادل والجائر ومن التمييزات التي وصفنا ينتج بوضوح أنّ الفعل العادل وسط بين الجور الذي ارتكبه مرتكب والجور الذي تحمله من وقع عليه الجور فلأحدهما الأكثر والآخر الأقلّ وأمّا العدالة فتوسّط ليس بالنوع الذي به الفضائل التي هي قبل بل من أجل أنّها في الوسط وأمّا الجور فمن الأطراف وأمّا العدالة وهو معطي العدل ولذاته من آخر ولآخر من آخر وليس على أن يعطي ذاته من المختار أكثر ولغيره أقلّ ومن الضارّ على خلاف ذلك بل يعطي المساوي الذي هو على قدر النسبة وكذلك يعطي لآخر من آخر (١٨) وأمّا الجور فعلى خلاف ذلك فإنّ الجائر يعطي ما ليس بعدل وهذا هو زيادة

---

7 فح : وح Bad || 8-11 فبين (...) فلأحدهما illegible F, Dun *there is no difference (...) for the one has* || 11 الفضائل corr. Bad : فضائل F || 13 first و om. Bad || 14 وكذلك corr. Bad, Dun : فلذلك F

is not just, i.e. excess and defect of the advantageous or the harmful proportionately.[161] Therefore injustice is excess and defect, since in it are excess and defect,[162] excess of the advantageous generally, and defect of the harmful. In the case of others, as for the whole the same applies,[163] and as for the greater, that one should act unjustly. (19) As regards justice and injustice, and what the nature of each is, let this be the manner of our speaking, and similarly in regard to the just and unjust in general.

6. Since it is possible that one not unjust may act unjustly, and that he may act unjustly with some kinds of injustice[164] and be unjust with every kind of injustice, e.g. a thief or adulterer or robber, in this way there is no difference at all. For if he has had intercourse with a woman, knowing what he was doing, yet not from a principle of choice but owing to passion, he acts unjustly but is not unjust. (2) Similarly it is possible that he may not be a thief though he has committed a theft, nor an adulterer, though he has committed adultery, and so on. (3) The nature of the case of reciprocity in relation to what is just has been spoken of previously. (4) We must not forget that the object of search, i.e. what is just in general, is political justice. This is the justice in which the others share,[165] so that there should be sufficiency to those who are free and equal, either proportionately or numerically. In that case all who do not have this, do not have political justice among themselves but a certain justice by a kind of resemblance. For justice also is for those who also have the possibility of law, and the law is for those who have the possibility of injustice. For judgement distinguishes[166] between justice and injustice. Those in whom is injustice have the possibility also of acting unjustly, and[167] injustice is not in all of those who have the possibility of acting unjustly. This is that they give to others less than they give themselves of good things in general, but more[168] of what are bad in general. (5) Therefore we do not allow a man to rule [but]

---

[161] Greek παρὰ τὸ ἀνάλογον wrongly translated by *ʿalā qadr al-munāsabah*, as at 1131b 32.

[162] The words ἐφ' αὑτοῦ are left untranslated.

[163] Here nearly two lines of the Greek dropped out.

[164] Arabic *bi-baʿḍ anwāʿ al-jaur*, mistranslating Greek ποῖα as indefinite (ποιά). The sentence then becomes embroiled.

[165] I.e. Greek ἐπὶ κοινωνῶν βίου is badly rendered.

[166] Arabic *yufaṣṣil*, Greek κρίσις.

[167] Here better 'but'.

[168] 'They give to others *less* [...] but *more*.' The Greek is different.

ونقص من النافع والضارّ على قدر المناسبة ومن أجل ذلك الجور زيادة ونقصان من أجل أنّ فيه زيادة ونقصاناً أمّا زيادة فمن النافع بنوع مبسوط ونقصاناً فمن الضارّ وأمّا في الأخرين أمّا الكلّ فمثل ذلك وأمّا الأكثر فأن يجور (١٩) فأمّا في العدالة ولا عدالة وما طبع كلّ واحد منهما فلنَقُلْ في هذا النوع وكذلك في العادل ولا عادل بنوع كلّي.

٦. وإذ يمكن أن يجور من ليس بجائر وأن يجور ببعض أنواع الجور ويكون جائراً بكلّ نوع من أنواع الجور مثل السارق أو الفاسق أو اللصّ فبهذا النوع لا يكون فرق البتّةَ فإنّه إن جامع امرأة وهو يعلم ما هو فاعل ولكن لا من أجل ابتداء اختيار بل لمكان الألم فإنّه يجور وليس هو بجائر (٢) وكذلك يمكن ألاّ يكون سارقاً وقد سرق ولا فاسقاً وقد فسق وكذلك سائر الأشياء (٣) فأمّا كيف حل مضادّة الألم إذا نسبت إلى العدل فقد قيل قبل هذا (٤) وينبغي ألاّ يذهب علينا أنّ المطلوب الذي هو العدل بنوع مبسوط هو العدل المدني وهذا هو العدل الذي يشترك فيه الغير لتكون كفاية للأحرار والمتساويان إمّا على قدر المناسبة أو على قدر العدد فإذاً جميع الذين ليس لهم هذا فليس لهم العدل المدني بعض في بعض بل عدل ما بنوع الشبه فإنّ عدلاً أيضاً للذين الناموس أيضاً إليهم والناموس للذين إليهم الجور فإنّ القضاء [٢/٣٥] يفصل بين العدل والجور والذين فيهم الجور إليهم أن يظلموا أيضاً والذين إليهم أن يظلموا فليس في فعل كلّهم الجور وهذا هو أنّهم يعطون غيرهم من الخيرات التي هي بنوع مبسوط أقلّ ممّا يعطون أنفسهم وأمّا من الرداءات التي بنوع مبسوط فأكثر (٥) ومن أجل ذلك لا ندع أن يرأس إنسان [بل]

3 الأخرين corr. Dun* (τῶν ἄλλων) : الأخذ F, Bad || 3 فأما F : وأما Bad || 5 بكل F : لكل Bad || 6 أو first corr. Bad*, Dun* (ἤ) : و F || 8 فسق F : فجر Bad || 11 للأحرار appar. Dun* (ἐλευθέρων) : للآخر F, Bad || 12 العدد appar. Dun (ἀριθμόν) : العدل F, Bad || 13 ما F*, Dun* (τὶ) : om. Bad || 13 عدلا F*, Dun* (δίκαιον) : هؤلاء Bad || 14 فإن القضاء F*, Dun* (δίκη) : om. Bad || 17 – p. 321, l. 1 [بل] الكلمة suppl. and corr. Ber,* Dun* (ἀλλὰ τὸν λόγον) : كلمة F; إنسانا Bad; mrg.: من أجل أنه يصير متغلبا فهو يقسم الخير لذاته أكثر كذا لخصه القاضي ترى الناس يتحلمون أي يرأس إنسان عليهم بالكلية

1134b reason,[169] because he does so for himself and becomes tyrannical. The chief is simply the guardian of what is just, and since he is the guardian of what is just he is the guardian of equality also. (6) He does not give himself[170] anything more, since he is just, for he does not give himself more of absolute good, unless it belongs to another to labour proportionately to his labour.[171] In that case he is not unjust.[172] Therefore he said[173] that justice is the good of another, as was said at first. (7) Accordingly let regard be shown [...] this is honour and a gift. (8) In this way among tyrants[174] despotic and practical[175] justice are not [...] alike. For there is no injustice in the things which belong to a man in an absolute sense. As for a child, because[176] it has grown up and is separated, it is as it were part of himself and his property,[177] and he does not choose to wrong it.[178] (9) Therefore no injustice is attributed to him nor anything unjust, nor political justice,[179] since it was according to law and in things[180] in the nature of which it is that there should be law in them, and these things[181] are those which have equality to rule and also to be ruled.[182]

7. As for political justice, some of it is natural and some of it is legal. What is natural is that which has the same force everywhere, whether that is thought of it or not. The legal is that which at the beginning is indifferent in this or another way, but when they have laid it down is not indifferent, e.g. that ransom should be a *mina*, or that one should sacrifice a goat and not sacrifice two sheep, and ev-

---

169 Arabic *al-kalimah*, Greek τὸν λόγον.

170 Greek δοκεῖ has disappeared, perhaps misread as δίδωσι.

171 The construction of διὸ ἑτέρῳ πονεῖ is wrong.

172 This is not in the Greek.

173 Arabic *qāla*, apparently ἔφη for φασίν.

174 Arabic *al-mutaghallibah*, cf. 1176b 13 (= X, 6, 3).

175 Arabic *al-fiʿlī*. But it is a bad mistranslation of τὸ πατρικόν as τὸ πρακτικόν. The whole passage is badly embroiled, with Greek ὅτῳ δὲ μὴ ἱκανὰ τὰ τοιαῦτα omitted, and the remainder of the sentence run together with the next words and apparently read: οὕτως γίνονται τύραννοις τὸ δεσποτικὸν δίκαιον καὶ τὸ πρακτικὸν [...].

176 Arabic *min ajl annahu*, but Greek is ἕως ἄν, 'until'.

177 This evidently renders τὸ δὲ κτῆμα, but is out of place in the sentence.

178 Arabic *ʿalaihi* = Greek αὐτόν for αὑτόν, 'himself'.

179 This also has gone wrong.

180 I.e. neuter for masculine.

181 See previous note.

182 This whole sentence is embroiled, and the following (3 lines): διὸ μᾶλλον [...] τοῦ πολιτικοῦ, are omitted.

الكلمة من أجل أنّه يفعل ذلك لذاته ويصير متغلّباً وإنّما الرئيس حافظ العدل وإذ كان حافظ العدل فهو حافظ المساواة أيضاً (٦) ولا يعطي ذاته شيئاً أكثر إذ كان عادلاً فإنّه لا يعطي ذاته من الخير المبسوط أكثر إلاّ أن يكون لآخر أن يتعب تعباً مناسباً لتعبه إذاً فليس بجائر من أجل ذلك قل إنّ العدالة خير لآخر كما قيل أوّلاً (٧) فإذاً فليكن إكراماً [...] هو كرامة وبرّ (٨) وعلى هذا النوع عند المتغلّبة العدل المسوّر والفعلي ليس [...] متشابه فإنّه ليس جور في التي هي له بنوع مبسوط وأمّا الولد فمن أجل أنّه قد اكتفى فيفارق كأنّه جزء منه وماله فليس يختار أن يجور عليه (٩) ومن أجل ذلك ليس ينسب الجور إليه ولا شيء جائر ولا العدل المدني من أجل أنّه على الناموس وفي التي في طبعها أن يكون فيها ناموس وهذه كانت التي لها مساواة أن ترأس وترأس أيضاً.

٧. وأمّا العدل المدني فبعضه طبيعي وبعضه ناموسي أمّا الطبيعي فالذي له قوّة واحدة في كلّ مكان ويظنّ به ذلك أو لا يظنّ وأمّا الناموسي الذي أمّا في الابتداء فليس فيه اختلاف بهذا النوع أو بنوع آخر وإذا وضعوه فيختلف مثل أن تكون المفاداة منا أو أن يذبح عنزاً

1 يصير Bad, Dun : illegible F || 2 second حافظ Bad, Dun : illegible F || 3 لتعبه F, Dun : لنفسه corr. Bad* (πρὸς αὑτόν) || 4 بجائر Bad, Dun : illegible F || 5 وبر وعلى F, Dun : على Bad || 7 وماله F*, Dun* (κτῆμα) : وما له Bad || 12 منا F : بمنا Bad

erything in regard to which there are prescribed rules in particular cases, e.g. sacrifices.[183] (2) Some people think that all these are related to reckoning,[184] because that which is natural does [not] vary,[185] and everywhere has the same force, for example, fire[186] both here and among the Persians,[187] for they saw that the things of justice vary. (3) This is not so, but it may be that it is what applies among the gods, not among us certainly.[188] There is also something[189] and a movement by nature,[190] so that both of them [vary],[191] except that some is natural, some unnatural,[192] (4) of the things which can be of another kind also, and it is not of a certain kind but is in agreement with law and convention, since both of them vary, and similarly[193] in other things. It is plain that this distinction[194] applies to them also, because the right hand is more excellent by nature, even if it was possible that all mankind should become ambidextrous. (5) What is
1135a by convention and what is better for the just man[195] resemble means,[196] because the measures of wine and wheat are not equivalent everywhere, but when they are bought are greater, and when they are sold are smaller, and similarly the natural just things,[197] except that they are alike[198] and are not the same everywhere, just as the ways of life of the city also do not everywhere agree, but there is everywhere one[199] which is natural. (6) As for the relation of each of the things

---

[183] A reference in the Greek to Brasidas is here omitted, together with the words καὶ τὰ ψηφισματώδη, 'decisions in the form of decrees'.

[184] Arabic *tunsabu ilā 'l-ḥisbah*. The Greek has simply τοιαῦτα, apparently read as τοσαῦτα.

[185] Reading *lā yataḥarrak* (Greek ἀκίνητον).

[186] Greek καίει, 'burns', is also omitted.

[187] Arabic *ʿinda 'l-ʿarsh*, 'at the Throne', evidently the mistake of a copyist for *ʿinda 'l-Furs*.

[188] The sense and construction of the sentence are not right (ἔστιν ὥς taken closely with παρά [...] τοῖς θεοῖς and οὐδαμῶς with παρ' ἡμῖν).

[189] The stop has been placed after παρ' ἡμῖν.

[190] The Arabic translator has construed φύσει with κινητόν contrary to the sense.

[191] Arabic *fa-kilāhumā*. Something may have dropped out, perhaps *tataḥarrakāni* (*tataḥarrak*), to correspond to Greek κινητὸν μέντοι πᾶν.

[192] Greek ποῖον δὲ φύσει is omitted (homoioteleuton).

[193] Greek ὁμοίως is wrongly construed with what follows.

[194] Greek δῆλον should not be construed with ὁ αὐτὸς [...] διορισμός.

[195] Arabic *akhyar li'l-ʿādil*, apparently rendering τὸ συμφέρον τῶν δικαίων.

[196] Arabic *al-ausāṭ*, i.e. μέσοις for μέτροις of the Greek text, cf. 1133b 16.

[197] This phrase is corrupt.

[198] Arabic *illā annahā tushbihu* represents Greek ἀλλ' ἀνθρώπινα.

[199] Arabic unclear, but perhaps *idhā*. In this case Greek ἡ ἀρίστη has not been rendered.

ولا يذبح شاتين وجميع التي بها النواميس الموضوعة في الأشياء الجزئية مثل الذبائح (٢) وبعض الناس يرى أنّ جميع هذه تنسب إلى الحسبة من أجل أنّ أمّا الذي بالطبع [فلا] يتحرّك وفي كلّ مكان فله قوّة واحدة مثل النار وها هنا وعند الفرس فإنّ كانوا يرون أنّ الأشياء العادلة تتحرّك (٣) وهذا ليس كذلك بل خليق أن يكون الذي عند الآلهة وليس هو عندنا البتّةَ وهي أيضاً شيء وتحرّك بالطبع فكلاهما [تتحرّكان] إلاّ أنّ بعضه بالطبع وبعضه ليس بالطبع (٤) من التي [٢/٣٦] يمكن أن تكون بنوع آخر أيضاً وليس بكيفية بل موافق للناموس والاتّفاق إذ كان كلاهما يتحرّك وكذلك في سائر الأشياء وبيّن أنّ هذا التفصيل يليق بها أيضاً من أجل أنّ اليد اليمنى أجود بالطبع وإن كان يمكن أن يصير جميع الناس ذا يمينين (٥) وأمّا التي تكون بالاتّفاق والذي هو أخير للعادل فإنّها تشبه الأوساط من أجل أنّ مكاييل النبيذ والحنطة ليست بمتساوية في كلّ مكان بل التي يشترى بها أكبر والتي يباع بها أصغر وكذلك الاشياء الطبيعية العادلة إلاّ أنّها تشبه وليست هي بعينها في كلّ مكان كما أنّ سير المدينة أيضاً ليست متّفقة في كلّ مكان بل إنّما تكون إذاً في كلّ مكان التي على الطبع فقط (٦) وأمّا نسبة كلّ واحد من الأشياء العادلة والناموسية فكنسبة الأشياء

1 ولا F, Dun : أو لا Bad || 2 أما F : om. Bad || 2 فلا suppl. Dun : فليس suppl. Bad || 3 يتحرك F, Dun : بمتحرك Bad || 3 second و om. Bad || 3 الفرس corr. Bad*, Dun* (Πέρσαις) : العرش F || 4 عند corr. Bad, Dun : عنده F || 5 وتحرك F : يتحرك Bad || 5 فكلاهما corr. Bad : فكليهما F, Dun || 5 تتحركان suppl. Dun || 5 إلا أن corr. Dun : الآن F, Bad || 6 بكيفية F, Dun : بطبيعية Bad || 11 الأشياء Bad, Dun : illegible F || 11 تشبه F, Dun : إنسية corr. Bad || 12 تكون : تكون معا suppl. Bad || 12 إذا Dun : uncertain F || 12 second كل F repeats: مكان بل إنما تكون إذا في كل أن سير المدينة أيضا ليست متفقة في كل

which are just and lawful, it is like the relation of universals to particulars, the things which are done being many and each of the former one, because it is a universal. (7) Between injustice and unjust and justice and just [there is a difference], for unjust is by nature,[200] and this actual deed, when done, is injustice,[201] and similarly justice, for we give the general name to what is just, because justice is called [the correction of] injustice. As for the things which are in each class,[202] and how many they are, and with what they deal, we must inquire later.

8. Since just and unjust acts are those which have been spoken of, a man acts unjustly and does justice only when he does them acting voluntarily. When he does them involuntarily, he neither acts unjustly nor does justice except accidentally, for they do the things that happen to be just or unjust. (2) Injustice and the doing of justice have been defined by the voluntary and involuntary. For when it is voluntary and is blamed, in that case it is not justice, so that there will be something not justice, but the man does not act unjustly if the voluntary is not present. (3) I say voluntary, as was said at first also, for the thing which when anyone knows that it is in his power, and that is not concealed from him,[203] he does, not being ignorant to whom he does it, nor with what, nor for what, as I might say, whom he strikes, and with what, and on account of what, and each of these also is not by accident and not by compulsion, like the man who takes another's hand and strikes a third man, involuntarily, for the blow is not in the power of the man whose hand it is. Again, it is possible that the one struck is the striker's father, and that the striker knows that he is one of the people present,[204] but does not know that he is his father. This distinction is made also in regard to the cause and in regard to the whole action. That is [in]voluntary which is not known, or which is known but is not in the agent's power, or is per-
1135b force. For we know many of the things in nature, and we do them, and they act on us, without any of them being either voluntary or involuntary, e.g. growing old, or death. (4) What is accidental is

---

[200] Greek ἢ τάξει has been omitted or has fallen out.

[201] Greek πρὶν δὲ πραχθῆναι, οὔπω, ἀλλ' ἄδικον is not rendered by the Arabic (*bi-nau' kull wāḥid minhumā*).

[202] Greek καθ' ἕκαστον [...] εἴδη is not rendered.

[203] Arabic *wa-lam yukhfa 'alaihi dhālika* is not in the Greek.

[204] Greek ἄνθρωπος ἤ is apparently left out. (Otherwise ἤ is left out, τῶν παρόντων being construed with ἄνθρωπος in error.)

الكلّية إلى الأشياء الجزئية أمّا التي تفعل فكثير وأمّا كلّ واحد من تلك فواحد لأنّه كلّي (٧) وفيما بين اللا اعتدال ولا عدل واعتدال وعدل [فاختلاف] فإنّ أمّا لا عدل فبالطبع وهذا بعينه إذا فعل هو لا اعتدال ومثل ذلك الاعتدال فإن نسمّي العامّ فعلى العدل من أجل أنّ الاعتدال يسمّى [تصحيحاً] لا اعتدالاً وأمّا التي بنوع كلّ واحد منهما وكم هي وفي أيّ شئ هي فنفحص أخيراً عن ذلك.

٨. وإذ كانت العادلة ولا عادلة التي قيلت فإنّما لا يعدل و يفعل العدل إذا فعلها فاعل بإرادته وأمّا إذا فعلها لا بإرادته فليس لا يعدل ولا يفعل العدل إلاّ بنوع العرض فإنّهم يفعلون بالتي عرض لها أن تكون عادلة أو لا عادلة (٢) وأمّا لا اعتدال وفعل الاعتدال فقد حدّ بالإرادي فإنّه إذا كان إرادياً يُذَمّ مع هذا يكون غير الاعتدال فإذاً سيكون شئ لا اعتدال وليس هو بلا عدل إن لم يكن معه الإرادي (٣) وإنّما أقول إرادي كما قيل أوّلاً أيضاً للشئ الذي إذا علم أحد أنّه من التي إليه ولم يخفَ عليه ذلك فعله إذا لم يخف لا لمن ولا بأيّ شئ ولا لأيّ شئ كقولي لمن يضرب وبأيّ شئ [٢/٣٧] ومن أجل أيّ شئ وكلّ واحد من هذه أيضاً لا بنوع العرض ولا بقهر مثل الذي يأخذ يد أحد ويضرب آخر بلا إرادة فإنّه ليس الضرب إلى صاحب اليد وقد يمكن أن يكون المضروب والده وأن يكون الضارب يعلم أنّه واحد من الناس الحضور ولا يعلم أنّه أب ولنفصّل هذا التفصيل وفي الذي من أجله وفي كلّ الفعل وأمّا الذي لا يعلم أو الذي يعلم إلاّ أنّه ليس إليه أو يكون بقهر فذلك [لا] إرادي فإنّا نعلم كثيراً لمن التي هي بالطبع فنفعلها ويفعل بنا وليس منها شئ لا إرادي ولا لا إرادي مثل التكبّر أو الممات (٤) والتي بنوع العرض متساوية في لا عدلية وفي عدلية

2 فاختلاف suppl. Dun* (διαφέρει) || 4 تصحيحا suppl. Dun* (ἐπανόρθωμα) || 4 عتدالا corr. Dun : عتدال F || 4 منهما F : منها Bad || 10 بلا عدل appar. corr. Dun* (ἀδίκημα) : بعدل F, Bad || 16 لا suppl. Dun || 17 منها F : فيها Bad

equally in unjust and just actions. For if an individual returns a deposit against his will and through fear, it is not said that he does what is just, nor is he called a doer of justice except accidentally. Similarly he who is compelled also not to return a deposit and does so[205] against his will, is said not to do justly accidentally. (5) Of the voluntary things some we do by choice previously made, and some we do without previous choice, with previous choice all the things to which we first turn our thought, and without choice all the things we do before thought is turned to them. (6) So then the injuries which occur in mutual dealings are of three kinds. (b)[206] The error which is from absence of knowledge when it is done to someone or for some purpose,[207] or with something or on account of something the agent never thought of. For either the agent thought that he would not wound this person,[208] or not for this cause,[209] or not whom he did wound, or not as he wished.[210] (7) For when the injury happens involuntarily, it is (a) a mishap, but when it happens not involuntarily yet without malice it is an error (b). For a man errs when the origin of the ignorance belongs to him, and when the origin is from without it is a mishap (a). (8) But when he knows, yet there was no previous direction of thought, it is called (c) injustice, e.g. all the things which are due to anger and all other acts of passion, compulsory or natural, which happen accidentally to mankind. For if they do injury by these or err by them, they act unjustly, and these are acts of injustice. But they are not yet unjust because of these, nor vicious, since the injury is not on account of wickedness. But when the unjust is from choice, then the doer of it is called unjust and vicious. (9) Hence for acts which are in consequence of anger,[211] since the beginning is not from the man who acts in anger, but from him who causes the anger. (10) And also the dispute is not with reference to the fact being so or not, but with reference to what is just and to evident injustice being more of a defect or anger.[212] For they do not dispute, as in business

---

205 Arabic *yaf'al dhālika*. We would say more naturally 'does not do so'.

206 The second term is given first.

207 Arabic *lā bimā dhāka* not right for Greek μήτε ὅ, 'nor the action itself', and the sentence appears to be repeated in the following phrase *lā min ajli aiy shai'in*.

208 Greek ἢ οὐ τούτῳ ἢ οὐ is omitted.

209 Greek ἀλλὰ συνέβη [...] ἵνα κεντήσῃ is now omitted.

210 Arabic *au laisa kamā arāda*, ᾧ read ὡς and the presumed sense expanded.

211 Greek καλῶς, then οὐκ ἐκ προνοίας κρίνεται, are not rendered, and the sense remains incomplete.

212 The Greek appears to have been read ἐπιφαινομένη [γὰρ] ἀδικία ἢ ὀργή.

فإنّه إن ردّ أحد الوديعة بكره ولمكان الفزع فليس يقل إنّه فعل العدل ولا يسمّى فاعل عدل إلاّ بنوع العرض وكذلك الذي يضطرّ أيضاً ألاّ يردّ الوديعة ويفعل ذلك بكره يقل إنّه لا يعدل بنوع العرض (٥) ومن الأشياء الإرادية ما نفعله باختيار قد تقدّم ومنها ما نفعله لا باختيار متقدّم أمّا باختيار متقدّم فجميع التي نجيل فيها الرأي أوّلاً وأمّا بلا اختيار فجميع التي نفعلها قبل أن يجل فيها الرأي (٦) فإذاً الضرّات التي تكون في المعاملات ثلاثة بأنواع الخطأ التي تكون من غير أن يعلم إذا فعلت لا لمن ولا بما ذاك ولا بأيّ شيء ولا من أجل أيّ شيء ظنّ الفاعل فإنّه إمّا أن يكون ظنّ الفاعل أنّه لا يجرح هذا أو لا بهذا السبب أو لا لمن أو ليس كما أراد (٧) فإنّ هذه إذا صارت من غير إرادة فهي شقاء وإذا لم تصِر من غير إرادة وكانت من غير شرّية فهي خطأ فإنّه يخطى إذا كان إليه بدء الجهالة وإذا كان البدء من خارج فذلك شقاء (٨) وإذا كان يعلم إلاّ أنّه لم يقدم جولان رأي فإنّه يقل لا اعتدال مثل جميع الأشياء التي تكون من أجل الغضب وجميع الآفات الأخر الاضطرارية أو الطبيعية التي تعرض للناس فإنّهم إذا ضرّوا بهذه أو أخطأوا بها فهم لا يعدلون وهي لا اعتدالات إلاّ أنّهم ليس هم بعد ذوي لا اعتدال بهذه ولا أشراراً من أجل أنّ المضرّة ليست لمكان الرداءة فإذا كانت من الاختيار فحينئذ يقل [٢/٣٨] لفاعلها لا عادل وشرير (٩) ومن أجل ذلك على التي تكون من الغضب من أجل [أنّه] ليس الابتداء من الذي يفعل بغضب بل من الذي يُغْضِب (١٠) وأيضاً ليست المشاجرة في أن يكون أو لا يكون بل في العادل وأنّ لا عدل الظاهرة أنقص شيء والغضب فإنّهم لا يشاجرون في المعاملات بأن

---

4 first متقدم corr. Bad : مقدم F || 5 الضرات F, Dun* (βλαβῶν) : الخيرات Bad || 6 غير ان Bad, Dun : illegible F || 6 بما F, Dun : لما Bad || 8 هذه Bad, Dun : illegible F || 10 شقاء F*, Dun* (ἀτυχεῖ) : شفاء Bad || 13-14 المضرة ليست corr. Dun (βλάβη) : المضوة ليس F; ليس الاضطرار Bad || 14 لمكان F : بمكان Bad || 15 انه suppl. Bad || 17 انقص F : النقص Bad || 17 والغضب F*, Dun* (ὀργή) : om. Bad

transactions, about the existence of that which necessitates[213] one of the parties being dishonest unless they did it without noticing. Rather they admit the fact and dispute about what is just—the one who has plotted does not know—,[214] so that one of them thinks that
1136a he is wronged while the other does not think so. (11) But if the man has done an injury voluntarily, then he has transgressed in these kinds[215] of injustice in which the man [who acts unjustly] is not said to be unjust, since it was contrary to propriety and contrary to equality. Similarly the just man also, when he has previously chosen to act justly,[216] acts justly only when he has not acted involuntarily. (12) As for the acts done in ignorance,[217] some of them are pardonable, others not pardonable. For all those sins committed by people not only because they were ignorant of them but on account of ignorance, are pardonable, but all those not on account of ignorance but because people were ignorant of them, not[218] on account of a natural or human passion, are not pardonable.

9. One may ask a difficult question in regard to distinguishing incontrovertibly having injustice done to one or doing injustice [...] first, if it is as Euripides strangely said:

> That I should kill my mother by my will and she willing,
> In short, or by her will[219] and I unwilling?

Is it truly possible that one should be wronged voluntarily, or on the contrary is all involuntary, as doing wrong is voluntary? And is all of the latter kind,[220] or is some voluntary and some involuntary? (2) Similarly also in the case of being justly treated. If there is volun-

---

[213] Arabic *bi-an yakūna 'lladhī yaḍrarru*, i.e. construing περὶ τοῦ γενέσθαι with ὧν ἀνάγκη.

[214] Arabic *lā yaʿlamu*, but the translator should have said 'is not ignorant' (Greek οὐκ ἀγνοεῖ).

[215] The construction is again wrong.

[216] This also has gone wrong. Greek δίκαιος is not the subject and lacks the article; δέ is left untranslated (Arabic *fa* in *fa'innamā* is *fa* of the apodosis, not the connective).

[217] Arabic *al-jahālāt*, but Greek τῶν ἀκουσίων is for *involuntary* actions.

[218] Greek μέν has apparently been rendered as μή.

[219] This is the old reading of the vulg.

[220] I.e. is all suffering injustice voluntary? The following words in Greek have been omitted: ἢ ἐκείνως ὥσπερ καὶ τὸ ἀδικεῖν πᾶν ἑκούσιον (Bywater bracketed ὥσπερ καὶ [...] ἑκούσιον).

يكون الذي يضطرّ أن يكون أحدهما ذا رداءة وإن لم يكونوا يفعلونه وهو لا يخفى بل كانوا يقرّون بالشيء وكانوا يشاجرون في العدل وكان الذي اغتل لا يعلم حتّى إنّ أحدهما يرى أنّه قد ظُلِم والآخر لا يرى ذلك (١١) وإن هو أضرّ بإرادة فقد جاوز بهذه أنواع الجور الذي لا يقل هو لا عادل إذ كان على غير ملاءمة وغير المساواة وكذلك العادل أيضاً إذا ما قدم الاختيار أن يعدل فإنّما يعدل إذا لم يكن يفعل من غير إرادة فقط (١٢) وأمّا الجهالات فبعضها ذوات عذر وبعضها لا ذوات عذر فإنّ جميع الذين يخطئون به الناس لا من أجل أنّهم يجهلونها فقط بل لمكان الجهل فإنّها ذوات عذر وأمّا جميع التي لا لمكانة الجهالة بل لأنّ الناس يجهلونها لا لمكان آفة طبيعية ولا إنسية فليست ذوات عذر.

٩. وخليق أن يسأل أحد مسئلة عويصة في تفضيل أن يجار عليه أو يجور و[...] أوّلاً إن كان كما قل أوريبيدس بنوع محل

أن أقتل والدتي بإرادتي وهي تريد
بقول فاصل أو بإرادتها وأنا لا أريد

فهل يمكن بالحقيقة أن يظلم أحد وهو يريد أم لا بل كلّ لا إرادي من الفعل بالجور إرادي وهل كلّ على هذه الحل أو البعض فإرادي والبعض لا إرادي (٢) مثل هذا أيضاً في

2 وكان F*, Dun* : وكأن Bad || 4 يقل corr. Dun : يقول F, Bad || 6 أجل F*, Dun* (διά) : اجهل Bad || 9 عويصة corr. Bad : عويص F || 12 أريد Bad, Dun : illegible F || 13 بل F, Dun : هل Bad || 14 مثل F : ومثل Bad

tary action,[221] then it must be that each should correspond in situation to the other in like fashion, viz. having injustice done to one or being justly treated, or that it should be voluntary or involuntary.[222] It may be thought that this is strange, and in being justly treated also, if all is voluntary. For some people do justly[223] involuntarily. (3) And also one may be perplexed as to this and also raise a difficult question, whether everyone who meets with injustice has injustice done to him, or is it simply as it is in acting (...)[224]

---

[221] Evidently an omission again here, cf. the Greek τὸ γὰρ δικαιοπραγεῖν πᾶν ἑκούσιον.

[222] The last part of the sentence has gone wrong.

[223] The Arabic verb can scarcely be passive. Greek is ἔνιοι γὰρ δικαιοῦνται οὐχ ἑκόντες.

[224] The rest of Book V is missing.

انفعل العدل فإن كان فعل إرادي فإذاً واجب أن يكون كلّ واحد مقابلاً بالوضع لصاحبه بنوع متشابه أيّ أن يجار عليه وأن ينفعل بالعدل أو أن يكون إرادياً أو لا إرادياً وخليق أن يظنّ أو ذلك محل وفي انفعل العدل أيضاً إن كان كلّ إرادياً فإنّ بعض الناس يعدلون وهم لا يريدون (٣) وأيضاً خليق أن يتحيّر أحد في هذا وأيضاً يسأل مسئلة عويصة هل كلّ من لقي الجور قد جير عليه أو إنّما هو كما هو في الفعل (...)

2 first ان suppl. mrg. || 2 first او corr. Dun : و F, Bad || 3 كل corr. Bad : كلا F || 4 عويصة corr. Bad : عويص F || 5 او corr. Bad*, Dun* (ἤ) : و F

BOOK VI

13.[1] [...] (5) [...] thought that [...] on account of [...] sciences. As for us, we say that they are with rational discourse.[2] (6) It is clear [...] has been said that it is impossible that a chief[3] should be [good] without intelligence or a practically wise man without ethical virtue. Reason[4] also reveals this, if any exceed the bounds, and makes clear that the virtues are separate from one another, because the individual is not of excellent nature as regards all of them, so that he will previously have attained some of them and not yet have attained others. For this is possible as regards the natural virtues, but as
1145a regards those in respect of which it is said that he is good in an unqualified sense, it is not possible, for they all exist with practical wisdom, which is one. (7) [...] clear that that is [...] practical wisdom [not] practical, because it must be a virtue [...] because there is no right choice without practical wisdom nor without virtue, because one of them brings to pass the complete result and the other [...] to the complete result. (8) Also, it is not [...] over wisdom and the good which [...] as medicine is not over health. For it does not employ it, but sees how it is to be [...] to it. Also it is like as if one said that civil government [...] the gods, because it gives orders in regard to everything in the state. And after this let us say: We make (have made) another beginning.[5]

The Sixth Discourse of the Ethics is completed, and praise [...].

---

[1] Book VI is only preserved in some few fragments.

[2] Arabic *kalimah*, here = Greek λόγος.

[3] Arabic *musawwad* represents Greek κυρίως, apparently read as κύριος.

[4] Greek λόγος is now rendered by Arabic *nuṭq*, if the reading is right.

[5] The reading and translation of the last two sentences—not in the Greek original—are uncertain.

المقالة السادسة

[...] [١/٨٧] كان يظنّ أنّ [...] علوم وأمّا نحن فنقول إنّها مع كلمة (٧) فبيّن [...] قيل أنّه لا يمكن أن يكون [...] من غير العقّل ولا ذو تعقل من غير الفضيلة الخلقية نطق أيضاً يعني هذا إن تجاوز به متجاوزون ويتبيّن أنّ الفضائل [...] بعض من أجل أنّه لا يكون الواحد جيّد الطبع في جميعها حتّى أنّه قد يكون [...] وبعضها لم يدركها بعد فإنّ هذا أمّا في الفضائل الطبيعية [...] أمّا في التي يقل أنّها خير بنوع مبسوط فليس يمكن فإنّها تكون جميعها مع التعقّل التي هو واحد (٨) [...] بيّن أنّ ذلك [...] التعقّل [غير] فعلي من أجل أنّه كان ينبغي أن تكون فضيلة ما كان [...] أجل أنّه [...] اختيار [...] من غير تعقّل ولا من غير فضيلة من أجل أنّ أحدهما يصيّر التمام والآخر يصيّر أن [...] يذهب الى التمام (٨) وأيضاً ليس هو [...] للحكمة ولا للخير التي [...] كمثل ما ليس [...] فإنّه لا يستعمله بل يرى كيف يكون [...] هو له وأيضاً مثل ما إن قل قائل إنّ للتدبير المدني [...] آلهة من أجل أنّه يأمر في جميع التي في المدنية [...] فلنقل إذاً [...]

تمّت المقالة السادسة من [...]

---

1 second [...] : illegible F, [...] *on account of* Dun || 2 [...] : illegible F, *a chief should be [good]* Dun || 2 نطق Dun : illegible F || 3 [...] : illegible F, *are separate from one* Dun || 4 [...] : illegible F, *previously have attained* Dun || 5 [...] : illegible F, *For this is possible* Dun || 6 غير suppl. Dun || 7 first [...] : illegible F, *there is no right* Dun || 10 second [...] : illegible F, *medicine is not over health* Dun || 9 first [...] : illegible F, *and after this* Dun || 11 second [...] : illegible F, *We make another beginning* Dun || 12 [...] : illegible F, *this Ethics is completed, and praise [...]* Dun

'SEVENTH BOOK'[1]

1. [...] the defect is cowardice, and the excess is rashness. [...] mean of these is bravery. This is also called courage. (2) [...] divine [...] is not of clear remorse [...], so that he is not afraid of anything, even those things which are higher than us, like [...] necessary. Nor is he afraid either of the things which most people are afraid of [...] who is afraid of the things which the madman is afraid of. (3) As for [...] he is the man who is called in Greek 'lofty',[2] and he is like Ibn ʿAus.[3] That belongs to the madman, and also ultimate in madness is he who fears the sky, if he is under it when [...] is bright.[4] [...] since there was nothing that caused him fear, for if things did not make him afraid he would not think and have knowledge of others. (4) Further, the horse which pricks up its ears if it [...] frightening to the water-animal,[5] and nothing else at all[6] [...] these things are like the hot things which cause heat and the cold things which cause cold, [...] they are small and few, they do not determine his enduring them. If they were many and great things, how is he not afraid, since he has much fear? (5) If he escapes from all of them, we [...] Said Alknāūn[7] [...] the courageous man is with us, and what things for us are terrible? And he said: As I describe [him], he is either a man whom all these things terrify [...] this man, which do not terrify the courageous, or a man whom these things will terrify but little. For the courageous man is not affected at all in regard to the things which are contemptible in the eyes of the rest of mankind, while in regard to the things by which the rest of mankind are affected excessively he is [...] little affected. In regard to those things which are higher than

[1] For this 'Seventh Book', see Introduction, pp. 55ff.

[2] The text has *ʿālī*, but this is not Greek.

[3] Not known. Perhaps some Greek name is intended. Odysseus?

[4] Several fragmentary lines follow here.

[5] Arabic *al-ḥaiwān al-māʾī*. This fragmentary sentence is of some significance for identifying the 'Seventh Book'.

[6] A fragmentary line and a half follow here.

[7] Apparently Alcmaeon of Croton, for which *Alknāūn* would seem to be the regular transcription in Arabic.

"المقالة السابعة"

[...] [١/٨٨] [...] النقصان [...] أمّا الزيادة فإقدام [...] توسّط لهذه جبر ويسمّى هذا أيضاً نجلة (٢) والتى [...] إلهية لا يكون بين الندامة حتّى أنّه لا يجزع من شئ لا من التي هي أرفع منّا مثل [...] ولا يجزع أيضاً من التي يجزع منها الكثير [...] يجزع من الأشياء التي يجزع منها الذاهب العقل (٣) وأمّا [...] الذي يقل له باليونانية عالي وهو شبيه ابن عوس فذلك للذاهب العقل وأيضاً الأكثر في ذهاب العقل المخوّف من السماء إن [...] صفاء [...] إذ لم يكن شئ يهوّله فإنّه إن لم تجزّعه الأشياء [...] غيره فليس يخبر (٤) وبعد فإنّ الفرس [...] يصير إن [...] هائلاً للحيوان المأي ولا شئ [...] هذه الأشياء كالأشياء الحارّة التي تحرّ والباردة التي تبرد كانت أشياء [...] فليس يصنع بهما تصبّره وإن كانت كثيرة وأشياء كبار فكيف ليس جزوعاً إذ كان له فزع كثير (٥) وأمّا إن قلت من كلّها فإنّا نكون [٢/٨٩] [...] سيّد الكناون [...] يكون عندنا النجد وأيّ الأشياء عندنا هائلة فقل كما أصف أنا أمّا فانّه إنسان تهوله هذه الأشياء كلّها [...] هذا التي لا تهول الأنجاد أو أنّه إنسان ستهوله هذه أيضاً هولاً يسيراً فإنّ النجد أمّا في التي تهون على سائر الناس فلا ينفعل البتّةَ وأمّا التي ينفعلون بها سائر الناس انفعالاً مفرطاً فإنّه ينفعل بها [...] قليلاً وأمّا في التي هي أرفع من طبع الإنسان فإنّه لا ينفعل ولا يجزع منها فإنّه غير جزوع من الموت بتوقّع

---

1 third [...] : illegible F, *cowardice* Dun || 3 first [...] illegible F, *and what, if seen, is avoided* Dun (partly) || 3 الأشياء Dun : illegible F || 4 الذي corr. : التي F || 4 هو corr. : هي F || 6 تجزعه Dun : uncertain F || 8 تبرد Dun : illegible F || 8 وإن Dun : illegible F || 10 النجد corr. Arberry, Dun : النجدة F, Bad || 11 تهوله هذه الأشياء كلها Dun : illegible F || 11 تهول F, Dun : تقول Bad

human nature, he is not affected and is not afraid of them, for he is not afraid of death in general. The kind of courage which is as it ought to be is like this. What is excellent in it is chosen for its own sake, not for anything else. (6) As for civic courage, it is that which is due to shame. For the laws induce people who feel shame and those who seek to avoid insult, to endure the destruction which is from wars and killing. This should not be so. Rather then should be the option of choosing destruction for the sake of the city, and they should not have to be like what is related of the people called the Scythians[8] who put on mourning garments when they had sharpened their weapons, but they should do something from free choice. (7) For Homer also says that the citizens are courageous, where he writes and says:

> Have shame before the young men of the Greeks,[9]

and in another place:

> I have shame before the Trojans,
> And the first to praise me will be Polydamas.[10]

(8) Civic courage like this then is obvious. As for that which is on account of anger, it is natural and it is that in respect of which they say that a wild animal also is courageous. [A man like this] endures alarms and disasters. For the angry man does not win, and hence young men and boys die in war more than grown men. (9) We say that the experienced are courageous, just as we say that soldiers, through experience, know the frightening things which are ventured upon. Also, because they have acquired bravery, they are not affected.[11] In this way wild animals and those who do not trust in the law are confident, for they are thought to endure things that are terrible to many. It is not [...][12] that the arrows come together gently.[13] The proof of that is that if they encounter brave men, there is flight. They know about the things that are frightening and venture upon them, and some they endure, and are steady in resisting. Other things they do not endure because they do not persevere in being coura-

---

[8] Arabic *Sqūthāyā*, the Scythians (1112a 28). Cf. also *Eudemian Ethics* III, 1, 25, where the Celts 'take arms and march against the waves'.

[9] Cf. Homer, *Iliad* V, 530 = XV, 562.

[10] Cf. Homer, *Iliad* XXII, 100, quoted somewhat differently above, III, 8, 2 = 1116a 23.

[11] Lit. 'the being affected is repelled from them'.

[12] A word or two are here illegible.

[13] I.e. in battle.

مبسوط فالنجدة التي هي على ما ينبغي فإنّها مثل هذه يختار ما فيها من الجيد لذاتها لا بغيرها (٦) وأمّا النجدة المدنية هي التي تكون للاستحياء فإنّ النواميس تصيّر ذوي الاستحياء والذين يهربون من المسبّة أن يصبروا على العطب الذي من الحروب والقتل ولا ينبغي أن يكون هذا كذلك بل على أنّه يختار أن يكون العطب دون المدينة وألاّ يكونوا كما يحكى عن القوم الذين يقل لهم سقوثايا أنّهم أحدّوا إذ قد حدّوا السلاح بل أن يكونوا يفعلون شيئاً يختارون (٧) فإنّ أوميرش أيضاً يقول إنّ المدنيين هم الأنجاد حيث يكتب ويقول

استحوا أحداث اليونانيين

وفي موضع آخر

أستحيي من أطراوس
فأوّل من مديحي بولودامس

(٨) فالنجدة المدنية التي مثل هذه فظاهرة وأمّا التي من أجل الغضب فطبيعية وهي التي بها يقولون البرّي أيضاً نجد ويصبر على التهاويل والمناحس فإنّ الغضب لا يغلب ومن أجل هذا يموت الأحداث الغلمان في الجهاد أكثر من الرجل (٩) ونقول إنّ أصحاب التجارب أنجاد مثلما نقول إنّ الجند بالتجربة يعرفون الأشياء الهائلة التي يتجرّأ عليها وأيضاً لأنّهم اكتسبوا الجرأة يدفع عنهم الانفعل وبهذا النوع يتفوّق السباع والذين [...] على الشرع فإنّه يظنّ بهم أنّهم يصبرون على التي هي هائلة لكثيرين وليست [...] أنّ السهام تأتي معاً بنوع لين والدليل على ذلك أنّهم [...] أنجاداً كان الهرب وهم [٢/٢٠] يعلمون الأشياء الهائلة ويتجرّأون عليها ويصبرون على بعضها وكانوا يقوون على المعونة ولا يصبرون على بعضها من أجل أنّهم لا يقوون على أن ينجدوا وأمّا بالنجد بالحقيقة

1 الجيد لذاتها appar. corr. Dun : الحياء ذلك أنها F, Bad || 2 هي : F فهي Bad || 4 يختار corr. mrg., Dun : يجيد || 5 سقوثايا Dun* : نفروا w.p. F; نفروا Bad || 5 أحدوا : اجبروا corr. mrg. || 6 يختارون : يبيدون corr. mrg. || 6 يقول corr. Bad : يقولون F || 7 يكتب Dun : illegible F || 12 طبيعية corr : طبيعة F || 13 التهاويل corr. Dun : التناول F || 15 يعرفون : F يعرف corr. Bad || 16 الجرأة Dun : partly illegible F || 16 اكتسبوا Dun : illegible F || 16 والذين Dun : illegible F || 18 [...] : illegible F, *if they encounter* Dun || 19 يتجرأون Dun : illegible F || 19 third و Dun : illegible F || 19 يقوون Bad, Dun : illegible F

geous. As for the truly courageous, he does not wish to be like this. (10) Those who have no experience show that they are courageous in the opposite way from experienced men. For children go towards wild beasts and towards fire, because they have no experience, and similarly in illnesses, and in the movements of the sea in winter when they are alarming. For those who are not experienced, not knowing what the result is, are often brave in regard to danger, while the experienced are apprehensive of it. (11) As for the fifth [kind of courage],[14] it is that which gives good hope. Like these are the young rather than the old, also those who are intoxicated with wine, because fear is anticipation of evil. Whoever does not consider anything of this is not fearful, like Odysseus, because it was not in his mind that he would perish some time. These also are said to be courageous. As for those who are truly [so], it is according to the fear which has already been mentioned,[15] for what has been said on this is not unknown.

2. It may be necessary that we should distinguish from what is common certain means in the species and goods and what among these sadden and gladden, and also those which are concerned with death. (2) Only the man who is concerned with these things when they are nearly anticipated is called the truly courageous man, because what is remote is not feared. For we all know that we shall die, yet we are not alarmed by this death, but by that which is close at hand. If anyone endures the different kinds of heat and cold, he is nearer to another virtue and similarly [i.e. in the opposite case] nearer to another vice. (3) The munificent and those whose lives are spent in good works, even if they are bold in fighting wars, like some of the Persians,[16] are [not] called courageous. But the courageous man aspires to a joyful death when young, not because [...] but because it is excellent, and because this word is true, and it is not [...] that it can be annulled, and he has now awakened from his sleep, because we do [not] call courageous those who endure death for the sake of certain pleasures or for the sake of [avoiding] pains, but we say that they are a different class of people, and for the most part we say that they are bad. (4) Also, he must be great with respect to courage and similarly every virtue. For all men, as far as words go, have acquired

[14] The others are civic courage (§ 6), courage due to anger (§ 8), courage of experience (§ 9) and courage of inexperience (§ 10).

[15] Cf. the earlier part of the chapter, especially § 5.

[16] The significance of this is not known to me.

فليس يريد أن يكون مثل هذا (١٠) والذين ليست لهم تجربة يظهرون أنّهم أنجاد على ضدّ ما هم عليه أصحاب التجارب فإنّ الصبيان يذهبون إلى السباع وإلى النار من أجل أنّه لا تجربة لهم وكذلك في الأمراض وفي حركات البحر في الشتاء إذا كانت هائلة فإنّ الذين لم يجرّبوا من أجل أنّهم لا يعلمون ما يكون من ذلك كثيراً ما يجترئون عليها وأمّا ذوو التجارب فإنّهم يجزعون من ذلك (١١) وأمّا الخامسة فالتي بها يكون يجيد الرجاء ومثل هؤلاء الأحداث أكثر من المشائخ والذين قد صاروا مخمورين بالخمر من أجل أنّ الفزع هو توقّع شرّ وأمّا الذي لا يزكن شيئاً من هذا فليس بجزوع مثل أودسيوس من أجل أنّه لم يكن عنده أن يهلك في وقت ما فإنّ هؤلاء أيضاً يقل إنّهم أنجاد وأمّا الذين هم بالحقيقة [كذلك] فالذي على قدر الهيئة التي قد قيلت فإنّ القول الذي هو لهذه ليس هو بمجهول.

٢. فقد ينبغي أن نفصّل من العامّ متوسّطات في الأنواع والخيرات وما في هذه من المحزنة والسارّة وأيضاً التي في الموت (٢) فإنّ النجد بالحقيقة إنّما يقل الذي في هذه إذا قربت من الرجاء من أجل أنّ ما كان يبعد لا يفزع فإنّا كلّنا نعلم أنّا سنموت ولكن لا نفزع من هذا الموت بل من الذي هو قريب وأمّا إن كان أحد يصبر على أنواع الحرّ والبرد فإنّه يكون أقرب من فضيلة أخرى وكذلك من رداءة أخرى (٣) فإنّ المنفقين والذين أعمارهم في البرّ وإن كانوا حرّيين على مجاهدة الحروب كبعض الفرس فإنّه [لا] يقل لهم أنجاد وأمّا النجد فإنّه إنّما يكون في ترجّي الموت السارّ حديثاً ليس من أجل أنّه [...] بل من أجل أنّه جيّد ومن أجل أنّ هذا القول صحيح ولا [...] أن يتحلّل ما فاق الآن لأنّا [لا] نقول أنجاد للذين يصبرون على الموت من أجل لذّات ما أو من أجل [٢/٢١] أحزان بل نقول إنّهم قوم ما غير أولئك وأكثر ذلك نقول إنّهم أشرار (٤) وأيضاً ينبغي أن يكون عظاماً للنجدة وكذلك كلّ فضيلة فإنّ جميع الناس بالقول قد اقتبسوا شيئاً من النجدة

8 يهلك corr. Dun : يهلل F, Bad || 9 كذلك suppl. Dun || 12 النجد corr. mrg. : النجم F || 16 وإن Dun, F : البرد إن Bad || 16 لا suppl. Dun || 18 ما فاق F, Dun : مما فات Bad || 19 لا suppl. Dun || 19 يصبرون Bad, Dun : illegible F || 21 عظاما F, Dun : عاما corr. Bad

something of courage, and likewise of continence, justice and the rest of the virtues. But there is nothing excellent in what is small, nor is it complete virtue, yet the aim is victory, and Homer said that for many men the evil fate of black death suffices.[17] (5) Also those who are at the extremes call the virtues by the opposite expressions. Cowards call the brave man rough, and rough people call him cowardly. For the intermediate man is in a sense both of the opposites, and in consequence of this 'rough' is applied in a sense to the courageous man, and similarly in regard to the other means, because he who is called by the opposite names of those who have the excess and the defect is intermediate. This is enough in regard to what is said about courage.

3. Let us speak about temperance. That it is concerned with the kinds of delight and pain and these matters of sense, is clear. (2) Yet it is not even in all of these. For we do not say that lovers of music and such spectacles are not temperate or temperate either, but we say that they are people different from those. We do not say that those who like sweetness and all similar qualities are intemperate, and those who like certain pleasures and those which are through touch, for these also appear in many ways. Some pleasures are complete to the last, e.g. those which belong to hot and smooth things and the like, and their opposites, because taste does not appear to lead to intemperance. For people of this kind[18] are in a way experts in the elegant management of a house as regards food and drink. (3) Those are named intemperate, for example who are inflamed by drink and eat many kinds of fare, and they think that there is temperance in and through these things, and they are partly right. As to what was said by Philoxenus, son of Eryxis,[19] he prayed that he might have a crane's gullet, since the pleasure is in this member, and with the descent of what is swallowed the delight is gone. Hence one may wonder at the slavish character which belongs to such a nature. For the pain caused by this kind of excess with the passage of time, involving other evil, appears to belong to a man of no understanding. These pleasures seem to belong to the member already spoken of, being through touch. (4) Similar also are the pleasures of love, for in them there is unrestraint. The natural pleasure here is from the com-

[17] 'The fates of black death' is a Homeric phrase, e.g. *Iliad* II, 834, but the whole quotation is not in our Homer.

[18] I.e. people who cultivate the pleasures of taste, gourmets.

[19] For him cf. *Eudemian Ethics* III, 2, 12. He is unnamed in EN III, 10, 10.

وكذلك من العفّة والعدالة وسائر الفضائل ولكن ليس شئ جيّد في صغير ولا هو فضيلة تامّة بل يراد أن يكون مغلبة فقد قال أوميرش إنّه كفى لكثير من الناس الأجل الردئ من الموت الأسود (٥) وأيضاً فإنّه يسمّيها بأسماء الأضداد أصحاب الأطراف فإنّ الجبناء يسمّون النجد فظّاً وذوو الفظاظة يسمّون النجد جباناً فإنّ المتوسّط هو بنوع ما كلّ واحد من الأضداد من أجل أنّ هذا فظّاً ما على النجد وكذلك في سائر المتوسّطات من أجل أنّ الذي يسمّى بالأسماء الضدّية من أصحاب الزيادة والنقصان هو متوسّط وفي هذا كفاية فيما قيل في النجدة.

٣. فلنقل في العفّة وأمّا أنّها في أنواع السرور والحزن وهذه الأشياء الحسّية فبيّن (٢) إلاّ أنّها ليست في كلّ هذه أيضاً فإنّا لا نقول إنّ محبّي الموسيقى والمناظر التي مثل هذه غير أعفّاء أو أعفّاء أيضاً بل نقول إنّهم قوم آخرون غير أولئك ولا نقول إنّ الذين يحبّون الحلاوة وجميع التي مثل هذه الكيفيات لا أعفّاء والذين يحبّون لذّات ما والتي تكون باللمس فإنّ هذه أيضاً تظهر بأنواع كثيرة وبعضها تامّة للآخر مثل التي للأشياء الحارّة واللّيّنة وأشباه هذه والتي تقابلها بالوضع من أجل أنّ الذوق لا يظهر أنّه يجرّ إلى لا عفّة فإنّ مثل هؤلاء بنوع ما أصحاب التدبير النقي البيتي في المطعم والمشرب (٣) وأمّا الذين يسمّون لا أعفّاء فمثل الذين يحرقهم الشراب ويكثرون أكل ألوان الطبيخ ويرون أنّ العفّة في هذه الأشياء وبها فإنّ بعض أقاويلهم ليس بخطأ وأمّا كما قال فيعلياس بن أدوسيوس دعا أن يكون له مرئ غرنوس من أجل أنّ اللذّة تكون في هذا العضو ومع نزول الشئ قد ذهب الفرح به ومن ها هنا خليق أن يعجب أحد من النوع العبودي الذي للطبيعة فإنّ [٢/٣٢] الجزع على الشئ بهذا النوع من الزيادة ومضي الزمان مع ما فيه من سائر الرداءة فإنّه يظهر أنّه لمن لا فهم له البتّةَ فهذه اللذّات يشبه أن تكون للعضو الذي قد قيل التي تكون باللمس (٤) ومثل هذا أيضاً والتي تكون من اللذّات الزهدية فإنّ فيها شيئاً من الحرّية فالطبيعية من هذه جماع المرأة والرجل والمقدر من ذلك فليس بمذموم وأمّا

9 ليست corr. Bad : ليس F || 9 محبي corr. Dun : محب F || 15 لا يسمون : يسمون appar. F || 16 فيعلياس w.p. F || 16 بن corr. Dun : فان F, Bad || 16 أدوسيوس w.p. F

ing together of the woman and the man, and a moderate amount of that is not blameworthy. The excess is an evil without cure. As for the pleasures that are unnatural and in things contrary to nature, they are a three-fold great misfortune, particularly when in excess. (5) Many incline to excess in pleasure, for the intemperate man is so not by reason of the quality of the pleasure only, but by reason of the quantity. He is rarely met who inclines to defect in it, and therefore he has no special name. These men would be like the rustics whom the poets[20] mention, who are called *qūmūdā*,[21] and they are satirists. (6) Here also rustics call the intermediate man his opposite,[22] e.g. one among them who has no feeling they call a man of no self-control, and one who is without self-control they call a man who has no feeling. They represent them in the middle place,[23] and argue about it as men argue about an excellent matter. They do so very rightly, since temperance is a mean for these things. It is the excellent form by which the temperate man is so—the temperate man, who delights in measure and in what is right and according to what is right and does not delight in anything which is not right. Temperance and similarly every one of the other virtues is simple and uniform. (7) As for the vices, they are multiform, as they are also in the forms of the body. As for the virtues, they are simple, and as for the vices, they have many forms. As for intemperance, it is spoken of in two senses, one of them the negative sense. That is, there is in man's nature a restraining factor, while the other sense is expressed by saying that although it is in his nature, he did not encounter the restraining factor. This is the opposite of temperance, because desire is naturally obedient to reflection and subject to its restraint. For the desire of the temperate man is for little, unimportant things, whereas the desire of the intemperate is opposed to these and resists them. (8) Intemperance has many names, and it is not difficult to distinguish them, e.g. there are the greedy and those who like many kinds of fare, also those who like drinking and like wine, and those whom drink inflames. Some things few like, or it may be one only, e.g. the man who loves tripe and buys always haunches and tripe and such scattered remains and things which are not well-cooked. If there

[20] Sc. the Arabic poets.
[21] Cf. Greek κωμῳδία.
[22] Cf. above, c. 2, § 5.
[23] The thought seems to be that countrymen will make mistakes in their ethical judgements, whereas (*wa*) they do not doubt that the mean is virtue, and the intermediate man virtuous.

المفرط فرداءة دون الشفاء فأمّا التي تكون على غير الطبيعة وفي أشياء مخالفة للطبيعة فهي كثيرة الشقاء ثلاثة أضعاف ولا سيّما التي تكون بإفراط (٥) وكثير من يميل إلى إفراط اللذّات فإنّ لا عفيف يكون ليس بكيفية اللذّة فقط بل وبالكمّية وقليل من يميل إلى النقصان فيها ومن أجل هذا ليس لهذا اسم وخليق أن يكون هؤلاء كالقرويين الذين يذكرهم الشعراء الذين يسمّون قومودا وهم الهجاؤون (٦) وها هنا أيضاً القرويون يسمّون المتوسّط مقابلاً بالوضع أمّا من كان منهم من لا حسّ له فإنّما يسمّيه ذا لا عفّة ومن كان منهم بلا عفّة يسمّيه ذا لا حسّ له ويصوّرونهم في الموضع المتوسّط ويشاجرون فيه كالمشاجرة في الشئ الجيّد ويفعلون ذلك بنوع صحيح جدّاً من أجل أنّ العفّة متوسّطة لهذه وهي الهيئة الجيّدة التي بها يكون العفيف الذي يلذّ بقدر وبما ينبغي وعلى ما ينبغي ولا يلذّ بالشئ الذي لا ينبغي فالعفّة وكذلك كلّ واحدة من سائر الفضائل مبسوطة وبنوع واحد (٧) وأمّا الرداءات فكثيرة الأنواع كما يكون في هيئات الجسم أيضاً أمّا الفضائل فمبسوطة وأمّا الرداءات فكثيرة الصور وأمّا لا عفّة فإنّها تقل بنوعين أحدهما بنوع السلب وهو أنّه في طبعه كظم والأخرى في طبعه ذلك إلاّ أنّه لم يصادف الكظم وهذه تقابل العفّة بالوضع من أجل أنّ الشهوة مطيعة للفكرة بالطبع ومتكظّمة لها فإنّ شهوة العفيف تشتهي الأشياء الصغار الدنيئة وأمّا شهوة لا عفيف فإنّها مضادّة لهذه وممانعة (٨) ولا عفّة كثيرة الأسماء وليس يعسر تجزّئها [٢/٢٣] مثل الشرهاء والذين يحبّون كثرة ألوان الطبيخ وأيضاً الذين يحبّون الشرب ويحبّون الخمر والذين يحرقهم الشراب وبعض الأشياء قليل من يحبّها أو خليق أن يكون واحداً مثل الذي يحبّ البطون والذي يشتري أبداً الأفخاذ والبطون وما يشبه ذلك من العناصر والأشياء التي لم تنضج فلو كان مثل هؤلاء كثيراً لقد كان ظهر لهم اسم ما مشترك وخليق ألاّ يكون ينبغي أن يفحص عن هذه.

1 الشفاء Bad, Dun : الشقاء F || 2 الشقاء F, Dun : الشفاء Bad || 5 القرويون corr. : القرويين F || 19 كثيرا corr. Bad : كثير F

were many such as these, some common name for them would have appeared. But perhaps it is not necessary to investigate these things.

4. Let us speak about equanimity. In anger there are excess and defect, and a mean state also. The excess is of several kinds, as indeed has already been said. The man who is disturbed at little things and for a short time is called hot-tempered. As for the man who lacks the share,[24] he is called a blamer, and he is [not] called a dissembler unless he cherishes his anger and keeps it up for a long period. (2) As for the man who is vengeful and who takes heavy vengeance in small matters and does not forgive, he is harsh and very bad. As for the opposite of this man, he has no name. Like these is he who feels no resentment at anything. If he is struck, he feels no resentment, and he is not angry when wrong is done to his children and his wife nor when his parents are maligned. This shows that he is a man dull of feeling on whom pain makes no impression. (3) While some of these exaggerate in excess and others are defective, there is an intermediate form by which resentment and anger may be according to what is right, at the right time and in the right way. That this form is intermediate and excellent is clear, and we lead back temperance to a form like this for the most part. (4) Whatever the mean in anger consists in, when resentment occurs at the wrong objects, there are pleasures and pains also involved, because he who is angry and bears resentment feels pain, and when he is able to take vengeance, or hopes to, he feels pleasure. The poet has said:[25]

> Truly, when a great blow has struck him
> the heart of man withers,
> But when he has taken vengeance it returns
> to its former state.

And as for the rest of what has been said, it is not difficult to refer it to each of the forms that have been mentioned.

5. As for liberality, magnificence and magnanimity, it is thought of them that they are near neighbours, and that one follows another, since the liberal man is not thought to be pusillanimous, nor is the magnificent man. (2) They suppose that for the most part illiberality is near to magnanimity, and they thought that some of the people who are called Laconians were magnanimous and were the reverse

---

[24] Something appears to have fallen out.
[25] Cf. Theognis, 361-362.

٤. فلنقل في الدعة فإنّ في الغضب إفراطاً ونقصاناً وتوسّطاً أيضاً فأمّا الإفراط فأنواع كثيرة وقد قيل ذلك قبل هذا أيضاً فالذي يختلط على أشياء صغار وزمان يسير يسمّى حادّ الغضب فأمّا الذي ينقص من القسم فيسمّى ذامّاً و[لا] يسمّى مداجياً ألاّ يجهر الغضب ويمتدّ به زماناً كثيراً (٢) وأمّا صاحب الانتقام والذي ينتقم نقمة شديدة عند أيشاء صغار ولا يعذر فصعب وذو رداءة جدّاً وأمّا ضدّ هذا فلا اسم له ومثل هؤلاء الذي لا يحرد على شيء وأمّا إن يلكم ولا يحرد ولا يغضب إذا انتقص ولده وامرأته ولا إذا افتري على أبويه فإنّ ذلك يظهر أنّه لإنسان كليل الحواسّ لا يحيك فيه الألم (٣) وإن بعض هؤلاء مفرطون في الزيادة وبعضهم ذوو نقص فهيئة ما متوسّطة التي بها يكون الحرد والغضب على ما ينبغي في الوقت الذي ينبغي وعلى النوع الذي ينبغي وأمّا أنّ هذه الهيئة متوسّطة وجيّدة فبيّن فإنّا نسوق العفّة إلى هيئة مثل هذه أكثر ذلك (٤) وفي أيّ شيء يكون التوسّط الذي في الغضب فإنّه إذا كان الحرد على ما لا ينبغي تكون لذّات وأحزان أيضاً فيها من أجل أنّ الذي يغضب ويحرد يحزن إذا هو قدر على الانتقام أو كان على الرجاء يلذّ فقد قل الشاعر:

إنّ قلب الرجل إذا أصابه ضرب كثير
يذبل
وإذا انتقم يعود
إلى الحال التي كان عليها

وأمّا سائر ما يقل فليس يعسر أن ينسب إلى كلّ واحد من الهيئات ممّا قد قيل.

٥. وأمّا الحرّية وعظم الاستئهل وعظم النفس فيظنّ بها أنّها متجاورة وأنّ بعضها [٢/٢٤] يتبع بعضاً من أجل أنّ ذا الحرّية لا يظنّ به أنّه صغير النفس ولا العظيم الاستئهل يظنّ به ذلك (٢) ويزعمون أنّ أكثر ذلك أنّ لا حرّية تقارب عظم النفس وكانوا يرون أنّ بعض

3 لا suppl. Bad, Dun || 3 مداجيا corr. : مداجي F || 5 يعذر Dun : يغدر Bad || 6 يلكم F, Dun : يكظم Bad || 6 second إذا F : إذ Bad || 21 أن لا corr. Bad : الا F

of liberal, since they judged of general principles and great matters very well, and in them did very well, but they pursue small gains owing to limited experience and lack of money.[26] To these matters belongs a special investigation as to how and in what state they are. At present we take the surface appearances and state what each is and what it consists of. (3) Let us then speak first of liberality. It is clear that it is concerned with the getting and giving of goods and with these also its opposite is concerned, yet in a different way, because the liberal man takes only from where it is fitting and as much as is fitting, and he acquires in this way, being more concerned with employing than acquiring wealth, because employment is a fulfillment and giving is more excellent than getting. For praise follows giving, not getting. (4) But he who gets all he can and as is not fitting, and in giving gives nothing—as one might say, 'neither when it is fitting, nor as much as is fitting'—, he is more concerned with not giving and not spending than the liberal man. This man too is of several kinds, including the ill-natured man who is defective [in liberality], and the stingy one, also the man who makes dishonest gains in business dealing. As for him who gives everything or him who gives to whom he ought not, or who gives the most,[27] he is a spendthrift and is not uncommon. Thus liberality and illiberality are opposites. (5) As for wealth, it can be employed in itself[28] and can be employed accidentally. As regards being employed in itself,[29] it is like the horse which is ridden. As regards being employed accidentally, it is [like a man] sitting on the horse in the house as he sits on a chair. Another case is when [the horse] is sold. In general, wealth and property consist in all the things which are subject to buying and selling. Therefore money was invented, for it would be difficult if exchange were made in something else than money, as the ancients did. So there was invented for the purpose a common something for which everything else could be exchanged by agreement.[30] For that reason money was called in Greek *nāmūsī mā*,[31] i.e. the law. (6) He who is illiberal desires money more than anything else. For this reason they do not have great possessions compared with others, but

---

[26] This perhaps refers to the Ephors at Sparta, cf. *Politics* II, 6, 16 (1270b 26ff.).
[27] Sc. of what he has.
[28] Or 'essentially', i.e. directly (Arabic *bi-dhātihā*).
[29] See previous note.
[30] Lit. 'on a condition' (Arabic *'alā sharīṭah*).
[31] I.e. Greek νόμισμα.

القوم الذين يقل لهم لاقونس كانوا عظماء الأنفس وكانوا غير ذوي حرّية إذ كانوا يقضون على الكلّيات والأشياء العظام قضاة جيّداً ويفعلون فيها فعلاً جيّداً وكانوا يصادون بأرباح قليلة لقلّة التجربة وعوز الدينار ولهذه الأشياء طلب خاصّ كيف هي وعلى أيّ حل وأمّا حيننا هذا فإنّا نأخذ الظاهرات ونخبر ما كلّ واحد منها وفي أيّ شيء هو (٣) فلنقل أوّلاً في الحرّية وهو بيّن أنّها في أخذ الأموال وإعطائها وفي هذه أيضاً ما يقابلها بالوضع إلاّ أنّها ليست بنوع متشابه من أجل أمّا ذو الحرّية فإنّما يأخذ من حيث ينبغي وبكمّية ما ينبغي وبمثل هذا النوع يقتني وهو في الاستعمل أكثر منه في القنية من أجل أنّ الاستعمل إتمام والإعطاء أجود من الأخذ فإنّه يتبع الإعطاء المدح ولا يتبع ذلك الأخذ (٤) بل الذي يأخذ بكلّ ما أمكنه وعلى النوع الذي لا ينبغي وأمّا في الإعطاء فإنّه لا يعطي شيئاً كقول القائل لا إذا كان ينبغي ولا كمّية ما ينبغي وهو في ألاّ يعطي ولا ينفق أكثر من صاحب الحرّية وهذا أيضاً على أنواع كثيرة فإنّه منه شكس وهو ينقص والشحيح ومنه القبيح الأرباح في المعاملة وأمّا الذي يعطي كلّاً أو الذي يعطي ليس لمن ينبغي أو الذي يعطي الأكثر فمتلاف وهو لا قليل ومن أجل هذا يقابلون بالوضع الحرّية ولا حرّية (٥) وأمّا الأموال فقد يمكن أن تستعمل بذاتها وقد يمكن أن تستعمل بنوع العرض أمّا بذاتها فمثل الفرس الذي يركب وأمّا بنوع العرض فإنّه [مثل من] يجلس على الفرس في المنزل كما يجلس على الكرسي ونوع آخر إذا بيع وبالجملة الأموال والقنية في جميع الأشياء التي فيها شراء وبيع ولذلك اتّخذ الدينار فإنّه لو كانت المبادلة بشيء آخر غير الدينار كما كان يفعل القدماء عسر [٢/٢٥] ذلك فاتّخذ لذلك شيء مشترك يمكن أن يبادل في جميع الأشياء على شريطة ولذلك يسمّى الدينار باليونانية ناموسي ما أيّ الناموس (٦) والذي ليس بحرّية يحرص على الدينار أشدّ من حرص غيره ومن أجل هذا ليس هم كثيري القنية من غيرهم

1 لاقونس w.p. F : لاقويين Bad || 2 يصادون F, Dun : يصارون Bad || 6 ليست corr. Bad : ليس F || 8-9 يأخذ بكل ما corr. Bad : يأخذ الأخذ بكل F || 12 كلا corr. Bad : كل F || 13 هو لا Dun : هولاء Bad || 15 فإنه appar. corr Dun : فإن F, Bad || 15 مثل من suppl. Dun || 16 القنية F, Dun : القينة Bad || 19 بحرية F : بذي حرية add. Bad || 20 القنية F, Dun : العطية Bad

they have much silver and gold. These are our remarks concerning liberality and its opposite.

(7) As for high merit,[32] it appears to be in expenditures which have the quality of greatness, particularly in cities, in which there is what is fitting. What is fitting is either as regards the man or in respect of the action and the work. For the merit of the rich man and the poor man is not identical, nor are the rich man and those of small means [alike] even in all the expenses authorised by law or custom, but each of them should spend according to what he possesses. (8) And it may be not only according to what he possesses, but also according to what power his fathers had and he now has, for we see that in everything action should be like extent of power, for that assimilates action and power, for it is not right that the food for a wedding-party should be like that of the sailors on a quadrireme, nor the decoration of a temple the same as that of a house, nor the beauty of form of four *mithqāls* other than a single property, so that in all considerable expenses the man of high merit brings what is fitting for himself and the actions. The man who comes short in all these things or in most of them, is said to be of little merit, while the man who spends and is lavish to excess and goes further than is fitting is called ostentatious.[33] It is not difficult to grasp this distinction from the individual cases. (9) It may be thought that the liberal man and the man of high merit are concerned with the same things, but this is not so. For one of them is concerned with acquiring and obtaining wealth, but mostly with giving it away, while the other is concerned with outgoings on cities and on followers. The man of high merit then appears to be as described. (10) We must now speak of magnanimity. It is thought to be concerned with honour and with honourable goods. It appears that the magnanimous man makes light of that, even great honour, yet he desires it from some. Hence Homer said, speaking in the person of Achilles:

> I need not this honour,
> Yet I deem that I am honoured by the
> allotment of Zeus.[34]

---

[32] Or 'magnificence'. Arabic *'uẓm al-isti'hāl* for Greek μεγαλοπρέπεια.

[33] Arabic *badhdhākh*, cf. II, 7, 6 = 1107b 19 and IV, 2, 4 = 1122a 31, where *al-badhakh* renders (wrongly) Greek βαναυσία.

[34] Homer, *Iliad* IX, 607-608. Arabic *bi-ḥaẓẓ Diyā* renders Greek Διὸς αἴσῃ; cf. 1124b 16: τῷ Διί = *li-Za'us*; 1165a 15: τῷ Διί = *bi-Diyā* (corr. *li-Diyā*).

بل هم كثيرو الفضّة والذهب فهذه الأقاويل التي تخصّ الحرّية والتي تقابلها بالوضع.

(٧) وأمّا عظم الاستئهل فإنّه يظهر أنّه في النفقات التي لها عظم ولا سيّما في المدن التي فيها ما ينبغي وما ينبغي إمّا عنده وإمّا من جهة الفعل والعمل فإنّه ليس استئهل الغني والفقير متشابهاً ولا الغني والذين قنيتهم قليلة ولا في سائر النفقات التي تطلب النواميس الإنفاق فيها أو العادات بل ينبغي لكلّ واحد منهم أن ينفق على قدر ما له من القنية (٨) وخليق ألاّ يكون على ما له من القنية فقط بل وعلى قدر ما لآبائه من القدر وله أيضاً فإنّا نرى أنّه في كلّ ينبغي أن يكون الفعل شبيهاً بعظم القدر فإنّ ذلك يشبه القدر ويشبه الفعل فإنّه لا ينبغي أن يكون طعام العرس مثل طعام ملاحي ذات الأربعة صفوف ولا زينة الهيكل والبيت زينة واحدة ولا حسن هيئة أربعة مثاقيل غير خاصّية واحدة ففي جميع الإنفاقات ذوات الأقدار فالعظيم الاستئهل يأتي فيها بما ينبغي لذاته والأفعل وأمّا الذي ينقص في جميع هذه أو في أكثرها فإنّه يسمّى صغير الاستئهل والذي ينفق ويسرف في الفرط ويتباهى على غير ما ينبغي يسمّى بذّاخاً وليس بعسير درك هذه أيّ هي من الجزئيات (٩) وخليق أن يظنّ أنّ ذا الحرّية والعظيم الاستئهل في أشياء واحدة بأعيانها وليس هذا كذلك فإنّ أحدهما في اقتناء الأموال وأخذها وأكثر ذلك في إعطائها والآخر ففي إنفاقات على المدن وعلى الأتباع فالعظيم الاستئهل قد يظهر أنّه إنسان ما مثل هذا.

(١٠) وقد ينبغي هذا القول في عظم النفس فقد يظنّ أنّه في الكرامة وفي الكرامة من الخيرات ويظهر أنّ كبير النفس يستخفّ بذلك وبالكرامة الكبيرة وهو يشتهيها من بعض [٢/٢٦] ومن ها هنا قال أوميرش عن إشيلوس

لا أحتاج إلى هذه الكرامة
بل أرى أن أكرم
بحظّ دياً

---

6 first على F : على قدر add. Bad || 12 يسمى F, Dun : ليس Bad || 12 هذه F : هني Bad || 14 أحدهما F : أحدما Bad || 16 third في om. Bad

For he cares for honour from Zeus, but takes no account of honour from the majority. (11) It is likely that he possesses all the virtues, for the man who masters the great pleasures appears to be great and magnanimous. Thus he assigns to himself and to others in great matters what is the best of it and according to his power. Similar is he who gives to his friends many great things. In the same way in the case of the remaining virtues the excesses are said to belong to the great-souled man. If magnanimity is such, it is then in agreement with the other perfect virtues,[35] and has something special as being concerned with honour. (12) As for the excess and defect in what is related to the forms, the magnanimous man then is concerned with the noble among the goods, unless it is possible that he who is worthy of great and noble things becomes entitled to such as these by considering himself entitled to them. For there is a great difference if they are his own in a sense, because it is clear that one of the two men acts correctly and has greatness since he considers himself entitled to great things, whereas is it not apparent that the other has no intelligence, since there is no great matter in respect of which he is not dispraised, because he acts contrary to what is necessary, differently from what is fitting and differently from what he is entitled to? Is it then that as a man is entitled to great things, so he is also not entitled or is entitled to more? For if the latter, does he deserve little? Since there is the man who is not entitled to great things and does not consider himself entitled to them, and there is the man who considers himself entitled to them, as regards him who is not entitled to great things and does not consider himself entitled to them,[36] it may be that [not] every single one is great, and in this sense it may be that he is neither to be praised nor blamed. But as for him who thinks he is worthy of great things, not being worthy of them, he is called remiss, for remissness is when the remiss man deserves nothing but thinks that he deserves great things. This is a bad state.

(13) The combinations of qualities being four, one of them seems to be mean though not blameworthy, since he who is not entitled to anything by no means does well. So then it is not right to make this a virtue, and then we say that this virtue is blameworthy remissness. Among those who are entitled to great things is the great man and then man who thinks aright. It is clear that he is magnanimous, since he was worthy of great things and considered himself entitled to

[35] I.e. as a mean between extremes.
[36] The text perhaps is here defective, with a lacuna.

فإنّه قد كان أمّا بكرامة دياً فيحفل وأمّا بكرامة الأكثر فقد كان يتهاون (١١) وقد يشبه أن يكون يقتني جميع الفضائل فإنّ الذي يقتنص اللذّات الكبار يظهر أنّه عظيم وعظيم النفس وكذلك يقيم لذاته ولغيره في الأشياء العظام ما هو أفضله وعلى قدره ومثل ذلك الذي يعطي الأصدقاء أشياء كثيرة عظيمة وعلى مثل هذا النوع في سائر الفضائل الزيادات يقل إنّها لكبير النفس فإن كان عظم النفس على هذه الحل فهو إذاً لسائر الفضائل التامّة موافق وله شيء خاصّ من أجل أنّه في الكرامة (١٢) وأمّا الزيادة والنقصان في التي تنسب إلى الهيئات فإذاً العظيم النفس في الكريمة من الخيرات أو الذي يستأهل الأشياء العظيمة والكريمة قد يمكن أن يكون أهلاً لمثل هذه بأن يؤهّلها ذاته فإنّه اختلاف عظيم إن يكون لذاته بنوع ما من أجل أنّه بيّن أنّ أمّا أحدها يفعل بصحّة وله عظم إذ يؤهّل ذاته لعظيمة والآخر فلا يظهر أنّه لا عقل له من أجل أنّه ليس شيئاً من الأشياء كبيراً إلاّ أنّه ليس بممدوح بهذه الجهة من أجل أنّه يفعل على خلاف ما يجب وعلى غير ما ينبغي وعلى غير ما يستأهل فهل كما أنّه يكون الإنسان يستأهل أموراً عظاماً كذلك يكون لا يستأهل أيضاً أو يستأهل أكثر فإن الأكثر يحقّ لهم القليل وإذ كان من لا يستأهل العظام ولا يؤهّلها ذاته وكان من يؤهّلها فالذي لا يستأهل العظام ولا يؤهّلها ذاته فخليق أن [لا] يكون كلّ واحد من الكبير وعلى هذا النوع خليق ألاّ يمدح ولا يذمّ وأمّا الذي يرى أنّه أهل للعظام وليس هو لها بأهل فإنّه يسمّى مسترخياً فإنّ الاسترخاء هو إذا لم يكن يستحقّ صاحبه شيئاً ويظنّ أنّه يستحقّ أشياء عظاماً وهذا من الحالات الرديئة.

(١٣) ولمّا كانت مقارنات الخطط أربعاً فإنّ أحدها يظهر أنّه وضيع وليس بمذموم من أجل أنّ الذي لا يستأهل [٢/٢٧] شيئاً ليس بجيّد البتّة فإذاً لا ينبغي أن توضع هذه فضيلة وإذاً قلنا إنّ هذه الفضيلة استرخاء مذموم وأمّا الذين يستأهلون العظام فمنهم العظيم والذي يرى رأياً مستقيماً وهو بيّن أنّه عظيم النفس إذ كان أهلاً للأشياء العظام وكان

1 الأكثر F, Dun : الكترا corr. Bad || 3 ما Dun : مما Bad || 6 second في F, Dun : ففي Bad || 7 فإذا F, Dun : وإذا Bad || 7 الذي يستأهل corr. Dun : التي تستأهل F, Bad || 10 كبيرا ... شيئاً corr. : كبير ... شيء F || 11 بممدوح F : بممدح Bad || 14 لا suppl. Dun || 16 مسترخيا corr. Bad : مسترخ F || 16 فإن F : لأن Bad || 20 وإذا F : ولذا corr. Bad || 20 العظيم Dun : الحكيم Bad

them. As for him who is entitled to great things and does not consider himself entitled to them, he is pusillanimous, since he is small and mean, not considering himself entitled to great things even if he is worthy of them. Greatness of soul appears to be a mean in honourable things between pusillanimity and remissness, for one of these is defective and the other excessive.

6. As for righteous indignation also, it ranks as a virtue. That is thought of it, for we say that righteous indignation is found in the best men, while the poets[37] attribute it also to the gods. With what is righteous indignation then concerned? Is it not that it is directed at excellent work, like envy also? But envy brings pain at what is in accordance with merit. That this character is bad and unjust is clear, and he who enjoys the unmerited misfortune of other people is called wicked and sinful. He is the man who enjoys what is bad, and he is blamed. (2) The envious is excessive in pains and defective in joy, since he who is pained at good things rejoices at nothing of which the condition is good, and he is blamed mostly with respect to this. Therefore he is named from this point of view. He who enjoys the bad, delights in what ought not be enjoyed. We should be pained at the misfortune of the good. (3) The following things also are what are praised, being in agreement with virtue:[38] modesty, truth-telling, a friend and friendship, and good behaviour. (4) Now he who is bashful about everything and dreads everything is called a weak man. He has no action and is almost an imbecile. As for him who cares for nothing, does not shrink from blame and has no shame, the imprudent man, he is unsound as regards virtue. As for him who shrinks from the blame which is attached to ugly things and is not pained at those to which no blame attaches, he is midway between these. He is called modest, and it is thought of this one that he is near to the temperate man. For shame appears to be partial temperance, for when it occurs, it is seen to be mingled therewith. (5) There is a kind of man who is hypocrite[39] respecting the goods, either those which are not or are for the most part.[40] This hypocrite is not concerned with all the goods, since they are not alike in soundness, and

[37] The Greek poets must here be meant.

[38] The connection with the foregoing is not clear, and something may have dropped out at this point.

[39] Arabic *murā'in*, Malcolm C. Lyons translates "pretentious" ("A Greek Ethical Treatise", in: *Oriens* 13-14 [1961], pp. 35-57, p. 40).

[40] Cf. 'Seventh Book', 5, 12, 'the noble among the goods'.

يؤهّلها ذاته فأمّا الذي يستأهل العظام ولا يؤهّلها ذاته فصغير النفس من أجل أنّه الصغير والوضيع لا يؤهّل ذاته للعظام وإن كان أهلاً لها فعظم النفس يظهر أنّه توسّط في الأشياء الكريمة فيما بين صغير النفس وبين الاسترخاء فإنّ أحد هذين ينقص والآخر يزيد

٦. وأمّا ناماسيس أيضاً وهي ترتّب فضيلة ما ويظنّ بها ذلك فإنّا نقول إنّ ناماسيس في الرجل الأفاضل فأمّا الشعراء فينسبون ذلك إلى الآلهة أيضاً فإذاً هو ناماسيس في أيّ شيء إلاّ أن يكون على جودة الصنع كالحسد أيضاً ولكن أمّا الحسد فإنّه يأتي بحزن على التي تكون على استحقاق وأمّا أنّ هذا الخلق رديء وغير عادل فبيّن وأمّا الذي يفرح بشقاء قوم على غير استحقاق فإنّه يسمّى جائراً فاسقاً وهو الذي يفرح بالرديء وهو مذموم (٢) وأمّا الحسود فإنّه يزيد في الأحزان وينقص في الفرح من أجل أنّ الذي يحزن على الخيرات لا يفرح على شيء لحسن حاله البتّة وهو بهذه الجهة مذموم أكثر ذلك ومن أجل هذا يسمّى من هذه الجهة فأمّا الذي يفرح بالرديء فإنّه يلذّ بالتي لا تنبغي فقد ينبغي أن نحزن عند شقاء الأخيار (٣) وهذه الأشياء أيضاً التي تمدح وهي موافقة للفضيلة من الاستحياء والصدق والصديق والصداقة وحسن التصرّف (٤) فإنّ الذي يستحيي من كلّ شيء ويتّقي كلّ شيء يسمّى البهيم وهو لا فعل له وهو قريب من الأحمق وأمّا الذي لا يهتمّ بشيء ولا يكع من الذمّ ولا حياء له وهو الوقاح فذو سقم عند الفضيلة وأمّا الذي يكع عن الذمّ الذي يكون بالأشياء السمجة ولا يحزن من التي لا ذمّ لها فإنّه متوسّط لهذه ويسمّى مستحياً ويظنّ بهذا أنّه مجاور للعفيف [٢/٢٨] فإنّ الحياء يظهر أنّه عفّة جزئية فإنّ حدوثها يرى أنّه يخالط بعضها بعضاً (٥) ومن الناس من هو مراء في الخيرات إمّا التي ليست وإمّا الأكثر وليس هذا المرائي في جميع الخيرات إذ ليست هي متشابهة في الصحّة والفضائل بنوع

4 ناماسيس (twice) corr. Bad, Dun : ماسيس F || 10 حاله F, Dun : ما له Bad || 12 شقاء suppl. mrg. || 15-16 الذم...ذم corr. Dun : السمو...سمو F, Bad || 17 مجاور appar. read. Dun : مجاوز F, Bad || 19 إذ Dun : أو Bad || 19 ليست corr. : ليس F

the virtues in a general way are concerned with the things which are exchanged. A man of this type is called ironical and is not praised at all. (6) As for the man who is defective and inclines to what is defective in its condition and does that with good, he appears not to be joyful. The Laconians[41] are thought to be like these. It was thought of Socrates also that he was ironical because he spoke ill of himself, yet in some things it appears that he was not joyless. In external things and those which happen frequently, there is ugliness involved and the mean for these is the truth which is not excessive and not defective. It is according to a condition and form of good, and in all its conditions is according to practical intelligence. (7) All that has been said is like the description of the virtues set down in books. As regards social life, there is a man who is difficult to associate with and hard, and who takes things always in the worst way.[42] These people may be called inimical, since they grow up in enmity. (8) The opposite of these, they who in all things share in pleasure and in merriment are called complaisant. Intermediate between hostility and complaisance is the man who does not share in merriment at everything. This is the moderate and excellent man. It does not escape us that he who is like this is also called a friend. For the sharing of pleasure according to what is right and in what is right, and the causing of it, belong to a friend and friendship. In conversing also there is a certain joy, and it has excess and defect, because some people[43] baseness for the sake of what is laughable, to the point that they bring embarrassments upon themselves and their parents and those who comprehend, shrink from nothing, if what is said is amusing, and endure hearing anything. The man who is like these is called a buffoon. It is thought that they are despicable. (9) The opposite of these say nothing, not even if they are reviled, enduring as did Sāwus[44] with the man who said he did something which he did not do, for rage carried him away. These people are usually called uneducated and frozen. The intermediate man says and hears nothing evil nor is he difficult, and his criticism is only of things which cause no pain to any sensible person. He only seeks and finds words to say

---

[41] Arabic *Lāqūn.s*, Greek Λάκωνες, cf. also c. 8, § 2.

[42] Translation not certain (Arabic *ma'khadhuhu ilā 'l-arda'*). For the form of the last word, cf. 1119b 32 (IV, 1, 4).

[43] Arabic verb is missing. One may compare the passage V, 8, 2-3.

[44] Possibly for Sāwus (Solon) or [Tha]sāwus (Theseus), but nothing is known of such an incident.

كلّي في التي تبدل ومن كان على مثل هذه الحل فيسمّى مستهزئاً وليس يمدح البتّةَ (٦) وأمّا الذي ينتقص ويميل إلى ما ينقص من حاله ويفعل ذلك بخير فيظهر أنّه ليس فرحاً ويظنّ بلاقونس أنّهم مثل هؤلاء وقد كان يظنّ بسقراطيس أيضاً أنّه كان مستهزئاً لأنّه كان ينقص ذاته وفي بعض الأشياء يظهر أنّه ليس لا فرح وأمّا في الأشياء الظاهرة والتي تكون كثيراً ففيها سماجة والمتوسّط لهؤلاء الصدق الذي لا يزيد ولا ينقص وهو على حالة وهيئة خير وهو في جميع حالاته على التعقّل (٧) وجميع ما قيل كأنّه صفة الفضائل موضوعة في كتب وأمّا في المعاشرة فمن الناس من هو صعب المعاشرة جاسٍ ومأخذه إلى الأردأ وخليق أن يسمّى هؤلاء ذوات عداوة إذ يربّون على العداوة (٨) والذين على مقابلة هؤلاء وهم في جميع الأشياء يشاركون في اللذّات وفي المدح فإنّهم يسمّون متأتّين والمتوسّط فيما بين العداوة والتأتّي الذي لا يشارك في مدح جميع الأشياء فهذا هو المتوسّط والجيّد وليس يذهب عنّا أنّ الذي مثل هذا يقل صديق أيضاً فإنّ اشتراك اللذّة على ما ينبغي وفيما ينبغي والتسبّب بها للصديق وللصداقة وفي المخاطبات أيضاً فرح ما وله زيادة ونقصان من أجل أنّ بعضهم دناءة للشئ المضحك حتّى إنّهم يعصون ذواتهم والآبه ومن أدركوا ولا يكعون عن شئ إذا كان المقول مضحكاً ويصبرون على أن يسمعوا كلّ شئ ويسمّى من كان مثل هؤلاء محاكياً ويرى أنّهم سفلاء (٩) وأمّا الذين على مقابلة هؤلاء فإنّهم لا يقولون شيئاً ولا إن اسمعوا يصبرون كما فعل ساوس بالذي قل إنّه يفعل شيئاً ممّا [٢/٢٩] لا يفعل فإنّه ذهب به الحسّ وقد اعتادوا يسمّون هؤلاء لا تعليم لهم وقوارس وأمّا المتوسّط فإنّه لا يقول ولا يسمع برداءة وليس هو صعب وإنّما ينتقص بأشياء لا تحزن أحداً من ذوي

2 ينتقص corr. Bad : ينقص F || 2 ينقص corr. Bad : نقص F || 3 فرحا corr. Bad : فرح F || 5 بلاقونس Dun : w.p. F; بلاقونين Bad || 7 ففيها corr. : ففيه F || 9 الأردأ F, Dun : الأنى Bad || 9 وهم F, Dun : هم Bad || 10 التاتي Dun : المتاتي F, Bad || 13 يعصون F, Dun : ينتقصون Bad || 17 الحس corr. Bad, Dun : الجنس F

which he thinks are lively[45] words. This form also resembles a virtue, and gives pleasure in conversations through a kind of badinage. The buffoon is thought to be lively, but one should not listen to him. Rather one should continually make a distinction—and it should be said that as regards the stories which are told and heard which the intermediate man might suitably tell, he is lively, and whoever goes beyond that is called a buffoon.

7. As for friendship, there is something excellent about it. It can be employed rightly and in the contrary way. What is the latter is not according to virtue. When it is correctly employed, it is a mean between being difficult and being complaisant. For the difficult person appears to be haughty in a way, ill to encounter, while the complaisant man is the opposite. Hence the people of Sicily called him [...],[46] i.e. waxing with drink. (2) As for the friend, he is intermediate in a way, not very demonstrative and not ill to encounter. (3) 'Aspiring' may be employed in both senses,[47] for when goods are equivalent to great things, then their possessor must be called aspiring, while if they are nothing excellent, then aspiration in this case appears to be foolishness. (4) If anyone distinguishes these things and their like in [other than] the way described and states them, he altogether fails to distinguish them and lacks direction. There follows this discussion the discussion of justice.

8. Much has been said about justice and written too. Some people think that it is the greatest of goods, such as the planet Venus is not when it appears in the evening after the setting of the sun, nor when it appears before the rising of the sun, and what annulled the wisdom of [...]goras[48] when he asked Plato: 'What is wisdom?', and he replied: 'It is justice.' (2) The directors[49] of the people called Laconians[50] assert that there should be training in justice, and some people judge the contrary, for they call justice the good of others, claiming that it is advantageous to him who is a stranger to it but injurious

---

[45] Arabic *haiyinat at-tanaqqul*, lit. 'light or easy to be moved'.

[46] Apparently Arabic *brṭīwāms*, perhaps for παροίνιος or πάροινος.

[47] It would appear more natural to say 'in two senses'. Perhaps something has dropped out.

[48] Probably Pythagoras in spite of the anachronism, cf. the form in the Arabic text with that in c. 9, § 10.

[49] Arabic *dhawī an-nahj*, apparently for the Spartan ephors.

[50] Arabic *Lāqūn.s*, cf. above c. 6, § 6 (n. 41).

الفهم وإنّما يتطلّب ويجد أقاويل يقولها الذي يظنّ بها أنّها أقاويل هيّنة التنقّل فهذه الهيئة أيضاً شبيهة بفضيلة ما وهي يهيئ في المخاطبات بهيله ما والمحاكي يرى أن يكون هيّن التنقّل ولكن لا ينبغي أن ينصت له بل ينبغي أن يصار إلى التفصيل وأن يكون يقل أمّا الذي يقل الأقاويل ويسمع التي خليق أن يقولها الرجل المتوسّط فإنّه هيّن التنقّل وأمّا الذي يزيد فيقل محاكي.

٧. وأمّا الصداقة فلها شيء جيّد ويمكن أن تستعمل بالصحّة وعلى ذلك وما كان على هذه الحال فليس هو على الفضيلة وأمّا إذا استعملت بالصحّة فإنّها تكون توسّطاً للصعوبة والمواتاة فإنّ الصعب يظهر أنّه مسامح ما سيء اللقاء وأمّا المواتي فمقابل لهذا ومن ها هنا أهل صقلية يسمّونه برطيوامس وهو المدلّل بالشرب (٢) وأمّا ذو الصداقة فمتوسّط ما ليس هو منشرح النفس جدّاً ولا هو سيء اللقاء (٣) ويمكن أن يستعمل عظيم الهمّة على كلي الوجهين فإنّه إذا كانت خيرات تساوي أشياء عظاماً فصاحبها ينبغي أن يقل عظيم الهمّة وأمّا إذا لم تكن شيئاً جيّداً فإنّ عظم الهمّة على هذا يظهر أنّه حمق (٤) هذه الأشياء وأشباهها إن فصلها أحد على النوع [غير] الموصوف وقالها فليس يفصلها بنوع ولا [...] فيه وقد يتبع هذا القول القول في العدالة.

٨. وقد قيل فيها قولاً كثيراً وقد كتب أيضاً وقد يظنّ بعض الناس أنّها أعظم الخيرات ما ليس كوكب الزهرة إذا كان يظهر بالعشي بعد غيوبة الشمس ولا إذا كان يظهر قبل طلوع الشمس والذي كان يحلّ حكمة [...]غورس لمّا سأل أفلاطون ما الحكمة فقل إنّها العدالة (٢) وذوي النهج من القوم الذين يسمّون لاقونس يزعمون أنّه ينبغي أن يتدرّب بالعدالة ومن الناس من يقضي بنقيض هذا [٢/٣٠] القول فإنّهم يسمّونها خيراً غريباً وأنّها نافعة

2 بهيله... يهيئ appar. read Dun : w.p. F || 4 الأقاويل : من الأقاويل add. Bad || 6 وما : F فما Bad || من : F, Dun حمق 12 || Bad يمكن : F, Dun لم تكن 12 || المذلل perh. read. Dun : F المدلل 9 || F يظن أن : يظن 15 || Dun lacks direction ,F illegible [...] 13 || suppl. Dun غير 13 || Bad partly : [...]غورس 17 || Bad يجل : F, Dun يحل 17 || Bad om. ما ليس (...) الشمس 15-17 || 18 Bad النضج : F, Dun النهج 18 || Bad إذ : F لما 17 || Bad افروطاغورس ;illegible F, Dun لاقونس Dun : لاقويين Bad

to its possessors. (3) As to the rest of the virtues, we have already spoken of them in the exoteric discourses, where sufficient has been said.[51] For these[52] being common doctrines applying to ethics in general, there are contained in them many excellent doctrines. But perhaps we seek special things more than concealed things. Someone may say that the reason for that is because we are loved because of honour more than because of philosophy. This applies also in other things, but in mathematics we do not do this, and we do not require inadequate proofs from those who investigate in an excellent as well as an inadequate manner. (4) As we said at first, we say now also: We take the just as equal. It is obvious that the equal is of two kinds, one of which divides honours, wealth and the like, while the other rectifies in mutual relations. Some mutual relations are voluntary, others involuntary. Let the voluntary be assumed, as we said at first, to be those in which the initiative is ours, e.g. hiring and every employment. When this does not apply, then the relation is involuntary. For some involuntary relations are perforce and some are due to fraud. The legislator in all this wished to rectify and to equalise between the man who falls short and the man who has an excess by what he exceeds and is defective [respectively]. (5) It seems that the Christians in this do not do well and that it is ludicrous, for they assert that he who is beaten with whips has more good. It does not appear so to the legislator, because the man has more evil, which means that he has less [good]. Therefore it must be made up to him in a good way. For he who beat with whips[53] and the man who was beaten should be increased,[54] and that should be compensated for by some evil. Similarly the loss of an eye [is compensated for] by the loss of an eye.

9. Since the equal is of two kinds, let us speak first of that which divides,[55] for the first thing said about the equal is that it is in two things at least, because the equal must be by things and for things. Because it divides things for things and the mean [divides] things

---

[51] Cf. e.g. *Protrepticus*, c. 6 (Valentin Rose, *Aristotelis Fragmenta*, Leipzig 1967, no. 57, p. 67).

[52] What is here said of ἐξωτερικοὶ λόγοι is of interest, giving Aristotle as author of all or at least some of them (cf. *Eudemian Ethics* II, 1, 1), since the speaker who mentions the 'esoteric discourse' is surely Aristotle.

[53] Apparently something has dropped out.

[54] Or reading *yujāzā* for *yuzāda* of the MS., 'should be recompensed'.

[55] Cf. c. 8, § 4.

لمن غرب منها وأنّها ضارّة لأصحابها (٣) فأمّا سائر الفضائل فقد قلنا فيها في الأقاويل الخارجة وقد قيل فيها قولاً كافياً فإنّه لمّا كانت أقاويل مشتركة تعمّ الأخلاق فقد سلّمت فيها أقاويل كثيرة جيّدة ولكن ربّما طلبنا الأشياء الخاصّية أكثر من الأشياء الخفية وخليق أن يقول قائل إنّ العلّة في ذلك من أجل أنّا محبوب للكرامة أكثر من حبّنا للفلسفة وهذا أيضاً في أشياء أخر وأمّا في التعليميات فليس نفعل ذلك ولا نطلب برهانات باطلة من الذين يطلبون بنوع جيّد وبنوع باطل (٤) فكما قلنا أوّلاً فكذا نقول الآن أيضاً فإنّا نأخذ العادل مساوياً وهو ظاهر أنّ المساوي على نوعين أحدهما مقسّم كرامات وأموالاً وما أشبه ذلك والآخر مصحّح في المعاملات وبعض المعاملات إرادية ومنها ما هو لا إرادي ولتوضع الإرادية كما قلنا أوّلاً التي أوائلها إلينا مثل الاستئجار وكلّ استعمل وأمّا عدم هذه فإنّ ذلك لا إرادي فإنّ بعض لا إرادية بالقهر وبعضها بالمخاتلة فواضع النواميس في جميع هذه يريد التصحيح وأن يساوي بين المنتقص وبين المتزيّد بما يزيد وينقص (٥) والمسائحة في هذا خليق أن تكون لا تحسن وأن تكون لعباً فإنّهم يزعمون أنّ المضروب بالسياط له البرّ أكثر وليس يظهر ذلك لواضع النواميس من أجل أنّ له أكثر الردئ وهذا هو أن يكون له أقلّ ومن أجل هذا ينبغي أن يساوى بنوع خير فإنّ الذي ضرب بالسياط وأن يزاد المضروب وأن يكافأ ذلك بردئ ما ومثل ذلك قلع العين بقلع عين.

٩. ولمّا كان المساوي على نوعين فلنقل أوّلاً في المقسّم فإنّ أوّل أقاويل المساوي إنّه أقلّ ما يكون في اثنين ما من أجل أنّه ينبغي أن يكون المساوي بأشياء ولأشياء ومن أجل أنّه يقسّم أشياء لأشياء والمتوسّط أشياء وبأشياء فالعدل المقسّم في أوائل أربعة كمثل التلاؤم

---

3 الخفية F, Dun : الحقية Bad || 10 بالقهر appar. Dun : illegible F; بالقصد Bad || 11 هذه F : هذا Bad || 12 المسائحة appar. read. Dun : F w.p.; المشاغبة Bad || 15 يزاد : يجازى perh. corr. Dun || 18 third أشياء appar. corr. Dun : شيئا F; شيء corr. Bad

and through things, distributive justice consists of four principles, like what is fitting, for it is concerned with the mean, and it may be for two, and just as the mean is two equals. We take this for granted, because the mean also is equal, and the equal is in two terms. (2) Since those things with which justice is concerned are four, and the things with which the division is concerned are divided and there is a relation among them, owing to some connection or owing to the virtue or honour of the agent or something else of this kind, it is possible that what is divided should be separated according to this same relation, and it is possible that it should be divided otherwise. (3) For if it is divided in a similar way the four come into relation, because it means that everything which is divided suits those among whom the division is made. When they are joined together with those which have the same relation, first to third and second to fourth, they all from the beginning have these same relations, each of the two being related to that with which it is joined. Equality of relations brings about just things, for when those who divide are in favour of him who is according to merit,[56] he being to them according to their relation, justice is done among them. (4) As to what it is, it includes both its kinds,[57] for people disagree, because some of them make judgement to be in accordance with virtue and others in a different way. (5) There should also be found here distributive justice which is in accordance with merit, and what is in accordance with merit can be judged. This relation is a mean for these things, because if what is divided is not portioned out according to one relation among those for whom the division is being made, and one relation is greater and another less, that which is divided among them will be unequal things, and one will have more and another less. So what is divided and what is just in these things, i.e. a natural mean, are as described. (6) As to the equal which is corrective,[58] it is shown by the legislator and the judge. For these balance and distinguish between those who do not act justly and those to whom justice is not done. For they, as we said, make this arrangement for some to be punished or corrected, and for some to take and employ what the legislator lays down and judges to be equal. (7) Excess and defect are estimated by the mean. For he who does wrong exceeds this, and he who is wronged falls short of it by an equivalent amount. For, as we said,

---

[56] I.e. meritorious.

[57] Cf. above, § 1 and c. 8, § 4.

[58] This is the second kind of the equal which is secured by corrective or rectificative justice, as the first kind (cf. § 1) is secured by distributive.

فإنّه في المتوسّط وخليق أن يكون لاثنين [٢/٣١] وكما أنّ المتوسّط اثنان متساويان ونحن نفرض هذا من أجل أنّ المتوسّط مساوٍ أيضاً والمساوي في حدّين (٢) ولمّا كانت التي فيها العدل أربعة وكانت التي فيها القسمة منقسمة ولها نسبة ما بعضها إلى بعض إمّا بالقرن وإمّا بفضيلة الفاعل أو بكرامته أو بشئ مثل هذه يمكن أن ينفصل المقسوم على هذه النسبة بعينها ويمكن أن ينقسم على غيرها (٣) فإنّه إن انقسم بنوع متشابه تصير الأربعة بالنسبة من أجل أنّه يريد أن يكون جميع الذي يقسّم موافقاً للذين يقسّم فيهم فإذا فرّقت معاً إلى التي هي على نسبة واحدة أمّا أوّلاً فللثالث وثانياً للرابع فلكلّها من الابتداء هذه النسب بعينها وكلّ واحد منهما إلى الذي فرّق إليه وإنّما تصير الأشياء العادلة مساواة النسب فإنّه لمّا كان له الذي على الاستئهل الذين يقسّمون إذا كان لهم على نسبتهم كان عندهم عدلاً (٤) فأمّا ما هو فإنّه يشمل قسميه فإنّهم يشاجرون من أجل أنّ بعضهم يصيّر القضاء على قدر الفضيلة وبعضهم بنوع آخر (٥) وينبغي أن يوجد ها هنا أيضاً العدل المقسوم الذي على قدر الاستئهل والذي على قدر الاستئهل يمكنه أن يقضى وهذه النسبة هي متوسّطة لهذه من أجل أنّ المقسوم إن لم يجزّأ على نسبة واحدة على الذين تكون فيهم القسمة وكان بعض النسب أكبر ودونها بعض فسيكون الذي يقسّم عليهم أشياء لا متساوية ويكون لبعضهم أكثر ولبعضهم أقلّ فالمقسوم والعادل في هذه وهو متوسّط بالطبع على هذا النوع (٦) وأمّا المساوي الصحيح فإنّما يظهره واضع النواميس والقاضي فإنّ هؤلاء يعدّلون ويصيرون بين الذين لا يعدلون وبين الذين لا يعدل عليهم فإنّهم كما قلنا يرتّبون هذا الترتيب أمّا بعض فعلى أن يعذّب أو يقوّم وبعض على أن يأخذ ويستعمل التي بها يضع النواميس ويقضي كالمساوي (٧) وإنّما يقدّر الزيادة والنقصان بالأوسط فإنّ الذي يجور يزيد على هذا والذي يجار عليه ينقص منه بكمّية متساوية فإنّه كما قلنا يستعمل المساوي في الجائر والذي يجار [٢/٣٢] عليه بالمساواة ويستعمل الدينار لكثرة

---

1 اثنان corr. Bad : اثنين F || 3 فيها F : قيها Bad || 4 الفاعل F, Dun : الفاقد corr. Bad || 6 موافقا F : موافقة corr || 10 قسميه F, Dun : قسيمه Bad || 14 الذي corr. Dun : الذين F, Bad || 18 يعذب F, Dun : يقرب Bad

[the legislator] employs the equal in respect of him who does wrong and him who suffers wrong equally, and employs money in the case of extensive wrongdoing and various kinds of injustice, because he has no more general measure than this. He increases the man who has suffered wrong in proportion to what he takes from the wrongdoer. When this has been done, the man who has suffered wrong exceeds the wrongdoer by two similar[59] amounts, and exceeds the intermediate man by one. Thus the legislator and the judge equalise according to the numerical relation. (8) On this account they pass to the judge as to the mean, and do not seek to influence the judge in a bad sense, because he divides if he wishes unpartially. They suppose that when they pass to the judge they pass to justice, for the judge in a transferred sense is animate justice, because he arranges what is just in accordance with what is possible. For it is not in every situation just that the agent should be punished with the like of what he has done, or that there should be taken from him according to what he has taken—for in this way there might be inequality—and according to what one of them is in excess over the mean and the other is exceeded and all the things which are a practice of the city, for in these also there is something in favour of him who has been the object of the action, as when the agent has not scourged with whips,[60] for in the case of these what is just lies between the indemnity and the gain. (9) Since what is just is the opposite of wrongdoing and the just man is the opposite of the wrongdoer, it follows that what we speak of is a mean. For the equal is the opposite of the unequal, as the just man is the opposite of the wrongdoer. And the mean is opposed to the extremes more than they are to each other, because the equal does not combine with the unequal. It is that which is more that combines with that which is less, for the rash man is cowardly and the foolish man is deceitful. (10) As for courage, it does not combine with anything, and what is just occurs in both relations.[61] The Pythagoreans[62] used to claim that what is just is requital, and that this is something ancient. It is said that it goes back to Rhada-

---

[59] Reading with the MS. *mithl hādhain*, 'like these', but perhaps correct to *mithl hādhā*, 'twice the amount'.

[60] Sc. and is punished with scourging.

[61] I.e. distributive and corrective justice.

[62] The reading of the Arabic *ahl ra'y Fīthāghūrās* is conjectural, but seems certain, cf. the Greek text of V, 5, 1-3 (the reference to the Pythagoreans has fallen out in the Arabic).

الجور وأنواع لا عدل من أجل أنّه ليس له قدر أعمّ منه وهو يزيد الذي قد جير عليه على قدر ما ينتزع من الجائر وإذا كان هذا يكون الذي قد جير عليه زائداً باثنين مثل هذين على الجائر وأمّا المتوسّط فبواحد فواضع النواميس والقاضي يساويان على قدر النسبة العددية (٨) ومن أجل هذا يمضون إلى القاضي كأنّهم إلى المتوسّط ولا يستميلون القاضي بنوع ردئ من أجل أنّه يقسم إذا شاء على النصف ويزعمون أنّهم إذا مضوا إلى القاضي أنّهم يمضون إلى العدل فإنّ القاضي بنوع الانتقل عدل متنفّس من أجل أنّه يرتّب العدل على قدر ما يمكن فإنّه ليس في كلّ موضع العدل أن ينتقم من الفاعل بمثل ما فعل ولا أن ينتزع منه على قدر ما انتزع فإنّه يكون بهذا النوع غير مساواة وعلى قدر ما يزيد أحدهما على الوسط والآخر يزاد عليه وجميع التي هي معاطاة المدينة فإنّه يكون في هذه أيضاً شئ ما للذي قد فعل به كما أنّه إذا لم يضرب الفاعل بالسياط فإنّه يكون حينئذ العدل في هؤلاء فيما بين الغرامة والربح (٩) فلمّا كان العدل ضدّ الجور وكان العادل ضدّ الجائر يتبع أن يكون المقول متوسّطاً فإنّ المتساوي ضدّ لا متساوي مثل أنّ العادل ضدّ الجائر والمتوسّط يقابل بالوضع الأطراف أكثر من مقابلة الأطراف بعضها لبعض من أجل أنّ المتساوي لا يخالط لا متساوي فأمّا الأكثر فإنّه يخالط الأقلّ فإنّه يكون المقدام جباناً ويكون المائق مماكراً (١٠) وأمّا النجد فليس يخالط شيئاً والعدل يقع على كلي النسبتين وأمّا أهل رأي فيثاغوراس فإنّهم كانوا يزعمون أنّ العدل هو الجزاء وأنّ هذا شئ قديم ويقل إنّه لزاذاميس وكانوا يحدّون كلّ واحد أنّه هو أوّل وغير الكثيرة وأمّا هذا أنّه في الأوائل من

---

1 يزيد appar. read. Dun : يريد F, Bad || 2 هذين F, Bad : هذا perh. corr. Dun || 12 المقول F, Dun : المقبول Bad || 12 و F, Dun : أو Bad || 14 first يخالط F, Dun : يخالف Bad || 14 second يخالط F, Dun : يخاله Bad || 15 يخالط F, Dun : يخالف Bad || 15-16 رأي فيثاغوراس read. and corr. Dun : راى الناغروس w.p. F; وادي الناغروس Bad || 17 لزاذاميس F, Dun : لذاقاميس Bad

manthys. They used to define each term as a principle[63] and not plurality. This is among the principles. On account of this they said that everything depends on numbers, because numbers are the principles of the identities. Six is injustice and the mixing of different things, while eight is justice,[64] because it is requital, and does not distinguish being and essence. Since there are many things belonging to things in themselves, they say that things in themselves are many. (11) Let us then leave aside how eight is justice, and let us investigate requital. Many a one who comes to it[65] does not seem at all to befit the law, nor to be one whose requital is according to the employment of virtue nor who is with merit. For there is no reversal in blameworthy acts unless it is according to what is valid. For it nowhere appears as if the requital which is made forcibly is made not for what they have done and not fairly, but many times over and unfairly, since they are punished for the vice. For wrong is done either wilfully, as did the father of Androtion, who wasted olive oil belonging to the city.[66] Mostly requital appears in voluntary actions, like selling, hiring and business dealing, for it is not possible that there should be life without taking and giving and exchanging.

10. The first exchange to exist is the exchange of special products, according to Plato.[67] For the weaver exchanges cloth, and the copper-smith household utensils. And since exchange was difficult, they established a single common measure for everything, for which they received the other things in exchange. Hence *dīnār* and *dirham* appeared, and the builder employed it for his work as the farmer did for his, each one giving his work to his neighbour, and they exchanged opposite things as if they corresponded with exactness[68] and requital was sought. And requital here is what is just, for according to what the doctor gives to the farmer, so the farmer gives to the doctor of his special work. (2) These things are related also to need, for according to Plato this is the final aim. For the final aim of building and of the house is protection from the heat and the cold and the

---

[63] Arabic *auwal*, plural *awā'il*, used in the same sense as in § 1 above.

[64] According to Alexander of Aphrodisias, quoted by Burnet on EN V, 5, 1 = 1132b 22, the Pythagoreans regarded the square numbers 4 and 9 as justice.

[65] Sc. requital, or perhaps justice, cf. § 8.

[66] Nothing seems to be known of such an incident. The father of Androtion is named by Demosthenes in his speech against the son owing money belonging to the state (*Oratio* XXII, 603).

[67] I.e. in the *Republic* II, 369B *et sqq*.

[68] Arabic *'alā qaṭr wāḥid*, lit. 'upon one drop'.

أجل هذا قالوا إنّ كلّ واحد في الأعداد من أجل أنّ الأعداد أوائل الهويات وكانت أمّا الستّة فلا عدل واختلاط آخر بآخر وأمّا الثمانية فالعدل من أجل أنّه جزاء ولم يكن [٢/٣٣] يفصّل ما هو وما أنيته ولمّا كانت أشياء كثيرة لأشياء بأعيانها قالوا إنّ أشياء بأعيانها كثيرة (١١) فلننزل كيف الثمانية العدل ولنفحص عن الجزاء فكثير من يصير إليه فإنّه لا يشبه البتّة أن يكون يليق بالناموس وما الذي يكون جزاءه في استعمل الفضيلة ولا الذي يكون باستئهل فإنّه لا لينعكس في الملاوم إلاّ أن يكون في المصحّح فإنّه لا يظهر في كلّه كأنّ الجزاء الذي يكون بالقهر يجازى به لأيّما عملوا ولا بالمساوي بل يجازى به مراراً كثيرة وعلى غير المساواة إذ كانوا يعذّبون على الرداءة فإنّه يظلم إمّا بإرادته كما فعل أبو أندروطيون بالذي كان يقطّر من الزيت للمدينة وأكثر ذلك إنّما يظهر الجزاء في الإرادية مثل البيع والأجرة والمعاملة المدنية فإنّه لا يمكن أن تكون حيلة من غير أخذ وإعطاء ومبادلة.

١٠. فأوّل ما يكون من المبادلة مبادلة الأعمل الخاصّة على نوع أفلاطون فإنّه يبادل أمّا الحائك فبالثياب وأمّا النحّاس فبالآلات ولمّا كانت المبادلة عسرة وضعوا قدراً واحداً عامّاً لجميع الأشياء قابلوا به وضع سائر الأشياء ومن ها هنا صار الدينار والدرهم ويستعمله البناء في عمله والفلاح في عمله ويعطي كلّ واحد منهما عمله لصاحبه ويتبادلون بالتي هي متقابلة بالوضع كالمتقابلة على قطر واحد وعلى المحاذاة فالمحاذاة ها هنا العدل فأنّه على قدر ما يعطي الطبيب الفلاح على قدر ذلك يعطي الفلاح من عمله الخاصّ الطبيب (٢) وتنسب هذه الأشياء أيضاً إلى الحاجة فإنّه على قدر نوع أفلاطون هذا هو التمام فإنّه تمام البناية وتمام البيت الكنّ من الحرّ والبرد وحرز الأموال وعلى ألاّ يرى فعلى قدر ما يستحقّ الاستعمال على قدر ذلك يجازى (٣) ويقل أيضاً الاستئهل عدل ويليق بما قد قيل

2 فلا عدل Dun : فولد له appar. F; فولولة Bad || 4 الجزاء F, Dun : الخبراء Bad || 6 لينعكس F : ليعكس Bad || 8 أبو corr. Bad : أب F || 9 يقطر corr. Bad : F uncertain; يفطر Dun || 16 فإنه F : وإنه Bad

possession of goods as safely as possible. Thus there is requital commensurately with what the employment deserves. (3) Merit also is called what is just, and suitably, from what has been said. Yet there is a doubt here as to whether it is not because some people employ 'merit' in expressions of praise and call those who search out the things contrary to the laws 'searchers out of justice' as being meritorious, and those who search out the true concerns of the laws they do not call meritorious. That is an indication that what is contrary to the laws is not just. Some people think of the merit which is contrary to the laws as contrary to what is just, and this looks like the fact. Some people judge of what is with merit that it is more just than the laws, and what is more excellent than the excellent is excellent in any case, and similarly what is more just than justice. (4) This should be known, that we know that there is something naturally just, which we may take as a model of words strong to convince and of the things which are given. But most do not have this opinion, owing to the difference of laws and to the correcting of laws, because they think that justice is for them, and it is likely that it is as it is in the city,[69] since the law there is fixed and has lasted a long time. (5) But consideration is more appropriate, and similarly also in the things which are with reliance and purpose, for some of them are naturally good and just, while others are the reverse of what they are thought to be, and one can only proceed through consideration, because that which is better cannot [otherwise] be comprehended. So at all times it is generally best that the situation of the law should be altered in accordance with the changing facts. Hence has come consideration and the rule of cities in accordance with the times. (6) As for democracies, they have laws of a kind, and most of their proceedings in the rule of the city are duly considered. (7) As for aristocracies, they always employ things in themselves.[70] It is not easy to describe[71] upon which of the two kinds action should be based, because each of them has some advantage, and it appears that both have certain defects. Yet it is likely that they are more excellent who desire that things should not be changed and altered, because there is no love and no friendship unless custom is like daily food, as Democritus said. This is liable to be better than what is more convenient at a particular time. On these matters something is said else-

[69] I.e. the conception which people have of justice is not general but in terms of the particular laws of their own city.

[70] I.e. things as they are.

[71] *Waṣf* of the MS. seems to be right, cf. I, 2, 3 (1094a 25).

إلاّ أنّ فيه تحيّراً ما من أجل أنّ بعض الناس يستعملون الاستئهل في أقاويل المدح ويسمّون الذين يستقصون الأشياء على خلاف النواميس مستقصي العدل كأنّهم مستأهلون الذين يستقصون أمور النواميس لا يصدقهم [٢/٣٤] مستأهلين وذلك دليل على أنّ الذي على غير النواميس ليس يعدل ومن الناس من يظنّ استئهل الذي على غير النواميس الذي هو على غير عدل وهذا يشبه الفعل ومن الناس من يقضي على التي تكون بالاستئهل أنّها أكثر عدلاً من النواميس والذي هو أجود من الجيّد هو جيّد على كلّ حل وكذلك الذي هو أكثر عدلاً من العدل (٤) وخليق أن يعلم هذا إنّ نحن علمنا أنّ شيئاً ما عدل بالطبع ويمكن أن يأخذ مثل أقاويل قوية الإقناع ومن الأشياء المعطلة فأمّا الأكثر فلا يرى هذا الرأي لاختلاف النواميس ولتصحيح النواميس من أجل أنّهم يرون أنّ العدل إليهم وقد يشبه أن يكون كما هو في المدينة فإنّ الناموس فيها محدود منذ زمان طويل (٥) وأمّا الحسبة فأحرى فبهذا النوع أيضاً يكون في التي تكون بالاعتماد والقصد فإنّ بعضها بالطبع جياد وعادلة وبعضها على غير ما يظنّ بها فإنّما صار طريق للحسبة من أجل أنّ الذي هو أخير لا يقدر أن يحاط به فالناموس في الزمان كلّه فكثيراً ما هو أجود أن ينقل وضعه على قدر تغيّر الأشياء فمن ها هنا أتت الحسبة وتدبير المدن على قدر الأزمنة (٦) فأمّا رياسات العوامّ فإنّها بنوع النواميس وأكثر تدبيراتها المدنية الحسبة (٧) وأمّا رياسات الأفاضل فإنّها أبداً تستعمل أشياء بأعيانها وليس يهون وصف على أيّ نوع من النوعين ينبغي أن يكون الفعل من أجل أنّ كلّ واحد شئ نافع ويظهر أنّ لكليهما عللاً ما إلاّ أنّه يشبه أن يكونوا أجود الذين يحرصون على ألاّ تستحيل الأشياء وتتغيّر من أجل أنّه لا تكون محبّة ولا ألفة إن لم تكن العادة كالغذاء كما قل ديموقريطس وخليق أن يكون هذا أجود من الذي يكون أوفق في زمان ما وفي هذه الأشياء قول آخر (٨) وأمّا أنّ عدلاً ما

2 خلاف corr. Dun : قدر F, Bad || 2 مستأهلون corr. Bad : مستأهلين F || 5 وهذا يشبه Dun : illegible F || 8 مثل Bad, Dun : illegible F || 12 غير Bad, Dun : illegible F || 16 وصف F, Dun : وسيط Bad || 17 أجل F, Dun : قبل Bad || 20 أجود F, Dun : القدر Bad

where. (8) As for there being a natural justice, that is confirmed also by what follows from the argument, and it is thought that general justice comes first and necessitates another. As for justice of [human] principles, it is not that which is thought to be by nature, and similarly in the equestrian art, seamanship and in all the sciences, for the best is (...)[72]

[72] The rest of the Book is missing.

طبيعياً فقد يليق ذلك ما يثمر من القول أيضاً فقد يظنّ أن العلل العامّ [...] أخر وأمّا المبدئي فليس هو الذي يظنّ به أنّه هو بالطبع وكذلك في صناعة الخيل وصناعة الملاحة وفي سائر العلوم فإنّ التي هي أجود هي (...)

1 first فقد F, Dun : بقدر Bad || 1 [...] : illegible F, *comes first and necessitates* Dun || 1 أخر corr. Dun : أخير F, Bad || 1 وأما om. Bad

BOOK VII

In the name of God, the Merciful, the Compassionate
God bless Muhammad and his family [and give them peace]

The Eight[1] Discourse of the Book of Aristotle on Ethics

Aristotle said: After these discussions let us pass to another beginning. We say that the kinds of moral qualities which are avoided are three—vice, incontinence and brutality. As to the opposites, two of them are evident: one we call virtue, the other continence. As for that which is said to be the opposite of brutishness, it is most proper that it should be said to be the virtue which is higher than us, and as it were related to heroes,[2] i.e. mighty men, and as it were like what Homer described in his poetry about Hector, when Priam said that he was very excellent, and it was not thought of him that he was the son of mortal man but the son of a god.[3] (2) So then if it is as they say, that some people are gods because of excess of virtue, it is plain then that it is a certain state like this which is opposed to[4] brutality. For as the beasts have neither vice nor virtue, so also God, but one of them[5] is nobler than virtue and the other[6] is a different kind of vice. (3) And since the divine is very rare among men, as the Laconians are accustomed to call him, when they admire any one very much, for they say: 'This is a divine man', so they suppose that the brutal is very rare among men. It is mostly found among barbarians, and sometimes through disease and disablement. To people who are excessively vicious in this way we give a bad mention.[7] (4) But let us mention this kind of condition later. In regard to vice, it has been
1145b 4 spoken of previously. As to [...][8] (5) proof of all the opinions regard-

---

[1] Actually Book VII, see Introduction pp. 55ff.

[2] Arabic *umūrin ussin* (apparently for *umūri ussin*), 'elemental things', but corr. *īrūīqā* (ἡρωϊκήν).

[3] Cf. Homer, *Iliad* XXIV, 258.

[4] Arabic *tuqābilu bi'l-waḍ'*, i.e. Greek ἀντιτιθεμένη.

[5] I.e. divine goodness (Rackham).

[6] I.e. bestial badness (Rackham).

[7] Greek οὕτως apparently taken with ὑπερβάλλοντας.

[8] Lacuna of five lines in the Arabic text.

المقالة الثامنة

[٣٨/١] بسم الله الرحمن الرحيم

صلّى الله على محمّد وعلى آله [وسلّم]

المقالة الثامنة من كتاب أرسطو في الأخلاق

١. قل أرسطو فلنصر بعد هذه الأقاويل إلى ابتداء آخر ونقول إنّ الأنواع التي للأشياء الخلقية التي يهرب عنها ثلاثة الشرّية ولا عفّة والسبعية والأضداد أمّا الاثنان منها فبيّنة فإنّنا نسمّي أمّا أحدهما ففضيلة والآخر عفّة وأمّا التي يقل إنّها ضدّ السبعية فينبغي أكثر ذلك أن يقل إنّها الفضيلة التي هي أرفع منّا وكأنّها منسوبة إلى إرويقا في الجبابرة وكأنّها كالذي وصف أوميرس في شعره عن أقطر حين قل عنه أبرياسوس إنّه كان جيّداً جدّاً وكان ما يظنّ به أنّه ابن رجل ميّت بل ابن إله (٢) فإذاً إن كان كما يزعمون أنّ من الناس قوماً يكونون آلهة بإفراط الفضيلة فبيّن إذاً أنّها تكون هيئة ما مثل هذه التي تقابل بالوضع السبعية فإنّه كما أنّه ليس للسبع شرّية ولا فضيلة كذلك للإله بل أحدهما أكرم من الفضيلة والآخر جنس آخر من الشرّية (٣) وإذ الإلهي في الرجل قليل جدّاً كما اعتادوا أن يسمّوه لاقونس إذا هم يعجبون من أحد جدّاً فإنّهم يقولون إنّ هذا رجل إلهي كذلك يزعمون أنّ السبعي في الناس قليل جدّاً وإنّما يكون أكثر ذلك في الأعجم [...] بعضاً بمرض وبزمانة والناس الذين يفرطون في الشرّية يوصفون بهذا الوصف سبعيون (٤) لكن الحالة التي نتحدّث عنها ستكون ممّا نذكر فيما بعد أمّا [...] [٣٨/٢] (٥) برهان جميع

---

2 وسلم suppl. Dun || 6 فإننا Dun : فلا Bad || 7 إرويقا corr. Dun* (ἡρωϊκήν) : أمور أس F, Bad || 8 عنه corr. Bad : ان F || 9 ابن corr. Bad*, Dun* : انه F || 10 يكونون corr. Bad : يكون F || 11 أحدهما corr. Bad : أحدها F || 14 الأعاجم corr. Bad : الاعجم F

ing these passions, or at least most of them and those which are really important. For if the difficulties are solved and the opinions remain, sufficient proof will have been brought. (6) It is thought that self-control and endurance are among the excellent and praiseworthy things, and it is thought that incontinence and softness are among the bad and blameworthy things, and that the self-controlled man and the man who constantly reflects are the same, and the man who is incontinent and he who is opposed to reflection are the same. For the man who is incontinent knows that he does bad deeds owing to an affliction of the soul.[9] The self-controlled man, when he knows that the desires are bad, does not follow them because of reflection. Some call the temperate man self-controlled and steadfast, and some call the man who is in this state temperate in everything, while some do not. Some call the temperate man incontinent and the incontinent man intemperate, through confusing the terms, while others say that these are different. (7) As regards the intelligent man of practical wisdom, sometimes they say that he cannot but restrain himself, and sometimes they say that some people are intelligent men of practical wisdom and inquiring mind.[10] It is said that they do not restrain themselves in respect of anger and honour and gain. These are the statements which are made.

2. One may be at a loss and ask how it is possible that one should see truly and not restrain oneself. Some people have supposed that this is impossible in one who has knowledge. For it is bad that anyone should possess knowledge, as Socrates thought, and that he does [not] restrain something else or is unjust against himself here and there, as if he were a slave. For Socrates was opposing the statement altogether and was affirming that lack of restraint does not exist, since no one thinks that he does anything other than good unless through ignorance. (2) This argument is at variance with the plain facts [...][11] that we should inquire into the condition,[12] if [...][13] himself. (3) They say that he who does not restrain himself does not have knowledge, so that the pleasures overcome him, rather what he

[9] Arabic *alam an-nafs*, Greek πάθος.
[10] Arabic *aṣḥāb faḥṣ*, Greek δεινούς.
[11] Short lacuna.
[12] Arabic *infiʿāl* (Greek πάθος) as also above, 1145b 5 ('passions'), and frequently.
[13] Lacuna of several lines.

الآراء التي في هذه الانفعالات وإلاّ فأكثرها والتي هي بالحقيقة مشهورة فإنّه إن حلّت الصعبة وبقيت الآراء يكون قد أتي من البرهان بما فيه الكفاية (٦) فقد يظنّ بالإمساك والعفّة أنّهما من الأشياء الفاضلة الممدوحة ويظنّ اللا عفّة واللّيّن من الأشياء الرديئة المذمومة وأنّ الممسك والدائم الفكرة واحد والذي لا عفيف ويضادّ الفكرة واحد وأمّا لا عفيف فإنّه يعلم أنّه يعمل أعمالاً رديئة لألم النفس وأمّا الممسك فإنّه لمّا علم أنّ الشهوات رديئة فلا يتبعها لمكان الفكرة ومن الناس من يسمّي العفيف ممسكاً وصبوراً ومن الناس من يسمّي من كان على هذه الحل عفيفاً في كلّ ومنهم من لا يسمّيه ويسمّي بعضهم لا عفيف لا ماسك ولا ماسك لا عفيف بقول مختلط ومن الناس من يقول إنّ ها هنا قوماً آخرين (٧) وأمّا المتعقّل فربّما قالوا إنّه لا يمكن أن يكون ألاّ يضبط نفسه وربّما قالوا إنّ بعض الناس متعقّلون وأصحاب فحص ويقل إنّهم لا يضبطون أنفسهم في الغضب والكرامة والربح فهذه الأقاويل التي تقل.

٢. وخليق أن يتحيّر أحد ويسأل كيف يمكن أن يرى أحد رأياً صحيحاً فلا يكون يضبط نفسه فقد زعم بعض الناس أنّ هذا لا يمكن أن يكون فيمن به معرفة فإنّه رديء أن يكون علماً لأحد كظنّ سقراطيس فيكون [لا] يضبط شيئاً أو يجور ذاته ها هنا وها هنا كأنّه مملوك فإنّ سقراطيس كان يضادّ القول بنوع كلّي وكان يثبت أنّه ليس لا ضبط من أجل أنّه لم يكن يظنّ واحد أنّه يفعل فعلاً غير الخير إلاّ أن يكون للجهل (٢) وهذا [...] يخالف الواقع وعلينا أن نفحص عن هذه الحالة فإن [...] [١/٣] (٣) قالوا إنّ الذي لا يضبط نفسه

1 مشهورة corr. Bad, Dun : مسودة appar. F || 2 بالإمساك F, Dun : بالاستمساك Bad || 5 فإنه يعلم Dun : F and Bad repeat فإنه يعلم أنه يعلم || 5 لألم النفس om. Bad || 6 فلا corr. Bad : ولا F || 9 لأخر F || 14 لأحد corr. Bad : يسل F || 12 يسأل corr. Bad : قوم آخرون F || قوما آخرين corr. Bad || 14 لا suppl. Bad, Dun || 16 واحد corr. : واحدا F || 16 غير الخير F, Dun : مخالفا للخير corr. Bad || 17 [...] : illegible F, *himself* Dun (partly)

1146a has is opinion. (4) But if there is opinion and not knowledge, and it[14] is not strong to resist but weak, as it is in those who are in doubt, they are pardonable in their maintaining[15] such opinions in the case of strong desire. But wickedness is not pardonable nor any other blameworthy thing. (5) So then it is practical intelligence which resists,[16] for it is very strong. But that is absurd, because the same man will be practically intelligent and lacking in restraint at the same time, and no one says that to do evil deeds voluntarily belongs to the practically intelligent man. At the same time it was proved earlier that the practically intelligent man is a man of action, because he is concerned with certain ultimates, and one who has the other virtues. (6) Also, if the restrained man is the one who has strong and wicked desires, then he is not the weak man, nor is the restrained man temperate, because the excessive man is not the temperate man, nor does he possess wicked desires, but he should possess none of these.[17] For if the desires are sound, then the state which prevents their attainment is bad, and if so, not all restraint is good. If they are weak and not wicked, they are not noble,[18] and if they are bad and weak, they are nothing much at all. (7) If restraint is abiding by every opinion, it is bad, or it is like,[19] and if lack of restraint causes the abandonment of every opinion, then there will be a good kind of lack of restraint—for instance Neoptolemus, mentioned by Sophocles in the discourse[20] *Philoctetes*, meaning 'loving possessions':[21] he is praised for *not* standing by what Odysseus persuaded him to. (8) For, on account of his grief, he was perplexed in his lying,[22] because, [since] he wished to rebut arguments inconsistent with the opinions,[23] in order that those who bring those arguments[24] might be clever, there

[14] Greek ὑπόληψις is not translated.

[15] But the Greek is 'in not maintaining them' (τῷ μὴ μένειν ἐν αὐταῖς).

[16] The interrogative is apparently unnoticed.

[17] The sense is misunderstood.

[18] Referring evidently to the desires, but the text appears to be wrong. Cf. 1155b 3 for another example of Arabic *karīm* for Greek σεμνός.

[19] Arabic *au ka'anna wa-in kāna*, but then Greek εἰ καὶ τῇ ψευδεῖ is missing.

[20] Arabic *maqālah*. The Arabic translator does not understand about stage plays.

[21] The last few words being a gloss not in the Greek text.

[22] Arabic *li-makān mā ḥazina* rendering Greek ἀπορία. The words ἔτι ὁ σοφιστικὸς λόγος ψευδόμενος are not translated (homoioteleuton), and the sentence is made to run on, in error.

[23] The whole phrase *aqāwīl khārijah 'an al-arā'i* stands for Greek παράδοξα, but the Arabic includes the words used above ('Seventh Book', c. 8, § 3) in the sense of Greek ἐξωτερικοὶ λόγοι.

[24] Apparently rendering the Greek words ὅταν ἐπιτύχωσιν.

ليس له علم فتغلب عليه اللذّات بل إنّ الذي له رأي (٤) ولكن إن كان رأي ولم يكن علم ولا كان قوياً يمانع بل ضعيفاً كما يكون في الذين يشكّون فلهم عذر في ثباتهم عليها عند الشهوة القوية ولكن ليس للرداءة عذر ولا لشئ آخر من المذمومات (٥) فإذاً التعقّل الذي يمانع فإنّه قوي جدّاً ولكن ذلك محل من أجل أنّه سيكون هو بعينه متعقّلاً ولا ضابطاً معاً ولا يقول أحد إنّ فعل الأشياء الرديئة بإرادة للمتعقّل ومع هذا فقد برهن أوّلاً أنّ المتعقّل فعلي من أجل أنّه من أواخر ما ومن الذي له الفضائل الأخر (٦) وأيضاً إن كان الضابط الذي له شهوات قوية ورديئة فليس هو الضعيف ولا الضابط عفيف من أجل أنّ الكثير جدّاً ليس هو العفيف ولا بدّ أن تكون له الرداءات بل ألاّ يكون له شئ من هذه فإنّه إن كانت الشهوات صالحة فالهيئة التي تمنع من إتيانها رديئة فإذاً ليس كلّ ضبط فاضلاً وإن كانت ضعيفة وليست برديئة فليست بكريمة وإن كانت رديئة وضعيفة فلا تكون شيئاً كثيراً البتّةَ (٧) إن كان الضابط في كلّ رأي الدوام كان الرأي رديئاً أو كأن وإن كان لا ضبط يزيل عن كلّ رأي فسيكون لا ضبط أمّا فاضل مثل ناوفطولاموس الذي يذكره سوفوقليس في مقالة فليواقطيطس الذي معناه محبّ القنية فإنّه ممدوح عندما لم يثبت على ما كان أقنعه به أودسيوس (٨) فإنّه لمكان ما حزن تحيّر في كذبه فإنّه من أجل أنّه [إذ] أراد أن يدفع أقاويلاً خارجة عن الآراء يكون الذين يصيرون تلك الأقاويل هناء صار تحيّر

---

2 يشكون corr. Bad*, Dun* (διστάζουσι) : يسكرون F || 10 ليست corr. Bad : ليس F || 10 وإن
corr. Dun : ولا إن F, Bad || 10 فلا corr. Bad : ولا F || 11 إن F : وإن suppl. Bad || 11 الراي
corr. Bad*, Dun* : الردئ F || 11 أو كأن F, Dun* : أيا كان corr. Bad || 12 ناوفطولاموس corr.
Bad : ناوفطولايومن F || 13 محب القنية corr. Dun* (Φιλοκτήτῃ) : محب الفتنة F, Bad || 13 عندما
corr. Bad : عند من F || 14 لمكان F, Dun : لكان Bad || 14 حزن corr. Dun : حرب F, جرب Bad ||
14 إذ suppl. Arberry || 15 يدفع Dun : uncertain F, يلمع Bad || 15 أقاويلا خارجة عن F, Dun : ولا
أما Bad

was perplexity in the resulting syllogism. For thought [...] that it should be stationary because [...][25] the argument. (9) There occurs [...][26] will do good deeds and [not] bad ones. (10) Also he who acts because he is persuaded and seeks for delightful things and chooses them will be thought to be better than the man who does [not] do so from reflection, but he who acts from lack of restraint is more easily cured,[27] since his conviction changes. As for the man who does not restrain himself, he must necessarily be contrary to the law,[28] and he says[29] contrary to the law: 'When water chokes a man, what must he
1146b drink after it?' For if he was convinced of what he was doing, when his conviction changed he would have refrained from that action. As it is, his conviction is by no means less than what it was, yet he does other things. (11) Again, if lack of restraint and restraint also are in everything, who is the man who in an absolute sense does not restrain himself? For not all lack of restraint is present in one man, yet we say that some men in an absolute sense are so.[30] The various kinds of the perplexity which occur, are certain kinds like these. Some of these must be removed and others left, for the solution of the perplexity is its discovery.[31]

3. So let us examine first whether they know or do not know, and how they know, then in respect of what the restrained man and the man who lacks restraint must be posited, I mean, whether the two of them must be posited in respect of every pleasure and pain,[32] or in respect of some separately, and whether the restrained man and the steadfast man are [the same] or different, and similarly in the other cases which are akin to this opinion.[33] (2) The start of the investigation is whether the restrained man and the man who lacks restraint are concerned with the same thing or have a distinction in some way, I mean, whether the restrained man and the man who lacks restraint

---

[25] Longer lacuna.

[26] Longer lacuna.

[27] What is wrong here is not completely set right by Arberry's tacit emendation *ʿilājan* for *ʿājilan* of the MS. (Greek ἀλλὰ δι' ἀκρασίαν is in fact wrongly construed with εὐϊατότερος and γάρ is taken out of place).

[28] I.e. the Arabic translator read παρανομία for παροιμίᾳ (Arberry).

[29] *Sic* text: *wa-yaqūlu* for Greek φαμέν.

[30] I.e. lacking in restraint.

[31] *Sic* text *wujūduhu* for Greek εὕρεσις.

[32] Strictly 'mental pain, grief', Arabic *ḥuzn*, cf. 1146a 21.

[33] Arabic *ra'y*, Greek θεωρίας.

في الجامعة التي [...] (٩) [...] [١/٤] سيفعل الخيرات [لا] ورداءات (١٠) وأيضاً الذي يفعل من أجل أنّه قنع ويطلب الأشياء السارّة ويختارها سيظنّ أنّه أجود من الذي [لا] يفعل ذلك بالفكرة فليكن الذي يفعل من أجل لا ضبط أهون علاجاً من أجل أنّه يتغيّر قنوعه وأمّا الذي لا يضبط ذاته فقد وجب عليه أنّه على خلاف الناموس ويقول في خلاف الناموس إنّه إذا كان الماء يخنق فما الذي ينبغي أن يشرب عليه فإنّه إن قنع بما كان يفعل فإذا تغيّر قنوعه أمسك عن ذلك العمل وأمّا الآن فليس قنوعه بدون ما كان البتّةَ ويفعل شيئاً آخر (١١) وأيضاً إن كان في جميع الأشياء لا ضبط وضبط أيضاً فمن الذي لا يضبط ذاته بنوع مبسوط فإنّه ليس يكون جميع لا ضبط في واحد ونقول إنّ بعض الناس بنوع مبسوط كذلك فأمّا أنواع التحيّر التي تعرض فهي أنواع ما مثل هذه وينبغي أن ينتزع بعض هذه وأن يترك بعضها فإنّ حلّ التحيّر هو وجوده.

٣. فلنفحص أوّلاً هل يعلمون أو لا يعلمون وكيف يعلمون ثمّ في أيّ شئ ينبغي أن يوضع الضابط ولا ضابط أعني هل ينبغي أن يوضعا في كلّ لذّة وحزن أو في بعضها بنوع مفصّل وهل الضابط والصبور [واحد] أو آخر وآخر وكذلك في سائر الأشياء التي هي مجانسة لهذا الرأي (٢) فأوّل الفحص هل الضابط ولا ضابط هما في شئ واحد أو لهما فصل بنوع ما أعني هل الضابط ولا ضابط هما في أشياء بأعيانها فقط أم لا بل هما في الذي من

1 first [...] : illegible F, *For thought [...] that it should be stationary because [...] the argument* Dun || 1 second [...] : illegible F, *There occurs [...] will do* Dun || 1 لا suppl. Dun || 2 لا suppl. Dun || 3 علاجا corr. Arberry* (εὐϊατότερος) : عاجلا F, Bad || 4 ذاته om. Bad || 6 أمسك corr. Bad : مسك F || 7 في om. Bad || 9 التي تعرض read. and corr. : الذي يعرض F, Bad || 11 يعلمون (three times) F, Dun : يعملون Bad || 12 first في repeated in Bad || 13 واحد suppl. Bad, Dun || 14 واحد F, Dun : وآخر Bad || 14 لهما corr. : لهم F

are concerned only with things-in-themselves or not,[34] but rather are concerned with what is from both, and also if lack of restraint and restraint are concerned with all things or not. For the man who [lacks] restraint is not concerned with all of them absolutely[35] but is concerned with the things in which the intemperate man is concerned. And he is not related[36] to these [...],[37] for that would be intemperance also, but he is [...].[38] (3) [...] that some of those who hold opinions do not doubt but think that they know entirely. (4) And if those who hold an opinion, through the weakness of their conviction, do more than those who know, they will act contrary to what is supposed[39] in what they think, and it is no less than what the others do in what they know. This is what Heraclitus shows. (5) But since we say that we know in two ways—for knowledge is said to be in him who has knowledge and does not use it, and it is said also that he who uses knowledge has knowledge—, there will be a difference between him who has knowledge and him who uses it.[40] For he who has knowledge and does not think that he must act upon it[41] is bad,[42]
1147a not he who has no opinion. (6) Also since there are two kinds of premisses, when a man has both there is nothing to prevent him acting contrary to knowledge, when he employs the universal premiss, not the particular, because it is the particulars that are done. And in the universal also there is a distinction, for sometimes it is with reference to the man himself and sometimes with reference to a part of the thing, as when I say that dry things are more suitable to every man and this is a man, or that the dry is this sort of thing. But as to whether it is this sort of thing, either he does not have [the knowledge] or does not act [upon it]. The difference will be according to these kinds, and there is no way of avoiding it.[43] So then this kind

---

[34] This is not what is said in the Greek.

[35] Arabic *bi-nauʿ mabsūṭ* is wrongly construed, cf. Greek ὁ ἁπλῶς ἀκρατής.

[36] The Greek construction (τῷ [...] ἁπλῶς ἔχειν) is disregarded.

[37] Lacuna in the MS.

[38] Lacuna of several lines.

[39] A line is here omitted in the Arabic translation (homoioteleuton with οὐθὲν [...] οὐδέν).

[40] This seems to render χρώμενος δέ, καὶ τὸ θεωροῦντα apparently having been omitted.

[41] This does not render the Greek.

[42] Arabic *radī*ʾ, Greek δεινόν, as also at 1145b 23.

[43] Arabic *wa-laisa fīhi ḥīlah* for Greek ἀμήχανον ὅσον.

كليهما وأيضاً إن كان في جميع الأشياء لا ضبط وضبط أم لا فإنّ [لا] ضابط ليس هو في كلّها بنوع مبسوط بل هو في الأشياء التي يكون فيها لا عفيف ولا ينسب إلى هذه [...] فإنّ هذا لا عفّة أيضاً بل هو [...] (٣) [...] [١/٥] أنّ بعض أصحاب الآراء لا يشكّون بل يظنّون أنّهم يعلمون بنوع استقصاء (٤) فإن كان أصحاب الرأي بضعف قنوعهم يفعلون أكثر من الذين يعلمون فإنّهم سيفعلون خلاف ما عليه الظنّ فيما يرونه وليس بدون فعل الآخرين فيما يعلمون وهذا هو الذي يدلّ به هرقليطس (٥) ولكن إذ نقول إنّا نعلم بنوعين فإنّ العلم يقل إنّه في الذي له العلم ولا يستعمله ويقل أيضاً إنّ الذي يستعمل العلم له علم فسيكون فصل فيما بين الذي له العلم والذي يستعمله فإنّ الذي له العلم ولا يرى أنّه ينبغي أن يعمل به إنّه ردئ لا الذي ليس عنده الرأي (٦) وأيضاً إذا كان نوعا المقدّمات إذا كان له كلاهما لم يكن شئ مانع أن يعمل على غير علم إذا هو استعمل المقدّمة الكلّية لا الجزئية من أجل أنّ الجزئيات مفعولة وفي الكلّي أيضاً فصل فإنّ بعضه في ذاته وبعضه في الجزء في الشئ كقولي إنّ اليابسة أوفق لكلّ إنسان وإنّ هذا إنسان أو إنّ اليابس مثل هذا ولكن إن كان مثل هذا إمّا ألاّ يكون له [علم] وإمّا إلاّ يفعل فالاختلاف سيكون على قدر هذه الأنواع وليس فيه حيلة فإذاً سيظنّ هذا النوع أنّه ليس تهل البتّة (٧) وأيضاً

1 لا suppl. Dun || 2 ينسب إلى هذه Dun : illegible F || 2-3 فإن هذا لا عفة أيضا بل هو Dun : illegible F || 4 بضعف read. Bad : يضعف F || 5 يرونه corr. Bad : يروه F || 5 الآخرين corr. Dun : الآخر F, Bad || 6 نقول read. Bad, Dun : يقول F || 10 له كلاهما appar. corr. Dun : لهما كليهما F, Bad || 12 الجزء في الشئ : الجزء corr. : الجزئ F, الشئ suppl. above line; الجزئ في Bad || 12 اليابس corr. Arberry : الناس F, Bad || 13 علم suppl. Dun

will be thought of as not absurd at all.[44] (7) Also it will be wondered at in another way[45] that men have knowledge according to another way different from those just mentioned. For we see the condition differing when it exists and is not used, so that it is said that the possessor has it and does not have it, e.g. the man asleep and mad and drunk. But exactly like this are the states of the victims of misfortunes, e.g. the different kinds of anger and the desires, some of which visibly alter the body.[46] Clearly it must be said that the state of those who do not restrain themselves is like these. (8) That it should be said that the words of wisdom are wisdom [...][47] they bring proofs [...][48] they should be imprinted[49] with it, and for that time is needed. So then it must be thought of those who do not restrain themselves that their words are like the words of these people who were spoken of earlier.[50] (9) Again, one may examine this cause naturally in this manner also. For one of the opinions is general, and the other is concerned with the particulars which are controlled by sense. When there results from them a single opinion, it must be said that the result here is chance,[51] whereas in practical[52] matters the action is immediate, for example, if every sweet must be tasted and if what is tasted is a sweet belonging to the particular things, then there must be a man able to do this, and there is nothing to prevent his doing it at once.[53] (10) So when the universal prevents the tasting and there is active that which says: 'Every sweet is [pleasant', and: 'This is

[44] Greek οὕτω μὲν εἰδέναι has disappeared, and Arabic *sa-yuẓannu hadhā 'n-nau' annahu laisa* [...] suggests that τοῦτο (τοιοῦτο) μὲν εἶναι was read instead.

[45] I.e. ἄλλως δὲ θαυμαστόν has been separated from the words it goes with and taken with the following sentence.

[46] Several words of the Greek are here omitted.

[47] Lacuna.

[48] Longer lacuna.

[49] The metaphor of the Greek is changed.

[50] The Arabic translator does not understand about actors (here τοὺς ὑποκρινομένους), cf. above, 1146a 20, also 1148b 8.

[51] I.e. τὴν τύχην for τὴν ψυχήν, as Arberry noted, wrongly construed with τὸ συμπερανθέν instead of with φάναι.

[52] Arabic *fī 'l-fi'līyah* for Greek ἐν [...] ταῖς ποιητικαῖς [sc. δόξαις] (Bywater) or προτάσεσι (Burnet). This is an exceptional rendering of ποιητικός (usually Arabic *fā'il*), as ποιητικός is exceptional in the sense of πρακτικός, which is evidently wanted here. If προτάσεσι ποιητικαῖς of the Greek text is an error and we should read πρακτικαῖς (Coraes, quoted by Rackham), it is clearly an old one.

[53] Arabic *ma'a hādha*, apparently reading the Greek ἅμα τοῦτο.

يتعجّب بنوع آخر أن يكون العلم للناس على نوع آخر غير الأنواع التي قيلت الآن فإنّا نرى الهيئة أنّها تختلف إذ كانت تكون ولا تستعمل حتّى إنّه يقل إنّها للذي هي له ويقل إنّها ليست له مثل النائم والمجنون والمخمور ولكن على هذا النوع تكون حالات أصحاب الآفات مثل أنواع الغضب والشهوات وبعض هذه تغيّر الجسم تغييراً بيّناً وهو بيّن أنّه ينبغي أن يقل إنّ حل الذين لا يضبطون أنفسهم مثل هؤلاء (٨) وأمّا أن [...] [١/٦] ينطبعون بها ويحتاج في ذلك إلى زمان فإذاً ينبغي أن يظنّ بالذين لا يضبطون أنفسهم أنّ أقاويلهم كأقاويل هؤلاء الذين قد قيلوا أوّلاً (٩) وأيضاً خليق أن يفحص فاحص عن هذه العلّة بنوع طبيعي على هذه الحل أيضاً فإنّ أحد الآراء كلّي والآخر ففي الجزئيات التي الحسّ مسوّدها وأمّا إذا صار منها رأي واحد فمضطرّ أن يقل إنّ المنتج ها هنا البخت وأمّا في الفعلية فالفعل من ساعته كقولي إن كان ينبغي أن يذاق كلّ حلو وأمّا إن كان الذي يذاق حلواً من الجزئيات فمضطرّ أن يكون القادر على ذلك ولا يمنعه مانع أن يكون فعله مع هذا (١٠) فإذا كانت الكلّية تمنع من الذوق وكانت تفعل التي تقول إنّ كلّ حلو [لذيذ وهذا حلو] وكان البخت في الشهوة فيقرب من أجل أنّها تقوى أن تحرّك كلّ واحد من

---

1 الآن : للآن Bad || 5 [...] : illegible F, *it should be said that the words of wisdom are wisdom [...] they bring proofs* Dun (partly) || 9 الحس corr. Bad, Dun : الخير F || 9 مسودها F : يسودها Bad || 9 البخت F, Dun : البحث read. Bad || 10 ساعته F : ساعة Bad || 12-13 وهذا حلو لذيذ suppl. Dun || 13 البخت F, Dun : البحث read. Bad

sweet'],[54] and chance is present in the desire,[55] it is approached, since desire is able to move each of the parts of the body. So then it hap-
1147b pens that one is lacking in self-restraint through a certain thought[56] and opinion, opposed not in itself but accidentally, (11) for it is the desire which is opposed to the true account,[57] not the opinion. Hence animals are not lacking in self-restraint, since they do not have universal thought but imagination of the particulars, and they have a certain memory. (12) How then is it possible[58] that he who does not restrain himself should know? This same argument also applies to the drunken man and the sleeper, and there is no separate account of this affliction. So we must listen to the students of natural science. (13) But since the last premise which is an opinion as to what is perceived and controller of the actions, the sufferer either does not have this or has it in such a way that he does not know how he has it, but repeats it as a drunk man repeats the words of Empedocles, because he does not have[59] a universal term nor one possessed of knowledge, since it was thought that the universal resembles the last term.[60] It seems that part of what Socrates was seeking.[61] (14) For the affliction does not occur since it is thought that knowledge in a true sense and not [...][62]

4. [...] in a partial way, and if so, in what sort of things, let it be said in what follows. That those who restrain themselves and those who are steadfast, and those who do not restrain themselves and the soft are concerned with pleasures and pains, is clear. (2) But since some of the things which produce pleasures are necessary, some of them

---

[54] Arabic omits Greek γλυκὺ ἡδύ, τουτὶ δὲ γλυκύ by homoioteleuton, which can hardly be due to the translator, but rather to the copyist.

[55] I.e. the Arabic translator read τύχῃ δ' ἐπιθυμίᾳ ἐνοῦσα (Arberry).

[56] Arabic *bi-fikratin mā*, but Greek πως, 'in a certain sense', has not been translated correctly.

[57] Arabic *al-qaul aṣ-ṣaḥīḥ*, one of several renderings used by the Arabic translator for Greek ὁ ὀρθὸς λόγος.

[58] Arabic omits Greek λύεται ἡ ἄγνοια καὶ πάλιν.

[59] This is apparently masculine for neuter, and the stop which whould have come after Greek τὰ Ἐμπεδοκλέους is wrongly placed after τὸν ἔσχατον ὅρον two lines later.

[60] The latter part of this sentence hardly yields a sense.

[61] Something has dropped out.

[62] Lacuna of several lines.

الأعضاء فإذاً يعرض أن يكون لا ضبط بفكرة ما ورأي ليس ضدّياً بذاته بل بنوع العرض (١١) فإنّ الشهوة ضدّية القول الصحيح لا الرأي من أجل هذا ليس للسباع لا ضبط من أجل أنّه ليس لها ظنّ كلّي بل لها فنطاسيات الجزئيات ولها ذكر ما (١٢) فكيف يمكن أن يكون عالماً الذي لا يضبط نفسه وهذا القول أيضاً بعينه في المخمور والنائم وليس لهذه الآفة قول خاصّ فينبغي أن نسمع من أصحاب الكلام الطبيعي (١٣) ولكن من أجل أنّ المقدّمة الأخيرة وهي رأي المحسوس والمسوّد من الأفاعيل فالذي في الآفة إمّا ألاّ يكون له هذا وإمّا أن يكون له بهذا النوع حتّى لا يعلم كيف هو له بل أن يكون يقوله كما يقول المخمور أقاويل أنبدقليس من أجل أنّه ليس له كلّي ولا ذو علم إذ كان يظنّ أنّ الكلّي شبيه بالحدّ الأخير ويشبه أنّ بعض ما كان يطلب سقراطيس (١٤) فالآفة لا تعرض إذ كان يظنّ أنّ علماً بنوع حقيقي ولا [...]

٤. [...] [١/٧] بنوع جزئي فإن كان ففي أيّ الأشياء هو فليقل فيما يتلو هذا وأمّا الذين يضبطون أنفسهم والذين يصبرون والذين لا يضبطون أنفسهم وذوي الليّن في اللذّات والأحزان فبيّن (٢) ولكن إذ بعض التي تفعل اللذّات مضطرّة وبعضها مختارة وبعضها

2 ضدية F : ضد Bad || 6 راي المحسوس corr. Dun* (δόξα τε αἰσθητοῦ) : راس السجلموس F, Bad || 9 فالآفة لا تعرض Dun : يمكن Bad || 9 يشبه F, Dun : في Bad, F || 6 second و corr. Dun : ففي F || 10 أن Dun : illegible F || 10 ولا Dun : illegible F || 11 فإن F : وإن Bad || 11 في corr. Bad : illegible F || 11 فليقل corr. Bad : فليقل F

chosen and some of them[63] by their nature[64] involving excesses, the necessary are the bodily functions, and I mean simply such as these which reside in food and in the use of sexual intercourse and the like bodily functions which we have described as involving intemperance and temperance. Others are necessary[65] and are chosen for themselves, as, for example, victory, honour, wealth and the like goods and pleasant things. The persons who are related to these,because they exceed the just account which is in them,[66] we do not call lacking in restraint absolutely, but we call them lacking in restraint, adding a qualification and saying 'lacking in restraint in regard to gain, honour and anger', but we do not call them that absolutely, nor do we say that they are like those called different[67] because of the re-
1148a semblance, like the man who was entirely[68] victorious, for the general expression for that differs but little from the special expression, yet in any case it was different. The proof of that is that the man who lacks self-restraint is blamed not because he commits an error only, but because he is unjust, either absolutely or partially,[69] but as for these, nothing is blamed and no one. (3) As for him who uses the bodily enjoyment with which the temperate and intemperate are connected, he is not called lacking in restraint who chooses[70] to pursue excesses of things delightful and avoids painful things, such as hunger, thirst and heat, and all that is related to touch and taste, but he is called lacking in restraint from[71] choice and reflection, not according to any presupposition[72] in regard to these things, as there is

---

[63] The last three words are not in the Greek text.

[64] Greek καθ' αὑτά is wrongly construed with ἔχοντα δ' ὑπερβολήν instead of with αἱρετὰ μέν.

[65] But this omits οὐχί (Arberry), and we should here have *ghair* or *lā muḍṭarrah*, i.e. unnecessary. It is perhaps a copyist's error.

[66] Arabic *hādhihi* [...] *annahā tazīdu [...] fīhā*, sc. the pleasant things, but this is incorrect. The MS. has the following note: *yatazaiyadu ʿalā 'l-qadr al-maqbūl* [?] *kadhā lakhkhaṣahu al-qāḍī*, i.e. Ibn Rushd, cf. Introduction, pp. 50ff.

[67] A mistake again here.

[68] Arabic *fī 'l-kullīyah*. This perhaps renders τὰ ὅλα for τὰ 'Ολύμπια which the translator did not know (Arberry). Yet in I, 8, 9 (1099a 2-3) where the name also occurs ('Ολυμπίασιν), the translator rendered *fī 'l-maidān*, 'at the race-ground', or 'in the contest' (which he may or may not have gathered from the context). Hardly, in any case, 'in the universal (premise)', cf. 1147a 2-3.

[69] This follows the order of words in the Greek, but modern translators (not Chase) connect ἢ ἁπλῶς οὖσα ἢ κατά τι μέρος explicitly with ἡ [...] ἀκρασία.

[70] The negative μή is omitted.

[71] But Greek παρά is here 'contrary to', and not 'along of, because of'.

[72] Arabic *taqdīm al-waḍʿ*, but Greek πρόσθεσιν is clearly 'addition'.

بذاتها لها زيادات فالمضطرّ الجسمية وإنّما أقول مثل هذه التي في الغذاء والتي في استعمل الجماع وما يشبه هذا من الجسمية التي وصفنا أنّ فيها لا عفّة وعفّة ومنها ما هي مضطرّة وهي بعينها مختارة كقولي مثل الغلبة والكرامة والغنى وما أشبه ذلك من الخيرات والأشياء اللذينة فالذين يضافون إلى هذه من أجل أنّها تزيد على القدر الذي هو فيها فليس نقول إنّهم لا ضابطون بنوع مبسوط بل نقول إنّهم لا ضابطون إذا زدنا وقلنا لا ضابطون في الربح والكرامة والغضب وأمّا بنوع مبسوط فلا نقول ذلك ولا إنّهم كالذين يقالون آخرين بالشبه كالإنسان الذي يغلب في الكلّية فإنّ كلمة ذلك العامّية كانت تخالف كلمة الخاصّية قليلاً وعلى أنّ قد كانت أخرى الدليل على ذلك أنّ لا ضبط يذمّ ليس بأنّه خطأ فقط وبل لأنّه ظلم إمّا بنوع مبسوط وإمّا بجزء ما وأمّا من هذه فليس شيء مذموم ولا واحد (٣) وأمّا الذي يستعمل التمتّع الجسمي الذي ينسب إليه العفيف ولا عفيف فليس يقل لا ضابط الذي يختار طلب زيادات الأشياء السارّة ويهرب من المحزنة مثل الجوع والعطش والحرّ وكلّ ما ينسب إلى اللمس والذوق بل يقل لا ضابط من الاختيار والفكرة وليس على قدر تقديم الوضع في هذه كما يكون في الغضب بل بنوع مبسوط فقط (٤) والدليل على ذلك أنّهم يتحدّثون عن الليّن لمكان هذه فأمّا لمكان الأخرى [...] ضبط ولا

4 القدر mrg.: يزيد على القدر المعقول كذا لخصه القاضي || 5 ضابطون (twice) corr. Bad : ضابطين F || 5 ضابطون corr. : ضابطين F, Bad || 7 الكليه F, Dun : الألمفية corr. Bad || 8 أخرى corr. Bad, Dun : أجزاء F || 8 الدليل F : والدليل add. Bad || 11 ضابط corr. Bad, Dun : ضبط F || 13 تقديم Dun : تقويم Bad

in anger, but absolutely. (4) The proof of that is that they are called soft with reference to these, but with reference to those others [...][73] restraint and intemperate [...][74] in the same way, but some of them [act] from choice.[75] For this reason we may rather call intemperate him who does not desire,[76] or who pursues excesses mildly, and avoids small pains, or[77] whoever of these[78] desires vehemently. And what might that man do, if there came to him vehement desire and violent pain in some[79] of the necessary things? (5) As for the desires and pleasures, some belong to a class of noble and excellent things,[80] for some pleasant things are naturally desirable, some are the opposite of these, and some are between the two, as we distinguished previously, e.g. wealth, gain, victory and honour, and at the same time[81] all like these and the intermediate things are not blamed[82] for being affected and being desired and loved. But they are blamed in a way and for exceeding the bounds. Hence all who seize on[83] more than is fitting, or seek one of the things which are naturally noble and good, like those who do all in their power[84] either for honour or for children and parents—these are good things, and those who strive after these are praised, but in any case[85] in these too there is a kind of excess, if one fights against the gods, as Niobe did, or as
1148b Satyrus did, who loved his father, when he prayed to his father,[86] and it was thought of him that he had been very foolish. In regard to these things there is not any wickedness, because of what has already

[73] Short lacuna.

[74] Longer lacuna.

[75] Greek οἱ δ' οὐ προαιροῦσανται omitted in Arabic.

[76] I.e. Greek ἐπιθυμῶν read as ἐπιθυμεῖ.

[77] Arabic *au*, but Greek ἤ is here 'than', not 'or'.

[78] I.e. τουτῶν has been read for τοῦτον (Arberry).

[79] I.e. ἐνίας for ἐνδείας.

[80] The Arabic translator who renders *fa'inna baʿḍahā min jins min jiyād wa-fāḍilah* has read the vulg. (without τῶν) and construed γένει with the following genitives καλῶν καὶ σπουδαίων.

[81] Arabic *maʿa hādha*, Greek πρός has been taken adverbially instead of with ἅπαντα [...].

[82] Cf. Gauthier, *ad locum*.

[83] Arabic *yamsikūna* for Greek κρατοῦνται, taken as middle, cf. 1149a 2.

[84] Greek μᾶλλον ἢ δεῖ is not translated.

[85] *ʿalā ḥāl*, cf. 1148a 2.

[86] Cf. Gauthier, *ad locum*.

عفّة [...] [١/٨] على حل واحدة بل بعضهم [يفعلون] باختيار ومن أجل هذا خليق أن نقول أكثر لا عفّة الذي لا يشتهي أو الذي يطلب الزيادات برفق ويهرب من الأحزان الصغيرة أو من كان من هؤلاء يشتهي شهوةً شديدةً فما عسى أن يفعل ذلك إن صارت له شهوة قوية وحزن شديد في بعض الأشياء المضطرّة (٥) وأمّا الشهوات واللذّات فإنّ بعضها من جنس من جيد وفاضلة فإنّ بعض اللذيذة مختارة بالطبع وبعضها مضادّة لهذه وبعضها فيما بين ذلك كما فصلنا أوّلاً مثل الأموال والربح والغلبة والكرامة ومع هذا فإنّ جميع ما كان مثل هذه والمتوسّطة فإنّها لا تذمّ بأنّها تنفعل وتشتهى وتحبّ بل تذمّ بنوع وبأنّها تفرط ومن أجل هذا جميع الذين يمسكون أكثر ممّا ينبغي أو يطلبون شيئاً من الأشياء التي هي بالطبع جياد وخيرات مثل الذين يجتهدون إمّا في الكرامة وإمّا في الأولاد والآباء فإنّ هذه من الخيرات فالذين يحرصون على هذه يمدحون ولكن على حل في هذه أيضاً إفراط ما إن حارب أحد الآلهة كما فعل أنيوبى أو كما فعل ظاطوروس المحبّ أبه حين دعا إلى أبيه فقد كان يظنّ به أنّه قد حمق جدّاً وليس في هذه ولا رداءة واحدة لما قد

1 يفعلون suppl. Dun || 10 الآباء F, Dun : الأبناء Bad || 11 فعل أنيوبى w.p. F : فعلت نيوبى read. and corr. Bad || 11 أبه F : أبيه Bad || 12 أبيه F, Dun : إلهيته Bad

been said, since each noble thing is naturally so for itself.[87] As for wicked deeds, they are to be avoided and are sins.[88] (6) And similarly intemperance,[89] for it is not merely to be avoided, but is also blameworthy. Since it is like the condition, they join to it intemperance[90] and apply it to each of them,[91] like a bad doctor.[92] We do not say that he is bad without qualification. And just as people do not speak here of vice, because each one of them is not a vice, but because they resemble vice [by analogy], so it must be thought here also that lack of restraint and restraint apply to the things to which [...][93]

5. [...] itself, to certain kinds of animals and men, and others are not so, but are in some cases owing to a chronic ailment, in others to custom and in others again to vicious natures. Now it is possible to see states of related kind in each of these cases, (2) I mean, the bestial, e.g. the female who was said to rend the wombs of pregnant women and eat the unborn children, and, as they assert, that certain savage people in the vicinity of the Pontic lands delighted to eat, some of them raw meat, others the flesh of men, and others to barter their unborn children for banquets, or what happened[94] in the case of Phalaris. (3) For these actions are brutish. Others of them arise owing to diseases and the madness of some, like the man who made his mother sit down[95] and ate her, and him who ate the liver of his fellow in slavery. As for those which are from the ill effects of diseases or custom, like plucking out the hair, biting the nails, eating charcoal

---

[87] Construction and translation have gone wrong. Greek here is φύσει τῶν αἱρετῶν as φύσει αἱρετά in 1143a 24 (there correctly rendered *mukhtārah bi'ṭ-ṭab'*), and these words form the complement of ἐστίν. Arabic *al-jiyād* is apparently for Greek αἱρετῶν.

[88] I.e. Greek φαῦλα δὲ καὶ φευκτὰ καὶ ἁμαρτήματα, the reading of K^b.

[89] The Greek negative (οὐδέ) is left untranslated. Arabic *lā 'iffah* is here for Greek ἀκρασία (as also at 1145a 16; 1145b 9; 1149a 2), usually *lā ḍabṭ* (below, 1148b 11; also 1146a 18, 19; 1146b 3, 4; 1149a 21). But *lā 'iffah* is regularly for ἀκολασία (1130a 30; 1147b 28; 1149a 5-6, 22; 1150a 10). The distinction is made very clear in the passage 1149a 18-22 where both expressions are twice used.

[90] See previous note.

[91] The construction is again wrong, for Greek περὶ ἕκαστον goes closely with τὴν ἀκρασίαν.

[92] The following words καὶ κακὸν ὑποκριτήν are omitted, cf. above, 1147a 23.

[93] Lacuna of several lines.

[94] The translator apparently read γενόμενον for λεγόμενον (Arberry).

[95] Apparently καθίσας for καθιερεύσας—so Arberry (letters omitted in a word of the Greek, cf. above, 1148a 21-22).

قيل من أجل أنّ كلّ واحد من الجياد إنّما هو بالطبع لذاته وأمّا الرداءات فالتي يهرب عنها والخطايا (٦) وكذلك لا عفّة فإنّها ليست مهروباً عنها فقط بل هي من المذمومات أيضاً ولمّا كانت تشبه الانفعل يركّبون عليها لا عفّة ويقولونها على كلّ واحد منها مثلما يقل طبيب سوء ولا نقول إنّه رديء بنوع مبسوط ومثل ما أنّهم لا يقولون ها هنا رداءة من أجل أنّه ليس كلّ واحد منهما رداءة وهي إنّما تتشبّه بالملاءمة كذلك ينبغي أن نقرّر هنالك أيضاً وألاّ ضبط وضبط هما في الأشياء التي [...]

٥. [...] [١/٩] بأجناس من الحيوان والناس وبعضها ليست كذلك بل يكون بعضها لمكان الزمانة وبعضها للعادة وبعضها للطبائع الرديئة فقد يمكن أن ترى هيئات في كلّ واحد من هذه بنوع مقارب (٢) وإنّما أقول السبعية مثل الإنسانية التي قيل إنّها كانت تشقّ بطون الحوامل وتأكل الأجنّة وكما يزعمون أنّ بعض الناس توحّشوا فيما يلي بلاد بنطس كانوا يحبّون أمّا بعضهم فأكل اللحوم النيئة وبعضهم لحوم الناس وبعضهم يبادل بعضاً بأجنّة أولادهم للولائم أو الذي كان من فالارس (٣) فإنّ هذه الأفعل سبعية بعضها تكون لمكان الأمراض وجنون بعضهم مثل الذي أقعد والدته وأكلها والذي أكل كبد رفيقه في العبودية وأمّا التي تكون من آفات الأمراض أو العادة مثل نتف الشعر وجرح الأظفار وأكل الفحم

3 كانت تشبه corr. and read. Bad : كان يشبه F || 3 لا عفة corr. Dun* (ἀκρασίαν) : اللا فضيلة F, Bad || 7 [...] : illegible F, *itself to* Dun (partly) || 7 بأجناس F : لأجناس Bad || 9 مقارب F : يقاربه Bad || 9 الإنسانية F : الإنسانة Bad || 9 قيل إنها om. Bad || 10 بنطس w.p. F || 10 كانوا : وكانوا add. Bad || 12 بعضها : وبعضها add. Bad

and earth, and also pederasty, these occur in some by nature, in others through habit, e.g. those who have been accustomed to gymnastics[96] from childhood. (4) Now no one would say of those who are ruled by nature, that they lack restraint, just as it is not said that women are lacking in restraint because they do not roast and do not cook, since they are a different thing,[97] and similarly those who have a diseased condition and through habit. (5) He who has each one of
1149a these is beyond the limits in vice, like brutishness. As for him who has patience[98] or mastery,[99] he does not have simple intemperance,[100] but that which bears a likeness to it, just as the man who in respect of anger is in this kind of condition, but he should not be called lacking in restraint, because all excessive folly, all excessive cowardliness, all intemperance and all vice are partly brutish and partly pathological. (6) One who is so by nature, e.g. he who shrinks from everything and is afraid at the sound of a mouse squeaking [...] because of disease and from nearness[101] [...] epilepsy or through different kinds of pathological madness. (7) At times it is possible that there should be something of this in a man without its dominating him, I mean, like Phalaris when he desired to eat a child, but restrained himself, or him in whose nature[102] was a desire for ugly sexual pleasure, and at times not only was this in the man, but he was conquered by it also, (8) like vice.[103] For some of it is called vice simply and outright,[104] some of it is called brutish with the addition of something, and some is called pathological, and it is not spoken of in one way simply. Thus it is clear that lack of virtue also is some of it brutish, some pathological, and that which is so absolutely is in-

[96] Arabic *alladhīna yaʿtādūna al-muthāqafah* for Greek τοῖς γυμναζομένοις of K^b, cf. X, 9, 14 = 1180b 3 Arabic *thaqīfah* = Greek γυμναστική, and X, 9, 14 = 1180b 14 Arabic *muthāqif* = Greek γυμναστής.

[97] This is far from the Greek.

[98] I.e. Greek καρτερεῖν (K^b) for κρατεῖν (Arberry).

[99] Arabic *taghallub*, i.e. Greek κρατεῖσθαι taken as middle instead of passive, cf. above, 1148a 29.

[100] Arabic *lā ʿiffah* for Greek ἀκρασία as elsewhere, e.g. 1145a 16, cf. on 1148b 5.

[101] Arabic *wa-min al-qarābah* (so Arberry) corresponding to Greek καὶ τῶν ἀφρόνων, then a lacuna of two lines.

[102] The words 'him in whose nature' (Arabic *alladhī fī dhātihi*) are not in the Greek, which mentions only Phalaris.

[103] Greek ὥσπερ οὖν καὶ μοχθηρίας is construed wrongly with the foregoing (with omission of οὖν).

[104] Arabic *bi'l-muwājahah*, i.e. κατ' ἄνθρωπον rendered 'man to man'.

والطين ومع هذا جماع الذكور فإنّ هذه تعرض أمّا لبعض فبالطبع ولبعض فبالعادة مثل الذين يعتادون المثاقفة منذ الصبا (٤) فالذين غلبتهم الطبيعة فليس يقول أحد إنّ هؤلاء غير ضابطين كما لا يقل إنّ النساء لا ضابطات لأنّهن لا يشوين ولا يطبخن إذ كنّ شيئاً آخر وكذلك الذين لهم شيء مرضي ومن أجل العادة (٥) فالذي له كلّ واحد من هذه فهو في الشرّية خارج عن الحدود كالسبعية وأمّا الذي له تصبّر أو تغلّب فليس فيه لا عفّة مبسوطة بل التي هي على شبه ذلك كمثل الذي له في الغضب على مثل هذا النوع من الانفعال فأمّا لا ضابط فلا ينبغي أن يقل من أجل أنّ كلّ حمق مفرط وكلّ جبن مفرط وكلّ لا عفّة وكلّ رداءة فإنّ بعضها سبعية وبعضها مرضية (٦) ومنهم من هو مثل هذا بالطبع مثل الذي يفزع من كلّ شيء حتّى من صوت فأرة إذا صوّتت [...] من أجل المرض ومن القرابة [...] [١٨٠] الصرع أو لأنواع الجنون المرضية (٧) وربّما أمكن أن يكون شيء من هذا في إنسان وألاّ يغلب عليه كقولي مثلما كان فلارس حين كان يشتهي أن يأكل طفلاً فضبط نفسه أو الذي في ذاته شهوة جماع قبيح وربّما لم يكن الشيء في الإنسان فقط بل يغلب منه أيضاً (٨) كالرداءة فإنّ بعضها يقل رداءة بنوع مبسوط بالمواجهة وبعضها يقل سبعية بزيادة شيء ما وبعضها يقل مرضية وليس يقل بنوع واحد مبسوط فبيّن أنّ لا فضيلة أيضاً بعضها سبعية وبعضها مرضية والتي هي بنوع مبسوط فالتي هي لا عفّة (٩) وأمّا أنّ لا

2 الصبا F : الصغر Bad || 3 النساء corr. Dun* (τὰς γυναῖκας) : السباع F || 4 ومن F : من Bad || 9-10 من أجل المرض ومن القرابة Dun : illegible F || 13 منه F : فيه Bad || 14 ألا فضيلة F : أن لا فضيلة corr. Bad

temperance.[105] (9) As to lack of restraint and restraint only being concerned with the same things as intemperance and temperance, and that in other things is another kind of lack of restraint, and that it is spoken of by a kind of metaphor,[106] not absolutely—all this is clear.

6. Let us now consider that lack of restraint with reference to anger is less ugly than lack of restraint in desires. For anger seems to have heard something of the language of reason but has not heard all of it,[107] like servants who make haste and run before they hear all that is said, then mistake the order, [and] like dogs who bark when they hear a sound, before they find out if it is a friend. So anger owing to the heat and quickness of its nature, when it hears without inquiring for the whole order, springs up to retaliate. For reason and imagination have shown[108] that there has been a calumny[109] or a slight, then anger, as if it has concluded[110] that it must make war on anyone of this kind, becomes difficult at once. But desire, when reason or sense
1149b intimates that something is pleasant, springs up to enjoy it. Anger in this way obeys reason in a way, but desire does not obey, so that it is uglier, as if one who does not restrain anger is conquered by reason in a way, but the other [...] is not [...] reason [...][111] (2) [...] and anger likewise, more than the desires which are related to excess and the necessary desires also, like the man who excused himself for striking his father, for he said: 'He struck his father, and *he*[112] struck *his* father', then pointing to his son he said: 'He too will strike me, when he becomes a man, for that is in our family', and like the man who was being dragged along by his son, and when he came to the door, told him to stop, because he also dragged his father to that point. (3) Again, the craftier men are, the more unjust[113] they are. Now the angry man does not act craftily, nor does anger, but is open. As for desire, as is said of Venus: 'The Cyprus-born contrives wiles', and

[105] I.e. with omission of κατὰ τὴν ἀνθρωπίνην and the nominative ἀκολασία instead of ἀκολασίαν. This translation of course fails to give the sense of the Greek.

[106] Text *intiqāl al-ism*, perhaps corr. *istiʿārat al-ism*, cf. 1149b 32.

[107] This translation of Greek παρακούειν is inexact.

[108] Arabic *qad dallat*. This translates the Greek aorist ἐδήλωσεν.

[109] Arabic *firyah* for Greek ὕβρις.

[110] Arabic *jamʿa jāmiʿatan*, cf. 1146a 24.

[111] Lacuna of several lines with a word here and there preserved.

[112] Lit. 'and that father also'.

[113] Or 'more tyrannical' (Arabic *ashaddu jauran*).

ضبط وضبط فقط في الأشياء التي فيها لا عفّة وعفّة وأنّ في سائر الأشياء نوع أخر من أنواع لا ضبط وأنّه يقل بنوع انتقل الاسم لا بنوع مبسوط فذلك بيّن.

٦. وأمّا أنّ لا ضبط الذي للغضب أقلّ سماجةً من لا ضبط الشهوات فلننظر في ذلك فإنّ الغضب يشبه أن يكون قد سمع شيئاً عن نطق الفكرة ولم يسمع كلّه كالخدم الذين هم أصحاب عجلة الذين يبتدرون قبل أن يسمعوا جميع ما قيل ثمّ يخطئون على الأمر [و] كالكلاب التي تنبح إذا سمعت طنيناً قبل أن تفحص إن كان ذلك من صديق كذلك الغضب لمكان حرارة الطبع وسرعته إذا سمع ولم يستقص جميع الأمر نهض في الانتقام فإنّ الفكرة والفنطاسيا قد دلّت على أنّه قد كانت فرية أو ضجر ثمّ أنّ الغضب كأنّه قد جمع جامعةً أنّه ينبغي أن يحارب من كان على هذه الحال فيتصعّب من ساعته وأمّا الشهوة فحين تخبر الفكرة أو الحسّ أنّ شيئاً لذيذ تنهض في التمتّع منه فالغضب على هذا النوع ينقاد للفكرة بنوع ما وأمّا الشهوة فلا تنقاد فهي إذاً أشدّ عاراً إذ كان الذي لا يضبط الغضب يغلب من الفكرة بنوع ما وأمّا الآخر [...] وليس [...] الفكرة [...] (٢) [...] [٣/١١] والغضب كذلك أكثر من الشهوات التي تنسب إلى الإفراط والمضطرّة أيضاً مثل الذي كان يعتذر عن ضرب أبيه فإنّه قل إنّ هذا ضرب أبه وذلك الأب أيضاً ضرب أبه ثمّ أشار إلى ابنه وقل هذا أيضاً سيضربني إذا صار رجلاً فإنّ ذلك في جنسنا ومثل الذي كان يجذبه ابنه فلمّا صار عند الباب أمره أن يكفّ من أجل أنه أيضاً جذب أبه إلى ذلك الموضع (٣) وأيضاً الذين هم أشدّ اغتيالاً هم أشدّ جوراً والغضوب لا يغتل ولا الغضب بل هو ظاهر وأمّا الشهوة فإنّها كما يقل في الزهرة إنّ المولود بقبرس يغتل الاغتيل وكما قل أوميرش

1 نوع أخر corr. Ar* (ἄλλο εἶδος) : أنواعا اخر F, Bad || 2 وأنه F : فإنه Bad || 5 على F : في Bad || 5 و suppl. Dun* (καί) : أو suppl. Bad || 7 second و F, Dun : أو Bad || 8 first أن F, Dun : إن Bad || 8 كأنه om. Bad || 9 يحارب F, Dun : نحارب read. Bad || 9 ساعته F : ساعة Bad || 18 المولود F : المولودة corr. Bad* || 18 يغتل F, Dun : فقتالة Bad

as Homer said of Kestus:[114] 'He stole the girdle, contriving a crafty plan.' So then since lack of restraint[115] is more unjust and worse than that which is connected with anger, and thus lack of restraint absolutely is not vice in a sense.[116] (4) Also, no one insults with pain, while every one who acts in anger acts with pain, and the man who calumniates[117] [acts] with pleasure. If then the things at which there is the most just anger are more unjust, in that case the lack of restraint which is on account of desire is so, for in anger there is no falsehood. (5) As to lack of restraint in desires being worse than that which is in anger,[118] and in respect of restraint and lack of restraint being concerned with desires and bodily pleasures—it is clear. (6) We must take the differences of these in themselves. For as was said at the beginning, some are human and natural, both in kind and magnitude, others are brutish, and others are owing to chronic diseases,[119] and it is only with the first of these that temperance and intemperance are concerned. For this reason we do not say that animals are either temperate or intemperate, except metaphorically and in general insofar as one animal species differs from another in ag-
1150a gression[120] and vengeance and in being [...].[121] (7) [...] goes beyond [...][122] the comparison of the wickedness of that which has no principle will be more hurtful.[123] As for the intelligence, it is a principle. So to make this comparison is like comparing injustice with the unjust man for their names are one. For each of them is bad,[124] and the bad man may do many times more harm than the beast.

---

[114] Wrongly taken as a proper name (Arberry). There is of course no such quotation as that which follows in Homer or anywhere else.

[115] But the Greek is 'this form of lack of restraint' (ἡ ἀκρασία αὕτη, viz. in regard to desire).

[116] Or translate 'it is lack of restraint in an absolute sense and not vice in a sense', reading *wa-lā* or *wa-* alone before *sharrīya* (*shurrīya*).

[117] Arabic *yaftārī* for Greek ὑβρίζει as elsewhere (1129b 22), and the translation also has *firyah* for ὕβρις (below, 1149b 23 and elsewhere).

[118] For the construction of the sentence, cf. 1149a 21ff., from which it is doubtful if Arabic *anna* inserted by Arberry after *fa-ammā* is necessary.

[119] Arabic *az-zamānāt* perhaps covers both Greek words, πηρώσεις and νοσήματα.

[120] Arabic *shatm* for Greek ὕβρις.

[121] Short lacuna.

[122] Longer lacuna.

[123] Arabic *akthar ḍararan*. The Greek has 'less hurtful' ('more harmless', ἀσινεστέρα).

[124] Arabic *radī*ʾ, but Greek is κάκιον.

عن كشطس إنّه سرق السير وهو يرى رأي اغتيل فإذاً إذ كان لا ضبط أشدّ جوراً وأقبح من الذي يكون في الغضب وكذلك يكون لا ضبط بنوع مبسوط لا شرّية بنوع ما (٤) وأيضاً ليس يشتم أحد ضدّ الحزن وكلّ من يفعل بغضب يفعل عند الحزن وأمّا الذي يفتري مع لذّة فإن كانت الأشياء التي بها يكون الغضب العادل أكثر ذلك هي أكثر جوراً فإذاً لا ضبط الذي يكون لمكان شهوة كذلك فإنّه ليس في الغضب فرية (٥) فأمّا اللا ضبط الذي في الشهوات أقبح من الذي في الغضب وبأنّ الضبط ولا صبط في الشهوات واللذّات الجسمية فبيّن (٦) فينبغي أن نأخذ فصول هذه بعينها فإنّه كما قيل في الابتداء بعضها إنسية وطبيعية وبالجنس والعظم وبعضها سبعية وبعضها لمكان الزمانات وفي أوائل هذه العفّة ولا عفّة فقط ومن أجل هذا لا نقول إنّ السباع أعفّاء ولا لا أعفّاء إلاّ باستعارة الاسم وبالجملة بالذي يتخالف جنس من جنس آخر من الشتم والانتقام وبأن [...] (٧) [...] قد خرج عن [...] [٣/١٢] سيكون قياس رداءة ما لا مبدأ أكثر ضرراً وأمّا العقل فمبدأ فقياس هذا كقياس الجور إلى الإنسان الجائر فاسمهما واحد فإنّ كلّ واحد منهما ردئ والإنسان الردئ خليق أن يفعل من الرداءة أكثر من السبع مراراً كثيرة.

2 وكذلك : F فكذلك Bad || 3 يفتري مع F, Dun : يفلانى فيتمتع ب Bad || 5 شهوة F : الشهوة Bad || 5 اللا ضبط corr. Dun : الاضبط F; لا ضبط Bad || 6 بأن F : أن Bad || 10 بالني F : التي بها Bad || 10 الشتم Dun : illegible F || 11 فمبدأ corr. Bad, Dun : بدئي F

7. In regard to the pleasures which are through touch and taste and in regard to the pains, desires and avoidance in which are intemperance and temperance, a distinction has already been drawn,[125] and perhaps it is the case that they are too high to be overcome, and perhaps they subdue what most are conquered by.[126] Of these, the man concerned with pleasures is restrained,[127] and the man concerned with pains is soft, though some of them are enduring.[128] Between most of them are [other] states,[129] and[130] people acquiesce more in the worst states. (2) For some pleasures are necessary, some are unnecessary, and for a certain time,[131] some are excesses, some defects,[132] and similarly in regard to the desires and pains, and he who [seeks] the excesses of pleasant things or exceeds the bounds[133] in regard to them by choice, for themselves, not for anything else which accrues, is intemperate, since this man must needs be unrepentant, and hence incurable, since he who does not repent is incurable. As for the man who is defective, he is the opposite, and the intermediate is the temperate man. Similarly he who avoids bodily pains, not because he is overcome but voluntarily. (3) As for those who flee[134] on account of what they did not choose, one yields on account of the pleasure, the other because he flees from the pain which is from the desire, so that between them there is a difference, and it may be thought that he is worse in every case[135] who does a disgraceful deed calmly,[136] not desiring, than him who does that with violent desire, and similarly if anyone strikes without anger he is worse than him who strikes in anger. And if not, could one say that if he were overcome [...][137] and hence the intem-

---

[125] I.e. Greek διωρίσθη is taken not with ἥ τε ἀκολασία καὶ ἡ σωφροσύνη as subject, but impersonally, as Arberry noted.

[126] The sentence by now of course is thoroughly embroiled.

[127] The translation should have said 'but the *other* man is restrained [...] but the *other* man is enduring'.

[128] See previous note.

[129] I.e. taking ἕξις as plural and disregarding ἡ.

[130] I.e. rendering καί simply for κἂν εἰ.

[131] Arabic *ilā waqt mā*, but the Greek μέχρι τινός is 'to a certain extent' ("up to a point", Ross; "jusqu'à un certain point", Gauthier).

[132] The words οὔ, οὐδέ are not translated, as Arberry noted.

[133] The translator finds a verb in the difficult expression ἢ καθ' ὑπερβολάς and omits the following ἤ.

[134] This is not in the Greek.

[135] Arabic *fī jamīʿ al-ḥālāt* for Greek παντί taken as neuter. But it is masculine and clearly goes with δόξειε, not with χείρων.

[136] Arabic *bi-rifq*, i.e. ἠρέμα for ἢ ἠρέμα (Arberry).

[137] Short lacuna.

٧. وأمّا في اللذّات التي تكون باللمس والذوق وفي الأحزان والشهوات والهرب التي فيها لا عفّة وعفّة فقد فصّل أوّلاً فربّما كانوا على هذه الحل حتّى يكونوا أرفع من أن يغلبوا وربّما ضبطوا الذي الأكثر من دونها ومن هؤلاء أمّا صاحب اللذّات فضابط وصاحب الأحزان فذو ليّن وبعضهم فصبور وفيما بين أكثرها هيئات ويسكنون في الهيئات الأردأ أكثر (٢) فإنّ بعض اللذّات اضطرارية وبعضها ليس باضطرارية وإلى وقت ما وبعضها زيادات وبعضها نقصانات وكذلك في الشهوات والأحزان والذي [طلب] زيادات الأشياء اللذيذة أو يفرط فيها بالاختيار لذاتها لا لشئ آخر يعرض فذلك لا عفيف من أجل أنّه اضطرّ ألاّ يكون هذا ذا ندامة ومن ها هنا لا برء له من أجل أنّ الذي لا يندم لا برء له وأمّا الذي ينقص فهو المقابل بالوضع وأمّا المتوسّط فالعفيف وكذلك الذي يهرب من الأحزان الجسمية لا لأنّه غلب بل لإرادته (٣) وأمّا الذين يهربون لمكان ما لم يختاروه فأحدهما ينقاد لمكان اللذّة والآخر لمكان أنّه يهرب عن الحزن الذي من الشهوة فإذاً فيما بينهما اختلاف وخليق أن يظنّ أنّه أردأ في جميع الحالات الذي يفعل فعلاً قبيحاً برفق وهو لا يشتهي من الذي يفعل ذلك بشهوة شديدة وكذلك إن كان أحد يضرب من غير غضب أردأ من الذي يضرب بغضب وإلاّ فما عسى أن يقول إذا غلبت عليه [....] ومن أجل

1 وفي corr. Dun : نفي F || 2 كانوا corr. Bad : كان F || 5 فإن F : وإن Bad || 6 طلب suppl. Dun || 12 أردأ F : اردني Bad || 12 الذي F, Dun : التي Bad || 14 يقول p uncertain F

perate man [...][138] (4) [...] restraint is in control and resistance is different from control, just as not to be conquered is different from
1150b conquering. On this account restraint is preferable to endurance. (5) As for him who is defective in regard to what most people resist and are able to do so, this man is soft and luxurious—and luxury is a kind of softness—, like him who trails his cloak so that he may not be tired by the pain of lifting it: he imitates a sick man and does not see that he is wretched since he is connected with the wretched. (6) Similarly in regard to restraint and lack of restraint. For it is not wonderful if someone is overcome by strong and excessive desires[139] or pains like these, rather it is excusable if he was resisting, like what the Philoctetes of Theodectes did, when he was bitten by vipers, and the dog which became a fox and was bitten by a crab,[140] and like those who desire to restrain their laughter and burst out laughing suddenly, like what happened to Xenophantus—but [it is wonderful if] someone cannot resist the things which most people can resist and is overcome by them,[141] on account of[142] a particular nature, like the softness in the kings of Scythia due to their birth, and like the distinction between female and male. (7) It is thought of the jester[143] that he is intemperate, when actually he is soft. Jesting is properly in lieu of rest, and the jester is one of those who are excessive in this. (8) Some lack of restraint is impetuosity, and some of it is weakness. For some people, when they have deliberated, do not abide by what they have resolved on because of passion, while others, because they have not deliberated, yield to passion. For some are like those who do [not] gargle,[144] because they have already experienced gargling.[145] Similarly after they have previously felt and known and, rousing up themselves and their reason, have gone forward, they are not overcome by passion, pleasant or painful. It is the hasty and excitable who are lacking in restraint with unrestrained impetuosity, for some

---

[138] Lacuna of several lines.

[139] Arabic *shahawāt*, evidently for *ladhdhāt*, 'pleasures' (Greek ἡδονῶν).

[140] According to Arberry a ludicrous mistranslation. The literary reference being unknown to the translator, he has supposed corruption of the text and emended according to his lights.

[141] Arabic *ghuliba minhā* (the marginal reading *ʿalaihā* is not an improvement, cf. 1150b 7 and 1151a 2).

[142] The negative μή ("except", Rackham) is left untranslated.

[143] Arabic *mazzāḥ* for Greek παιδιώδης.

[144] So apparently, the translator having confused Greek γαρχαλίζω, 'tickle', with γαργαρίζω, 'gargle'.

[145] See previous note.

هذا لا عفيف [...] (٤) [...] [٣/١٣] والضبط في الإمساك والمدافعة غير الإمساك كما أنه لا يُغلَب غير أن يَغلب ومن أجل هذا يختار الضبط أكثر من الصبر (٥) وأمّا الذي ينقص عن التي يدافع عنها أكثر الناس ويقدرون على ذلك فإنّ هذا ذو ليّن وصاحب ترف والترف ليّن ما كالذي بجرّ ثوبه لكيلا يتعب في حزن حمله ويتشبّه بالمريض ولا يرى أنّه شقي إذ كان يشبه بالشقي (٦) وكذلك في الضبط ولا ضبط فإنّه ليس بعجب إن غلب أحد من شهوات قوية مفرطة أو أحزان مثل هذه بل يعذر إذا كان يدافع مثلما فعل فلقطيطس ثيودقطس حين لسع من الأفاعي والكلب الذي صار ثعلباً ولسع من سرطان وكالذين يرومون أن يضبطوا الضحك فيقهقهون بغتةً كالذي عرض لأكسونوفنطس بل [يعجب إن] لم يقدر أحد أن يدافع الأشياء التي يقدر على مدافعتها أكثر الناس وغلب منها لمكان طبع خاصّ مثل الليّن الذي في ملوك الإسقوثا من الجنس وكالفصل الذي بين الأنثى والذكر (٧) ويظنّ بالمزّاح أنّه لا عفيف وهو ذو ليّن والمزاح أحرى بأن يكون يدلّ من أن يكون راحة فالمزّاح من الذين يفرطون في هذه (٨) وبعض لا ضبط إقدام وبعضه ضعف فإنّ بعضهم لمّا أجالوا الرأي لا يقتحمون على ما أجالوا الرأي لمكان الانفعل وبعضهم لأنهم لم يجلبوا [الرأي] انقادوا للانفعل فإنّ بعضهم كالذين [لا] يدغدغون لأنهم قد جرّبوا الدغدغة وكذلك لمّا قدّموا الحسّ والعلم وتقدّموا في نهوض ذاتهم وفكرهم لا يغلبون من الانفعل كان لذيذاً أو كان محزناً وإنّما يكونون لا ضابطين بإقدام لا ضبط

---

1 عفيف Dun : illegible F || 1 في corr. Dun : غير F, Bad || 3 التي F, Dun : الني Bad || 4 ثوبه يجر F, Dun : يجذبونه Bad || 4-5 شقي ... بالشقي Bad, Dun : شفى ... بالشفي F || 5 يشبه corr. Dun : ينسب F || 6 يعذر F, Dun : يعوز Bad || 6 إذا corr. Dun : إذ Bad, F || 6 فلقطيطس 3rd letter w.p. F || 7 ثيودقطس w.p. F || 8 يعجب إن suppl. Dun || 9 الأشياء corr. Dun : والأشياء Bad, F || 9 منها corr. mrg.; Bad inserts it after خاص || 10 الإسقوثا read. Arberry : w.p. F || 14 عليها F, Dun : الرأي suppl. Bad || 14 لا suppl. Dun* (où) || 14-15 يدغدغون ... الدغدغة corr. Bad : يغدغدون ... الغدغدة F

of them owing to quickness and others owing to vehemence do not wait for reason, because they follow imagination.

8. Nor [...][146] is not repentant, and the one who [...][147] cannot be cured, and the other less [...][148] different in kind from vice. For vice
1151a is concealed, but lack of restraint is not concealed. (2) Of the latter themselves, those whose understandings change are better than those who possess reason and do not abide by it. For they are overcome by a slight affliction and do not go forward after deliberation,[149] like others. For the man who lacks restraint is like those who get drunk quickly from a little dilute[150] wine, not like what intoxicates most people. (3) It is plain [that] lack of restraint is not a vice, though in a sense it is so, because the one is without choice, the other with choice. Yet they resemble each other[151] in the actions, like the saying of Demodocus about the Milesians,[152] when he said: 'The Milesians are not fools, but they act like fools through lack of experience', and those who do not restrain themselves are not unjust, though they act unjustly. (4) Since the man who is such is not like him who[153] employs[154] bodily pleasures to excess and contrary to the right rule, and the other, because he is like this, is convinced that he should pursue them, [it may be that] the conviction [of the former] is altered,[155] but not [the conviction] of the latter. For of virtue and vice, the one destroys the principle, while the other preserves it, and in the actions the final cause is a principle, like the principles[156] in mathematical matters. It is not then discourse[157] which teaches the goods[158] either

[146] Short lacuna.
[147] Lacuna.
[148] Longer lacuna.
[149] Arabic *wa-laisa yataqaddamūna baʿd jaulān ar-raʾy*, but the sense is wrong (Greek ἀπροβούλευτοι).
[150] Arabic *mabsūṭ*. This meaning is not given in most dictionaries, but of Dozy, s.v. I. *basaṭa*.
[151] Arabic *illā annahum mutashābihūna*, i.e. Greek ὅμοιον has been read as ὅμοιοι.
[152] Arabic *ahl Mīlisūs*. The translator does not know the name Miletus and forms the substantive from the Greek adjective incorrectly.
[153] Arabic *laisa mithl alladhī* mistranslates Greek ὁ μὲν τοιοῦτος οἷος μή, and the following words διὰ τὸ πεπεῖσθαι are simply omitted.
[154] Arabic *yastaʿmilu*, Greek διώκειν, 'pursues'.
[155] Arabic *bi-an yataghayyara qunūʿuhu*, cf. 1149b 25.
[156] Arabic *mabādiʾ*, Greek ὑποθέσεις.
[157] Arabic *al-kalimah*, Greek ὁ λόγος.
[158] Arabic *al-khairāt*, which, as Arberry notes, seems to render ἀγαθῶν for ἀρχῶν.

أصحاب الحدّة والمرّة السوداء فإنّ بعضهم لمكان السرعة وبعضهم لمكان الشدّة لا ينتظرون النطق لأنّهم يميلون إلى اتّباع الفنطاسيا.

٨. فلا [...] لا يعرض له الندم والذي [...] لا برء له والآخر أقلّ [...] [٣/١٤] غير جنس الشرّة فإنّ الشرّة تخفى وأمّا لا ضبط فلا يخفى (٢) ومن هؤلاء بأعيانهم فإنّ الذين تغيّرت عقولهم أجود من الذين لهم النطق ولا يثبتون عليه فإنّهم يغلبون من آفة صغيرة وليس يتقدّمون بعد جولان الرأي كغيرهم فإنّ لا ضابط شبيه بالذين يسكرون سريعاً من خمر مبسوط قليل لا كالذي يسكر أكثر الناس (٣) فبيّن [أنّ] لا ضبط ليس هو رداءة وإلاّ أن يكون بنوع ما من أجل أنّ بعضه بلا اختيار وبعضه بلختيار إلاّ أنّهم متشابهون بالأفعل كقول ديمودوقس في أهل ميلسوس حين قل إنّ أهل ميلسوس ليس هم بجهّل وهم يفعلون فعل الجهّل لقلّة التجربة والذين لا يضبطون أنفسهم ليس هم جائرين وهم يجورون (٤) وإذ كان الذي هو على هذه الحل ليس مثل الذي يستعمل اللذّات الجسمية بالإفراط وعلى غير القياس الصحيح وكان الآخر من أجل أنّه مثل هذا قد قنع أن يطلبها بأن يتغيّر قنوعه وأمّا هذا فلا فإنّ الفضيلة والرداءة إحداهما تتلف البدء والأخرى تسلّمه وفي الأفعل الذي من أجله هو بدء كالمبادئ في الأشياء التعليمية فليست الكلمة معلّمة

3 والذي Dun : illegible F || 3 لا برء له والآخر اقل Dun : illegible F || 7 أن suppl. Bad || 7-8 وإلا أن يكون : F وإن [كان] يكون [كذلك] corr. and add. Bad || 8 بلا اختيار corr. Bad : بالاختيار F || 8 بلختيار : F فلختيار Bad || 9 ديمودوقس corr. Bad : نوديقس F || 9 وهم : F وإنهم Bad || 12 أجل om. Bad || 13 تسلمه corr. Dun* (σῴζει) : سليمة F, Bad || 14 فليست corr. : فليس F

there or here, but virtue, natural or of the senses,[159] for it is the cause of correctness of opinion as regards the principle, so that he who is such is temperate and his opposite intemperate. (5) And perhaps there is one who diverges from the right rule because of some affliction, so that he does not do what he does according to the right rule through the affliction overcoming him. When such a man is able to convince himself that he is right that he should pursue these pleasures freely, [not] forcibly,[160] this is he who lacks restraint. He is better than the intemperate man and is not bad absolutely, since the principle which is best and sound[161] and is the opposite of this man, stands firm [...][162] and it is clear that [...][163] and the other is bad.

9. Is then [...][164] and right choice, as we were finding at first with difficulty?[165] Or is it possible accidentally, whichever of them it is, though essentially one of the two men holds to the true word and the
1151b right choice and the other does not? For if anyone chooses or seeks a thing for something else, [he gets][166] the thing accidentally. We only say 'without qualification' of what is so in itself. So then it is possible that there is the man who holds to any opinion whatever, and that there is the man who diverges from it and the man who holds to the true opinion.[167] (2) Some people hold to their opinion, and they call them 'strong in resolution'. They are those who are difficult to convince, and one does not change them[168] from their conviction. They have a likeness to the restrained man, as the prodigal is like the liberal man and the audacious like the brave man. But between them is much difference, for the restrained man does not change because of passion and desire, since, being restrained, he is excellent at being

---

[159] Arabic *ḥassīyah*, i.e. apparently Greek αἰσθητική for ἐθιστή (Arberry).

[160] Greek κρατεῖ is taken as dative of κράτος (Arberry), and the sentence has gone wrong.

[161] Arabic *salīm* for Greek σῴζεται.

[162] Short lacuna.

[163] Short lacuna.

[164] Longer lacuna.

[165] Arabic *bi-nauʿ al-ʿawīṣ*, used with *najidu* to translate ἠπορήθη. Greek ἀπορέω is elsewhere rendered by Arabic *shakka* (1095a 32 and 1096a 34).

[166] Arabic *akhadha* has dropped out after *ash-shaiʾ*. Greek καθ' αὑτὸ [...] διώκει is left untranslated (homoioteleuton), αἱρεῖται is construed with what follows, and δέ is disregarded.

[167] I.e. Greek ὁ τῇ ἀληθεῖ, as the vulg. As Arberry notes, ἁπλῶς has dropped out.

[168] Reading *wa-lā yughaiyiruhum* (Greek εὐμετάπειστοι, cf. VII, 8, 4 = 1151a 14) for *wa-lā yaʿṣūhum* of the text. Cf. also below, 1151b 14-15.

الخيرات لا هناك ولا ها هنا بل الفضيلة إمّا الطبيعية وإمّا الحسّية فإنّها علّة صحّة الرأي في البدء فالذي هو مثل هذا عفيف وضدّه لا عفيف (٥) وربّما كان أحد يخرج عن القياس الصحيح لآفة ما حتّى إنّه لا يفعل ما يفعل على القياس الصحيح لغلبة الآفة عليه فإذا كان مثل هذا يقوى على أن يقنع ذاته أنّه ينبغي أن يطلب هذه اللذّات بقحة و[لا] بقوّة فهذا هو لا ضابط وهو أجود من لا عفيف وليس يقدم فيها بنوع مبسوط من أجل أنّ البدء الذي هو أجود وسليم [...]

٩. [...] [٣/١٥] والاختيار الصحيح كما نجد أوّلاً بنوع العويص ويمكن بنوع العرض أيّهما كان وأمّا بذاته فأحدهما يثبت على الكلمة الصادقة والاختيار الصحيح والآخر لا يثبت فإنّ اختيار أو طلب أحد شيئاً لشئ أخر [أخذ] الشئ بنوع العرض وإنّما نقول بنوع مبسوط الذي هو بذاته فإذاً يمكن أن يكون من يثبت على أيّ رأي كان وأن يكون من يخرج عنه ومن يثبت على الرأي الصدق (٢) ومن الناس من يثبت على الرأي ويسمّونهم أقوياء العزم وهم الذين يعسر قنوعهم ولا يغيّرهم عن قنوعهم وبهم شبه ما من الضابط كشبه المسترخي للذي الحرّية وشبه المقدام للجرئ وبينهم اختلاف كثير فإنّ الضابط لا يتغيّر لمكان الانفعل والشهوة ومن أجل أنّه إذا كان ضابطاً يكون جيّد القنوع وأمّا هؤلاء فلا

2 ضده F, Dun : هذه Bad || 4 لا suppl. Dun* (où) || 4 بقوة corr. Dun : قوة F || 6 [...] illegible F, Dun *and is the opposite of this man, stands firm [...] and it is clear that [...] and the other is bad* || 7 [...] illegible F, Dun (partly) *is then* || 8 فإن corr. Dun : فإنه F, Bad || 9 [من أجل] شئ آخر [وهذا الأخير هو الذي طلب أو اختير بذاته ولكن أخذ الشئ [الأول] : F أحد شيئا لشئ أخر اخذ شئ Bad || 9 اخذ suppl. Dun || 12 يغيرهم corr. Dun : يعصوهم appar. F; يتيسر corr. Bad

convinced.[169] As for these, they do not yield to reason but cling to desires, and many a one yields to pleasures. (3) They only are strong in resolution who have special resolution,[170] on account of pleasure or pain. For they rejoice in victory if their conviction is not changed, and they are pained when their words, which are in their opinion like a reckoning,[171] are not confirmed, so that they are liker to[172] the restrained man. (4) Among men there is the one who does not hold to what he has opined, not because of lack of restraint, as Neoptolemus did, who is described in the work done by him[173] who called it *Philoctetes*, although[174] he did not hold fast on account of pleasures, and Odysseus had convinced him[175] [...] it is pleasure, he is intemperate [...] (5) [...] it appears that it also [...][176] few things,[177] its appearance is rare, and as it is thought of temperance that it is the opposite of intemperance only, so it is thought of restraint that it is the opposite of lack of restraint. (6) Since many things are said by similitude, the restraint of the temperate person must be spoken of by
1152a similitude also. For the restrained man as it were does nothing contrary to reason[178] on account of bodily pleasures,[179] but one of the two possesses bad desires, and the other[180] does not. One of them is like the man who does not feel pleasure contrary to reason, and the other is like him who feels pleasure.[181] The man who does not restrain himself also [...][182] resembling the intemperate, yet they are

[169] Arabic *jaiyid al-qunūʿ*, Greek εὔπειστος. The following words ὅταν τύχῃ are omitted. The sentence is wrongly construed (ὁ ἐγκρατής is of course the subject), and the sense is lost.

[170] Several words are here omitted through homoioteleuton.

[171] I.e. an exact tally, Arabic *ka'l-ḥisbah* for Greek ψηφίσματα, which was not understood in the sense of decrees passed in a legislative assembly.

[172] The words τῷ ἀκρατεῖ ἐοίκασιν ἤ are left untranslated, or perhaps rather the Arabic equivalent has been left out by a copyist, giving a contrary sense.

[173] I.e. Sophocles.

[174] Arabic *wa-'in*, Greek καίτοι.

[175] The text of the next few lines is frequently illegible, and there follows a lacuna of several lines.

[176] Short lacuna.

[177] *Sic* (Arabic *ashyā' qalīlah*) for Greek ἐν ὀλίγοις (masculine).

[178] Arabic *ʿalā khilāf an-nuṭq*, cf. 1152a 3.

[179] The vital words καὶ ὁ σώφρων are omitted, and the contrast intended fails to be expressd clearly.

[180] I.e. the temperate man, mention of whom has dropped out.

[181] Greek ἀλλὰ μὴ ἄγεσθαι is not in the Arabic translation.

[182] Short lacuna.

ينقادون للكلمة بل يتشبّثون بالشهوات وكثير من ينقاد للذّات (٣) وإنّما يكونون أقوياء العزم الذين لهم عزم خاصّ لمكان اللذّة أو الحزن فإنّهم يفرحون عند الغلبة إن لم يتغيّر قنوعهم ويحزنون إذا لم تثبت أقاويلهم التي هي عندهم كالحسبة فإذاً هم أشبه بالضابط (٤) ومن الناس من لا يثبت على ما قد رأى لا من أجل لا ضبط كما فعل ناوبطولاموس الذي يوصف في كتاب قد فعله الذي يسمّيه فليقطيطس وإن كان لم يثبت لمكان لذّات جيّداً وقد أقنعه أودوسوس [...] كان اللذّة ليس هو عفيف [...] [٣/١٦] (٥) [...] تظهر أنّها أيضاً [...] أشياء قليلة يكون ظهورها قليلاً وكما أنّه يظنّ بالعفّة أنّها ضدّ لا عفّة فقط كذلك يظنّ بالضبط أنّه ضدّ لا ضبط (٦) وإذ يقل بالتشبيه الأشياء الكثيرة فإنّه ينبغي أن يقل ضابط العفيف بالتشبيه أيضاً فإنّ الضابط لا يفعل على خلاف النطق لمكان اللذّات الجسمية ولكن أحدهما له الشهوات الرديئة والآخر ليس له هذه وأحدهما كالذي لا يلذّ على خلاف النطق والآخر كالذي يلذّ ولا ضابط أيضاً [...] يشابه لا عفيف وهما آخر وآخر

3 كالحسبة corr. Dun : كالحسنة F, Bad || 4 ناوبطولاموس w.p. F || 5 فليقطيطس w.p. F || 5 لذات F : لذة Bad || 6 تظهر أنها F : تظهران Bad || 8-9 أن يقل ضابط F, Dun : للضابط Bad

quite different. Both of them pursue bodily pleasures,[183] but one of them thinks that that is right, while the other does not think so.

10. It is not possible that the same man is intelligent and also lacking in restraint at the same time. It has been proved that a man is at once intelligent[184] and good in character. (2) Also the intelligent[185] man is not so through knowledge alone but also[186] through action. As for the man who lacks restraint, he is not practical. As for the clever man, nothing prevents him being lacking in restraint. On account of this it is sometimes thought of some people that they are intelligent but lack restraint, since between cleverness and intelligence there is a distinction according to the way which has been spoken of in the first discussions. In significance the two are closely akin, yet they differ in respect of choice. (3) There is no difference between[187] him who knows and him who possesses opinion, except as between[188] the sleeping man and the man drunk by his own will,[189] for he knows in a way what he does and why, and is not bad[190] [...] a city which reckons all[191] [...]. (4) [...] the opposite of this holds out more and the other less strongly than most people can. The most quickly cured of the types of lack of restraint is that belonging to melancholic persons, for they are more quickly cured than those who deliberate and do not stand firm. Similarly those who do not restrain themselves owing to habit are more quickly cured than those whose lack of restraint is natural. For change of habit is easier than change of nature, and habit is hard [to change] simply because it resembles nature, as Evenus said:

> He said:[192] Practice from length of time
> Is soon complete nature to men.

---

[183] Lit. 'pleasant and bodily things'.

[184] See previous note.

[185] See previous note.

[186] Arabic *bal wa-* for Greek ἀλλὰ καί.

[187] Evidently a mistake (δέ read as διαφέρει, or διαφέρει supplied from the preceding διαφέρειν, and the first ὡς —line14 of the Greek—omitted).

[188] The Arabic translation again goes wrong, vid. previous note.

[189] Arabic *al-makhmūr bi-irādatihi*, i.e. καὶ ἑκὼν μέν construed with what precedes.

[190] The text of the next few lines becomes illegible as a continuity.

[191] Arabic *madīnah taḥsubu bi-jamīʿ* (Arberry). This must render the first words of the verse ἡ πόλις ἐβούλεθ' [...]. For *taḥsubu* cf. 1151b 15-16.

[192] Greek is φημί.

فكلاهما يطلب الأشياء اللذيذة والجسمية ولكن أحدهما يرى أنّه ينبغي ذلك والآخر لا يرى ذلك.

١٠. ولا يمكن أن يكون هو بعينه عاقلاً ولا ضابطاً معاً أيضاً فقد برهن أنّه معاً العاقل والفاضل الخلق (٢) وأيضاً ليس العاقل بالعلم فقط بل وبالفعل وأمّا لا ضابط فليس هو ذا فعل وأمّا الداهي فليس شيء يمنع أن يكون لا ضابط ومن أجل هذا ظنّ ببعض الناس أنّهم عقلاء مع أنّهم لا ضابطون لمكان أنّ بين الدهاية والعقل فصلاً على قدر النوع الذي قد قيل في الأقاويل الأوّل وهما أمّا بالكلمة فيتقاربان ويختلفان لمكان الاختيار (٣) ولا بين الذي يعلم وذي الرأي اختلاف إلاّ كما بين النائم والمخمور بإرادته يفعل فإنّه يعلم بنوع ما ما يفعل ومن أجل ماذا يفعل وليس هو رديئاً [...] المدينة تحسب بالجميع [...] (٤) [...] [١/٧٣] أكثر ثباتاً والآخر أقلّ في قوّة أكثر الناس والذي هو أسرع برءً من أنواع لا ضبط النوع الذي لأصحاب مرّة سوداء فإنّهم أسرع برءً من الذين يجيلون الرأي ولا يثبتون وكذلك الذين لا يضبطون أنفسهم لمكان العادة أسرع برءً من الذين لا ضبط لهم طبيعي فإنّ انتقل العادة أهون من انتقل الطبيعة وإنّما صعبت العادة من أجل أنّها تشبه الطبيعة كما قل أوينيوس:

قل إنّ الدراس بكثرة الزمان
يكون للناس سريعاً بطبع تامّ

---

3 يكون : F يتفق Bad || 3 هو : F هذا Bad || 5 ظن ببعض : F, Dun فقد يظن بعض Bad || 7 يختلفان corr. : يختلفون F, Bad || 8 الذي corr. Bad : الذين F || 8 بإرادته F, Dun : بإرادته Bad || 10 [...] illegible F, Dun (partly) *the opposite of this holds out* || 11 لأصحاب مرة سوداء F, Dun : لأهل المرة السوداء Bad || 13 صعبت Dun : ثبتت Bad || 14 أوينيوس Bad : اوسوجس appar. F || 16 سريعا F, Dun : شبيها Bad

(5) It has now been said what restraint and lack of restraint, endurance and softness, are, and how these states are in relation to one another.

1152b 11. Examination of pleasure and pain belongs to the political philosopher, for this man is the chief architect of the end, and to it we look and say of everything that it is good or bad absolutely. (2) Also, to inquire about them[193] is one of the obligatory matters. For we have already posited that moral virtue and vice are related to pains and pleasures. Most people think that happiness is with pleasure, and for that reason they call a man blessed because he enjoys. (3) Some people think that not a single pleasure is good [...][194] accident, since good and pleasure are not the same. Other people think that some pleasures are goods, but that most of them are bad. Also there are other people who have a third opinion, that all of them are good, yet pleasure is something which cannot be the best. (4) Pleasure in general is not a good, since every pleasure is a process[195] in a nature perceived by the senses,[196] and no single process[197] resembles the ends, as when I say that no[198] [...] the temperate man avoids pleasures, and also the intelligent man seeks what the weak man does not wish for.[199] Also pleasures are a hindrance to thinking [...][200] the sexual pleasures, for it is not possible for anyone to understand anything in them. Also there is no art which seeks for pleasure, although every good is [...][201] (5) [...] since some pleasures[202] cause disease. Pleasure is not excellent,[203] since it is not an end but a process. These are most of the opinions which have been given on the matter.

---

[193] I.e. pleasure and pain.

[194] Short lacuna.

[195] Arabic *kaun* in sense of 'a coming into existence' (Greek γένεσις). Cf. below, n. 199, also 1173a 30, 1173b 4, 1174b 10, etc.

[196] Arabic *ṭabʿ maḥsūs*, i.e. apparently εἰς φύσιν αἰσθητή wrongly construed together.

[197] See note 197.

[198] Illegible word follows.

[199] This is no doubt a paraphrase of the Greek.

[200] Words illegible.

[201] Three lines illegible.

[202] Arabic *al-ladhdhāt*, i.e. rendering τῶν ἡδονῶν rather than τῶν ἡδέων.

[203] This represents the old reading of the Greek οὐκ ἄριστον, corrected by Spengel followed by the editors.

(٥) فقد قيل ما الضبط وما لا ضبط وما الصبر وما اللين وكيف هذه الهيئات بعضها إلى بعض.

١١. وأمّا النظر في اللذّة والحزن فلصاحب الفلسفة المدنية فإنّ هذا هو رئيس بحار الغاية وإليه النظر والقول على كلّ واحد من الأشياء إنّه جيّد أو ردئ بنوع مبسوط (٢) وأيضاً الفحص عنها من الأشياء المضطرّة فإنّا قد وصفنا أنّ الفضيلة والشرّية الخلقية ترتبط بالأحزان واللذّات وأكثر الناس يقولون إنّ السعادة مع اللذّة ومن أجل هذه العلّة سمّوه المغبوط من أجل أنّه يفرح (٣) فمن الناس من يرى أنّ لا خير في اللذّة [...] العرض من أجل أنّ ليس الخير واللذّة شيئاً واحداً ومن الناس من يرى أنّ بعض اللذّات خيرات وأنّ معظمها ردئ وأيضاً من الناس من يرى رأياً ثالثاً أنّ كلّها خير إلاّ أنّها لا يمكن أن تكون الأفضل (٤) فاللذّة أمّا بنوع كلّي فليس تكون خيراً لأنّ كلّ لذّة هي كون في طبع محسوس وليس ولا كون واحداً هو من جنس غاية كقولي إنّه ليس [...] العفيف يهرب عن اللذّات وأيضاً العاقل يطلب الذي لا يطلبه الضعيف وأيضاً إنّ اللذّات تشغل عن التعقّل [...] لذّات الجماع لأنّه لا يمكن أحداً أن يفهم بها شيئاً وأيضاً ليس توجد صناعة واحدة للذّة وإن كان كلّ خير [...] (٥) [...] [١/٧٤] أنّ بعض اللذّات تمرض وإمّا أنّ اللذّة ليست فاضلة من أجل أنّها ليست تماماً بل كوناً فهذه جلّ الأقاويل التي تقل في ذلك.

---

3 الغاية appar. Dun : العلم Bad || 8 خيرات F : خير Bad || 14 خير F, Dun : شئ Bad

12. That it results[204] for these opinions that [pleasure] is not a good, and that it is not the best, is plain from the following. First, since the good is of two kinds, part in an absolute sense and part for a particular thing,[205] the natural states[206] follow it, as do the movements and processes.[207] The bad pleasures,[208] which are thought to be bad absolutely and for a particular thing,[209] are not so. But they are chosen for this one thing[210] and some not even for this,[211] except at a particular time and for a short time. As for choosing them[212] no. Some of them are not hateful,[213] but appear so, viz. all those which involve pain and are for healing [and health], like those of the sick. (2) Also, since some good is action and some a state incidentally,[214] they are subservient to[215] the natural state, since they are actions in the desires of the state and nature,[216] because [the sweetest] pleasures are without pain and without desire also, like [...][217] since they enjoy sharp and bitter
1153a things and none of these is sweet by nature or absolutely. So then
[...][218] and from one another, so the pleasures arising from these differ. Also [...][219] (3) [...] necessary that there should be something better than pleasure, as some people assert. Rather [...][220] with a process [...][221] happen to be an end coming into being, but an end

---

[204] Arabic *annahu yaʿriḍ*. The negative has been left out, cf. the Greek: Ὅτι δ' οὐ συμβαίνει.

[205] Greek τινί taken as neuter.

[206] For Greek αἱ φύσεις καὶ αἱ ἕξεις, i.e. the natures and the states.

[207] Cf. above, n. 197.

[208] Strictly the Arabic translation should speak of the 'processes' or 'movements and processes' (αἱ κινήσεις καὶ αἱ γενέσεις) just mentioned.

[209] See note 197.

[210] Greek τῷδε (twice in line 30 of the Greek text) is masculine, like τινί above.

[211] See previous note.

[212] This involves reading αἱρεταί [or αἵρεται] δ' οὔ for αἱρεταὶ <ἁπλῶς or ἀεὶ> δ' οὔ.

[213] Arabic *bi-baghīḍah* for Greek οὐδ' ἡδοναί, read apparently as οὐ (οὐδὲ) δειναί.

[214] Arabic *bi-nauʿ al-ʿarḍ*, i.e. Greek κατὰ συμβεβηκός wrongly construed with the foregoing τὸ δ' ἕξις.

[215] Arabic apparently *khādimah*. This should render Greek καθιστᾶσαι, rather than ἡδεῖαι, which appears to be omitted.

[216] Greek ὑπολοίπου is not rendered, and τῆς [...] ἕξεως καὶ φύσεως is wrongly construed with ταῖς ἐπιθυμίαις (instead of with <ἐνέργεια> supplied).

[217] Several lines illegible.

[218] Words illegible.

[219] Words illegible.

[220] Words illegible.

[221] Words illegible.

١٢. وأمّا أنّه يعرض لهذه الأقاويل ألاّ تكون خيراً وألاّ تكون الأفضل فبيّن من هذه أمّا أوّلاً فمن أجل أنّ الخير على نوعين فإنّ بعضه بنوع مبسوط وبعضه لشئ ما فالهيئات الطبيعية مستتبعة أو تستتبع الحركات والأكوان والرديئة التي يظنّ بها رديئة بنوع مبسوط وأمّا لشئ ما فلا بل إنّها مختارة لهذا الواحد وبعضها فلا لهذا أيضاً إلاّ في وقت ما وفي زمان قليل وأمّا اختيارها فلا وبعضها ليست ببغيضة ولكن تظهر وهي جميع التي تكون مع حزن ولمكان علاج بالبرء كالتي للمرضى (٢) وأيضاً إذ كان بعض الخير فعلاً وبعضه هيئة بنوع العرض على الهيئة الطبيعية خادمة من أجل أنّها أفعل في شهوات الهيئة والطبيعة ومن أجل لذّات لا تنطوي على حزن أو شهوة أبداً مثل [...]

1 يعرض لهذه F, Dun : تعني هذه Bad || 4 first لهذا F, Dun : تختار Bad || 8 – p. 413, l. 1 [...] : illegible F, *since they enjoy [...] injurious to health* Dun

employed.[222] And also [...][223] other things [...][224] nature, and hence[225] [...] the natural state [...] and it is something else. (4) As for the view that they[226] are bad because some [...][227] the same, because some healthy things also are bad for enrichment.[228] In this way [...] but they are not bad,[229] for investigation at that time[230] is injurious to health. (5) No one prevents or understands[231] the pleasure which is from each of them, but foreign pleasures prevent it. And since from those who think and learn they produce thought and instruction[232] [...]. (6) [...] incidentally that no single pleasure is the work of an art [...], because there is no art of another work but of the capacity only, although it is thought of the art of applying perfume and that which produces the different kinds of cooking that they are for pleasure. (7) That the temperate man avoids doing that which the intelligent man does not pursue,[233] whereas children and animals pursue it—all this is solved by one and the same thing. Since it has been said how all[234] pleasures are goods in an absolute sense, and how they are not goods, and that children and animals seek the like of these and those of them that are painless,[235] and the intelligent man seeks such pleasures as involve desire and pain, and are bodily pleasures,[236] for these are so, and he avoids excess of these, in respect of which the intemperate man is intemperate. Hence the temperate man avoids these, since the temperate man has pleasures also.

---

[222] Apparently γινόμενον [...] χρώμενον has been read, the latter word taken as passive.

[223] Words illegible.

[224] Words illegible.

[225] An illegible line follows.

[226] Sc. pleasures.

[227] Lacuna.

[228] Arabic *ījād* for Greek χρηματισμόν.

[229] Greek κατά γε τοῦτο apparently left untranslated.

[230] I.e. τότε for ποτέ (Arberry).

[231] *Sic* (Arabic *wa-laisa yamnaʿ wa-lā yafham wāḥid*), i.e. φρονήσει has been taken as a verb.

[232] This is only a distant approximation to the Greek. A short lacuna follows.

[233] Greek τὸν ἄλυπον βίον omitted in Arabic and the negation (*lā*) inserted (Arberry).

[234] Greek πᾶσαι is misplaced.

[235] Arabic *mā lā yuḥzin minhā*, i.e. Greek τὴν τούτων ἀλυπίαν wrongly translated and construed. These words are parenthetic going closely with [διώκει] ὁ φρόνιμος.

[236] This of course is the opposite of what the Greek says.

[٣/١٧] [...] (٥) وليس يمنع ولا يفهم واحد اللذّة التي تكون من كلّ واحد منها بل تمنع الغريبة وإذ يصيرون من الذين يرون ويتعلّمون الرأي والتعليم [...] (٦) [...] عرض ألاّ تكون ولا لذّة واحدة فعل المهنة [...] من أنّه ليس المهنة تفعل آخر البتّةَ [...] القوّة وإن كان يظنّ بمهنة لطبخ العطر والصانعة ألوان الطبخ أنّها للذّة (٧) وبأنّ العفيف يهرب من العمل الذي لا يطلبه العاقل وبأنّ الصبيان والسباع تطلبه فحلّ جميع هذه شئ واحد هو هو وإذ قيل كيف جميع اللذّات خيرات بنوع مبسوط وكيف ليست بخيرات وأنّ الصبيان والسباع تطلب ما كان مثل هذه وما لا يحزن منها والعاقل يطلب ما كان منها بشهوة وحزن والتي هي جسمية فإنّ هذه كذلك ويهرب من إفراط هذه التي بها يكون لا عفيف ومن أجل هذا يهرب العفيف من هذه من أجل أنّ للعفيف لذّات أيضاً.

3 second [...] : illegible F, *but of (...) only* Dun || 4 لطبخ العطر والصانعة ألوان F, Dun : للذات
العاقل 5 || Bad الطبخ والعطر أنها صانعة Bad || 4 الطبخ أنها للذة Dun : illegible F || 4 بأن F : أن
العمل الذي لا يطلبه F, Dun : اللذة وأن العاقل يطلب الخلو من الألم corr. Bad

1153b 13. Also it is agreed that pain is bad and to be avoided. If there exists absolutely bad or good,[237] then necessarily pleasure is a good. For it does not turn out that the solution is like the solution of Speusippus, that the greater is the opposite of the lesser and the equal, for it is impossible that he should say that pleasure is like what is evil. (2) Nothing prevents a particular pleasure being good,[238] and since some pleasures are bad,[239] just as a particular knowledge of a particular thing is bad,[240] and it may be that that is a necessity, since the actions of every state are unimpeded, whether the action of all of them is happiness or the action of some one of them, when unimpeded, and[241] it is most desireable, I mean, when it is pleasure. So then it will be a certain pleasure which is the best, even if [...][242] one of the things impeded from being complete. As for happiness with [...][243] the pleasure which is in the body and which is from without, and which belongs to the soul,[244] in order that these things may not prevent him.[245] (3) As for those who say that he who is rich and he who has fallen into great misfortune is happy, if he is not[246] good, they say nothing, whether they are speaking voluntarily or involuntarily, (4) since, if[247] it requires luck, some people think that good luck and happiness are the same. But it is not so, for this also, when excessive, is an impediment, and it may be that it is not right that it should remain 'good luck', since its definition is related to happiness. (5) Also in the fact that all, men and beasts, seek pleasure, is a proof that it is somehow good:

---

[237] A number of words have been omitted after ἡ [read as εἰ, Arberry] μὲν γὰρ ἁπλῶς κακόν ἡ [read as ἥ = corr.^{2} K^b] by homoioteleuton.

[238] Arabic *khairan*, i.e. τἄριστον of codd. as against Spengel's ἄριστον, 'the (supreme) good'.

[239] The clause should be construed with the foregoing, cf. the Greek.

[240] This fails to render the Greek.

[241] This 'and' is a mistake. The words αἱρετωτάτην εἶναι are dependent on the foregoing ἀναγκαῖον.

[242] The text for a line or two is very defective.

[243] A word or two is still missing.

[244] I.e. ψυχῆς for τύχης (Arberry).

[245] I.e. the old reading of the Greek, but it is mistranslated: ταῦτα is accusative, 'in these ways', cf. Burnet *in loco*, not subject.

[246] But the Greek is ἐὰν ᾖ ἀγαθός, 'if he is good'. Arberry suggested that ἐὰν μὴ ἀγαθός was read.

[247] Arabic *in*; apparently δέ is read as εἰ.

١٣. وأيضاً ممّا يقرّ به أنّ الحزن ردئ مهروب عنه فإن كان بنوع مبسوط ردئ أو خير فمضطرّ أن تكون اللذّة خيراً ما فإنّه لا يعرض أن يكون الحلّ كحلّ أسبوسبوس كما أنّ الأكبر ضدّ الأصغر والمساوي إذ لا يمكن أن يقول إنّ اللذّة كالشئ الردئ (٢) وليس يمنع مانع أن تكون لذّة ما خيراً ولمّا كانت بعض اللذّات رديئة كما أنّه علم ما لبعض ما هو ردئ وخليق أن يكون ذلك اضطراراً إذ كانت أفعل كلّ هيئة غير ممنوعة كان فعل كلّها سعادة أو كان فعل بعضها إذا كان غير ممنوع وكان [...] كان لذّة فإذاً سيكون لذّةً ما التي هي أجود وإن [٣/٨] [...] واحد من الأفعل الممنوعة يمكن أن يكون كاملاً [...] اللذّة في الجسم والتي من خارج والتي للنفس لكيلا تمتنعه هذه (٣) وأمّا الذين يظنّون أنّ الذي أيسر والذي قد وقع في رداعة بخت يكون سعيداً إن لم يكن خيراً فليس يقولون شيئاً لا إن كانوا يقولون بإرادتهم أو كانوا يقولون بغير إرادتهم (٤) فمن أجل أنّه إن يحتاج إلى البخت ظنّ بعض الناس أنّ جودة البخت والسعادة شئ واحد وليست كذلك فإنّ هذه أيضاً إذا أفرطت تكون ممانعة وخليق ألاّ يكون واجباً أن يبقى جودة بخت من أجل أنّ حدّها يضاف إلى السعادة (٥) وأيضاً في طلب جميع الناس والسباع اللذّة دليل ما أنّها جيّدة بنوع ما

4 لما : لو Bad || 5 اضطرارا : باضطرار Bad || 6 [...] : illegible F, *most desirable, I mean, when* Dun || 6 ما om. Bad || 6 التي corr. Bad : الذ F || 7 second [...] : illegible F, *as for happiness with* Dun (partly) || 8 تمتنعه هذه F, Dun : ممتنعة بهذه Bad || 9 سعيدا corr. Bad : سعيد F || 9 لم يكن F, Dun : كان Bad* (ﯨ) || 12 يبقى F, Dun : يلفى Bad || 12 حدها corr. Dun : أحدها F; أحدهما corr. Bad

I say:[248] No pleasure is unrestricted in all cases
But that which is the most.[249]

(6) But since no nature and no state is excellent in itself alone, nor is thought to be so, similarly all men do not seek exactly the same pleasure, but they may all seek pleasure, not that which they think nor that which they would say, but that which is one, since all things have something divine. But the bodily pleasures have been allotted the name, since we come to them frequently and since all men share
1154a them, since they alone are known.[250] (7) It is plain that if the pleasure, which is in the activity, is not a good, it is not possible that one should live in pain either.[251] Pain is neither a good nor an evil, since pleasure also is neither a good nor an evil, so then why does he avoid it? Also, the life of the excellent man is not pleasanter unless it is in the activity.

14. We must investigate the bodily pleasures and the statements which are made concerning them. For it is said that [some] pleasures are very desirable, such as the noble ones, not the bodily pleasures to which the intemperate man is related. (2) Why then are the contrary pains bad? For the contrary of bad is good.[252] Up to what point[253] does good[254] reach? For all the states and movements which do not admit of excess in what is better, do not admit of excess in pleasure either [...][255] what is better, admit of excess in pleasure also. The bodily goods admit of excess [...][256] is so by his seeking excess, not by his seeking the necessary things. For all love in some way the different kinds of food and wine and sexual intercourse, but not all as they ought. As regards pain, it is the contrary case. For he does not avoid the excess but [pain] in general, for there is no pain con-

[248] I.e. φημί for φήμη, as Arberry noted. Here at least the Arabic translator or annotator did not consult a copy of Hesiod, cf. 1095b 10ff. (= I, 4, 7), apparently not recognising that this was a quotation (*Works and Days*, 763). (In the other passage the poet's name is mentioned.)

[249] Or 'that which belongs to the majority', reading the Arabic *li'l-akthar*.

[250] οὖν has already been omitted, several words are left out.

[251] The translator has telescoped the passage, as Arberry noted. It is, as so often, another case of homoioteleuton (ζῆν in 1154a 2 and again in 4).

[252] Text *khairan*, corr. *khairun*, after which several words of the Greek are omitted (ἢ οὕτως [...] ἀγαθόν ἐστιν).

[253] Translates the Greek του as τοῦ.

[254] Arabic *al-khair*, i.e. ἀγαθόν for ἀγαθαί.

[255] Short lacuna.

[256] Short lacuna.

أقول ليس لذّة ما مرسلة في جميع الحالات

بل التي هي الأكثر

(٦) ولكن إذ ليس لا طبع ولا هيئة بجيّدة هي بعينها واحدة ولا يظنّ أنّها كذلك ليس يطلبون أجمعين ولا لذّة واحدة بعينها ولكن خليق أن يكونوا أجمعين يطلبون لذّة ليس الذي يظنّون ولا التي خليق أن يقولوا بل التي هي واحدة من أجل أنّ لجميع الأشياء شيئاً إلهياً ولكن أخذت اللذّات الجسمية قديمة الاسم من أجل أنّا نصير إليها كثيراً ومن أجل الجميع يقتسمونها من أجل أنّها وحدها معروفة (٧) وهو بيّن أنّه إن لم تكن اللذّة التي بالفعل خيراً لا يمكن أن يحيا بحزن أيضاً والحزن لا خير ولا شرّ إذ كانت اللذّة أيضاً لا خير ولا شرّ فإذاً لِمَ يهرب عنها وأيضاً لا يكون عمر الفاضل ألذّ إن لم يكن له بالفعل.

١٤. فينبغي أن نبحث عن اللذّات الجسمية والأقاويل التي تقل عليها فإنّه يقل إنّ لذّات مختارة بمنزلة اللذّات الجميلة لا الجسمية التي ينتسب إليها لا عفيف (٢) فلِمَ صارت الأحزان الضدّية رديئة فإنّ ضدّ الشرّ خير وإلى أين ينتهي الخير فإنّ جميع الهيئات والحركات التي [٣/١٩] ليس لها إفراط في الأجود ليس لها إفراط ولا في اللذّة [...] الأجود لها إفراط اللذّة أيضاً وإنّما الإفراط للخيرات الجسمية [...] هو بطلبه الإفراط لا بطلبه الأشياء المضطرّة فإنّ الجميع يحبّون تذوّق ألوان الطبيخ والخمور والجماع ولكن ليس على ما ينبغي وأمّا في الحزن [...] ضدّي فإنّه ليس يهرب من الإفراط بل [الحزن] بنوع

2 الأكثر F, Bad, Dun : للأكثر perh. corr. Dun || 3 second ليس F : فليس Bad || 5 اجل أن لجميع corr. Bad, Dun : أجل الجميع F || 6 أنا نصير read. Dun : أنها تصير F, Bad || 8 بحزن ... والحزن corr. Bad, Dun : والجود ... بجود F || 9 ألذ إن F, Dun : إذ Bad || 9 له F, Dun : له في Bad || 11 الجميلة corr. Bad*, Dun* (αἱ καλαί) : الحية F || 11 فلم corr. Bad, Dun : فلو F || 12 خير corr. Bad, Dun : خيرا F || 12 أين corr. mrg., Dun : أن F, Bad || 14 لها F : فلها Bad || 14 اللذة F : اللذة Bad || 16 الحزن suppl. Dun

trary to the excess but[257] for him who seeks excess specially. (3) Since not only must the truth be told, but also the cause of the lie, for that agrees with[258] persuasion, for when the necessity, apparently true of any cause, appears, it does not produce conviction of what is not true any more than what is true,[259] so then let us say why the bodily pleasures appear more to be chosen than others. (4) The reason for that is, in the first place (A), because they expel pain. Since pleasure is a cure for excess of pain,[260] men seek excessive pleasures and, in general, bodily pleasure. The cure is potent, hence it is sought for, since it appears without the contrary.[261] It is thought that pleasure is not good for these two reasons, as has already been said, in consequence of (a) some pleasures being actions of a nature bad from birth, like the action of a wild beast, and (b) others being from habit, like the cures of bad men,[262] because they have a defect,[263] and
1154b it is better than to be.[264] Some of them[265] occur for those which are being complete,[266] and they are not[267] perfect accidentally. (5) Further (B), they are sought because they are potent on the part of those who are unable to like any others—people whose pleasures[268] are so many kinds of thirst.[269] When they are not harmful, they are not forbidden. When they are harmful, that is bad, because

---

[257] Arabic *bal* for Greek ἀλλά as in the previous line, i.e. ἤ is left untranslated.

[258] Arabic *muwāfiq* does not appear to render Greek συμβάλλεται correctly.

[259] The sentence 'it does not produce conviction [...]' has been 'emended' by omission of ὂν ἀληθές, and τῷ ἀληθεῖ is construed with μᾶλλον as if it were a genitive of comparison rather than with πιστεύειν.

[260] The translation is not exact.

[261] Arabic *min ghair aḍ-ḍidd* for παρὰ τὸ ἐναντίον, but παρά here is 'in comparison with'.

[262] I.e. reading αἱ τῶν φαύλων ἀνθρώπων ἰατρεῖαι with omission of αἱ δέ.

[263] I.e. reading apparently ὅτι ἐνδεεῖς.

[264] I.e. apparently 'it is better to have a defect than to be bad'.

[265] For αἳ δέ—the mistake is natural.

[266] Arabic *li'llatī tatimmu* for Greek τελεουμένων.

[267] I.e. οὐ for οὖν of the Greek (Arberry).

[268] Arabic *fa-hum ladhdhātuhum*. A marginal note reads *ṣalāḥ ẓ[āhir]*, the corrector evidently felt that something (i.e. παρασκευάζουσιν, which, as Arberry noted, is untranslated) was lacking and altered the reading in the text. But this of course does not mean that he had the Greek original before him (i.e. obvious correction *fa-bihim li-ladhdhātihim*).

[269] This is not right; the Greek speaks of people creating thirsts for themselves.

كلّي فإنّه ليس للإفراط حزن ضدّي بل للذي يطلب الإفراط بنوع خاصّ (٣) وإذ لا ينبغي أن يقل الصدق فقط بل ينبغي أن تقل علّة الكذب فإنّ ذلك موافق للإقناع فإنّه إذا ظهر الوجوب لأيّ علّة يظهر أنّه صدق لا نصير أن نقنع بالذي ليس صدقاً أكثر من الذي هو صدق فإذن فلنقل لأيّ علّة تظهر اللذّات الجسمية أنّها في الاختيار أكثر من غيرها (٤) والعلّة في ذلك أمّا أوّلاً من أجل أنّها تدفع الحزن ولمّا كانت اللذّة برءً من إفراط الحزن طلبوا اللذّة المفرطة وبالجملة الجسمية وتكون البرئية قوية ومن أجل هذا تطلب من أجل أنّها تظهر من غير الضدّ ويظنّ باللذّة أنّها ليست فاضلة لمكان هاتين العلّتين كما قد قيل من أنّ بعضها أفعال طبيعة رديئة من المولد كفعل السبع وبعضها من أجل العادة كعلاجات أشرار الناس من أجل أنّ لهم نقصاً وهو أجود من أن يكون وبعضها يعرض للتي تتمّ فهي ليست بفاضلة بنوع العرض (٥) وأيضاً تطلب لأنّها قوية من الذين لا يقدرون أن يحبّوا غيرها فهم لذّاتهم أنواع عطش ما فإذا كانت لا تضرّ لا تمنع وإذا كانت ضارّة كان ذلك رديئاً من أجل أنّه ليس لهم أشياء أخر يسرّون بها إذا لم يكن ولا واحد

---

1 للذي corr. Dun : الذي F, Bad || 8 طبيعة corr. Dun : طبيعية F, Bad || 9 second من om. Bad || 10 ليست corr. Bad : ليس F || 11 لذاتهم corr. Dun : لذاتها F || 11 second لا F : فلا Bad

they have no other things to delight in, since neither of them[270] is painful to many owing to their nature. For it is said that an animal is naturally tired, according to the witness of the physiologists[271] also, since they say that sight and hearing cause pain, but we have become accustomed to that, as they say (6) generally[272] of youth on account of growth, like the condition of drunkards, and youth is pleasant. But as for those whose nature is that of the black bile,[273] they need treatment, for their temperament[274] is tormented [...][275] much, and they are forever in a state of violent desire, and pleasure [...][276] has supervened strongly. For this reason they are intemperate and are bad.[277] (7) Those pleasures which are without pains have no excess. These are among the things pleasant naturally, not accidentally. I mean by pleasant accidentally the things which cure, for it happens to him who persists in being treated that he does an action by way of health, hence it is thought to be pleasant because of such pleasant action as it does.[278] (8) There is nothing always pleasant in itself of this sort of nature,[279] since our nature is not simple, but in it is something else also through which it errs.[280] So then if one of the two does something, that is opposed to the other nature, and when it is equivalent, then what is done is thought to be neither painful nor pleasant. For if

---

[270] Arabic *idhā lam yakun wa-lā wāḥid minhā* (corr. *minhumā*), but Greek τε is omitted and *idhā*, 'if, when', is not in the Greek, also τὸ μηδέτερον, 'that which is neither', must here mean 'the neutral (state)'. The Arabic translator has rendered μηδέτερον, disregarding τό.

[271] Arabic *aṣḥāb al-aqāwīl aṭ-ṭabīʿīyah*, apparently the φυσιολόγοι of Aspasius (Arberry) rather than φυσικοί (K^{b}). *Al-aqāwīl aṭ-ṭabīʿīyah* alone is an exact translation of vulg. οἱ φυσικοὶ λόγοι.

[272] I.e. rendering ὅλως instead of ὁμοίως (Arberry). Two sentences have been run together here.

[273] I.e. excitable people, cf. above, 1152a 19. Arabic omits ἀεί.

[274] Arabic *al-mizāj* here not for Greek σῶμα, which is not rendered, but for τὴν κρᾶσιν taken as subject.

[275] Short lacuna.

[276] Short lacuna.

[277] Arabic *takūn lā ʿafīfah wa-takūn radīʾah*. Evidently pleasures are meant. But this is impossible with the masculine forms ἀκόλαστοι and φαῦλοι.

[278] The sentence has gone wrong: Greek ἰατρεύεσθαι is wrongly construed with τοῦ ὑπομένοντος and the contrast between 'things pleasant naturally' and 'things pleasant accidentally' is disregarded. Greek φύσει, 'actually', is not even translated, nor is 'in itself' good as a translation of τὸ αὐτό.

[279] Arabic *min mithl hādhihi 'ṭ-ṭabīʿah*, i.e. τῆς τοιᾶσδε φύσεως from the preceding paragraph.

[280] Arabic *alladhī bihi takhṭiʾu*, Arberry's brilliant conjecture is καθ' ὃ ἁμάρτοι read for καθὸ φθαρτοί.

منهما يحزن كثيرين لمكان الطبع فإنّه يقل إنّ الحيوان يتعب بالطبع كشهادة أصحاب الأقاويل الطبيعية أيضاً إذ يقولون إنّ النظر والسماع محزن لكنّا قد اعتدنا ذلك كذلك (٦) بنوع كلّي حل الشباب لمكان النمو كحل المخمورين والشباب لذيذ وأمّا الذين هم بالطبيعة ذوو مزاج حادّ فإنّهم في حاجة مستمرة إلى العلاج فإنّ [٣/٢٠] المزاج [...] يلذع لذعاً كثيراً وهم أبداً في شهوة شديدة واللذّة [...] تكون قوية ولهذه العلّة تكون لا عفيفة وتكون رديئة (٧) والتي تكون من غير أحزان فليس لها إفراط وهذه هي من الأشياء اللذيذة بالطبيعة لا بنوع العرض وإنّما أقول لذيذة بنوع العرض الذي يبرئ فإنّه يعرض للذي يصير على العلاج أن يفعل فعلاً بنوع الصحّة ومن أجل هذا يظنّ به أنّه لذيذ لمكان ما يفعل من الفعل اللذيذ (٨) وليس شئ لذيذاً بذاته من مثل هذه الطبيعة أبداً من أجل أنّ طبيعتنا ليست بمبسوطة بل فيها شئ آخر أيضاً الذي به تخطئ فإذاً إن فعل أحدهما شيئاً يكون ذلك للطبيعة الأخرى مخالفاً وإذا كان متساوياً فحينئذ لا يظنّ بالمفعول لا أنّه محزن

---

1 منهما corr. Dun : منها F, Bad || 2 إذ Dun : illegible F || 4 المزاج Dun : illegible F || 5 عفيفة F, Dun : تكون لا عفيفا : يكون لا Bad || 6 والتي Dun : illegible F || 10 طبيعتنا corr. Dun* (ἡμῶν τὴν φύσιν) : طبيعتها F, Bad || 10 تخطئ F, Dun : نفنى Bad

the thing's nature were simple, the same action would be pleasant. Hence God enjoys always a single, simple pleasure, for action does not belong to movement only but to rest also, and the pleasure in rest is more than in movement, as the poet says:[281] All things most sweet[282] change through some defect, for this is like the man swift to change [and bad],[283] since it is not simple and not good.[284] (9) Restraint and lack of restraint have now been spoken of, as also pleasure and pain and what each of them is, and how some of them are good things and others bad things. It remains also that we speak of friendship.

End of the Eigth Discourse of the Ethics, and praise be to God and peace upon His servants whom He has chosen.

[281] Cf. Euripides, *Orestes*, 234.

[282] Arabic *al-ḥalwah jiddan*, i.e. Greek γλυκύτατον (K^b, L^b) as against γλυκύ (Aspasius) has been wrongly construed with πάντων.

[283] Arberry supplied *wa-radī'*. The following Greek words καὶ ἡ φύσις ἡ δεομένη μεταβολῆς are then omitted.

[284] Arabic *dhā isti'hāl*, lit. 'deserving', for Greek ἐπιεικής as at 1155b 35, etc.

ولا أنّه لذيذ فإنّه إذا كانت طبيعة الشيء مبسوطة فالفعل بعينه يكون لذيذاً ومن أجل هذا الإله يسرّ أبداً بلذّة واحدة مبسوطة فإنّ الفعل ليس هو للحركة فقط بل للسكون أيضاً واللذّة في السكون أكثر منها في الحركة كقول الشاعر إنّه يتغيّر جميع الأشياء الحلوة جدّاً لرداءة ما فإنّه كالإنسان السريع التغيّر [والرديء] من أجل أنّه ليس بمبسوط ولا ذا استئهل (٩) فقد قيل في الضبط ولا ضبط وفي اللذّة والحزن وما كلّ واحد منها وكيف بعضها خيرات وبعضها رداءات فقد أيضاً بقي أن نقول في المحبّة.

آخر المقالة الثامنة من الأخلاق والحمد للّه وسلّم على عباده الذين اصطفى

---

3 جميع om. Bad || 4 والردئ suppl. Arberry || 6 فقد F : وقد Bad || 6 أيضا om. Bad

BOOK VIII

In the name of God, the Merciful, the Compassionate
God bless Muhammad and his family and give them peace

The Ninth Discourse of the Book of Ethics of Aristotle

1155a Aristotle said: There follows these discussions the discussion of friendship,[1] for it is one of our virtues.[2] It is one of the things very needful, moreover, no one who had all the remaining good things would choose life without friends. For [...][3] leading positions and possessors of power see the need[4] for friends [...][5] the benefit in the excellence of this condition, if it be deprived of the doing of kindness [...][6] mostly among friends and is much praised in respect of them? And how can it be guarded and kept safe without one's friends? For the greater it is, the more danger is present. (2) Also in poverty and the other misfortunes [there] is not thought to be any refuge except friends. They are the refuge of the young that they should not err, and the help[7] of the old in the attention which they need in lack of activity owing to their weakness, and [a friend] helps those in the prime of life in good actions. For 'two when they come together',[8] are better able to act and to understand. (3) It seems that it is natural, and that it is like the relation of parent to child,[9] not among men only but also among birds[10] and like the relation to one another which is among those of a single race, especially mankind, whence we praise those who love mankind. In different kinds of

---

[1] Arabic *maḥabbah*, strictly 'love', 'affection', for Greek φιλία.

[2] Greek ἢ μετά is taken as an abbreviation (Arberry).

[3] Short lacuna.

[4] Arabic *yarauna al-ḥājah*. i.e. δοκεῖ is taken closely with πλουτοῦσι and κεκτημένοις.

[5] Short lacuna.

[6] Short lacuna.

[7] Arabic *wa-ma'ūnah*, i.e. βοήθεια, the reading of M^{b} (Arberry).

[8] I.e. a poetical quotation (Homer, *Iliad* X, 224).

[9] Arabic omits πρὸς τὸ γεγεννημένον τῷ γεννήσαντι, as K^{b} and Γ.

[10] The following words καὶ τοῖς πλείστοις τῶν ζῴων are omitted (Arberry, Badawī).

المقالة الثامنة

بسم الله الرحمن الرحيم

صلّى الله على محمّد وعلى آله وسلّم

المقالة التاسعة من كتاب الأخلاق لأرسطو

١. قل أرسطو وقد يتلو هذه الأقاويل القول في المحبّة فإنّها فضيلة ما من فضائلنا وهي من الأشياء المضطرّة جدّاً في العمر [...] وأيضاً فإنّه ليس يختار أحد الحية [٣/٢١] من غير الأصدقاء و [...] الرياسات وذوي الأقدار يرون الحاجة إلى الأصدقاء [...] المنفعة بحسن هذه الحل إذا انتقص منها [...] اصطناع المعروف أكثر ذلك في الأصدقاء ويكون بهم ممدوحاً جدّاً وكيف يمكن أن يبقى ويسلم من غير أصدقائه فإنّه على قدر كثرته كذلك الخطر فيه (٢) وأيضاً في الفقر وسائر رداءات البخت لا يظنّ أنّ [هناك] ملجأً آخر ما خلا الأصدقاء وهم ملجأ الأحداث لئلا يخطئوا ومعونة المشائخ فيما يحتاجون إليه من المصلحة فيما بهم من نقص الفعل لضعفهم ويعين الشباب في الأفعل الجيد فإنّ الاثنين إذا اجتمعا كانا أقوى على الفعل والفهم (٣) ويشبه أن يكون بالطبع وأن يكون كإضافة الوالد للمولود ليس في الناس فقط بل وفي الطائر وكالإضافة التي هي من أمّة واحدة بعضها إلى بعض ولا سيّما الناس ومن ها هنا نمدح محبّي الناس وفي أنواع التحيّر

5 جدا في العمر (...) وايضا فانه ليس يختار Bad, Dun : illegible F || 6 first [...] : illegible F, *for* Dun (partly) || 7 اصطناع المعروف Dun : illegible F || 8 يبقى Bad, Dun : illegible F || 9 هناك suppl. Bad || 10 يخطئوا corr. Bad : يخطئون F || 11 ويعين F : المحبة تعين suppl. and read. Bad || 14 إلى بعض F : لبعض corr. Bad || 14 نمدح read. Bad, Dun : يمدح F

[...] : illegible F, *who had all the remaining good things* Dun

perplexity[11] also one may see that every man is special[12] for the other, and his friend. (4) It seems sometimes that it is friendship which is the special characteristic of[13] cities, and that the effort of the lawgivers is directed to it more than their effort [to justice], and it is indebted to it and resembles their effort in justice, and it seems that agreement in opinion is a surety[14] of friendship. This is their desire most of all and they remove difference of opinion most of all because it is enmity. When they are friends they do not need justice, but when they are just they need friendship. It seems that the just most of all have friendship.[15] (5) And it is not necessary only, but also it is excellent. For we praise friends,[16] and it is thought that to have many friends is one of the excellent things. Some people think that good men and friends are one thing among the excellent things, and some people think that good men and friends are one and the same things in themselves. (6) In regard to that, there is no little doubt. For some lay down for friendship a kind of likeness, and lay down [...][17] they say: 'Like is like like', and: 'The most beautiful[18] is
1155b like the most beautiful[19] [...][20] is like these.' Others say the opposite, and that all who [...][21] to one another, like potters.[22] In regard to these same things, inquiry is made at a higher level and in a more natural way, like Euripides when he spoke of the 'raising of the earth' which has dried from the rain and 'the raising[23] of the high-ranking sky which is filled with rain to fall upon the earth', and Heraclitus when he says: 'It matches like the opposite in equality', and: 'From different things comes excellent harmony', and: 'All things are at strife.'

---

[11] Arabic *fī anwāʿ at-taḥaiyur* rendering Greek ἐν ταῖς πλάναις (Arberry).

[12] Arabic *khāṣṣ* rendering Greek οἰκεῖον.

[13] Arabic *takhuṣṣ* for Greek συνέχειν, as at 1132b 32 and 1133a 27.

[14] Arabic *ḥirzan*, but the Greek is ὅμοιον read as ὅμερον.

[15] The Greek is construed similarly in Rackham's alternative rendering of the passage: "And the just are thought to possess friendliness in its highest form."

[16] Arabic *al-aṣdiqā'*, i.e. Greek φίλους, the reading of K^b and M^b (Arberry). Cf. 1159a 34.

[17] Lacuna.

[18] Arabic *ajmal*. But this is for κάλλιον, as Arberry saw, rather than the κολοιόν of the text (= jackdaw).

[19] See previous note.

[20] Short lacuna.

[21] Short lacuna.

[22] Arabic *al-q.wm.ra* for Greek κεραμεῖς.

[23] Arabic *rufiʿat* for Greek ἐρᾶν. The Arabic translator knows the meaning of ἐρᾶν (which he renders by *ʿashiqa* 1158a 11, 1167a 4ff.), but he here seems to have read αἵρειν.

أيضاً يمكن أحداً أن يرى أنّ كلّ إنسان خاصّ بالإنسان وصديق له (٤) وقد يشبه أن تكون المحبّة التي تخصّ المدن وأن يكون اجتهاد واضعي النواميس فيها أكثر من اجتهادهم [في العدالة] ومديناً له وقد يشبه اجتهادهم في العدالة فقد يشبه أن يكون اتّفاق الرأي حرزاً ما للمحبّة وهذا هو شهوتهم أكثر ذلك وينفون اختلاف الرأي أكثر ذلك لأنّه عداوة وإذا كانوا أصدقاء فليس يحتاجون إلى العدالة وأمّا إذا كانوا عدولاً فقد يحتاجون إلى المحبّة ونرى أن يكون العدول أكثر ذلك ذوي محبّة (٥) فإنّ ذلك ليس بمضطرّ فقط بل هو جيّد أيضاً فإنّا نمدح الأصدقاء ويظنّ بالتكثير من الأصدقاء أنّه واحد من الأشياء الجيّدة وبعض الناس يرى أنّ الرجال الأخيار والأصدقاء هم شئ واحد من الأشياء الجيّدة وبعض يرى أنّ الرجل الأخيار والأصدقاء هم شئ واحد بعينه بأعيانهم (٦) وفي ذلك تشكيك ليس بقليل فإنّ بعضهم يضع لها مشابهة ما ويضع [٣/٢٢] [...] قالوا إنّ الشبيه كالشبيه والأجمل كالأجمل [...] شبيه هذه ومنهم من قل خلاف ذلك بأنّ جميع من كان [...] بعضهم لبعض كالقومرة ويطلب في هذه بعينها طلباً أرفع وأوفر طبيعة كأوريبيوتوس حين قل ورفعت الأرض التي قد جفّت من المطر ورفع السماء الكريمة التي تملأ من المطر لتقع على الأرض وإيرقليطس حين يقول إنّه يكون كالمخالف في التساوي مشاكلاً ويكون من المختلفة تأليف جيّد ويكون جميع الأشياء على المشاجرة وقل قوم آخرون ضدّ ما قل

1 أيضا om. Bad || 1 بالإنسان corr. : بلإنسان F; بل نسان Bad || 2-3 في العدالة suppl. Dun || 12 كالقومرة F : كالقرمدة corr. Bad* (κεραμεῖς) || 12 وأوفر corr. Bad : أفضل F || 12 طبيعة F, Dun : رفع F; رفع corr. : ورفعت 12 || corr. Bad كاوريفيدس : F partly w.p. كأريبيوتوس 12 || Bad بالطبع Bad || 13 الكريمة corr. Dun* (σεμνόν) : الكرية F, Bad || 13 تملا Bad : ملى F || 14 وابرقليطس partly w.p. F || 14 حين om. Bad

Other people said the opposite of what these said. Thus Empedocles said: 'Like desires like.' (7) Let us then leave the difficult natural questions,[24] for they are not consonant with this inquiry. As for those of them which are[25] connected with character and the emotions, let us inquire about them, as for instance: Is friendship in everyone, or is it impossible that men should be friends when they are vicious?, and: Is there one sort of friendship or more than one? For those who think that it is one because it admits of increase and decrease,[26] are convinced with unconvincing proofs, because things different in kind admit of increase and decrease.[27] A special discussion on these has already been given previously.

2. It may be that the account of them will be clear if the lovable is known. For it is thought that not everything is loved, but the lovable is, and that this is the good, or the pleasant, or the useful. It may be thought that the useful is that from which some good or pleasure comes. So then the good and the pleasant will be loved.[28] (2) Do men love the good, or that which is good for them? Sometimes there is a difference in these, and similarly also in what is near to these.[29] It is thought that each one loves the pleasant which is pleasant for him, and the good similarly,[30] and that the good without qualification is lovable,[31] and that for each one it is what it is for him.[32] For each one, on the assumption that it is of the nature of good,[33] loves not the good which is for him good but that which appears to him so. There is no difference at all here, since the lovable is what appears so.

---

[24] Arabic *masā'il al-ʿawīṣ*, evidently for Greek ἀπορήματων—a good translation, lit. 'questions of the obscure, the abstruse', cf. 1136a 10 and 23.

[25] Some Greek words are omitted (ἐστὶν ἀνθρωπικὰ καί).

[26] Corr. Arabic *az-ziyādah wa'n-nuqṣān* for Greek τὸ μᾶλλον καὶ τὸ ἧττον as at 1173a 17. Elsewhere the phrase is rendered *al-akthar wa'l-aqall* (cf. 1115b 10, 1173a 24-25, 27-28).

[27] See previous note.

[28] Greek ὡς τέλη omitted (Arberry).

[29] *Wa-fīmā yalī hādhihi*, apparently καὶ περὶ τοιαῦτα for καὶ περὶ τὸ ἡδύ.

[30] The Greek represented by 'loves the pleasant [...] the good similarly' is different (τὸ αὑτῷ ἀγαθὸν φιλεῖν, 'loves the *good* which is *good* for him').

[31] There seems to be a slight difference here from the Greek ἁπλῶς μὲν τἀγαθὸν φιλητόν, i.e. the good is lovable without qualification.

[32] A literal and not exact rendering of ἑκάστῳ δὲ τὸ ἑκάστῳ.

[33] This assumes that the text is right: *ʿalā annahu khairīyun* (the last word carefully vocalised with *sukūn*). In any case the words are an addition to the Greek.

هؤلاء وكذلك قال أنبدقلس إنّ الشبيه يشتهي الشبيه (٧) فلندع مسائل العويص الطبيعية فإنّها ليست موافقة لهذا الفحص وأمّا ما كان منها ينتسب إلى الأخلاق والآفات فلنفحص عنها كقولي هل تكون المحبّة في كلّ أم لا يمكن أن يكونوا محبّين إذ كانوا ذوي رداءة وهل نوع المحبّة واحد أو أكثر من واحد فإنّ الذين يظنّون أنّه واحد لأنّه يقبل الزيادة والنقصان فليس قنوعهم بدلالة مقنعة لأنّ المختلفة بالنوع تقبل الزيادة والنقصان وقد قيل في هذه قولاً خاصّاً فيما تقدّم.

٢. وخليق أنّه سيظهر القول فيها إذا علم المحبوب فإنّه يظنّ أنّه لا يحبّ كلّ بل يحبّ المحبوب وأنّ هذا هو الخير أو اللذيذ أو النافع وخليق أن يظنّ أنّ النافع هو الذي منه يكون خير ما أو لذّة فإذاً سيكون محبوبين الخير واللذيذ (٢) فهل يحبّون الخير أو الذي هو خير لهم فربّما كان في هذه اختلاف وكذلك وفيما يلي هذه ويظنّ أنّ كلّ أحد يحبّ اللذيذ الذي هو عنده لذيذ والخير كذلك وأن يكون الخير بنوع مبسوط محبوباً ويكون عند كلّ واحد الذي هو عنده فإنّ كلّ واحد على أنّه خيري يحبّ ليس الخير الذي هو له خير بل الذي يظهر له وليس في ذلك اختلاف البتّة من أجل أنّه يكون المحبوب الظاهر

1 أنبدقلس partly w.p. F || 3 إذ F : إذا Bad || 5 النقصان (...) لأن corr. and suppl. Dun* (δέχεται γὰρ τὸ μᾶλλον καὶ τὸ ἧττον καὶ τὰ ἕτερα τῷ εἴδει) : لأنه يقبل الزيادة والمختلفة بالنوع F, Bad || 12 خيري corr. Dun : حائر F, Bad

(3) Since those who love[34] are three, as regards love for what has not breath, it is not called love, because in those things[35] there is no reciprocity in love and no wish for good, so that it would deserve ridicule to speak of the good man wishing for good things, unless he wishes that they should be preserved in order to be his, and they say that a friend must wish for good things on his account.[36] As for those who wish for good things in this way, they call them sincere,[37] if the same is not forthcoming from the other. For sincerity[38] is love of those who are reciprocal in feeling. (4) There must be added to this 'when it is not concealed'.[39] Many give sincere advice to those whom they have not seen, and it is thought of them that they are
1156a deliberate and meritorious, not useful.[40] This is the same thing, and if one of those is requited on the part of these with sincere advice,[41] these appear[42] to one another, and how can they be called friends, the condition of each of whom is concealed from the other? So then one of them must advise the other sincerely and wish for good things for the other, and not conceal anything of what is said about them.[43]

3. Since these[44] differ from one another in form, the affections and friendships differ accordingly. Thus the kinds of friendship are three, equal in number to the lovable things. In each one of them there is reciprocity in friendship which is not concealed, and those who love

---

[34] This is perhaps the reading of K^b which omits δία. But the Arabic translation is wrong. Aristotle is here speaking of the three grounds for friendship which he has already mentioned.

[35] Arabic *fī tilka* for Greek ἐκείνων (the vulg.).

[36] Arabic *yanbaghī an yurīda aṣ-ṣadīq al-khairāt min ajlihi*, i.e. the construction is wrong.

[37] Or 'disinterested', Arabic *nuṣaḥā'* (so also 1157b 18, 1167a 2), hardly equivalent to Greek εὔνους.

[38] Arabic *naṣīḥah* for Greek εὔνοιαν, which should be construed with ἀντιπεπονθόσι. As it stands, the sentence is wrong.

[39] The question with Greek ἤ is here disregarded.

[40] The sentence is evidently misunderstood, with μή for ἤ in the last words (Arberry).

[41] I.e. Greek τοῦτο δὲ τὸ αὐτό is construed apart from the rest of the sentence. πρὸς τούτων has been read instead of πρὸς τοῦτον, and εὖνοι (cf. Arabic *bi-naṣīḥah*) is brought in from the next sentence.

[42] The sentences coalesce.

[43] Arberry's suggestion δὲ ἕν read for δι' ἕν seems right, and 'about them' (Arabic *ʿanhum*) is an addition.

[44] I.e. the three grounds for friendship or loveable things mentioned already above, first in c. 2, § 1 (not distinctly indicated in the Arabic translation of the last sentence of c. 2).

(٣) فلمّا كان الذين يحبّون ثلاثة أمّا في محبّة ما ليست لها نفس فليست تقل محبّة [٣/٢٣] لأنّه ليس يكون في تلك تكافؤ في المحبّة ولا إرادة الخير بل سيكون أهلاً أن يضحك بالقول الذي يقول إنّ الخير يريد الخيرات إلاّ أن يكون يريد أن يسلم ليكون له قد زعموا أنّه ينبغي أن يريد الصديق الخيرات من أجله فإنّ الذين يريدون الخيرات بهذا النوع فإنّهم يسمّونهم نصحاء إن لم يكن من ذلك أيضاً مثل هذا فإنّ النصيحة محبّة المتكافئين في الانفعل (٤) وينبغي أن يزاد على هذا إذا لم يخفَ فكثير من ينصح من لم يرَ ويظنّ بهم أنّهم ذوو روية واستئهل لا منفعة وهذا هو بعينه فإن كوفئ أحد أولئك من هؤلاء بنصيحة فإنّ هؤلاء يظهرون بعض لبعض وكيف يمكن أن يسمّى محبّين الذين يختفي عنهم حل كلّ واحد منهما عن صاحبه فإذاً ينبغي أن ينصح بعضهم بعضاً ويريد الخيرات لصاحبه وألاّ يخفي شيئاً ممّا قيل عنهم.

٣. وإذ تختلف هذه بعضها من بعض بالصورة تختلف إذاً الأحبابات والمحبّات فإذاً أنواع المحبّة ثلاثة مساوية بالعدد للمحبوبات وفي كلّ واحد منها تكافؤ في المحبّة لا يخفى

2 بل سيكون Bad, Dun : illegible F || 3 الخير يريد F, Dun : الخمر نريد (!) Bad || 3 second يريد F : نريد read. Bad || 3 له F : لنا Bad || 3 قد زعموا F, Dun : وقول هذا Bad || 4 يريد الصديق F, Dun : نريد للصديق Bad || 4 فإن F, Dun : ولكن Bad || 6 الانفعل F, Dun : الإحسان Bad || 6 إذا لم يخف فكثير F, Dun : إذ أنه يلقى كثير Bad || 6 first من corr. Dun : ممن F, Bad || 7 لا F, Dun : و Bad

each other wish for good things for each other, for this very friendship which they have. For those who love each other for advantage, do not love for themselves but because they have some mutual good from each other. Similarly those who love for some pleasure do not love [those who easily] change[45] because of their possessing a quality, but because they are pleased with them. (2) Thus those who love for some advantage love simply for the good which they get, and those who love for pleasure love simply for what is pleasant for them. The loved person is not loved,[46] but he who is useful or pleasant.[47] These friendships are accidental, for they are not loved for what[48] the person is loved for, but because[49] they provide, the one of them a certain good, the other pleasure. (3) Those which are such are easily dissolved by their [not] remaining[50] as they were. For if they are [not] pleasant in respect of anything[51] or useful, they cease[52] from friendship. As for the useful, it does not remain but changes at all times, and becomes something different. So when the cause of their being friends is dissolved, the friendship is dissolved also, since the friendship was something superadded on that account. (4) It is thought of this kind of friendship that it is mostly among old men, for people like these seek not the pleasant but the useful, and the young also and those who are at this stage of growth—all of them who seek that which is best[53] likewise. Those who are of this type mostly [do not][54] live together, and sometimes are not pleasant, and do not need this life together, if they are not mutually useful. For they are pleasant to the extent that they have hope[55] of good therein. And youthful[56] friendship you would place here also. (5) The friend-

---

[45] I.e. Arberry's addition of *al-haiyinī* before *at-tanaqqul*, comparing 1157a 6.

[46] I.e. omitting ᾗ in both cases.

[47] See previous note.

[48] The adverbial use of ᾗ, 'in so far as', is not understood, and the word is mistranslated.

[49] See previous note.

[50] The negative is omitted.

[51] The Arabic translation appears to have read Greek μηκέτι ἡδεῖς as μή τι ἡδεῖς (with omission of the negative by a copyist).

[52] Arabic *fa'innahā takuffu*, but the subject here are the friends (παύονται φιλοῦντες).

[53] Arabic *al-akhyar*, not *al-akhīr*, cf. 1157a 28, 1160a 10, b 2, 1168a 12. Arberry's conjecture τὸ ὕστερον for τὸ συμφέρον is therefore needless. τὸ συμφέρον elsewhere is *an-nāfi*ʿ (1104b 31, 1126b 29).

[54] Arabic again omits the negative.

[55] Text *rajā'a* [sic], i.e. Greek ἐλπίδα, which is the reading of K^b (Arberry).

[56] Arabic *al-ḥadīthah* perhaps for τὴν ξενικήν read as τὴν νεανικήν (Arberry).

والذين يحبّون بعضهم بعضاً يريدون الخيرات بعضهم لبعض لهذه المحبّة التي يحبّون بعينها فإنّ الذين يحبّون بعضهم بعضاً لمنفعة فليس يحبّون لذاتهم بل بأن يكون لهم خير ما بعضهم من بعض وكذلك الذين يحبّون للذّة ما فإنّهم لا يحبّون [الهيني] التنقّل لأنّهم ذوو كيفية بل لأنّهم يلتذّون بهم (٢) فالذين يحبّون لمنفعة ما إنّما يحبّون للخير الذي هو لهم والذين يحبّون للذّة إنّما يحبّون لللذيذ عندهم وليس يحبّ الذي هو محبوب بل النافع أو اللذيذ وهذه المحبّات بنوع العرض فإنّها لا تحبّ بالذي يحبّ المحبوب بل لأنّها تكسب أمّا إحداهما فخيراً ما والأخرى لذّة (٣) والتي تكون مثل هذه تكون هشّة النخلي على أنّها [لا] تبقى على حالها فإنّها إن [ما] كانت لذينة بشيء ما أو نافعة فإنّها تكفّ عن المحبّة فأمّا النافع فلا يبقى بل يتغيّر في كلّ وقت ويصير شيئاً آخر فإذا انحلّ الذي بسببه كانوا الأحبّاء تنحلّ المحبّة أيضاً كانت المحبّة من المضاف من كان (٤) [...] كان المحبّة التي تكون [٣/٢٤] أكثر ذلك [...] فإنّ مثل هؤلاء لا يطلب اللذيذ بل يطلب النافع والأحداث أيضاً والذين هم على هذا السنّ وجميع من كان منهم يطلب الذي هو الأخير كذلك والذين هم على مثل هذه الحل [لا] يعيش بعضهم مع بعض أكثر ذلك فربّما لم يكونوا ألذّاء ولا يحتاجون إلى هذه المعاشرة إن لم يكونوا ذوي منفعة فإنّهم ألذّ بالقدر الذي لهم فيه رجاء الخير والصداقة الحديثة تضع في هذا أيضاً (٥) وصداقة

---

1 الذين يحبون corr. Bad : الني يحب F || 1 يريدون corr. Bad : يريد F || 3 الهيني suppl. Arberry || 3 التنقل F, Dun : العقل Bad || 5 للذيذ corr. Dun : اللذيذ F, Dun || 7 فخيرا F : فخير Bad || 8 لا suppl. Dun || 8 ما suppl. Dun || 10 [...] : illegible F, *It is thought of this kind of* Dun || 11 [...] : illegible F, *among old men* Dun || 12 يطلب الني F, Dun : يطلب النافع والني suppl. Bad || 13 لا suppl. Dun || 15 الحديثة تضع F, Dun : الجودية توضع corr. Bad

ship of the young is thought to be for the sake of pleasure, since they live by the emotions.[57] Mostly they seek what is pleasant for them and such of it as is present. But when the age alters, the pleasant things change also. Hence they become friends quickly and break off
1156b quickly, for friendship changes with what is pleasant, and this[58] pleasure changes quickly. The young also are amorous, since the most of love is emotion and pleasure.[59] Hence they love and leave off quickly many times in one day, and change,[60] and wish that they were together all day and all their life. For such is friendship for them.[61] (6) Perfect friendship is that of good men who are alike in virtue, for these wish good things for each other in a similar manner,[62] being good in themselves.[63] As for those who wish good things for the bad,[64] they are friends mostly for their sake and it is [a friendship] in this case for their sake,[65] not by chance. The friendship of these continues as long as they continue good, and virtue is lasting. Each of the two is good absolutely to the friend,[66] for the good who are good absolutely[67] are profitable to one another. Similarly too they find pleasure in one another. For the good find pleasure absolutely [and] in one another, since for each one his own special actions are pleasant and the actions which are like these belong to the good,[68] and similar actions. (7) The friendship which is like this is rightly lasting, since it unites in itself[69] all that there should be to mutual friends. For all friendship is on account of good, or for pleasure, either absolutely or for the one who loves, and by reason of a

---

[57] Arabic *bi 'l-āfāt* rendering Greek κατὰ πάθος.

[58] I.e. ταύτης read for τοιαύτης, as often elsewhere, e.g. 1157a 2.

[59] Greek κατά and δία are left untranslated.

[60] Arabic *wa-yantaqilūna*. But Greek μεταπίπτοντες should be construed with πολλάκις τῆς αὐτῆς ἡμέρας.

[61] The Arabic translator fails to give the sense of γίνεται and τὸ κατὰ φιλίαν. Cf. Ross: "[...] for it is thus that they *attain* the *purpose* of their friendship."

[62] Arabic *bi-nauʿ at-tashābuh*, Greek ὁμοίων.

[63] Arabic *ʿalā annahum akhyār bi-dhātihim*, i.e. ἀγαθοὶ δ' εἰσί has dropped out.

[64] Arabic *li-dhawī 'r-ridā'ah*, i.e. φαύλοις for φίλοις (Arberry).

[65] Arabic *li-makānihim* (used immediately above for Greek ἐκείνων ἕνεκα) is here for δι' αὑτούς apparently misread as δι' αὐτούς.

[66] Arabic *li 'ṣ-ṣadīq*, but Greek is '*and* to the friend' (καὶ τῷ φίλῳ).

[67] Arabic *fa'inna al-akhyār alladhīna hum akhyār bi-nauʿ mabsūṭ*. But we need 'the good are both good absolutely and [...]'.

[68] The construction is faulty, αἱ τοιαῦται being taken with τῶν ἀγαθῶν.

[69] Arabic *yajmaʿ fī dhātihā*. This is also Rackham's translation: "[...] it combines in itself". But there is no variant αὑτῇ, and συνάπτει is untranslated.

الأحداث يظنّ بها أنّها لمكان اللذّة من أجل أنّ هؤلاء يحيون بالآفات وأكثر ما يطلبون اللذيذ عندهم وما حضر منه وإذا انتقل القرن تغيّرت اللذّة بهذه أيضاً ومن أجل هذا يصيرون أصدقاء سريعاً ويتقاطعون سريعاً فإنّ المحبّة تتغيّر مع اللذيذ وتغيّر هذه اللذّة سريعة والأحداث أيضاً ذوو عشق من أجل أنّ أكثر العشق آفة ولذّة ومن أجل هذا يحبّون ويكفّون سريعاً مراراً كثيرة في يوم واحد وينتقلون ويريدون أن يكونوا متواصلين نهارهم وحياتهم فإنّه تكون لهم الصداقة على هذه الحل (٦) والتامّة هي صداقة الأخيار المتشابهين بالفضيلة فإنّ هؤلاء يريدون الخيرات بعضهم لبعض بنوع التشابه على أنّهم أخيار بذاتهم وأمّا الذين يريدون الخيرات لذوي الرداءة فإنّهم أصدقاء أكثر ذلك لمكانهم وهي على هذه الحل لمكانهم لا بنوع العرض فصداقة هؤلاء تدوم ما داموا هم أخياراً وأمّا الفضيلة فباقية وكلّ واحد منهما خير بنوع مبسوط للصديق فإنّ الأخيار الذين هم أخيار بنوع مبسوط هم نافعون بعضهم بعضاً وكذلك أيضاً يلذّ بعضهم بعضاً فإنّ الأخيار ملذّون بنوع مبسوط وبعضهم بعضاً من أجل أنّ عند كلّ واحد الأفعل الخاصّية به لذيذة والتي هي مثل هذه للأخيار والشبيهة (٧) والمحبّة التي هي مثل هذه بحقّ تكون باقية من أجل أنّه يجمع في ذاتها جميع ما ينبغي أن يكون للمخلصين فإنّ كلّ المحبّة تكون لمكان خير أو لذّة إمّا بنوع [٣/٢٥] مبسوط وإمّا للمحبّ وبشبه ما وبهذه الموالاة جميع التي قيلت

---

1 يحيون بالآفات appar. corr. Dun* (κατὰ πάθος γὰρ οὗτοι ζῶσι) : يحبون الآفات F, Bad || 2 القرن corr. Dun : الغرب F, العمر corr. Bad || 3 تغير F, Dun : تصير Bad || 4 أن repeated in F || 10-12 مبسوط (...) للصديق om. Bad || 12 وبعضهم corr. Dun : بعضهم F, Bad || 12 كل واحد F, Dun : كلها نجد Bad || 13 للأخيار F, Dun : الأخيار Bad || 14 ما corr. Bad : مما F || 15 الموالاة corr. Dun : الموالات F, الحل Bad

certain resemblance,[70] and in this friendship are all the things which have been mentioned by themselves,[71] since all the others are alike[72] in this, i.e. the absolute good and the absolute pleasant.[73] These are the most loved things, and friendship and mutual love are most in these,[74] and they are best.[75] (8) It may be that these are rare, since such men[76] are few. Also they require time and custom, like the proverb which says: 'People must first know that they are as it is said of them',[77] and one must not at first accept from them that they are friends until it appears that each of them is lovable for the other, and it is accepted that he is so. (9) As for those who hastily assume the actions of a friend with each other, they wish to be friends, but cannot, unless they are loved[78] also. That is the same thing,[79] for the quick wish is friendship,[80] but friendship is not so.

4. As for this [friendship], it is perfect, both in time and the other matters, and in all these things[81] there are also similar [benefits] for each of the two from each of them, which is what should be for
1157a friends. One of them[82] has a resemblance to this on account of what is pleasant. For the good are pleasant for one another,[83] and similarly those who are friends on account of the useful,[84] for these[85] are good to one another for the most part.[86] Friendship is established among

---

[70] Or 'analogy', cf. VII, 9, 6.

[71] Arabic *bi-dhātihā* for Greek καθ' αὑτούς.

[72] Arabic *al-ukhar mutashābiha*, i.e. Greek ὅμοια rather than ὅμοιοι (the reading of K^b).

[73] Arabic *ai al-khair al-mabsūṭ wa'l-ladhīdh al-mabsūṭ*, which fails to represent the Greek (τό τε ἁπλῶς ἀγαθὸν καὶ ἡδὺ ἁπλῶς ἐστίν).

[74] Arabic *fī hādhihi*, but the Greek pronoun (ἐν τούτοις) is masculine plural.

[75] Arabic *wa-hiya afḍal*, i.e. καὶ ἀρίστη, 'and best', is wrongly construed.

[76] Arabic has *hā'ulā'i* in error for οἱ τοιοῦτοι.

[77] Greek πρὶν τοὺς λεγομένους ἅλας συναναλῶσαι has baffled the translator.

[78] Or 'lovable'.

[79] Arabic *mutasāwiyan*, i.e. ἴσόν ἐστιν for ἴσασιν.

[80] I.e. perhaps φιλία for φιλίας.

[81] I.e. ταῦτα (for ταὐτά) wrongly construed with κατὰ πάντα. For ταῦτα, see L^b, M^b and Γ. According to Bywater, K^b omits.

[82] Arabic *li-baʿḍihā* rendering ἡ δέ which should be (but is not) construed with διά τὸ ἡδύ ("friendship for the sake of pleasure", Ross).

[83] Arabic *ladhīdh baʿḍuhum ʿinda baʿḍ*, cf. 1156b 29 *maḥbūb ʿinda ṣāḥibihi*.

[84] Arabic *alladhīna hum aṣdiqā' li-makān an-nāfiʿ*, i.e. rendering οἱ διὰ τὸ χρήσιμον with K^b, L^b and M^b (Arberry).

[85] I.e. οὗτοι (K^b) for τοιοῦτοι of the Greek vulg. (Arberry).

[86] I.e. μάλιστα is construed with the foregoing words (Arberry) and οἱ ἀγαθοί is clearly subject, not complement.

بذاتها من أجل أنّ سائر الأخر متشابة بهداة أيّ الخير المبسوط واللذيذ المبسوط وهذه هي المحبوبة أكثر ذلك والمحبّة والتجاوب في هذه أكثر ذلك وهي أفضل (٨) وخليق أن تكون هذه نزرة من أجل أنّ هؤلاء قليلون وأيضاً تحتاج إلى زمان وعادة كالمثل الذي يقول ينبغي أن يعلموا أوّلاً أنّهم على ما يقل فيهم ولا ينبغي أن يقبل منهم أوّلاً أنّهم أصدقاء قبل أن يظهر أنّ كلّ واحد منهم محبوب عند صاحبه ويصدّق أنّه كذلك (٩) وأمّا الذين يسرعون في أفعل المحبوب بعضهم لبعض فإنّهم يريدون أن يكونوا أصدقاء لكنّهم ليس لهم إن لم يكونوا محبوبين أيضاً ويكون ذلك متساوياً فإنّ الإرادة السريعة تكون صداقة ولا تكون صداقة كذلك.

٤. فأمّا هذه فإنّها تكون تامّة وبالزمان وبسائر الأسباب وبجميع هذه الأشياء تكون أيضاً [منافع] متشابهة لكلّ واحد منها من كلّ واحد منها وهو الذي ينبغي أن يكون للأصدقاء ولبعضها تشابه من هذه لمكان اللذيذ فإنّ الأخيار لذيذ بعضهم عند بعض وكذلك الذين هم أصدقاء لمكان النافع فإنّ هؤلاء أخيار بعضهم لبعض أكثر ذلك وتثبت المحبّة في

1 أجل Bad, Dun : illegible F || 1 الأخر متشابة Dun : الأصدقاء تتشابه Bad || 2 first أكثر corr. mrg., Bad : لكثر F || 4 و om. Bad || 7 تكون F, Dun : لتكوين Bad || 7 second و F, Dun : قد Bad || 10 منافع suppl. Dun || 12 أخيار F, Dun : اختيار Bad || 12 المحبة F, Dun : الحجة Bad

these when one and the same thing is from both of them, like pleasure, and not only this, but when it will have been from one and the same thing, like what is for those who easily change, not as it is for the lover and the beloved, since these do not find pleasure in one thing but one of them finds pleasure in seeing the other, and the other in the lover serving him. When the hour[87], i.e. the condition, abates, often the friendship abates also, since the sight is not pleasant to the one nor the service to the other. Many remain[88] [friends], if they love the characters through length of association,[89] when they have become alike by association. (2) Something pleasant is cut off[90] when the change comes.[91] But the useful is among lovers,[92] and they have little friendship and constancy.[93] And since those who are friends on account of the useful separate in a situation which is more useful,[94] they are not friends of one another but of that which is better,[95] for it is either on account of pleasure or on account of utility.[96] It is possible that wicked men should be friends to one another and good men friends of bad men, and those who are something of both of these,[97] [friends] to either of the groups. As for those who are friends in themselves, it is plain that they are the good only, since the bad do not enjoy this,[98] if there is no utility. (3) The friendship of the good alone is not angered and does not admit slander, since it is not easy to admit anything against one who has been tested during much time. The confirmation in these things[99] is that there is no injustice at any time whatever, and all the other things of this kind, for they are the best preservers of[100] true friendship. As for the others, there is

---

[87] I.e. ὥρας rendered literally in its later sense.

[88] Greek αὖ is not translated.

[89] Arabic *fa-muthāfina* for Greek συνηθεία rendered above (1156b 26) by Arabic *ʿādah*.

[90] The Arabic *wa'nqaṭaʿa* [*al-qaṭʿ*, MS.] *shai' ladhīdh* suggests that for οἱ δὲ μὴ τὸ ἡδύ the translator read τεμνεταὶ δὲ [or καὶ τεμνεταί] τι ἡδύ.

[91] Arabic *ʿinda 't-tabaddul*, representing ἀντικαταλλαττόμενοι.

[92] Greek ἐν τοῖς ἐρωτικοῖς wrongly construed with τὸ χρήσιμον, is taken as masculine.

[93] The sense is completely misunderstood.

[94] But the sense of the Greek is 'when the profit ceases'.

[95] Arabic *akhyar* for Greek τοῦ λυσιτελοῦς, cf. above 1156a 27.

[96] 'For it is [...].' These words should be construed with what follows.

[97] The sense of the Greek is given, though, as Arberry says, Greek μηδέτερον is the opposite of 'both of these'.

[98] Arabic *bi-hādhā*, but Greek ἑαυτοῖς.

[99] Neuter for masculine.

[100] This represents Greek ἀξιοῦται, 'are expected of, required of'.

هؤلاء إذا كان يكون شيء واحد بعينه لكليهما مثل اللذّة وليس هكذا فقط وإذا كان يكون من شيء واحد بعينه مثلما يكون للهيني التنقّل لا كما يكون للعاشق والمعشوق من أجل [أنّ] هؤلاء لا يلذّان بشيء واحد بل أحدهما يلذّ بأنّه يرى الآخر والآخر بأنّ العاشق يخدمه وإذا نقصت الساعة يعني الحل ربّما نقصت المحبّة أيضاً من أجل أنّه لا يكون النظر لأحدهما لذيذاً ولا تكون الخدمة للآخر وكثير من يثبت إذا هم أحبّوا الأخلاق بطول المثافنة إذا صاروا متشابهين بالمثافنة (٢) وانقطع شيء لذيذ عند التبدّل ولكن النافع في ذوي العشق وهم قليلو الصداقة والثبات ومن أجل أنّ الذين هم أصدقاء لمكان النافع ينحلّون في حل الذي [٣/٢٦] هو أنفع فإنّهم لم يكونوا أصدقاء بعضهم لبعض بل الذي هو أخير فإنّه إمّا لمكان اللذّة أو لمكان المنفعة. فقد يمكن أن يكون الأشرار أصدقاء بعضهم لبعض والأفاضل أصدقاء للأشرار والذين هم شيء من هذين لأيّ الفريقين كان وأمّا الذين يكونون أصدقاء بذاتهم فبيّن أنّهم الأخيار فقط من أجل أنّ الأشرار لا يفرحون بهذا إن لم تكن منفعة (٣) ومحبّة الأخيار وحدها لا تغضب ولا تقبل السعاية من أجل أنّه ليس يهون قبول شيء على الذي قد جرّب زماناً كثيراً فالتصديق في هذه ألاّ يكون جور في وقت ما البتّة وجميع الأخر التي هي مثل هذه فإنّها أبقى للمحبّة التي هي بالحقيقة فأمّا في

1 لكليهما corr. Bad : كليهما F || 2 التنقل F, Dun : التعقل Bad || 3 أن suppl. Bad || 6 بالمثافنة ... المثافنة F, Dun : المشافهة ... المشافهة Bad || 6 وانقطع corr. Dun : والقطع F || 8 في حل corr. Dun : فحل F, Bad || 8 هو أنفع F, Dun : بينهما نفع Bad || 9 فإنه F : وإنه Bad || 12 تغضب F, Dun : تنضب Bad || 13 فالتصديق appar. corr. Bad : فالصديق F; إلى الصديق وخليق suppl. and corr. Bad

nothing in them to prevent these things existing. (4) Since men call people friends on account of utility, like possessors of cities,[101] and it is thought that help in fighting[102] is in the cities on account of what is better,[103] and similarly those who love each other on account of pleasure, like children, it may be that we should call friends those who are like these. The kinds of friendship are many,[104] and the first of them in truth[105] is the friendship of good men *qua* good, while the rest are so by resemblance, since they are friends depending on what is a certain good and a certain resemblance, since the pleasant is a certain good[106] in the opinion of lovers of pleasure. (5) These do not come together very much, nor do the same friends become so[107] on account of the useful and on account of the pleasant. So then things
1157b that are accidental do not come together much. (6) Since the kinds of friendship are divided into these, bad people will be friends on account of pleasure or profit since they are alike.[108] As for the good, they are friends for themselves, in virtue of their being good, and these[109]

5. For just as in the case of the virtues it is said that some people are good as regards a state and others as regards an action, and similarly in the case of friendship also. For some of them associate with others in life and rejoice in one another, and aquire[110] good, and some of them, when they are asleep and separated in different places, are not active, yet their state is like the state of one who is active in a kind of friendship, since the places do not annul the friendship absolutely but annul the action. Yet if the absence is for a long time, it is thought that it produces forgetfulness of the friendship also, and hence it is said: 'Journeying is devoid of many friendships.' (2) It

---

[101] Arabic *aṣḥāb al-mudun*. Arberry suggests that οἱ πολῖται was read instead of αἱ πόλεις.

[102] Arabic *mu'āwanah fī'l-qitāl* for Greek αἱ συμμαχίαι.

[103] Arabic *akhyar*, Greek τοῦ συμφέροντος, as at 1156a 27.

[104] The construction (dependent on λέγειν) seems to be disregarded.

[105] Arabic *wa-auwaluhā bi'l-ḥaqīqah* does not render adequately Greek πρώτως μὲν καὶ κυρίως.

[106] Arabic *khairun mā* for Greek ἀγαθόν as for ἀγαθόν τι in the previous line.

[107] Arabic *lā yaṣirūna aṣdiqā'uhum bi-a'yānihim*, i.e. the translator has apparently construed οἱ αὐτοὶ φίλοι together.

[108] Greek ταύτῃ is omitted.

[109] A line and a half are omitted, apparently through homoioteleuton (οὗτοι [...] τούτοις).

[110] I.e. taking Greek πορίζουσι as medium.

الأخر فليس شيء ممتنع أن يكون هذه (٤) وإذ يسمّى الناس أصدقاء لمكان المنفعة كأصحاب المدن فقد يظنّ أنّ المعاونة في القتل تكون في المدن لمكان الذي هو أخير وكذلك الذين يحبّ بعضهم بعضاً لمكان اللذّة كالصبيان فخليق أن يكون ينبغي لنا أن نسمّي أصدقاء الذين هم مثل هؤلاء وأنواع المحبّة كثيرة وأوّلها بالحقيقة محبّة الأخيار على أنّهم أخيار وأمّا الباقية فبالتشبّه من أجل أنّهم يكونون أصدقاء على ما هو خير ما وشبه ما من أجل أنّ اللذيذ خير ما عند محبّي اللذّة (٥) وهذه لا تجتمع اجتماعاً شديداً ولا يصيرون أصدقاءهم بأعيانهم لمكان النافع ولمكان اللذيذ فإذاً التي تكون بنوع العرض لا تجتمع كثيراً (٦) وإذ كانت أنواع المحبّة تنقسم في هذه فإنّ أهل الرداءة سيكونون أصدقاء لمكان اللذّة أو النافع إذ كانوا متشابهين وأمّا الأخيار فإنّهم يكونون أصدقاء لذاتهم بأنّهم أخيار فهؤلاء

٥. فإنّه كما أنّ في الفضائل يقل إنّ بعضهم أخيار بالهيئة وبعضهم بالفعل فكذلك في الصداقة أيضاً فإنّ بعضهم يعاشر بعضاً في الحية ويفرح بعضهم ببعض ويكسبون الخير وبعضهم إذا كانوا نياماً ومفرّقين في المواضع فإنّهم أمّا بالفعل فلا يفعلون وهيئتهم كهيئة من يفعل بينهم الصداقة من أجل أنّ المواضع لا تحلّل الصداقة [٣/٢٧] بنوع مبسوط بل تحلّل الفعل فإن صارت الغيبة مزمنة يظنّ أنّها تصيّر نسيان الصداقة أيضاً ومن هنا قيل إنّ السياح خالي صداقات كثيرة (٢) وليس يظهر أنّ المشايخ والضعفى المرارة يكونون ذوي

---

5 و corr. Dun* (καί) : أو F, Bad || 8 إذ corr. : إذا F, Bad || 9 إذ corr. : إذا F, Bad || 12 يكسبون F : يكتسبون Bad || 13 first و F, Dun : أو Bad* (ἤ) || 16 السياح F, Dun : السياج read. Arberry || 16 خالي F, Dun : حلل Bad || 16 ليس Bad, Dun : illegible F || 16 والضعفى corr. Dun : الضعفى F; الضعيفي Bad || 16 ذوي corr. Dun : ذا F

does not appear that old men and bilious[111] people are friendly, since pleasure in them is slight, and no one is able to spend his days in association with what is painful or not pleasant. It appears that nature for the most part avoids what is painful, and that it desires what is pleasant. (3) As for those who accept one another and do not come together in life, they are more like sincere advisers[112] than friends, since for friends there is nothing like companionship in life. For the needy wish for benefiting, and the fortunate wish for companionship, since the latter must seldom be solitary. And it is not possible that there will be companionship one with the other, unless they find pleasure in one another and enjoy the same things, as is thought for a friendship of comrades. (4) The friendship which is most a friendship is the friendship of good men, as has been said many times. It is thought that the absolutely good or pleasant is the lovable and excellent and the like of this[113] for each individual person, what is so for him. The good man is like the good in all of these.[114] (5) It seems[115] that liking is a feeling, while friendship is a state of character. For liking not seldom is for things which have no life, while reciprocity in friendship is from choice, and choice is from a state of character. They wish good things for those who are lovable in their opinion,[116] not because of the feeling but because of the state of character. And when they love a friend, they love the good which is for themselves, since when the good man becomes a friend, the friend becomes a good. Each of the two loves his own good and makes an equal return in will and kind.[117] The expression 'friendship of equality' is used,
1158a and this is mostly for the friendship of the good.

6. Among the bitter[118] and old, friendship rarely develops in accordance with their being difficult and the small amount of pleasure

[111] Arabic *aḍ-ḍaʿfā al-marārah*, Greek στρυφνοί.

[112] Arabic *nuṣaḥā'* for εὔνοις as previously (1155b 32).

[113] I.e. the good and pleasant.

[114] Arabic *yushbih al-khair bi-kull hādhihi*. Apparently ἔοικε has been taken from the following sentence, but the text here is uncertain (vid. next note).

[115] For *wa-yashtahīhi* of the text, leg. either *wa-yashtabih* or corr. *wa-yushbih* of mrg., Greek ἔοικε evidently having been taken twice.

[116] Arabic *al-maḥbūbīn ʿindahum*, in error for Greek τοῖς φιλουμένοις ἐκείνων ἕνεκα.

[117] Arabic *wa 'n-nauʿ*, i.e. εἴδει (first hand L^b and Γ) for ἡδεῖ (Arberry).

[118] Arabic *dhawī al-ʿafāṣah* for Greek στρυφνοῖς, translated above (1157b 14), cf. n. 110, *aḍ-ḍaʿfā al-marārah*, 'bilious people' (*al-ʿafāṣah* is a rare form for *al-ʿufūṣah*, vid. Dozy).

صداقة من أجل أنّ اللذّة فيهم يسيرة وليس يقدر أحد أن يفني أيّامه بمعاشرة ما الحزن أو ما ليس بلذيذ وقد يظهر أنّ الطبيعة أكثر ذلك إمّا تهرب من الحزن وأنّها تشتهي اللذيذ (٣) وأمّا الذين يقبل بعضهم بعضاً وليس يجتمعون في الحيلة فإنّهم أحرى أن يشبهوا النصحاء من أن يشبهوا الأصدقاء من أجل أنّه ليس للأصدقاء شيء يشبه المعاشرة في الحيلة فإنّ المحاويج يشتهون المنفعة والمغبوطين يشتهون المعاشرة من أجل أنّ هؤلاء ما ينبغي لهم أن يكونوا ذوي وحدة وليس يمكن أن تكون معاشرة بعض مع بعض وهم ليس يلذّ بعضهم بعضاً ولا يفرحون بأشياء بأعيانها كما أنّه يظنّ للصداقة الصحابية (٤) فالصداقة التي هي أكثر ذلك صداقة الأخيار كما قيل مراراً كثيرة فقد يظنّ أنّ المحبوب الفاضل الخير بنوع مبسوط أو اللذيذ ولكلّ واحد مثل هذا الذي هو عنده كذلك وأمّا الخير فإنّه يشبه الخير بكلّ هذه (٥) ويشبه أمّا المصادقة فانفعال وأمّا الصداقة فهيئة فإنّ المصادقة ليست قليلاً في التي لا نفس لها وإنّما تكون في التكافؤ في الصداقة من اختيار والاختيار من هيئة ويريدون الخيرات للمحبوبين عندهم ليس من أجل الانفعال بل من أجل الهيئة وإنّما أحبّوا الصديق يحبّون الخير الذي هو لذاتهم من أجل أنّ الخير إذا صار صديقاً يصير الصديق خيراً فكلّ واحد منهما يحبّ الخير الذي هو له ويكافئ بالتساوي بالإرادة والنوع فقد يقل صداقة المساواة وهذا هو أكثر ذلك لصداقة الأخيار.

٦. وأمّا عند ذوي العفاصة والكبر فقلّما تكون الصداقة على قدر صعوبتهم وعلى قدر قلّة

1 first ما om. Bad || 4 أنه F : أن Bad || 8 كما F, Dun : وكما Bad || 10 ويشبه corr. mrg., Dun : ويشتهيه F, Bad || 13 وإنما F : وإذا Bad || 16 العفاصة F, Dun : العقامة corr. Bad

they find in society, since it is thought that these things[119] are mostly friendship and productive of friendship. For this reason the young are friends quickly while old men are not, since they are not friends to those in whom they do not find pleasure, but are like bitter[120] slaves.[121] But these are good mutual advisers,[122] for they wish good things [for each other] and meet each other in necessities. But as for friends, they are not entirely that,[123] since they do not continue the association all day and do not find pleasure in each other, which is friendship[124] more than anything else. (2) It may not be possible that a great number[125] should be friends with perfect friendship, just as it is not possible that one person should love many at the same time. For it is like excess, and it is in the nature of this that it should be related to one. That one should be very greatly pleased with many at the same time is not easy, and it may be that it is not possible that they should even be good. (3) It is sometimes necessary that experience should be had, and that there should be much intimacy and familiarity. That is very difficult. But for utility and pleasure it is possible that one person should be pleased with many, since these are many and they are tests[126] in a short time. (4) It is likely that the friendship of these[127] is mostly that which is on account of the pleasant, when these things are incumbent on both[128] and one finds pleasure in the other, or they find pleasure in the same things, like the friendships of the young, for mostly in these are the generous. As for friendship for utility, it is the friendship of market people. The happy do not at all need sources of usefulness. They need pleasant things, because they wish for association with some people. They bear what is painful for a short time, but it may be that none can endure pain

---

[119] I.e. "good temper and sociability" (Rackham).

[120] Arabic *al-ʿafiṣīn*, another rendering of Greek οἱ στρυφνοί, cf. n. 117.

[121] Arabic *ka'l-abīd*, i.e. Greek δ' οὐδ' οἱ read as δοῦλοι (Arberry). 'Like', Arabic *ka-*, is given by Greek ὁμοίως.

[122] Greek εὔνοι as previously.

[123] Arabic *laisa hum kull dhālika* for Greek οὐ πάνυ.

[124] Reading *ṣadāqa* with the MS., i.e. Greek φιλία for φιλικά.

[125] Reading *kathratun*. It looks, however, as if πολλοὺς δ' εἶναι φίλους has been read instead of πολλοῖς δ' εἶναι φίλον.

[126] Arabic *mujarrabāt*. Arberry suggests that αἱ ὑπηρεσίαι has been 'emended' to ἡ πεῖρα [or πεῖραι] ἔσται. A marginal note reads: *wa-taḥṣulu at-tajribah bi-him fī zamān qalīl kadhā lakhkhaṣahu al-qāḍī*, i.e. Ibn Rushd.

[127] I.e. construing τούτων taken as masculine with φιλία, the vulg. reading (not φιλίᾳ).

[128] I.e. Greek ταὐτὰ ἀπ' ἀμφοῖν (Arberry).

فرحهم بالمعاشرة من أجل أنّه يظنّ بهذه أنّها أكثر ذلك صداقة وفاعلة الصداقة ومن أجل هذا أمّا الأحداث فسريع ما يكونون وأمّا المشايخ فلا من أجل أنّهم [٣/٢٨] لا يكونون أصدقاء للذين [...] فيهم بل هم كالعبيد العفصين بل هؤلاء فإنّهم نصحاء بعضهم لبعض فإنّهم يريدون خيرات ويتلاقون في الحوائج وأمّا أصدقاء فليس هم كلّ ذلك من أجل أنّهم لا يلمون المعاشرة نهارهم ولا يفرح بعضهم ببعض التي هي صداقة أكثر من غيرها (٢) وخليق ألاّ يمكن أن يكونوا كثرة أصدقاء بالصداقة التامّة كما أنّه لا يمكن أن يعشق الواحد كثيراً معاً فإنّه يشبه الإفراط وفي طبع هذا أن يكون مضافاً إلى واحد وأمّا أن يكون واحد يرضى بكثيرين معارضاً شديداً فذلك ليس ببيّن وخليق ألاّ يمكن أن يكونوا أيضاً خياراً (٣) فقد ينبغي أن توجد التجربة وأن تكون مخالطة كثيرة ومؤانسة وذلك عسير جدّاً وأمّا من أجل المنفعة واللذّة فقد يمكن أن يرضى الواحد بكثير من أجل أنّ هؤلاء كثيرون ويكونون مجرّبات في زمان قليل (٤) وقد يشبه أن تكون صداقة هؤلاء أكثر ذلك التي تكون لمكان اللذيذ إذا كانت تكون هذه عن كليهما وكان يفرح بعض ببعض أو كانوا يفرحون بأشياء بأعيانها كصداقات الأحداث فإنّ أكثر ما في هذه ذوو الحرّية وأمّا الصداقة التي تكون للمنفعة فصداقة السوقيين. وذو الغبطة فإنّهم لا يحتاجون إلى الأشياء التي هي ذوات منفعة البتّةَ ويحتاجون إلى اللذيذة لأنّهم يريدون معاشرة بعض الناس فأمّا المحزن فإنّهم يحتملونه زماناً يسيراً فخليق ألاّ يصبر أحد صبراً دائماً على المحزن ولا على الخير بعينه

3 [...] : illegible F, *they do not find pleasure* Dun || 7 معا F : om. Bad || 9 توجد F, Bad, Dun : توخذ read. Arberry || 10 first ان repeated in F || 11 مجربات mrg.: قليل كذا لخصه القاضي || 12 او corr. Dun* (ῆ) : و F, Bad || 12 على F : عن corr. above line || 12 وتحصل التجربة لهم في زمان فصداقة 14 || Dun : unclear F; بصداقة Bad || 15 لأنهم corr. Dun : لا F, Bad || 16 المحزن F : الحزن Bad

continuously nor the good itself if it is painful to him. Hence they seek that their friends should be pleasant and good at the same time. It may be that they are good for themselves, when they are pleasant, and thus they have all that is necessary for friends. (5) Those who are in various positions of power and authority appear to use their friends separately, since friends for utility are for them different from friends for pleasure. That both of them should be the same does not often happen, since they do not seek friendships of pleasure with virtue nor friendships of utility from noble things.[129] Rather they desire people easy to change[130] for the sake of pleasure and wish for clever men for the doing of what they are ordered. These qualities are not often in one and the same man. (6) It has been said that the good man is at the same time pleasant and useful. But this man is not a friend to his superior in rank, unless he also is superior in virtue. Otherwise he is not equal to him in comparison,[131] since that other exceeds him. But it is not usual that people like these are very many.
1158b (7) The friendships which have already been mentioned are with equality, since there are in both friends the same things. Each of them wishes for his friend something for something else[132] like pleasure for utility. It has already been said that these are friendships less[133] and that they remain. Because of the similarity and dissimilarity it is thought of them that they are friendships by the similarity of virtue,[134] since some of them have what is pleasant and others have what is useful, and these are things in which that other[135] also is superior.[136] But since that does not change and is constant, while these change quickly and are different from one another, on this account

---

[129] The text is 'friendships of pleasure [...] friendships of utility' (Arabic *dhawāt lidhdhah* [...] *dhawāt manfa'ah*), but the Greek speaks of persons (ἡδεῖς [...] χρησίμους). This mistake leads to mistranslation of Greek εἰς τὰ καλά as *min al-ashyā' al-khairah*.

[130] Arabic *al-haiyini at-tanaqqul*. Mrg. has *au ṣ<aḥīḥ> al-haiyin wa-kādhā lakhkhaṣahu al-qāḍī*, i.e. Ibn Rushd read the expression as singular.

[131] Arabic *fī 't-tashbīh* for Greek ἀνάλογον, now usually construed with ὑπερεχόμενος.

[132] The construction has gone wrong through omission of ἤ and the verb ἀντικαταλλάττονται.

[133] Arabic *dūn* for Greek ἧττον, which should also be construed with the following words (*wa-innahā tathbut*).

[134] Arabic *at-tashābuh al-faḍlī*, before and after which some words have been dropped.

[135] I.e. the friendship of good men, which is true friendship.

[136] Arabic *tatazaiyadu*, i.e. ὑπερέχει for ὑπάρχει.

إن كان عنده محزناً ومن أجل هذا يطلبون أن يكونوا الأصدقاء ذوي لذّة وأخياراً معاً وخليق أن يكونوا أخياراً لذواتهم إذا كانوا ذوي لذّة وكذلك يكون لهم جميع ما ينبغي أن يكون للأصدقاء (٥) وأمّا الذين في أنواع المقدرة والسلطان فإنّهم يظهرون أنّهم يستعملون الأصدقاء بنوع التفضيل من أجل أنّ أصحاب المنفعة عندهم غير أصحاب اللذّة وأمّا أن يكون كلاهما شيئاً واحداً فليس يكون ذلك كثيراً من أجل أنّهم لا يطلبون ذوات لذّة مع فضيلة ولا ذوات منفعة [٣/٢٩] من الأشياء الخيرة بل يشتهون الهيّن التنقّل لمكان اللذّة ويريدون الدهاة بفعل ما يأمرون به وهذه لا تكون كثيراً في الواحد بعينه (٦) وقد قيل إنّه يكون الفاضل معاً لذيذاً ونافعاً ولكن هذا لا يكون صديقاً للمتزيّد في الفضيلة إلاّ أن يكون هو أيضاً يتزيّد في الفضيلة وإلاّ فليس يساويه في التشبيه إنّما كان ذلك يزيد عليه وليس في العادة أن يكون مثل هؤلاء كثيرين جدّاً (٧) فالمحبّات التي قد قيلت بالمساواة من أجل أنه يكون في كليهما أشياء بأعيانها وكلّ واحد منهما يريد لصاحبه شيئاً آخر بدل شئ آخر كاللذّة بدل المنفعة وقد قيل إنّ هذه محبّات دون وإنّها تثبت بل كان التشابه ولا تشابه يظنّ بها أنّهما محبّات بالتشابه الفضلي من أجل أنّ لبعضها اللذيذ ولبعضها النافع وهذه هي التي تتزيّد بها تلك أيضاً وأمّا بأنّ تلك لا تتغيّر وأنّها ثابتة وبأنّ هذه تتغيّر سريعاً ويختلف

---

1 يكونوا F : يكون corr. Bad || 5 لذة F : om. Bad || 6 الهين mrg.: الهين وكذا لخصه القاضي || 6 الهين التنقل Dun* (τοὺς εὐτραπέλους) : partly illegible F; الهين الأصل Bad || 9 التشبيه F : النشب Bad || 10 مثل F : om. Bad || 10 أنه F : أن Bad || 11 في كليهما F : لكليهما Bad || 13 بها corr. Dun : به F, Bad; om. Arberry

many do not see[137] that they are friendships, because they do not resemble that other.[138]

7. Among the kinds of friendship there is another kind,[139] like the friendship of the father to the son, and in general the elder to the young man, the man to the woman and every chief to the subject. These differ, since there is not one and the same friendship of fathers with children and chiefs with subjects, nor[140] of father with son, nor son with father, nor of man with woman, nor woman with man, because the virtue of each one of these is different, and the action is different, and the reasons for which they love are different, hence the reasons for[141] the friendships and mutual love are different. (2) For these[142] do not belong to each of them from each, nor are they sought for.[143] When the child is kind to his parents, as is right for parents, and the parents are kind to the children, as is right, the friendship of these is permanent and meritorious. It should be proportional[144] in every one whose friendship is preponderant, as for instance that the better should be loved rather than love, and similarly the more useful and each of the others. For when love is according to merit, there is then a certain equality, which is thought to belong to friendship. (3) It does not appear that what is equal is alike in matters of justice and in friendship, for the equal, in the first place, in matters of justice, is what is according to merit and what is according to quantity in the second place, but in friendship what is according to quantity in the first place and what is according to merit in the second place. (4) It is clear then that[145] there is much difference between virtue and vice, or wealth or anything else, since they are not after that friends, nor do they think they merit it. That is very evident in the case of the gods, for these have much preponderance over all good things. That
1159a is plain in the case of the kings also, since those who are beneath them do not think themselves worthy to be their friends. Similarly

---

[137] I.e. Greek πολλοῖς taken with οὐ φαίνονται (Arberry).

[138] I.e. the friendship of good men which is true friendship.

[139] Greek τὸ καθ' ὑπεροχήν is omitted.

[140] The nuance in Greek ἀλλ' οὐδέ, 'nor even, nor indeed', is disregarded.

[141] Arabic *fa'llatī lahā* [...] *ukhar*, i.e. Greek ἕτερα οὖν καὶ δι' ἅ, the reading of K[b], as Arberry noted (*fa* = οὖν).

[142] I.e. ταῦτα for ταὐτά.

[143] Arabic fails to render Greek δεῖ (perhaps misread as δή).

[144] Greek καὶ τὴν φίλησιν is not translated.

[145] Arabic *annahu*, but Greek ἐάν with a conditional clause.

بعضها من بعض فمن أجل هذا كثير من لا يرى أنّها محبّات لأنّها لا تشبه تلك.

٧. ومن أنواع المحبّة نوع آخر كمحبّة الأب للابن وبالجملة الشيخ للشابّ والرجل للمرأة وكلّ رئيس للمرءوس عليه وهذه فيما بينها اختلاف من أجل أنّه ليست المحبّة واحدة بعينها للآباء في الأولاد والرؤساء في المرؤسين عليهم ولا للأب في الابن ولا للابن في الأب ولا الرجل في المرأة ولا المرأة في الرجل لأنّ فضيلة كلّ واحدة من هذه أخرى والفعل آخر والتي يحبّون لها آخر فالتي لها تكون المحبّات والتحابّ آخر (٢) فإنّ هذه لا تكون لكلّ واحد منهما من أحدهما ولا تطلب وإذا برّ الولد والديه على ما ينبغي للوالدين وبرّ الوالدين للأولاد على ما ينبغي تكون محبّة هؤلاء ثابتة وذات استئهل وينبغي أن يكون في جميع [ما] تكون محبّته هي بالتزيّد على نسبة ذلك كقولي إنّه ينبغي أن يُحَبّ الأجود أكثر من أن يحِبّ وكذلك الأنفع وكلّ واحد من الأخر فإنّ الحبّ إذا صار على قدر الاستئهل تكون حينئذٍ مساواة ما التي يظنّ أنّها للمحبّة (٣) وليس يظهر المتساوي أنّه متشابه [٣/٣٠] في العدلية والمحبّة فإنّ المساوي بنوع أوّل أمّا في العدلية فالذي على الاستئهل وأمّا على التي على الكمّية فبنوع ثانٍ وأمّا في المحبّة فالذي على الكمّية بنوع أوّل وأمّا الذي على الاستئهل فبنوع ثانٍ (٤) فبيّن أنّه يكون بُعْد كثير فيما بين الفضيلة والرداءة أو الوجد أو شيء آخر من أجل أنّهم لا يكونون بعد ذلك أصدقاء ولا يوهّلون وذلك ظاهر جدّاً في الآلهة فإنّ تزيّد هؤلاء على جميع الخيرات كثير وذلك بيّن في الملوك أيضاً من أجل أنّ الذين دونهم لا يؤهّلون أنفسهم أن يكونوا أصدقاء لأولئك

1 فمن : F من Bad || 3 ليست corr. Bad : ليس F || 9 ما suppl. Bad || 9 هي corr. Bad : هو F || 11 ما مساواة : F مساواتها Bad || 12 المتساوي : F perh. corr. المساوي || 12 first في : F مع Bad || 15 الوجد corr. Dun : الوجود F, Bad

those who merit nothing are not friends of the best and[146] wisest men. (5) There is not in this an exact limit up to what point they are friends.[147] For if many things are removed, [friendship] remains even so,[148] but when one is separated by much, as God is, it does not remain. (6) Hence there is deep perplexity as to whether perhaps friends do not wish great goods for their friends, as for instance that they should be gods. For if so, they will not afterwards be friends nor will they be good things,[149] since friends are kinds of good, just as[150] it is said that a friend wishes good things for his friend on his account, and that they should continue to him, if necessary,[151] as long as that is so. He will wish for him, since he is a man, that he should have great goods.[152]

8. Many a man is thought through love of honour to wish to be loved rather than to love. On account of this the lovers of the compliant are many, for the compliant is a friend who exceeds in pretence.[153] He himself[154] pretends to love more than he is loved, and to be loved is thought to be near to being honoured by those who desire it not for itself.[155] (2) They seem to choose honour not for itself,[156] but incidentally. Often a man rejoices when he is honoured by those in power, on account of hope: they think that they will obtain from them what they need. They rejoice in honour as if it was a proof of devoted obedience.[157] As for those who desire honour from men of worth [and] knowledge, they desire that they should confirm their own opinion regarding themselves,[158] and they rejoice that they are

---

[146] Arabic *wa-*, 'and', for Greek ἤ, 'or'.

[147] Arabic *ilā mādhā al-aṣdiqā'*. This is the vulg. reading οἱ φίλοι literally rendered in Arabic.

[148] Arabic *aiḍan* for Greek ἔτι, as often.

[149] Greek αὐτοῖς is left out, and the sense is lost.

[150] I.e. ἀγαθὰ εἴδη καλῶς [καὶ ὡς, Arberry], read for ἀγαθὰ. εἰ δὴ καλῶς.

[151] The construction is clearly wrong, for δέοι goes closely with μένειν: the friend has to remain himself.

[152] This sentence is misunderstood and the following sentence omitted probably through homoioteleuton.

[153] Apparently for ἢ προσποιεῖται (Arberry).

[154] Arabic *wa-huwa bi-ʿainihi*, i.e. καὶ αὐτός for τοιοῦτος καί (Arberry).

[155] Arabic *mimman yashtahīhi lā li-dhātihi*, i.e. οὗ is taken as masculine, οἱ πολλοί has fallen out and ἐφίεται (for ἐφίενται) is construed with οὐ δι' αὐτό from the following sentence.

[156] Arabic *lā bi-dhātihā*, but the phrase has already been rendered.

[157] Arabic *jūdat aṭ-ṭaʿah*, i.e. εὐπειθείας for εὐπαθείας of the text (Arberry).

[158] I.e. Greek δέ for δή.

وكذلك الذين لا يستأهلون شيئاً لا يكونوا أصدقاء للأفاضل والحكماء جدّاً (٥) وليس في هذا حدّ مستقصى إلى ماذا الأصدقاء فإنّه إن انتزعت أشياء كثيرة تبقى أيضاً فأمّا إذا فارق شيئاً كثيراً مثل الإله فليست تبقى (٦) ومن ها هنا يتحيّر بنوع عويص لهل الأصدقاء لا يريدون لأصدقائهم الخيرات العظيمة كقولي أن يكونوا آلهة فإنّه إن كانوا ذلك لا يكونون من بعد ذلك أصدقاء ولا يكونون خيرات من أجل أنّ الأصدقاء أنواع خيرية كما قيل إنّ الصديق يريد الخيرات لصديقه من أجله وأن تثبت له إن كان ينبغي ذلك ما دام ذلك كذلك فيسير بذلك إذ هو إنسان أن تكون له الخيرات العظام.

٨. وكثير من يظنّ به بمحبّ الكرامة أنّه يريد أن يحَبّ أكثر من أن يحِبّ ومن أجل هذا محبّو المتأتّي كثيرون فإنّ المتأتّي صديق متزيّد على ما يؤاتي وهو بعينه يؤاتي أن يحِبّ أكثر ممّا يحَبّ وأن يحَبّ يظنّ أنّه قريب من أن يكون الذي يكرم ممن يشتهيه لا لذاته (٢) فقد يشبه أن يكونوا يختارون الكرامة لا بذاتها بل بنوع العرض فكثيراً ما يفرح إذا أكرم من أصحاب السلطان لمكان الرجاء ويظنّون أنّهم يصيبون منهم ما يحتاجون إليه فيفرحون بالكرامة كأنّها دلالة على جودة الطاعة وأمّا الذين يشتهون الكرامة من الذين هم ذوو استئهال ومعرفة فإنّهم يشتهون أن يؤكّدوا رأيهم فيهم ويفرحون أنّهم أخيار ويصدّقون

2 فأما F : أما Bad || 3 فليست corr. Bad : فليس F || 3 لهل F : هل Bad || 4 آلهة read. Bad, Dun : ألهة F || 4 كانوا corr. Bad : كان F || 4 يكونون corr. Bad, Dun : يكونوا F || 5 يكونون corr. Bad, Dun : يكونوا F || 6 وأن تثبت corr. Dun : وإن ثبت F, Bad || 7 فيسير F : يشير Bad || 7 إذ F : إن Bad || 8 first من F : ممن corr. Bad || 8 بمحب corr. Dun : محب F, Bad || 9 محبو corr. Bad : محبي F || 9 محبو المتأتي corr. mrg.* (φιλοκόλακες) : محبي التاتي F || 14 ومعرفة corr. Bad, Dun : معرفة F || 14 يؤكدوا corr. Bad, Dun : يؤكدون F

good[159] and believe in the judgement of the speakers.[160] Thus they rejoice in being loved,[161] since friendship is chosen for itself. (3) It is thought that it is more likely to be in the one who loves than the one who is loved. The proof of that are mothers, who take pleasure in loving. For some of them allow that what is theirs should be less.[162] They love with knowledge and do not seek a requital of love, if both are not possible, but it seems that it is sufficient for them to see the good state of the children, and they love the children, even if they are not kind to the mother in any of the things in respect of which she ought to be treated kindly, on account of ignorance. (4) As friendship is more in the one who loves,[163] and the one who loves his friends[164] is praised, it seems that the exercise of friendship is the virtue of friends. So then those who possess this according to merit
1159b are firm friends, and the friendship of these is firm. (5) These and those who are equal[165] should be friends in equality,[166] for equality and similarity are friendship, and especially similarity of excellent people,[167] since, as they are constant in themselves, they are constant also with each another, and do not require base things,[168] nor do they do such things, but, one might say, prevent that even, as they neither go wrong in regard to good things[169] nor order their friends to go wrong in them. As for wicked men, they do not possess firmness, since they are not constantly alike in their conditions. They become friends for a little time, and each of them delights in the wickedness of the other. (6) As for those who are useful and pleasant, they are very constant as long as they provide pleasures and utilities for each

---

[159] So also Gauthier: "[...] leur joie, c'est d'être bons."

[160] A marginal note reads: *wa-bi-taṣdīq al-mukramīn lahum fa-dhālika idh lā yukrimu 'l-akhyāra illā 'l-akhyāru kadhā lakhkhaṣahu 'l-qāḍī*, i.e. Ibn Rushd.

[161] Greek καθ' αὑτό has dropped out, as well as διὸ δόξειεν [...] τιμᾶσθαι, noted by Arberry.

[162] Arabic *dūn*, possibly τρέπεσθαι, 'be changed', was read for τρέφεσθαι, 'to be nourished'.

[163] Arabic *fī 'lladhī yuḥibbu* for Greek ἐν τῷ φιλεῖν.

[164] Arabic *alladhī yuḥibbu 'l-aḥibbā'*, i.e. the vulg. (φιλοφίλων) as against K^b (φίλων). Cf. 1155a 29.

[165] Arabic *fa-hā'ulā'i wa'l-mutasāwūn*. Arberry suggests that οὗτοι δ' ἄν was read for οὕτω δ' ἄν.

[166] Arabic *bi'l-musāwāt* for Greek ἰσάζοιντο γὰρ ἄν.

[167] Arabic *ahl al-faḍl* but Greek is τῶν κατ' ἀρετήν [sc. ὁμοίων], i.e. 'those alike in virtue'.

[168] I.e. services (Ross).

[169] The construction is wrong (τῶν ἀγαθῶν taken as neuter, is construed as dependent on ἁμαρτάνειν).

بقضية القائلين وكذلك يفرحون [٣/٣٦] بأن يحَبّوا من أجل أنّ المحبّة مختارة بذاتها (٣) ويظنّ بها أنّها أحرى أن تكون في النى يحِبّ من النى يحَبّ والدليل على ذلك الأمّهات التي تفرح أن تحِبّ فإنّ بعضهن يعطين أن يكون ما لهنّ دون وهن يحبّن بعلم ولا يطلبن التكافؤ بالمحبّة إذا لم يكن كلاهما بل يشبه أن يكون عندهن مقنعاً أن يرين حسن حل الأولاد وهن محبّات للأولاد وإن كانوا لم يردوا الوالدة بشئ ممّا ينبغي أن تبرّ به لمكان الجهالة (٤) وإذا كانت المحبّة أكثر في النى يحِبّ وكنّا نمدح النى يحبّ الأحبّاء فقد يشبه أن يكون استعمل الصداقة فضيلة الأصدقاء فإذاً الذين يكون هذا فيهم على الاستئهل فهؤلاء أصدقاء ثابتون على الصداقة وصداقة هؤلاء ثابتة (٥) فهؤلاء والمتساوون أحرى أن يكونوا أصدقاء بالمساواة فإنّ المساواة والتشابه صداقة ولا سيّما تشابه أهل الفضل من أجل أنّهم إذا كانوا ثابتين في ذاتهم ثبت أيضاً بعضهم مع بعض وليس يحتاجون إلى الأشياء الرديئة ولا يفعلون مثل هذه بل كقول القائل يمنعون من ذلك أيضاً إذ كانوا لا يخطئون عن الخيرات ولا يأمرون الأصدقاء أن يخطئوها فأمّا الأشرار فليس لهم التأكيد من أجل أنّهم لا يثبتون على حالاتهم متشابهين وإنّما يصيرون أصدقاء زماناً قليلاً وكلّ واحد منهم يفرح برداءة الآخر (٦) وأمّا في المنفعة واللذّة فإنّهم يثبتون كثيراً ما دام

1 القائلين mrg.: وبتصديق المكرمين لهم فذلك إذ لا يكرم الاخيار وإلا الاخيار كذا لخصه القاضي || 3 ان يكون F, Dun : om. Bad || 6 في النى يحب Dun : illegible F || 11 إذ corr. Bad : إذا F

other. It is mostly thought that friendship is from opposites on account of utility, like the friendship of the poor man with the rich and the ignorant man with the learned. For he does not oppose,[170] being a poor man,[171] and he desires and is given instead something else. One might bring in here the lover also and the beloved, and the handsome and the ugly. Hence it appears ridiculous in lovers when they wish at some time to be loved.[172] Similarly[173] when they are lovable, they would be considered worthy in this way, but when they have nothing like this, they would deserve to be laughed at. (7) Perhaps the mutual desire of opposite for opposite is not essential, but accidental, and desire is for the mean. For this is good, as for instance the good for the dry is [not] that it should be wet but that it should reach an intermediate state, and similarly for the hot and the other things. But let these matters be left aside, for they are extraneous.

9. It is likely, as was said at the beginning, that friendship and justice are concerned with what is between us and among us,[174] and since it is thought that in every partnership and association there is a certain justice and[175] friendship. They call friends those who accompany one another on ships[176] and in the army, and similarly in other shared associations, and the measure of their friendship is according to their sharing in the association, for justice and the proverb is true,[177] that what belongs to friends is shared in common, since friendship is a sharing. (2) All that belongs to brothers and comrades is shared in common, but others have what is measured out,[178] to some more, to others less, since some friendships are more and some less. In justice
1160a too there is a difference, since they are not the same [things] for

---

[170] Arabic *lā yuḍāddu*, as Arberry indicates, is like οὐ γὰρ ἐναντιοῦται which was apparently read for οὐ γὰρ τυγχάνει τις of the Greek text.

[171] Arabic *wa-hādhā faqīr*, Greek ἐνδεὴς ὤν. It seems that οὗτος has been read for is for τούτου.

[172] Greek ὡς φιλοῦσιν is here omitted.

[173] Arabic *ka-dhālika*. But Greek ὁμοίως goes closely with φιλητούς.

[174] Arabic *fīmā bainanā wa-fīnā* for Greek περὶ ταὐτὰ καὶ ἐν τοῖς αὐτοῖς.

[175] The force of καὶ φιλία δέ is not attended to.

[176] Arberry's *as-sufun* seems preferable to the reading ot the MS. *as-safr*, cf. 1161b 13 where Greek αἱ συμπλοϊκαὶ <φιλίαι> is rendered by *allatī takūn bi-ṣuḥbat as-safīnah*.

[177] Arabic *fa'inna 'l-'adl wa'l-mathal ṣaḥīḥ*. The construction of ἡ παροιμία with τὸ δίκαιον is wrong.

[178] Arabic *muqaddar*, 'hardly' = ἀφωρισμένα.

يكتسبون اللذّات والمنافع بعضهم لبعض ويظنّ أكثر ذلك أنّ المحبّة تكون من الأضداد لمكان المنفعة كمحبّة الفقير للغني والجاهل للعالم فإنّه لا يضادّ وهذا فقير وهو يشتهي وهو يعطى بدله شيئاً آخر وخليق أن يجذب أحد إلى ها هنا العاشق أيضاً والمعشوق والجميل والقبيح ومن أجل هذا يظهر أنّه أهل أن يُضحك بالعشّاق إذ يريدون في وقت ما أن يحَبّوا وكذلك إذا كانوا محبوبين خليق أن يؤهّلوا على هذا النوع وإذا لم يكن لهم شئ مثل هذا خليق أن يكونوا يضحك بهم (٧) وخليق اشتياق الضدّ إلى الضدّ [أن يكونا] [٣/٣٢] لا بذاته بل بنوع العرض والشهوة للمتوسّط فإنّ هذا هو خير كقولي إنّه الخير لليابس ألا يصير رطباً بل أن يصير إلى الوسط وكذلك للحارّ وللأشياء الأخر فلنترك هذه فإنّها غريبة عن موضوعنا.

٩. ويشبه كما قيل في الابتداء أن تكون المحبّة والعدل فيما بيننا وفينا ومن أجل أنّه يظنّ أنّ في كلّ اشتراك ومعاملة عدلاً ما وصداقة ويسمّون أصدقاء المرافقين في السفن والجيش وكذلك في سائر المعاملات المشتركة ومقدار صداقتهم على قدر شركتهم المعاملة فإنّ العدل والمثل صحيح أنّ ما للأصدقاء مشترك من أجل أنّ الصداقة بشركة (٢) بجميع ما للإخوة والأصحاب مشترك وأمّا ما للأخر فمقدّر أمّا لبعض فأكثر وأمّا لبعض فأقلّ من أجل أنّ بعض الصداقات أكثر وبعضها أقلّ وفي العدل أيضاً اختلاف من أجل

2 فإنه F : فإن Bad || 2 يضاد F : تضاد Bad || 2 وهذا F : فهذا Bad || 5 first و F : om. Bad || 5 يؤهلوا
F, Dun : يرسلوا Bad || 6 يكونوا يضحك F : يكونوا أهلا أن يضحك suppl. Bad || 6 أن يكون suppl.
Dun || 8 لليابس corr. Dun : اليابس F, Bad || 8 ألا corr. Dun : أن F, Bad || 11 السفن corr.
Arberry : السفر F || 14-15 ولبعض فأقل corr. Dun : ولبعض أقل F; بعض فأقل Bad

fathers and[179] sons and brothers to one another, nor comrades and those who are from one city, and similarly in the case of other friends.[180] (3) For justice[181] also is different for each one of them, and it is more likely[182] to receive the increase among friends, as for instance taking money from a comrade is worse than taking it from a fellow-citizen, and not helping a brother is worse than not helping a stranger, and similarly striking a father is worse than striking anyone else. It appears[183] that justice increases with friendship, as if they[184] are both in the same things, and it extends equally.[185] (4) All partnerships in common resemble the parts of the political form, for they all pass to something which is better,[186] and provide something of what is advantageous in life. And it is thought that the political association delights in[187] what is more advantageous and goes with it from the beginning and continues also. This is the aim of legislators, and they suppose that justice is the common advantage.[188] (5) For the rest of the partnerships desire the partial advantage, as those who take ship desire the more advantageous in taking ship for gaining wealth or for something like this, and companions in arms desire the more advantageous in fighting either owing to their desire for money or owing to their desire for victory or for taking a city, and similarly members of one of the people's tribes.[189] It is thought that some partnerships are for the sake of pleasure, like[190] the partnership of the chiefs of communities,[191] and the chiefs of those who contribute equal shares, for these are on account of sacrifice. It is likely that all these are under the political form, for the political [form] does not desire what is

---

[179] The Greek is 'to sons' (πρὸς τέκνα).

[180] Arabic *al-aṣdiqā'*, but Greek is φιλιῶν (Arberry).

[181] Reading τὰ δίκαια (L^b and Γ) for τὰ ἄδικα of the vulg. (Arberry).

[182] Arabic *aḥrā*. This apparently represents τῷ μᾶλλον, cf. 1159a 27.

[183] Arabic *yaẓhar*, i.e. φαίνεται, the reading of K^b, rather than πέφυκεν (Arberry).

[184] Arabic *ka-annahumā*, i.e. Greek ὥσπερ, 'as if', giving a different sense from ὡς of the text. And Greek ἐν τοῖς αὐτοῖς is masculine.

[185] Arabic *wa-yantahī bi 'l-masāwāt* for Greek καὶ ἐπ' ἴσον διήκοντα.

[186] Arabic *akhyar* for Greek συμφέροντι, cf. 1156a 27.

[187] Arabic *tafraḥu bi 'lladhī*, i.e. apparently χαίρειν for χάριν (Arberry).

[188] MS. *li 'l-ʿāmm*, but corr. *al-ʿāmm*. The difficulty of the MS. reading was felt, and mrg. corrects to *li 'l-ʿilm*, 'for science', which is of no help. Cf. 1096b 32-33 τὸ κοινῇ κατηγορούμενον ἀγαθόν rendered by Arabic *al-khair al-ʿāmm al-maḥmūl*, also the parallel phrase here *al-aufaq al-juz'ī*, 'the partial advantage'.

[189] Arabic *afyā'*, appears to be a plural of *fi'ya*, 'company', cf. Lane, s.v.

[190] This is similar to Richards' emendation <διον> before θιασωτῶν.

[191] Arabic *ishtirāk ru'asā' al-jamāʿāt*. The Arabic translator does not understand θιασωτῶν (members of a religious guild) from θίασος.

أنّها ليست [الأشياء] بأعيانها للآباء والأبناء والإخوة وبعضهم إلى بعض ولا الأصحاب والذين من مدينة واحدة وكذلك في سائر الأصدقاء (٣) فإنّ العدل أيضاً آخر لكلّ واحد منهم وأحرى أن تقبل الزيادة عند الأصدقاء كقولي إنّ انتزاع الأموال من الصاحب أردأ من انتزاعها من المشارك في المدينة وترك معونة الأخ أردأ من ترك معونة غريب وكذلك شدخ الأب أردأ من شدخ آخر من كان ويظهر أنّ العدل يتزيّد مع المحبّة كأنّهما في أشياء بأعيانها وينتهي بالمساواة (٤) وجميع اشتراكات العامّة تشبه أجزاء الهيئة المدنية فإنّها تمضي جميعاً إلى شئ هو أخير وتكسب شيئاً ممّا هو موافق في العمر ويظنّ بالشركة المدنية أنّها تفرح بالذي هو أوفق وتنطلق معها من البدء وتثبت أيضاً وهذا هو غرض واضعي النواميس ويزعمون أنّ العدل هو الأوفق العامّ (٥) فإنّ سائر الاشتراك يشتهي الأوفق الجزئي كالذين يركبون الماء يشتهون الأوفق في ركوب الماء لكسب الأموال أو لشئ مثل هذا والمشاركين في الجندية يشتهون الأوفق في القتل إمّا لشهوتهم الأموال وإمّا لشهوتهم الغلبة [٣/٣٣] أو لأخذ مدينة وكذلك ذوو الفئية من أفياء الناس ويظنّ ببعض الاشتراكات أنّها تكون لمكان اللذّة كاشتراك رؤساء الجماعات ورؤساء الذين يتخارجون فإنّ هذه تكون من أجل الذبيحة ويشبه أن تكون هذه كلّها تحت الهيئة المدنية

1 الأشياء suppl. Bad || 3 الزيادة corr. Dun* (αὔξησιν) : الردامة F, Bad || 3 إن Bad : إنه F || 6 مع || 9 العامة corr. Arberry : العاملة F, Bad || 7 مما F : ما Bad || 8 معها : perh. corr. Arberry مع || 9 العام corr. Dun : للعام F, Bad; للعلم corr. mrg. || 12 الفئية corr. Dun : القنية F, Bad || 12 افياء من Bad, Dun : illegible F || 13 الذين F, Dun : الدين Bad

more advantageous[192] but those who render sacrifice during all their life[193] and honour God in the assemblies.[194] For they gain rest for themselves, with pleasure. And it appears that ancient sacrifices and assemblies were after the gathering of the fruits, in the sense of offerings, because their leisure was mostly in these times. (6) Thus it has appeared that all the partnerships are parts of the political form, and friendships of these types tend to follow partnerships of these types.

10. There are three kinds of the political form[195] and their declensions are equal also in number, I mean, their perversions. The political kinds are kingship, aristocracy, and the third, which depends on honours. It appears that it is likely to be called the timocracy, while most people are accustomed to name it *politeia*, i.e. way of life.[196] (2) The best of these is kingship, and the worst of them is democ-
1160b racy.[197] As for the declension of kingship, it is tyranny. Both of them are monarchies, but between them is much difference, because the aim of the tyrant is what is best for him, while the aim of the king is what is best for those under his rule. For he is not a king who is not self-sufficient[198] and perfect[199] in all good things and does not need anything, so that his aim is [not] his personal interests but the interests of his subjects. Whoever is not so, would be king by lot. As for tyranny, it is the opposite of this, because the tyrant seeks his own good, and it more evidently is worse, because the opposite of the good is also bad.[200] (3) It changes from kingship to tyranny, because tyranny is the vice of single rule, and the bad king becomes a tyrant. And it changes from aristocracy to oligarchy, which is the worst of

[192] Arabic *alladhī huwa aufaq*. Something has dropped out, corresponding to Greek παρόντος.

[193] Arabic *bal* [...] *fī jamī' al-umūr*, i.e. Greek ἀλλ' εἰς ἅπαντα τὸν βίον construed with the following words.

[194] The Arabic translator has apparently read and construed: καὶ περὶ τὰς συνόδους τιμὰς ἀπονέμοντες τῷ θεῷ.

[195] Arabic *al-hai'ah al-madanīyah* for Greek πολιτείας; above c. 9, §§ 4, 5 and 6, the same Arabic expression renders ἡ πολιτική [sc. κοινωνία].

[196] This explanation is, of course, an addition to the Greek.

[197] Arabic *riyāsat al-'awāmm*, i.e. δημοκρατία for τιμοκρατία (Arberry).

[198] Arabic *makfīy*, passive participle of *kafā*, I, lit. 'sufficed, satisfied', i.e. not quite Greek αὐτάρκης.

[199] Arabic *fāḍil* for Greek ὑπερέχων.

[200] Perhaps for καὶ κάκιστον (Arberry).

فإنّ [الهيئة] المدنية ليست تشتهي الذي هو أوفق بل الذين يصيّرون الذبيحة في جميع العمور ويكرمون الإله في الاجتماعات فإنّهم يكتسبون راحة لذواتهم مع لذّة فقد يظهر أنّ الذبائح القديمة والاجتماعات كانت تكون عند جمع الثمار كأنّها قرابين من أجل أنّ فراغهم كان أكثر ذلك في هذه الأوقات (٦) فقد ظهر أنّ جميع الاشتراكات أجزاء الهيئة المدنية وتستتبع صداقات مثل هذه اشتراكات مثل هذه.

١٠. فأنواع الهيئة المدنية ثلاثة وزوالاتها مساوية أيضاً أعني فسلاداتها فالأنواع المدنية الملك ورياسة الأخيار والثالث الذي يكون من كرامات ويظهر أنّه يشبه أن يقل رياسة الكرامة وقد اعتاد أكثر الناس أن يسمّيها بولوطيا أيّ سيرة (٢) فأخير هذه الملك وأشرّها رياسة العوامّ وأمّا زوال الملك فالتغلّب فكلاهما ذوو رياسة واحدة وبينهما اختلاف كثير من أجل أنّ المتغلّب غرضه ما هو أخير له وغرض الملك ما هو أخير لمن تحت رياسته فإنّه ليس يملك الذي ليس بمكفي وفاضل في جميع الخيرات فليس يحتاج إلى شئ فإذاً غرضه [ليس] منافع ذاته بل منافع رعيته ومن لم يكن كذلك فخليق أن يكون ملكاً بالقرعة وأمّا التغلّب فضدّ هذا من أجل أنّه يطلب الخير لذاته وهو أشدّ ظهوراً أنّه أردأ من أجل أنّه ضدّ الخير شرير أيضاً (٣) وينتقل من الملك إلى التغلّب من أجل أنّ التغلّب رداءة لرياسة وحدانية والملك الردئ يصير متغلّباً وينتقل من رياسة الأخيار إلى رياسة قليلين وهي أردأ الرؤساء الذين يقسمون مل المدنية على غير استئهل ويصيّرون جميع الخيرات

1 الهيئة المدنية suppl. and corr. Dun* (ἡ πολιτική) : المدينة F || 1 أوفق F, Dun : الآن Bad || 2
العمور corr. Dun : العمر F, Bad || 2 ويكرمون corr. Bad : ويكرموا F || 7 الذي يكون corr. : التي تكون
F, Bad || 9 وأما F : فأما Bad || 9 فالتغلب corr. Dun : والتغلب F; بالتغلب corr. Bad || 9 ذوو F : ذو
Bad || 12 ليس suppl. Bad, Dun || 12 ملكا corr. Bad : ملك F || 13 أردأ F, Dun : الردئ Bad ||
15 الردئ corr. Dun* (φαυλότης) : الذي F

the chiefs[201] who divide among themselves the wealth of the city contrary to merit, and appropriate all the goods or most of them, and work to secure that the offices should always be to the same people.[202] The chiefs are few and vicious, instead of the deserving among the best men. It changes also from timocracy to democracy, for these two forms of rule are conterminous with each other, since timocracy also means that it is majority rule,[203] and that all are equal in honour. Democracy is not very bad, since its declension from the form of *politeia*[204] is not great. It is in this way that the forms mostly alter, for in this way their change is easy and trifling. (4) It is possible for one to get likenesses of these, as it were examples of them, in households also, because the dealing of the father with his sons is like the dealing of the king with his subjects. For the father cares for the sons, and therefore Homer named [Zeus] 'father', because the king's rule has to be paternal. Among the Persians the rule of the father is tyrannical, for they take their sons as slaves. And the master's rule of slaves is tyrannical also, since in it he employs them insofar as it is better[205] for the master. The latter, it seems, is right, but the Persian form is wrong, since the forms of rule are different things.[206] (5) For aristocracy in man and woman seems to be different,[207] because the man rules by merit over the things which he should rule over, and he hands over to the woman all that is appropriate for her. If the man has control and command over everything,
1161a it becomes oligarchy, and he does that contrary to merit, not by his being better.[208] And sometimes women rule, when that is by lot,[209] and the rule[210] is not then according to virtue but on account of wealth and power, like what is in oligarchies. (6) The rule of broth-

---

[201] Arabic *wa-hiya arda' ar-ra'usā'* [sic], i.e. apparently κακίστη for κακίᾳ.

[202] The words περὶ πλείστου ποιούμενοι τὸ πλουτεῖν have dropped out (Arberry).

[203] Arabic *riyāsat kathrah* Greek ἐν τῷ τιμήματι.

[204] Arabic *as-sīrah*, i.e. timocracy, cf. § 1.

[205] Arabic *ajwad* for Greek συμφέρον, cf. infra § 6.

[206] We could read, for *al-mukhtalifah* of the text, *al-mukhtalifah mukhtalifah*, and get a good sense, but apparently this was not what the Arabic translation had originally, vid. next note.

[207] I.e. διάφοροι from the previous sentence is construed with ἀνδρὸς δὲ καὶ γυναικὸς ἀριστοκρατική (Arberry).

[208] Arabic *ajwad* for Greek ἀμείνων.

[209] Arabic *bi 'l-qurʿah*, i.e. the Arabic translator read ἐπὶ κλήρῳ. This seems more probable than that he renders ἐπίκληροι, 'heiresses', as if = κληρωτοί, cf. 1160b 6.

[210] Arabic is plural (*ar-riyāsāt*) corresponding to the Greek (αἱ ἀρχαί).

[٣/٣٤] أو أكثرها لذاتهم ويجتهدون أن تكون الرياسات أبداً لقوم بأعيانهم ويكون الرؤساء قليلين وذوي رداءة بدل مَن يستأهل ذلك من الأفاضل وتنتقل من رياسة الكرامة إلى رياسة العامّة فإنّ هاتين الرياستين متقاربتا الحدود من أجل أنّ رياسة الكرامة أيضاً تريد أن تكون رياسة كثرة وأن يكونوا أجمعين الذين في الكرامة متساوين ورياسة العامّة قليلة الرداءة من أجل أنّ زوالها من نوع السيرة قليل. بهذا النوع تتغيّر السير أكثر ذلك فإنّه يهون انتقالها بهذا النوع وتقلّ (٤) ويمكن أن يأخذ آخذ أشباه هذه كأمثالها في البيوت أيضاً من أجل أنّ معاملة الأب للأولاد كمعاملة الملك للرعية فإنّ الأب يعنى بالأولاد ولذلك سمّى أوميروش [ديا] أباً لأنّ الملك يحتاج أن تكون رياسته أبوية وأمّا عند الفرس فرياسة الأب تغلّبية فإنّهم يتّخذون أولادهم كالعبيد ورياسة المولى للعبيد تغلّبية أيضاً من أجل أنه إنّما يستعملهم فيها ما هو أجود للمولى فأمّا هذه فيظهر أنّها مصيبة وأمّا الفارسية فمخطئة من أجل أنّ الرياسات من المختلفة (٥) فإنّ رياسة الأخيار في الرجل والمرأة يظهر أنّها مختلفة من أجل أنّ الرجل يرئس بالاستئهال على التي ينبغي أن يرئس عليها ويسلّم إلى المرأة جميع ما يليق بها فإذا قدر الرجل وساد على جميع الأشياء يصير إلى قلّة رياسة ويفعل ذلك بلا استئهل لا بأنّه أجود وربّما رأست النساء إذا كان ذلك بالقرعة ولا تكون الرياسات على الفضيلة حينئذ بل تكون لمكان الغنى والقوّة كما يكون في رياسات القليلين (٦) ورياسة الإخوة تشبه رياسة الكرامة من أجل أنّهم متساوون وليس يختلفون ما خلا اختلاف الأسنان ولهذا السبب إن كان اختلافهم في الأسنان متقارباً لا تكون المحبّة

---

1 أو corr. Dun : و F, Bad || 8 ديا suppl. Dun : زيوس suppl. Bad || 10 فيها ما F : فيما Bad corr. || 14 راست corr. Bad : راس F || 14 بلا استئهل corr. Dun* (παρά) : بالاستئهل F, Bad ||

ers resembles timocracy, because they are equal and do not differ apart from the difference of age. For this reason, if their difference in age is wide, the friendship is not fraternal. Democracy is mostly in dwellings which have no master, for here [all] are equal, and in those of which the chief is weak, and each man has power.

11. In each of the ways of life friendship appears to the extent to which justice also appears. As for the friendship of the king towards those over whom he rules, it is to the extent of the superiority in doing good. For the king, if he is good, does good to those over whom he rules, and takes care of them in order that their actions must be just,[211] as the shepherd takes care of his sheep, and for that reason Homer called Agamemnon 'the shepherd of the people'. (2) Exemplary[212] rule is like this also, and differs only in the greatness of the benefits. For it is thought of him that he is the cause of the existence[213] and being, and the nurture and instruction, and by these requites[214] previous generations, since the father is the head of the sons by nature and similarly past generations heads of their descendants, and so the king of his subjects. (3) These friendships involve superiority, and hence parents are honoured. Justice regarding these is not one and the same, but depends on merit, and similarly the friendship (4)[215] in an aristocracy also is according to virtue: to the better there is more in good things and to each one according to what is right, and similarly justice also. (5) As for the friendship of brothers, it is like the friendship of comrades. For they are equal and near to one another, and those who are such have emotions in common and their characters resemble each other for the most part. These are like people under a timocracy, since what is wanted is that the citizens should be equal, and meritorious, and that the rule should be partial[216] and with equality, and so friendship also. (6) In the declensions, however, as there is little justice so also [little] friendship, and least of what there is in the worst of them. For in

---

[211] I.e. 'that they may do good' for Greek εὖ πράττωσιν.

[212] Arabic *al-amthal* for Greek πατρική.

[213] The mrg. has *ʿillah li-innīyah* [sic] *al-aulād kadhā lakhkhaṣahu al-qāḍī* [sc. Ibn Rushd].

[214] Arabic *yukāfī bi-hādhihi* appears to suit neither προσνέμεται, the vulg. reading, nor ἀπονέμεται (M^b and Rackham).

[215] Nearly a line of Greek is omitted by homoioteleuton, and the construction goes wrong.

[216] Arabic *juz'īyah* for Greek ἐν μέρει, but the meaning is 'in turn'.

أخوية فأمّا رياسة العوامّ فإنّها تكون أكثر ذلك في المساكن التي لا سيّد لها فإنّ [الكلّ] ها هنا بالسواء وفي التي رئيسها ضعيف ولكلّ [٣/٣٥] واحد تسلّط.

١١. وفي كلّ واحدة من السير تظهر محبّة على قدر ما يظهر العدل أيضاً أمّا محبّة الملك في الذين يملك عليهم فعلى قدر تفاضل الإحسان فإنّ الملك إذ كان خيراً يحسن إلى من يملك عليه ويتعهّدهم لتكون أفعالهم عادلة كتعاهد الراعي غنمه ولذلك سمّى أوميروش غانمين راعي الناس (٢) والرياسة الأمثل مثل هذه أيضاً وإنّما تختلف بعظم المنافع فإنّه يظنّ به أنّه علّة للإنّية والكون والتربية والأدب ويكافئ بهذه من سلف من الآباء من أجل أنّ الأب رئيس الأولاد بالطبع وكذلك من سلف من الآباء رئيس من ولد منهم وكذلك الملك على الذين يملّك عليهم (٣) وهذه المحبّات [...] ومن أجل هذا يكرمون الآباء والعدل من هؤلاء ليس هو واحد بعينه بل على الاستئهل وكذلك المحبّة (٤) في رياسة الأخيار أيضاً فإنّها تكون على قدر الفضيلة ويكون للأجود في الخيرات أكثر وعلى قدر ما ينبغي لكلّ واحد وكذلك العدل أيضاً (٥) وأمّا محبّة الإخوة فتشبه محبّة الأصحاب فإنّهم متساوون ومتقاربون والذين مثل هؤلاء فإنّ انفعالاتهم معاً ومتشابهو الأخلاق أكثر ذلك وهؤلاء يشبهون أصحاب رياسة الكرامة من أجل أنّه يراد أن يكون المدنيون متساوين ذوي استئهل وأن تكون الرياسة جزئية بالسوية وكذلك المحبّة أيضاً (٦) وأمّا في الزوالات فكما أنّ العدل قليل فكذلك المحبّة أيضاً وأقلّ ما تكون في أردئها فإنّ في التغلّب ليس شيئاً من المحبّة إلاّ ان يكون قليلاً فإنّ في الأشياء التي ليس فيها شئ مشترك للرئيس

1 الكل suppl. Dun || 7 للإنية Bad, Dun : illegible F || 7 للإنية mrg.: لانية الاولاد كذا لخصه القاضي || 8 علة third من F : لمن Bad || 9 [...] : illegible F, *involve superiority* Dun || 11 للأجود F, Bad || 13 الأجود : corr. Dun || 13 انفعالاتهم corr. Bad : انفعالتهم F || 15-16 وأما في (...) أيضا F, Dun : om. Bad || 17 شيئا F : شئ Bad

tyranny there is no friendship except a little. For in the things in which there is nothing in common for ruler and subject, there is no friendship either, nor any justice either,[217] like craftsman and tool,
1161b soul and body, and master and slave. For all these profit from the user, but there is no friendship for what is inanimate, nor any justice either, nor from those things which have souls, however it happened,[218] like an ox in its character of being an ox,[219] or a slave in his character of being a slave,[220] because the slave is an animate tool, and the tool an inanimate slave. (7) Thus *qua* slave, friendship is not related to him, but *qua* man, and it is sometimes thought that there is a certain justice for every man towards anyone who is able to share with him in law and contract,[221] and friendship also, according as he is a man. (8) And in tyrannies also friendships are slight, and justice similarly, but in democracies they are more numerous, since common[222] things are many, and they are equal in regard to them.

12. Every friendship then, as has already been said, is in a common[223] association. One may separate between the friendship of relations and the friendship of comrades. As for the friendships of fellow-townsmen, fellow-tribesmen, fellow-voyagers and all like these, they are liker to the associations which arise through partnership, since it appears as if they were a kind of parity and agreement. It may be that one should place among these friendships friendship with strangers. (2) The friendship of relations seems very variegated, except that all of it goes back to paternity. For parents love their children because they are something of themselves, and children love their parents because they are from them. The parents' knowledge of what is from them is more than the children's knowledge that they are from these, and the parent is more specially concerned with his offspring than the offspring with its begetter, since what is produced from something belongs specially to that from which it is

---

[217] Greek γάρ before δίκαιον is not rendered.

[218] The words 'nor from those things [...] happened' are an addition. To afford a tolarable sense—generalising—'from', Arabic *min*, should evidently be 'for'.

[219] Arabic *ka-thaur bi'th-thaurīyah*, which, as Arberry says, implies Greek πρὸς βοῦν ᾗ βοῦς read for πρὸς ἵππον ἢ βοῦν.

[220] Arabic omits Greek οὐδὲν γὰρ κοινόν ἐστιν.

[221] Arabic *ash-sharīṭah*, Greek συνθήκης.

[222] Arabic *ʿāmmīyah*, Greek κοινά.

[223] See previous note.

والمرءوس عليه ليست ولا محبّة أيضاً ولا عدل أيضاً كالصانع والآلة والنفس والجسد والمولى والعبد فإنّ جميع هذه ينتفع من الذي يستعملها ولكن ليس محبّة لما لا نفس له ولا عدل أيضاً ولا من التي لها أنفس كيفما وقع كثور بالثورية أو عبد بالعبودية من أجل أنّ العبد آلة متنفّسة والآلة عبد لا متنفّس (٧) فبأنّه عبد لا تنتسب [٣/٣٦] المحبّة إليه بل بأنّه إنسان ويظنّ أنّ عدلاً ما لكلّ إنسان إلى كلّ من يقدر أن يشاركه بالناموس والشريطة والمحبّة أيضاً على أنّه إنسان (٨) وفي التغلّبات أيضاً المحبّة يسيرة والعدل كذلك وأمّا في رياسات العوامّ فأكثر من ذلك من أجل أنّ الأشياء العامّية كثيرة وهم متساوون فيه.

١٢. فكلّ محبّة كما قد قيل ففي معاملة عامّية وخليق أن يفرز أحد بين المحبّة الجنسية والمحبّة الصحبية وأمّا المحبّات المدنية والعشيرية والتي تكون بصحبة السفينة وجميع ما يشبه هذه فإنّها أشبه بالمعاملات التي تكون بالشركة من أجل أنّه يظهر كأنّها تكافؤ ما واتّفاق وخليق أن يصيّر أحد في هذه المحبّات المحبّة الغريبية (٢) وقد تظهر المحبّة الجنسية أنّها كثيرة الأشخاص إلاّ أنّ كلّها تنسب إلى الأبوية فإنّ الوالدين يحبّون الأولاد من أجل أنّهم شيء منهم ويحبّ الأولاد الوالدين من أجل أنّهم منهم ومعرفة الوالدين بالذي كان منهم أكثر من معرفة الأولاد فإنّهم من أولئك والوالد أكثر خصوصية بالمولود من المولود بفاعله من أجل أنّ الذي هو من شيء خاصّ لذلك الذي هو منه كالسنّ والشعر وما كان مثل هذا وأمّا تلك فليست بخاصّة لشيء ممّا يكون منها وهي أيضاً دون بكثرة

4 تنتسب read. Bad : ينتسب F || 5 ويظن Dun : illegible F; من أجل Bad || 5 الشريطة F, Dun : الشريعة Bad || 13 منهم F : فيهم Bad || 14 بالذي corr. Bad : بالتي F

produced, as a tooth, a hair and the like, whereas the former[224] do not belong specially to anything which is produced from them, and they are also less in the amount of time,[225] since fathers love their children as soon as they are born, while the children only love after time passes,[226] and they know their parents either by the understanding or by sense. It is plain from this that mothers love more than others. (3) Thus parents love their children for themselves,[227] because that which is of them is as it were another of them, except that they are separate. As for children, they love their parents because their being is from them, and brothers love one another because their being is from the same people, and what makes their connection with one another is their connection with the latter. Hence it is said that: 'The blood is one', and: 'The origin is one', and the like, since they[228] are one thing in a manner, and some of them[229] is in different people. (4) Being educated together is also a great harmoniser of friendship and similarly nearness of age in one existence,[230] for contemporaries like each other and associates are friends. Therefore the friendship of
1162a brothers is like that of comrades, and the special character of cousins and other relations is from these,[231] since they are from the same people, some of them closer and some farther, according to nearness to and remoteness from the first ancestor. (5) The friendship in children for their parents and among men for the gods[232] is as it were to that which is good and superior, since in their action is the greatest benefit, they being the cause of existence and nurture and, after existence, the cause of education. (6) Friendship like this possesses more pleasure and utility than what is in friendship with strangers, according to their sharing in the common action of life. In the friendship of brothers there is that which is in comradely friendship, and particu-

[224] Arabic *tilka*. This should refer to the producers, but the sense has obviously been lost.

[225] Greek ἧττον is wrongly construed with τῷ πλήθει [...] τοῦ χρόνου in the following sentence (Arberry) and further confusion arises.

[226] Arabic *zamān* without article, as in K^b (προελθόντος χρόνου).

[227] Arabic *li-dhātihim*, perhaps for *ka-dhātihim* (Greek ὡς ἑαυτούς).

[228] Arabic is feminine singular for masculine plural of the Greek text.

[229] See previous note.

[230] Arabic *ijtimāʿ al-jīl bi-kaun wāḥid*. A marginal note adds: *al-khail lakhkhaṣahu al-qāḍī* [*wa-yumkin*] *an yakūna kadhālika wa-yumkin aiḍan an yakūna* [...] (reference again to Ibn Rushd).

[231] I.e. brothers.

[232] Reading *li'l-ālihah*. Greek καὶ ἀνθρώποις πρὸς θεούς, regarded by some as interpolated (Gauthier *in loco*), is retained in the Arabic translation.

الزمان من أجل أنّ الآباء يحبّون الأولاد حين تولّد من ساعتها وأمّا الأولاد فإنّها تحبّ بعد أن يمضي زمان وتعرف الوالدين إمّا بالفهم وإمّا بالحسّ ويتبيّن من هذا أنّ الأمّهات أكثر محبّة من غيرهم (٣) فالوالدان يحبّون الأولاد لذاتهم من أجل أنّ الذي هو منهم كأنّه آخرهم ما خلا أنّهم مفارقون وأمّا الأولاد فإنّهم يحبّون الوالدين من أجل أنّ كونهم منهم ويحبّ الإخوة بعضهم بعضاً من أجل أنّ كونهم من قوم بأعيانهم والذي يصيّر اتّصل بعضهم ببعض اتّصالهم بأولئك ومن ها هنا قيل إنّ الدم واحد والأصل واحد وما أشبه ذلك من أجل أنّها شئ واحد بنوع ما وبعضها في مفترقين (٤) واجتماع التربية أيضاً كثير [٣/٣٧] الموافقة في المحبّة وكذلك اجتماع الجيل بكون واحد فإنّ القرين يحبّ قرينه والخلطاء أصحاب ومن أجل [ذلك] تشبه محبّة الأخوية [محبّة] الصحبة وأمّا خصوصية بني العمّ وسائر المقرابة فإنّها من هؤلاء من أجل أنّهم من قوم بأعيانهم ويكون بعضهم أخصّ وبعضهم أبعد على قدر قرب الأوّل الذي هم منه وبعده (٥) والمحبّة التي تكون في الأولاد للوالدين وفي الناس للآلهة كالشئ الخير الفاضل من أجل أنّ في فعلهم أعظم الإحسان وهم علّة للكون وللتربية وبعد الكون علّة الأدب (٦) وهذه المحبّة من اللذّة والمنفعة أكثر ممّا هو في محبّة الغرباء على قدر مشاركتهم في معاملة العمر وفي المحبّة الأخوية ما في المحبّة الصحبية ولا سيّما في ذوي الاستئهل وبالجملة في المتشابهين على قدر أكثر خصوصيتهم من مولدهم ومحبّة بعضهم لبعض وعلى قدر مشابهة بعضهم بعضاً في الأخلاق الذين هم من قوم بأعيانهم وتدرّبوا معاً وتأدّبوا معاً وقد طالت فيهم التجربة

4 آخرهم ما corr. Dun : آخرهم هم ما F, Bad || 4 منهم F : فيهم Bad || 8 الجيل بكون Dun : illegible
F; من في سن Bad || 8 الجيل mrg.: أن يكون كذلك ويمكن أيضا أن يكون ويمكن القاضي لخصه الخيل || 9
ذلك suppl. Dun || 9 first محبة corr. : المحبة F, Bad || 9 second محبة suppl. Dun || 9 الصحبة
corr. Dun : الصحيحة F, Bad || 12 للآلهة F : للآلهة Bad || 12 كالشئ : perh. corr. كللشئ || 12
فعلهم F, Dun : تسليم Bad || 13 وهم F : فهم Bad || 13 first علة F, Dun : om. Bad || 13 وهذه F :
ولهذه Bad || 15 first في repeated in F

larly among the meritorious, and in general among those who resemble each other, according to the closer degree of special connection from their birth and mutual love, and according as those who are from the same people and have been reared together and instructed together, resemble each other in character. In their case the test of time has been very long and reliable. (7) Similarly in the other things[233] those who belong to one family are according to the proportion of their friendship. As for the friendship between man and woman it is thought that it is natural friendship, because man is naturally in a family[234] more than in a city, according as the household is before the city and more necessary, and similarly the procreation of children is commoner to animals. For association in the other things[235] is to this extent, but in mankind cohabitation is not merely for their procreating children but also for what is involved in life. For the works of man and woman are separate, and the works of the one are different from the works of the other. When the special works are made common, there is then sufficiency. For these reasons it is thought that in this friendship there is usefulness as well as pleasure. For if it is excellent, it consists of[236] meritorious people, since each one of the two has a virtue, and it is likely that each of them will take pleasure in this kind of bond.[237] It is thought that the bond is children, and hence the annulment of the childless marriage is quicker. For children are a good shared by both of them, and what is shared unites and binds together. (8) The question how the life of man should be with woman, and in general the life of friend with friend, appears to contain nothing else except how there is justice here, since it does not appear that the life of a friend with his friend must be like his life with a stranger, and similarly life with a comrade and with a schoolmate.

13. Since friendships are of three kinds, as was said at the beginning, and in each one of them there are some friends on equal terms and

---

[233] Arabic *fī sā'ir al-ashyā'*. But Greek ἐν τοῖς λοιποῖς refers to persons.

[234] Arabic *fī 'l-'ashīrah*, but not right for Greek συνδυαστικόν.

[235] Arabic *al-ashyā'*. Again neuter for masculine. The translator has apparently failed to see the contrast here continued between man and the other animals.

[236] Arabic *fa-hiya*, perhaps originally followed by *ṣadāqah* or by *min*. But the Arabic translator has gone wrong.

[237] I.e. translating Greek τῷ τοιούτῳ συνδέσμῳ. σύνδεσμος.

الزمانية وثبتت جدّاً (٧) وكذلك في سائر الأشياء على قدر مناسبة المحبّة الذين هم من جنس واحد وأمّا المحبّة التي هي للرجل والمرأة فإنّه بما أنّها محبّة طبيعية من أجل أنّ الإنسان في العشيرة بالطبع أكثر منه في المدينة على قدر ما أنّ البيت قبل المدينة وأشدّ اضطراراً وكذلك توليد الأولاد أعمّ للحيوان فإنّ المعاشرة أمّا في سائر الأشياء فعلى هذا القدر وأمّا في الناس فإنّ المساكنة ليست من أجل فعلهم الأولاد فقط بل تكون من أجل ما في العمر أيضاً فإنّ أعمل الرجل والمرأة مفترقة وأعمل هذا غير أعمل تلك وإذا صيّرت الأعمل الخاصّية عامّية كان في ذلك كفاية ومن أجل هذه الأشياء يظنّ أنّ في هذه المحبّة النافع واللذّة فإنّها إن كانت فاضلة فهي ذات استئهل من أجل أنّ لكلّ واحد منهما فضيلة وخليق أن يفرح كلّ واحد منهما بمثل هذا الرباط ويظنّ أنّ الرباط هو الأولاد ومن أجل هذا فتحلّل من لا ولد له [٣/٣٨] يكون أسرع فإنّ الأولاد خير مشترك لكليهما والمشترك يجمع ويربط (٨) وأمّا الطلب كيف ينبغي أن يكون عمر الرجل مع المرأة وبالجملة عمر الصديق مع الصديق فإنّه يظهر أنّه ليس في هذا الطلب شئ آخر ما خلا كيف العدل في هذا من أجل أنّه لا يظهر أنّه ينبغي أن يكون عمر الصديق مع صديقه كعمره مع الغريب وكذلك العمر مع الصاحب ومع القرين في التعليم.

١٣. ولمّا كانت المحبّات على ثلاثة أنواع كما قيل في الابتداء وكان في كلّ واحدة منها بعض الأصدقاء بالتساوي وبعضهم بالزيادة فإنّ الأخيار يكونون أصدقاء بالسوية ولا يكون الأجود صديقاً للأردأ ويكونان أيضاً كذلك ملتذّين ويكونون متساوين في الصداقات لمكان

8 النافع F : المنافع Bad || 8 فاضلة F : حاصلة Bad || 8 ذات corr. Bad : ذوا F || 10 فتحلل corr. Dun* (διαλύονται) : فناء لنة F, Bad || 12 يظهر F, Dun : يظن Bad || 17 يكونان : perh. corr. يكون || 17 الصداقات F : الصداقة Bad

others with a superiority[238] —for good men are friends equally, and
1162b the best man is not[239] a friend to the worst, and they are also similarly[240] found pleasant[241] and are equals in the friendships[242] on account of utility, and different also—for it is necessary for equals that their friendship should be equal, and that they should be equal in all the other things. As for those who are not equal, it is necessary that they should be[243] in regard to the excess[244] according to[245] the relation of one to the other. (2) Various kinds of complaint arise on account of[246] blame also, in the friendship which is on account of utility, and rightly[247] arise in this alone, or arise in it more. For those who are friends on account of virtue want to do good to one another, since this belongs to virtue and friendship, and the disagreement of these is not complaining or fighting, since no one is difficult to his friend and the doer of kind deeds, but if he brings happiness,[248] he requites him with kindness. If he exceeds, he does not complain of his friend, when he has obtained what he desires, since every man desires the good. (3) Nor does this occur much either in the friendship which is for the sake of pleasure, since both of them together possess the thing which they desire, for they rejoice in their being together, and it might appear that he who does not complain and does not bring happiness also[249] deserves to be laughed at, since it is possible also not to remain all day with him. (4) Among the friendships there is one which is censorious on account of utility.[250] For those who em-

---

[238] Arabic *bi 'z-ziyādah*. Greek ὑπεροχή is often so translated (1133a 21, etc.), but we also have ἐν ὑπεροχῇ (1124a 22) translated *dhawū faḍl*, 'superior persons'.

[239] The negative is not in the Greek.

[240] Arabic *ka-dhālika* for Greek ὁμοίως rendered differently in the previous line (*bi 's-sawīyah*).

[241] Arabic *multadhdhīn* (passive participle) for Greek ἡδεῖς.

[242] Arabic *aṣ-ṣadāqāt*, i.e. φιλίαις read for ὠφελείαις of the Greek text (Arberry).

[243] Greek ἀποδιδόναι is left untranslated and the sense is lost.

[244] Arabic *fī 'z-ziyādah* for Greek ταῖς ὑπεροχαῖς, which, however, should go closely with ἀνάλογον.

[245] I.e. κατὰ τό the reading of Γ.

[246] I.e. apparently κατὰ μέμψεις for καὶ αἱ μέμψεις (Arberry).

[247] Arabic *bi-ḥaqqin*, cf. 1156b 18.

[248] Arabic *sārran* (for Greek χαρίεις) appears to refer to the friend.

[249] Apparently rendering ὁ μὴ ἐγκαλῶν καὶ μὴ τέρπων.

[250] The same Arabic expression *li-makān al-manfa'ah* is used to translate διὰ τὸ χρήσιμον at 1157a 16 and ἐπ' ὠφελείᾳ here.

المنفعة ويختلفون أيضاً فإنّه ينبغي أمّا للمتساوين فأن تكون محبّتهم متساوية وأن يكونوا متساوين في جميع سائر الأشياء وأمّا الذين ليسوا بمتساوين فينبغي أن يكونوا في الزيادة على قدر نسبة بعضهم إلى بعض (٢) وأنواع الشكاية تكون لمكان اللوم أيضاً في المحبّة التي تكون لمكان المنفعة وبحقّ تكون في هذه فقط أو تكون فيها أكثر ذلك فإنّ الذين هم أصدقاء لمكان الفضيلة يحبّون أن يحسن بعضهم إلى بعض الفعل من أجل أنّ هذا هو للفضيلة والمحبّة ومشاجرة هؤلاء ليست شكاية ولا قتالاً من أجل أنّه لا يتصعّب أحد على المحبّ والذي هو حسن الفعل بل إن كان سارّاً فإنّه ينتقم منه بحسن الفعل فإن كان مفرطاً فإنّه إذا أصاب ما يشتهي لا يشكو الصديق من أجل أنّ كلّ إنسان يشتهي الخير (٣) ولا يكون هذا كثيراً أيضاً في التي لمكان اللذّة من أجل أنّه يكون لكليهما معاً الشئ الذي يشتهونه فإنّهم يفرحون بكينونتهم معاً وخليق أن يظهر أنّ الذي لا يشكو ولا يسرّ أيضاً أهل لأن يضحك به إذ كان يمكن ألاّ تقيم معه يومه أيضاً (٤) ومن الصداقات صداقة لوّامة لمكان المنفعة فإنّ الذي يستعمل بعضهم بعضاً لمكان المنفعة يحتاجون أبداً إلى الأكثر ممّا ينبغي ويلومون من أجل أنّهم لا يصادقون على قدر [٣/٣٩] ما بهم إليه الحاجة إذ كانوا أهل ذلك ورأوا الإحسان الفضل لا يقدر على أداء جميع ما يحتاجون إليه المنفعلون (٥)

9 التي corr. : النني F, Bad || 11 يمكن corr. Dun : يمكنه F; لك Bad || 13 إذ corr. Dun : إذا F, Bad

ploy each other on account of utility[251] always require more[252] than what is necessary and find fault because they do not obtain according to what they need, since they deserve that, and those who are doing the kindness are not able to provide all that the recipients require. (5) It seems that friendship is like justice, and as justice is of two kinds—for some justice is unwritten and some is in accordance with the law—, so the friendship[253] which is related to utility is some of it moral and some of it legal. The various kinds of complaint arise for the most part when the friendship is not according to merit,[254] but is altered. (6) Legal friendship[255] is that which is stated distinctly,[256] some of it being of the market place entirely—that which is from hand to hand—, while the more liberal is at a particular time and acknowledges something in exchange for something. The entitlement in this case is clear, there is no doubt in regard to it, and cash[257] is involved rather than friendship. Hence there is no legal judgement for these in the opinion of some people, but they think that he who makes a contract on credit must be honoured.[258] (7) The moral contract is not in things which are stated distinctly, but one gives as to a friend, or something else like this. [The giver] thinks that he will receive the equivalent or more, as if he has not given but as if it were a loan, and his complaint in making the contract and ending it is dissimilar.[259] (8) That happens simply because all men, or most of them, wish for the good and choose the useful. The good is to do a good
1163a deed not for requital, the useful to do good to one who is able[260] (9) to requite according to the worth of what was received by him.[261] For it is not right to make a friend unwillingly, as if they made an

---

[251] See previous note.

[252] Arabic *al-akthar*. The Greek καὶ ἔλαττον ἔχειν οἴονται, 'and think that they get less', is omitted.

[253] Arabic *al-maḥabbah*, i.e. for Greek φιλίας, the reading of K^b and Aspasius.

[254] I.e. κατὰ τὴν ἀξίαν for κατὰ τὴν αὐτήν (Arberry).

[255] Arabic *al-maḥabbah an-nāmūsīyah*, i.e. the reading of M^b.

[256] Arabic *yunṭaqu* for Greek ἐπὶ ῥητοῖς.

[257] Arabic *an-nājiz*, 'ready (money)', apparently for καταβολήν rather than ἀναβολήν (Arberry).

[258] Arabic *yukrama* is hardly right for στέργειν, which does not, in any case, govern τοὺς κατὰ πίστιν συναλλάξαντας.

[259] Here οὐχ ὁμοίως is construed wrongly with the main verb ἐγκαλέσει instead of with the participles.

[260] The Arabic translation runs on, construing δυναμένῳ [...] with τὸ εὐεργετεῖσθαι.

[261] The words καὶ ἑκόντι are omitted, as in K^b and Aspasius (Arberry).

وقد يشبه أن تكون المحبّة كالعدل فكما أنّ العدل على نوعين فإنّ بعض العدل لا يكتَب وبعضه على قدر الناموس كذلك المحبّة التي تنسب إلى المنفعة فإنّ بعضها خلقية وبعضها ناموسية فأنواع الشكاية تكون أكثر ذلك إذا لم تكن المحبّة على قدر الاستئهل بل كانت متغيّرة (٦) فالمحبّة الناموسية التي ينطق بها بعضها سوقية بكلّيتها وهي التي تكون من يد إلى يد وأمّا التي هي أكثر حرّية فإنّها تكون بزمان وإعطاء شئ بدل شئ والاستئهل في هذه بيّن لا يشكّ فيه والناجز فيها دون محبّة ومن أجل هذا ليس بهذه حكومة عند بعض الناس بل يبدون أنّه ينبغي أن يكرم من عامل معاملة بالدين (٧) وأمّا المعاملة الخلقية فليست في أشياء ينطق بها بل يعطى كالصديق أو شئ آخر مثل هذا ويرى أن يأخذ المتساوي أو الأكثر كأنّه لم يعط بل كأنّه عارية وليست شكايته في المعاملة والمفارقة متشابهة (٨) وإنّما يعرض ذلك من أجل أنّ جميع الناس أو أكثرهم يريدون الخير ويختارون النافع والخير هو أن يصنع الإحسان بالمجازاة والنافع أن يحسن إلى من يقوى (٩) أن يجازي على قدر استئهل ما صار إليه فإنّه لا ينبغي أن يصيّر صديق على الكره كأنّهم قد أخطأوا في البدء وأصابهم خير من الذي لم يكن ينبغي من أجل أنّه لم يكن ذلك من صديق ولم يكن فعلهم لهذا بعينه فإنّه كمثل ما ينبغي أن تكون معاملة من اصطنع إليه المعروف في أشياء ينطق بها كذلك خليق أن يكون ينبغي أن يقرّ بالمعروف

5 وإعطاء Bad, Dun : illegible F || 9 المتساوي : F المساوي Bad || 9 ليست corr. Bad : ليس F || 9 F, Dun : الكره 12 || Bad يصر : F يصير 12 || F, Bad ما : corr. Dun من 11 || Bad شكاية : F شكايته Bad الفكرة

error[262] at the beginning and obtained good from one from whom they should not, since that was not from a friend and their action was not for its own sake. For just as it is necessary to break with the man to whom the benefit was done[263] in matters which are stated distinctly, so[264] it may be necessary to acknowledge the kindness which he is able to do and is unable to requite. If he does not do so because he is unable to,[265] then it would have been obligatory for him, if he had the power to do it, to have done it. We must investigate to begin with by what[266] the benefit is done to him and on what terms, and how he is patient,[267] and if he is patient or not. (10) In regard to this there is a difference to the advantage of the recipient and that the requital should be according to this, or that the measure[268] should be according to the benefit conferred by the agent. For the recipients say that they have received from the benefactors things which were of little account to them and what could be obtained from others, and that is little in their estimation. The benefactors, however, say the opposite—that they gave most of what they possessed and what could not have been obtained from others, except by various kinds of punishment or similar kinds of thing. (11) So when the friendship is for the sake of utility, its measure is the utility of the recipient, for he is the one who needs it, and he has sufficiency in that[269] because he brings the equivalence, so that the help is according to whatever this man is benefited by, and he should hand back to him according to what has been obtained,[270] or more, for that is more excellent. As for the friendships which are according to the virtues, in them there are no kinds of complaint. The choice of the agent is like a measure, for the greater part of virtue and character lies in choice.

14. It is different in the friendships which are excessive, because each one thinks that he should have more, and when that happens the

---

262 Reading διήμαρτον τό for διαμαρτόντα.

263 But εὐεργετηθέντα is not the object of διαλυτέον.

264 The construction is wrong: καὶ ὁμολογήσαι does not take up καθάπερ in the foregoing. The Arabic translator appears to have read ὁμολογῆσαι ὅ.

265 δ' οὐδ' ὁ διδοὺς ἠξίωσεν ἄν of the Greek has disappeared.

266 Arabic *bi-mādhā*, but ὑφ' οὗ is masculine.

267 I.e. reading καὶ ὅπως and ignoring the subjunctive (ὑπομένῃ) in the dependent clause. This difficult paragraph was not understood by the Arabic translator.

268 Arabic *qiyās* representing Greek μετρεῖν.

269 Arabic *wa-lahu fī dhālika kifāyah*, i.e. Greek ἐπαρκεῖ αὐτῷ taken as 'it suffices for him'—correctly '(the other) helps him'.

270 Arabic *uṣība*. The sense of the Greek ἐπηύρετο is not expressed.

الذي يقدر عليه ولا يقدر على المكافأة وإذا لم يفعل ذلك لمكان أنّه لا يقدر عليه فخليق أن يكون قد أوجب أنّه لو كان يقوى على ذلك لما كان قد فعله وينبغي أن نفحص في البدء بماذا يكون الإحسان إليه وعلى ماذا وكيف يصبر عليه أو إن كان يصبر أو لا يصبر (١٠) وفي هذا [٣/٤٠] مشاجرة هل ينبغي أن يكون القياس على قدر منفعة المنفعل وأن تكون المجازاة على قدر هذه أو أن يكون القياس على قدر إحسان الفاعل فإنّ المنفعلين يقولون إنّهم أخذوا من المحسنين أشياء كانت عندهم صغاراً وما كان يمكن أن يؤخذ من غيرهم ذلك قليل في أعمارهم وأمّا المحسنون فيقولون خلاف ذلك وأنّهم أعطوا أكثر ما كان عندهم وما لم يكن يمكن أن يؤخذ من غيرهم إلاّ بأنواع العقاب أو أنواع مثل هذه (١١) فإذا كانت الصداقة لمكان المنفعة فقياسها منفعة المنفعل فإنّ هذا هو المحتاج وله في ذلك كفاية من أجل أنّه يأتي بالمساواة فالمعونة تكون على قدر ما ينتفع به هذا وينبغي أن يسلم إليه على قدر ما أصيب أو أكثر منه فإنّ ذلك أجود وأمّا المحبّات التي تكون على قدر الفضائل فليست فيها أنواع شكاية وإنّما يشبه القياس اختيار الفاعل فإنّ جمهور الفضيلة والخلق في الاختيار.

١٤. وهو يختلف في الصداقات التي تكون على الإفراط من أجل أنّ كلّ واحد يرى أنّ له الأكثر وإذا كان ذلك تحلّل الصداقة فإنّ الأجود يرى أنّه ينبغي أن يكون له الأكثر من أجل أنّه ينبغي أن يعطى الأكثر الخير وكذلك يرى أنّه أنفع ولا يزعمون أنّه ينبغي أن يكون

---

2 لما كان corr. Bad, appar. Dun : لمكان F || 3 يصبر أو : F يصبر عليه أو suppl. Bad || 4 قدر F, Dun : قد Bad || 7 ذلك قليل corr. Dun : قليل قليل F; لأجل التقليل Bad || 7 أعمارهم F, Dun : أعمالهم Bad || 8 العقاب F, Dun : الغضب Bad || 12 فليست corr. : فليس F, Bad || 16 يزعمون mrg.: ولا يزعم أحد أنه ينبغي أن يكون مساويا للفاضل كذا لخصه القاضي

friendship is dissolved. For the best man thinks that more should be his, since the good man should be given more, and similarly he thinks that he is more useful.[271] They do not suppose that the bad man[272] should have equality with them[273] and that unless the matters of friendship[274] are according to the merit of the actions, it seems that they are servitude, not friendship. For as in a partnership of money he who is more concerned[275] takes more, so it should be in friendship also, and that the deficient and worse partner is in the opposite case, for the good friend is he who helps the needy to sufficiency. For they suppose that there is utility[276] in being a friend of a good man or of
1163b one who is powerful, though not benefiting by it at all. (2) It is likely that the opinion in the case of both of them is right, for each of the two should be given more from the friendship of his comrade, but that the more excellent should be given more honour and the baser more gain, since honour is the reward of virtue and the reward of well-doing, while gain is assistance for various kinds of need.[277] (3) It appears that that is so in political constitutions[278] also, for he who does [not] obtain some good for the community is not honoured. For what is common is given to him who benefits the community, and his honour is common. It is impossible that one should make money at the same time and be honoured from the common stock.[279] For it is impossible that one should be content with diminution in all things. They give honour to him who is diminished in wealth, and to him who is bribed money, for the merit equalises matters and preserves the friendship, as has been said. So also it should be said[280] in regard to those who are not equal and in regard to him who is benefited in wealth or virtue, and that honour should be given

[271] Arabic *yarā annahu anfa*ʿ, but the Greek is wrongly taken (ὁμοίως δὲ καὶ ὁ ὠφελιμώτερος).

[272] Arabic *li'r-radī*ʾ, i.e. Greek αἰσχρόν rather than ἀχρεῖον (Arberry).

[273] Mrg. has: *wa-lā yazʿumu aḥad annahu yanbaghī an yakūna musāwīyan li'l-fāḍil kadhā lakhkhaṣahu al-qāḍī*, i.e. Ibn Rushd.

[274] Arabic *umūr*, i.e. Greek τὰ ἐκ τῆς φιλίας.

[275] Arabic *alladhī qād ʿuniya akthar* does not well express Greek οἱ συμβαλλόμενοι πλεῖον.

[276] The interrogative τί was read as τι (Arberry).

[277] Arabic *anwāʿ al-ḥājah* which is like ταῖς ἐνδείαις of K^b (Arberry).

[278] Arabic *as-siyar al-madanīyah*, Greek ταῖς πολιτείαις.

[279] Arabic *min al-ʿāmmīyah*, Greek ἀπὸ τῶν κοινῶν, which is construed with τιμᾶσθαι.

[280] Arberry's conjecture ὁμολογητέον for ὁμιλητέον seems right.

للرديء السوية ما لهم وأنّ أمور المحبّة إن لم تكن على قدر استئهل الأفعل يظنّ بها أنّها تكون خدمة لا محبّة فإنّه كما أنّ في اشتراك الأموال إنّما يأخذ الأكثر الذي قد عني أكثر ذلك ينبغي أن يكون في المحبّة أيضاً وأن يكون الناقص والأردأ على خلاف ذلك فإنّ الصديق الخير الذي يعين المحاويج على الكفاف فإنّهم يزعمون أنّ منفعة بأن يكون صديقاً لفاضل أو لذي مقدرة ولا يتمنّع به أصلاً (٢) وقد يشبه أن يكون الرأي في كليهما بنوع صحيح فإنّه ينبغي أن يعطي كلّ واحد منهما الأكثر من صداقة صاحبه ولكن أن يعطي إمّا الأفضل والأكثر من الكرامة وإمّا الأخسّ والأكثر من الربح من أجل أنّ الكرامة [٣/٤١] جزاء الفضيلة وجزاء حسن الصنيع وأمّا الربح فإنّه معونة على أنواع الحاجة (٣) ويظهر أنّ ذلك كذلك في السير المدنية أيضاً فإنّه لا يكرم الذي [لا] يكتسب خيراً ما للعامّة فإنّ العامّ يعطى للذي ينفع العامّة وإكرامه عامّ وليس يمكن أن يتحوّل أحد معاً ويكرم من العامّية فإنّه في جميع الأشياء لا يمكن أن يصبر أحد على النقصان وإنّما يعطون الكرامة الذي ينتقص بالأموال والذي يرتشي بالأموال فإنّ الاستئهل يصيّر الأشياء متساوية ويحفظ الصداقة كما قيل وكذلك ينبغي أن يقل في الذين ليس لهم على التساوي وفي الذي ينتفع بالأموال أو بالفضيلة وأن تعطى الكرامة من الذي يعطي ما يمكن (٤) فإنّ الصداقة إنّما عليها ما أمكن لا ما على الاستئهل فإنّ الاستئهل ليس في جميع الأشياء هو كما في الكرامات التي تكون في الآلهة وفي االآباء من أجل أنّه لا يؤدي أحد فيهم الاستئهل أبداً

1 السوية corr. Dun : أسوة F, Bad || 4 منفعة F, Dun : منفعته corr. Bad || 5 يتمنع F : يمنع corr. Bad; ينتفع mrg. || 8 على corr. Bad, Dun : كل F || 9 لا suppl. Bad, Dun || 13 first في corr. Bad, Dun : و F || 16 يؤدي F : يؤدي في suppl. Bad

by him who gives what is possible.[281] (4) For friendship's search is for what is possible, not what is according to merit. For merit does not exist in all things, as in the case of the honours paid to the gods and to parents, since no one ever pays in their case what they merit. When one serves them according to his ability he is thought to be meritorious. Hence it may be thought that it is not permissible for a son to contradict[282] his father, and that it is obligatory for the son to pay his father what he owes.[283] When he does anything, he does a good deed which [the father] began. He is like the man who has a debt owing to his creditor.[284] It cannot be that anyone has authority to leave his father,[285] for no one thinks that he should flee from one who is not excessively wicked. For, apart from natural friendship, it is in human nature not to grudge help, and what is better to be avoided[286] rather than desired is assistance to the wicked,[287] since most people wish that good be done them, and they themselves avoid doing good, as not profitable to them. This is the extent of what is said on these topics. In all friendships[288] which are of different kinds, it is suitability[289] which equalises the friendship, as has already been said.[290]

End of the Ninth Discourse of the Ethics, and praise be to God, and peace upon His servants whom He has chosen.

---

[281] Arabic *wa-an tuʿṭā al-kirāmah min alladhī yuʿṭī mā yumkin*. Greek τιμὴν ἀνταποδοτέον is wrongly construed with what follows instead of with the foregoing καὶ τῷ εἰς χρήματα ὠφελουμένῳ [...].

[282] Arabic *an yujāwiba qaul al-ab*. But this is Greek ἀντειπεῖν, not ἀπείπασθαι (Arberry).

[283] I.e. the words in the Greek πατρὶ δ' υἱόν· ὀφείλοντα γὰρ ἀποδοτέον are taken together (Arberry).

[284] Greek ὥστ' ἀεὶ ὀφείλει. οἷς δ' ὀφείλεται is run together.

[285] This is for Greek ἐξουσία ἀφεῖναι· καὶ τῷ πατρὶ δή run together (Arberry) and the sense of the rest of the sentence has been completely lost.

[286] I.e. τῷ δὲ φευκτόν read as τὸ δὲ φευκτόν.

[287] Greek οὐ with σπουδαστόν is omitted and τὸ ἐπαρκεῖν wrongly construed with μοχθηρῷ ὄντι.

[288] Arabic *fī* has apparently dropped out of the text before *jamīʿ*.

[289] Arabic *al-mulāʾamah* which the Arabic translator has previously used (1136a 3) for τὸ ἀνάλογον.

[290] The last sentence actually represents the beginning of Book IX, where it appears again.

وإذا هو خدم على قدر الطاقة يظنّ به أنّه ذو استئهل ومن أجل هذا خليق أن يظنّ أنّه لا يحلّ للابن أن يجاوب قول الأب وأنّه يجب على الابن أن يؤدي ما قد وجب عليه الأب وإذا فعل شيئاً فقد فعل خيراً ما ابتدأ به وهو كالذي عليه حقّ واجب للذي الحقّ وخليق ألاّ يكون لأحد سلطان على أن يترك الأب فإنّه لا يرى أحد أن يهرب من الذي ليست شرّيته مفرطة فإنّه مع ما في ذلك من الصداقة الطبيعية إنّ في أخلاق الناس ألاّ يضنّ بالمعونة والذي هو أحرى بأن يهرب منه من أن يحرص عليه معونة ذوي الرداءة من أجل أنّ أكثر الناس يريدون أن يصنع بهم خير ويهربون من أن يفعلوا هم ذلك كأنّ ذلك ليس بنافع لهم فهذا قدر ما يقال في هذه وأمّا في جميع المحبّات التي أنواعها مختلفة فإنّ الملاءمة تساوي المحبّة كما قد قيل.

آخر المقالة التاسعة من الأخلاق والحمد لله وسلّم على عباده الذين اصطفى

2 الأب : F للأب Bad || 6-7 first ان (...) يحرص F, Dun : om. Bad

BOOK IX

In the name of God, the Merciful, the Compassionate
God bless Muhammad and his family and give them peace

The Tenth Discourse of the Book of Ethics of Aristotle

1. He said: [In] all friendships which are of different kinds, it is suitability[1] which equalises and preserves the friendship, as has already been said, just as in the political form also. For in it the shoemaker exchanges his shoes for what he is entitled to, and similarly the
1164a weaver and others of the craftsmen. (2) Here a common measure has been found, namely money, and to it all these things are related and by it are reckoned. But in the form of love sometimes the lover complains, when he loves to excess and is not loved in return, and there is nothing lovable[2] in him, if it is so, and the beloved complains much, because the other at first made all sorts of promises and does not now fulfil any of them. (3) These things occur when the lover loved the beloved for the sake of pleasure and the beloved loved the lover for the sake of utility, and these were not in either of them. For the friendship exists because of these things, and its dissolution takes place when the things because of which their friendship existed have ceased to exist, since they were not loving each other's self[3] but things[4] which did not last, and hence the friendships became the same. But the friendship depending on character lasts, since it is for itself, as has already been said. (4) The friendship differs also when the two of them have it[5] and it is not as they desire. For when the lover is not afforded the thing by virtue of which he loves, it is for him like what does not exist at all,[6] resembling one who promises the singer that he will increase his joy according to the excellence of

---

[1] Again Arabic *al-mulā'amah* which the Arabic translator has previously used (1136a 3) for τὸ ἀνάλογον.

[2] Arabic *maḥabbī* exceptionally for Greek φιλητόν usually rendered by Arabic *maḥbūb*.

[3] Arabic *dhātahumā*, i.e. αὑτούς, the reading of Bekker (Arberry).

[4] Arabic *ashyā'*, which hardly attemps to translate Greek τὰ ὑπάρχοντα.

[5] Greek ἕτερα is omitted (Arberry).

[6] All this diverges evidently from the Greek.

المقالة التاسعة

[٣/٤٢] بسم الله الرحمن الرحيم
صلّى الله على محمّد وعلى آله وسلّم

المقالة العاشرة من كتاب الأخلاق لأرسطو

١. قال وأمّا [في] جميع المحبّات التي أنواعها مختلفة فإنّ الملاءمة تساوي وتسلّم المحبّة كما قد قيل مثلما يكون في الهيئة المدنية أيضاً فإنّه يبادل الإسكاف فيها الخفاف بما يستحقّ وكذلك الحائك وغيرهما من الصنّاع (٢) وأمّا ها هنا فقد أصيب مقدار مشترك وهو الدينار وإليه ينسب جميع هذه وبه يقدّر وأمّا في هيئة العشق فربّما شكا العاشق إذا أحبّ محبّة مفرطة ولم يحَبّ مثلما فليس له شئ محبّي إن كان ذلك وكثيراً ما يشكو المعشوق من أجل أنّه كان يعد أوّلاً جميع المواعيد وليس يفعل منها شيئاً الآن (٣) وإنّما تعرض هذه الأشياء إذا كان يحبّ العاشق المعشوق لمكان اللذّة ويكون المعشوق يحبّ العاشق لمكان المنفعة ولم تكن هذه في كليهما فإنّه من أجل هذه تكون المحبّة ويكون تحلّلها إذا لم تكن الأشياء التي من أجلها كانت محبّتهما من أجل أنّهما لم يكونا محبّين ذاتهما بل أشياء ليست بباقية ومن أجل هذا صارت المحبّات مثلها وأمّا المحبّة الخلقية فمن أجل أنّها بذاتها فإنّها تبقى كما قد قيل (٤) وهي تختلف أيضاً إذا كانت لهما ولم تكن على ما يشتهون فإنّ المحبّ إذا لم يصِر الشئ إليه على ما يحبّ كان عنده شبيهاً بالذي لا يكون البتّة مثل الذي يعد المغنّي بأنّه يزيد في سروره على قدر جودة غنائه فإذا

4 في suppl. Dun || 6 وغيرهما : F وغيرها Bad || 6 الصنّاع corr. Dun : الصنائع F, Bad || 8 فليس : F وليس Bad || 9 كان يعد : Dun لا يعد F || 9 المواعيد corr. Bad : المواعين appar. F || 12 محبّتهما : F محبّتها Bad || 15 يصر corr. Bad : يصير F || 15 يحبّ read. Dun : يجب F, Bad || 16 جودة : F جود Bad

his song, but when[7] he regains from him the fulfilment of the promises, he says to him that he has already sufficed him with pleasure for pleasure. Now if this had been the wish of both of them, it would be sufficient. But if one of them wanted simply amusement and the other gain, and one of them has got what he wanted, but not the other, then the association is not right, since a man's concern is for the things which he needs, and he only gives what he gives on account of them.[8] (5) To which of them should be assigned the degree of merit?[9] To the one who gave[10] that it should be like the thing which he got,[11] as they say Protagoras did? For when he taught anything he bade the learner honour[12] what he learned according to what he thought it was worth, and he used to take a fee to this amount. (6) Some people in cases like these are pleased with the reward,[13] and some take the silver[14] and do nothing of what they said owing to the excess of their promises. They rightly become exposed to various kinds of complaint, on account of their not doing what they agreed to and promised of themselves. (7) It may be that our luminaries[15] are bound to do this because no one gives[16] them his silver[17] for what they know. As for these, since they do not do that for which they have already taken pay, they are rightly exposed to various kinds of complaint. But in the things in which there is no stipulation for doing them, it has already been said that to those who give that for
1164b themselves[18] no complaint attaches, for the friendship which is from

---

[7] Arabic *fa-idhā*. Mention of morning has disappeared in this translation. Arberry suggests that εἰς ἕως was read.

[8] Lit. 'gives these things on account of those', when *min ajl tilka* (plural) is for ἐκείνου χάριν.

[9] Arabic *martabat al-istiʾhāl*, which looks like a rendering of τῆς ἀξίας [...] τάξις instead of τὴν ἀξίαν [...] τάξαι.

[10] Some words have dropped out through homoioteleuton.

[11] Arabic *an yakūna ka'l-amri 'lladhī akhadha* is far from the Greek (ἔοικ' ἐπιτρέπειν ἐκείνῳ).

[12] Arabic *yukrima* (*yukarrima*). The sense of Greek τιμῆσαι, 'assess', was evidently not understood, and the sentence goes wrong.

[13] As Arberry noted, the reference to Hesiod (*Works and Days*, 370: μισθὸς δ' ἀνδρί) is not recognised by the translator. Cf. above 1153b 27 (= VII, 13, 5).

[14] Arabic *fiḍḍah*, 'silver', renders Greek ἄργυρος rather than ἀργύριον, which is hardly used = 'money'. Cf. 1109a 27, 1127b 13 (*bis*).

[15] Arabic *ash-shihābūn*, a remarkable rendering of the sophists, difficult to explain.

[16] Arabic *yaʿṭīhim*, i.e. ἄν is apparently disregarded.

[17] See n. 14.

[18] I.e. Greek αὐτούς, the common reading.

اقتضاه المواعيد قل له إنّه قد كافاه بدل اللذّة بلذّة فلو كانت هذه إرادة كلّ واحد منهما لكان في ذلك كفاية وأمّا إن كان إنّما يريد أحدهما النزهة والآخر الربح فكان لأحدهما ما أراد ولم يكن للآخر ذلك فإذاً لا تكون المعاملة على ما ينبغي من أجل أنّه إنّما محبّته إلى التي يحتاج إليها وإنّما يعطي هذه الأشياء من أجل تلك (٥) ولأيّهما ينبغي أن تكون مرتبة الاستئهال للذي أعطى أن يكون كالأمر الذي [٣/٤٣] أخذ كما زعموا أنّه كان يفعل فروطاغورس فإنّه كان إذا علّم شيئاً ما كان يأمر المتعلّم أن يكرم على قدر ما يرى أنّه يستأهل ما تعلّم فكان يأخذ على هذا القدر (٦) وبعض الناس برضيهم في مثل هذه الأجرة ومنهم من يأخذ الفضّة ولا يفعل شيئاً ممّا قل لإفراط المواعيد وبحقّ يصيرون إلى أنواع الشكاية من أجل أنّهم لا يفعلون ما قد أقرّوا به ووعدوا من أنفسهم (٧) وخليق أن يكون الشهابون يضطرّون أن يفعلوا هذا من أجل أنّه لا يعطيهم أحد فضّة لما يعلمون وأمّا هؤلاء إذ لا يفعلون ما قد أخذوا [له] الأجر فبحقّ هم في أنواع الشكاية وأمّا في الأشياء التي لا يكون شرط على فعلها فقد قيل إنّ الذين يفعلون ذلك من أجل ذاتهم لا تلزمهم الشكاية فإنّ المحبّة التي تكون عن الفضيلة مثل هذه وتصير المكافأة على الاختيار من أجل أنّ

4 ولأيهما corr. Arberry : ولأيتهما F || 7 برضيهم F, Dun : يرضيهم Bad || 8 يأخذ [القضية] : F يأخذ suppl. Bad || 8 الفضة corr. Dun* (ἀργύριον) : المفضة appar. F; المقررة perh. Bad || 10 الشهابون F, Dun, Arberry : السفسطائيون corr. Bad* (οἱ σοφισταί) || 11 له (or من أجله) suppl. Dun : عليه suppl. Bad || 12 شرط corr. Arberry, Bad : شرطا F || 13 من corr. Bad, Dun : ومن F, Arberry

virtue is like this and requital depends on choice, because the requital of a friend and virtue are the same.[19] It seems that sharing and working together with another at philosophy is of this type, since merit is not reckoned in money, and there is no one in this working together who is equivalent in weight.[20] But perhaps sufficiency here is what is possible, as in the case of parents also.[21] (8) For even if the gift is not like these, but in some things there must be requital[22] for the most part with equality according to what both of them think is according to merit, and if that did not happen, then it may be not only necessary that he to whom it belongs[23] should assess the value, but also right, for according as the latter benefited or according as he preferred pleasure to something else, so he takes a recompense from the other according as that merits. (9) For it appears in the things which are sold that it is so, and in some things[24] there are no laws either,[25] since there is no judgement in voluntary contracts, as if it were necessary that he should leave this man or rather him [with whom][26] he was content even as he associated with him. For it is thought that he who is gladdened[27] by him is worthier of the grade of deserving[28] than him who gladdens,[29] because for the most part those who possess something and [those] who wish to receive it do not value it equally. For the special things and those which each of the givers gives appear to be worth much, yet the recompense is according to the value assessed by the receivers, and honour should not be according as it seems the thing is worth[30] but according to what merit is in it.[31]

---

[19] Arabic *mukāfa'at aṣ-ṣadīq wa 'l-faḍīlah wāḥidah*, i.e., as Arberry saw, αὕτη is taken as referring to ἀμοιβήν, not to προαίρεσιν.

[20] Arabic *man yusāwī bi 'l-wazn*. Greek τιμή has disappeared.

[21] Greek πρὸς θεούς has dropped out.

[22] The construction is wrong, and there is no main clause.

[23] Arabic *alladhī huwa lahu*, i.e. apparently προσέχοντα for προέχοντα.

[24] Arabic *fī baʿḍ al-ashyā' laisat nawāmīs aiḍan*, i.e. the translation has understood ἐνιαχοῦ as ἔνια τ' οὐκ (Arberry).

[25] The construction is again wrong: Greek νόμοι must be taken with the following words.

[26] Supplying *bihi* after *qaniʿa*, evidently a misunderstanding of Greek ἐπίστευσε.

[27] Arabic *surra bihi*, *sarra*, representing Greek ἐπετράφθη [...] ἐπιτρέψαντος, but the translator read ἐπετέρφθη [...] ἐπιτέρφαντος.

[28] Arabic *manzilat al-istiḥqāq*. But Greek is τάξαι, 'fixing the value'.

[29] See n. 27.

[30] Greek ἔχοντι is omitted.

[31] Arabic *mā fīhi min al-isti'hāl*, i.e. ἔχει τιμήν or ἔνεστι τιμή for πρὶν ἔχειν ἐτίμα of the text.

مكافأة الصديق والفضيلة واحدة ويشبه أن تكون مشاركة ومعاملة عامل على الفلسفة على هذه الحل من أجل أنّ الاستئهل لا يعدّ بالأموال ولا يكون في هذه المعاملة من يساوى بالوزن بل خليق أن يكون الكفاف فيها الممكن كما هو في الآباء أيضاً (٨) فإنّه وإن كانت العطية ليست مثل هذه ولكن ينبغي في بعض الأشياء أن تكون المكافأة أكثر ذلك بالمساواة على قدر ما يرى كلاهما أنّها على الاستئهل وأمّا إن لم يعرض ذلك فخليق ألاّ يكون مضطرّاً فقط أن يرتب فيه الذي هو له بل أن يكون واجباً أيضاً فإنّه على قدر ما انتفع هذا أو على قدر ما اختار اللذّة على غيرها على قدر ذلك مكافأة يأخذ منه على قدر ذلك من الاستئهل (٩) فإنّه يظهر في الأشياء التي تشترى أنّه يكون ذلك وفي بعض الأشياء ليست نواميس أيضاً من أجل أنّه ليس قضاء في المعاملات الإرادية كأنّه ينبغي أن يفارق هذا بل الذي قنع [به] كما خالطه أيضاً فإنّه يرى أنّ الذي سرّ به أولى بمنزلة الاستحقاق من الذي سرّ من أجل أنّ أكثر ذلك لا يكرمون بالمساواة الذين لهم ذلك و[الذين] يريدون أن يأخذوه فإنّ الأشياء [٣/٤٤] الخاصّية والتي يعطيها كلّ واحد من المعطين يظهر أنّها أهل للكثير إلاّ أنّ المكافأة تكون على قدر ما يرتبون الذين يأخذون وينبغي ألاّ تكون الكرامة على قدر [ما] يظهر أنّه يستأهل الشئ بل على قدر ما فيه من الاستئهل.

---

2 يكون F, Dun : تكون Bad || 6 first ان corr. Bad : إن F || 7 اختار Bad, Arberry, Dun : اختيار F || 10 به suppl. Dun || 11 بالمساواة corr. Arberry* (ἴσου) : المواسة F, Bad || 11 الذين suppl. Dun || 12 يعطيها corr. : يعطيهم F, Bad || 13 للكثير F, Bad : الكثير Arberry || 14 ما suppl. Bad

2. In these things too there is a difficulty of an awkward kind, as for instance: 'Should one hand over everything to one man, e.g.[32] a father, and be content with what he says, or should a sick man be content with[33] what the doctor says? Or should the fighting general be appointed?[34] Similarly should the friend or[35] the good man be served? And is it preferable to requite him who has done a kindness or another,[36] and if it is impossible to do good to both of them, is it preferable to do good to him who first did the favour?' (2) Or perhaps it is not easy to elaborate all questions completely, for there are many differences in regard to them according to the abundant difference of kinds in importance and unimportance and excellence and necessity. (3) That one should not hand over all things to one person is clear, for it is not right that kindness should be done,[37] for the most part,[38] to another than the man who began the kindness to the exclusion of the latter, or that it should be preferable to grant it to another[39] to his exclusion (but it is preferable to requite the latter with that which is his), as the loan[40] which he lent,[41] so that he should be given it more than another.[42] Perhaps this is not so always. (4) For example, should a man who has been ransomed from brigands ransom him who has ransomed him and requite him thereby, whoever
1165a he was, or not ransom him when it has happened? Should he give to the man who has demanded it, or should he ransom his father? Perhaps it may be thought that to ransom his father is more incumbent upon him than to ransom himself even. (5) For, as was said, in general one should pay the obligatory debt, but if the gift is of what is

---

[32] Perhaps reading τῳ [= τινί] τῷ πατρί (dittography).

[33] Arabic *yaqnaʿa* for Greek πιστεύειν, as above, c. 1, § 9.

[34] Arabic *yuṣaiyara* (Arberry's reading of the MS.) does not give the sense of Greek χειροτονητέον, 'be elected by vote'.

[35] Arabic *au*, i.e. μᾶλλον is omitted.

[36] I.e. ἑτέρῳ read for ἑταίρῳ (Arberry).

[37] But we miss the meaning of Greek ἀνταποδοτέον, 'repay'.

[38] The next four words of the Greek (μᾶλλον ἢ χαριστέον ἑταίροις) are greatly expanded in the Arabic translation—to 'that which is his' four lines below. It appears to be a matter of alternative versions, the second beginning or 'that it should be preferable' down to 'his exclusion'. This is followed by a restatement of the thought (in brackets, not in the original). The necessity for all this appears to have been in the negation introduced incorrectly at the beginning of the § (with Greek ἀνταποδοτέον).

[39] I.e. ἕτερος again confused with ἑταῖρος (Arberry), cf. n. 36.

[40] This is presumably Greek ὥσπερ δάνειον, the reading of K^b.

[41] Arabic *aqraḍahu*, but Greek ὀφείλει, 'owes'.

[42] See n. 39.

٢. وفي هذه أيضاً تحيّر بنوع عويص كقولي هل ينبغي أن تسلم جميع الأشياء إلى إنسان واحد مثل الأب ويقنع بقوله أو ينبغي للمريض أن يقنع بقول الطبيب أو يصيّر قائد الجيش المحارب وكذلك هل ينبغي أن يخدم الصديق أو الفاضل وهل أحرى أن يكافئ الذي اصطنع المعروف أو غيره وإن لم يمكن أن يصطنع الخير كليهما كان أحرى أن يصطنع إلى الذي ابتدأ بالإحسان (٢) وخليق ألاّ يهون تفصيل جميع الأشياء على الاستقصاء فإنّ فيها اختلافات كثيرة على اختلاف أنواع كثيرة بالعظم والصغر والجيّد والمضطرّ (٣) وأمّا أنّه لا ينبغي أن يسلم بجميع الأشياء إلى واحد فبيّن فإنّه لا ينبغي أن يصير اصطناع المعروف أكثر ذلك إلى غير من قد ابتدأ بالمعروف دون هذا أو أن يكون أحرى أن يهب لغير هذا دونه بل أحرى أن يكافئ هذا بذلك الذي هو له كالقرض الذي أقرضه فينبغي أن يعطه أكثر من غيره وخليق ألاّ يكون هذا أبداً (٤) مثل الذي قد خلّص من اللصوص هل ينبغي أن يخلّص الذي خلّصه ويكافئه بذلك من كان أم لا يخلّصه إذا وقع وهل ينبغي أن يعطى لمن اقتضاه أو ينبغي أن يخلّص أباه فخليق أن يظنّ أنّ خلاص أبيه أوجب عليه من خلاص ذاته أيضاً (٥) فإنّه كما قيل بالجملة ينبغي أن يؤدّي الحقّ

3 يخدم F : نخدم read. Bad || 10 ابدا corr. Dun* (ἀεί) : ايضا F, Bad

excellent or obligatory,[43] then one should pay heed to it. Sometimes there is no equal requital of what was a gift, when the agent was acting towards one whom he knows to be a good man, and it[44] is to one who thought to be bad. And sometimes it would not be right to lend to him who has lent and thereby make requital, for he who has lent simply did so thinking that he will receive it in full,[45] since not to hope to get what is his own is characteristic of a very wicked man.[46] If this is really so, the merit[47] is not equal, and if it is not so, but is thought to be so, perhaps it would not be thought of him[48] that he is doing what he should not, (6) just as it has been said[49] many times that men[50] in their emotions and actions are equal, and they are defined[51] in respect of what they are concerned with. (7) That all should not be given the same things and that a father should not be given all things, just as sacrifice is not to Zeus alone, is plain. For fathers are given some things and brothers other things, and they give yet other things to comrades, and to those who have done them a kindness what is theirs, and they requite them with what they should.[52] It appears that they do so, for they invite to wedding their kinsmen and those who[53] share the same family and the same actions,[54] and they want the presence of their likes in special matters[55] mostly, for that should be. (8) Hence they would think that it is incumbent upon them to feed the parents who are the cause of their being,[56] and that that is more excellent in them than [doing] what is for themselves and that they should provide them sufficiently with

---

[43] Arabic *in kānat al-ʿaṭīyah li'l-jaiyid au al-muḍṭarr*, i.e. Greek ὑπερτείνῃ is not rendered.

[44] I.e. the requital.

[45] Greek ἐπιεικεῖ ὄντι is left untranslated here and rendered in the next clause as if it were οἰκεῖα ὄντα (Arabic *mā huwa lahu khāṣṣ*).

[46] Arabic *khāṣṣ khulq ash-sharīr*. Perhaps παρὰ πονηπῷ was read instead of παρὰ πονηροῦ.

[47] Arabic *isti'hal*, but Greek ἀξίωμα is 'demand, claim'.

[48] I.e. Greek δόξειεν of M^b as against δόξαιεν.

[49] The Arabic sentence runs on beyond Greek ἄτοπα ποιεῖν.

[50] Greek λόγοι is omitted (Arberry).

[51] Arabic *wa-hum maḥdūdūn*, representing Greek ἔχουσι τὸ ὡρισμένον.

[52] The construction is again wrong, with Greek ἑκάστοις omitted.

[53] But the Greek is explanatory: 'for these [...].'

[54] Greek is αἱ περὶ τοῦτο δὴ πράξεις, 'actions concerning the family (γένος), family affairs'.

[55] Arabic *al-ashyā' al-khāṣṣīyah*, but we miss the equivalent of Greek κήδη = 'funerals'.

[56] The words μάλιστα and ὡς ὀφείλοντας are not translated.

الواجب وأمّا إن كانت العطية للجيّد أو المضطرّ فينبغي أن يحل إليها فربّما لم تكن المكافأة مساوية لما قد كان من العطية إذا كان الفاعل يفعل بمن يعلم أنّه فاضل ويكون للذي يظنّ به أنّه ذو رداءة فربّما لم ينبغ أن يقرض الذي أقرض ويكافئ بذلك فإنّ الذي أقرض إنّما أقرض وهو يرى أنّه سيستوفيه من أجل أنّ الذي لا يرجو أن يأخذ ما هو له خاصّ خلق للشرير جدّاً فإن كان هذا هكذا بالحقيقة لا يكون الاستئهل [٣/٤٥] يساوي وإن لم يكن كذلك وكان يظنّ به فخليق ألاّ يظنّ به أنّه يفعل ما لا ينبغي (٦) وكما قيل مراراً كثيرة أنّهم في الانفعالات والأفعل بالسوية وهم محدودون فيما هم فيه (٧) وأمّا أنّه لا ينبغي أن يعطوا أجمعين أشياء بأعيانها ولا أن يعطى الأب جميع الأشياء كما أنّه ليس الذبيحة لديا فقط فبيّن فإنّ الآباء يعطون أشياء أخر والإخوة أشياء أخر وآخرون يعطون للأصحاب والذين اصطنعوا المعروف ما هو لهم ويكافئونهم بما ينبغي ويظهر أنّهم يفعلون كذلك فإنّهم إنّما يدعون في الأعراس مجانسيهم والذين يعمّهم الجنس وتصيبهم أفعل ويريدون حضور أشباههم في الأشياء الخاصّية أكثر ذلك فإنّ ذلك ينبغي أن يكون (٨) ومن أجل هذا خليق أن يروا أنّه يجب عليهم أن يقوتوا الآباء الذين هم علّة كونهم وأن يكون ذلك فيهم أجود ما يكون لذاتهم وأن يكفواهم هذه الأشياء وأن يكرم الآباء كالآلهة

---

6 يفعل corr. above line : ينفعل F || 6-7 مرارا كثيرة أنهم Dun* (πολλάκις) : مرارا كثيرة أن F*;
F أخرون : Bad corr. اخر second 9 || Bad أن : F فإن 9 || om. Bad : فيما هم فيه 7 || Bad وإذا النقاش
بما 10 || Bad أخر : F ما هو 10 || Bad والأصحاب : F للأصحاب 10 || F يعطوها : corr. Bad يعطون 9 ||
F : بها Bad || 10 ويظهر F*, Dun* (φαίνονται) : أيضا Bad || 14 يكفواهم F : يكفوا Bad

these things, and that parents should be honoured like the gods, yet not with all honours. For honour to a father is not honour to a mother nor honour to a wise man honour to a general, but a father is honoured with a father's honour and a mother similarly with that due to a mother, (9) and every old person with the honour which is due to his age, by rising up for him and by giving him a cushion[57] and the like, and also[58] friendliness[59] to comrades and brothers and those who mingle with us.[60] To all of them, i.e. kindred, tribesmen,[61] people of one's city and all the rest, one should always desire to give them what is special to them and compare what belongs to each of them in regard to special claim or virtue or [utility]. (10) For comparison of those who have a common genus is easy, but comparison of those who differ in genus is difficult.[62] Yet the question must not be given up on this account, [but] must be decided according to what is possible.

1165b 3. In that there is a difficulty also, whether friendships are dissolved or not in the case of those who are not constant. Or for those who are friends for the sake of the useful or the pleasant, when these things do not exist, is it no shame[63] that their friendships should be dissolved, because they were friends of these things, and when they vanished, the people are bound not to love? One might complain if the pretence was made in love for the sake of the useful or the pleasant that it was for character. For, as was said at the beginning, there are many differences among friends when their thoughts are not similar and they are friends.[64] (2) For when anyone is deceived and thinks that he is loved for the sake of character and the other man was doing nothing of the kind, he should impute it to himself. But when he is sought by pretence, he is right to complain of him who sought[65] him more than of those who debase the *dīnār*[66] according to

---

[57] Arabic *bi 't-tausīd*, but Greek κατακλίσει is rather to offer a chair or couch.

[58] Supplying something like 'we should show', quite as in the Greek.

[59] Arabic *mu'ānasah* scarcely renders Greek παρρησίαν.

[60] Arabic *wa 'l-khulaṭā'*, i.e. Greek καὶ ἁπάντων κοινότητα is badly mistranslated here.

[61] Arabic *al-ʿashīrah* alone renders Greek φυλέταις.

[62] Greek is ἐργωδεστέρα, i.e. comparative. The superlative is similarly neglected at 1171b 32 (Greek αἱρετώτατον rendered by Arabic *mukhtār*).

[63] Arabic *laisa bi-qabīḥ* for Greek οὐδὲν ἄτοπον.

[64] The construction of ὁμοίως with οἴωνται and ὦσι has not been understood.

[65] I.e. ἀπατηθῇ and ἀπατήσαντι read as ἀπαιτηθῇ and ἀπαιτήσαντι (Arberry).

[66] Arabic singular in the text. The plural *danānīr* is common = 'money'.

ولكن ليس جميع الكرامات فإنّ كرامة الأب ليست كرامة الأمّ ولا كرامة الحكيم كرامة قائد الجيش بل يكرم الأب الكرامة الأبوية والأمّ كذلك بالأمّية (٩) وكلّ كبير الكرامة التي تجب بقرنه بالوقوف له وبالتوسيد وما أشبه ذلك وأيضاً مؤانسة الأصحاب والإخوة والخلطاء بكلّهم أيّ القرابة والعشيرة وأهل مدينته وجميع باقي هؤلاء فقد ينبغي أبداً أن يدام إعطاؤهم ما هو لهم خاصّ وأن يقايس ما لكلّ واحد منهم بالخاصّية أو الفضيلة أو الا[نتفاع] (١٠) فإنّ قياس الذين يعمّهم الجنس هيّن وأمّا قياس الذين يختلفون بالجنس فعسير ولكن لا ينبغي أن يترك ذلك من أجل هذه السبيل [بل] ينبغي أن يفصّل على ما يمكن.

٣. وفي ذلك تحيّر أيضاً إن كانت المحبّات تتحلّل أم لا في الذين لا يثبتون أو الذين هم أصدقاء لمكان النافع أو اللذيذ إذا لم تكن هذه الأشياء ليس بقبيح أن تتحلّل صداقاتهم لأنّهم إنّما كانوا أصدقاء لهذه الأشياء التي إذا فنيت يجب ألاّ يحبّوا وخليق [٣/٤٦] أن يشكو شاك إذا كان يرائي بالمحبّة لمكان النافع أو اللذيذ الخلقي فإنّه كما قيل في البدء يكون في الأصدقاء اختلافات كثيرة إذا لم تكن ظنونهم متشابهة وكانوا أصدقاء (٢) فإنّه إذا كذب أحد وظنّ أنّه يحَبّ لمكان الخلق وكان ذلك لا يفعل شيئاً مثل هذا فخليق أن يتّهم ذاته وأمّا إذا طلب بمرايات بذلك فواجب أن يشكو الذي طلب أكثر من شكاية الذين

2 الأبوية corr. mrg. : الابية F || 3 بقرنه corr. Dun* (ἡλικίαν) : بقوته F || 3 الوقوف Bad*, Dun* (ὑπαναστάσει) : بالقوة F || 3 وبالتوسيد F*, Dun* (κατακλίσει) : وبالتوسيع Bad || 4 أي F : اما corr. Bad || 6 الانتفاع corr. and suppl. Bad : الا F || 7 بل suppl. Bad || 9 أو F, Dun : أما corr. Bad || 10 ليس F : فليس Bad || 10 بقبيح F, Dun : بعجيب Bad || 12 يشكو corr. Bad*, Dun* (ἐγκαλέσειε) : يشك F || 12 إذا F : أما Bad || 12 بالمحبة F*, Dun* (ἀγαπῶν) : في باطنه Bad || 13 second إذا Bad, Dun : إنما F || 14 يحب read. Bad, Dun : يجب appar. F || 15 يشكو F, Dun : نشكو Bad

the baseness of the action in that which is nobler. (3) But if the other is accepted[67] as good, then becomes bad and is thought to be so, should he be loved also?[68] Or is that impossible, since not everything should be loved, apart from the good and he did not love that? For evil should not be loved,[69] nor should one become like the bad, and it has already been said that like loves like. Should then the friendship be dissolved immediately, or should that not be in all cases, but in the case of those for whose wickedness there is no cure? As for those in whom improvement is possible, they should rather be helped in character than property[70] according as it is better than the latter [and] perhaps it is more connected with friendship. It may be thought of him who dissolves [the friendship] that he does not do anything he should not do, for he was not a friend to this man nor the like of him,[71] and when he has changed and it is impossible to bring back what is gone, [he turns away][72] from him. (4) If one of them has remained the same and the other has become better and developed greatly in virtue, should the former be taken as a friend, or is that impossible? This becomes very clear in the case of a great interval, e.g. boyhood friendships, for if one of the two has remained a boy in mind, and the other came to have the powerful mind of a man, how are they friends, since they do not approve of the same things, and are not happy and sad at the same things? For these same things are not to them like what they were to each of them,[73] and it is impossible that they should be friends without these, as has been said, nor is it possible that the life of both should be in a single intimacy. These things have already been spoken about. (5) So then, even if he had not been his friend at one time, no greater change is possible for him than this.[74] The intimacy which previously existed should be remembered, and just as we think that friends should be given more than strangers, so we should give to those who have been friends for

---

[67] Greek ἀποδέχηται is apparently taken as passive, which is not likely.

[68] Arabic *aiḍan* = Greek ἔτι.

[69] The words οὔτε δεῖ· φιλοπόνηρον have been omitted by homoioteleuton.

[70] Arabic *min al-māl*, i.e. ἤ taken as = 'than', with Chase, Rackham, Thomson and Gauthier (Ross ἤ = 'or').

[71] I.e. τούτῳ ἤ, the reading of K^b and M^b (Arberry).

[72] Arabic *'anna* added by Arberry. Some verb with the sense of ἀφίσταται, 'separate from', has to be supplied. Elsewhere the translation uses *haraba* = ἀφίσταται (1163b 23 and 1166b 10), but *'anna* could easily drop out before *'anhu*.

[73] Greek περὶ ἀλλήλους is not well rendered.

[74] The Arabic translator rendered ἆρα as ἄρα disregarding the question, and ἢ εἰ as καὶ εἰ (*wa-lau*), so that the sense is entirely lost.

يغشون الدينار على قدر رداءة الفعل في الذي هو أكرم (٣) وأمّا إن كان يقبل ذلك على أنّه خير ثمّ صار رديئاً يظنّ به ذلك فهل ينبغي أن يحَبّ أيضاً أو لا يمكن ذلك إذ كان لا ينبغي أن يحبّ كلّ شيء ما خلا الخير وكان لا يحبّ ذلك إذ لا ينبغي أن يكون يحبّ الشرير ولا أن يتشبّه بردئ وقد قيل إنّ الشبيه محبّ للشبيه فهل ينبغي أن تحلّ الصداقة من ساعتها أو لا ينبغي ذلك في كلّهم بل في الذين لا شفاء لشرّيتهم وأمّا الذين يمكن فيهم الإصلاح فأحرى بأن ينبغي أن يعانوا في الخلق من المال على قدر ما هو أجود من هذا وربّما هو أخصّ بالمحبّة وخليق أن يظنّ بالذي يحلّ أنّه لا يصنع شيئاً لا ينبغي فإنّه لم يكن صديقاً لهذا ولا بمثل هذا وإذا تغيّر فلا يمكن أن يعيد ما قد ذهب [عنّ] عنه (٤) وأمّا إن ثبت أحدهما وصار الآخر أفضل وتبدّل في الفضيلة كثيراً فهل ينبغي أن يتّخذ صديقاً أو لا يمكن ذلك وإنّما يتبيّن ذلك كثيراً في البعد العظيم مثل الصداقات الصبيانية فإنّه إن ثبت أحدهما صبياً في العقل وصار الآخر له عقل رجلي قوي فكيف يكونون أصدقاء إذ لا يرتضون بأشياء بأعيانها ولا يفرحون ويحزنون بأشياء بأعيانها فإنّه لا تكون لهم هذه الأشياء بأعيانها كما هي لكلّ واحد منهما وليس يمكن أن يكونوا أصدقاء من غير هذه كما قيل ولا يمكن أن يكون عمرهما في خلطة واحدة وقد قيل في هذه (٥) فإذاً ولو لم يكن صار له صديقاً في وقت ما لم يمكن له من التغيّر أشدّ من هذا وينبغي أن تكون تذكر الخلطة التي كانت فكما نرى أنّه ينبغي أن يوهب [٣/٤٧] الأصدقاء أكثر من الغرباء كذلك ينبغي أن

1-2 أنه خير Dun : أنه أخر F; الأخر Bad || 2 أو لا يمكن F*, Dun* (ἢ οὐ δυνατόν) : لا نظن Bad || 6 أن corr. Bad : بأن F || 6 و suppl. Dun || 6 ربما F : وبما Bad || 7 يحل read. Bad* (διαλυόμενος) : تخل F || 7 يصنع read. Dun : يضيع F, Bad || 8 عن suppl. Arberry* (ἀφίσταται) || 11 العقل corr. Dun* (τὴν διάνοιαν) : الفعل F, Bad || 11 الأخر له عقل رجلي قوي وصار with ظ (= ظاهر) above line || 11 يكونون corr. Bad : يكون F || 15 تكون تذكر F, Dun : نذكر نكون Bad || 16 كذلك F : فكذلك Bad

the sake of previous friendship, if it has not been dissolved on account of excessive wickedness.

1166a 4. The matters of friendship are defined by their relationship to the friends,[75] and it is likely that all the friendships which are defined have come from their relationship to them.[76] For they posit as friend him who wishes good things and does them, or things which appear to be good, for the sake of friendship itself,[77] or him who wishes to be and to choose for the sake of his friends,[78] like what affects mothers in regard to their children and friends who have done a wrong. Some people posit as friend the associate and him who agrees in choice, or him who is pained by the friend's pain and rejoices with his joy for the most part.[79] This occurs also with mothers. Some define a friend with reference to each of these, because they belong to the virtuous man.[80] (2) As for the rest, they think that they are like these.[81] And it is likely, as has already been said, that virtue and the virtuous man are the measure of each of them.[82] (3) For the virtuous man shares in will[83] and desires the same things with all his soul and wishes for himself goods and what appear to be goods, and he does this, for the good man is roused up[84] for the sake of the good and for himself. For it is on account of thought that each man is thought to be what he is.[85] He wishes for life for himself and security, and especially the security of that by which he understands. (4) Existence[86] is good for the virtuous man, and everyone wishes for goods for him-

---

[75] As Arberry notes, this implies vulg. (τοὺς φίλους), i.e. not τοὺς φίλους πέλας.

[76] Arabic *ilaihā* apparently for Greek πρὸς ἑαυτόν.

[77] But the Greek is ἐκείνου ἕνεκα with no variant.

[78] Arabic *yurīdu an yakūna wa-an yakhtāra min ajl aṣdiqā'ihi*. The last part of this is τῶν φίλων χάριν for τὸν φίλον αὐτοῦ χάριν and perhaps also ζητεῖν for ζῆν.

[79] I.e. μάλιστα is wrongly construed with the foregoing συγχαίροντα τῷ φίλῳ rather than with what follows (Arberry).

[80] This sentence results from running together the two sentences τούτων δέ τινι [...] and πρὸς ἑαυτὸν δέ [...] and altering or omitting words.

[81] I.e. for Greek τοῖς δὲ λοιποῖς [...] εἶναι, badly mistranslated.

[82] Arabic *bi-kull wāḥid minhum*, i.e. rather ἑκάστῳ, vulg., than ἑκάστων, the reading of K^b.

[83] For Greek ὁμογνωμονεῖ.

[84] Arabic *yub'athu*, apparently for Greek διαπονεῖν.

[85] The dependent (relative) clause with ὅπερ is not recognised as such.

[86] The connection (γάρ) between this and the previous sentence is not noticed.

يعطون الذين صاروا أصدقاء لمكان الصداقة المتقدّمة إذا لم تتحلّل لمكان إفراط الرداءة.

٤. وإنّما تحدّ الأشياء الصداقية بإضافتها إلى الأصدقاء ويشبه أن تكون جميع الصداقات التي تحدّ إنّما جاءت من إضافتها إليها فإنّهم يفرضون الصديق الذي يريد الخيرات ويفعلها أو التي تظهر أنّها خيرات من أجل الصداقة بعينها أو الذي يريد أن يكون وأن يختار من أجل أصدقائه كالذي يصيب الأمّهات نحو الأولاد والذين أخطؤوا من الأصدقاء ومن الناس من يفرض الصديق المعاشر والموافق في الاختيار أو الذي يألم بألم الصديق ويفرح بفرحه أكثر ذلك ويعرض هذا أيضاً للأمّهات ومنهم من يحدّ الصديق بالإضافة إلى كلّ واحد من هذه لأنّها للفاضل (٢) وأمّا الباقون فإنّهم يرون أنّهم مثل هؤلاء فقد يشبه كما قد قيل أن تكون الفضيلة والفاضل قدراً بكلّ واحد منهم (٣) فإنّ الفاضل يشارك في الإرادة ويشتهي الأشياء بأعيانها بكلّ نفسه ويريد لذاته الخيرات والتي يظهر أنّها خيرات ويفعل ذلك فإنّ الخير يبعث لمكان الخير ومن أجل ذاته فإنّه من أجل الفكرة يظنّ كلّ واحد ما هو ويريد الحياة لذاته والسلامة ولا سيّما سلامة هذا الذي يعقل به (٤) والإنّية خير للفاضل وكلّ واحد يريد لذاته الخيرات وليس يريد ذلك أحد إذا صار إليه ما خلا الذي

3 إليها F, Dun : إلينا Bad || 3 الصديق F, Dun : الصديق بانه add. Bad || 5 نحو Bad, Dun : illegible F || 9 بكل F : لكل Bad

self. No one would wish[87] for that, if it came to him, except him who desires that he should have all things, for he wishes that he should have that. For God now has excellence in another way,[88] whatever it is, and it may be thought that every one is that which understands, (5) and especially if[89] such a man as this wished to live with himself. For he does that with pleasure, for he desires the recollection of what he has done, and that rejoices him, and he desires also the hope of good things in future and ideas[90] like this, for he controls them by thought.[91] He shares with himself pain and pleasure for the most part, for always the one thing is painful and pleasant and not other things at a different time, as the saying is:[92] 'He has no regrets.' Each of these must be for the good man as each of them is in itself, and must be in the friend as it is in himself, since the friend is another self, if[93] it is thought that friendship is something, and friends are those who have the same things.[94] (6) As to whether or not there is friendship,[95] let us leave that for the present. Perhaps it may be thought that this friendship is friendship and[96] that there are two
1166b friendships or more, from what has been said also, and that the excess of friendship is alike with reference to him.[97] (7) It appears that what has been said applies to the many also, even if they are bad. Do they measure themselves[98] by their being pleased with themselves and think that they are good? For nothing of this is in those who are extremely bad and wicked in their actions, and does not even appear to be. That scarcely appears in bad people. (8) For there is an essential difference here,[99] and they desire some things, like those who do

---

[87] 'No one would wish [...].' The sentence has been misunderstood, but apparently ἐκεῖνο τὸ γενόμενον was read, as Arberry saw.

[88] I.e. ἄλλως instead of ἀλλ' ὤν (Arberry).

[89] Greek μάλιστα is wrongly construed with what follows. ἤ is not = 'and', and Arabic *in*, 'if', is not in the Greek.

[90] I.e. τ' ἰδέαι for δ' ἡδεῖαι (Arberry).

[91] Arabic *fa'innahu yaqdiru 'alaihā bi'l-fikrah*, which fails to render Greek καὶ θεωρημάτων δ' εὐπορεῖ τῇ διανοίᾳ.

[92] Arabic *ka-qaul al-qā'il* for Greek ὡς εἰπεῖν.

[93] Apparently καί is read as εἰ.

[94] I.e. ταὐτα for ταῦτα, frequently confused.

[95] Greek πρὸς αὑτὸν δέ is omitted in the Arabic translation (Arberry).

[96] Greek καί read for ᾗ.

[97] Greek τῇ omitted before πρὸς αὑτόν read as πρὸς αὐτόν. The idea of a man's friendship with himself is nowhere expressed by the Arabic translator.

[98] Greek μετροῦσιν αὑτούς, suggested by Arberry, is read for μετέχουσιν αὐτῶν.

[99] Arabic *fa'inna fīhi ikhtilāfan fī 'dh-dhāt*, but Greek διαφέρονται γὰρ ἑαυτοῖς, 'they are at variance with themselves'.

يشتهي أن يكون له جميع الأشياء فإنّه يريد أن يكون له ذلك فإنّ للإله الآن الجود بنوع أخر ما كان من شيء وخليق أن يظنّ أنّ كلّ واحد هو الذي يفهم (٥) ولا سيّما إن أراد مثل هذا أن يعاشر ذاته فإنّه يفعل ذلك بلذّة فإنّه يشتهي مذاكرة ما قد عمل به ويسرّه ذلك ويشتهي أيضاً رجاء الخيرات فيما يستأنف وما كان مثل هذا من الآراء فإنّه يقدر عليها بالفكرة ويشارك ذاته بالألم واللذّة أكثر ذلك فإنّه أبداً الشيء الواحد محزن ولذيذ وليس آخر وآخر في زمان مختلف كقول القائل ليس فيه ندامة. [٣/٤٨] ينبغي أن يكون الفاضل كلّ واحد من هذه كما أنّ كلّ واحد منها بذاته وأن يكون عند الصديق كما هو عند ذاته من أجل أنّ الصديق آخر هو هو إن كان يرى أنّ الصداقة شيئاً ما والأصدقاء الذين لهم أشياء بأعيانها (٦) وأمّا هل الصداقة أو هل ليست فلنترك ذلك حيننا هذا فخليق أن يظنّ بهذه الصداقة [أنّها] صداقة وأنّهما اثنان أو أكثر ممّا قيل أيضاً وأنّ إفراط الصداقة إنّما يشابه بالإضافة إليه (٧) ويظهر أنّ الذي قد قيل يكون للكثيرين أيضاً وإن كانوا ذوي رداءة فهل يقيسون ذواتهم بأنّهم يرتضون بذواتهم ويرون أنفسهم أفاضل فإنّه ليس شيء من هذا في الذين هم شديدو الشريّة رديئو الأعمل ولا يظهر ذلك أيضاً ويكاد ألاّ يظهر ذلك في ذوي الرداءة (٨) فإنّ فيه اختلافاً في الذات ويشتهون أشياء أخر كالذين لا يضبطون أنفسهم فإنّهم يختارون

---

2 second ان F : بان Bad || 3 به : om. Bad || 8 شيئا F : شيء Bad || 8 الذين corr. Dun : والذين F, Bad || 10 أنها suppl. Dun || 13 رديئو Bad, Dun : illegible F

not restrain themselves. For they choose instead of what they think is good for them the pleasant things which are harmful. Some of them avoid doing what they think is good for them, through cowardice or idleness. Those who have done many wicked deeds are hated for their wickedness and flee from life and kill themselves. (9) Wicked men seek people to spend their days with them and flee from their wickedness. For they recall many unpleasant things and anticipate other things like these, when they are alone, but when they are with other people they forget that. For not possessing anything to be loved, they are not affected by any [feeling of love] towards themselves, and people like these do not take pleasure in themselves, but[100] they are pained in themselves, since their souls are at variance, and some part of their souls is pained at wickedness when it abstains from certain things, and another part is pleased, part drawing in this direction and part in that, as if tearing them asunder. (10) And if it is impossible that a man should feel pain and be glad at the same time, yet he feels pain a little[101] because he was glad and did not wish[102] that these things should become pleasant for him. For bad people are filled with remorse. Hence the condition of the wicked man towards himself does not appear to be that of friendship, and he does not love himself, since he does not have anything lovable. If anything like that is so,[103] he is excessively wretched, and[104] one should avoid wickedness seriously, and [...] virtuous, for in this way one can take pleasure in oneself and be a friend to another.

5. As for goodwill, it resembles friendship, but it is not friendship, since goodwill is felt towards those whom one does not even know and is even concealed. Friendship, on the other hand, is not. Statements of this kind[105] have already been made. Nor is it affection either, since it has no tension and no desire, and these things follow affection. (2) And affection is with intimacy, while goodwill is an

---

[100] Arabic *bal* does not convey Greek οὐδέ.

[101] Arabic *qalīlan*, i.e. μικρόν for μετὰ μικρόν (Arberry).

[102] Arabic *lam yakun yurīdu an taṣīra hādhihi lahu ladhīdhah*. Greek ἄν seems to be disregarded. It is not clear that Arabic (*lam yakun yurīdu*) has the same meaning as Greek οὐκ [...] ἐβούλετο, 'wished that [...] not'.

[103] Arabic *wa-in kāna mithl dhālika*, i.e. reading apparently εἰ δὲ οὕτως ἔχειν, breaking up the protasis of the conditional sentence, the apodosis of which is φευκτέον [...].

[104] Not in the Greek, see previous note.

[105] Arabic *aqāwīl mithl hādhihi*, i.e. τοιαῦτα for ταῦτα.

بدل ما يرون أنّها خيرات لهم اللذينة التي هي ضارّة ومنهم من يهرب عن فعل ما يرى أنّه له جيّد للجبن أو للبطالة وأمّا الذين عملوا أعمالاً كثيرة رديئة فإنّهم يبغضون لمكان الرداءة ويهربون من الحيوة ويقتلون أنفسهم (٩) وذوو الرداءة يطلبون قوماً يقضون نهارهم معهم ويهربون من رداءتهم فإنّهم يتذاكرون أشياء كثيرة صعبة ويترجّون أشياء أخر مثل هذه إذا كانوا وحدهم وإذا كانوا مع قوم آخرين نسوا ذلك فإنّهم لمّا لم يكن لهم شيء يحبّ صاروا لا ينفعلون بشيء نحو ذواتهم والذين مثل هؤلاء لا يفرحون بذواتهم بل يألمون بذواتهم من أجل أنّ أنفسهم مشاغبة فبعض أنفسهم تألّم للرداءة إذا تباعد عن أشياء وبعض يلذّ وبعض يحدث إلى ها هنا وبعض إلى ثمّ كالشيء يشقّ بالجذب باثنتين (١٠) وإن كان لا يمكن أن يحزن ويفرح معاً إلاّ أنّه يحزن قليلاً لأنّه فرح ولم يكن يريد أن تصير هذه له لذينة فإنّ ذوي الرداءة مملوءون من الندامة. من أجل هذا يظهر ذو الرداءة أنّه ليست حاله في ذاته حال [٣/٤٩] صداقة ولا يحبّ ذاته من أجل أنّه ليس له شيء محبوب وإن كان مثل ذلك فإنّه شديد الشقاء وينبغي أن يهرب من الرداءة جدّاً وأن [...] فاضلاً فإنّه بهذا النوع خليق أن يكون سارّاً لذاته ويكون صديقاً لغيره.

٥. وأمّا النصيحة فقد تشبه الصداقة وليست صداقة من أجل أنّ النصيحة تكون في الذين لا يعرف أيضاً و[...] أيضاً وأمّا الصداقة فلا وقد قيلت أقاويل مثل هذه قبل هذا أيضاً وليست محبّة أيضاً من أجل أنّه ليس لها امتداد ولا شهوة وهذه الأشياء تتبع المحبّة (٢) والمحبّة مع الخلطة وأمّا النصيحة فإنّها تكون تراثاً قديماً مثل الذي يعرض في

1 عن F : من Bad || 3 الحيوة Dun : reading uncertain F || 3 يقتلون read. Bad*, Dun* (ἀναιροῦσιν) : يقبلون F || 4 يترجون corr. Dun* (ἐλπίζουσι) : يتدرجون F, Bad || 5 وحدهم corr. above line : وجودهم F || 6 نحو Dun : محيي Bad || 8 بالجنب w.p. F || 11 إن F : إذا Bad || 12 فانه F : أنه Bad || 12 فانه بهذا F : فإن هذا Bad || 13 صديقا Bad, Dun : illegible || 15 يعرف F, Dun : نعرف Bad || 15 [...] : illegible F, *is concealed* Dun || 15 و[...] (...) هذا أيضا : om. Bad || 16 من أجل Bad, Dun : illegible F || 17 مع الخلطة Dun* (μετὰ συνηθείας) : مخالطة Bad; F illegible || 17 ترائا قديما F, Dun : أيضا فجة Bad* (προσπαίου)

1167a old inheritance,[106] like what happens in the case of competitors. For people have goodwill towards them and sympathise with them, but would not by any means share with them in action, so that, as we have said, they become well-wishers by pretence and love in appearance, as if pretending.[107] (3) It is likely that the beginning of friendship, like passionate love, is the pleasure which arises through sight. For no one loves if he is not pleased through the sight first, and he who takes delight in what is pleasant[108] does not love anything more than it,[109] but when he is affected[110] by its absence, he desires its nearness also. Similarly it is not possible that men should be friends if they have not already become well-wishers. But well-wishers do not love more,[111] for they only wish for good things for those to whom they are well-wishers, and they would not agree with them on a particular action, not even if it were concerning themselves.[112] Hence one may transfer this name and say that goodwill is tardy friendship, and when it has lasted long and become habitual it is friendship—not for the sake of what is useful nor for the sake of what is pleasant, for goodwill does not exist on these terms. For he who is well treated requites with goodwill in return for the benefit which he has received, and is just in his action. He who wishes to do good to a benefactor and hopes to receive what he wishes from doing good to him is not likely to be a well-wisher on that account, but he is rather a well-wisher to himself, just as he is not a friend either, and simply serves him for some use. (4) In general, goodwill arises by reason of a certain virtue and merit, when a man [appears to be in another's eyes] good[113] or brave or something like this,[114] as we said in the case of competitors also.

---

[106] Arabic *turāth qadīm*, i.e. apparently παλαιοῦ read for προσπαίου (Arberry).

[107] Arabic *ka'l-tamwīh*, an obvious gloss on *maḥabbatan ẓāhiratan* for Greek ἐπιπολαίως, which was not understood.

[108] Arabic *bi'l-ladhīdh*, i.e. τῷ ἡδεῖ for τῷ εἴδει (Arberry), cf. 1173b 28.

[109] I.e. οὐδὲν μᾶλλον construed not as a phrase (= 'any the more'), but separately.

[110] I.e. πάθῃ for ποθῇ (Arberry).

[111] Again οὐδὲν μᾶλλον is not correctly taken (= 'any the more').

[112] Greek οὐδ' ὀχληθεῖεν ὑπὲρ αὐτῶν, misread as something like οὐδ' ὅταν εἶεν ὑπὲρ αὐτῶν (Arberry). The meaning of ὀχληθεῖεν was unknown, apparently, cf. 1171b 19.

[113] Arabic *ṣāliḥ* for Greek καλός.

[114] The English translation follows Arberry's Arabic text: *idhā ẓahara insān an yakūna ʿinda ākhar ṣāliḥan au najidan au shai'an mithl hādhā*, which requires further explanation. The MS. has apparently: *idhā ẓahara* [or rather *idh aẓhara*] [...] *ṣāliḥ au najid au shai' mithl hādhā*, where the lacuna has room for seven or eight letters at most (*insān an yakūna ʿinda ākhara* contains nearly twenty letters).

المجاهدين فإنّهم يناصحونهم ويوافقونهم بالإرادة وخليق ألاّ يشاركوهم في الفعل البتّةَ فكما قلنا يصيرون نصحاء بالمراءة ويحبّون محبّة ظاهرة كالتمويه (٣) فقد يشبه أن يكون ابتداء الصداقة اللذّة التي تكون بالبصر كمحبّة العشق فإنّه لا يعشق أحد إن لم يلذّ بالبصر أوّلاً والذي يفرح باللذيذ لا يعشق شيئاً أكثر منه بل إذا أصيب بتباعده اشتهى قربه أيضاً وكذلك لا يمكن أن يكونوا أصدقاء إن لم يكونوا قد صاروا نصحاء وأمّا النصحاء فلا يحبّون حبّاً أكثر فإنّهم يريدون الخيرات فقط للذين هم لهم نصحاء وخليق ألاّ يوافقوهم على فعل ما ولا إن كان عن ذواتهم ومن أجل هذا يمكن أحداً أن ينقل هذا الاسم ويقول إنّها صداقة بطيئة فإذا أزمنت وصارت في العادة تكون صداقة لا من أجل النافع ولا من أجل اللذيذ فإنّ النصيحة لا تكون على هذه الأشياء فإنّ الذي أحسن إليه يكافئ بالنصيحة بدل ما اصطنع إليه وهو عادل في فعله وأمّا الذي يريد إحسان محسن ويرجو أن ينال ما يريد من الإحسان به فليس يشبه أن يكون مناصحاً لذلك بل أحرى أن يكون ناصحاً لذاته كما أنّه لا يكون صديقاً أيضاً وإنّما يخدمه لاستعمل ما (٤) وبالجملة إنّما تكون نصيحة بفضيلة واستئهل كما إذا ظهر [٣/٥٠] إنسان [أن يكون عند آخر] صالحاً أو نجداً أو شيئاً مثل هذا كما قلنا في المجاهدين أيضاً.

---

2 بالمراءة corr. Arberry : بالمرأيات F || 2 فقد F : فهو Bad || 5 فلا corr. Bad : لا F || 7 يمكن corr. Dun* : لا يمكن F, Bad || 7 أحدا corr. Bad : أحد F || 8 أزمنت F, Dun : ادمنت Bad || 13 إنسان Bad, Dun : illegible F || 13 أن يكون عند آخر suppl. Arberry || 13 صالحا corr. Arberry : صالح F, Bad || 13 نجدا corr. Arberry : نجد F; مجد Bad || 13 شيئا corr. Arberry : شئ F, Bad

6. It appears that agreement of opinion is friendly also. Hence it is not agreement in intention, for this exists among those who do not even know each other. And people do not say that those who have the same wish in regard to the same thing agree in opinion[115] when the agreement of their wish in regard to something[116] is better, and they choose these[117] and carry out their common intentions. (2) In regard to actions their opinions agree, and[118] in great matters, and in what is possible to be for both of them, or all of them, as cities, when all see that the offices shall be virtues,[119] and that the people of Lacedaimon[120] should be taken as partners in the war and helped,[121] or that Pittacus should rule, who[122] wanted it himself also, and when each of the two wishes himself also,[123] like what happened among the people of Phoenicia,[124] when they became at variance.[125] For the goodwill[126] of each of them cannot possibly be the agreement in opinion of each of them with reference to something or other, but with reference to one and the same thing, like what happens when
1167b the common people and the better class[127] wish that the best men should rule, for by this the desire of all of them is brought about. Agreement in opinion seems to be political friendship, as is said also in regard to[128] the things which are better and in regard to the things which are needed in life. (3) This agreement in opinion is in meritorious men, for these are agreed in opinion in themselves and with one another also, since they are concerned with the same things, as

---

[115] See following note.

[116] A lacuna is here noted by Arberry. It should rather be placed earlier, after 'in opinion', being due to homoioteleuton of ὁμονοεῖν φασίν in lines 24f. and 26.

[117] Arabic *hādhihi*, but Greek is ταὐτά.

[118] Greek τούτων is left untranslated.

[119] I.e. ἀρετάς for αἱρετάς (Arberry). The Arabic text seems to need some correction: *ajma'ūn an takūn* for *ajma'īn an*.

[120] Arabic *ahl Lāqādūmūnyā*, cf. 1102a 11, 1112a 29, also 1180a 25.

[121] Above (1157a 27) *al-mu'āwanah fī 'l-qitāl* renders αἱ συμμαχίαι.

[122] Apparently ὅτε = 'when' is misunderstood.

[123] Arabic *kull wāḥid minhumā yurīdu dhātahu aiḍan*, i.e. Greek ἑκάτερος καὶ ἑαυτόν, the reading of K^b (Arberry).

[124] Arabic *ahl Fūh Nīqā* for Greek οἱ ἐν ταῖς Φοινίσσαις, 'the men in the *Phoenissai*', a play of Euripides, which the Arabic translator evidently does not know, though he appears to know the Greek name Φοινίκη = Phoenicia.

[125] Arabic *'indamā shaghabū*, i.e. Greek στασιάζουσιν construed with οἱ ἐν ταῖς Φοινίσσαις.

[126] Arabic *naṣīḥah*, i.e. Greek εὐνοεῖν, the reading of K^b, L^b and Γ.

[127] Arabic *al-afāḍil*, exceptionally for Greek οἱ ἐπιεικεῖς.

[128] I.e. καθάπερ καὶ λέγεται is run on to the following sentence, disregarding γάρ.

٦. ويظهر أنّ اتّفاق الرأي محبّي أيضاً ومن أجل هذا ليس هو اتّفاقاً في العزيمة فإنّ هذا يكون بين من لا يعلم بعضهم بعضاً أيضاً ولا يقولون إنّ الذين يريدون إرادة واحدة في شئ واحد متّفقون في الرأي إذا كان اتّفاق إرادتهم في الشئ أصلح وكانوا يختارون هذه ويفعلون العزائم العامّية (٢) وأمّا في الأفعل فإنّ آراءهم تتّفق وفي التي هي ذات عظم منها وفيما يمكن أن يكون لكليهما أو لكلّهم كالمدن إذا رأوا أجمعون أن [تكون] الرياسات فضائل وأنّه ينبغي أن يشارك أهل لاقادومونيا في الحرب ويعانوا أو أن يرؤس فطاقوس الذي كان يريده هو أيضاً وإذا كان كلّ واحد منهما يريد ذاته أيضاً مثلما كان في أهل فوه نيقى عندما شغبوا فإنّ نصيحة كلّ واحد منها ليس يمكن أن تكون اتّفاق كلّ واحد منهما بالرأي لشئ ما بل للواحد بعينه مثل ما يكون إذا أرادت العامّة والأفاضل أن يرأس الأخيار فإنّ هذا يكون شهوة كلّهم واتّفاق الرأي يظهر أنّه محبّة مدنية كما يقل أيضاً في الأشياء التي هي أخير وفي التي يحتاج إليها في العمر (٣) وهذا الاتّفاق بالرأي في ذوي الاستئهل فإنّ هؤلاء متّفقو الرأي في ذواتهم وبعضهم لبعض أيضاً إذ كانوا في أشياء بأعيانها كالقول

1 اتفاق الرأي محبي Bad, Dun : illegible F || 2 بين من Bad, Dun : illegible F || 3 إرادتهم F, Dun : إرادي Bad || 3 الشئ Bad : الشئ هي F || 3 أصلح F, Dun : الأصلح Bad || 4 ذات corr. Arberry : ذو F, Bad || 5 أجمعون corr. Dun : أجمعين F, Bad || 5 تكون suppl. Dun || 6 لاقادومونيا : last three letters w.p. F || 6 يرؤس F*, Dun* (ἄρχειν) : يروا من Bad || 7 ذاته F, Dun : لذاته Bad || 7-8 فوه نيقى corr. Bad, Dun : قوة نيعى second part w.p. F || 8 شغبوا read. Bad*, Dun* (στασιάζουσιν) : سعبوا F || 11 بالرأي or في الرأي corr. Bad, Dun : الرأي F

the saying is[129] that the wish of these people is steady and does not flow from thing to thing and change, like the flow of the Euripus,[130] and they wish for justice and the things which are more fitting, and desire these things with a common desire. (4) As for the bad, it is impossible that their opinion should agree except a little, as that they should be friends, because of their desire for much gain in those things which are profitable, while in different kinds of work and service they are defective. Each of them wishes these things for himself and makes inquiries about his neighbour and hinders him. For if they do not guard the common interest, it is lost. This dissension occurs among them because they try to compel one another, but are not willing to do that in which justice lies.

7. It is thought that those who benefit others have more love for those who have been benefited than those to whom a kindness has been done have for those who have done it. This is investigated as something which is contrary to reason. For the most part that is clear. Also some of them love,[131] and that is incumbent on the others, as it is in the case of loans. For those against whom a claim stands wish that those to whom the claim is due should not exist, but as for those who have lent, they take care of and are concerned for the welfare of their debtors. Similarly those who have done a kindness wish that those to whom the kindness has been done should be like those who bring their favours.[132] As for those who are concerned to requite them, Epicharmus[133] might say of them: 'From the fact that they say these things, it is likely that a wicked man sees them.'[134] For most people have no memory, and their desire that good should be done them is more than their desire to do it. (2) It may be thought that the

---

[129] Arabic *ka'l-qaul*, Greek ὡς εἰπεῖν.

[130] Arabic *Ūrībus*. The Arabic translator knows (from previous knowledge, or from some paraphrase or commentary on the *Ethics*), or perhaps has guessed, that the Euripus is a waterway, since he adds *sailān*, 'flow', cf. above *Fūh Nīqī* = Φοινίκη.

[131] I.e. Greek ὀφείλουσι read as φιλοῦσι (Arberry).

[132] Arabic *ka'lladhīna ya'tūna bi-aidīhim*. This entirely fails to translate Greek ὡς κομιουμένους τὰς χάριτας, when the participle is future and with ὡς expresses a purpose, to be construed with τοὺς εὐεργετήσαντας, not with τοὺς παθόντας, i.e. the benefactors wish those who haven been benefited to exist, in order to receive the favours which express their gratitude.

[133] Text apparently *yataḥarramūn*, corr. *Abīkharmūs*, Greek Ἐπίχαρμος.

[134] Arabic *shabīh* (corr. *yushbih* for *bi-sabab* over *shabīh* in the MS.). This is for Greek ἐκ πονηροῦ θεωμένους badly translated, with ἔοικε δ' ἀνθρωπικῷ following, read apparently ἔοικεν ἀνθρώπου. The sense is hopelessly lost.

بأنّ إرادة هؤلاء ثابتة ولا تسيل من شئ إلى شئ وتنتقل كسيلان أوريبس وهم يريدون العدالة والتي هي أوفق ويشتهون هذه الأشياء شهوة عامّية (٤) وأمّا ذوو الرداءة فلا يمكن أن يتّفق رأيهم إلاّ قليلاً كما يكونون أصدقاء لشهوتهم في كثرة قنية في التي هي نافعة وأمّا في أنواع التعب والخدمة فإنّهم نقّص وكلّ واحد منهم يريد هذه لذاته ويستقصي على القريب ويمنعه فإنّهم إذا لم يحفظوا العامّ هلك وإنّما يعرض لهم هذا الشغب لأنّهم يضطرّون بعضهم بعضاً فهم لا يريدون أن يفعلوا ما فيه العدل.

٧. ويظنّ أنّ المحسنين أكثر حبّاً [٣/٥١] للذين أحسن إليهم من الذين اصطنع إليهم المعروف للذين اصطنعوا ذلك ويطلب ذلك كالشئ الذي يكون على غير قياس وأمّا الأكثر فإنّ ذلك ظاهر وأيضاً فإنّ بعضهم يحبّ وبعضهم يحقّ ذلك عليه كما يكون في القروض فإنّ الذين يجب الحقّ عليهم يريدون ألاّ يكون الذين يجب لهم الحقّ وأمّا الذين أقرضوا فإنّهم يتعاهدون ويهتمّون بسلامة غرمائهم وكذلك يريدون الذين اصطنعوا المعروف أن يكونوا الذين اصطنع إليهم كالذين يأتون بأيديهم وأمّا الذين يهتمّون بأن يكافئوهم فخليق أن يقول فيهم أبيخرموس بأنّهم يقولون بهذه الأقاويل يشبه أن يكون يراهم إنسان شرير فإنّ أكثر الناس ليس بذوي ذكر وشهوتهم أن يصطنع إليهم الخير أكثر من شهوتهم في أن يفعلوا ذلك (٢) وخليق أن يظنّ أنّ العلّة في ذلك طبيعية وليس فيه

1 أوريبس corr. Dun : اوريس F; اوربس Bad || 3 قنية w.p. F || 4 نقص corr. Arberry* (ἐλλείποντας) : بغض F, Bad || 5 القريب corr. Dun* (τὸν πέλας) : الغريب F, Bad || 9 ظاهر F*, Dun* (φαίνεται) : واحد Bad || 9 second و : om. Bad || 10 first الذين corr. : الذي F, Bad || 10 يكون corr. Bad : يكونوا F || 11 أقرضوا F*, Dun* (δανείσαντες) : أعطوا Bad || 11 يريدون F : يريد Bad || 12 يكونوا corr. Dun : يكون F, Bad || 12 يأتون Bad, Dun : illegible F || 13 ابيخرموس Dun : illegible F || 13 يشبه corr. Dun : شبيه F; بسبب corr. above line, Bad

cause of that is natural and there is no similarity to creditors, for in these there is no friendship, but rather a wish for the welfare [of the debtor] for the sake of recovering the debt. As for those who have done a kindness, they love and desire those to whom the kindness was done, even though no profit has been made from them of any kind, nor will there be any advantage from them afterwards, like what happens in the case of craftsmen also. (3) For every craftsman loves what he has made more than he would be loved by his handi-
1168a work, even if his handiwork were animate. This perhaps appears more in the case of poets, for these last go to excess in love of what is more poetical, like love of children. (4) The like of this occurs to those who do good in doing a kindness. For their work is the doing, sc. of the kindness,[135] and they love this more than the doer loves his action.[136] The reason for that is that existence is chosen by all and loved also, and we are by action, for we exist by living and acting, so that the doer of a work is by action. He loves the work for the sake of existence,[137] and this is natural. The work shows in action what this man is in potentiality. (5) At the same time for the doer of the kindness the action is noble, so that he to whom this belongs[138] rejoices, but for the man to whom the kindness was done there is nothing good in the agent unless there is what is profitable,[139] and this is less in pleasure and love.[140] (6) Pleasure[141] in what is present is in action, in what is to come is in hope, in what has been is in memory, and that which is in action is said to be necessary, like as with reference to an action the agent remains.[142] For the excellent lasts its time, while the benefit of him to whom the kindness was done passes away from him. Memory of good is pleasant, but memory of benefits is very slight,[143] while hope is likely to be the opposite of that. It seems that love is like action and being loved like being acted upon,

---

[135] Arabic *al-iṣṭinā'*, not right for τὸ [...] εὖ πεπονθός.

[136] Arabic *akthar min maḥabbat al-fā'il li-fi'lihi*. But in the expression μᾶλλον ἢ τὸ ἔργον τὸν ποιήσαντα, τὸ ἔργον is clearly subject, not object as in the Arabic.

[137] Arabic *li-makān al-annīyah* for Greek διότι καὶ τὸ εἶναι is not right.

[138] Or 'applies', Arabic *alladhī lahu hādha*, but the sense is wrong, the clause depending on the verb (χαίρειν, 'rejoices').

[139] Arabic *akhyar* for Greek συμφέρον.

[140] I.e. less pleasant and lovable.

[141] Arabic *al-ladhdhah*, but Greek is ἡδεῖα, not ἡδονή.

[142] Arabic *ka-mithl mā li-fi'l fa-baqiya al-fā'il*, i.e. ὁμοίως taken with what follows and then mistranslation (Arberry).

[143] Greek ἢ ἧττον is here omitted.

تشبيه بأصحاب القرض فإنّه ليس في أولئك محبّة بل إرادة السلامة لمكان الأخذ وأمّا الذين اصطنعوا المعروف فإنّهم يحبّون ويريدون الذين اصطنع إليهم وإن لم يكن ينتفع بهم في شيء ولا تكون منهم منفعة فيما بعد كالذي يعرض في أصحاب الصناعات أيضاً (٣) فإنّ كلّ ذي صناعة يحبّ ما صنع أكثر ممّا يحبّ من المصنوع ولو كان المصنوع متنفّساً وخليق أن يظهر هذا أكثر في الشعراء فإنّ هؤلاء يفرطون في محبّة ما أشعروا كمحبّة الأولاد (٤) فمثل هذا يعرض للمحسنين في اصطناع المعروف فإنّ عملهم الاصطناع ويحبّون هذا أكثر من محبّة الفاعل لفعله والعلّة في ذلك أنّ الإنّية مختارة عند الكلّ ومحبوبة أيضاً ونحن بالفعل فأنا نحيا ونفعل ففاعل العمل هو بالفعل ويحبّ العمل لمكان الإنّية وهذا طبيعي ويدلّ العمل بالفعل [على] ما هو هذا بالقوّة (٥) ومع هذا فإنّ الفعل عند صانع المعروف جيّد حتّى إنّه يفرح الذي له هذا وليس للذي اصطنع إليه المعروف خير ما عند الفاعل إلاّ أن يكون الذي هو أخير وهذا هو أقلّ في اللذّة والمحبّة (٦) واللذّة [٣/٥٢] أمّا فيما هو مقيم ففي الفعل وأمّا فيما يأتي ففي الرجاء وفي الذي قد كان في الذكر والذي في الفعل قالوا واجب كمثل ما لفعل فبقي الفاعل فإنّ الجيّد يطول زمانه وأمّا منفعة الذي اصطنع إليه المعروف فإنّها تفرّ عنه وذكر الخير لذيذ وأمّا ذكر المنافع فقليل جدّاً وأمّا الرجاء فيشبه أن يكون على خلاف ذلك ويشبه أن تكون المحبّة كالفعل

---

2 فإنهم يحبون ويريدون F, Dun : فيحبون ويودون Bad || 4 و : om. Bad || 5 أشعروا corr. Dun : أشعر F, Bad || 8 نحن F, Dun : نحيا Bad || 8 فأنا F : بأنا Bad || 8 ففاعل F, Dun : نعامل Bad || 9 على suppl. Bad || 11 إلا F*, Dun* (ἀλλ' εἴπερ) : يمكن Bad || 11 الذي corr. Dun : للذي F, Bad || 12 first ففي F, Dun : على Bad || 12 second ففي F, Dun : مع Bad || 13 ما لفعل F : بالفعل Bad || 13 فبقي F : يبقى Bad || 14 تفر w.p. F

and that the things loved[144] are compared with the things that follow the action. (7) And also all men love what has come to them with trouble more than anything else, like money, for those who have made money love it more than those who have received it freely. It may be thought that to have good done to one involves no trouble, but to do good is a trouble. Hence mothers love their children more, because birth was more painful, and they love the children more than themselves.[145] This might be thought to be a special characteristic also of those who do a kindness.

8. There is a difficulty also as to whether one who loves should love himself most, or that he should love another. For some people forbid[146] those who love themselves most and call them 'self-lovers', as it were a bad thing. It is thought also that a bad man does all that he does for himself and increases therein, according as he increases in badness, and we blame him simply because he does nothing except for himself.[147] As for the good man, he acts for the sake of the excellent and increases in doing good, according as he increases in excellence, and he acts also for the sake of a friend and sets aside what is his own interest. (2) The actions oppose these statements, not without cause. For people say that one should love best him who is a friend,[148] and he is best for a friend who wishes for good things, or who[149] wishes for good things for his friend for his sake, even if no one knows that. These things are mostly for him with reference to himself, and all the rest of the things by which a friend is defined. It has already been said that all the things of friendship pass from him to others. All the proverbs express the same wish, e.g. what is said as to one soul and the [goods] of friends being shared equally and the knee being nearer than the shin. For all these things would best be related to him,[150] since he is his best friend, and it is best that he

---

[144] Arabic *al-ashyā' al-muḥabbah* for τὰ φιλικά, omitting τὸ φιλεῖν with K^b. The Greek sentence appears to have been much modified before translation.

[145] Arabic *yuḥibbūn* [sic] *al-aulād akthar min dhātihim* [masculine]. Greek has καὶ μᾶλλον ἴσασιν ὅτι αὑτῶν, and the words have been rejected as out of place here (Rackham and Gauthier).

[146] Arabic *yanhā* for Greek ἐπιτιμῶσι, 'criticize, censure'. 'Forbid' from what?

[147] Arabic *illā li-dhātihi*, which is not the same as Greek ἀφ' ἑαυτοῦ, "of his own accord" (Ross).

[148] But Greek is τὸν μάλιστα φίλον.

[149] Apparently for ἣ ὧ of K^b according to Bywater (ἢ ᾧ, Rackham).

[150] Greek πρὸς αὑτόν.

والاستحباب كالانفعل وأن تقاس بالأشياء التي تلي الفعل الأشياء المحبّة (٧) وأيضاً جميع الناس يحبّون ما صار إليهم بتعب أكثر من غيره كالأموال فإنّ الذين اكتسبوها يحبّونها أكثر من الذين سلّمت إليهم عفواً وقد يظنّ بأنّ حسن الانفعل لا تعب فيه وأمّا حسن الفعل فتعب ومن أجل هذه الأشياء الأمّهات أكثر حبّاً للأولاد من أجل أنّ الولادة أشدّ ألماً ويحبّون الأولاد أكثر من ذاتهم وخليق أن يظنّ هذا خاصّاً أيضاً للذين يصطنعون المعروف.

٨. وقد يتحيّر أيضاً هل ينبغي أن يحبّ محبّ ذاته أكثر ذلك أو أن يحبّ آخر ما فإنّ من الناس من ينهى الذين يحبّون ذواتهم أكثر ذلك ويسمّيهم محبّي ذواتهم كأنّه شئ قبيح ويظنّ أيضاً أنّ ذا الرداءة يفعل جميع ما يفعل لذاته ويزيد في ذلك على قدر زيادته في الرداءة وإنّما نلومه من [أجل] أنّه لا يفعل شيئاً إلاّ لذاته وأمّا الفاضل فإنّما يفعل من أجل الجيّد ويزيد في فعل الخير على قدر زيادته في الجودة ويفعل أيضاً من أجل الصديق ويدع ما هو له (٢) والأفعل تخالف هذه الأقاويل ليس من غير علّة فإنّهم يزعمون أنّه ينبغي أن يحبّ أحرى الذي هو صديق وأحرى أن يكون صديقاً الذي يريد الخيرات أو الذي يريد الخيرات لصديقه من أجله وإن لم يعلم ذلك أحد وله هذه الأشياء أكثر ذلك عنه وجميع سائر الأشياء التي يحدّ بها الصديق فقد قيل إنّ جميع الأشياء الصديقية منه تصير إلى الآخر وجميع الأمثل توحّد الإرادة مثلما يقل إنّ نفساً واحدة وإنّ الذي للأصدقاء مشترك بالتساوي وإنّ الركبة أقرب من [٣/٥٣] الساق فإنّ جميع هذه الأشياء أحرى أن تضاف إليه

3 الانفعل F*, Dun* (πάσχειν) : الإحسان Bad || 4 الولادة corr. Dun : الاولاد F; الولاد Bad || 7 محبّ ذاته read. Dun : محبّ ذاتِه F || 8 ينهى F*, Dun* (ἐπιτιμῶσι) : ينعى Bad || 10 أجل suppl. Dun || 12 فإنهم corr. Bad : فإنه F || 16 توحد read. Bad*, Dun* (ὁμογνωμονοῦσιν) : توجد F

should love himself. It is right that[151] there should be a difference of opinion as to which of the two views we must follow, when both of
1168b them are convincing. (3) It may be that we should divide the statements which are like these and should distinguish the value of the statement of both,[152] and perhaps it will become more clear. (4) Those who cite it[153] reproach it, for they call 'lovers of themselves' those who appropriate to themselves the most wealth and honours and bodily pleasures. For the majority desire these things and covet them, as if they were better, hence they are contended for, and those who abound in desire rejoice[154] in desires and in all the passions of the soul and in the good[155] of the soul, i.e. the animal part. (5) Most people are like these, and on account of this it has got its name from the great amount of its badness, and whoever is in this condition is rightly reproached as being a lover of self. That most people are accustomed to call those who think themselves worthy of these things lovers of self is clear. For if one were constantly eager to act justly more than all men[156] and to do the things in which temperance consists, or other actions related to the virtues, and were always in general doing good in oneself,[157] such a man would not be called a lover of himself, and would not be blamed. (6) It might be more appropriate that he should be thought a lover of self who assigns to himself the best and greatest of good things, and who rejoices[158] in what is truly his and is ever persuaded by it. Just as the city is thought to be the real thing[159] for the most part [rather] than[160]

---

[151] Arabic *yaḥuqqu an* for Greek εἰκότως, elsewhere *bi-ḥaqqin* without *an* (1164a 29, 33, 1169a 31, 1172a 1) which also renders Greek δικαίως, cf. 1168b 22.

[152] A line of Greek (καὶ πῇ [...] ἑκάτεροι) has been omitted through homoioteleuton.

[153] Sc. the expression 'self-love', which was among the omitted words, cf. previous note.

[154] Arabic *yafraḥūna*, i.e. Greek χαίρουσιν (or χαίρονται, a later form) read for χαρίζονται.

[155] Apparently Greek ἀλόγῳ read as ἀγαθῷ (Arberry).

[156] Arabic *akthar min jamīʿ an-nās*, i.e. Greek μάλιστα πάντων is taken as masculine with most modern translations.

[157] Arabic *yafʿalu fī dhātihi al-khair* hardly renders Greek τὸ καλὸν ἑαυτῷ περιποιοῖτο.

[158] Arabic *yafraḥu*, again the wrong rendering of Greek χαρίζεται, cf. n. 154.

[159] Arabic *ash-shai' al-ḥaqqī*, i.e. τὸ κυριώτατον (rendered in the line above *al-ladhī huwa lahu bi'l-ḥaqīqah*), but what is the complement in the Greek sentence (πόλις) is taken as the subject.

[160] Apparently ἢ for καί of the Greek, but we need to supply *akthar* with *min*, perhaps from the preceding *akthar dhālika*, with suppresion of *dhālika*.

من أجل أنّه له صديق أحرى وأحرى أن يحبّ ذاته ويحقّ أن يتحيّر في أيّهما ينبغي أن يتبع إذا كان كلاهما ثقة (٣) وخليق أن يكون ينبغي أن نقسّم الأقاويل التي تشبه هذه وأن نفصّل قدر قول كليهما فلعلّ أن يتبيّن أكثر (٤) فإنّ الذين يأتون به يعيّرون به فإنّهم يسمّون محبّي أنفسهم الذين يخصّون أنفسهم بأكثر الأموال والكرامات واللذّات الجسمية فإنّ الأكثر يشتهون هذه الأشياء ويحرصون عليها كأنّها أفضل من أجل ذلك هي تنازعية والذين يكثرون في الشهوة يفرحون بالشهوات وبجميع الآلام النفسانية وبالخير النفسي أيّ البهيمي (٥) وأكثر الناس مثل هؤلاء ومن أجل هذا صار اسمه من كثرة شرّيته ونحن نعيّر من كان على هذه الحل بأنّه محبّ ذاته وأمّا أنّ أكثر الناس قد اعتاد أن يسمّي الذين يؤهّلون أنفسهم هذه الأشياء محبّي ذواتهم فبيّن فإنّه إن كان أحد يحرص أبداً على أن يفعل بالعدل أكثر من جميع الناس وأن يفعل الأشياء التي فيها العفّة أو أفعالاً أخر تنسب إلى الفضائل وكان أبداً بالجملة يفعل في ذاته الخير لا يقل هذا محبّ ذاته ولا يذمّ (٦) وخليق أن يكون أحرى أن يظنّ أنّه محبّ ذاته الذي يخصّ ذاته بأجود الخيرات وأعظمها والذي يفرح بالذي هو له بالحقيقة ويقنع به أبداً. كما أنّ المدينة يظنّ أنّها الشئ الحقّي أكثر ذلك [أكثر] من كلّ جمع آخر كذلك الإنسان أيضاً وأحرى أن يكون محبّ ذاته الذي

---

1 يحق F : بحق Bad || 5 كأنها F*, Dun* (ὡς) : كلها Bad || 6-7 النفسي أي البهيمي F, Dun : وبالجزء اللانطقي في النفس Bad* (τῷ ἀλόγῳ τῆς ψυχῆς) || 10 بالعدل corr. Dun* (τὰ δίκαια) : بالعمل F, Bad || 14 أكثر suppl. Dun

any other grouping, so man also. He is most fittingly a lover of self, who loves this[161] and delights[162] in it. The expressions 'controlled' and 'uncontrolled' and 'his mind controls him' or 'it does not con-
1169a trol him', in each case mean this. It is thought that people do certain actions voluntarily, and especially those which are done for a reason.[163] That each one of them is this, or mostly, is clear, and that the good man most fittingly loves this, and hence would be a lover of self in another way different from the man who is reproached, and he possesses a difference like the difference between life as it ought to be[164] and life which is painful.[165] And just as it is more fitting to desire what is nobler,[166] (7) all men accept of those who are eager for noble actions, as it should be,[167] and praise them, and if all strove for the good and were eager to do the best, all the things which should be would exist in common, and there would exist in particular for each man the greatest of goods,[168] since the virtues are so. Thus the good man should be a lover of self, for he is benefited in himself through his doing good deeds, and he benefits others. But the bad man should not be so, for he injures himself and whoever comes near him, when he follows evil passions. (8) Between what is incumbent on the bad man and what he does there is a difference. The good man simply does what he ought, since every intelligence chooses the best,[169] and the good man obeys the intelligence. (9) It is also true that the good man does many things for the sake of friends and for the sake of the country, and if he needs to die for them,[170] he will give up wealth and honours and in general all the goods which

---

[161] I.e. his true self (τὸ κυριώτατον).

[162] Arabic *wa-yusarru bihi*, i.e. once more confusion between χαρίζεται and χαίρει (χαίρεται).

[163] The turn here with the transposition ἑκουσίως καί is not in the Greek.

[164] Arabic *al-ḥaiyāt allatī takūn ʿalā mā yanbaghī* for Greek τὸ κατὰ λόγον ζῆν.

[165] Arabic *allatī takūn ta'lam* involving a misunderstanding of κατὰ πάθος.

[166] I.e. Greek καί ὀρέγεσθαι [...] συμφέρειν modified and taken with what follows.

[167] Arabic *ʿalā mā yanbaghī* scarcely 'above what is necessary', for Greek διαφερόντως. It is better to retain the meaning of the same phrase immediately above 'as it ought to be, as it should be'. The sense of the sentence has of course already been lost.

[168] Arabic *akthar al-khairāt*, but read *akbar*, for Greek τὰ μέγιστα τῶν ἀγαθῶν.

[169] Greek ἑαυτῷ omitted (Arberry).

[170] The construction is wrong: Arabic takes κἂν δέῃ ὑπεραποθνήσκειν closely with προήσεται [...] as apodosis, but γάρ of course is against this.

يحبّ هذا ويسرّ به ويقل ضابط ولا ضابط فضبطه عقله أو إنّه لا يضبطه كلّ واحد منهما هو هذا ويظنّ بهم أنّهم فعلوا بالإرادة ولا سيّما الأفاعيل التي تفعل لعلّة وأمّا أنّ كلّ واحد منهم هو هذا أو أكثر ذلك فبيّن وأنّ الفاضل أحرى أن يحبّ هذا ومن أجل هذا خليق أن يكون محبّ ذاته بنوع آخر غير الذي يعيّر وله اختلاف كاختلاف الحيلة التي تكون على ما ينبغي والحيلة [٣/٥٤] التي تكون تألم وكما أنّه أوفق أن يشتهي الذي هو أجود (٧) فإنّ الذين يحرصون على الأفعل الجياد على ما ينبغي جميع الناس يقبل منهم وتمدّحهم وإذا تنازعوا الخير أجمعين وحرصوا على فعل الأجود تكون جميع الأشياء التي ينبغي كائنة وتكون خاصّية لكلّ واحد أكبر الخيرات إذ كانت الفضائل كذلك فإذاً ينبغي أن يكون الخير محبّ ذاته فإنّه ينتفع بذاته عند فعله الخيرات وينفع غيره ولا ينبغي الرديء أن يكون كذلك فإنّه يضرّ ذاته ومن قرب منه إذا اتّبع الآفات الرديئة (٨) فبين ما يجب على ذي رداءة وبين ما يفعل اختلاف وأمّا الفاضل فإنّما يفعل ما ينبغي من أجل أنّ كلّ عقل يختار الأجود والفاضل مطيع للعقل (٩) وهو حقّ أيضاً أنّ الفاضل يفعل أشياء كثيرة من أجل الأصدقاء ومن أجل الوطن وإن احتاج إلى أن يموت دونهم فإنّه يبذل الأموال والكرامات وبالجملة

---

3 ذلك Bad, Dun : illegible F || 3 وان F, Dun : فإن Bad || 3 أجل F, Dun : جل Bad || 5 تألم F*, Dun* (κατὰ πάθος) : بالم Bad || 6 يقبل Dun : تقبل Bad || 7 كائنة om. Bad || 8 اكبر read. Dun* (τὰ μέγιστα) : اكثر F || 10 إذا F, Dun : لانه Bad corr. || 10-11 فبيّن ... وبيّن F, Dun : وبيّن ... فبيّن Bad || 11 اختلاف F : اختلافا Bad || 12 second الفاضل corr. Dun : الفاعل F, Bad || 12 يفعل Bad, Dun : illegible F

are contended for, in order to obtain the goods[171] for himself, for it would perhaps be best that he would choose to experience an intense joy for a short time or[172] that he should experience a mild joy for a long time, and that he should live a noble life for one year or[173] many years, according to what he has attained,[174] and that he should do one great and noble deed or[175] many small deeds. And perhaps these things happen with those who die for others, for they think that there accrued to them a great memorable good, and they give up money by the most accruing to friends. For in this there is money for the friend, and for himself he secures the noble and the best good.[176] (10) He employs this same manner in the different kinds of honours and offices. For he gives up all these to his friend, and he thinks of this as good, and as praiseworthy for him. And we do that, since it is thought that he is virtuous, and that he chooses the noble above all things. It is possible that he may give up the actions to his friend, and that the action of the friend may be nobler in him than his own action, and that the friend should be the cause of that.[177] (11) It ap-
1169b pears then that the good man in all the things that are praised gives himself most good. It is in this way that one should be a lover of oneself, as was said, but according as most people think one certainly should not.

9. There is doubt also in regard to the happy man, whether he needs friends or not. People have asserted that the fortunate do not need friends at all, nor do the self-sufficient, because they possess the good things and, since they are self-sufficient, with their self-sufficiency do not need anything, while a friend is another self and provides what a man is unable to provide by himself. Hence he should be [...]:[178]

> [...] the happy man for friends.

(2) It seems absurd if we are to assign all good things to the happy man and should not assign to him friends, when this is thought to be

---

[171] Arabic *al-khairāt*, as immediately above; Greek is τὸ καλόν (in the previous line *al-khairāt* is for τὰ [...] ἀγαθά).

[172] As elsewhere, ἤ (= 'than') is misunderstood.

[173] See previous note.

[174] Arabic *ʿalā mā adraka* for Greek τυχόντως.

[175] See n. 172.

[176] Arabic *al-jaiyid wa'l-khair al-ajwad*, Greek τὸ καλόν simply.

[177] Greek τὸ αἴτιον is wrongly construed.

[178] Lacuna, including part of the line of poetry from Euripides, *Orestes*, 1046.

جميع الخيرات التي يتنازع فيها ليكتسب الخيرات لذاته فإنّه خليق أن يكون أحرى بأن يختار أن يسرّ سروراً شديداً زماناً قليلاً أو أن يسرّ زماناً طويلاً سروراً ضعيفاً وأن يحيا حية جيّدة سنة واحدة أو سنين كثيرة على ما أدرك وأن يفعل فعلاً واحداً جيّداً وعظيماً أو أفعالاً كثيرة صغاراً وخليق أن تعرض هذه الأشياء للذين يموتون دون غيرهم فإنّهم يرون أنّه يصير إليهم خير عظيم مؤثّر ويبذلون الأموال بأن يصير الأكثر للأصدقاء فإنّه يكون أمّا للصديق فأموال وأمّا لذاته فالجيّد والخير الأجود يصير لذاته (١٠) ويستعمل هذا النوع بعينه في أنواع الكرامات والرياسات فإنّه يبذل جميع هذه لصديقه ويرى هذا أنّه خير وأنّه مديحة له ونحن نفعل ذلك إذ كان يظنّ أنّه فاضل وأنّه يختار الجيّد على جميع الأشياء وقد يمكن أن يبذل الأفعال للصديق وأن يكون أجود عنده من فعله فعل صديقه وأن يكون الصديق علّة ذلك (١١) فقد يظهر الفاضل في جميع الأشياء الممدوحة [٣/٥٥] أنّه يعطي ذاته من الخير الأكثر فبهذا ينبغي أن يكون محبّ ذاته كما قيل وأمّا على رأي أكثر الناس فلا ينبغي ذلك.

٩. ويشكّ أيضاً في السعيد إن كان يحتاج إلى الأصدقاء أم لا فقد زعموا أنّ ذوي الفطنة لا يحتاجون البتّة إلى الأصدقاء ولا ذوو الكفاية من أجل أنّ لهم الخيرات وأنّهم ذوو كفاية لا يحتاجون مع الكفاية إلى شئ وأمّا الصديق وهو ذات أخرى فيتكفّل بتقديم ما لا يقدر أن يكتسب بذاته ومن ها هنا

ينبغي أن يكون [...]

إلى الأصدقاء

(٢) وقد يشبه المحل إذا كنّا نصيّر للسعيد جميع الخيرات ولا نعطي أن يكون له أصدقاء

---

2 first أن : وأن Bad || 2 أو corr. Dun : و F, Bad || 3 second و corr. Dun : أو F, Bad || 5 يكون
F : يكون هذا Bad || 8 إذ : F إذا Bad || 13 وانهم ذوو كفاية F*, Dun* (αὐτάρκεις οὖν ὄντας) :
فإنهم في الأهم الأكثر Bad || 14 وهو ذات أخرى فيتكفل بتقديم Bad, Dun : illegible F || 18 يكون Bad,
Dun : illegible F

the greatest[179] of external goods. And if [...] to do good rather than have good done to one, then[180] it belongs to the good and excellent man[181] to do a kindness more, and the doing of a kindness to friends is nobler than doing it to strangers, and[182] the excellent man needs some one to do good to, hence the question is raised [...] good fortune needs those to whom he is to do good, just as whoever is in distress needs those who are to do good to him. (3) Also it would be absurd to make the happy man a solitary. [No] one would choose to have all the good things with solitude, since man is political, and it is in his nature to share in life. This also is the happy man, for he has the goods which are owing to nature. And it is clear that it is better that his days should be spent with friends and good men than with strangers and whoever he has met up with.[183] So then the happy man must have friends. (4) What then is it that the ancients[184] say, and wherein are they right? Is it not[185] that most people think that friends are those who are useful? The ideally happy man does not need at all the like of these, since he possesses the good things and does not need a friend for the sake of the pleasant, since the pleasure of life is small,[186] and he does not need at all adventitious pleasure from outside. And since he does not need friends like these, it is thought of him that he does not need friends. (5) It may be that this is untrue. It has already been said at the beginning that happiness is an activity, [and] it is clear that an activity comes into existence, and is not a possession. And if happiness is life and action, and the action of a good man is excellent and pleasant in itself, as was said at the beginning, and what is one's own also is among the pleasant things, we[187] are able to see whoever is near better than ourselves, and to see their actions better than our own actions, and the actions of good men,
1169b 35 when they are friends (...)[188]

[179] Arabic *akthar*, as previously, 1169a 10 = IX, 8, 7.

[180] Arabic *fa-*. But we have not yet reached the apodosis, which should come at [*wa*] *'l-fāḍil yaḥtāju* [...], 'the excellent man needs [...]'.

[181] Arabic *li 'l-jaiyid wa'l-fāḍil*, but Greek τοῦ ἀγαθοῦ καὶ τῆς ἀρετῆς.

[182] Arabic *wa-* is not in the Greek.

[183] Arabic *man adraka*, cf. 1169a 24 = IX, 8, 9, 1173b 5 = X, 3, 5.

[184] Arabic *al-qudamā'* for Greek οἱ πρῶτοι (= the holders of the first view, viz. that the fortunate do not need friends).

[185] Arabic *lā* not in the Greek.

[186] I.e. ἐπὶ μικρόν taken with ἡδὺς γὰρ ὁ βίος (Arberry), γάρ being disregarded as elsewhere.

[187] Greek δέ is omitted.

[188] One folio is missing.

وهذا يظنّ به أنّه أكثر الخيرات التي تكون من خارج وإذا [...] أن يحسن من أن يحسن إليه فإنّ للجيّد والفاضل أن يصطنع المعروف أكثر واصطناع المعروف إلى الأصدقاء أجود من اصطناعه إلى الغرباء والفاضل يحتاج إلى أن يحسن إليه من أجل هذا يطلب [...] سعادة البخت إلى الذين يحسن إليهم كما يحتاج من كان في الشقاء إلى الذين يحسنون إليه (٣) وأيضاً خليق أن يكون محالاً أن يصيّر المغبوط وحدانياً فخليق ألاّ يختار أحد أن يكون له جميع الخيرات مع الوحدة من أجل أنّ الإنسان مدني وفي طبعه أن يكون يشارك في الحياة وهذا هو أيضاً السعيد فإنّ له الخيرات التي للطبيعة فبيّن أنّه أحرى أن تكون أيّامه مع أصدقاء وأفاضل من أن تكون مع غرباء ومن أدرك فإذاً ينبغي أن يكون أصدقاء لذوي السعادة (٤) فما الذي يقوله القدماء وبأيّ شيء يصدقون إلاّ بأنّ أكثر الناس يرون أنّ الأصدقاء هم الذين ذوو منفعة والمغبوط لا يحتاج البتّةَ إلى من كان مثل هؤلاء من أجل أنّ له الخيرات ولا يحتاج إلى الصديق لمكان اللذيذ من أجل أنّ لذّة العمر قليلة وهو لا يحتاج إلى لذّة دخيلة من خارج البتّةَ وإذ لا يحتاج إلى مثل هؤلاء الأصدقاء يظنّ به أنّه لا يحتاج إلى الأصدقاء (٥) وخليق ألاّ يكون هذا حقّاً [٥٦/٣] فقد قيل في الابتداء إنّ السعادة فعل ما وهو بيّن أنّ الفعل يكون وليس هو كيفية ما فإن كانت السعادة الحياة والفعل وكان فعل الخير فاضلاً ولذيذاً بذاته كما قيل في البدء وكان الخاصّ أيضاً من اللذّات أمكننا أن نرى ما قرب أكثر من ذاتنا وأن نرى أفعل أولئك أكثر من أفعالنا وأفعل الأفاضل الذين هم أصدقاء (...)

---

4 الشقاء Bad, Dun : illegible F || 5 ألا corr. Dun* (οὐθείς) : أن F, Bad || 5 أحد F : أحد له Bad || 6 second يكون om. Bad || 11 أن لذة Bad, Dun : illegible F || 14 first و suppl. Bad || 15 من اللذات corr. Dun : التي للذات F, Bad || 16-17 الذين هم أصدقاء Dun : illegible F

1170b 20 10. (...) should it be said, as is said in regard to hospitality? For as[189] it is thought that [...][190] with him who 'multiplies hospitality for strangers', and not that he should 'not entertain a single stranger', so should it be that[191] [...] friendship, and not be without a single friend, nor have an excessive number of friends either? (2) This statement is thought to be very like as if it was said of those who [...][192] for profit. For requital of service to very many is difficult, and life is not sufficient for one to do this actual thing.[193] The majority are always busy[194] with what [...][195] their lives, and they work[196] and strive to live at ease and not do anything themselves.[197] Of the friends whom people take for the sake of pleasure a few are enough, like spices in food. (3) As for good friends, should they be many in number, or is there any measure for the size of a friendship, as there is for a city? For a city is not made up of ten men, nor is a city ten times ten thousand either, and perhaps the amount is not always the same, but whatever is between certain fixed limits. (4) So then there is a cer-
1171a tain number for friends also[198] for they are sharing [...][199] (5) [...] in joy and grief and in many special things,[200] and it might happen at the same time to share in the pleasure of one and the sorrow of another. It may be better that they should not seek that they should be great friends,[201] but seek those who are adequate to sharing life. It may be thought that it is impossible to be a great friend of many people, and this [...][202] that one should be in love with several people,

---

[189] Arabic *fa'innahu* (disregards the question with Greek ἤ).

[190] Short lacuna.

[191] MS. *yanbaghī an* followed by a short lacuna.

[192] Short lacuna.

[193] Arabic *hādhā bi-ʿainihi*, i.e. αὐτὸ τοῦτο, the reading of K^b (Arberry).

[194] Mistranslation of Greek ἱκανῶν, and the construction is wrong.

[195] Short lacuna.

[196] Arabic *yaʿmalūna wa-yajtahidūna*, i.e. Greek περίεργοι καὶ ἐμπόδιοι—out of construction and the last word wrongly translated.

[197] The Arabic version badly mistranslates Greek.

[198] Greek καὶ ἴσως οἱ πλεῖστοι has fallen out.

[199] The limits of the considerable lacuna indicated by Arberry seem to be from συζῆν (1171a 2) to γίνεται καὶ τό (1171a 6) (similarity of συζῆν and συγχαίρειν).

[200] Arabic *fī ashyāʾ kathīrah khāṣṣah*. This is Greek οἰκείως πολλοῖς read as οἰκείοις πολλοῖς.

[201] Arabic *allā yaṭlubū an yakūnū aṣdiqāʾ jiddan*, Greek μὴ ζητεῖν ὡς πολυφιλώτατον [read apparently by the translator as πολυφιλωτάτους] εἶναι. Cf. below 'a great friend of many people', *ṣadīqan jiddan li-kathīrīn*, where Greek is πολλοῖς εἶναι φίλον σφόδρα.

[202] Short lacuna.

١٠. (...) أن يقل كما يقل في الضيافة فإنّه كما يظنّ أنّه [...] أكثر الضيافة للغرباء ولا ألاّ تضيف البتّةَ غريباً كذلك ينبغي أن [...] الصداقة ولا يكون لا صديق له ولا أن يكون أيضاً كثير الأصدقاء بإفراط (٢) وهذا القول يظنّ به أنّه يشبه أن يقل جدّاً في الذين [...] منفعة فإنّ المكافأة في الخدمة لكثيرين فيها تعب وليس في العمر كفاية لأن يفعل هذا بعينه والأكثر متشاغل أبداً فيما فيه [...] أعمارهم ويعملون ويجتهدون في أن يحيوا نعماء وألاّ يفعلوا شيئاً بذواتهم والأصدقاء الذين يتّخذون لمكان اللذّة يكفي منهم القليل كالأبذار في الطعام (٣) وأمّا الأصدقاء الأفاضل فهل ينبغي أن يكونوا كثرة بالعدد أو عدد ما للكثرة الصداقة مثلما هو للمدينة فإنّه لا تكون مدينة من عشرة رجل وأيضاً لا تكون مدينة من عشر مريدات وخليق ألاّ تكون الكمّية شيئاً واحداً بل كلّ ما هو ما بين أشياء محدودة (٤) فإذاً عدد ما للأصدقاء أيضاً فإنّهم يكونون يشاركون [...] (٥) [...] في الفرح والألم وفي أشياء كثيرة خاصّة وخليق أن يعرض معاً أمّا لأحدهما فأن يشارك في اللذّة وأمّا للآخر فأن يشارك في الحزن وخليق أن يكون أجود ألاّ يطلبوا أن يكونوا أصدقاء جدّاً بل يطلبون الذين هم على هذا القدر الذي فيه كفاية [...] فخليق أن يظنّ أنّه لا يمكن أن يكون صديقاً جدّاً

2 ينبغي أن Bad, Dun : illegible F || 2 first ولا F : فلا Bad || 4 فيها Bad, Dun : illegible F || 4 والأصدقاء Bad, Dun : illegible F || 6 يفعلوا corr. Bad : يفعلون F || 6 وليس Bad, Dun : illegible F || 7 أما الأصدقاء Bad, Dun : illegible F || 7 بالعدد F*, Dun* (κατ’ ἀριθμόν) : بالعدل Bad || 8 الصداقة مثلما Bad, Dun : illegible F || 9 عشر F : عشرة Bad || 10 first في Bad, Dun : illegible F || 12 يطلبوا corr. Bad : يطلبون F || 13 [...] : illegible F, *sharing life* Dun || 13 صديقا corr. Bad : صديق F

because love means that it is [...] friendship [...], and warm friendship is for few. (6) Possibly this lies in the facts also, for there is not abundance of friends in comradely[203] friendship. As for the friendship that has precedence in honour, it is said to be between two persons. Those who have many friends[204] and meet all properly are thought to be friends of no one, like[205] those who are called obsequious. For politically it is possible to be a friend to many and not be obsequious but as one ought. But to be a friend for the sake of virtue to many persons, and for themselves, is not possible, and what is loved among these also is not much.[206]

11. Is there most need for a friend in prosperity, or in adversity? They are sought for in both conditions, since those whose conditions are bad need help, and those who are prosperous need people to associate with and to do good to, for they wish to do kindness, except that in misfortune there is more necessity for that, and hence there is need then for whoever is useful. But in good fortune that is nobler, and hence they seek good men who are worthy.[207] For it is preferable to do good to these rather than others, and similarly to be with them. (2) For the presence of friends itself is cheering[208] in the time of prosperity and in the time of adversity, since those who are sad find it consoling to this sadness when friends share with them in their sadness. Hence perhaps one might raise the question and ask whether friends at that time actually take part in the sadness which affects their friends, as one might release a man with a burden some of his load and lighten him, or rather,[209] as their association was cheerful and their presence was pleasant, the thought was formed[210] in regard to their presence: Was the sadness less?[211] As to whether

---

[203] Arabic *as-saḥābīyah*. Mrg. has *al-ʿāmmah kadhā lakhkhaṣahu al-qāḍī* [sc. Ibn Rushd].

[204] Arabic *al-kathīrū al-aṣdiqā'*, Greek πολύφιλοι, cf. n. 201.

[205] Greek πλὴν πολιτικῶς is not rendered here, apparently substituted for by Arabic *mithl*.

[206] I.e. the Greek read very differently, perhaps ἀγαπητὸν δὲ καὶ ὀλίγον ἐν τούτοις.

[207] *Sic*, unless the meaning is 'and hence good men seek those who are worthy' (Arabic *wa-min ajl hādhā yaṭlubūna al-afāḍil dhawī 'l-isti'hāl*), but the Greek is against this.

[208] Arabic *sārr* for Greek ἡδεῖα.

[209] Arabic *bal*, Greek ἢ τοῦτο μὲν οὔ [...] δέ.

[210] Arabic *ṣuyyirat* here much like *ṣuwwirat*, but the Arabic translation goes wrong.

[211] Arabic *ā- 'l-ḥuzn aqallu*, divergence again from the Greek.

لكثيرين ولهذا [...] لواحد معشوقون كثيرون لأنّ العشق [...] وشدّة القليلين (٦) وقد يمكن أن يكون هذا في الأشياء أيضاً فإنّه لا تكون كثرة أصدقاء في الصداقة الصحابية [٣/٥٧] وأمّا التي تقوم بالشرف فيقل إنّها في اثنين وأمّا الكثيرو الأصدقاء ويلقون الجميع بما ينبغي فيظنّ بهم أنّهم ليسوا أصدقاء لأحد مثل الذين يسمّون مواتين فإنّه أمّا بنوع مدني فقد يمكن أن يكون صديق لكثيرين وألاّ يكون مواتياً بل أن يكون كاللذي ينبغي وأمّا أن يكون صديق لمكان الفضيلة لكثيرين ولذاتهم فليس يمكن ذلك والمحبوب عند هؤلاء أيضاً قليل.

١١. فهل يحتاج إلى الصديق عند حسن الحال أكثر ذلك أو عند سوء الحال فإنّهم يطلبون في كلتي الحالين من أجل أنّ الذين حالاتهم سيئة يحتاجون إلى المعونة والذين في حسن الحال يحتاجون إلى من يؤنسهم ومن يحسنون إليه فإنّهم يريدون اصطناع المعروف إلاّ أنّه في سوء الحال أكثر ضرورة إلى ذلك ومن أجل هذا يحتاج حينئذ إلى من عنده منفعة وأمّا في حسن الحال فإنّ ذلك أجود ومن أجل هذا يطلبون الأفاضل ذوي الاستئهل فإنّه يختار الإحسان إلى هؤلاء أكثر من غيرهم وكذلك الكينونة معهم (٢) فإنّ حضور الأصدقاء بعينه سارّ في وقت حسن الحال وفي وقت سوء الحال من أجل أنّ الذين هم في حزن يسلي ذلك حزنهم إذا شاركهم الأصدقاء في الحزن ومن أجل هذا خليق أن يتحيّر متحيّر ويسأل هل الأصدقاء حينئذ يقتسمون شيئاً من الحزن الحل بأصدقائهم كما يأخذ الآخذ عن ذي الثقل بعض ما عليه من الثقل فيخفّ عنه بل إذا كانت معاشرتهم سارّة وحضورهم لذيذاً صيّرت الفكرة في حضورهم آلحزن أقلّ وأمّا إن كانوا يسلون لهذه الأشياء أو لشئ

1 second [...] : illegible F, *means that it is [...] friendship* Dun || 2 تكون Bad, Dun : illegible F || 2 الصحابية mrg.: التامة كذا لخصه القاضي || 4 بما corr. Bad, Dun : ما F || 4 ليسوا corr. Bad : ليس F || 4 فإنه F : وإنه Bad || 5 first أن corr. Dun : إذ F, Bad || 9 كلتي F : كلتا Bad || 10 يؤنسهم corr. Bad*, Dun* (συμβίων) : يؤسيهم F || 10 يحسنون corr. Bad : يحسنوا F || 14 بعينه F*, Dun* (αὐτή) : هو Bad || 15 حزنهم Bad, Dun : illegible F

they are consoled for these reasons or for another, let the inquiry into that be left aside. At all events[212] what has been said appears to happen. (3) It seems that the presence of friends is a shared one.[213] The
1171b very sight of friends is cheering to him who is in another condition[214] and him who is in misfortune, and there comes to him from that a kind of help[215] against grieving, since the friend consoles both by sight and words, when he is as he should be, for he then knows the character of his friend and the things in which he takes pleasure and also at which he feels pain. (4) To see someone pained at his[216] ill fortune is painful, and everyone seeks to avoid being a cause of pain to his friends. Hence those whose nature it is to be manly avoid their friends being pained by their being pained for them, even if they are not excessive in not feeling pain,[217] but they take upon themselves[218] the pain which affects those others, and, in general, they do not desire anyone to share with them in mourning, since they also are [not] given to mourning. On the other hand, women and men who resemble them take pleasure in those who enter with them into their sufferings.[219] It is plain that one should imitate in all things him who is best. (5) To the presence of friends in times of prosperity belong a pleasant association and a cheering thought, since[220] they take pleasure in the good things belonging to their friends. For this reason we may think that in prosperity one should be eager to bring in one's friends, since to do a kindness is noble, but in misfortune one should not be eager for that, since one should minimise the sharing of evil, and hence I say[221] that a sufficiency of consolation is necessary in misfortune. Consolation[222] should mostly be when it is among those

---

[212] Arabic *illā anna* renders Greek δ' οὖν.

[213] Arabic *mushtarakan mā* for Greek μικτή τις.

[214] I.e. ἄλλως taken out of the phrase ἄλλως τε καί which goes closely with ἀτυχοῦντι.

[215] Arabic *bi-maʿūnatin mā*. If this is right, the grammatical subject is still *an-naẓr*, but with *min dhālika* perhaps we should read *maʿūnah mā*.

[216] Arabic *ʿalā sūʾ ḥālihi*, i.e. ἐπὶ ταῖς αὐτοῦ ἀτυχίαις was read.

[217] The sense is not clear. The clause should be taken with the words that follow, no with what precedes.

[218] 'But' is not in the Greek, which has οὐχ ὑπομένει (Arberry).

[219] Here some words have dropped out.

[220] Arabic *min ajl an*, i.e. Greek ὅτι taken as 'because'.

[221] Arabic *aqūlu*, suggesting ἅλις λέγω read for ἅλις ἐγώ (Arberry).

[222] Arabic *at-taʿziyah*, but Greek παρακλητέον is to be taken as 'should summon', not 'should console'.

آخر فلنترك الطلب لما يكون ذلك إلاّ أنّ الذي قد قيل يظهر أنّه يعرض (٣) وقد يشبه أن يكون حضورهم مشتركاً ما. في النظر إلى الأصدقاء بعينه سارّ للذي في حل أخرى والذي في سوء حل ويكون له من ذلك بمعونة ما على ألاّ يحزن من أجل أنّ الصديق يعزّي بالنظر وبالكلام إذا كان كما ينبغي فإنّه حينئذ يعرف خلق صديقه والأشياء التي يسرّ بها ويحزن بها أيضاً [٣/٥٨] (٤) وأمّا إن أحسّ أحداً يحزن على سوء حاله حزن وكلّ يهرب من أن يكون للأصدقاء علّة حزن ومن أجل هذا أمّا الذين طبعهم الترجّل فيجتنبون تحزّن الأصدقاء بحزنهم فيهم وإن لم يفرطوا في ترك الحزن لكنّهم يتقلّلون الحزن الذي يصيب أولئك وبالجملة لا يشتهون من يشاركهم في النوح من أجل أنّهم أيضاً [ليسوا] بذي نوح وأمّا النساء والرجل الذين مثلهم فإنّهم يسرّون بالذين يشاركونهم في الآلام وهو بيّن أنّه ينبغي أن يتشبّه في جميع الأشياء بالذي هو أجود (٥) وأمّا حضور الأصدقاء في حسن الحالات فإنّ له معاشرة لذيذة وفكرة سارّة من أجل أنّهم يلذّون بالخيرات التي لأصدقائهم ولهذا السبب خليق أن يظنّ بأنّه ينبغي أمّا في حسن الحالات فأن يحرص على اجتلاب الأصدقاء من أجل ذلك اصطناع المعروف جيّد وأمّا في سوء الحل فينبغي ألاّ يحرص على ذلك من أجل أنّه ينبغي أن يقلّل شركة الرداءة ومن ها هنا أقول إنّه ينبغي الكفاف من

2 سار F, Dun : صار Bad || 3 بمعونة : perh. corr. معونة Dun || 4 كما Bad, Dun : illegible F || 4 حينئذ F, Dun : جيدا Bad || 4 يسر Bad, Dun : illegible F || 5 أحس mrg. corr. : أحسن F || 5 وكل F : فكل Bad || 6 فيجتنبون Bad : يجتنبون F || 7 يتقللون mrg. corr., Dun : يتقللون F, Bad || 8 ليسوا suppl. Bad || 10 يتشبه F, Dun : نتشبه Bad || 12 فان corr. : ان F; فإن Bad || 13 المعروف corr. Bad : معروف F

who acknowledge that it is of much profit to the unfortunate.[223] (6) As to the loving, perhaps it should be the contrary and people should console him who is suffering misfortune without invitation and eagerly, for to do a kindness is the part of a friend, especially to those who need it and to him who has not asked for it. For that is nobler for both of them and more agreeable. In prosperity there should be diligent help, since in circumstances like this[224] a man needs friends. Yet when it is a case of a kindness being done to him, he should be slow, for greediness for profit to oneself is not noble. One should no doubt avoid the suspicion of what is not agreeable which sometimes belongs to the troublesome man.[225] The presence of friends, however, in all circumstances appears to be desirable.

12. It is the case then that, as for lovers sight is very dear, and they prefer this sense rather than the other senses, because love depends on it mostly and also comes through it, so for friends association in life is preferable? For friendship is an association, and as the friend is in himself, so he is for his friend, and the perception is in him, because he is chosen,[226] and it [sc. friendship] is in his friend also.
1172a The activity itself[227] occurs through association, so that rightly they desire this. (2) And when[228] each one of them has an existence or that for which they choose life, they wish to be in this with their friends. Hence some of them drink with others, some of them play with others at backgammon, etc., some of them come together for athletic exercises and hunting,[229] and they spend their days in what each of them loves with those whom they love of all the people in the world.[230] For they do that at pleasure[231] with the good,[232] and they

---

[223] Greek ὀχληθέντες was not understood by the Arabic translator, cf. 1167a 10 = IX, 5, 3, and this has obliged him to take great liberties with the text where μέλλωσιν is apparently read as μέλλουσιν (participle).

[224] Arabic *fī mithl hādha* does not give the nuance of Greek καὶ [...] εἰς ταῦτα.

[225] The sense is lost.

[226] Text *fa-ḥiss*, corr. *wa 'l-ḥiss*, Greek is ἡ αἴσθησις. The following words are wrongly construed, with περὶ αὐτόν taken as περὶ αὐτόν, and ὅτι rendered 'because', so that the sense breaks down.

[227] I.e. apparently αὐτή for αὐτῆς.

[228] Arabic *idhā*, i.e. ὁπότε for ὅ ποτέ (Arberry).

[229] Greek ἢ συμφιλοσοφοῦσιν has dropped out (Arberry).

[230] I.e. Greek τῶν ἐν τῷ βίῳ taken as masculine.

[231] Arabic *li-jaulān ar-ra'y*, lit. 'at the motion of the thought'. It is evident for βουλόμενοι, but Greek συζῆν γάρ has been omitted, and the construction is again wrong.

[232] Arabic *ma'a 'l-akhyār* for Greek μετὰ τῶν φίλων, apparently through inadvertence.

التعزية عند سوء الحل وإنّما ينبغي أن تكون التعزية أكثر ذلك إذ كان عند الذين أذعنوا لها منفعة كثيرة لذوي سوء الحل (٦) وأمّا المحبّي فخليق أن يكون ينبغي على خلاف ذلك وأن يكون ينبغي أن يعزّي أمّا الذي في سوء الحل من غير دعوة مجتهدين فإنّ اصطناع المعروف للصديق ولا سيّما إلى الذين يحتجون إليه وإلى الذي لم يسأل ذلك فإنّ ذلك أجود لكليهما أو أسرّ وأمّا في حسن الحل فينبغي المعونة بلختيار من أجل أنّه يحتاج في مثل هذا إلى الأصدقاء وأمّا في أن يصطنع المعروف إليه فينبغي أن يكون بطئ فإنّ الحرص على المنفعة لذاته ليس بجيّد وخليق أن يكون ينبغي أن يختلف فوقهم ما ليس بسارّ الذي ربّما لذي الثقل وأمّا حضور الأصدقاء في جميع الأشياء فإنّه يظهر أنّه مختار.

١٢. فهل كما أنّ النظر محبوب جدّاً عند العشاق وهم مختارون هذا الحسّ أكثر من سائر الحواسّ لأنّ العشق به هو أكثر ذلك وبه يكون أيضاً كذلك عند الأصدقاء [٥٩/٣] المعاشرة في الحياة مختارة فإنّ الصداقة معاشرة والصديق كما أنّه في ذاته كذلك هو عند صديقه والحسّ هو فيه من أجل أنّه مختار وهو في الصديق أيضاً وأمّا الفعل بعينه فإنّه يكون في المعاشرة فإذاً نحن مشتهون هذا (٢) وإذا كانت الإنّية لكلّ واحد منهم أو الذين يختارون الحياة فإنّهم يحبّون أن يكونوا في هذا مع الأصدقاء ومن أجل هذا بعضهم يشاربون بعضاً وبعضهم يلاعب بعضاً بالنرد وغيره وبعضهم يجتمعون في الرياضة والصيد ويفنون أيّامهم بما يحبّ كلّ واحد منهم مع من يحبّ ممّن في العالم فإنّهم يفعلون ذلك لجولان الرأي

---

1 إذ : F إذا Bad || 3 يعزي corr. Dun : يحزن F, Bad || 5 أسر وأما corr. Bad : أسروا F || 5 بلختيار : F corr. Bad مختار 8 || Bad دعا : F, Dun ربما 8 || Bad بطر ;F بطؤ : corr. Dun بطئ 6 || Bad بلختياره 13 || Bad معنى ;F من : corr. Dun هو first 12 || F, Bad فحس : corr. Dun والحس 12 || F مختارة : ومع : F مع 16 || Bad يقضون : F يفنون 15 || F غيرهم : corr. Bad غيره 15 || F الذي : corr. Bad الذين Bad

share with those[233] whom they think[234] to share with in life. (3) So the friendship of bad people is bad, for they associate with the bad and those who have no stability, and they become wicked through becoming like one another. But the friendship of men of merit is meritorious, for it increases in association, and it is thought of them that they become more excellent when they act, since they correct each other's faults, because one of them takes on the likeness from the other in the things which they approve—'Good deeds are from the good'. (4) This is the extent of what is said on friendship. There follows the discussion on pleasure.

End of the Tenth Discourse of the Ethics, and praise be to God and peace upon His servants whom He has chosen.

---

[233] Arabic *wa-yushārikūna 'lladhīna*, i.e. Greek τούτων has been taken as masculine and read τούτους.

[234] I.e. οἷς οἴονται of vulg. rather than ὡς οἷόν τε (K^b).

مع الأخيار ويشاركون الذين يرون أن يشاركوا في الحيلة (٣) فيكون أمّا صداقة ذوي الرداءة فرديئة فإنّهم يعاشرون ذوي الرداءة والذين لا ثبات لهم ويصيرون أشراراً بتشابه بعضهم ببعض وأمّا صداقة ذوي الاستئهال فذو استئهل فإنّه يزيد في المعاشرة ويظنّ بهم أنّهم يصيرون أجود إذا فعلوا من أجل أنّهم يقوّم بعضهم [بعضاً] لأنّهم يتمثّل بعضهم من بعض بالتي يرتضون بها الخيرات من الخير (٤) فهذا قدر ما يقل في المحبّة ويتبع ذلك القول في اللذّة.

آخر المقالة العاشرة من الأخلاق والحمد للّه وسلّم على عباده الذين اصطفى

---

4 بعضا suppl. Bad || 4 يتمثل F : بتمثل Bad || 5-6 فهذا (...) اللذة om. Bad || 5 ما repeated in F

BOOK X

In the name of God, the Merciful, the Compassionate
God bless Muhammad and his family and give them peace

The Eleventh Discourse of the Book of Ethics of Aristotle

He said: And after this there should perhaps follow the discussion of pleasure, since it is thought for the most part[1] that our species is particularised by it. Hence the young are educated by being accustomed[2] to pleasure and pain. And it is thought that to enjoy what one ought and to feel pain at what one ought is a great thing in ethical virtue. For the continuance of these things extends through the whole of life, since they have a tendency and power in life,[3] for people choose the pleasant and avoid the painful. (2) It may be thought that these matters should scarcely be omitted, and also[4] since in regard to them there is much controversy. For some say that pleasure is a good and others on the contrary that all pleasure is bad. Perhaps some of them have been convinced that it is so too, while others have thought it is better in our life that pleasure should be judged to be one of the bad things, even if it is not so. For most people incline to it and the desires enslave them, and for this reason they have to be brought in the opposite direction, and it may be that in this way they will come to the mean. (3) It may be that this is not well said. For words about emotions and actions are less convincing than deeds, so when they are opposed to the things of sense, people despise them
1172b and choose[5] the truth also. For if he who blames pleasure is seen at any time desiring it, it is thought that he inclines to it, and that all pleasure in his opinion is like this, for discrimination does not belong to most. (4) Thus it seems that true statements are useful not merely in regard to knowledge, but also in regard to life. For since they agree with the facts they are confirmed, and hence they advise

---

[1] Arabic *akthar dhālika*, Greek μάλιστα. This should be construed with συνῳκειῶσθαι, not with δοκεῖ.

[2] Arabic *ya'tādū*, Greek οἰακίζοντες was not understood.

[3] The Greek words ἀρετήν τε καὶ τὸν εὐδαίμονα have dropped out (Arberry).

[4] Arabic *wa-aiḍan*. We should expect *wa-lā siyāma* for Greek ἄλλως τε καί.

[5] Apparently reading προαιροῦνται for προσαναιροῦσιν.

المقالة العاشرة

بسم الله الرحمن الرحيم

صلى الله على محمّد وعلى آله وسلّم

المقالة الحادية عشرة من كتاب الأخلاق لأرسطو

١. قل وبعد هذه خليق أن يكون يتلو القول في اللذّة من أجل أنّه يظنّ أكثر ذلك أنّها قد خصّ جنسنا بها ومن أجل هذا يؤدّبون الأحداث على أن يعتادوا اللذّة والحزن ونظنّ أنّ الفرح بما ينبغي والحزن لما ينبغي شئ كبير في فضيلة الخلق فإنّ مكث هذه يمتدّ في جيمع العمر إذا كان لها [٣/٦٠] ميل وقوّة في العمر فإنّهم يختارون اللذيذ ويهربون عن المحزنة (٢) وخليق أن يظنّ أنّ ترك هذه الأشياء قلّما ينبغي أن يستعمل وأيضاً إذ كان فيها مشاجرة كثيرة فإنّ بعض الناس يقولون إنّ اللذّة خير وبعض الناس على خلاف ذلك إنّ كلّ لذّة رديئة فخليق أن يكون بعضهم قد قنع أنّها كذلك أيضاً وبعضهم قد رأى أنّه أخير في سيرنا أن نقضي على اللذّة أنّها من الرداءات وإن لم تكن كذلك فإنّ أكثر الناس يميل إليها وتتعبّدهم اللذّات ولهذا ينبغي أن يؤتى بهم إلى ضدّ ذلك فخليق أن يصيروا بهذا النوع إلى الوسط (٣) وخليق ألاّ يكون يقل هذا نعماً فإنّ أقاويل الانفعالات والأفعل أقلّ إقناعاً من الأعمل فإذا خالفت الأشياء الحسّية تهاونوا بها ويختارون الصدق أيضاً فإنّ الذي يذمّ اللذّة إن رؤى في وقت ما أنّه يشتهيها يظنّ به الميل إليها وأنّ كلّها عنده مثل هذه فإنّ التفصيل ليس للأكثر (٤) فقد يشبه أن تكون الأقاويل الصادقة نافعة لا في المعرفة

---

5 يعتادوا F, Dun, Ax : يضادوا Bad || 5 نظن F, Ax : يظن Bad || 6 الخلق F*, Dun*, Ax* (τοῦ ἤθους) : الحق Bad || 8 المحزنة F : الحزينة Ax; المحزن Bad || 10 أيضا corr. Arberry : يقل إنها F, Ax, Bad || 11 سيرنا F, Bad : عمرنا Ax || 12 تتعبدهم corr. Dun : تتعبده F, Ax, Bad || 13 يقل om. Bad || 14 و corr. Dun* (καί) : أن F, Ax, Bad || 14 يختارون F, Ax : يختاروا corr. Bad || 15 رؤى F, Dun : ري corr. Ax, رأى Bad

those who understand to manage their lives in accordance with them.[6] Since these statements have been made on what is for the most part,[7] let us begin to mention pleasure.

2. Eudoxus thought that pleasure is the good since he saw everything, reasonable and unreasonable, desiring it. For the meritorious and the very strong[8] know[9] that which is desirable and that all moves in itself.[10] For better than all things[11] is the existence[12] of the good in itself,[13] like the existence of food also, and what is good for all and all desire, is good.[14] The arguments were confirmed by the virtue of his character rather than by themselves. He was thought to be duly[15] temperate and was not saying these things because he loved pleasure, but because they were true so, (2) and that that was plain[16] from its opposite no less, for pain[17] in the opinion of all is to be avoided, and its opposite also in their opinion is desirable. And what is desirable is for the most part what we choose not for the purpose of something else, nor on account of something else, and they admit that pleasure is such, for no one asks for what purpose he is pleased—as if pleasure by itself is desirable. When it is added to any one of the goods, it renders it more desirable, e.g. acting with justice and temperately, and good occasions[18] itself. (3) This argument seems to necessitate that [pleasure] is among the goods and that it is nothing else at all,[19] for whatever comes with another good is more to be chosen than when it is alone. With the like of this Plato refutes the view that pleasure is good,[20] since the pleasant life is more to be chosen when it is with intelligence than when it is without intelli-

[6] Arabic *bihā*, with change of person (Greek κατ' αὐτούς).

[7] I.e. μάλιστα read for ἅλις (Arberry).

[8] Arabic *al-qawī jiddan*, i.e. Greek τὸ μάλιστα κράτιστον construed together.

[9] Greek εἶναι read as εἰδέναι (Arberry).

[10] Arabic *fī dhātihi* for Greek επὶ ταὐτό.

[11] Greek μηνύειν and ἕκαστον are not translated.

[12] I.e. Greek εὑρίσκειν taken as passive, 'to be found'.

[13] Arabic *al-jaiyid bi-dhātihi* is wrong for Greek τὸ αὐτῷ ἀγαθόν.

[14] *Sic*, Arabic *khair*, not 'the good' (Greek τἀγαθόν).

[15] Arabic *ʿalā mā yanbaghī* is not a good translation for Greek διαφερόντως. The whole paragraph scarcely yields a sense.

[16] The sentence runs on, and Greek ᾤετο is left untranslated.

[17] Greek καθ' αὑτό is not translated or has fallen out.

[18] Corr. *yusabbiha* for Greek αὔξεσθαι = 'increases'.

[19] I.e. οὐδὲν μᾶλλον ἑτέρου (Arberry).

[20] The translation should render 'the good' (τἀγαθόν), cf. n. 14.

فقط بل في العمر أيضاً فإنّهم إذا كانوا موافقين للأعمل يصدقون ومن أجل هذا يشيرون على ذوي الفهم أن يدبّروا حياتهم بها وإذ قيلت هذه الأقاويل فيما يكون أكثر ذلك فلنأخذ في ذكر اللذّة.

٢. فإنّ أمّا أودقسس فقد يظنّ أنّ اللذّة هي الخير من أجل أنه رأى كل شئ يشتهيها ما له نطق وما لا نطق له فإنّه يعلم المختار ذو الاستئهل والقوي جدّاً وأنّ الكلّ يتحرّك في ذاته فإنّه أجود من جميع الأشياء وجود الجيّد بذاته كوجود الغذاء أيضاً وإنّ الذي هو خير للجميع وكلّ يشتهيه فهو خير وكانت تصلق الأقاويل بفضيلة الخلق أحرى من أن تصلق لذاتها وقد كان يظنّ به أنّه عفيف على ما ينبغي ولم يكن يقول هذه الأشياء لأنّه كان محبّاً للذّة بل لأنّها من الحقيقة كذلك (٢) وإنّ ذلك يتبيّن من ضدّها تبييناً ليس بدون فإنّ الحزن عند الكلّ يهرب منه وضدّها [٣/٦١] أيضاً عندهم مختار وإنّ المختار أكثر ذلك الذي يختاره لا لشئ آخر ولا من أجل شئ آخر وهم يقرّون به أنّ اللذّة مثل هذه فإنّها لا يسأل أحد لماذا يلذّ كأنّ اللذّة بذاتها مختارة وإذا زيدت على شئ ما من الخيرات تصيّره أكثر مختاراً مثل الفعل بالعدول أو التعفيف وإنّ الخير يسبّه ذاته (٣) وقد يشبه هذا القول أن يقضي عليها أنّها من الخيرات وأنّها ليست شيئاً آخر البتّةَ فإنّ كلّ ما يكون مع خير آخر أحرى أن يختار منه إذا كان وحده وبمثل هذا ينفي أفلاطون أن تكون اللذّة خيراً من أجل أنّ العمر اللذيذ أحرى أن يختار إذا كان مع عقل منه إذا كان بلا عقل فإن كان أجود فليست

---

2 فيما F, Bad, Dun : فيها Ax || 4 اودقسس F w.p. : اودقسيس Ax || 4 راى F, Bad : راى [ن] suppl. Ax || 7 بفضيلة corr. Bad : الفضيلة F, Ax || 8 به om. Bad || 11 هم corr. Bad : هو F, Ax || 11 ان به F, Ax, Dun : بان corr. Bad || 12 لماذا F, Ax, Dun : إذا corr. Bad || 12 يلذ F, Bad, Dun : نلذ Ax || 12 كأن F*, Dun* (ὡς) : كان corr. Ax; كانت corr. Bad || 13 يسبه corr. Dun* (αὔξεσθαι) : بسبب F, Ax, Bad || 14 يقضي F, Bad, Dun : نقضي Ax || 14 second انها F, Bad : انه Ax || 16 احرى suppl. mrg.

gence. If it[21] is better, then pleasure is not good,[22] for the good in
itself[23] is not more desirable than anything else before that good is
laid down.[24] And it is clear that the good is not anything else than[25]
the things which, when they are with those which are in themselves
good, are chosen more than others. (4) The thing which is such[26] is
that which is common to us also, for what is sought is such. Those
who reject this statement and say that what everyone desires is not a
good, would seem to say nothing. For we say that it is what we all
1173a think, and he who destroys this conviction brings no better conviction than they. Only[27] irrational creatures desire what is contrary[28] to
this statement, and if anyone makes this statement intelligently,[29] let
him make it. And it may be that there is a certain natural good in bad
things, better than they, and that it loves the good which is appropriate to it. (5) It is likely that they do not speak well about the contrary
either, for they do not say that if pain is bad, pleasure is good, since
evil is by hypothesis[30] opposed to evil and both to that which is neither of them. And they do not well[31] in saying this, nor do they speak
the truth regarding these things which have already been spoken of.
For if they are both evils, then they should both be avoided, and as
for the things which are neutral, neither is to be avoided, or they are
alike. But now it is obvious that men avoid some of them as evil and
choose others as good, and are opposed in this choice.[32]

3. It does not follow either, if pleasure is not one of the qualities, it is not for this reason one of the goods. For the actions of virtue are not qualities, nor is good fortune either. (2) People suppose that the good is definite, while pleasure is indefinite, because it admits of increase and decrease. The way in which they make this judgement in regard to pleasure from being pleased is the same as that in which they

---

[21] Greek τὸ μικτόν is omitted.

[22] See note 20.

[23] Arabic *al-khair bi-ʿainihi*, i.e. rendering αὐτὸ τἀγαθόν, the reading of the first hand in K^b.

[24] Arabic *mauḍūʿan*, i.e. Greek προστεθέντος was read προτεθέντος.

[25] The sense is missed. 'Than' is not in the Greek.

[26] The question in Greek τί οὖν ἐστὶ τοιοῦτον [...] is not noticed (Arberry).

[27] Greek εἰ is not read by the Arabic translator, and the sentence goes wrong.

[28] Arabic *alladhī yuḍādd*. This is ἄν τι read as ἀντι- (Arberry).

[29] Arabic *bi-ra'y mā*, representing Greek τὰ φρόνιμα.

[30] Arabic *bi 'l-waḍʿ*, cf. 1133b 21: *bi-nauʿ al-waḍʿ*.

[31] I.e. reading οὐ καλῶς for οὐ κακῶς (Arberry).

[32] The sense has been missed.

اللذّة خيراً فإنّه لا يكون الخير بعينه مختاراً أكثر من غيره قبل أن يكون ذلك الخير موضوعاً فبيّن أنّه لا يكون الخير شيئاً آخر البتّةَ من الأشياء التي إذا كانت مع التي هي بذاتها خيرات كانت تختار أشدّ من غيرها (٤) والشيء الذي هو مثل هذا هو الذي يعمّنا نحن أيضاً فإنّ المطلوب مثل هذا وأمّا الذين يردّون هذا القول ويقولون إنّ الذي يشتاق إليه كلّ ليس بخير خليق ألاّ يكونوا يقولون شيئاً فإنّه إنّما نقول إنّه الذي نراه أجمعون والذي ينقض هذا الإقناع ليس يأتي بإقناع أكثر منهم وإنّما يشتهي الذي يضادّ هذا القول ما لا يفهم وإن كان يقول قائل هذا القول برأي ما فليقل فخليق أن يكون في الأشياء الرديئة خير ما طبيعي أخير منها وأن يكون يحبّ الخير الذي هو له خاصّ (٥) ويشبه ألاّ يكونوا يجيدون القول في الضدّ أيضاً فإنّهم لا يقولون إنّه إن كان الحزن رديئاً فإنّ اللذّة خير من أجل أنّهم يقولون إنّه يقابل بالوضع رديء برديء وكلاهما للذي لا واحد منهما وليس يحسنون في هذا القول ولا يصدقون في هذه التي قد قيلت فإنّه إذا كانا كلاهما رديئين فقد كان ينبغي أن يكونا كلاهما يهرب منه وأمّا اللواتي لا واحد منهما فلا يهرب ولا من واحدة منها وتكون متشابهة وأمّا الآن فإنّه ظاهر أنّهم يهربون من بعضها على [٣/٦٢] أنّها رديئة ويختارون بعضها على أنّها خير وهم يتضادّون هذا الاختيار.

٣. ولا يكون هذا أيضاً ولا إن لم تكن اللذّة من الكيفيات وكانت لهؤلاء من الخيرات فإنّ أفعال الفضيلة ليست بكيفيات ولا سعادة البخت أيضاً (٢) ويزعمون أنّ الخير محدود وأمّا اللذّة فليست بمحدودة لأنّها تقبل الزيادة والنقصان والنوع الذي يقضون [به] بهذه القضية على اللذّة من التلذّذ هو الذي يقضون به على العدل وسائر الفضائل التي يزعمون أنّ

5 فإنه : F فإننا Bad || 5 نراه : F, Bad تراه Ax || 7 فليقل : F, Bad فلنقل Ax || 9 يقولون corr. Bad : F, Ax يقولوا || 9 فإن corr. Bad : F, Ax إن || 10 إنه corr. Bad, Dun : F, Ax إنهم || 10 بالوضع F, Ax, Dun : الوضع Bad || 12 لا F, Ax, Dun : فلا corr. Bad || 12 واحدة corr. Bad : F, Ax واحد || 13 تكون F, Bad : Ax يكون || 14 هذا F, Bad : Ax بهذا || 15 لهؤلاء F, Bad, Dun : Ax لهذا || 17 به suppl. Dun

judge in regard to justice and the rest of the virtues, which they suppose admit of increase and decrease to a certain extent. In this way it is possible that the same thing should have qualities, since some people are more just and more brave, and it is possible to be more and less concerned with just action and with temperance, and to be concerned with pleasures[33] also. It may be that they do not make known the reason in regard to how some pleasures are unmixed and some are mixed. (3) And what hinders that, just as health, which is definite, admits of more and less, pleasure is so also? For the proportion is not one in all things, and in one and the same thing there is not always a single proportion, but it decreases to a certain extent and differs by more and less. It is possible that there is something like this in pleasure also. (4) People assume that the good is perfect and that movements and processes are not perfect, trying to determine pleasure to be a movement and a coming into existence. It is likely that the view is wrong, and that pleasure is not a movement. It is thought that all things[34] have a special speed and slowness also, and if it is not in itself, like that of[35] the world, it is in relation to something else. As for pleasure, it has neither of these. It is possible
1173b for us to feel pleasure quickly, just as it is possible to be angry, but that pleasure should be perfect, is not possible nor that it should be related to anything else,[36] while walking, growing, and everything like this can change[37] to pleasure quickly and slowly. But to produce pleasure[38] quickly also is not possible, (5) and I mean that to be pleased is a coming into existence[39] in a way.[40] It is thought that anything that one has come upon[41] does not result from anything that one has come upon,[42] but a thing dissolves into that from which it comes into being. Pain is the corruption of that of which pleasure is

[33] The construction is wrong here.

[34] Greek πάσῃ, correctly 'every movement', rendered in the Arabic by *kull wāḥid min jamīʿ al-ashyāʾ*.

[35] The movement of the world is meant, but this is obscured by the faulty Arabic translation. Cf. previous note.

[36] Arabic *wa-ammā an takūna 'l-ladhdhah tāmmatan fa-lā yumkin wa-lā an taḍāfa ilā shaiʾ ākhar*—expands but fails to render Greek ἥδεσθαι δ' οὔ, οὐδὲ πρὸς ἕτερον (masculine).

[37] I.e. running on with μεταβάλλειν [...] after πάντα τὰ τοιαῦτα (Arberry).

[38] Arabic *an yafʿalū 'l-ladhdha* for Greek ἐνεργεῖν κατ' αὐτήν.

[39] Again running on with γένεσίς τε [...] after λέγω δ' ἥδεσθαι (Arberry).

[40] I.e. πώς for πῶς, the question being disregarded.

[41] I.e. any chance thing (Ross), Greek τὸ τυχόν, cf. 1169a 24 and 1169b 21.

[42] See previous note.

الزيادة والنقصان فيها بين بين فبهذا النوع يمكن أن تكون الكيفيات للشئ بعينه من أجل أنّه يكون قوم أكثر عدلاً وأكثر نجدة وقد يمكن أن يكون الأكثر والأقلّ في الفعل العادل وفي العفّة وأن يكون في اللذّات أيضاً وخليق ألاّ يكونوا يخبرون بالعلّة في ذلك كيف بعضها من غير اختلاط وبعضها مختلط (٣) وما المانع أن يكون كما أنّ الصحّة المحدودة تقبل الأكثر والأقلّ أن تكون اللذّة أيضاً كذلك فإنّ الاعتدال ليس بواحد في جميع الأشياء ولا يكون في الشئ الواحد بعينه اعتدال واحد ما أبداً بل ينقص إلى قدر ما ويختلف بالأكثر والأقلّ فيمكن أن يكون شئ مثل هذا في اللذّة أيضاً (٤) وهم يصفون أنّ الخير تامّ وأنّ الحركات والتكوينات ليست بتامّة يرومون أن يقضوا أنّ اللذّة حركة وكون وقد يشبه ألاّ يكونوا يقولون قولاً جيّداً وألاّ تكون اللذّة حركة فقد يظنّ أنّ لكلّ واحد من جميع الأشياء سرعة خاصّية وإبطاء أيضاً وإن لم تكن بذاتها مثل التي للعالم فإنّه مضاف إلى غيره وأمّا اللذّة فليس بها ولا واحد من هذين فقد يمكن أن نلذّ بسرعة كما يمكن أن نغضب وأمّا أن تكون اللذّة تامّة فلا يمكن ولا أن تضاف إلى شئ آخر وأمّا المشي والنشوء وجميع ما كان مثل هذه فيمكن أن يتغيّر إلى اللذّة بسرعة وإبطاء وأمّا أن يفعلوا اللذّة بسرعة أيضاً فلا يمكن (٥) فإنّي أقول إنّ التلذّذ يكون كوناً بنوع ما فقد يظنّ أنّه لا يكون كلّ ما أدرك من كلّ ما أدرك بل الذي يكون منه الشئ [٣/٦٣] فيه يتحلّل والذي كونه

3 third في F, Dun : قي Bad || 3 كيف F, Ax : كيفية Bad || 7 يصفون corr. Bad : يصفوا F; يضعوا Ax || 10 وإبطاء أيضا F*, Ax*, Dun* (βραδυτής) : وأيضا أيضا Bad || 11 بها F : لها Bad, Ax || 12 ولا om. Arberry || 12 تضاف F, Dun : تصير Bad || 13 فيمكن corr. Bad : يمكن F, Ax || 13 يتغير read. Dun : تتغير F, Ax; تصير Bad || 14 فإني F : وإني Bad || 14 التلذذ F, Bad, Dun : التاذذ Ax || 15 من كل ما أدرك suppl. mrg. || 15 يتحلل corr. Ax : يتحل F; فيتحل Bad

the coming into being. (6) People say that pain is a defect of the natural thing, while pleasure is the making good of the defect, and these effects are bodily. If pleasure is the making good of a natural defect, then that in which the making good of the defect takes place is that which feels pleasure, and it is the body which feels pleasure. But that is not thought to be so. Consequently pleasure is not the making good of the defect, but when the making good of the defect was taking place, the man felt pleasure, and when he was being cut, he felt pain. It is thought of this opinion that it has arisen from the pains and pleasures which arise in connection with food, since when people need food, and they have previously been pained in consequence of that, they feel pleasure in the making good of the defect. (7) This does not occur in all pleasures, since in the pleasures of learning there is no pain, nor in those of touch[43] and smell and hearing, and what is looked at is when the objects are numerous,[44] and hope for the like of these[45]—of what are they the coming into existence? For they have not come into existence through a lack,[46] nor[47] is there any word in that case of making good a defect. (8) As for those who adduce the pleasures which we reprobate, one may say, as regards them, that these are not pleasant, for even if they are pleasant to those whose constitution is defective, it should not be thought that they are pleasant besides except to these only, just as it should not be thought that things which in the eyes of a sick man are healthy, or sweet, or bitter, actually are so, or that what appear to be white [things] to the man with ophtalmia are white. (9) Otherwise it might be said in this way that pleasures are desirable, not, however, by these means, just as it is said that wealth is desirable, but not desirable for the betrayer, and health is desirable but not for the man who has eaten a certain thing. (10) It may be that pleasures differ in pleasure,[48] since the pleasures which are from noble sources are different from those which are from base sources, and it is impossible for any who is not just to feel the pleasure of the just man, and for

---

[43] Arabic *allatī takūn bi'l-lams* mistranslates Greek τῶν κατὰ τὰς αἰσθήσεις.

[44] Arabic *wa-mā yubṣaru ilaihi yakūn idhā kāna kathīrah* [sic]. These words which are weak grammatically and hardly yield a sense are a surprising expansion of Greek ὁράματα πολλά.

[45] Arabic *wa-rajā' mithl hādhihi*, i.e. Greek μνῆμαι καί read as τοιαῦται (Arberry).

[46] Arabic *fa-innahā lam takun min naqṣ*, i.e. Greek ἔνδεια is read as ἐνδείᾳ, and the subject becomes 'these pleasures' (*hādhihi*, above).

[47] Arabic *wa-lā*, i.e. Greek οὗ read as οὐ.

[48] Arabic *bi'l-ladhdhah* for Greek εἴδει read as ἡδεῖ (Arberry), cf. 1167a 5.

اللذّة فساد الحزن (٦) ويقولون إنّ الحزن نقصان للشئ الطبيعي وأمّا اللذّة فتمام النقصان وهذه الانفعالات جسمية وإن كانت اللذّة تمام نقصان طبيعي فالذي فيه يكون تمام النقصان هو الذي يلذّ فإنّ الجسم الذي يلذّ ولكن لا يظنّ ذلك فإنّما ليس اللذّة تمام النقصان بل إذا كان يكون تمام النقصان يلذّ الإنسان وإذا كان يقطع يحزن وقد يظنّ هذا الرأي إنّما كان من الأحزان واللذّات التي تكون فيما يلي الغذاء من أجل أنّهم إذا احتاجوا وتقدّم حزنهم في ذلك يلذّون بتمام النقصان (٧) وهذا لا يعرض في جميع اللذّات من أجل أنّ اللذّات التعليمية ليس فيها حزن ولا التي تكون باللمس والشمّ والسماع وما يبصر إليه يكون إذا كان كثيرة ورجاء مثل هذه فهذه لأيّ شئ تكون كوناً فإنّها لم تكن من نقص ولا يقال إذاً تمام النقصان (٨) وأمّا الذين يحتملون اللذّات التي نعيّرها فخليق أن يقول أحد فيهم إنّ هذه ليست بلذيذة فإنّها وإن كانت لذيذة عند الذين هيئتهم هيئة رديئة لا ينبغي أن يظنّ بها أنّها لذيذة وأيضاً ما خلا عندهم ولا فقط كما أنّه لا ينبغي أن يظنّ أنّ التي عند المرضى مبرّأة أو حلوة أو مرّة فهي كذلك ولا أنّ [الأشياء] البيض التي تظهر لمن كان به رمد أنّها بيض (٩) وإلاّ فإنّه هو على هذا النوع خليق أن يقل إنّ اللذّات مختارة إلاّ أنّها ليست بهذه كمثل ما يقل إنّ الغنى مختار ولكن ليس هو مختاراً للذي يغتل والصحّة مختارة ليس إن أكل شيئاً ما (١٠) وخليق أن يكون تختلف اللذّات باللذّة من أجل أنّ اللذّات التي من الأشياء الحسنة غير التي تكون من القبيحة ولا يمكن أن يلذّ

2 تمام نقصان طبيعي corr. Dun* (τοῦ κατὰ φύσιν ἀναπλήρωσις) : تمام ونقصان طبيعي F, Ax; تماما ونقصانا طبيعيا corr. Bad || 3 فإنما appar. corr. Dun : فاما F || 4 هذا F, Bad : بهذا Ax || 7 باللمس F, Bad, Dun : بالحس Ax || 8 كثيرة F*, Ax*, Dun* (πολλά) : تذكرة Bad || 8 لأي F*, Dun* (τίνος) : لا في Bad, Ax || 10 أحد فيهم F, Ax, Dun : أحدهم Bad || 11 عندهم corr. Dun : عندها F || 12 الأشياء suppl. Bad, Dun || 14 بهذه F, Ax, Dun : فهذه Bad || 15 إن F, Bad, Dun : لمن Ax || 16 أن om. Arberry

any who is not musical[49] to feel the pleasure of the musical man, and similarly in the other things. (11) It is thought also to be evident[50] that a friend is different from a flatterer, and that their pleasure is not the same[51] but different. For one of them is thought to associate for
1174a good, the other for pleasure, and one of them is reprobated, and the other is praised because he associates with another intention. (12) It may be that no one would choose the noble of life,[52] having the intelligence of a child, and take pleasure during his life[53] in what children can take pleasure in, most decidedly[54] even if there is no pleasure at all in that, e.g. sight, thought, memory, and knowledge of the virtues.[55] If pleasures attend these necessarily, there is no difference at all in that. We may choose these, even if there is no pleasure from them. (13) That not every good[56] is pleasure and not every pleasure desirable, is plain, for[57] among them what is desirable in itself is different in form.[58] The things that are said about pleasure and pain have now been spoken of sufficiently.

4. What pleasure is or what kind of thing it is may become clearer if we proceed to mention it again from the beginning also. It is thought that sight at any time is effective, since it does not need anything at all supervening later to complete its form. It seems that pleasure is like this, since it is something complete, and no one can at any time perceive a pleasure in regard to which it is possible for it to be in a longer time, so that its form may be completed.[59] (2) Hence pleasure is not a movement either, because every movement is in time and for an end, like building. For it[60] is complete when it has done what it

---

[49] Arabic *mūsīqūs* = Greek μουσικός, for which there was no equivalent in Arabic.

[50] But Greek ἐμφανίζειν is transitive. The sense is missed.

[51] Arabic *laisa bi-wāḥidin*, but Greek is οὐκ οὖσαν ἀγαθόν, hence Arberry suggested that ἕν was read for ἀγαθόν.

[52] Arabic *al-jamīl al-ḥaiyāt*, Greek ζῆν simply. Probably *al-jamīl* is to be deleted.

[53] The phrase διὰ βίου seems to be wrongly construed.

[54] Greek οὐδὲ χαίρειν [...] ποιησαίμεθ' ἄν has here dropped out (Arberry). Arabic *akthar al-battah* for Greek ὡς οἷόν τε μάλιστα. Otherwise *al-battah* refers back to *aḥad*, 'no one at all'.

[55] Greek εἰδέναι construed wrongly with τὰς ἀρετάς and ἔχειν left untranslated.

[56] Arabic *kull khair*, but Greek τἀγαθόν.

[57] Arabic *fa'inna*, i.e. καὶ ὅτι is misunderstood.

[58] Greek ἣ ἀφ' ὧν has dropped out (Arberry).

[59] The Arabic here is notably cumbrous and obscure as a translation of the Greek.

[60] Arabic *fa'innahā takūn tāmmah* implying Greek καὶ τελεία, the reading of K^b.

بلذّة العادل من ليس بعادل ولا بلذّة الموسيقوس من ليس بموسيقوس وكذلك في سائر الأشياء (١١) ويظنّ أيضاً أنّه ظاهر أنّ الصديق غير المتأتّي وأنّ لذّتهما ليس بواحد بل مختلف فإنّ أحدهما يظنّ به أنّه يعاشر للخير والآخر للذّة وأحدهما يعيّر والآخر يمدح لأنّه يعاشر لمعنى آخر (١٢) وخليق ألاّ يختار أحد الجميل الحياة وله عقل صبي ويلذّ [٣/٦٤] عمره بما يمكن أن يلذّ به الصبيان أكثر البتّةَ وإن لم يكن في ذلك شئ من اللذّة البتّةَ مثل النظر والفكرة والذكر والمعرفة بالفضائل وأمّا إن كانت اللذّات تلحق هذه بالضرورة فليس في ذلك اختلاف البتّةَ فخليق أن يختار هذه وإن لم تكن منها لذّة (١٣) وأمّا أنّ ليس كلّ خير لذّة ولا أنّ كلّها مختارة فبيّن فإنّ فيها ما هو مختار بذاته مختلف بالصورة فالتي تقل في اللذّة والحزن فقد قيلت قولاً فيه كفاية.

٤. فأمّا ما هي اللذّة أو أيّ شئ هي فخليق أن يصير أبين إن أخذنا في إعادة ذكره من البدء أيضاً فقد يظنّ أنّ البصر في وقت ما نافذ من أجل أنّه لا يحتاج إلى شئ البتّةَ يكون من بعد لتتمّ صورته وقد يشبه اللذّة أن تكون مثل هذا من أجل أنّها شئ تامّ ولا يمكن أحداً أن يدرك لذّة ما في زمان يمكن فيها أن تكون في زمان أكثر لتتمّ صورتها (٢) ومن أجل هذه ليست حركة أيضاً لأنّ كلّ حركة في زمان وتمام ما مثل البناية فإنّها تكون تامّة إذا فعلت ما

1 first بلذة corr. Bad : بلذ F, Ax || 2 يظن read. Bad, Dun : نظن F, Ax || 5 عمره F*, Ax*, Dun* (βίου) : غيره Bad || 8 مختلف F, Bad : مختلفة Ax || 9 تقل read. Bad : يقل F, Ax || 12 ولا corr. Bad, Dun : لا لا F, Ax || 12 أحدا corr. Bad : أحد F, Ax || 13 فيها F, Ax, Dun : فيه Bad

intended, rather than[61] its completion being in all this time in which[62] this action is being done. In the parts of the time[63] all movements are incomplete, and they differ in form from the total movement and from one another. For the putting together of the stones is different from the setting up[64] of the columns, and between these things also and the preparation of the temple there is a distinction. For the preparation of the temple is complete, since it needs nothing for its object to be complete, whereas the preparation of the foundation and the frieze is not complete, since each of them is partial. They differ in form, and it is not possible for there to be a movement at any time complete in form, except it be in the whole time. (3) Similarly in walking and so on, for[65] locomotion is a movement from one thing to another, and the difference of its kinds,[66] walking, leaping and the like. And not only so, but there is also the difference in walking itself, for movement from thing to thing is not the same in the race-course and part [of it, nor] in one part [and another,] nor is passing
1174b along this line and that the same, since one does not pass along a line only but along a line in a place also, and one moves differently on this line from one's movement on the other line. We have already dealt exhaustively with motion in other discussions. It seems that it is not complete at all times, but that many movements are incomplete, different in form also, since that which moves from thing to thing is a quality in the form.[67] (4) As for the form of pleasure it is at all times complete, and it is clear in that case that the pleasures will be different from one another,[68] for pleasure is among the things that are complete and whole. This may be thought in regard to it also and from the fact that it is impossible to be moved by being pleased in time,[69] since of it[70] that which is now is a complete whole. From

---

[61] Mistranslation of ἤ, putting the sense awry.

[62] I.e. Greek ἥ translated now as ᾗ, with τοῦτο (for τούτῳ).

[63] Arabic *fī ajzā' az-zamān*. This is the vulg. ἐν [...] τοῖς μέρεσι τοῦ χρόνου as against the reading of K^b ἐν [...] τοῖς μέρεσι καὶ τῷ χρόνῳ.

[64] Arabic *intiṣāb*, i.e. for Greek ῥαβδώσεως meaning 'fluting', but not understood.

[65] Greek εἰ is disregarded.

[66] Greek πτῆσις, 'flying', has here dropped out (Arberry).

[67] Arabic *kaifīyah bi'ṣ-ṣūrah* for Greek εἰδοποιόν.

[68] Not right. What is said in the Greek to be different are not pleasures, but pleasure contrasted with movement.

[69] I.e. Greek ἐν χρόνῳ, ἥδεσθαι is construed together, and the following δέ is disregarded.

[70] Sc. pleasure.

أرادت أكثر من تمامها في جميع هذا الزمان الذي يفعل فيه هذا الفعل وأمّا في أجزاء الزمان فجميع الحركات ليست بتامّة وتختلف بالصورة من الحركة الكلّية وبعضها من بعض فإنّ تأليف الحجارة غير انتصاب الأساطين وهذه أيضاً بينها وبين تهيئة الهيكل فرق تامّاً من أجل أنّها لا تحتاج إلى شيء ليكون به الموضوع تامّاً وأمّا تهيئة الأساس والإفريز فليس بتامّ من أجل أنّ كلّ واحد منهما جزئ وهم يختلفون بالصورة ولا يمكن أن توجد حركة في زمان ما تامّة بالصورة إلاّ أن تكون في الكلّ (٣) وكذلك في المشي وسائر ذلك فإنّ النقلة حركة ما من شيء إلى شيء واختلافات أنواعها المشي والوثوب وما كان مثل هذه فليس هكذا فقط بل الاختلاف أيضاً في المشي بعينه فإنّ الحركة من شيء إلى شيء ليست شيئاً واحداً بعينه في العلوة والجزء [منه ولا] في جزء [وآخر] ولا العبور على هذا الخطّ فذلك واحد من أجل أنّه لا يعبر على خطّ فقط بل [٣/٦٥] على خطّ هو في مكان أيضاً فالذي يتحرّك في هذا الخطّ غير حركته في الخطّ الآخر وقد استقصينا القول في الحركة في أقاويل غير هذه وقد يشبه ألاّ تكون تامّة في كلّ زمان بل أن تكون كثيرة منها ليست بتامّة مختلفة بالصورة أيضاً إذ كان الذي تحرّك من شيء إلى شيء كيفية بالصورة (٤) فأمّا صورة اللذّة ففي كلّ زمان تامّة فبيّن إذاً أنّ اللذّات ستكون مخالفة بعضها لبعض فإنّ اللذّة من الأشياء التامّة ذوات الكلّ وخليق أن يظنّ بها هذا أيضاً ومن أنّها لا يمكن أن تتحرّك بأن تلذّ في زمان من أجل أنّ الذي هو منها الآن كلّ تامّ ومن هذه بيّن أيضاً أنّهم لعلّة ما

1 أرادت F, Bad : اردت Ax || 1 first هذا suppl. mrg. || 3 فرق F, Ax : فروق corr. Bad || 5 جزئ Dun : F reading uncertain; حرف Bad || 6 تكون Bad : يكون read. Ax || 6 المشي F*, Ax*, Dun* (βαδίσεως) : الشئ Bad || 9 العلوة F*, Bad*, Dun* (τῷ σταδίῳ) : العدوة Ax || 9 و[آخر] F, والجزء في جزء : (καὶ ἐν τῷ μέρει, καὶ ἐν ἑτέρῳ μέρει) suppl. Dun* والجزء [منه ولا] في جزء Ax; والجزي جدا Bad || 14 أن F, Ax : من Bad || 14 مخالفة corr. Ax : مخالفا F, Bad || 16 تلذ Bad : يلذ read. Ax

these considerations it is clear also that people for some reason[71] say that pleasure is a movement or a coming into existence, since these things are not said about all, but are said about those which are divided up and are not [wholes].[72] For neither sight, nor a point, nor a unit has a coming into existence, nor is any of these a movement or a coming into existence, nor has pleasure either, since it is a whole. (5) Every sense acts according to what is perceived, and the sense of which the condition is excellent acts in a complete manner with the most excellent[73] of what comes under the sense. It is thought of the complete action for the most part that it is something like this, and it is said that there is a distinction[74] between saying that the sense is active and saying that it is active in that in which it resides.[75] For in each case the best action is the action of the thing of which the condition is best, with the strongest[76] of what pertains to it. And it may be that this is a complete movement and pleasant in all the senses.[77] Pleasure is in all,[78] and similarly in thought and reflection. The most pleasant is the most complete, and the most complete is that which has the best condition in comparison with[79] the most excellent of the things that come under it, for what completes the action is the pleasure. (6) But pleasure does not complete the action in the same way as the object of sense and sense complete it, even if they are good things, just as health[80] and the doctor are not causes of health[81] equally and in a similar way. (7) That there is pleasure in all of the senses is clear, and we say that sights and sounds are pleasant. It is

---

[71] Arabic *li-ʿillah mā*, perhaps meiosis for Greek οὐ καλῶς.

[72] Text has *wa-laisat wujūduhā*. Arberry emends *wa-laisat wuḥūduhā* for Greek καὶ μὴ ὅλων. Since, however, Greek ὅλος is rendered in three other places in this passage by Arabic *kull*, one should not expect a different rendering here. Nor has *wuḥūdahā*, lit. 'their oneness', quite the right meaning. Perhaps therefore *wujūduhā* should be retained with omission of a following *kullan* or *kullīyatan* or (cf. 1174a 17) *shaiʾan tamāman*.

[73] Arabic *ajwad* for Greek κάλλιστον.

[74] Arabic *faṣl*, but we need the negative (Greek μηθέν), and the nuance 'let no distinction be made' (Greek διαφερέτω) is not taken into account.

[75] Arabic *innahā tafʿal fī alladhī hiya fīhi*, but we want the sense 'that in which the sense resides is active'.

[76] Arabic *aqwā* for Greek κράτιστον.

[77] I.e. running on: ἥδιστη κατὰ πᾶσαν γὰρ αἴσθησιν, γάρ being disregarded.

[78] Arabic *fī jamīʿ* not in the Greek. 'In all' repeats κατὰ πᾶσαν (Arberry).

[79] Arabic *ʿinda*, representing Greek πρός, 'in relation to'.

[80] Arabic *barʾ*, lit. 'recovery'.

[81] See previous note.

يقولون إنّ اللذّة حركة أو كون من أجل أنّ هذه الأشياء لا تقل على الجميع بل تقل على التي تنقسم وليست وجودها [كلّية] فإنّه ليس كون للبصر ولا للنقطة ولا للوحدة وليس شيء من هذه حركة ولا كون واللذّة أيضاً من أجل أنّها شيء كلّ (٥) وكلّ حسّ يفعل على قدر المحسوس ويفعل بنوع تامّ الحسّ الذي حاله حال جيّدة مع أجود ما يجب للحسّ فقد يظنّ بالفعل التامّ أكثر ذلك أنّه شيء مثل هذا ويقال إنّه بين القول الذي يقول إنّها تفعل وبين القول الذي يقول إنّها تفعل في الذي هي فيه فصل فإنّ في كلّ واحد من الأشياء الفعل الأجود هو فعل الشيء الذي حاله أجود الحالات ما أقوى ما يكون منه فخليق أن تكون هذه حركة تامّة ولذينة في كلّ الحواسّ. اللذّة في جميع كذلك في الفكرة والرأي وألذّها التامّة جدّاً والتامّة جدّاً التي هي له أحسن الحل عند الفاضل جدّاً من التي تحتها فإنّ ما يتمّ الفعل اللذّة (٦) ولكن لا تتمّ الفعل اللذّة والمحسوس والحسّ بنوع واحد وإن كانت أشياء فاضلة كما أنّ البرء والطبيب ليس ممّا عللاً أن يكون برء بالسوية ونوع متشابه (٧) وأمّا أنّ اللذّة تكون في كلّ من الحواسّ فبيّن فقد نقول إنّ مناظر ومسامع للذينة وهو

1 اللذة perh. corr. للذة Dun || 1 تقل Bad (twice) : يقل read. Ax || 2 كلية suppl. Dun* (ὅλων) || 3 اللذة F, Bad, Dun : لا لذة Ax || 3 كل F, Ax, Dun : وكل Bad || 5 شيء F : شيء ما Bad || 6 فصل F*, Dun* (διαφερέτω) : فضل Ax; فعل Bad || 7 first ما F, Ax : لا Bad || 8 اللذة F, Bad : واللذة Ax || 8 كذلك F : فكذلك Ax; وكذلك Bad || 9 first التامة F*, Ax*, Dun* (ἡ τελειοτάτη) : العامة Bad || 9 تحتها read. Dun* (ὑπ' αὐτήν) : يحبها F, Ax, Bad || 11 مما F, Dun : هما Ax; يرى Bad || 12 فقد نقول F, Ax, Dun : من القول Bad || 12 للذينة Dun corr. : اللذينة F, Ax

clear also that pleasures are most acute when the sense is strong[82] and is active according to its strength.[83] When the object of sense and that which perceives are such, there is always pleasure, since when there is an agent and an object, (8) pleasure completes the action,[84] not like the form within, but like an end which supervenes afterwards, e.g. the beauty which appears in the young. As long as the object of sense and the object of understanding continue as they
1175a should be and that which judges or reflects continues as it was, there will be pleasure in the action. For when the object and the agent are alike, and the relation of each of them to the other is unaltered, naturally the same thing arises. (9) For somehow[85] no one feels continuous pleasure nor continuous pain, since all human things are incapable of acting continuously, so that pleasure also is not continuous, since it follows the action. Some things afford pleasure when new, but afterwards they are not so for these reasons.[86] For at first reflection knows[87] and acts on them much and powerfully, like those who look at a distant object with the sense of sight, then afterwards no action like that comes into existence, but there may come into existence an action which is despised,[88] hence the pleasure becomes weak. (10) Perhaps one might think[89] that all men love life also. Life is an activity, and each man works at those things which are best[90] and in them his activity mostly is like the musician who employs hearing in regard to tunes, the lover of learning[91] who employs reflection in regard to opinions, and similarly each of the rest of these. Pleasure completes actions and life, for which the desire is. Thus those who desire life rightly desire pleasure also, since it completes in each the life which is desirable. (11) For the sake of pleasure[92]

---

[82] Arabic *qawī*, Greek κρατίστη, cf. 1174b 19 = X, 4, 5.

[83] Arabic *ʿalā qadr qūwatihi* for Greek πρὸς τοιοῦτον, understood with reference to the meaning already given to κρατίστη.

[84] The sentence runs on: ὑπάρχοντός γε [...] πεισομένου τελειοῖ δὲ τὴν ἐνέργειαν [...], disregarding δέ.

[85] I.e. πώς for πῶς (Arberry).

[86] Arabic *li-hādhihi 'l-ʿilal*, i.e. Greek διὰ ταῦτα, the reading of L^b.

[87] Arabic *al-fikrah qad taʿrifu*. But Greek is παρακέκληται, 'is stimulated, roused up'.

[88] Arabic *qad yuhawwanu bihi* for Greek παρημελημένη.

[89] Greek ὀρέγεσθαι δὲ τῆς ἡδονῆς is not rendered.

[90] Arabic *allatī hiya akhyar*, apparently ἀγαθά for ἀγαπᾷ (Arberry).

[91] Arabic *al-muḥibb fī 't-taʿlīm*, strictly 'lover of instruction', cf. *al-ladhdhāt at-taʿlīmīya* (1173b 16-17), there translated 'the pleasures of learning'.

[92] Several words have been omitted by homoioteleuton (τὸ ζῆν [...] τὴν ἡδονήν), and the meaning as usual in such cases is lost.

بيّن أيضاً أنّه تكون لذّات أشدّ إذا كان الحسّ قوياً وكان يفعل على قدر قوّته [٣/٦٦] وإذا كانت مثل هذه المحسوس والذي يحسّ تكون اللذّة أبداً من أجل أنّه إذا كان الفاعل والمنفعل (٨) تمّمت اللذّة الفعل لا كهيئة هي فيه بل كتمام ما يصير فيه من بعد كالجمل الذي يصير في الشباب فما دام المحسوس والمعقول على ما ينبغي والذي يقضي أو يرى على حاله فاللذّة تكون في الفعل فإنّه إذا كان المنفعل والفاعل متشابهين وإضافة كلّ واحد منهما إلى صاحبه على حل واحدة يكون بالطبع شئ واحد بعينه (٩) فإنّه بنوع ما لا يلذّ ملذ لذّة متّصلة ولا يتأذّى أذى متّصلاً من أجل أنّ جميع الأشياء الإنسية لا تقوى على أن تفعل فعلاً متّصلاً فإذاً لا تكون ولا لذّة من أجل أنّها تتبع الفعل وبعض الأشياء تسرّ وهي جدد وأمّا من بعد فليست كذلك لهذه العلل فإنّ أوّلاً تكون الفكرة قد تعرف وتفعل فيها فعلاً كثيراً قوياً مثل الذين يبصرون البعيد بحسّ البصر ثمّ بعد ذلك لا يكون فعل مثل هذا بل قد يكون فعل قد يهوّن به من أجل هذا تضعف اللذّة (١٠) وخليق أن يظنّ ظانّ أنّ أجمعين يحبّون الحية أيضاً والحية فعل ما وكلّ واحد يفعل في التي هي أخير وما يكون فعله أكثر ذلك كالموسيقوس الذي يستعمل السمع في الألحان وكالمحبّ في التعليم الذي يستعمل الفكرة في الآراء وكذلك كلّ واحد من سائر هؤلاء واللذّة تتمّ الأفعل والحية التي تكون بها الشهوة فالذين يشتهون الحية بحقّ يشتهون اللذّة أيضاً من أجل أنّها تتمّ في كلّ الحية التي هي مختارة (١١) فهل ينبغي أن نترك الفعل حيننا هذا لمكان

1 أنه F, Bad : ان Ax || 1 أشد F*, Dun* (μάλιστα) : أفخر Bad || 2 أبدا corr. above line : الذ F || 3 كالجمل F, Ax, Dun : كالحل Bad || 6 يكون Bad : تكون Ax (Dun?) || 6 لا om. Bad || 7 ملذ om. Bad || 12 ما F, Bad : بها Ax || 16 مختارة F*, Ax*, Dun* (ὀρέγονται) : سارة Bad

should we leave action at this present time? For it appears that they are joined together and do not admit of separation, for without action there is no pleasure and pleasure completes every action.

5. Hence it is thought of pleasure that it is different in form, and it is thought of things different in form that they are completed by other, different things. Such appear to be natural objects and those which come under art, like animals, plants,[93] a painting,[94] idols,[95] a house, households vessels. (2) Similarly the activities of different form are completed by things of different form. The activities of thought differ from those of the senses, and these differ from one another in respect of form, and similarly the pleasures which perfect them. That appears also from the fact that every pleasure is borne resemblance to[96] by the activity which completes it. For the special pleasure promotes the activity by its growth, for those who do what they do with pleasure are more exact in investigation[97] in all things and more inquiring, as is the case with those who employ mensuration[98] and take delight in measuring and inquiring into each of the parts of mensuration more, and similarly lovers of music and lovers of building and all the others increase in their special activities in which they take delight. The pleasures grow[99] along with the activities and what
1175b grows[100] with things is special to them. Things that are other in respect of form have properties other in respect of form. (3) Also that might well appear from the fact that the pleasures which are from other things interfere with the activities. For those who love themselves[101] are unable to listen quietly to discourse, and if they hear somebody playing the flute, they delight in the flute more than the special[102] activity, and the pleasure which is from the flute spoils the activity which is from speech. (4) This happens similarly to others

[93] Arabic *naṣb* for Greek δένδρα, ‘plants’, is perhaps colloquial.

[94] Arabic *tazwīq*, Greek γραφή.

[95] I.e. reading ἀγάλματα of vulg. (ἄγαλμα, K^b).

[96] Arabic *yushākiluhā*, 1178a 15. The Arabic translation has already had difficulty with Greek συνοικειόω, 1161b 21, 1162a 2, 1172a 20.

[97] Arabic text has *istiqṣā’*, but Greek κρίνουσι suggests a form from *qaḍā*, ‘judge’.

[98] Arabic *yasta‘milūna al-masāḥah* for Greek γεωμετρικοί, but the construction is wrong.

[99] The Greek verb is transitive (συναύξω).

[100] See previous note.

[101] I.e. Greek φίλαυλοι read as φίλαυτοι (Arberry).

[102] Arabic *al-khāṣṣ*, apparently a copyist’s error for *al-ḥāḍir* (Greek παρούσης).

اللذّة فإنّه يظهر أنّها قد تقاربت معاً فلا تقبل فرقة فإنّه لا تكون لذّة من غير فعل وإنّما تتمّم كلّ فعل اللذّة.

٥. ومن ها هنا يظنّ بها أنّها مختلفة بالصورة فقد يظنّ بالمختلفة في الصورة أنّها تتمّ بأشياء أخر مختلفة وكذلك تظهر الأشياء الطبيعية والتي تحت المهنة كالحيوان والنصب والتزويق والأصنام والبيت والإنية (٢) وكذلك الأفعل المختلفة الصورة تتمّ بالمختلفة الصورة والتي للفكرة تخالف التي للحواسّ وهذه [٣/٦٧] يخالف بعضها بعضاً بالصورة وكذلك اللذّات المتمّمة ويظهر ذلك أيضاً من أنّ كلّ واحد من اللذّات يشاكلها بالفعل الذي يتمّمها فإنّ اللذّة الخاصّية ينمي الفعل بنموها فإنّ الذين يفعلون ما يفعلون بلذّة أشدّ استقصاءً في جميع الأشياء وأكثر فحصاً مثلما يكون في الذين يستعملون المساحة ويفرحون بأن يمسحوا ويفحصوا عن كلّ واحد من الأجزاء التي للمساحة أكثر وكذلك محبّو الموسيقى ومحبّو البناء وكلّ واحد من غيرهم يزيدون في أعمالهم الخاصّية التي يفرحون بها واللذّات تنمي معها والتي تنمي مع أشياء هي خاصّ بها والتي هي أخر بالصورة فخواصّها أخر بالصورة (٣) وأيضاً خليق أن يظهر ذلك من أنّ اللذّات التي تكون من أشياء تكون مانعة للأفعل فإنّ الذين يحبّون ذواتهم لا يقدرون أن ينصتوا للكلام وإن سمعوا أنّ امرءً يزمر فرحوا بالزمر أكثر من الفعل الخاصّ واللذّة التي تكون من الزمر تفسد الفعل الذي يكون من القول (٤) وكذلك يعرض هذا للأخر أيضاً إذا كان الفعل معاً

1 معا F, Bad : بها Ax || 1 وإنما F, Bad : فإنها Ax || 2 تتمم Bad : يتمم Ax || 3 في om. Bad || 6 يخالف F, Bad, Dun : تخالف Ax || 7 بالفعل F, Bad : الفعل Ax || 8 ينمي F, Ax, Dun : تنمي Bad || 12 أشياء F, Ax, Dun : الأشياء Bad || 14 ذواتهم F, Bad, Dun : زمارتهم Ax* (φίλαυλοι)

also, when the activity is at the same time concerned with two things. For the more pleasant repels the other, and it is more likely to do that when it exceeds greatly in pleasure, so that the other leaves off being active. For this reason, when we delight in something, we mostly do nothing else, but what we do[103] pleases others by doing quietly,[104] just as applauders[105] in the meetings which assemble for viewing,[106] when the contestants are bad, for at that time they contend in applause. (5) Since the special pleasure makes the actions exact and renders them more lasting, longer and better, while the unfamiliar pleasures [are hurtful],[107] it is plain that between them there is much difference. The unfamiliar pleasures do nearly what the special pains do. For the special pains spoil the actions, as, for instance, if someone who does not take pleasure in writing is pained by thought,[108] for he does not write and does not think,[109] since the action is painful. The opposite occurs from the special pleasures and pains in the actions, for the special pleasures are those which come into existence after the action itself. The unfamiliar pleasures have already been said to have something like the effect of pain, since they spoil [the action], only not in the same way. (6) Since the actions differ in merit and badness, and some of them are to be desired, some to be avoided, and some neither one nor the other, pleasures also are similar. For each action has a special pleasure: the good is special to the meritorious, while the bad is hurtful.[110] For the desires also for noble things are praised and those for bad things are blamed. The pleasures which arise along with actions are more special to the actions than the desires, since the desires are separated in times and in nature, whereas the pleasures are closely connected with the actions and are not separated from them, to this extent that there is doubt in regard to them as to the activity and the pleasure being the same. (7) But it is not likely that the pleasure is a thought or that it is

[103] Arabic *bal alladhī naf'al*, i.e. ἀλλ' ἃ ποιοῦμεν for καὶ ἄλλα ποιοῦμεν (Arberry).

[104] Arabic *bi-sukūn*, Arberry's correction for *sa-yakūn* of the MS., rendering ἠρέμα, but the Greek has been wrongly construed.

[105] Arabic *aṣḥāb al-qaṣf* for Greek οἱ τραγηματίζοντες, which was not understood.

[106] The circumlocution for Greek ἐν τοῖς θεάτροις is noticable.

[107] The Arabic equivalent of Greek λυμαίνονται has dropped out.

[108] The Arabic omits or misunderstands Greek ἤ (Arberry), but also appears to misunderstand Greek λογίζεσθαι, which is rendered by Arabic *al-fakirah*.

[109] Arabic *lā yufakkir* for Greek λογίζεται. See previous note.

[110] Arabic *wa 'r-radī'ah mu'dhiyah*, i.e. apparently for τῇ φαύλῃ μοχθηρά.

في اثنين فإنّ الألذّ يرفع الآخر وأحرى أن يفعل ذلك إذا كان مفرطاً في اللذّة جدّاً حتّى يترك الآخر أن يفعل ولهذا السبب إذا فرحنا بشيء ما لا نفعل شيئاً آخر أكثر ذلك بل الذي نفعل رضا آخرين بسكون كما فعل أصحاب القصف في المجامع التي تجتمع للنظر إذا كان المجتهدون ذوي رداءة فإنّهم حينئذ يجتهدون في القصف (٥) فإذا اللذّة الخاصّية تستقصي الأفعال وتصيّرها أدوم في زمان أطول وأجود واللذّات الغريبة [مؤذية] فبيّن أنّ بينها فرقاً كثيراً فقد يكاد أن تفعل اللذّات الغريبة ما تفعل الأحزان الخاصّية فإنّ الأحزان الخاصّية تفسد الأفعال كقولي إن كان الذي لا يلتذّ بالكتابة يحزن بالفكرة فإنّه لا يكتب ولا يفكّر إذ كان الفعل محزناً ويعرض في الأفعال الضدّ من اللذّات الخاصّية والأحزان فإنّ الخاصّية التي تكون بعد الفعل بعينه وأمّا اللذّات الغريبة فقد قيل إنّها تفعل شبيهاً بفعل الحزن من أجل أنّها تفسد إلاّ أنّها ليس بنوع [٣/٦٨] متشابه (٦) فلمّا كانت تختلف الأفعال بذي الاستئهال والرداءة وكان بعضها مختارة وبعضها يهرب [منها] وبعضها لا شيء من هذين صارت اللذّات أيضاً متشابهة فإنّ لكلّ فعل لذّة خاصّية فالفاضلة خاصّية ذي استئهال والرديئة مؤذية فإنّ الشهوات أيضاً أمّا التي للأشياء الجيلا فممدوحة والتي للقبيحة فمذمومة واللذّات التي تكون مع الأفعال أخصّ بالأفعال من الشهوات من أجل أنّ الشهوات منفصلة بالأزمنة والطبيعة وأمّا اللذّات فقريبة من الأفعال فليس تنفصل منها على هذه الحال حتّى إنّه يشكّ فيها بأنّ الفعل واللذّة شيء واحد (٧) ولكن لا يشبه أن تكون

2 نفعل Dun : يفعل Ax, Bad || 3 رضا F, Bad, Dun : يرضي Ax || 3 بسكون corr. Dun* (ἠρέμα) : سيكون F, Ax || 3 فعل corr. Bad : فعلوا F, Ax || 3 القصف F, Bad, Dun : القصب Ax || 3 تجتمع Dun, Ax : يجتمع Bad || 4 القصف F, Bad, Dun : القصب Ax || 5 مؤذية suppl. Dun* || 6 first تفعل Bad : يفعل Ax || 7 بالكتابة corr. Dun : بالكتاب F, Ax || 9 بعينه F, Dun : تعينه read. Bad, Ax || 9 شبيها F, Dun : شبها Ax; شيئا Bad || 11 منها suppl. Bad || 12 صارت اللذات corr. Dun : صارت واللذات F, Ax || 12 متشابهة Ax : متشابها F, Bad || 12 ذي corr. Dun : ذو F, Ax || 15 فقريبة F, Ax, Dun : القريبة Bad

a sensation, for that is absurd, but since they are not separate, it appears to some people that both are one. Just as actions are different
1176a then, and pleasures are different also. Sight is distinct from touch in clearness,[111] hearing and smell are distinct from taste, and similarly the pleasures are distinct also. Those which are in reflection are distinct from them also, and each of them is so with reference to the other. (8) It is sometimes thought that each of the animals has a special pleasure also, like the special function which is in the activity.[112] This appears to anyone who thinks of each of the things. For the pleasure of the horse is different, and similarly the pleasure of the dog is different, and so the pleasure of man, as Heraclitus said: The intelligence[113] would prefer perceptions[114] to gold. For to the intelligence[115] food is pleasanter than gold. The pleasures therefore of things which are different in form are different in form, whereas the pleasures of those which are the same are rightly not different. (9) They change in the case of men, to no small extent, since the same things delight some and distress others, and are painful to some and hated, while to others they are pleasant and welcome. This happens in sweet things also, since the fevered and the healthy man have not the same opinion in regard to them, nor is that which is hot the same in the opinion of the weak and the strong, and this occurs similarly in the case of other people[116] also. (10) It is thought in regard to all things like these that they are what appears to the good man. If this is so, then it is well said[117] that virtue is the measure of everything, as is thought,[118] and is the good qua good,[119] and that which appears to this man to be so is pleasure, and the things which he delights in are pleasant. That what is difficult of these[120] should appear

---

[111] Arabic *bahā'* for Greek καθαρειότητι.

[112] Arabic *ka 'l-ʿamal al-khāṣṣ alladhī yakūn ʿinda 'l-fiʿl*. But this mistranslates ἡ γὰρ κατὰ τὴν ἐνέργειαν, which must refer to the pleasure.

[113] I.e. misreading ὄνους of the text (ὄνον, Rackham without explanation) as ὁ νοῦς (Arberry).

[114] I.e. misunderstanding σύρματα, 'sweepings'.

[115] Again ὄνοις confused with some case of νοῦς.

[116] Arabic *qaum ākharīn*, but the Greek ἐφ' ἑτέρων is no doubt neuter.

[117] The construction here (καλῶς λέγεται separated from εἰ δὲ τοῦτο) is wrong.

[118] The phrase (Arabic *kamā yuẓannu*) should be construed with Greek καλῶς λέγεται, 'it is well said'.

[119] Again misconstruction. Arabic *al-khair bi-annahu khair* goes with Greek ἡ ἀρετή, 'virtue and the good man as such are the measure of everything'.

[120] I.e. τούτων for τούτῳ.

اللذّة فكرة ولا أن تكون حسّاً فإنّ ذلك محال ولكن من أجل أنّها لا تنفصل يظهر لبعض الناس أنّهما شيء واحد فكما أنّ الأفعل أخر فاللذّات أخر أيضاً وينفصل البصر من اللمس بالبهاء والسمع والشمّ من الذوق وكذلك تنفصل اللذّات أيضاً والتي في الفكرة ومنها أيضاً وكلّ واحد منها لصاحبه (٨) وقد يظنّ أنّ لكلّ واحد من الحيوان لذّة خاصّية أيضاً كالعمل الخاصّ الذي يكون عند الفعل ويظهر هذا لمن يظنّ في كلّ واحد من الأشياء فإنّ لذّة الفرس أخرى وكذلك لذّة الكلب أخرى وكذلك لذّة الإنسان كما قل إيرقلطس إنّ العقل أحرى يختار الإدراكات على الذهب فإنّ للعقل غذاءً ألذّ من الذهب فالتي للأشياء التي تختلف بالصورة فهي تختلف بالصورة وأمّا التي لأشياء بأعيانها فبحقّ ألاّ تكون مختلفة (٩) وهي تتبدّل في الناس تبديلاً ليس بصغير من أجل أنّها بأعيانها تفرح بعضاً وتحزن بعضاً وهي لبعض محزنة وبغيضة ولبعض لذيذة ومحبوبة ويعرض هذا في الأشياء الحلوة أيضاً من أجل أنّه لا يرى المحموم والصحيح رأياً واحداً فيها وليس الحارّ عند الضعيف والقوي واحداً وكذلك يعرض هذا في قوم آخرين أيضاً (١٠) ويظنّ في جميع أشباه هذه أن تكون ما يظهر للفاضل وإن هذا كذلك فنعم ما يقل إنّ الفضيلة مقدار كلّ شيء كما يظنّ ويكون [٣/٦٩] الخير بأنّه خير واللذّة التي تظهر لهذا أنّها كذلك وتكون لذيذة التي يفرح هذا بها وأمّا ما صعب من هذه فليس يعجب أن يظهر أيضاً أقلّ في اللذّة.

---

2 أنهما F, Bad : انها Ax || 2 فاللذت F, Bad : واللذت Ax || 6 إيرقلطس F w.p. : ارقلطس Ax || 9 تفرح Bad : يفرح Ax || 10 تحزن Bad : يحزن Ax || 11 رايا corr. Ax, Dun : دائما F, Bad || 15 يعجب F, Ax : يعجبه Bad || 15 في F, Ax, Dun : و Bad

also less in pleasure[121] is not to be wondered at. For in mankind there are many corruptions and much evil,[122] and they[123] are not pleasant, except to this man and to those who[124] are in a similar condition. (11) As for the pleasures which are admitted to be bad, plainly they are not called pleasures except among those who are corrupt. As for those thought to be worthy, which of them or which from among them[125] should be said to be for man, save those[126] which are from the activities? For it is plain[127] that the pleasures follow the activities, and whether there is one pleasure or several for the complete, happy man, the pleasures which complete these are rightly said to be pleasures of man. As for the rest of them, they are often[128] spoken of as activities.

6. Since we have now spoken of the virtues and the forms of friendship and pleasure, it now remains to speak of happiness,[129] since we posit it to be the end[130] of human things. If what has already preceded is repeated, it will prove a shorter discussion. (2) We have already said that happiness is not a state, otherwise it would belong to him who slumbers away his life and lives the life of the non-existent,[131] [or to] him who is in great misfortune. If these statements
1176b are not acceptable, but it is better that pleasure should be posited in an activity, as was said at first, and some activities are necessary and desirable for the sake of something else, and others are so for themselves, then it is clear that happiness should be posited as being one of the things which are desirable in themselves, not one of those which are desirable for something else, since happiness is not in need of anything but is self-sufficient. (3) The things desirable in themselves are those from which nothing else is sought, save the

[121] Arabic *an yaẓhar aiḍan aqalla fī 'l-ladhdhah* for Greek εἴ τῳ φαίνεται ἡδέα. But τῳ is omitted (or read καί) and ἧττον is added before ἡδέα in this rendering.

[122] Arabic *ḍarrar* for Greek λῦμαι.

[123] The change of subject in the Greek is apparently not noted.

[124] I.e. Greek τούτῳ καὶ τοῖς (Arberry).

[125] Arabic *aiyuhā au aiyu minhā*, pleonastic (Greek ποίαν ἢ τίνα).

[126] The Arabic translator again has difficulties with ἤ and his construction is wrong.

[127] Greek δῆλον is taken with the following ταύταις γὰρ [...], but it is an error.

[128] I.e. πολλάκις for πολλοστῶς (Arberry), δευτέρως καί being evidently omitted.

[129] Greek τύπῳ has dropped out (Arberry).

[130] Arabic *timām*, Greek τέλος, as elsewhere (1152b 2, 23, 1176b 28, etc.).

[131] Arabic *al-ma'dūm*. Arberry conjectured very plausibly that the Arabic translator read φθιτῶν for φυτῶν, or rather φθιτοῦ for φυτοῦ (read by O^b and Γ).

فإنّه يكون في الناس فسادات كثيرة وضرر كثير وليست لذينة إلاّ لهذا واللذين على حل ما مثل هذه (١١) وأمّا المقرور أنّها قبيحة فبيّن أنّها لا تقل لذّات إلاّ عند الذين قد فسدوا وأمّا التي يظنّ بها أنّها من ذوات الاستئهل فأيّها أو أيّ منها ينبغي أن يقل إنّها للإنسان ما خلا التي من الأفعل فإنّه بيّن أنّ اللذّات تتبع الأفعال وإن كانت لذّة واحدة أو لذّات كثيرة للرجل التامّ المغبوط فاللذّات التي تتمّم هذه بحقّ يقل إنّها لذّات إنسان وأمّا سائرها فربّما قيلت كالأفعل.

٦. وإذ قد قيلت أقاويل في الفضائل والمحبّات واللذّة فقد بقي القول في السعادة من أجل أنّا نضعها تمام الأشياء الإنسية وإن أعيد ما تقدّم كان قولاً واجزاً (٢) وقد قلنا إنّها ليست هيئة وإلاّ فستكون للذي ينام عمره ويحيا حياة المعدوم [أو] للذي في شقاء عظيم وأمّا إن كانت هذه الأقاويل ليست ترضى بل أحرى أن توضع في فعل ما كما قيل أوّلاً وكان بعض الأفعل مضطرّاً ومختاراً لمكان شيء آخر وبعضها لذاتها فبيّن أنّه ينبغي أن توضع السعادة أنّها شيء من التي هي مختارة بذاتها لا من التي تختار لشيء آخر من أجل أنّ السعادة ليست محتاجة إلى شيء بل مكتفية (٣) وإنّما المختارة بذاتها التي لا يطلب منها آخر خلا الفعل

2 المقرور F*, Bad*, Dun* (ὁμολογουμένως) : المقدور Ax || 5 فاللذات F, Ax, Dun : باللذات Ax || اوجز F; واجز : Bad corr. || 8 واجزا perh. corr. Dun* (ἡδονάς) || واللذات : F || 7 واللذة Bad || 9 أو suppl. Dun || 9 second للذي Dun : الذي F, Bad, Dun : فسيكون الذي Ax || 9 فستكون للذي Ax, Bad || 11 لمكان suppl. mrg. || 13 خلا Dun : خلى F; على Ax, Bad

activity, and it is thought that the like of these deeds are those which are related to virtue, for noble, virtuous deeds are among[132] those which are chosen for themselves. And similarly pleasant amusements, for people do not choose them for any other thing. The harm which affects people in consequence of them is more than the profit, and often a man who loves happiness neglects[133] bodies and possessions, and has recourse to[134] making use of the conditions which are like this,[135] since[136] those[137] who behave in this kind of way, enjoy the favour of tyrants. For they render themselves pleasant in those things which the tyrants desire, and they need these people. It is thought that these amusements afford happiness because the possessors of power are occupied with them. (4) It may be that these do not afford an example, since virtue and intelligence from which virtuous actions proceed do not depend on power. Therefore, since they have not tasted pure unmixed pleasure, they have recourse to the bodily pleasures, and therefore these are thought more desirable. For boys think that the best[138] things are those which are honoured among themselves, and it may well be that, as valuable things appear different among boys and men, so it is with the vicious and the meritorious. (5) The valuable and pleasant things, as has been said many times, are those which are such in the opinion of the good, and in the opinion of every one a most desirable activity is that which corresponds to his special state, and in the case of the good man too[139] that which is in accordance with virtue. So then happiness does not lie in amusement. (6) It is absurd that the end should be amusement, and that one should spend one's life in actions and should toil all one's life.[140] For in general we seek all that we seek for the sake of something else—except happiness, because it is an end, and to strive and toil for the sake of amusement is vain and superficial and very child-

---

[132] MS. *hiya* with *ẓ* (*ẓāhir*) written above it, corr. mrg. *min*, cf. Greek τῶν δι' αὑτὰ αἱρετῶν.

[133] Corr. *yatahauwanu* for *yutahāwanu* of the text.

[134] Corr. *ilā* with mrg., but of course the Arabic translation has gone wrong.

[135] Greek τῶν εὐδαιμονιζομένων οἱ πολλοί has dropped out (Arberry).

[136] Greek διό, 'on which account', scarcely rendered by Arabic *min ajl an*.

[137] Greek εὐτράπελοι has dropped out (Arberry).

[138] Arabic *aqwā*, lit. 'strongest', for Greek κράτιστα, as usual.

[139] Arabic *aiḍan* for Greek δή probably read as δέ.

[140] Greek τοῦ παίζειν χάριν has dropped out (Arberry).

ويظنّ أنّ مثل هذه الأعمل التي تنسب إلى الفضيلة فإنّ الأعمل الجيلد الفاضلة من التي تختار لذاتها وكذلك اللذينة من أنواع اللعب فإنّهم لا يختارونها لشئ آخر والضرر الذي يلخل عليهم منها أكثر من المنفعة وكثيراً ما محبّ السعادة يتهوّن بالأجساد والقنية ويهرب إلى تصرّف الحالات التي مثل هذه من أجل أنّ الذين في مثل هذا التصرّف يحظّون عند المتغلّبة فإنّهم يصيّرون ذواتهم لذينة في التي يشتهونها المتغلّبة وهم يحتاجون إلى هؤلاء وإنّما يظنّ بهذه أنّها ذات سعادة من أجل [٣/٧٠] أنّ أصحاب المقدرة يشتغلون بها (٤) وخليق ألاّ يكونوا لهؤلاء مثل ما من أجل أنّه ليست في المقدرة والعقل التي منها الأفعل الفاضلة ومن أجل هذا لمّا كانوا لم يذوقوا اللذّة المحضة الخالصة يهربون إلى اللذّات الجسمية ومن أجل هذا يظنّ بها أنّها أكثر اختياراً فإنّ الصبيان يرون أنّ أقوى الأشياء التي عندهم مكرمة فخليق أن يكون كما أنّ ظهور الأشياء الكريمة عند الصبيان غيرها عند الرجل كذلك يكون عند ذوي الرداءة وذوي الاستئهل (٥) فالأشياء الكريمة واللذينة كما قيل مراراً كثيرة التي هي مثل هذه عند الأفاضل وعند كلّ واحد فعل مختار جدّاً الذي يكون على موافقة هيئته الخاصية وعند الفاضل أيضاً الذي يكون على الفضيلة فإذاً ليست السعادة في اللعب (٦) فمحل أن يكون التمام لعباً وأن يتصرّف في الأعمل ويتعب في جميع العمر فإنّا بالجملة نروم كلّ ما نرومه من أجل شئ آخر ما خلا السعادة لأنّها تمام والحرص والتعب من أجل اللعب باطل وظاهر ولائق بالصبيان جدّاً فأمّا الحرص على

---

1 هذه corr. Dun : هؤلاء F, Ax, Bad || 1 من corr. mrg. : هي F, Ax, Bad || 3 يتهون corr. Dun : يتهاون F, Ax, Bad || 4 إلى corr. mrg., Ax, Dun : من F, Bad || 4 من F, Ax, Dun : ومن Bad || 5 يشتهونها F, Ax : يشتهيها Bad || 5 وهم corr. Bad : وهو F, Ax || 6 ذات corr. Bad : ذو F, Ax || 7 لهؤلاء مثل F, Ax, Dun ; لها ولامثل Bad || 15 نروم w.p.

ish. As for striving after amusement,[141] it is at first[142] thought to be right, since amusement resembles rest, and those who are not strong
1177a enough to continue to labour, need rest. So rest is not the end of happiness, since it is for the sake of the activity. It is thought that the happy life is according to virtue, and this is only with virtue,[143] not in amusement. (7) And we say that the virtuous things are more excellent than the laughable things connected with amusement, and we say that the activity of the more excellent part of the body and the more excellent man is always more virtuous, and the activity of the more excellent is more excellent and happier. (8) Perhaps the bodily pleasures can be enjoyed by any one, and the enjoyment of the slave is not less than that of the best man, but no one attributes happiness to the slave, whose life is not his own.[144] So then happiness does not lie in the like of these doings, but is in virtuous actions, as was said also at first.

7. If happiness is an activity in accordance with virtue, then it is right that it should be in accordance with the best virtue,[145] and that this should be of what is best, whether that is intelligence or something else, thought to rule and have precedence by nature and to possess reflection concerning excellent and divine things, whether it is also divine, or is the divinest part of what is in us. So then the activity of this in accordance with its particular virtue is complete happiness. That it is theoretical[146] has already been said. (2) It may be thought that this is agreed among the ancients[147] and the speakers of truth,[148] since this activity is best,[149] and that it is intelligence of what is in us and of the knowable things which the intelligence embraces.[150] And it is most continuous, since it is intelligence, and we are better able

---

[141] Arabic *fa-ammā al-hirṣ ʿalā ʾl-laʿb*. Greek παίζειν δ' ὅπως σπουδάζῃ is misunderstood.

[142] Arabic *fī ʾl-ibtidāʾ*. This is for κατ' Ἀνάχαρσιν translated as κατὰ τὴν ἀρχήν (Arberry).

[143] Greek σπουδή, as well as ἀρετή, is here rendered by the same Arabic word, *faḍīlah*.

[144] Arabic *alladhī laisa ʿumruhu ilaihi* is not right for Greek εἰ μὴ καὶ βίου.

[145] Arabic *al-faḍīlah al-qawīyah*, cf. n. 138.

[146] The subject must be 'happiness'.

[147] Arabic *al-qudamāʾ* for Greek τοῖς πρότερον, perhaps read as τοῖς προτέροις.

[148] Arabic *aṣ-ṣādiqīna* for Greek τῷ ἀληθεῖ.

[149] Arabic *qawī*, lit. 'strong' (Greek κρατίστη), cf. n. 138.

[150] The ellipse of κράτιστος, κράτιστα has been missed by the Arabic translation.

اللعب فيظنّ به في الابتداء أنّه صحيح من أجل أنّ اللعب يشبه الراحة والذين لا يقوون على دوام التعب يحتاجون إلى الراحة فليست الراحة تمام السعادة من أجل أنّها تكون لمكان الفعل ويظنّ بالعمر السعيد أنّه على الفضيلة وإنّما يكون هذا مع فضيلة لا في اللعب (٧) ونقول إنّ الفاضلة أجود من المضحكة التي مع اللعب ونقول إنّ فعل العضو الأجود والإنسان الأجود أفضل أبداً وفعل الأجود أجود وأكثر سعادةً (٨) وعسى أن يتملّى من اللذّات الجسمية من أدرك وليس بدون تملّي المملوك والأخير وليس ينسب أحد السعادة إلى المملوك الذي ليس عمره إليه فإذاً ليست السعادة في مثل هذه التصرّفات بل هي في الأفعل الفاضلة كما قيل أيضاً أوّلاً.

٧. وإن كانت السعادة فعلاً على الفضيلة فبحقّ أن تكون على الفضيلة القوية وأن تكون هذه للأجود كان ذلك عقلاً أو شيئاً آخر يظنّ به أنّه يرأس بالطبع [٣/٨١] ويتقدّم وله فكرة في الجياد والإلهية كان هو أيضاً إلهياً أو كان الإلهي جدّاً ممّا فينا فإذاً فعل هذا على فضيلته الخاصية هو السعادة التامّة وأمّا أنّها رائية فقد قيل (٢) وعسى أن يظنّ بهذا أنّه مقرّ به عند القدماء والصادقين من أجل أنّ هذا الفعل قوي وأنّه عقل ما فينا والمعلومات التي يحيط بها العقل وهو متّصل جدّاً من أجل أنّه العقل وأحرى أن يقوى على استعمل الرأى

---

2 دوام F, Ax : دوامة Bad || 2 ليست corr. : ليس F || 4 المضحكة F, Bad, Dun : الضحكة Ax || 6 الأخير corr. Dun* (τοῦ ἀρίστου) : الاسير F, Bad; الامير Ax || 10 يراس F, Ax : يرئس Bad || 12 رائية corr. Arberry (θεωρητική) : ذاتية F, Ax, Bad || 13 عقل F, Ax, Dun : عقلي Bad

to employ reflection continuously than we are to act at some time.[151] (3) We think that happiness must be mingled with pleasure. It is admitted that the most pleasant of the activities which are related to virtue are those which are according to wisdom, and it is sometimes thought that philosophy has pleasures marvellous for intelligence and permanence, and it is right that they should be for those who know in a special manner[152] among those who seek, (4) and that what is called self-sufficiency[153] is mostly concerned with what is near to theory. For the wise man and the just man and the rest need the things which are necessary for life, and when these are sufficiently supplied, the just man needs those among whom and with whom to act justly, and similarly the temperate man also, and the brave man, and each of the others. But the wise man is able to employ theory[154] when he is alone, and also the wiser he is, the more adequately he does that. Perhaps it is better when he has helpers in
1177b the action, yet he is most self-sufficient. (5) Perhaps it may be thought that this alone is loved for itself, for nothing comes of it, save the employment of theory, while from practical pursuits[155] we gain either more or less than what belongs to the action.[156] (6) Happiness is thought to depend on leisure, since we are busy in order to be at leisure, and we make war in order to have security and peace. The actions of the virtues[157] are those which are related to operation in political matters and[158] those which are related to war. But the operations which are related to them are thought to be those which are busy.[159] Warlike actions are so entirely, for no one chooses to make war in order to make war, or is the cause of preparations for war. Perhaps it would in any case be thought that to the man who renders friends enemies so that there should be wars and killing, there attach the contamination and guilt of slaughter. The activity of the fighting man[160] is that he should be busy, and gain by his politi-

---

[151] Arabic *fī waqt mā*, apparently misreading ὁτιοῦν as ὅτε οὖν.

[152] Arabic *bi-ḍarb khāṣṣī*, represents Greek ἡδίω τὴν διαγωγήν, the construction of ἡδίω (with τῶν ζητούντων) not being understood.

[153] The Arabic sentence runs on.

[154] Arabic *istiʿmāl ar-raʾy*, Greek θεωρεῖν.

[155] Arabic *dhawāt al-fiʿl*, apparently i.e. τῶν πρακτικῶν, the reading of K[b].

[156] Arabic *mimmā li'l-fiʿl* for Greek παρὰ τὴν πρᾶξιν (not 'of what').

[157] Greek πρακτικῶν has been omitted.

[158] The Greek is ἤ, 'or'.

[159] I.e. lack leisure, for Greek ἄσχολοι εἶναι.

[160] Arabic *al-muḥārib*, evidently mistranslating τοῦ πολεμικοῦ for τοῦ πολιτικοῦ (Arberry).

بالاتّصل من أن يفعل في وقت ما (٣) ويرى أنّه ينبغي أن تخالط السعادة اللذّة ويقرّ به أنّ ألذّ الأفعل التي تنسب إلى الفضيلة التي تكون على الحكمة فقد يظنّ بالفلسفة أنّ لها لذّات عجيبة بالذكاء والثبات وبحقّ أن تكون للذين يعلمون بضرب خاصّي من الذين يطلبون (٤) وأن تكون التي تقل كفاية أكثر ذلك فيما يلي الرأي فإنّ الأشياء التي يضطرّ إليها للحياة يحتاج إليها الحكيم والعادل وسائر ذلك وإذا رزق هؤلاء الكفاف فالعادل منهم يحتاج إلى الذين يعدل فيهم ومعهم وكذلك العفيف أيضاً والنجد وكلّ واحد من الأخر وأمّا الحكيم فإنّه يقوى على استعمل الرأي إذا كان وحده وأيضاً كلّما كان أحكم كان أحرى أن يفعل ذلك وعسى أن يكون ذلك أجود إذا كان له أعوان في الفعل إلاّ أنّه ذو كفاية جدّاً (٥) وعسى أن يظنّ هذه فقط تحبّ لذاتها فإنّه لا يكون منها شئ ما خلا استعمل الرأي وأمّا من ذوات الفعل فإنّا نتّخذ إمّا أكثر وإمّا أقلّ ممّا للفعل (٦) ونظنّ أنّ السعادة في البطالة من أجل أنّا نشتغل لنبطّل ونحارب لنكون في سلامة وصلح فأفعل الفضائل التي تنسب إلى العمل في الأشياء المدنية والتي تنسب إلى الحرب وأمّا الأعمل التي تنسب إليها فيظنّ بها أنّها التي تشتغل وأمّا الحربية فبنوع كلّي فإنّه لا يختار أحد أن يحارب ليحارب ولا يكون علّة تهيئة حرب فعسى يظنّ على كلّ حل أنّ الذي يصيّر الأصدقاء أعداء حتّى تكون حروب وقتل تلزمه نجاسة القتل ومضرّته وفعل المحارب

---

3 تكون Bad : يكون Ax || 4 يضطر Ax, Dun : نضطر Bad || 9 تحب read. Dun* (ἀγαπᾶσθαι) : تجب F, Ax, Bad || 14 تكون Ax : يكون Bad || 14 فعسى [أن] suppl. Ax : فعسى F, Bad

cal activity[161] itself power and honours, or gain for himself and for the citizens the happiness which is different from the political activity,[162] and which we plainly seek as being different. (7) If the political and warlike actions surpass the actions which are related to the virtues[163] in nobility and greatness, and these are unleisured and aim at a certain end and are not desirable for themselves, and the activity of the intelligence is thought to be distinguished in seriousness, since it employs theory, and does not desire to have any other end at all except itself, and if it has its own pleasure, and by the growth of this pleasure the activity grows, and the self-sufficiency, leisure and rest,[164] to the extent to which these are alike, and all the other things which are related to the fortunate man and are thought to be owing to the same activity, then[165] complete happiness is this, when it has received a complete period of the life of man, for nothing belonging to happiness is not complete. (8) Such a life is higher than that it should be related to man. For man's life is not the condition[166] *qua* man, but in so far as there is in him something divine, and according as this is distinct from the composite, so is its activity distinct from the activity of the other virtues,[167] and according as the intellect is divine by comparison with man, so also the life which is related to it is divine, when it is annexed to human life. And the thoughts of man should not be human, even if he is man, as certain people advise, nor should his thoughts be mortal, since he is subject to death, but he should render them immortal, as far as possible, and do everything with a
1178a view to living life according to the best that is in him,[168] and if

---

[161] Arabic *ḥarakah*, lit. 'movement'.

[162] Arabic *al-madanīyah*, elsewhere used alone for ἡ πολιτική [sc. ἐπιστήμη], cf. 1180b 31-32, 1181a 23. In the present passage *al-ḥarakah* is probably to be understood with *al-madanīyah* in accordance with the context, cf. the translators (Ross: "a happiness different from political action", Gauthier: "bonheur qui est autre que l'activité politique").

[163] I.e. Greek προέχουσιν is taken as governing τῶν [...] πράξεων.

[164] Arabic *ar-rāḥah* for Greek ἄτρυτον is not right. Gauthier now gives "la durée illimitée".

[165] Arabic *fa'innahu*. The Arabic translator perhaps did not realise that here began the apodosis of the whole long sentence.

[166] Arabic *'alā hādhihi* seems to have dropped out before *al-ḥāl*, lit. 'upon this condition', rendering οὕτω, for which cf. 1164b 2.

[167] Arabic *sā'ir al-faḍā'il* for Greek τὴν ἄλλην ἀρετήν. This translation is given by Rackham ("the other forms of virtue") and Gauthier ("les autres vertus"), but it seems to be wrong and "the other kind of virtue" (Ross) to be right. Cf. below, 1178a 9, when the same Greek phrase is rendered differently.

[168] Arabic *aqwā mā fīhi* for Greek κατὰ τὸ κράτιστον τῶν ἐν αὑτῷ.

[٣/٧٢] أنّه يشتغل ويكتسب بحركته للمدينة التي بعينها قدرة وكرامات أو يكتسب السعادة لذاته وللمدنيين التي هي غير المدنية وبيّن أنّا نطلبها على أنّها أخرى (٧) وأمّا إن كانت الأعمل المدنية والحربية تفوق الأعمل التي تنسب إلى الفضائل بالحسن والعظم وكانت هذه مشغولة وتشتهي تماماً ما وليست مختارة لذاتها وكان يظنّ بفعل العقل أنّه ينفصل بالاجتهاد إذ كان يستعمل الرأي ولا تشتهي أن يكون له تمام آخر البتّةَ غير ذاته وإن له لذّة خاصّية وهذه اللذّة بنموها ينمي الفعل والكفاية والبطالة والراحة على ما هي تشبه وجميع سائر الأشياء التي تنسب إلى ذي الغبطة ويظنّ أنّها بالفعل بعينه فإنّه تكون السعادة التامّة هذه إذا ظلّت مدّة تامّة من عمر الإنسان فإنّه ليس شئ ممّا للسعادة ليس بتمام (٨) والعمر الذي مثل هذا أرفع من أن ينسب إلى إنسان فإنّه ليس عمره [على هذا] الحل على أنّه إنسان بل على أنّ فيه شيئاً إلهياً وعلى قدر انفصل هذا من المركّب كذلك انفصل فعله من فعل سائر الفضائل وعلى قدر ما أنّ العقل إلهي بإضافته إلى الإنسان كذلك والعمر الذي ينسب إليه إلهي إذا أضيف إلى العمر الإنسي فينبغي ألاّ تكون همم الإنسان إنسية وإن كان إنساناً كما يشير المشيرون بذلك ولا أن تكون هممه ميّتة إذ هو ميّت بل ينبغي أن يصيّرها علامة موت على قدر ما يمكن وأن يفعل كلّ شئ على أن يحيا

1 يشتغل read. above line : w.p. F || 1 للمدينة F, Bad, Dun : للمدنية Ax || 1 بعينها F, Dun : يعينها read. Ax, Bad || 2 هي F, Bad : من Ax || 2 اخرى read. Ax*, Dun* (ἑτέραν) : أحرى F, Bad || 3 بالحسن Ax, Dun : بالجنس F, Bad || 4 ما om. Bad || 5 ينفصل F*, Ax*, Dun* (διαφέρειν) : ينفعل Bad || 6 تشبه F, Bad, Dun : يشبه Ax || 7 يظن Bad : نظن Ax || 7 بالفعل F, Ax, Dun : الفعل Bad || 8 إذا ظلت F*, Bad*, Dun* (λαβοῦσα) : اذ اقلت Ax || 9 على هذا suppl. Dun || 10 انفصل corr. mrg. : انفعل F || 13 كان corr. Bad, Dun : كانت F, Ax

it is small in bulk, yet in power and excellence it surpasses all by far. (9) It may be thought that every man is this, since it is the ruling and better part, and it would be absurd that one should not choose his own life but the life of another. What was said at first must be said now also, that what is special for each is best by nature and pleasant for each, and so for man likewise the life which is related to the intellect, since this is man most of all. So then this life is the happiest also.

8. The life which is related to another virtue[169] is happy in a secondary way, since its activities are human. For just and courageous actions and the rest of the doings which we do to each other according to the virtues in transactions and wants and all the actions and emotions through safeguarding each of the things,[170] for it appears that all these are human. (2) It is thought of some of them that they arise from the body, and that moral virtue resembles very much the emotions[171] (3) and temperance itself,[172] since the first principles of practical wisdom[173] are according as practical wisdom envisages them, and through the emotions they are concerned with what is composite. The virtues of what is composite are human and the individual's life also and similarly his happiness.[174] The happiness of the intellect[175] is separate. So much is said about it; an investigation into that is beyond our present purpose. (4) Perhaps it may be thought that it needs ethical acquirement[176] from outside, slight or small.[177] As for the necessities, both require them, and the need is[178] equal. The political man toils more in what is connected with the body and everything similar, and differs only a little. In the activities, however, there is a great difference, because the free man needs money

---

[169] Arabic *faḍīlah ukhrā*, but Greek is 'the other virtue' (τὴν ἄλλην ἀρετήν).

[170] Arabic *li-ḥafẓ kull wāḥid min al-ashyā'*. Something has apparently dropped out corresponding to τὸ πρέπον.

[171] Greek συνέζευκται [...] ἤθους ἀρετῇ is omitted, as noted by Arberry, owing to homoioteleuton

[172] Arabic *wa 'l-ʿiffah bi-ʿainihā*, i.e. Greek αὕτη read as αὐτῇ, but also *wa 'l-ʿiffah* (= σωφροσύνη) appears to have been written in error for *at-taʿaqqul* (= φρόνησις).

[173] Greek τὰς ἠθικάς [...] κατά has dropped out (homoioteleuton in κατά).

[174] I.e. omitting ὁ and reading κατὰ ταῦτα for κατὰ ταύτας.

[175] Arabic *saʿādat al-ʿaql*. This is also Rackham's translation, but it seems that what is meant is the virtue or excellence of the intellect (so Ross and Gauthier).

[176] I.e. τῆς ἠθικῆς taken with χορηγίας (Arberry).

[177] Arabic *ṣaghīr au qalīl* for Greek ἐπὶ μικρὸν ἢ ἐπ' ἔλαττον. The meaning is of course lost already through construing τῆς ἠθικῆς wrongly (see previous note).

[178] Arabic *wa-takūn*. The force of ἔστω is lost.

حية أقوى ما فيه وإن كان صغيراً بالعظم لكنّه بالقوّة والكرم يفوق الجميع كثيراً (٩) وخليق أن يظنّ أنّ كلّ واحد هو هذا إذا كان المسود الأجود ويكون محالاً ألاّ يختار مختار عمر ذاته بل يختار عمر غيره وينبغي أن يقل الآن أيضاً ما قيل أوّلاً إنّ الخاصّ عند كلّ واحد أقوى بالطبع ولذيذاً عند كلّ واحد فإذ سيكون عند الإنسان كذلك العمر الذي ينسب إلى العقل إذ كان هذا إنساناً أكثر ذلك فإذاً هذا هو السعيد جدّاً أيضاً.

٨. وأمّا الذي [٣/٧٣] ينسب إلى فضيلة أخرى فسعيد بنوع ثانٍ من أجل أنّ أفعالها إنسية فإنّ الأفعل العادلة والنجدية وسائر الأعمل التي نستعملها فيما بيننا على الفضائل في المعاملات والحوائج وجميع الأفعل والانفعالات لحفظ كلّ واحد من الأشياء فإنّه يظهر أنّ جميع هذه إنسية (٢) ويظنّ أنّ بعضها أيضاً يعرض من الجسم وأنّ فضيلة الخلق تشاكل الانفعالات كثيراً (٣) والعفّة بعينها إذ كانت أوائل التعقّل على قدر التعقّل بها وبالانفعالات تكون في المركّب وفضائل المركّب إنسية وعمره أيضاً وسعادته كذلك وأمّا سعادة العقل فمنفصلة والقول فيها بهذا القدر وأمّا الفحص في ذلك فلعرض أكثر من هذا (٤) وعسى أن يظنّ أنّه يحتاج إلى اكتساب خلقي يكون من خارج صغيراً أو قليلاً أمّا الأشياء المضطرّة فبكلّيتها إليها حاجة وتكون بالسوية والمدني أكثر تعباً فيما يلي الجسد وجميع ما يشبهها وإنّما يخالف اختلافاً قليلاً وأمّا في الأفعل فكثير الاختلاف فإنّ ذا

2 عمر corr. Ax, Bad : عمره F || 4 أقوى corr. Dun : قويا F, Ax; قوي Bad || 9 بعضها F, Bad : ببعضها Ax || 9 يعرض Bad : تعرض Ax || 10 العفة F, Ax, Dun : الفطنة Bad || 11 first و F*, Ax*, Dun* (καί) : أو Bad || 12 فلعرض F, Bad : فلغرض Ax || 14 المدني F : البدني corr. mrg. || 15 يخالف Bad : تخالف Ax

in order to do the actions of freedom, and similarly the just man needs it in requiting, since wishes are not clear, and those who are not just pretend that they wish to do justly. The brave man needs strength, if he is to do that in which there is virtue. The temperate man needs power,[179] in order that it may be clear if he is so, and if one of the rest is.[180] (5) The question is asked whether the choice is
1178b more worthy of[181] virtue, or the actions, as if it depended on both. The perfection, it is plain, is in both, but for it to be in the actions there is need for many discussions, and the greater and more excellent the actions, there is need for more. (6) He who employs reflection has no need for anything like this for the sake of the activity. Rather it may be said that that hinders the employment of reflection. If[182] he is a man and chooses[183] that his life should be with a large number, he will need to[184] do the actions of virtue in order to live the life of mankind, and will not need such.[185] (7) That complete happiness is a reflective activity will appear from this also. We think that the gods are most of all fortunate and happy. What actions then must be attributed to them? For if just acts are attributed to them, that will appear ridiculous, since they will have commercial transactions, repayment of deposits and everything like that. And if there are attributed to them courageous actions, they will encounter alarms and danger, and if it is good that something of the actions of freedom should be attributed to them,[186] it will be absurd in them to have *dīnārs* or anything like this. And if temperate actions are attributed to them, what is this except a detraction from praise, since they have no evil desires? If all actions are reckoned, it will appear that they are contemptible and unworthy to be mentioned of the gods. Yet everyone thinks that they have life, and then they have activity, be-

[179] Arabic *tasalluṭ* for Greek ἐξουσίας.

[180] The interrogation is missed (Arberry).

[181] Arabic *aḥaqq* (Greek κυριώτερον).

[182] Arabic *in*, i.e. ᾖ read as εἰ.

[183] I.e. the Arabic translator has taken αἱρεῖται with συζῇ which he has read as συζῆν (Arberry).

[184] Greek δεήσεται is construed (wrongly) with πράττειν and again with τῶν τοιούτων ('will not need such').

[185] The mistake is due to a misreading of δεήσεται οὖν as δεήσεται δ' οὐ (Arberry).

[186] Arabic *wa-in kāna jaiyidan an yunsaba ilaihim shai' min af'āl al-ḥurrīyah*, i.e. running together ὅτι καλόν [...] δώσουσιν and forcing the translation. The words *shai' min af'āl* are from mrg. and perhaps an unnecessary addition, cf. a few lines above 'just acts', Arabic *al-'adlīyah*, for Greek τὰς δικαίας [sc. πράξεις].

الحرّية يحتاج إلى أموال ليفعل أفعل الحرّية وكذلك العادل يحتاج إليها فيما يجازي به من أجل أنّ الإرادات ليست بيّنة والذين ليسوا بعدول يراؤون أنّهم يريدون العمل بالعدل ويحتاج النجد إلى قوّة إذ كان يفعل ما فيه الفضيلة والعفيف يحتاج إلى التسلّط لكي يكون بيّناً إن كان كذلك وإن كان أحد الباقية (٥) ويطلب هل الاختيار أحقّ بالفضيلة أو الأفعل كأنّها كلاهما وأمّا التمام فبيّن بأنّه يكون في كليهما وأمّا في أن يكون في الأفعل فإنّه يحتاج إلى أقاويل كثيرة وكلّما كانت الأفعل أكبر وأجود يحتاج إلى أكثر (٦) وأمّا الذي يستعمل الرأي فليس يحتاج إلى شئ مثل هذا لمكان الفعل بل يمكن أن يقل إنّ ذلك يمنع من استعمل الرأي وإمّا إن كان إنساناً وكان يختار أن يكون عمره مع كثرة فإنّه سيحتاج أن يفعل أفعل الفضيلة ليتصرّف تصرّف الناس ولا يحتاج إلى مثل هذه (٧) [٣/٧٤] وأمّا أنّ السعادة التامّة فعل ما رأيي فسيظهر من هذا أيضاً فإنّا نرى أنّ الآلهة أكثر ذلك ذوو غبطة وسعادة فأيّ أفعل ينبغي أن ينسب إليهم فإنّه إن نسب إليهم العدلية فسيظهر ذلك أنّه أهل أن يضحك به إذ تكون لهم معاملات وردّ ودائع وسائر ما يشبه هذه الأشياء وإن نسب إليهم الأفعل النجدية كانوا يلقون الأشياء المفزعة وما فيه العطب وإن كان جيّداً أن ينسب إليهم شئ من أفعل الحرّية فسيكون فيهم شيئاً محالاً أن تكون لهم دنانير أو شئ مثل هذا وإن نسبت إليهم الأفعل العفّية فما هذا إلاّ نقلاً من المدح من أجل أنّهم ليست لهم شهوات رديئة فإن أحصيت جميع الأفعل فسيظهر أنّها صغيرة لا تستأهل أن تقل على الآلهة ولكن كلّ يرى أنّ لهم حيلة فإذاً لهم فعل من أجل أنّهم لا ينبغي أن يكونوا نياماً

3 || Bad تحتاج : Ax يحتاج first 3 || F, Ax ليس : corr. Bad ليسوا 2 || Ax ببينة : F, Bad بينة 2
F, Ax إذ : corr. Dun إن first 4 || Bad تفعل : Ax, Dun يفعل 3 || F, Ax, Bad النجدة : Dun النجد
F, يمنع 7 || F, Ax, Bad أكثر : read. Dun أكبر 6 || Ax انه : F, Bad بانه 5 || om. Bad و first 4 ||
تنسب : Ax ينسب 11 || Bad فايما : F, Ax فأي 11 || F, Ax ذو : corr. Bad ذوو 10 || Bad يمتنع : Ax
15 || Ax يكون : Bad تكون 14 || suppl. mrg. شئ من افعل 14 || Ax يكون : Bad تكون 12 || Bad
Ax يقل : Bad تقل 16 || Ax يستاهل : Bad تستأهل 16 || F, Bad فعلا : corr. Ax, Dun نقلا

cause they must not be asleep, like Endymion, since there is removed from them the activity of the living,[187] and what remains to them of activity more than the employment of reflection?[188] So then the activity of God which excels in felicity will be reflective, and the human activity resembling this activity is happiness.[189] (8) The proof of that is that the other animals do not have happiness like that, since they completely lack an activity like this, because the life of those who are perfect[190] affords felicity, since the activity is like this also, and among men, according to the extent to which there is in them a likeness to this activity. But there is nothing happy among the other animals, since they do not employ reflection in anything whatsoever.[191] Happiness also is among those who employ reflection more and those who are happy [not] by chance but by the employment of reflection, for this in itself is very much a matter of thinking.[192] So then happiness will be a kind of reflection. (9) Being a man, one will need external wellbeing, for there is not in man's nature a sufficiency for the employment [of reflection], but he needs also health
1179a of body and a supply of food and the remaining services. But it must not be supposed, if it is impossible that he should enjoy felicity without external goods, that the possessor of happiness needs many and great things. For sufficiency is not in excess,[193] nor judgement, nor actions.[194] (10) One who is not a ruler by land and sea can do virtuous actions, for a man can be of humble origins[195] and perform the deeds of virtue. That can be clearly seen, for it is not thought that humble men do less of what they ought than the powerful, but they do virtuous deeds more than the others. In these things when they exist there is sufficiency, since the life of the man who is active with virtue will be happy. (11) Solon perhaps spoke well when he judged

---

[187] Arabic *idh nufiya ʿanhum fiʾl al-aḥyāʾ*, i.e. disregarding the stop after τὸν Ἐνδυμίωνα and construing τῷ ζῶντι τοῦ πράττειν together as a single phrase. The sentence goes wrong.

[188] Greek ἐτὶ δὲ μᾶλλον τοῦ ποιεῖν is construed with the following words τί λείπεται πλὴν θεωρία rather than (correctly) with the preceding τοῦ πράττειν ἀφαιρουμένου.

[189] Arabic *saʿādah*, weak for Greek εὐδαιμονικωτάτη.

[190] Arabic *dhawī ʾt-tamām*, i.e. τοῖς μὲν γὰρ τελείοις for τοῖς μὲν γὰρ θεοῖς (Arberry). The change may be intentional.

[191] Greek ἐφʼ ὅσον δὴ διατείνει ἡ θεωρία has dropped out by homoioteleuton.

[192] Arabic *fikrīyah* for Greek τιμία taken as = 'depending on estimation'.

[193] Arabic *isrāf* for Greek ὑπερβολῇ.

[194] I.e. οὐδʼ ἡ κρίσις οὐδʼ αἱ πράξεις, the reading of M^b (Arberry).

[195] Arabic *min al-auḍāʿ*. It is noticeable that Greek ἀπὸ μετρίων is so rendered, perhaps because the translator belonged to the upper ranks of society.

كحل أنلمين إذ نفي عنهم فعل الأحياء وما الذي يبقى أن يكون لهم من الفعل أكثر من استعمل الرأي فإذاً فعل الإله الذي يفضل بالغبطة سيكون رأياً والفعل الإنسي المجانس لهذا الفعل يكون سعادة (٨) والدليل على ذلك أنّ سائر الحيوان ليست له سعادة مثل ذلك إذ قد عدم فعلاً مثل هذا علماً تامّاً من أجل أنّ عمر ذوي التمام يغتبط به إذ كان الفعل مثل هذا أيضاً وأمّا في الناس فعلى قدر ما فيهم مثل ما من هذا الفعل وأمّا سائر الحيوان فليس فيه شيء سعيد من أجل أنّه لا يستعمل الرأي في شيء من الأشياء والسعادة أيضاً في الذين يستعملون الرأي أكثر والذين هم سعداء [لا] بنوع عرضي بل استعمل الرأي فإنّ هذه بذاتها فكرية جدّاً فإذاً ستكون السعادة رأياً ما (٩) وسيحتاج إذا كان إنساناً إلى حسن الحال الخارجي فإنّ الطبيعة ليس فيها كفاية لاستعمل بل ويحتاج إلى صحّة الجسم وأن يكون له غذاء وسائر الخدمات له ولكن لا ينبغي أن يتوهّم أنّ صاحب السعادة يحتاج إلى أشياء كثيرة عظيمة إذ كان لا يمكن أن يكون مغبوطاً من غير الخيرات الخارجة فإنّ [٣/٧٥] الكفاية ليست في الإسراف ولا للقضاء ولا الأعمل (١٠) فقد يمكن أن يفعل الأفعل الجياد من ليس بالوالي على الأرض والبحر فإنّه يمكن أن يكون إنسان من الأوضاع وأن يعمل أعمل الفضيلة ويمكن أن يرى ذلك بيّناً فإنّه لا يظنّ بالأوضاع أنّهم أقلّ فعلاً ممّا ينبغي من ذوي القدرة بل هم أكثر فعلاً لها من أولئك وفي هذه كفاية إذا كانت من أجل أنّه سيكون عمر الفاعل بالفضيلة سعيداً (١١) وعسى أن يكون صولن نعم ما قل حين

1 كحل F, Bad, Dun : مثل Ax (ὥσπερ) || 1 أنلمين w.p. F : اندومين Ax || 1 إذ F, Ax : إن Bad || 1 وما F, Ax : فما corr. Bad || 4 يغتبط F, Bad : مغتبط Ax || 7 لا suppl. Ax*, Dun* (οὐ) || 8 فكرية F, Bad, Dun : كريمة Ax* (τιμία) || 8 إذا F, Bad : اذ Ax || 9 بل F, Ax : وبل Bad || 10 الخدمات corr. Dun : الخادمات F, Ax || 12 الإسراف read. Bad*, Dun* (ὑπερβολῇ) : الإشراف F, Ax || 12 للقضاء F, Bad, Dun : القضاء Ax || 15 ذوي F, Ax : أولي Bad || 15 القدرة F, Bad : المقدرة Ax || 16 الفاعل F*, Ax*, Dun* (ἐνεργοῦντος) : الفاضل Bad

that the happy are those who have been provided with a moderate amount of external goods and have done noble actions, as if[196] their life were temperate. And it is possible to do what is right though one possesses little. It seems that Anaxagoras also did not think that the happy man was rich or powerful, when he said that he would not be surprised if he appeared to the majority as ridiculous, for they define by the things which are external, since those are the only things they perceive. (12) It seems that the decisions[197] of the wise are in agreement with the arguments, for in these is conviction. The truth in deeds, however, only becomes clear from actions and life, for what is certain depends on these. So we must consider what was said at first, when it has been brought to [the test of] actions and life, and if [our arguments] are in agreement with the facts, they are to be accepted. If they disagree, they are to be thought of as mere words. (13) He who is intellectually active and cultivates the intellect and whose condition is excellent[198] is likely to be a great lover[199] of God. For if there is care for humanity[200] on the part of the gods, as is thought, and according to what is right,[201] and they rejoice in what is most excellent and they rejoice in what is most akin, and this is the intellect. So then it is most fitting that they should do good to those who love them most, and honour them[202] and take care of them, like friends and because their activity is a right and noble activity. That all this belongs mostly to the wise man is not unknown and is not concealed. So then he is a great lover of God, and it is right that he himself should be most happy also. So then if the wise man is in this situation, it is most fitting that he should be happy.

9. Is there enough then[203] in what has been said about these matters and about the virtues and also about friendship and pleasure? Must it

---

[196] This is apparently ὥσπερ read for ὡς ᾤετο.

[197] Arabic *ʿazāʾim*, Greek δόξαι.

[198] The Greek καὶ διακείμενος ἄριστα is similarly taken, i.e. as a clause parallel to κατὰ νοῦν ἐνεργῶν and καὶ τοῦτον θεραπεύων and part of the subject, by Rackham, but apparently wrongly.

[199] Arabic *muḥibban li'llāh jiddan*, i.e. θεοφιλέστατος is taken as active.

[200] Arabic *taʿāhud li'n-nās*, i.e. τῶν ἀνθρώπων read for τῶν ἀνθρωπίνων.

[201] I.e. Greek καὶ εἴη ἂν εὔλογον construed with the foregoing words. Modern translators begin the apodosis here.

[202] Arabic *yuḥibbūnahum akthar wa-yukrimūhum*, the latter word subjunctive, depending on the preceding *an*, but Greek is τοὺς ἀγαπῶντας μάλιστα τοῦτο καὶ τιμῶντας.

[203] Greek εἰ is not rendered.

قضى أنّ السعداء الذين قد رزقوا القصد من الأشياء الخارجة وفعلوا الأفعال الجيّدة كأنّ عمرهم بعفّة فقد يمكن أن يفعل ما ينبغي الذي يقني القليل وقد يشبه أن يكون أنكساغورس أيضاً لا يرى أنّ السعيد غنيّ ولا ذو مقدرة حين قل إنّه لا ينبغي أن يتعجّب إن ظهر للأكثر أنّه محل ما قل هؤلاء يحلّدون بالتي من خارج إذ كانوا يحسّون بهذه فقط (١٢) وقد يشبه أن تكون عزائم الحكماء موافقة للأقاويل فإنّ في هذه قنوعاً وأمّا الحقّ في الأعمل إنّما يبين من الأفعل والعمر فإنّ في هذه المحقّق وينبغي أن ننظر ما قيل أوّلاً إذ نقلت إلى الأفعل والعمر فإن هي وافقت الأعمال قبلت وإن هي خالفت ظنّ بها ما يظنّ بالكلمة (١٣) وأمّا الذي يفعل بعقل وكانت خلمته للعقل وحاله جيّدة فقد يشبه أن يكون محبّاً للّه جدّاً فإنّه إن كان يكون تعاهداً للناس من الآلهة كما يظنّ وعلى ما يحقّ وكانوا يفرحون بالأفضل وإنّهم يفرحون بالمجانس جدّاً وهذا هو العقل وإذاً أحرى أن يحسنوا إلى الذين يحبّونهم أكثر ويكرمونهم ويتعاهدونهم كالأصدقاء ومن أجل أنّ فعلهم فعل صحيح جيّد وأمّا أنّ جميع هذا للحكيم أكثر ذلك فليس بمجهول ولا خفي فإذاً هو محبّ للإله جدّاً ويحقّ أن يكون هو بعينه سعيداً جدّاً أيضاً فإذاً إذ كان الحكيم على هذه الحل فأحرى أن يكون سعيداً.

٩. فهل فيما قيل في هذه وفي الفضائل وأيضاً في الصداقة واللذّة كفاية وينبغي أن يظنّ أنّه

1 الخارجة F, Ax : الخارجية Bad || 1 كأن F, Dun : كان Bad || 2 يقني F, Bad : يقتني Ax || 3 يتعجب F, Ax, Dun : نتعجب Bad || 4 للاكثر corr. Ax, Dun : الأكثر F, Bad || 4 يحلدون F*, Ax*, Dun* (κρίνουσι) : يجودون Bad || 4 إذ كانوا يحسون F*, Ax*, Dun* (αἰσθανόμενοι) : إذا كان يحيون Bad || 6 إنما F, Ax, : فإنما Bad || 6 وينبغي F, Bad : فينبغي Ax || 10 بالأفضل : F repeats بالأفضل فإنهم يفرحون بالمجانس || 10 بالمجانس Dun : بالمحاسن F, Ax, Bad || 11 كالأصدقاء F, Ax, Dun : والأصدقاء Bad || 15 fourth و F, Ax : أو Bad

be thought that there must be choice of the various types[204] or, as is
1179b said, in what is practical it is not an end that reflection should be employed in all of them and that it should be known, but that there should be action in them? (2) For there is not enough in knowledge of virtue, but it must be possessed, and we must seek to employ it, or employ something else in order to become good somehow, unless[205] there is enough in discourses.[206] (3) And rightly many great pledges would be brought[207] in obtaining them, as Theognis and Adarnās[208] said. As it is, it appears that they have the power to stir and rouse up to movement generous youth, and make [a young man] equally[209] noble and loving the excellent in truth, since they impart virtue to him.[210] As for the majority, they have no power to rouse them up to excellence, (4) since they do not obey the sense of honour but fear, and do not refrain from evil deeds on account of their baseness but on account of the penalty. For because they live by passions, they seek their own pleasures and the things through which these pleasures come and avoid the corresponding pains. But of the excellent and the truly pleasant they have not even an idea, since they have not tasted it. (5) What argument then can alter these men? For it is not possible, or not easy, that what has become rooted in longstanding habits over a period should be altered by talk, and perhaps we must be content, when all the things are ours which are considered most excellent, to get a glimpse[211] of virtue. (6) It is thought that some people are naturally good[212] and some through instruction. As to what is by nature, plainly its existence does not depend on us, but is owing to some divine care for those whose luck is really good. But the operation of argument and teaching is not effective[213] in all. Rather the soul of him who is to listen to instruction must have been

---

[204] I.e. τὴν προαίρεσιν construed with τοῖς τύποις (Arberry).

[205] I.e. the Arabic translator has read εἰ μὲν οὐκ ἦσαν for εἰ μὲν οὖν ἦσαν (Arberry) and has construed wrongly.

[206] Greek πρὸς τὸ ποιῆσαι ἐπιεικεῖς is omitted.

[207] Perhaps πίστεις (or πιστούς, Arberry) for μισθούς (MS. *tuḥmal īmānun*).

[208] Text uncertain. The corruption 'and Adarnās [?]' may have arisen from καὶ ἔδει ἄν. The rest of the phrase <ἐν> τούτους πορίσασθαι apparently gave rise to Arabic *fī iktisābihā*.

[209] Arabic *bi's-sawīyah*, no doubt ἴσως read for ἰσχύειν (Arberry).

[210] Arabic *idhā 'khtabarat ʿalaihi al-faḍīlah*. Greek κατοκώχιμον hardly seems rendered.

[211] Arabic *naqtabis*, lit. 'obtain a light from a fire already burning'.

[212] The words οἱ δ' ἔθει have dropped out (Arberry).

[213] The force of μή [...] οὐκ is disregarded.

ينبغي أن يكون [٣/٧٦] بالاختيار بالرسوم أو كما يقل ليس فيما يفعل تمام أن يستعمل الرأي في كلّها وأن يعلم بل إنّما يكون العمل فيها (٢) فإنّه ليس في معرفة الفضيلة كفاية بل ينبغي أن تقتنى وأن يرام استعمالها أو استعمل شئ آخر لنصير أخياراً بنوع ما لو لم يكن في الأقاويل كفاية (٣) فبحقّ ما كانت تحمل أيمان كثيرة وعظيمة في اكتسابها كما قل ثاوغونس وأدرناس وأمّا الآن فقد يظهر أنّها تقوى على أن تهيج وتنهض بالحركة ذوي الحرّية من الأحداث ويصيّر بالسوية شريف الجنس ومحبّ الجيّد بالحقيقة إذا اختبرت عليه الفضيلة وأمّا الأكثر فلا يقوى على أن ينهض حركتهم إلى جودة الخير (٤) من أجل أنّهم لا ينقادون بالحياء بل بالفزع ولا يمتنعون من الرداءات لمكان القبيح بل لمكان العذاب فإنّه لمّا كانوا يحيون بالانفعل طلبوا لذّات أنفسهم والأشياء التي بها تكون هذه ويهربون من الأحزان المقابلة بالوضع وأمّا الجيّد والذي هو بالحقيقة لذيذ فليس عندهم ولا فكرة له إذ لم يذوقوه (٥) بأيّ قول يمكن أن يغيّر هؤلاء فإنّه لا يمكن أو ليس بهيّن أن يغيّر بالكلام ما قد ثبت بالأخلاق القديمة زماناً كثيراً وعسى أن نكون نحبّ إذا كانت لنا جميع الأشياء التي يرى أنّها تكون أفاضل أن نقتبس الفضيلة (٦) ويظنّ أنّ بعض الناس يكونون أخياراً بالطبع وبعضاً بالتعليم وأمّا ما يكون من الطبيعة فبيّن أنّه ليس كونه إلينا بل إنّما يكون بعناية ما إلهية للذين بختهم جيّد بالحقيقة وأمّا القول والتعليم ففعل لا يقوى في كلّ بل ينبغي أن تكون نفس الذي يستمع التعليم قد استعملت بالعادة لتحبّ

---

2 يكون corr. Bad : فيها F, Ax || 2 العمل F, Ax : بالعمل Bad || 2 فإنه F, Bad : فإنها Ax || 3 أو F*, Dun* (ἤ) : و corr. mrg., Ax || 4 أيمان F, Ax, Dun : أثمان Bad || 5 ثاوغونس w.p.; ثاوغنوس Ax || 5 وأدرناس F, Bad, Dun : وارد ناس Ax || 6 يصير Bad : تصير Ax || 7 يقوى Ax, Dun : تقوى Bad || 9 بالانفعل corr. Dun* (πάθει) : بالأفعل F, Ax, Bad || 11 بأي F, Bad : فأي Ax || 11 first أن Ax, Dun : أو F, Bad, Dun || 13 يظن Bad : نظن Ax || 14 وأما F, Ax, Dun : فأما Bad

habitually employed to love and hate aright, as the earth loves the seed which it nourishes. (7) For he who lives by passion does not hear any argument which would turn him aside from something nor does he understand it, and how can the conviction of one who is in this case be altered? In general, it is not thought that these passions yield to reason but to force. (8) Character must precede virtue and have an affinity for it in some way, and love the good and avoid the base. But for true virtue to be attained[214] from a young man's life[215] is difficult without his being brought up under like laws, since the practice of temperance with hardiness is not pleasant to the majority.[216] Also the food and exercises of the young should be measured by laws also, for they are not painful when a habit has been formed
1180a and the actions follow. (9) Perhaps it is not enough that the young should get the right food and attention, but should employ them,[217] when they have grown up,[218] and should become accustomed to them, and we shall need laws here and in general in the whole of life. For the majority obey necessity more than they obey reason, and their obedience is to loss[219] rather than the noble. (10) Hence some persons think that lawgivers should aim at the reception of virtue and prescribe that for the sake of the noble, since the deserving[220] who have had the custom previously would obey them, and should impose various punishments and penalties on whoever does not obey and is intractable by nature, and that whoever is absolutely incurable should be driven away. For the deserving man who lives for the noble is convinced by reason, while the bad man who desires pleasure must be chastised by pain, like a beast of burden. For this reason they say that the pains must be such as are most opposed to the pleasures which they love. (11) So, as has been said, he who will be good must employ what is necessary for life,[221] and not do what is bad either willingly or unwillingly. These things are only for those

---

[214] Arabic *an tuṣābu faḍīlah ṣaḥīḥa*. But the Greek is ἀγωγῆς ὀρθῆς [...] πρὸς ἀρετήν, "a right training for virtue" (Ross).

[215] Arabic *min sīrat ḥadath*, Greek ἐκ νέου.

[216] Greek ἄλλως τε καὶ νέοις has dropped out.

[217] Arabic *yasta'milūhā*, i.e. with αὐτά of the vulg. as against ἄττα, a conjectural reading, approved by Thomas, Susemihl and Gauthier (i.e. *certain* rules).

[218] Arabic *idhā tarajjalū*. This translates Greek ἀνδρωθέντας; ἐπειδή is not translated.

[219] Arabic *khasārah*, but ζημίαις here is for 'penalties', cf. 1132a 10 = V, 4, 4.

[220] Arabic *dhawū 'l-isti'hāl*, but this translates Greek τῶν ἐπιεικῶς.

[221] Greek τραφῆναι καλῶς, 'to be well brought up', is evidently left untranslated, also καὶ ἐθισθῆναι, εἶθ' οὕτως (Arberry).

وتبغض نعماً كمحبّة الأرض الزرع الذي تربّيه (٧) فإنّ الذي يعيش بالانفعال لا يسمع قولاً يردّ عن شئ ولا يفهمه ومن كان على هذه الحال فكيف يمكن أن يغيّر قنوعه وبالجملة لا يظنّ أنّ هذه الآلام الخلقية تنقاد للكلام بل للقهر (٨) وينبغي أن يكون الخلق قبل الفضيلة وأن يكون خاصّاً بها بنوع ما وأن يحبّ الجيّد وينفر عن القبيح وأمّا أن تصاب [٣/٧٧] فضيلة صحيحة من سيرة حدث فعسير إلاّ أن يكون قد ربّي بنواميس مثل هذه من أجل أنّ استعمل العفّة بنوع الصبر ليس بلذيذ عند الأكثر وأيضاً ينبغي أن يقدّر غذاء الأحداث وأفعالهم بالنواميس أيضاً فإنّها لا تكون محزنة إذا كانت العادة قد جرت بها (٩) وعسى ألاّ يكون في اتّخاذ الغذاء والتعاهد الصحيح للأحداث كفاية بل ينبغي إذا ترجّلوا أن يستعملوها وأن يعتادوها ويحتجون في ذلك إلى نواميس وبالجملة في جميع العمر فإنّ الأكثر ينقادون لضرورة أكثر من انقيادهم للقول وللخسارة أكثر من انقيادهم إلى الجيّد (١٠) ومن أجل هذا يرى بعض الناس أنّه ينبغي لواضع النواميس أن يطلبوا في قبول الفضيلة وأن يفرضوا ذلك من أجل الجيّد إذ كان يطيعهم ذوو الاستئهال الذين قد تقدّمت فيهم العادة وأن يضعوا أنواع العذاب والنقمة على من لم يطع وكان صعب الطبيعة ومن كان لا برء له البتّةَ أن ينفى فإنّ ذا الاستئهال الذي يحيا للجيّد يقنع بالقول وأمّا الردئ الذي يشتهي اللذّة فينبغي أن يعاقب بالحزن كالدابّة ولهذا قالوا إنّه ينبغي أن تكون أحزان مثل هذه التي أحرى أن تضادّ للذّات المحبوبة (١١) فكما قيل ينبغي للذي سيكون خيراً أن يستعمل ما ينبغي للحيلة وألاّ يفعل الردئ لا بإرادته ولا بغير إرادته وإنّما تكون هذه الأشياء

1 يسمع Ax*, Dun* (ἀκούσειε) : يسيغ F, Bad || 2 يفهمه F*, Ax*, Dun* (συνείη) : يقيمه Bad || 5 ربي corr. Ax*, Dun* (τραφέντα) : رضي F, Bad || 9 يحتجون corr. Bad : يحتجوا F, Ax || 10 لضرورة F, Bad : للضرورة Ax || 11 الناس F, Bad : اناس Ax || 12 ذلك Dun* : ذلك ولا F || 12 كان يطيعهم F, Ax, Dun : بطبيعتهم Bad || 13 النقمة F*, Ax*, Dun* (κολάσεις) : النفقة Bad || 14 يحيا للجيد corr. Arberry* (πρὸς τὸ καλὸν ζῶντα) : يحب الجيد F, Ax; يحمى للجيد corr. mrg. Ax || 15 يعاقب F*, Bad*, Dun* (κολάζεσθαι) : يهذب Ax || 16 تضاد F, Bad : تضادا Ax

who live by intelligence and a right order possessing force. (12) There is not in the command of a father either power or compulsion nor in the command of any man at all, unless he is a king [or] like a king. The law, however, has constraining power, since it is a statement derived from a certain intelligence and understanding. Men are the enemies of those who oppose them in their actions,[222] even if they do so rightly. But the law is not a burden when it enjoins what is right. (13) It is thought that the lawgiver has ordered the care of sustenance and the disposal of actions with small means[223] in the city of the Lacedaemonians only. In most of the cities consideration of things of this kind has been missed, and everyone lives as he wishes and cares for his children and his wife in the manner of the Cyclops. (14) The most decisive[224] thing is that there should be proper general supervision, such that it can be employed.[225] When it is missed from the community, each individual should be concerned[226] for his children and his friends, and that they should be helped to virtue, and that they should choose it. A man would best be able for these things, from what has already been said, who has become a lawgiver, for it is plain that general supervision exists only through the laws, and good men[227] exist through good laws, whether
1180b written or unwritten. For perhaps there is no difference in regard to that, nor in regard to whether one person or many[228] are to be educated by means of them, just as there is no difference in the case of music and gymnastic skill[229] and the other activities. For just as matters of the law and customs[230] are powerful in cities, so in the household words of the fathers and customs, and they are stronger also on account of the family relationship and the various benefits, and even before that the people honour them and obey nature. (15) Also, be-

---

[222] Arabic *bi'l-af'āl* for Greek ταῖς ὁρμαῖς, "impulses" (Ross).

[223] Arabic *maʿa ashyāʾ qalīlah*, but Greek μετ' ὀλίγων is usually taken to mean 'along with a few (others)', i.e. ὀλίγων is masculine.

[224] Arabic *aṣram* for Greek κράτιστον; elsewhere κράτιστον is rendered *qawī*, *aqwā*, 'strong', 'strongest' (1174b 19, 29, 1176b 22, 1178a 5-6, etc.). Probably a misreading of the copyist.

[225] Arabic *yumkin an yustaʿmala*, i.e. the words καὶ δρᾶν αὐτὸ δύνασθαι are in the traditional place in the text.

[226] Arberry's conjecture *munhamman* seems right, but the Arabic falters as a translation of the Greek.

[227] The Arabic translator takes ἐπιεικεῖς as masculine and omits αἱ.

[228] MS. *au kathīr*, Greek ἢ πολλοί.

[229] Arabic *thaqāfah*. Elsewhere Greek γυμναστική is rendered *riyāḍah* (1112b 5), *ʿilm ar-riyāḍah* (1096a 34).

[230] I.e. the translator read ἔθη (M^b) for ἤθη.

للذين يعمرون بعقل ونظم صحيح ذي قوّة (١٢) وليس في أمر الآباء القوّة ولا الضرورة ولا في أمر رجل واحد البتّةَ إلاّ أن يكون ملكاً [أو] كما الملك وأمّا الناموس فإنّ له قوّة تقهر إذا كان قولاً من عقل ما وفهم وهم يعادون الذين يضادّونهم بالأفعال وإن فعلوا ذلك بنوع صحيح وأمّا الناموس فليس يثقل إذ كان يرتّب ما ينبغي (١٣) ويظنّ بواضع النواميس أنّه أمر باهتمام الغذاء وتصرّف الأعمال مع أشياء قليلة في مدينة لاقلادامونيا فقط وأمّا في أكثر المدن فقد ضيّع النظر في مثل هذه ويحيا كلّ واحد كما يريد ويهتمّ كاهتمام كلاوش بأولاده وامرأته (١٤) وأصرم الأشياء أن يكون تعاهد عامّ صحيح ما يمكن [٣/٧٨] أن يستعمل وإذا ضيّع من الجماعة فينبغي أن يكون كلّ واحد مهمّاً بأولاده وأصدقائه وأن يعانوا الفضيلة وأن يختاروها وأحرى أن يقوى على هذه الأشياء ممّا قد قيل الذي صار واضع نواميس فإنّه بيّن أنّ التعاهد العامّي إنّما يكون بالنواميس وذوو الاستئهل يكونون بالأشياء الفاضلة كانت مكتوبة أو غير مكتوبة فإنّه عسى ألاّ يكون في ذلك اختلاف ولا في التي يؤدب بها واحد أو كثير كما أنّه لا اختلاف في الموسيقى والثقافة وسائر الأعمال فإنّه كما أنّ الأشياء الناموسية والعادات قوية في المدن كذلك في البيت أقاويل الآباء والعادات وهو أقوى أيضاً لمناسبة الجنس وأنواع المنفعة وهم قبل ذلك يكرمون وينقادون للطبيعة (١٥) وأيضاً فيما

---

1 الأباء F, Bad : الأب Ax || 1 القوة corr. Bad : لقوة appar. F; بالقوة Ax || 2 واحد F*, Ax*, Dun* (ἑνός) : آخر Bad || 2 أو suppl. Bad, Dun || 4 يثقل corr. Bad : ثقل F; بثقل Ax || 5 باهتمام الغذاء F, Ax, Dun : بالاهتمام بالغذاء Bad || 5 لاقلادامونيا corr. Ax, Bad, Dun : لاملحامونيا F || 6 كلاوش F, Ax : قوقلوفس corr. Bad || 7 أصرم F : اجزم corr. mrg.; أقوى Ax; أهرم Bad || 7 third و om. Ax || 8 مهما corr. Arberry : منهم F, Ax, Bad || 8 وأن om. Bad || 8 يعانوا corr. : يعانون F, Ax, Bad || 9 وإن يختاروها F : وان يختارونها corr. Ax; ويختارها corr. Bad || 10 ذوو corr. Bad : ذو F, Ax || 11 يؤدب corr. Ax*, Dun* (παιδευθήσονται) : يوجب F, Bad || 14 لمناسبة corr. Ax : المناسبة F, Bad, Dun

tween partial and universal studies there is a difference, just as there is in medicine. In general, abstinence from food and rest are better for the man with a fever, but perhaps are not best for someone. The wrestling master, it may be, does not arrange the same fight for everyone. It would rather seem[231] that the partial receives thorough investigation when the supervision is special, since to each there accrues what there should.[232] But everyone provides excellent supervision,[233] whether he be physician or trainer, and everyone who has acquired universal knowledge of what is for all rather than[234] he who has learned what is for the like of these people, since the sciences are said to be, and are, concerned with what is general. (16) Yet it may be that no single thing is prevented from excellent supervision, even if its supervisor is not scientific, but has set down[235] accurately owing to experience what occurs in each one, like some doctors[236] who are thought to be very good in regard to themselves while unable to suffice others in anything. So perhaps it would be thought that whoever wishes to be master of a skill and a theory must take the path of what will lead him to the universal, none the less, and let him know that also as far as possible. It is with this, as has already been said, that the sciences are concerned. (17) Perhaps he who wishes to render people better through care, whether they are many or few, should try to be a legislator, if we become good through laws. For not every chance person is able to make a good arrangement, even the one which is described.[237] Rather, if that exists for anyone, it is for him who knows, as in the case of medicine and the rest of the skills there is a certain supervision and understanding. (18) After this is it necessary to examine whence or how a man becomes a legislator, since that is in regard to political matters[238] as it is in all others matters? It was thought that legislation was a part of the political art. Or does it not seem that it is alike in politics and the rest of the sciences and

---

[231] I.e. Greek μᾶλλον is construed with δόξειεν ἄν instead of with ἐξακριβοῦσθαι.

[232] Greek μᾶλλον in the following line is left untranslated, or has dropped out.

[233] Greek καθ' ἕν is not rendered.

[234] Arabic *mā li'l-kull akthar min* for Greek τί πᾶσιν ἢ τοῖς τοιοιδί [or τοιοῖσδε], 'what is for all or for people of a certain kind [for such people]'. Confusion of ἤ = 'or' and ἤ = 'than' is not infrequent, cf. 1148a 19, 1164b 32, 1169a 23.

[235] Arabic *qad waḍaʿa*, i.e. τιθέμενον or θέμενον for τεθεαμένον.

[236] Arabic *baʿḍ al-aṭibbā'*. The construction is wrong.

[237] Arabic *wa-lā al-mauṣūf aiḍan*. This is apparently for ὅντινα [read as οὐδένα] [...] καὶ τὸν προτεθέντα, or ὅντινα is simply omitted.

[238] Arabic *min al-ashyā' al-madanīyah* for Greek παρὰ τῶν πολιτικῶν which is masculine. The second question introduced by ἤ is disregarded.

بين الآداب الجزئية والعامّية اختلاف كما هو في الطبّ فبالجملة ترك الطعام والسكون هو أجود للمحموم وعسى ألاّ يكون أجود لبعض وصاحب الصراع عسى ألاّ يصنع لكلّ مقاتلة واحدة وأحرى أن يظنّ بالجزئي في الاستقصاء فيه إذ كان يكون التعاهد خاصّياً من أجل أنّه يصير إلى كلّ واحد ما ينبغي ولكن إنّما يتعاهد كلّ واحد تعاهداً جيّداً طبيباً كان أو مثاقفاً فكلّ واحد من الذي يعلم علماً كلّياً ما للكلّ أكثر من الذي يعلم ما لمثل هؤلاء من أجل أنّ العلوم يقل إنّها للعامّي وهي للعامّي (١٦) إلاّ أنّه خليق ألاّ يمنع شئ واحد تعاهداً جيّداً وإن متعاهده ليس بعالم إلاّ أنّه قد وضع باستقصاء ما يعرض في كلّ واحد لمكان التجربة كبعض الأطبّاء الذين يظنّون أنّهم يجيدون في أنفسهم ولا يقدرون على أن يكفوا غيرهم بشئ فعسى أن يكون يظنّ أنّه ينبغي للذي يريد أن يكون ذا مهنة ورأي أن يسلك سبيل ما يصير به إلى الشئ الكلّي ليس بدون وليعلّم ذلك أيضاً على ما يمكن فقد قيل إنّ العلوم في هذا (١٧) وعسى أن يكون ينبغي للذي يريد أن يصيّر بالتعاهد قوماً أجود إمّا كثيرين وإمّا قليلين أن يروم ليكون واضع نواميس إن كنّا نصير أخياراً بالنواميس فإنّه ليس يقدر كلّ من أدرك أن يضع وضعاً [٣/٧٩] جيّداً ولا الموصوف أيضاً بل إن كان ذلك لأحد فإنّه للذي يعلم كما في الطبّ وسائر المهن تعاهد ما وفهم (١٨) فهل بعد هذا ينبغي أن نفحص من أين أو كيف يكون إنسان واضع نواميس إذ ذلك يكون من الأشياء المدنية كما يكون في سائر الأشياء فقد كان يظنّ بوضع النواميس أنّه جزء للصناعة المدنية إذ لا يظهر أنّ ذلك يشبه في المدنية سائر العلوم والقوى فإنّ في سائر الأشياء يظهر أنّ الذين

3 مقاتلة corr. Dun* (πυκτικός) : معالجة F, Ax, Bad, معاجلة Arberry || 3 يظن Bad : نظن Ax || 3 بالجزئي corr. Ax, Dun : بالجزء في F, Bad || 5 الذي يعلم F : التي تعلم Ax, Bad || 5 second يعلم F, Bad : تعلم Ax || 7 متعاهده F, Bad : تعاهده Ax || 7 يعرض corr. Ax*, Dun* (συμβαίνοντα) : يفرض F, Bad || 8 كبعض F*, Ax*, Dun* (ἔνιοι) : كفعل Bad || 8 يجيدون corr. Ax*, Dun* (ἄριστοι εἶναι) : يجيلون F, Bad || 9 يكفوا F*, Bad*, Dun* (ἐπαρκέσαι) : يكنفوا Ax || 9 و F*, Ax*, Dun* (καί) : أو Bad || 14 تعاهد F, Ax : بتعاهد Bad || 15 نفحص Bad : يفحص Ax || 17 first أن suppl. above line || 17 المدنية Ax, Dun : المدينة Bad

faculties? For in all other things it appears that those who teach the faculties are those who practise them, e.g. doctors and writers,[239]
1181a whereas in politics the experts[240] promise to teach it, and not one of them practises it. Rather it is thought that those who are engaged in politics practise it by a certain faculty, and they would seem to practise it by experience rather than thought, for it does not appear that they write or speak anything on these matters, and perhaps that is better than to compose controversial and obscure[241] speeches, and it would rather be incumbent on them to compose political speeches,[242] if they could do so,[243] since that might afford the cure of themselves[244] or others of their friends. (19) For they would not have left to the cities anything better, to be a substitute for them,[245] than this faculty,[246] nor to their friends either. It is not that the concurrence of experience is negligible. Without it no one would have been a politician from habit, therefore people[247] who desire to know the political art require to have experience. (20) As for those experts[248] who promise to teach politics, it appears that they are very far from doing so. For they absolutely do not know what it is nor with what matters it is concerned. Otherwise they would not think that it and rhetoric are the same, or that it is inferior to rhetoric, nor would they think that legislation is easy for him who collects successful laws. For as to the choice of the best,[249] they think that the choice also does not occur except through the understanding, and to judge correctly is a great thing,[250] as in the different kinds of music. For it is those who have experience[251] in everything who judge correctly of the works,

---

[239] Arabic *al-kuttāb* for Greek γραφεῖς, 'painters'.

[240] Arabic *al-muḥakkimīn* for Greek οἱ σοφισταί.

[241] Arabic *'awīṣah* for Greek δημηγορικούς.

[242] I.e. πολιτικούς wrongly construed with λόγους.

[243] The words 'it would rather [...] if they could do so' are from § 19: εὔλογον δ' ἦν, εἴπερ ἐδύναντο construed with the foregoing.

[244] Arabic *bur' dhawātihim* (ὑγιεινούς for υἱεῖς, Arberry).

[245] Arabic *li-yakūna lahā 'iwaḍan*, apparently ἀνθ' αὑτῶν for οὔθ' αὑτοῖς (Arberry).

[246] Greek προέλοιντ' ἄν is left untranslated.

[247] Arabic apparently *li-hā'ulā'i*. As Arberry notes, the translator seems to have read τούτοις instead of διό.

[248] I.e. the Sophists (Greek σοφισταί), as above, n. 240.

[249] Arabic *fa'inna 'l-ikhtiyār li'l-afāḍil*, i.e. Greek ἐκλέξασθαι γὰρ εἶναι τοὺς ἀρίστους, but the sentence goes awry.

[250] Leg. *kabīr* (renders μέγιστον).

[251] Arabic *tajārib* is plural.

يعلّمون القوى هم الذين يفعلون بها مثل الأطبّاء والكتّاب وأمّا الأشياء المدنية فإنّ المحكمين يعدون أن يعلّموها وليس أحد منهم يفعلها بل يظنّ أنّ الذين يستعملون السيرة المدنية يفعلون ذلك بقوّة ما وأحرى أن يفعلوا ذلك بالتجربة من أن يفعلوا ذلك بفكرة فإنّه لا يظهر أنّهم يكتبون أو يقولون شيئاً في هذه وعسى أن يكون ذلك أجود من وضع أقاويل خصومية وعويصة وقد كان أحرى أن يجب عليهم وضع الأقاويل المدنية لو كانوا يقدرون عليها إذ في ذلك برء ذواتهم أو ذوات آخرين من الأصدقاء (١٩) فإنّهم لم يكونوا يخلفون للمدن شيئاً أجود البتّةَ ليكون لها عوضاً منهم من هذه القوّة ولا للأصدقاء أيضاً وليس بأنّ موافقة التجربة صغيرة ولو لا ذلك لم يكن أحد مدنياً من العادة لهؤلاء الذين يشتهون يعملون الصناعة المدنية ينبغي أن تكون لهم تجربة (٢٠) وأمّا الذين يعدون أنّهم يعلّمون من المحكمين فيظهر أنّهم بعيدون من ذلك جدّاً فإنّهم لا يعلمون البتّةَ ما ذلك ولا في أيّ الأشياء ولو لا ذلك لم يكونوا يرون أنّها والريطوريقى شئ واحد ولا أنّها أردأ من الريطوريقي ولم يكونوا يرون أنّ وضع النواميس هيّن على الذي يجتمع ما ينجح من النواميس. فإنّ الاختيار للأفاضل يرون أنّ الاختيار أيضاً لا يكون إلاّ بالفهم والقضاء بالصحّة كبير كالتي تكون بأنواع الموسيقى فإنّ أصحاب التجارب في كلّ شئ الذين

---

2 يعلموها F*, Ax*, Dun* (διδάσκειν) : يفعلوها Bad || 5 خصومية read. Ax, Bad, Dun : حضومية F || 5 لو corr. Dun : إذ F, Ax || 6 برء F, Ax, Dun : بدء Bad || 7 أجود om. Bad || 8 مدنيا Ax*, Dun* (πολιτικοί) : مدينا F, Bad || 8 لهؤلاء F, Ax, Dun : فهؤلاء Bad || 13 للأفاضل F, Ax, Dun : الأفاضل corr. Bad || 14 كبير read. Dun* (μέγιστον) : كثير F, Ax, Bad

and know by what means they come into existence[252] and how and which agrees with which, while from the inexperienced it is to be wished that they should not[253] know if the performance of the work is good or bad, as is the case with writing.[254] As for the laws, they
1181b are like political works. How then from these does a legislator come into existence or judge in regard to the best? (21) For that does not appear [in the case of doctors, whose experience] is not [from] scrolls of books.[255] And if[256] they desire to speak not merely of treatments but also of how the cure takes place and how each individual should be treated, and classify the states—this is thought to be useful to the man of experience but for those who do not know unnecessary—, perhaps political assemblies[257] and laws also are suitable to those who are capable of reflection and judgement on the good or its opposite, or it is easy[258] to employ whichever of them is necessary for whichever occasion. As for those who begin on these without a state of knowledge, they are not capable of judging aright, unless it is from instinct, and it may be that those who are more intelligent will be more successful in[259] these matters. (22) Since the ancients have left the examination and inquiry about legislation, perhaps it would be better to investigate that[260] and the city[261] in a general way, in order to complete as far as possible the philosophy of human affairs. (23) First of all then, we wish[262] to give an account of any partial good that has been spoken of by the ancients, then to see from the collected polities[263] which of them destroys cities or preserves them, and which of them preserves and destroys each of the

---

[252] Or 'exist' (Arabic *takūn*), which scarcely renders Greek ἐπιτελεῖται.

[253] The negative implied (Arabic *yakhfā*) is due to a misunderstanding of the Greek.

[254] Arabic *li'l-kitābah*, should be 'painting' (Greek γραφικῆς).

[255] Arabic *lā yaẓhar dhālika wa-lā yakūn dhālika qarāṭīs min al-kutub*. Some such reconstruction as that indicated by the words in brackets is necessary. *Qarāṭīs* (plural of *qirṭās*) is evidently for Greek ἐκ τῶν συγγραμμάτων.

[256] Arabic *wa-in*, i.e. καὶ εἰ for καίτοι.

[257] Arabic *ijtimā'āt al-madīnah*, Greek πολιτειῶν has apparently been read as πολίτων.

[258] The construction has gone wrong.

[259] Lit. 'suitable for', Arabic *aufaq*. The Greek is somewhat expanded in the Arabic.

[260] Greek αὐτούς, 'ourselves' is not expressed.

[261] Arabic *al-madīnah*, but read *al-madanīyah*, 'politics', i.e. Richards' emendation.

[262] Arabic *narūma*, Greek πειραθῶμεν is subjunctive, 'let us try'.

[263] Arabic *siyar*, Greek πολιτειῶν.

يقضون بالصحّة على الأعمل ويعلمون بأيّ شئ تكون وكيف وأيّ موافق أيّاً وأمّا الذين لا تجربة لهم فيراد منهم [٣/٨٠] أن يخفي عنهم إن كان فعل العمل نعماً أو بئساً ما كان لكتابة وأمّا النواميس فتشبه الأعمل المدنية فكيف يكون من هؤلاء واضع لنواميس ما أو يقضي على الأفاضل (٢١) فإنّه لا يظهر ذلك ولا يكون ذلك قراطيس من الكتب وإن كانوا يرومون أن يقولوا ليس العلاجات فقط بل وكيف يصير البرء وكيف ينبغي أن يعالج كلّ واحد ويفصّلون الهيئات وهذه يظنّ بها أنّها أمّا لني التجربة فنافعة وأمّا الذين لا يعلمون فليس يحتاجون إليها فعسى أن تكون اجتماعات المدينة والنواميس أيضاً موافقة للذين يقوون على الرأي والقضاء الجيّد أو ضدّ ذلك أو يكون يهون استعمل أيّها ينبغي لأيّ وأمّا الذين يأخذون في هذه من غير هيئة معرفة فليس لهم أن يقضوا نعماً إلاّ أن يكون ذلك من الذات وخليق أن يكونوا أوفق في هذه الذين أكثر فهماً (٢٢) وإذ قد ترك القدماء الفحص والطلب عن وضع النواميس فعسى أن يكون أجود النظر في ذلك وفي المدينة بنوع كلّي ولكي نتمّم على قدر طاقة الفلسفة في الأشياء الإنسية (٢٣) فأوّلاً نروم أن نخبر عن كلّ جيّد جزئي قاله القدماء ثمّ أن نرى من السير المجموعة أيّها يفسد المدن أو يسلّمها وأيّها

---

1 تكون F : يكون Ax, Bad || 2 فيراد F, Ax, Dun : فيرى Bad || 2 بئسا F, Bad, Dun : بئسما Ax || 3 لكتابة read. Ax : لكتابه F, Dun; لكتمانه corr. Bad || 3 لنواميس F, Bad : النواميس Ax || 6 لني Dun : الني F, Ax; لنوي Bad || 7 يحتاجون corr. Ax, Bad : يحتاج F || 7 تكون Bad : يكون Ax || 7 المدينة F, Bad, Dun : المدنية Ax || 11 المدينة F, Dun (πολιτείας) : المدنية corr. Ax, perh. corr. Dun (corr. Richards, πολιτικῆς) || 12 لكي corr. Dun : لكن F, Ax, Bad || 12 طاقة F : الطاقة Ax, Bad || 13 نرى Bad : يرى Ax

polities,[264] and for what causes some of the constitutions become excellent and some the reverse. For when investigation has been made into these things, perhaps we may know more which of the constitutions is better also, and how each of them is laid down, and what it is like[265] in its employing the customs.

The Eleventh Discourse of the book of Aristotle on Ethics which is called *Nīqūmākhiyā* is completed. Praise be to God and peace upon His servants whom He has chosen, and that on Wednesday, 27th *Shaʿbān* the Ennobled of the year 619.

---

[264] See previous note.

[265] Arabic *li-mādhā yushbih*, i.e. Greek καὶ τίσι νόμοις read as καὶ τίσιν ὁμοίοις [or ὅμοιος] (Arberry).

يسلّم ويفسد كلّ واحد من السير ولأيّ علل صارت سير بعضها جيداً وبعضها على ضدّ ذلك فإنّه إذا نظر في هذه فعسى أن يعلم أكثر أيّ السير أجود أيضاً وكيف وضع كلّ واحد منها ولماذا يشبه عند استعمالها العادات.

تمّت المقالة الحادية عشرة من كتاب أرسطو في الأخلاق وهو المسمّى نيقوملخيا والحمد للّه وسلّم على عباده الذين اصطفى وذلك في يوم الأربعاء السابع والعشرون من شعبان المكرّم عام تسعة عشر وستمائة.

---

3 يشبه F, Ax : تشبه Bad || 3 العادات Dun : العادات فلنبدأ ونقل F, Ax, Bad || 5 شعبان F, Bad : شعبن Ax

SELECTIVE BIBLIOGRAPHY

Editions of EN

Aristotle, *Ethica Nicomachea*, ed. Ingram Bywater, Oxford 1890.

—, *The Ethics of Aristotle*, ed. John Burnet, London 1900 (reprinted New York 1973).

—, *Nicomachean Ethics*, ed. and transl. Harris Rackham, London 1926, revised edition 1934 (reprinted London 1999).

—, *L'Éthique à Nicomaque*, ed. and transl. René A. Gauthier and Jean Y. Jolif, 2 vols., Louvain/Paris ²1970.

—, *Ethica Nicomachea* (Aristoteles Latinus; XXVI, 1-3), Leiden/Brussels 1972-1974.

Arīsṭūṭālīs, *Kitāb al-aḫlāq, tarǧamat Isḥāq Ibn Ḥunain*, ed. ʿAbdarraḥmān Badawī, Kuwait 1979.

Axelroth, Dorothy G., *An Analysis of the Arabic Translation of Book Ten of Aristotle's Nicomachean Ethics*, Unpublished PhD thesis with an edition of Book X, The Dropsie College, Philadelphia 1968.

Other Primary Sources

ʿAbd al-Laṭīf al-Baghdadī, *Kitāb al-ifādah wa'l-iʿtibār (The Eastern Key)*, transl. Kamal Hafuth Zand and John A. and Ivy E. Videan, Cairo/London 1204/1964.

Abū 'l-Faraj ibn al-ʿIbrī (Bar Hebraeus), *Ta'rīkh mukhtaṣar ad-duwal*, ed. Anṭūn Salḥānī, Beirut ²1958.

Abū Ḥaiyān at-Tauḥīdī, *Kitāb al-imtāʿ wa'l-mu'ānasah*, ed. Ahmad Amin and Ahmad az-Zain, 3 vols., Beirut n.d.

—, *al-Muqābasāt*, ed. Ḥasan as-Sandūbī, Cairo 1374/1929.

Abū Sulaimān al-Sijistānī, *Muntakhab ṣiwan al-ḥikmah*, ed. Douglas M. Dunlop, The Hague 1979.

al-ʿĀmirī, *Kitāb as-saʿādah wa'l-isʿād*, ed. Mojtaba Minovi (University of Tehran Publications; 435 / The Mahdavi Fund Series; 5), Wiesbaden 1377/1957.

Aristotle, *Ars Rhetorica: The Arabic Version*, a new edition, with commentary and glossary by Malcolm C. Lyons, 2 vols., Cambridge 1982.

—, *Ethica Eudemia*, ed. Franz Susemihl, Leipzig 1884 (reprinted Amsterdam 1967).

—, *Magna Moralia (with Metaphysics, X-XIV, and Oeconomica)*, ed. and transl. G. Cyril Armstrong, London 1958.

Arisṭūṭālīs, *Fī 'sh-shi'r (Aristotle's Poetics)*, ed. Shukrī Muḥammad ʿAyyād, Cairo 1387/1967.

Aspasius, *In Ethica Nicomachea commentaria*, ed. Gustav Heylbut (Commentaria in Aristotelem Graeca; 19/1), Berlin 1889.

Averroes, *La béatitude de l'âme*, ed. Marc Geoffroy and Carlos Steel, Paris 2001.

al-Balādhurī, *Futūḥ al-buldān*, ed. Ṣalāḥ ad-Dīn al-Munajjid, Cairo 1956.

—, *Futūḥ al-buldān (Liber expugnationis regionum)*, ed. Michael J. de Goeje, Leiden 1866.

Dominicus Gundisalvus, *De scientiis*, ed. Manuel Alonso, Madrid/Granada 1954.

Elias, *In Porphyrii Isagogen et Aristotelis Categorias Commentaria*, ed. Adolf Busse (Commentaria in Aristotelem Graeca; 18), Berlin 1900.

al-Fārābī, *Falsafat Arisṭūṭālīs*, ed. Muḥsin Mahdī, Beirut 1961.

—, *Al-Farabi on the Perfect State (Mabādi' ārā' ahl al-madīna al-fāḍila)*, ed. and transl. Richard Walzer, Oxford 1985.

—, *Alfarabius de Platonis Philosophia*, ed. Franz Rosenthal and Richard Walzer (Plato arabus; 2), London 1943.

—, *Fuṣūl al-madanī (Aphorisms of the Statesman)*, edited with an English translation, introduction and notes by Douglas M. Dunlop (University of Cambridge Oriental Publications; 5), Cambridge 1961.

—, *Kitāb al-ḥurūf*, ed. Muḥsin Mahdī, Beirut 1969.

—, *Kitāb iḥṣā' al-ʿulūm (Catálogo de las ciencias)*, ed. Ángel González Palencia, Madrid/Granada ²1953.

—, *Kitāb al-milla wa-nuṣūṣ ukhrā (Book of Religion and Related Texts)*, ed. Muḥsin Maḥdī, Beirut 1968.

—, *Kitāb at-tanbīh ʿalā sabīl as-saʿādah*, Haidarabad 1346/1927.

—, *Der Musterstaat*, transl. Friedrich Dieterici, Leiden 1900 (reprinted Frankfurt am Main 1999).

—, *Philosophische Abhandlungen*, transl. Friedrich Dieterici, Leiden 1892 (reprinted Frankfurt am Main 1999).

—, *Philosophische Abhandlungen aus Londoner, Leidener und Berliner Handschriften*, ed. Friedrich Dieterici, Leiden 1890 (reprinted Frankfurt am Main 1999).

—, *Philosophy of Plato and Aristotle*, translated, with an introduction by Muhsin Mahdi, New York 1962.

—, *Risālah fī 'l-ʿaql*, ed. Maurice Bouyges (Bibliotheca Arabica Scholasticorum; 8/1), Beirut 1938.

—, *Risālah fī arā' ahl al-madīnah al-fāḍilah*, ed. Friedrich Dieterici, Leiden 1895 (reprinted Frankfurt am Main 1999).

—, *As-Siyāsāt* [sic] *al-Madanīyah*, Haidarabad 1346/1927.

Ḥunayn ibn Isḥāq, *Sittensprüche der Philosophen (Kitâb Âdâb al-Falâsifah)*, transl. Karl Merkle, Leipzig 1921.

Ibn al-Abbār, *al-Takmilah li-Kitāb al-ṣila*, ed. ʿIzzat al-ʿAṭṭār al-Ḥusainī, 2 vols., Cairo 1956.

Ibn Abī ʿUṣaibiʿah, *ʿUyūn al-anbāʾ fī ṭabaqāt al-aṭibbāʾ*, ed. Imruʾu l-Qais b. aṭ-Ṭaḥḥan (August Müller), 2 vols., Cairo 1299/1882.

Ibn al-Athīr, *al-Kāmil fī ʾt-tāʾrīkh*, ed. Carolus J. Tornberg, 13 vols., Leiden 1851-1876 (reprinted Beirut 1385/1965-1386/1966).

Ibn Bājjah, *Fī Ittiṣāl al-ʿaql bi ʾl-insān (Tratado sobre la unión del intellecto con el hombre)*, ed. and transl. Miguel Asín Palacios, in: *al-Andalus* 7 (1942), pp. 1-47.

—, *Rasāʾil falsafīyah li-Abī Bakr Ibn Bājjah*, ed. Jamāl ad-Dīn al-ʿAlawī, Beirut/Casablanca 1983

—, *Rasāʾil Ibn Bājjah al-ilāhīya (Opera Metaphysica)*, ed. Majid Fakhry, Beirut 1968.

—, *Risālat al-wadāʿ (La Carta de adiós de Avempace)*, ed. and transl. Miguel Asín Palacios, in: *al-Andalus* 8 (1943), pp. 1-87.

—, *Tadbīr al-mutawaḥḥid* (*El régimen del solitario)*, ed. and transl. Miguel Asín Palacios, Madrid/Granada 1946.

Ibn Juljul, *Ṭabaqāt al-aṭibbāʾ waʾl-ḥukamāʾ* (*Les générations des médecins et des sages*), ed. Fuʾād Sayyid, Cairo 1955.

Ibn Khaldūn, *The Muqaddimah. An Introduction to History*, translated from the Arabic by Franz Rosenthal (Bollingen Series; 43), 3 vols., New York 1958.

—, *Les Prolégomènes d'Ebn Khaldoun (Muqaddimah)*, ed. Étienne Marc Quatremère, 3 vols., Paris 1858.

Ibn an-Nadīm, *The Fihrist of al-Nadīm. A Tenth-Century Survey of Muslim Culture*, transl. Bayard Dodge (Records of Civilization: Sources and Studies; 83), 2 vols., New York/London 1970.

—, *Kitāb al-Fihrist*, ed. Gustav Flügel, 2 vols., Leipzig 1871-1872.

Ibn Rushd, *Averroes' Middle Commentary on Aristotle's Nicomachean Ethics in the Hebrew Version of Samuel ben Judah*, ed. Lawrence Berman, Jerusalem 1999.

—, *Tafsīr mā baʿd aṭ-ṭabīʿa*, ed. Maurice Bouyges (Bibliotheca Arabica Scholasticorum; 5-7), 4 vols., Beirut 1938-1952.

Ibn Ṣāʿid al-Andalusī, *Kitāb ṭabaqāt al-umam (Les catégories des nations)*, ed. Louis Cheikho, Beirut 1912.

—, *Livre des catégories des nations (Kitâb Ṭabaqât al-Umam)*, transl. Régis Blachère, Paris 1935.

Ibn Sīnā, *Kitāb al-ishārāt waʾt-tanbīhāt*, ed. Jacques Forget, Leiden 1892.

—, *Livre des directives et remarques (Kitāb al-išārāt waʾt-tanbīhāt)*, transl. Amélie-Marie Goichon, Beirut/Paris 1951.

—, *Majmūʿ rasāʾil ash-Shaikh ar-Raʾīs*, Haidarabad 1354/1935.

—, *Rasāʾil* (*Traités mystiques)*, August F. Mehren, 4 fasc., Leiden 1889-1899.

Ibn Ṭufail, *Philosophus Autodidactus or Ḥayy ibn Yaqẓān*, transl. Simon Ockley, London 1708 (reprinted Cairo 1905).

—, *Risālat Ḥayy ibn Yaqẓān fī asrār al-ḥikmah al-mushriqiyyah*, ed. and transl. Léon Gauthier, Beirut [2]1936.

Ibn az-Zubair, Abū Ja'far, *Ṣilat aṣ-ṣilah*, ed. Évariste Lévi-Provençal, Paris 1937.

Ibn Zur'ah, *Vingt traités philosophiques et apologétiques d'auteurs arabes chrétiens*, ed. Paul Sbath, Cairo 1929.

al-Kindī, *Rasā'il al-Kindī al-falsafīyah*, ed. Muḥammad 'Abd al-Hādī Abū Rīdah, 2 vols., Cairo 1369/1950-1372/1953.

—, "Studi su al-Kindi I. Uno scritto introduttivo allo studio di Aristotele", ed. Michelangelo Guidi and Richard Walzer, in: *Atti dell'Accademia Nazionale dei Lincei. Memorie. Classe di Scienze Morali, Storiche e Filologiche* 6/5 (1940), pp. 375-419.

Mas'ūdī, *Murūj adh-dhahab wa-ma'ādin al-jauhar (Les prairies d'or)*, ed. and transl. Barbier de Meynard, 9 vols., Paris 1861-1876.

—, *Les prairies d'or (Murūj adh-dhahab wa-ma'ādin al-jauhar)*, transl. Barbier de Meynard and Pavet de Courteille, revised by Charles Pellat, 5 vols., Paris 1962-1997.

Miskawaih, *Tahdhīb al-akhlāq*, ed. Qusṭanṭīn Zuraiq, Beirut 1966.

Moses Maimonides, *Le guide des égarés (Dalālat al-ḥā'irīn)*, ed. and transl. Salomon Munk, 3 vols., Paris 1865-1866 (reprinted Osnabrück 1964).

—, *The Guide of the Perplexed (Dalālat al-ḥā'irīn)*, transl. Shlomo Pines, Chicago 1963.

al-Mubashshir b. Fātik, *Mukhtār al-ḥikam wa-maḥāsin al-kalim*, ed. 'Abdarraḥmān Badawī, Madrid 1958.

Nicolaus Damascenus, *On the Philosophy of Aristotle*, ed. Hendrik J. Drossaart Lulofs, Leiden 1965.

Porphyry, *Porphyrii philosophi fragmenta*, ed. Andrew Smith, fragmenta arabica David Wasserstein interpretante, Stuttgart 1993.

Pseudo-Aristotle, *Die sogenannte Theologie des Aristoteles aus arabischen Handschriften*, ed. Friedrich Dieterici, Leipzig 1882 (reprinted Frankfurt am Main 2000).

al-Qifṭī, *Ta'rīkh al-ḥukamā'*, ed. Julius Lippert, Leipzig 1320/1903.

Simplicius, *Commentaire sur les Catégories*, ed. Ilsetraut Hadot, transl. Philippe Hoffmann, fasc. I, Leiden 1990.

aṭ-Ṭabarī, *Ta'rīkh ar-rusul wa 'l-mulūk (Annales)*, ed. Michael J. de Goeje *et al.*, 15 vols., Leiden 1879-1901.

Theophrastus of Eresus, *Sources for His Life, Writings, Thought and Influence*, ed. and transl. William W. Fortenbach *et al.*, 2 vols., Leiden 1992.

al-Ya'qūbī, *Ta'rīkh (Historiae)*, ed. Martijn Th. Houtsma, 2 vols., Leiden 1883.

Yāqūt, *Jacut's Geographisches Wörterbuch [Mu'jam al-buldān] aus den Handschriften zu Berlin, St. Petersburg, Paris, London und Oxford*, ed. Ferdinand Wüstenfeld, 6 vols., Leipzig 1866-1870.

Secondary Literature

Akasoy, Anna A. / Fidora, Alexander, "Hermannus Alemannus und die *alia translatio* der *Nikomachischen Ethik*", in: *Bulletin de philosophie médiévale* 44 (2002), pp. 79-93.

Arberry, Arthur J., "An Arabic Treatise on Politics", in: *The Islamic Quarterly* 2 (1955), pp. 9-22.

—, "The *Nicomachean Ethics* in Arabic", in: BSOAS 17 (1955), pp. 1-9.

Badawi, Abdarrahman, *Neoplatonici apud Arabes* (Islamica; 19), Cairo 1955.

—, *La transmission de la philosophie grecque au monde arabe* (Études de philosophie médiévale; 66), Paris 1968.

Berman, Lawrence V., "Excerpts from the Lost Arabic Original of Ibn Rushd's *Middle Commentary* on the *Nicomachean Ethics*", in: *Oriens* 20 (1967), pp. 31-59.

—, "Ibn Rushd's *Middle Commentary* on the *Nicomachean Ethics* in Medieval Hebrew Literature", in: Jean Jolivet (ed.), *Multiple Averroès: Actes du Colloque International organisé à l'occasion du 850e anniversaire de la naissance d'Averroès, Paris 20-23 septembre 1976*, Paris 1978, pp. 287-321.

—, "A Note on the Added Seventh Book of the *Nicomachean Ethics* in Arabic", in: JAOS 82 (1962), pp. 555-556.

Berti, Enrico, *La filosofia del "primo" Aristotele*, Milan [2]1997.

Brandon, Samuel G. F. (ed.), *A Dictionary of Comparative Religion*, London 1970.

Brockelmann, Carl, *Geschichte der arabischen Litteratur* (Studi e Testi; 133), 5 vols., Leiden 1937.

Bywater, Ingram, *Contributions to the Textual Criticism of Aristotle's Nicomachean Ethics*, Oxford 1892 (reprinted New York 1973).

d'Alverny, Marie-Thérèse, "Remarques sur la tradition manuscrite de la *Summa Alexandrinorum*", in: AHDLMA 49 (1982), pp. 265-272.

Dunlop, Douglas M., "Divine Ascriptions in the *Summa Alexandrinorum*", in: *Hamdard Islamicus* 6/3 (1983), pp. 43-45. [Also in: *Essays on Islam*, Felicitation Volume in Honor of Dr. Muhammad Hamidullah, ed. Hakim Mohamed Said, Karachi 1992, pp. 102-105.]

—, "The Manuscript Taimur Pasha 290 Aḫlāq and the *Summa Alexandrinorum*", in: *Arabica* 21 (1974), pp. 252-263.

—, "A Masterpiece of Translation from the School of Ḥunain: Aristotle's *Nicomachean Ethics*", in: *Ephrem-Hunayn Festival, 4-7/2/1974*, Baghdad 1974, pp. 571-588.

—, "The *Nicomachean Ethics* in Arabic, Books I-VI", in: *Oriens* 15 (1962), pp. 18-34.

—, "Observations on the Medieval Arabic Version of Aristotle's *Nicomachean Ethics*", in: *Oriente e occidente nel medioevo, Filosofia e scienza* (Convegno internazionale, 9-15 aprile 1969), Rome 1971, pp. 229-250.

—, "Remarks on a Text of Avempace", in: Renato Traini (ed.), *Studi in onore di*

Francesco Gabrieli nel suo ottantesimo compleanno, vol. I, Rome 1984, pp. 291-300.

Fidora, Alexander, "Die Behandlung der Unbeherrschtheit in der *Summa Alexandrinorum*", in: Tobias Hoffmann, Jörn Müller and Matthias Perkams (eds.), *Akrasia und incontinentia – Das Problem der Willensschwäche in der Philosophie des Mittelalters*, Leiden 2005, in print.

—, "Ética y Política en el *De divisione philosophiae* de Domingo Gundisalvo", in: *Mediaevalia* 22 (2003), in print.

Fowler, George B., "Manuscript Admont 608 and Engelbert of Admont (c. 1250-1331). Appendix 14: *Summa Alexandrinorum*", in: AHDLMA 49 (1983), pp. 195-252.

Franceschini, Ezio, "Il *Liber Philosophorum moralium antiquorum*", in: *Atti dell' Accademia Nazionale dei Lincei. Memorie. Classe di Scienze Morali, Storiche e Filologiche*, Rome 1930, pp. 355-399.

Gauthier, Léon, *Ibn Thofaïl, sa vie, ses œuvres* (Publications de l'École des Lettres d'Alger; 43), Paris 1909.

Graf, Georg, *Geschichte der christlichen arabischen Literatur* (Studi e Testi; 133), 5 vols., Vatican City 1944-1953.

Hadot, Ilsetraut, "The Role of the Commentaries on Aristotle in the Teaching of Philosophy According to the Prefaces of the Neoplatonic Commentaries on the *Categories*", in: Henry Blumenthal and Howard Robinson (eds.), *Aristotle and the Later Tradition*, Oxford 1991, pp. 175-189.

Harvey, Steven, "The Sources of the Quotations from Aristotle's *Ethics* in the *Guide* and in the *Guide to the Guide*", in: *Jerusalem Studies in Jewish Thought* 9 (1998), 87-102 (Hebrew with English summary).

Ivry, Alfred, "Averroes' Three Commentaries on *De anima*", in: Gerhard Endreß and Jan A. Aertsen (eds.), *Averroes and the Aristotelian Tradition, Sources, Constitution and Reception of the Philosophy of Ibn Rushd (1126-1198)*, Leiden 1999, pp. 199-216.

Jacoby, Felix, *Fragmente der griechischen Historiker* (*F. gr. Hist.*), vol. I-, first Berlin, now Leiden 1923-.

Jaeger, Werner, *Aristotle*, English translation by Richard Robinson, Oxford ^{2}1967.

Jeffery, Arthur, *The Foreign Vocabulary of the Qur'ān*, Baroda 1938.

Jourdain, Amable, *Recherches critiques sur l'âge et l'origine des traductions latines d'Aristote. Nouvelle édition revue et augmentée par Charles Jourdain*, Paris 1843 (reprinted New York 1960 [Burt Franklin Bibliographical Series; 19]).

Kraus, Paul, "*Kitāb al-akhlāq li-Jālīnūs*", in: *Majallat Kullīyat al-ādāb bi'l-Jāmi'a al-miṣrīya (Bulletin of the Faculty of Arts of the University of Egypt)* 5 (1937), Arabic Section, pp. 1-51.

Lacombe, Georges, *Aristoteles Latinus – Codices I*, Rome 1939.

Lyons, Malcolm C., "A Greek Ethical Treatise", in: *Oriens* 13-14 (1961), pp. 35-57.

Mansfeld, Jaap, *Prolegomena Mathematica. From Apollonius of Perga to the Late Neoplatonism. With an Appendix on Pappus and the History of Platonism*, Leiden 1998.

—, *Prolegomena. Questions to Be Settled Before the Study of an Author*, Leiden 1994.

Marchesi, Concetto, *L'Etica Nicomachea nella traduzione latina medievale*, Messina 1904.

Margoliouth, David Samuel (ed.), *Analecta orientalia ad Poeticam Aristoteleam*, London 1887.

McCarthy, Richard J., *Al-taṣānīf al-mansūbah ilā Failasūf al-ʿarab, baḥth bi-munāsabat iḥtifālāt Baghdād wa'l-Kindī*, Baghdad 1382/1962.

Millás-Vallicrosa, José María, *Las traducciones orientales en los manuscritos de la Biblioteca Catedral de Toledo*, Madrid 1942.

Ramón Guerrero, Rafael, "La *Ética a Nicómaco* en la obra de Alfarabi", in: Luis Méndez Francisco (ed.), *Ética y sociología. Estudios en memoria del prof. José Todolí Duque O.P.*, Salamanca 2000, pp. 201-212.

Rescher, Nicholas, *Al-Fārābī. An Annotated Bibliography*, Pittsburgh 1962.

Rosenstein, Michael, *Abū-Nassr Alfarabii De intellectu intellectisque*, Sulzbach 1858.

Rosenthal, Erwin I. J., *Averroes' Commentary on Plato's 'Republic'*, Cambridge 1956 (reprinted Cambridge 1969).

—, "The Place of Politics in the Philosophy of Ibn Bajja", in: *Islamic Culture* 25 (1951), pp. 187-211.

Rosenthal, Franz, "Ishaq b. Hunayn's *Ta'rīkh al-aṭibbā'*", in: *Oriens* 7 (1954), pp. 55-80.

—, "Al-Mubashshir Ibn Fâtik, Prolegomena to an Abortive Edition", in: *Oriens* 13-14 (1961), S.132-158.

Salman, Dominique, "The Mediaeval Latin Translations of Alfarabi's Works", in: *The New Scholasticism* 13 (1939), pp. 245-261.

Schacht, Joseph, "Über den Hellenismus in Baghdad und Cairo im 11. Jahrhundert", in: ZDMG 90 (1936), pp. 526-545.

Smith, William (ed.), *Dictionary of Greek and Roman Biography and Mythology*, 3 vols., London 1844.

Steinschneider, Moritz, *Die arabischen Übersetzungen aus dem Griechischen*, Leipzig 1893 (reprinted Graz 1960).

—, *Die europäischen Übersetzungen aus dem Arabischen* (Sitzungsberichte der Kaiserlichen Akademie der Wissenschaften in Wien, Philosoph.-histor. Klasse; 149/4-151/1), Vienna 1904-1905 (reprinted Graz 1956).

—, *Al-Farabi (Alpharabius), des arabischen Philosophen Leben und Schriften, mit besonderer Rücksicht auf die Geschichte der griechischen Wissenschaft unter den Arabern* (Mémoires de l'Académie Impériale des Sciences de St.-Pétersbourg, VIIe série; XIII, 4), St. Petersburg 1869.

—, *Hebraeische Übersetzungen des Mittelalters und die Juden als Dolmetscher*, Berlin 1893 (reprinted Graz 1956).

Théry, Gabriel, *Autour du décret de 1210: II. Alexandre d'Aphrodise, Aperçu sur l'influence de sa noétique*, Kain 1926.

Tkatsch, Jaroslaus, *Die arabische Übersetzung der Poetik des Aristoteles und die Grundlage der Kritik des griechischen Textes* (Akademie der Wissenschaften in Wien. Philosophisch-historische Klasse. Kommission für die Herausgabe der arabischen Aristoteles-Übersetzungen; 1), Vienna/Leipzig 1928.

Vansteenkiste, Clemens, "Études critiques", in: *Laval théologique et philosophique* 7 (1951), pp. 202-217.

Westerink, Leendert G., *Anonymous Prolegomena to Platonic Philosophy*, Amsterdam 1962.

Dictionaries

Dozy, Reinhart P., *Supplément aux dictionnaires arabes*, 2 vols., Leiden ^{2}1927.

Endreß, Gerhard / Gutas, Dimitri, *A Greek and Arabic Lexicon (GALex). Materials for a Dictionary of the Mediaeval Translations from Greek into Arabic*, vol. I-, Leiden 1992-.

Lane, Edward William, *Arabic-English Lexicon in Eight Parts (Derived from the Best and the Most Copious Eastern Sources)*, 8 vols., London/Edinburgh 1863 (reprinted New York 1955-1956).

Ullmann, Manfred, *Wörterbuch zu den griechisch-arabischen Übersetzungen des 9. Jahrhunderts*, Wiesbaden 2002.

—, *Wörterbuch der klassischen arabischen Sprache*, vol. I-, Wiesbaden 1970-.

GRAECO-ARABIC GLOSSARY

A

τὸ ἀγαθόν	حسنة 1199a 22
	خير 1094a 3, 22 / 1094b 7 / 1095a 16, 27 / 1096b 6, 14, 34 / 1097a 1, 18, 23 / 1097b 8, 27 / 1098a 16 / 1098b 13 / 1099a 6 / 1102a 14 / 1113a 16 / 1114a 32 / 1114b 7 / 1130b 27 / 1134b 5 / 1152b 26, 33 / 1153b 17 / 1154a 15 / 1155b 19 / 1169a 21 / 1173a 5
	cf. لذة 1153b 17
ἀδικία	جور 1134b 12
	لا عدالة 1129a 3
αἴσθησις	حس 1098b 3 / 1109b 23 / 1113a 1 / 1126b 4 / 1147a 26 / 1161b 26 / 1170a 17 / 1170b 10 / 1171b 43 / 1172a 36 / 1175a 27
	حواس 1103a 29 / 1118b 1
αἰτία	بدء 1135b 19
	سبب 1098b 1 / 1099b 23 / 1110b 2, 32 / 1112a 25, 31
	علة 1174b 26
ἀκολασία	تبذير 1119b 31
	شره 1107b 6 / 1114a 28 / 1118b 1 / 1119a 20, 33
	لا عفة 1130a 30 / 1147b 28 / 1149a 5, 20, 22 / 1149b 30 / 1150a 10 / 1151b 31
ἀκούσιος	ليس إرادي / لا 1131a 3 / 1131b 26, 31 / 1132b 31 / 1135a 33 / 1135b 2 / 1136a 16
	ليس طوعا 1110b 18 / 1111a 24
	كرها 1109b 35 / 1111a 2, 28

ἀκρασία	لا ضبط 1150b 19 لا عفة 1145a 16f. / 1149a 2
ἀλήθεια	حق 1108a 20 / 1124b 28 حقيقة 1128b 23 صدق 1128b 6
ἄλλος αὐτός	آخر هو 1166a 32
ἄλογος	بهيمية 1111b 1 من غير علة 1168b 1 على غير قياس 1120b 18 غير ناطق 1102a 28 / 1102b 13 / 1108b 29 لا نطق له 1172b 10
ἀνάγκη	ضرورة 1112a 24, 32 / 1180a 4 اضطر 1116b 2
ἀνθρώπινον ἀγαθόν	الخير الذي يخص الإنسان 1094b 7 / 1098a 16 الخير الإنساني 1102a 14
ἀντιπεπονθός	مضادة الألم 1132b 21
ἀξία	أهل 1123b 3, 17 استئهل 1131a 24, 26 / 1158b 27, 31 / 1159a 35 / 1160b 13, 33 / 1161a 22 / 1163a 2, 30 / 1163b 11 / 1164a 22 / 1164b 4 استحقاق 1119a 20 / 1163b 35 cf. مقدار 1122b 29 / 1123a 18 على ما يجب 1122a 26
ἀξίωμα	أصل موضوع يعمل عليه 1117a 24 استئهل 1165a 11 استحقاق 1123b 25 قدر 1122b 33 (ذو) أقدار / ذو قدر 1123a 2 / 1123b 19 / 1124b 19 / 1126b 36
ἀπάθεια	سكون العوارض 1104b 24
ἄπειρος	الذين لا تجربة لهم 1181a 21

	غير خبير 1095a 3
	(ما) لا نهاية (له) 1097b 13 / 1106b 29 / 1113a 2
ἁπλῶς	بنوع مبسوط 1129b 3, 26 / 1130a 13 / 1146b 21 / 1148a 4, 11 / 1149a 23 / 1151b 2 / 1152b 27 / 1155b 24 / 1157b 27
	على الإطلاق 1095b 3 / 1105b 33
	بجهة واحدة 1106b 35
ἀπόδειξις	برهان 1094b 27
ἀρετή	فضيلة 1098a 15, 17 / 1102a 6, 14 / 1102b 3, 12 / 1103a 4, 9, 14f. / 1104b 9 / 1106a 17, 22 / 1106b 36 / 1113b 5 / 1115b 13 / 1120a 7 / 1122a 19 / 1122b 15 / 1124a 7, 28 / 1129b 26, 31 / 1130a 9, 13 / 1145a 19 / 1151a 18 / 1152b 5 / 1159a 35 / 1164b 1 / 1172a 22 / 1172b 15 / 1173a 14 / 1177a 17 / 1177b 6 / 1178a 16
ἀριστοκρατία	رياسة الأخيار 1160a 32 / 1160b 10 / 1161a 23
τὸ ἄριστον	أخيار 1167b 1
	أفاضل 1129b 16
ἀρχὴ πράξεων	مبدأ للأفعال 1112b 32 / 1113b 18
ἀρχιτεκτονικός	رئيسية 1094a 14
αὐτάρκεια	كفاية 1134a 27 / 1177a 27
	مكتفية 1097b 7

B

βασιλεύς	ملك / ملوك 1113a 8 / 1150b 14 / 1159a 1 / 1161 a 11 / 1180a 20
βία	قسر 1109b 35
	قهر 1135a 33 / 1179b 29
βλάβη	ضرر / ضار / ضرات 1094b 18 / 1126b 34 / 1135b 11
βούλευσις	روية 1112b 22
βούλησις	حب 1157b 36

	يريدون / إرادة / إرادات 1155b 29 / 1156b 31 / 1178a 30
	هوى 1111b 11 / 1113a 15

Γ

γένεσις	كون 1103a 16 / 1152b 13, 23 / 1173a 30 / 1173b 4 / 1174b 10, 12
	وجود 1112b 24
γένος	جنس / أجناس 1094b 25 / 1098a 8 / 1106a 12 / 1123a 11 / 1130b 1 / 1145a 27 / 1148a 23 / 1149b 28 / 1150b 35
γνῶσις	علم 1095a 6 / 1097a 6
	فحص 1102a 22
γυμναστική	علم الرياضة / رياضة 1096a 34 / 1112b 5
	ثقافة 1180b 3

Δ

δεινότης	دهاية 1152a 11
τὸ δέον	ما يجب / واجب 1107a 4 / 1121a 1 / 1121b 12 / 1122b 29
δεσπότης	مولى 1160b 29 / 1161a 35
δημοκρατία	رياسة العامة / العوام 1160b 17, 20 / 1161a 6 / 1161b 9
διάθεσις	حل / أحوال 1107b 16, 30 / 1108a 24 / 1145a 33
διάνοια	عقل 1112a 16 / 1165b 26
	فكرة 1148a 10 / 1174b 21 / 1175a 7 / 1175b 34 / 1176a 3 / 1181a 2
τὸ δίκαιον	عدل / عدول 1129a 5 / 1155a 28 / 1159b 26 / 1161a 11 / 1162b 21
δικαιοσύνη	عدل / عدالة 1120a 20 / 1129a 3f. / 1130b 6 / 1155a 24, 27 / 1173a 18

δόξα
رأي / أراء 1111b 11, 31/ 1145b 36 / 1147a 25 / 1147b 1, 3, 9 / 1159a 23
ظن 1128b 24
cf. عزائم 1179a 17

δύναμις
cf. صناعة 1094a 10, 26
أعوان 1099b 2
قوة / قوى / قوات 1102a 34 / 1102b 5 / 1103a 26 / 1105b 20f. / 1129a 12f. / 1130b 1 / 1134b 26 / 1153a 25 / 1161a 3 / 1168a 7 / 1172a 24 / 1180a 21 / 1180b 32

E

ἐγκράτεια
ضبط / ضابط (النفس) 1128b 34 / 1146a 14, 17 / 1146b 18 / 1150a 34
عفة 1145a 18
إمساك 1145b 8

ἔθος
أخلاق 1095b4
عادة 1103a 17, 26 / 1148b 17, 27, 30, 34 / 1152a 30 / 1154a 33/ 1180a 8 / 1180b 5 / 1181b 22

εἶδος
صورة 1096a 13 / 1156a 6 / 1174a 16, 19, 22, 28 / 1174b 5 / 1175a 22, 28 / 1175b 1 / 1176a 9
نوع 1096b 10 / 1155b 15 / 1174a 30

εἰρωνεία
مزح / مزاح 1108a 22 / 1124b 30

ἑκών
طوعا 1110b 20, 23 / 1113b 14 / 1114a 13, 21
بإرادة / إرادي 1136a 23 / 1146a 7

ἔλεος
رحم / رحمة 1105b 23 / 1109b 32 / 1111a 1

ἐμπειρία
حنكة 1116b 3
كثرة الحيلة 1116b 9
تجربة / تجارب 1115b 4 / 1158a 14 / 1180b 18 / 1181a 2, 10, 20
دربة 1103a 16

ἐνέργεια
فعل / أفعل / أفاعيل 1094a 4 / 1098a 7 / 1098b 33 / 1099a 29 / 1103a 27 / 1103b 21f. / 1104a 29 /

	1113b 5 / 1115b 20 / 1119b 9 / 1122b 1 / 1153b 10 / 1154b 27 / 1157b 6 / 1168a 6, 13 / 1169b 29/ 1173a 15 / 1174b 16 / 1175b 6, 24 / 1176b 2 / 1177a 10 / 1177b 7, 19 / 1178b 21
ἕξις	حال 1103b 21, 23 / 1104b 19 / 1105b 20f. / 1114a 10 / 1114b 2, 31 / 1115b 21 / 1122b 1 / 1126b 21 / 1128b 11 ملكة 1098b 33 هيئة / هيئات 1103a 9 / 1117a 20 / 1129a 14 / 1147a 12 / 1150a 15 / 1152b 33f. / 1154a 13 / 1157b 6, 29, 32 / 1174b 32 / 1181b 10
ἕξις προαιρετική	حال مختارة 1106b 36
ἐξωτερικοὶ λόγοι	الأقاويل الخارجة 1102a 26
ἐπαγωγή	استقراء 1098b 3
ἐπανορθωτικὸν δίκαιον	عدل صحيح / ذو تصحيح 1132a 18 / 1132b 24
ἐφ' ἡμῖν	(كان) إلينا 1111b 30, 32 / 1112a 31 / 1113b 7 / 1114a 29
ἐπιείκεια	استئهل 1175b 24 نزاهة 1121b 24
ἐπιθυμία	شهوة / شهوات 1103b 18 / 1111a 25 / 1111b 11 / 1117a 1 / 1118b 8f. / 1119a 4 / 1119b 5 / 1147a 15 / 1148a 21 / 1149a 26
ἐπιστήμη	علم / علوم 1094a 7, 26 / 1096 a 30 / 1097a 4 / 1106b 8 / 1112b 1, 7 / 1116b 5 / 1129a 13 / 1146b 32 / 1147a 2 / 1147b 15 / 1153b 8 / 1180b 15, 23, 32
ἔργον	مصنوع 1167b 34 / عمل / أعمال 1122b 15f. / 1123a 8 / 1133a 9 / 1162a 22 / 1168a 9 / 1172b 6 فعل / أفعال 1097b 24, 29 / 1098a 7, 13 / 1106a 18, 23 / 1106b 10 / 1113b 28 / 1120b 13 / 1129b 20 / 1153a 23 / 1168a 35 / 1172a 35 / 1179a 21 مفعولات 1094a 5

τὸ ἔσχατον أخير / أواخر 1112b 19, 23 / 1146a 9

ἕτερος αὐτός آخرهم 1161b 28f.
ذات أخرى 1169b 7

εὐδαιμονία سعادة 1095a 18f. / 1129b 18 / 1152b 6 / 1153b 11 / 1169b 29 / 1176a 31f.

εὔνοια نصيحة 1155b 33 / 1166b 30f.

εὐπραξία جميل أفعل 1098b 22

Z

ζημία خسارة / خسران 1132a 10 / 1132b 18 / 1180a 5

ζήτησις بحث 1096a 12 / 1112b 22
طلب وفحص 1102a 13

ζωή حياة 1175a 12
سيرة 1098a 13

ζῷον حيوان 1104b 35 / 1111a 26 / 1111b 9 / 1119a 8 / 1148b 16 / 1154b 7 / 1162a 19 / 1176a 3 / 1178b 24, 28
سباع 1118b 3

H

ἡδονή لذة / لذات 1096b 18, 24 / 1099a 15 / 1101b 28 / 1104a 23, 34 / 1104b 4, 6 / 1107b 4 / 1109b 8 / 1113a 34 / 1118b 21, 27 / 1126b 30 / 1147b 24 / 1148a 22 / 1149b 26 / 1150a 9, 16 / 1151b 35 / 1152b 1f. / 1153b 34 / 1156a 12f. / 1172a 19f. / 1176b 20
لذيذ 1119a 5
ملذوذ 1156b 16
التذ 1126b 13

ἦθος خلق / أخلاق / خلقي 1095a 7 / 1111b 6 / 1121a 26 / 1121b 6 / 1128a 11 / 1145a 16 / 1155b 10 / 1163a 23 / 1164a 12 / 1165b 6 / 1172a 22 / 1172b 15 / 1178a 16f. / 1179b 17

Θ

θάνατος	قتل 1115a 11 / 1116b 20
	موت 1128b 13 / 1131a 8
θεός	إله 1145a 23, 26 / 1154b 26 / 1159a 5 / 1160a 24 / 1166a 22
	الله 1096a 24 / 1099b 11 / 1101b 30 / 1122b 20 / 1123a 10 / 1123b 18 / 1179a 25
	الآلهة 1134b 28 / 1158b 35 / 1159a 7 / 1162a 5 / 1178b 8
	متألهون 1101b 19, 23
θεωρητικὸς βίος	سيرة صاحب / أهل النظر 1095b 19 / 1096a 4
θεωρία	نظر 1103b 26 / 1122b 17
	رأي 1174b 21 / 1178b 5
θηριότης	سبعية 1145a 17 / 1149a 1
θυμός	غضب 1105a 8 / 1111a 25f. / 1111b 11, 18 / 1116b 23 / 1126a 21 / 1135b 21, 26 / 1145b 20 / 1147a 15 / 1147b 34 / 1149a 3, 26

I

ἰδέα	بصر 1167a 5
	صور 1096a 17f.
τὸ ἴσον	مساوي / متساوي 1106a 27 / 1129a 34 / 1130b 9f. / 1131a 11f. / 1153b 6 / 1158b 30
	مساواة 1136a 3
ἰσότης	مساواة 1131a 22, 31 / 1132b 33 / 1133b 4 / 1134b 15 / 1157b 36 / 1158b 1, 28
	متساوي 1162b 3
	بالتساوي 1162a 35 / 1168b 8

K

καθ' ἕκαστον	جزئية / جزئيات 1109b 23 / 1110b 6, 8, 33 / 1126b 4 / 1147a 3, 26 / 1147b 5

καιρός — وقت 1096a 32 / 1110a 14

κακία — شرور 1114a 22

καλοκαγαθία — كبير النفس 1124a 4
جودة الخير 1179b 10

τὸ καλόν — جميل 1104b 32 / 1115b 12
صواب 1121a 1

καρτερία — صبر 1150b 1
عفة 1145b 8

κατηγορία — مقولة / مقولات 1096a 29, 32

κεραμεῖς — قومرة 1155a 35

κέρδος — ربح 1122a 3, 8 / 1130b 4 / 1132a 10 / 1132b 12, 18 / 1145b 20 / 1147b 33 / 1148a 26 / 1163b 3, 5 / 1164a 19

κίνησις — حركة / حركات 1102b 9 / 1112a 23 / 1125a 13 / 1128a 11f. / 1152b 28 / 1154a 13 / 1154b 27f. / 1173a 29f. / 1174a 19, 28 / 1174b 13

κοινωνία — اشترك / اشتراك / اشراكات 1108a 11 / 1128b 6 / 1130a 2 / 1132b 31 / 1133a 17 / 1133b 6 / 1159b 27 / 1160a 9 / 1163a 31
معاشرة 1133a 24 / 1162a 20 / 1171b 32
معاملة / معاملات 1135b 12 / 1160b 24 / 1161b 11 / 1164a 20

κόσμος — جمل 1123a 7
زينة 1124a 1
عالم 1112a 22 / 1173a 33

κρατεῖν — صبر 1150a 35
ضبط 1145b 24 / 1150a 12 / 1168b 34 / 1145b 35
غلبة 1151a 22
أمسك 1148a 29

κρίσις — حكم / أحكام 1109b 23 / 1119b 24
فصل 1134a 31

	قضية 1159a 24
	ميز 1126b 4
κωμῳδία	هجاء 1128a 22

Λ

λογισμός	فكر / فكرة 1111a 34 / 1117a 21 / 1119b 10 / 1145b 11f. / 1146a 33 / 1150b 24
λόγος	عقل 1180a 21
	علم 1105b 13
	فكر / فكرة 1104b 23 / 1149a 32 / 1149b 1, 3
	قول 1107a 1 / 1109b 21
	قياس 1131b 21
	كلمة 1134a 35 / 1151a 17 / 1151b 10
	تمييز 1112a 16 / 1117a 21 / 1119b 11
	نطق 1102b 15 / 1145b 14 / 1150b 28 / 1151a 1
	نطق الفكرة 1149a 26
λύπη	أذى 1119a 23

M

μαθηματικός	(صاحب) التعاليم 1094b 26 / 1112b 22
	التعليمية 1151a 17 / 1173b 17
μάθησις	علم 1099b 15
	تعلم 1099b 19
μακάριος	سعيد / سعادة 1098a 19 / 1099b 2 / 1113b 15f.
	ذو الغبطة 1158a 22 / 1169b 4 / 1177b 23 / 1178b 9
	مغبوط 1152b 7 / 1157b 21 / 1176a 27 / 1179a 2
	غبط به 1099b 18
	اغتبط به 1178b 26
μεγαλοπρέπεια	كرم 1107b 17 / 1122a 18f. / 1125b 3
μεγαλοψυχία	كبر / كبير النفس 1107b 22, 26 / 1123a 34f. / 1125a 33f. / 1125b 3

μέθοδος
بحث 1129a 6
مذهب 1094a 1
صناعة 1098a 29
طريق 1094b 11

τὸ μεσόν
وسط / أوسط 1132a 19 / 1133b 33
أوساط الناس 1124b 20
توسط / متوسط 1105b 28 / 1116a 6 / 1121a 21 / 1121b 12

μεσότης
توسط / متوسط 1104a 26 / 1106b 12, 36 / 1107a 33 / 1108a 15 / 1133b 32

μικροψυχία
صغر النفس 1107b 23 / 1125a 33

μουσικός
غناء 1105a 21
موسيقوس 1173b 30f. / 1175a 13
موسيقى 1180b 2 / 1181a 19

μοχθηρία
رداءة 1110b 32 / 1113b 16 / 1129b 24 / 1130a 7 / 1130b 24 / 1135b 24 / 1148b 2 / 1149a 16f. / 1163b 36 / 1166b 20, 27
شرة / شرية 1150b 32 / 1163b 23 / 1165b 18

N

νίκη
ظفر 1097a 20
غلبة 1094a 9 / 1148a 26 / 1160a 17

νόμιμος
أشياء ناموسية 1135a 6 / 1180b 4
متمسك بالناموس 1129a 33

νόμισμα
دينار / دنانير 1133a 20 / 1133b 11 / 1164a 1 / 1165b 12 / 1178b 15
دينار ودرهم 1119b 26

νομοθετεῖν
وضع / واضع النواميس 1109b 34 / 1180a 6 / 1181a 16
نواميس موضوعة 1134b 23

νόμος
شريعة 1094b 16
ناموس / نواميس 1102a 10 / 1113b 34 / 1116a 19 /

	1128a 32 / 1129b 14, 19 / 1130a 24 / 1132a 5 / 1132b 16 / 1133a 30 / 1134a 30f. / 1134b 14 / 1161b 7 / 1164b 13 / 1179b 32, 34 / 1180a 3, 21, 24, 34 / 1180b 25 / 1181a 17, 23 / 1181b 7, 22 أشياء ناموسية 1130b 24
νοῦς	عقل 1096a 25 / 1096b 29 / 1097b 2 / 1110a 11 / 1112a 33 / 1150a 5 / 1168b 35 / 1169a 17f. / 1177a 13 / 1177b 30 / 1178a 7 / 1178a 22 / 1179a 27 / 1180a 18 عاقل 1112a 21 / 1115b 9

Ξ

ξενία	ضيافة 1170b 21

Ο

ὀλιγαρχία	رياسات القليلين / رياسة قليلين 1160b 12 / 1161a 3 قلة رياسة 1160b 35
ὁμιλία	معاشرة / معاشرات 1126b 11, 31 / 1127b 34 / 1128b 2, 9 / 1156a 29 / 1158a 3 / 1172a 11
ὁμοδοξία	متفقون في الرأي 1167a 23
ὁμόνοια	اتفاق الرأي 1167a 22f.
ὄνειδος	عير / عار 1116a 29 / 1122a 3, 9 / 1123a 32 / 1168b 15 هوان 1116a 19
ὄργανον	آلة / آلات 1094a 12 / 1097a 27 / 1099b 1 / 1111a 5 / 1112b 29 / 1161a 34 / 1161b 4
ὀργή	غضب 1103b 18 / 1105b 22 / 1108a 4 / 1125b 26, 30 / 1126a 16, 22 / 1126b 10 / 1130a 31 / 1135b 29 / 1148a 11 / 1149b 20
ὀρθὸς λόγος	تمييز صواب 1103b 32f. قول صحيح 1147b 3
ὅρος	حد / حدود 1097b 12 / 1147b 14 / 1149a 1 / 1153b 25

οὐσία	ذات 1096a 20
	جوهر 1107a 6 / 1119a 18
	مل 1120a 1 / 1120b 7, 9, 12 / 1121a 18 / 1165b 20

Π

πάθος	آلام خلقية 1179b 27
	شهوة / شهوات 1095a 4, 8 / 1135b 21 / 1136a 8 / 1156a 32 / 1168b 20
	عوارض 1105b 20f. / 1111b 1
	انفعل 1126b 23 / 1128b 11, 15, 17 / 1132a 9, 13 / 1179b 13
παιδεία	أدب / آداب 1130b 26 / 1161a 17 / 1180b 8
	سلوك 1104b 13
παιδιά	مداعبة / مداعبات 1127b 34 / 1128a 14, 20 / 1128b 4, 6
	لعب 1176b 9, 28
	مزاح 1150b 17
	هزل 1108a 13, 23
παράνομος	مخلاف / مخالف / خالف الناموس 1129a 32 / 1129b 11 / 1130b 8
	ليس بناموس 1129b 1
παρουσία	حضور 1171a 28 / 1171b 13, 27
	قرب 1167a 6
πίστις	قنوع 1179a 17
	إقناع 1154a 23 / 1173a 1
	معاملة بالدين 1162b 30
πλεονέκτης	ذو قنية كثيرة 1129a 32 / 1129b 1 / 1130a 26
ποίησις	تهيئة 1174a 24
πόλεμος	حرب 1096a 32 / 1115a 30, 35 / 1177b 10
	قتل 1160a 17
πόλις	مدينة / مدن 1094b 8 / 1103b 3 / 1123a 2 / 1162a 19

	/ 1167a 30 / 1168b 31 / 1170b 30f. / 1180a 27 / 1180b 4 / 1181a 7 / 1181b 18
πολιτεία	بولوطيا 1160a 34 سيرة / سير 1160b 20f. / 1161a 10 سياسة / سياسات 1103b 6 / 1113a 8 سير المدينة / مدنية 1135a 5 / 1163b 5 هيئة مدنية 1160a 31
πολιτικὸς βίος	سيرة صاحب تدبير المدن 1095b 18
πονηρός	ردئ 1113b 15 / 1152a 16 / 1165b 15 شرير / أشرار 1122a 6 / 1135b 24 / 1167b 26
πρᾶξις	فعل / أفعل 1110b 6 / 1113b 18 / 1114a 8 / 1151a 16 / 1154a 32 / 1169a 33 / 1178b 17
τὸ πρέπον	واجب / ما يجب 1122a 34 / 1127a 2 ما يليق 1123a 9
προαίρεσις	اختيار 1094a 1 / 1095a 14 / 1097a 21 / 1110b 31 / 1111b 5f. / 1113b 5 / 1134a 20 / 1135b 25 / 1151a 30f. / 1163a 23 إرادة / إرادات 1106a 3 / 1136a 1
προπέτεια	إقدام 1150b 19

Ρ

ῥητορική	خطابة 1094b 3 ريطوريقى 1181a 15

Σ

σοφία	حكمة 1098b 24 / 1103a 5 / 1177a 24
σοφισταί	محكمين 1180b 35 / 1181a 12 شهابون 1164a 31
σπουδαῖος	فاضل 1145b 8 / 1146a 15, 19 / 1148a 23 / 1154a 31 / 1154b 2 / 1163a 35 / 1164b 25 / 1165a 6

σπουδή	اجتهاد 1177b 19 فضيلة 1177a 2
στρατηγική	تدبير الحرب 1094a 9, 13 / 1096a 32 / 1097a 19 صناعة الحرب 1094b 3
συλλογισμός	جامعة 1146a 24
συμβεβηκός	شيء عارض 1096a 21 (بنوع الـ...) عرض 1135a 18 / 1135b 3f. / 1154b 17 / 1157a 35
συμμετρία	اعتدال 1173a 26
συναλλάγματα	معاشرات 1131b 25 معاملات 1131a 1 / 1131b 33 / 1135b 29 / 1178a 12
σύνεσις	فهم 1103a 5 / 1161b 26 / 1181a 18
τὸ σύνθετον	مركب 1177b 28 / 1178a 20
σχῆμα	شكل 1125a 30 تشكل 1133b 1
σωτηρία	تحفظ 1096a 14 سلامة 1110a 10 / 1111a 5 / 1115b 2 / 1116b 20 / 1130b 2 / 1167b 23
σωφροσύνη	عفة 1103a 6 / 1104a 19, 25 / 1107b 5 / 1147b 28 / 1149a 22 / 1149b 30 / 1151b 31

T

τὸ τέλειον	تام 1174b 15 تمام 1178b 1 كامل 1102b 2
τέλος	آخر 1114b 31 تمام 1152b 23 / 1174b 33 غاية / غايات 1094a 4 / 1097a 28f. / 1110a 13 / 1111b 26 / 1112b 12, 15, 33 / 1113b 3 / 1114b 4, 6, 21, 24 / 1115b 20, 22 / 1152b 2, 14

τέχνη	صناعة / صنائع / صناعات 1094a 1, 7 / 1097a 17 / 1098a 24 / 1099b 23 / 1103a 32 / 1104a 7 / 1105a 22, 26 / 1106b 14 / 1112b 7 / 1132b 9 / 1152b 18f.
	مهنة 1153a 23, 25f.
τύραννος	تغلب / متغلب / متغلبة 1110a 5 / 1120b 25 / 1122a 5 / 1134b 1, 8 / 1160b 2, 11 / 1176b 13
τύχη	اتفاق 1096b 27 / 1099b 10 / 1105a 23 / 1112a 27, 32
	بخت 1120b 17 / 1153b 22

Υ

ὕβρις	cf. تحدد 1125a 9
	شتم 1149b 33
	عار 1115a 22
	فرية 1149a 32 / 1149b 23
ὕλη	مادة 1094b 12 / 1098a 28 / 1104a 3
ὑπερβολή	إسراف 1179a 3
	إفراط 1145a 24 / 1164a 29 / 1165b 36 / 1166b 1
ὑπόληψις	ظن 1147b 4

Φ

φαντασία	تخيل 1114b 3
	يتخيل 1114a 32
	فنطاسيا / فنطاسيات 1147b 5 / 1149a 32 / 1150b 28
φαντάσματα	تخيل 1102b 10
φαῦλος	ردئ / رداءات / ذوي الرداءة 1128b 25 / 1169a 14 / 1176b 24
	اردا 1121a 25
	شرير / شرار / أشرار 1113b 14 / 1132a 2 / 1145b 10 / 1148b 4 / 1157a 17
φίλαυτος	محب ذاته / محبي ذواتهم 1168a 30 / 1169a 3
	محبي أنفسهم 1168b 15

φιλία	محبة 1105b 22 / 1126b 20, 22 / 1155a 3f.
	قبول 1108a 28
φιλοσοφία	فلسفة 1096b 31 / 1164b 3 / 1177a 25 / 1181b 15
φιλοτιμία	محبة للكرامة 1107b 31 / 1125b 22f.
	محب الكرامة 1159a 13
φόβος	خزع 1110a 4
	خوف 1105b 22 / 1107a 33 / 1115a 7, 9 / 1116a 31 / 1128b 11f.
	فرق 1121b 28
	فزع / أمور مفزعة 1117a 29 / 1135b 5 / 1179b 11
φρόνησις	ذهن 1103a 6
	عقل 1152a 12 / 1172b 30
	تعقل 1146a 4 / 1178a 16
	فهم 1096b 24 / 1098b 24 / 1180a 22 / 1180b 28
φύσις	طبع / طبيعي / طبيعة / طبائع 1094b 16, 25 / 1096a 21 / 1099b 21 / 1102b 13 / 1103a 19f. / 1104b 20 / 1106b 15 / 1112a 25 / 1113a 21 / 1114b 14, 16 / 1118b 18 / 1119a 24 / 1133a 30 / 1134b 25 / 1135a 10 / 1148b 18, 30f. / 1152a 30 / 1152b 13, 27, 36 / 1153b 29 / 1154a 32 / 1154b 17, 23 / 1179b 20

X

χάρις	شكر 1120a 15
	هبة 1133a 3f.
χρῆσις	استعمل / استعمل 1098b 32 / 1120a 8 / 1129b 31 / 1130b 20 / 1167a 18
	منفعة 1170b 23
χρόνος	زمان / أزمنة 1098a 23 / 1156b 33 / 1162b 27 / 1174a 22 / 1174b 8 / 1175b 31
	وقت 1096a 26

Ψ

ψήφισμα حسبة 1151b 16

ψόγος ذم 1109b 31 / 1110a 33

ψυχή نفس / أنفس / نفسي / نفسانية 1098a 7 / 1098b 14, 19 / 1102a 5, 17, 23f. / 1102b 8 / 1104b 19 / 1105b 17, 20 / 1114a 22 / 1161a 35 / 1166a 14 / 1166b 19 / 1168b 7, 21

Ω

ὠφέλεια منفعة 1108a 29 / 1157a 20 / 1157b 20 / 1162b 2, 17 / 1163a 10, 17

REVERSED GLOSSARY

أخير / أواخر τὸ ἔσχατον
آخر τέλος
آخرهم ἕτερος αὐτός
آخر هو ἄλλος αὐτός
أدب / آداب παιδεία
أذى λύπη
أصل موضوع يعمل عليه ἀξίωμα
آلام خلقية πάθος
إله θεός
الله θεός
الآلهة θεός
متألهون θεός
(كان) إلينا ἐφ' ἡμῖν
أهل ἀξία
استئهل ἀξία, ἀξίωμα
آلة / آلات ὄργανον
بحث ζήτησις, μέθοδος
بخت τύχη
بدء αἰτία
مبدأ للأفعال ἀρχὴ πράξεων
تبذير ἀκολασία
برهان ἀπόδειξις
بنوع مبسوط ἁπλῶς
بهيمية ἄλογος

بولوطيا πολιτεία
تام τὸ τέλειον
تمام τὸ τέλειον, τέλος
ثقافة γυμναστική
تجربة / تجارب ἐμπειρία
الذين لا تجربة لهم ἄπειρος
جزئية / جزئيات καθ' ἕκαστον
جامعة συλλογισμός
جميل τὸ καλόν
جميل أفعل εὐπραξία
جنس / أجناس γένος
اجتهاد σπουδή
جودة الخير καλοκαγαθία
جور ἀδικία
جوهر οὐσία
حب βούλησις
محبة φιλία
محب ذاته / محبي ذواتهم φίλαυτος
محبي أنفسهم φίλαυτος
حد / حدود ὅρος
تحدد cf. ὕβρις
حرب πόλεμος
تدبير الحرب στρατηγική

صناعة الحرب στρατηγική
حركة / حركات κίνησις
حس αἴσθησις
حواس αἴσθησις
حسبة ψήφισμα
حسنة τὸ ἀγαθόν
حضور παρουσία
حق ἀλήθεια
حقيقة ἀλήθεια
استحقاق ἀξία, ἀξίωμα
حكم / أحكام κρίσις
حكمة σοφία
محكمين σοφισταί
حنكة ἐμπειρία
حال / أحوال διάθεσις, ἕξις
كثرة الحيلة ἐμπειρία
حياة ζωή
حيوان ζῷον
غير خبير ἄπειρος
خزع φόβος
خسارة / خسران ζημία
خطابة ῥητορικη
مخلاف / مخالف / خالف الناموس
παράνομος
خلق / أخلاق / خلقي ἦθος
أخلاق ἔθος
خوف φόβος
خير τὸ ἀγαθόν
الخير الذي يخص الإنسان
ἀνθρώπινον ἀγαθόν
الخير الإنساني ἀνθρώπινον
ἀγαθόν
أخيار τὸ ἄριστον
اختيار προαίρεσις
حال مختارة ἕξις προαιρετικη
تخيل φαντασία,
φαντάσματα
يتخيل φαντασία
دربة ἐμπειρία
درهم νόμισμα
مداعبة / مداعبات παιδιά
دينار / دنانير νόμισμα
دهاية δεινότης
ذم ψόγος
مذهب μέθοδος
ذهن φρόνησις
ذات οὐσία
ذات أخرى ἕτερος αὐτός
رئيسية ἀρχιτεκτονικός
رياسة الأخيار ἀριστοκρατία
رياسة العامة / العوام
δημοκρατία
رياسات القليلين / رياسة قليلين
ὀλιγαρχία
راي / أراء δόξα, θεωρία
ربح κέρδος
رحم / رحمة ἔλεος
ردي πονηρός, φαῦλος
أردا φαῦλος
رداءة μοχθηρία
مركب τὸ σύνθετον

يريدون / إرادة / إرادات βούλησις, προαίρεσις

بإرادة / إرادي ἑκών

ليس إرادي ἀκούσιος

علم الرياضة / رياضة γυμναστική

ريطوريقى ῥητορικη

روية βούλευσις

زمان / أزمنة χρόνος

سبب αἰτία

سباع ζῷον

سبعية θηριότης

إسراف ὑπερβολή

سعادة εὐδαιμονία, μακάριος

سكون العوارض ἀπάθεια

سلوك παιδεία

سلامة σωτηρία

سياسة / سياسات πολιτεία

مساوي / متساوي τὸ ἴσον

متساوين ἰσότης

مساواة τὸ ἴσον, ἰσότης

بالتساوي ἰσότης

سيرة ζωή, πολιτεία

سير المدينة / مدنية πολιτεία

سيرة صاحب / أهل النظر θεωρητικὸς βίος

شتم ὕβρις

شرة / شرية μοχθηρία

شرير / أشرار πονηρός, φαῦλος

شرور κακία

شريعة νόμος

اشترك / اشتراك / اشراكات κοινωνία

شره ἀκολασία

شكل σχῆμα

تشكل σχῆμα

شهابون σοφισταί

شهوة / شهوات ἐπιθυμία, πάθος

صبر καρτερία

عدل صحيح / ذو تصحيح ἐπανορθωτικὸν δίκαιον

صدق ἀλήθεια

صغر النفس μικροψυχία

صناعة μέθοδος, τέχνη, cf. δύναμις

مصنوع ἔργον

صواب τὸ καλόν

صورة εἶδος, ἰδέα

ضبط / ضابط (النفس) ἐγκράτεια

لا ضبط ἀκρασία, κρατεῖν

مضادة الألم ἀντιπεπονθός

ضرر / ضار / ضرات βλάβη

ضرورة ἀνάγκη

اضطر ἀνάγκη

ضيافة ξενία

طبع / طبيعي / طبيعة / طبائع φύσις

طريق μέθοδος

على الإطلاق ἁπλῶς

طوعا ἑκών

ليس طوعا ἀκούσιος

ظفر νίκη

ظن ὑπόληψις

عدل / عدول τὸ δίκαιον

عدل / عدالة δικαιοσύνη

لا عدالة ἀδικία

اعتدال συμμετρία

شيء عارض συμβεβηκός

(بنوع الـ...) عرض συμβεβηκός

عوارض πάθος

عزائم cf. δόξα

معاشرة κοινωνία, ὁμιλία, συναλλάγματα

عفة ἐγκράτεια, καρτερία, σωφροσύνη

لا عفة ἀκολασία, ἀκρασία

عقل διάνοια, λόγος, νοῦς, φρόνησις

عاقل νοῦς

تعقل φρόνησις

علة αἰτία

من غير علة ἄλογος

علم γνῶσις, ἐπιστήμη, λόγος, μάθησις

(صاحب) التعاليم μαθηματικός

التعليمية μαθηματικός

تعلم μάθησις

عالم κόσμος

عمل / أعمال ἔργον

معاملة / معاملات κοινωνία, συναλλάγματα

معاملة بالدين πίστις

استعمل / استعمال χρῆσις

عادة ἔθος

أعوان δύναμις

عير / عار ὄνειδος, ὕβρις

ذو الغبطة μακάριος

مغبوط μακάριος

غبط به μακάριος

اغتبط به μακάριος

غضب θυμός, ὀργή

غلبة νίκη

تغلب / متغلب / متغلبة τύραννος

غناء μουσικός

غاية / غايات τέλος

فحص γνῶσις

إفراط ὑπερβολή

فرق φόβος

فرية ὕβρις

فزع / أمور مفزعة φόβος

فصل κρίσις

أفاضل τὸ ἄριστον

فاضل σπουδαῖος

فضيلة ἀρετή, σπουδή

فعل / أفعل / أفاعيل ἐνέργεια, ἔργον, πρᾶξις

مفعولات ἔργον

انفعال πάθος

فكرة διάνοια, λογισμός, λόγος

فلسفة φιλοσοφία
فنطاسيا / فنطاسيات φαντασία
فهم σύνεσις, φρόνησις
قبول φιλία
قتل θάνατος
قتل πόλεμος
قدر ἀξίωμα
(ذو) أقدار / ذو قدر ἀξίωμα
مقدار cf. ἀξία
إقدام προπέτεια
قرب παρουσία
استقراء ἐπαγωγή
قسر βία
قضية κρίσις
قلة رياسة ὀλιγαρχία
قنع πίστις
قنوع πίστις
إقناع πίστις
ذو قنية كثيرة πλεονέκτης
قهر βία
قول λόγος
قول صحيح ὀρθὸς λόγος
مقولة / مقولات κατηγορία
قومرة κεραμεῖς
قوة / قوى / قوات δύναμις
على غير قياس ἄλογος
كبير النفس
καλοκαγαθία, μεγαλοψυχία
كرم μεγαλοπρέπεια
محبة للكرامة φιλοτιμία
محب الكرامة φιλοτιμία
كرها ἀκούσιος
كفاية αὐτάρκεια
مكتفية αὐτάρκεια
كلمة λόγος
كامل τὸ τέλειον
كون γένεσις
لذة cf. τὸ ἀγαθόν
لذة / لذات ἡδονη
لذيذ ἡδονη
ملذوذ ἡδονη
التذ ἡδονη
لعب παιδιά
ما يليق τὸ πρέπον
مادة ὕλη
مدينة / مدن πόλις
مزح / مزاح εἰρωνεία,
παιδιά
أمسك κρατεῖν
إمساك ἐγκράτεια
ملك / ملوك βασιλεύς
ملكة ἕξις
مهنة τέχνη
موت θάνατος
موسيقوس μουσικός
موسيقى μουσικός
مال οὐσία
ميز κρίσις

تمييز λόγος

تمييز صواب ὀρθὸς λόγος

نصيحة εὔνοια

نطق λόγος

غير ناطق ἄλογος

لا نطق له ἄλογος

نطق الفكرة λόγος

نظر θεωρία

نفس / أنفس / نفسي / نفسانية ψυχή

منفعة χρῆσις, ὠφέλεια

ناموس / نواميس νόμος

أشياء ناموسية νόμιμος, νόμος

متمسك بالناموس νόμιμος

ليس بناموس παράνομος

(ما) لا نهاية (له) ἄπειρος

نوع εἶδος

هجاء κωμῳδία

هزل παιδια

هوان ὄνειδος

هوى βούλησις

هيئة / هيئات ἕξις

تهيئة ποίησις

هيئة مدنية πολιτεία

على ما يجب ἀξία

ما يجب / واجب τὸ δέον,
τὸ πρέπον

وجود γένεσις

بجهة واحدة ἁπλῶς

وسط / أوسط τὸ μεσόν

توسط / متوسط τὸ μεσόν,
μεσότης

وضع / واضع النواميس
νομοθετεῖν

نواميس موضوعة νομοθετεῖν

اتفاق τύχη

اتفاق الرأي ὁμόνοια

متفقون في الرأي ὁμοδοξία

وقت καιρός, χρόνος

مولى δεσπότης

هبة χάρις

INDEX NOMINUM

The Index refers to the Introduction only.

ʿAbd al-Laṭīf al-Baghdadī 76
Abū ʿl-Faraj ibn al-ʿIbrī 72ff., 76
Abū Ḥaiyān at-Tauḥīdī 19, 69ff.
Abū Rīdah, Muḥammad ʿAbd al-Hādī 6ff., 20, 60
Abū Sulaimān al-Sijistānī 26, 57, 68ff., 75, 77, 99f.
Achilles 61
Achillinus, Alessandro 89
Aertsen, Jan A. 78
al-ʿAlawī, Jamāl ad-Dīn 89
Albertus Magnus 93
Alcmaeon 61
Alexander of Aphrodisias 89ff.
Alonso, Manuel 18
Amin, Ahmad 19
Ammonius 34
al-ʿĀmirī 19ff., 31, 58, 86, 93
Anaxagoras 66
Androtion 56, 61
Arberry, Arthur J. 2ff., 19, 22, 42f., 47, 86, 97f., 105
Aristotle *passim*
Armstrong, G. Cyril 15
Asín Palacios, Miguel 35ff., 40ff., 46f.
Aspasius 98, 107
Atreus 61
Avempace see Ibn Bājjah
Averroes see Ibn Rushd
Avicenna see Ibn Sīnā
ʿAyyād, Shukrī Muḥammad 105

Badawī, ʿAbdarraḥmān 22, 75, 105
al-Balādhurī 78
Bar Hebraeus see Abū ʿl-Faraj ibn al-ʿIbrī
Bekker, Immanuel 97
Berman, Lawrence V. 4f., 18, 51ff.
Bernays, Jacob 57, 97
Berti, Enrico 57
Blachère, Régis 17, 32f.
Blumenthal, Henry 16
Bouyges, Maurice 77, 91
Brandon, Samuel G. F. 44
Brockelmann, Carl 9
Burnet, John 43, 57, 96f., 107
Busse, Adolf 14
Bywater, Ingram 96f., 107

Cheikho, Louis 17

d'Alverny, Marie-Thérèse 62
David the Armenian 14
de Courteille, Pavet 72
de Goeje, Michael J. 10, 78
de Meynard, Barbier 72
Demosthenes 56
Dieterici, Friedrich 10ff., 20, 48, 91
Dietrich, Albert 73
Diogenes Laertius 33
Dodge, Bayard 72f., 76
Dominicus Gundisalvus 18
Drossaart Lulofs, Hendrik J. 76

Elias 14
Endreß, Gerhard 78
Epicurus 66
Eudemus 7

Fakhry, Majid 35ff., 39f., 46ff., 93
al-Fārābī, Abū Naṣr 1, 8ff., 23, 25f., 28, 32ff., 36, 39ff., 45f., 48ff., 60, 82, 86ff., 106
Flügel, Gustav 10, 73, 106
Forget, Jacques 31
Fortenbach, William W. 33
Fowler, George B. 29, 62, 67, 69, 82f.

Franceschini, Ezio 63

Galen 76, 78, 91
Gauthier, Léon 20, 44, 48f.
Gauthier, René A. 3, 28, 32, 53, 57, 94f., 97, 107
Geoffroy, Marc 90
Gerard of Cremona 18
al-Ghazālī, Abū Ḥāmid 41ff.
Ghūras (Protagoras?) 61
Gilson, Étienne 91
Goichon, Amélie-Marie 20, 44f.
González Palencia, Ángel 9
Graf, Georg 9f.
Guidi, Michelangelo 6ff.

Hadot, Ilsetraut 16
Heraclitus 66
Hermannus Alemannus 53, 62, 64, 68f., 79
Hermes Trismegistus 37
Hermias of Atarneus 37, 47
Hesiod 99ff., 104
Heylbut, Gustav 107
Hippocrates 57, 78
Hoffmann, Philippe 16
Homer 56, 61, 64, 67, 98, 101, 104
Houtsma, Martijn Th. 11
Ḥunain b. Isḥāq 27, 33f., 60, 73, 106
al-Ḥusainī, ʿIzzat al-ʿAṭṭār 6

Ibn al-Abbār 6
Ibn Abī ʿUṣaibiʿah 17f., 26, 33, 37, 70, 76ff., 86, 90, 92, 105f.
Ibn al-Athīr 78, 106
Ibn ʿAus 57, 61
Ibn Bājjah 1, 18, 35ff., 45ff., 52f., 86, 88ff., 92f.
Ibn Buṭlān 72ff., 77
Ibn Faḍlān 74
Ibn Harīdūs, ʿAlī 6
Ibn Juljul 105
Ibn Khaldūn 5, 78, 106
Ibn an-Nadīm 1, 10, 12, 17f., 23, 25ff., 31, 47, 60, 70, 72ff., 78, 86f., 93, 106
Ibn Nāʿimah, ʿAbd al-Masīḥ 9f., 90
Ibn Rushd 18, 50ff., 62, 77f., 89f., 92f.
Ibn Saʿdān, Abū ʿAbd Allāh 70
Ibn Ṣāʿid al-Andalusī, Abū Qāsim 11, 16f., 32ff., 106
Ibn Sīnā 20, 31f., 44f., 91
Ibn aṭ-Ṭaḥḥan, Imru'u l-Qais see Müller, August
Ibn Ṭufail 18, 44, 48f., 52, 88
Ibn Zurʿah 53, 68ff., 74f., 79
Ibrāhīm b. Adham 37
Isḥāq b. Ḥunain 26f., 60, 75, 77f., 89f., 94, 100
Ivry, Alfred 78

Jacoby, Felix 77f.
Jackson, Henry 15
Jaeger, Werner 33, 57
Jeffery, Arthur 44
Jolif, Jean Y. 3, 28, 32, 57, 94f., 97, 107
Jolivet, Jean 51
Jourdain, Amable 51, 62
Julian, Emperor 72f.

al-Kindī 1, 6ff., 14f., 20, 60f., 85, 90, 94
Kraus, Paul 79

Lacombe, Georges 62
Lévi-Provençal, Évariste 6
Lippert, Julius 27, 73
Lyons, Malcolm C. 2ff., 8, 58, 76, 105

Mahdī, Muḥsin 16ff., 20, 48
al-Ma'mūn 9f.
Mansfeld, Jaap 14f.
Marchesi, Concetto 22, 62, 67, 82
Masʿūdī 72, 78
McCarthy, Richard J. 6
Mehren, August F. 44
Merkle, Karl 34
Millás-Vallicrosa, José María 52
Minovi, Mojtaba 19f., 23, 31
Miskawaih, Abū ʿAlī Aḥmad 23, 26, 28ff., 68, 70, 82, 86
Moses Maimonides 12, 15, 18, 49, 52f., 87, 91f.
al-Mubashshir b. Fātik 22, 30f., 34, 38f., 62f., 85f., 106
Müller, August 17, 26
al-Munajjid, Ṣalāḥ ad-Dīn 78

Munk, Salomon 50
al-Muʿtaṣim 9f., 90

Nicolaus 3, 5
Nicolaus Damascenus 76ff.
Nicolaus of Laodicea (?) 72ff.

Ockley, Simon 48f.
Odysseus 61

Pellat, Charles 72
Philoponus 34, 75
Philoxenus 56, 61
Pines, Shlomo 50, 92
Plato 8, 11, 13, 16f., 19, 50, 61, 67
Plotinus 90
Polydamas 61
Porphyry 10ff., 23ff., 31, 37, 41, 45, 47f., 50, 55, 58, 60, 86ff., 93f., 100, 104
Proclus 74ff.
Protagoras 61
Pseudo-Aristotle 10, 90
Pythagoras 56, 61, 67

Quatremère, Étienne Marc 78
al-Qifṭī, Jamāl ad-Dīn 1, 26f., 31, 60, 70, 72ff., 76

Rackham, Harris 96ff.
Rescher, Nicholas 34
Rhadamanthys 56, 61
Robinson, Howard 16
Robinson, Richard 33
Robson, James 44
Rosenstein, Michael 91
Rosenthal, Erwin I. J. 92f.
Rosenthal, Franz 5, 16, 34, 62, 77
Ross, William David 13, 96

Saiyid, Fu'ād 105
as-Saiyid Pasha, Lutfi 1
Sbath, Paul 71
Salḥānī, Anṭūn 73
Salman, Dominique 52, 54, 93
Ṣamṣām ad-Daulah 70
as-Sandūbī, Ḥasan 69
Sā'ūs 57, 61
Schacht, Joseph 74
Schmölders, F. Augustus 34
Simplicius 16, 34
Smith, Andrew 23
Smith, William 14, 76
Socrates 40, 61, 67
Stahr, Adolf 14
Steinschneider, Moritz 10, 26, 33f., 41, 46, 74, 76ff., 89f., 92
Steel, Carlos 90
Susemihl, Franz 14

aṭ-Ṭabarī, Abū Jaʿfar Muḥammad ibn Jarīr 6, 10, 78
Themistius 12, 26f., 87
Theognis 56, 61
Theophrastus of Eresus 33
Théry, Gabriel 89f.
Tkatsch, Jaroslaus 105
Tornberg, Carolus J. 78
Traini, Renato 49

Ullmann, Manfred 105
Uwais al-Quranī 37

Vansteenkiste, Clemens 32
Videan, Ivy E. 76
Videan, John A. 76

Walzer, Richard 3, 6ff., 16, 25, 28
Wasserstein, David 23
Westerink, Leendert G. 34
Wüstenfeld, Ferdinand 74

Yaḥyā b. ʿAdī 26f., 74
al-Yaʿqūbī 8, 10f., 17
Yāqūt 74ff.

az-Zain, Ahmad 19
Zand, Kamal Hafuth 76
az-Zauzanī 73
Zeus 62
Zuraiq, Qusṭanṭīn 26, 28f.

ARISTOTELES SEMITICO-LATINUS

Founded by
H.J. Drossaart Lulofs

General Editors
H. Daiber
R. Kruk

* *Volumes 1 to 4 are available directly from the Royal Netherlands Academy of Arts and Sciences, P.O. Box 19121, 1000 GC Amsterdam, The Netherlands / edita@bureau.knaw.nl*

*1. Ḥunain ibn Isḥâq.– *Ein kompendium der aristotelischen Meteorologie in der Fassung des Ḥunain ibn Isḥâq.* Hrsg. mit Übers., Komm.und Einl. von H. Daiber. 1975. (viii, 117 [18 Arabic t.] pp., 4 [facs.] pl.). ISBN 07 20 48302 6
*2. Aristotle.– *The Arabic version of Aristotle's Parts of Animals. Books* XI-XIV *of the Kitāb al-Ḥayawān.* Critical ed. with introd. and sel. glossary by R. Kruk. 1979 (96 [4 fasc.], 156 Arabic t. pp.). ISBN 07 20 48467 7
*3. Gätje, H. *Das Kapitel über das Begehren aus dem Mittleren Kommentar des Averroes zur Schrift über die Seele.* [Mit Text u. Übers.] 1985. (viii, 100 [10 Arabic t.] pp.). ISBN 04 44 85640 4
*4. Nicolaus Damascenus, *De Plantis.* Five translations. Ed. with introd. by H.J. Drossaart Lulofs and E.L.J. Poortman. 1989. (xvi, 732 [incl. Syriac, Arabic, Hebrew, Latin, Greek t. and num. fasc.] pp.). ISBN 04 44 85703 6
5. Aristotle. *De Animalibus. Michael Scot's Arabic-Latin translation.* Three parts.
Part 1. Books I-X : History of Animals. Ed. by A.M.I. van Oppenraaij. *In Preparation.*
Part 2. Books XI-XIV : Parts of Animals. Ed. by A.M.I. van Oppenraaij. 1998. ISBN 90 04 11070 4
Part 3. Books XV-XIX : Generation of Animals. Ed. by A.M.I. van Oppenraaij. With a Greek index to *De Generatione Animalium* by H.J. Drossaart Lulofs. 1992. (xxvi, 504 [243 Latin p.] pp.). ISBN 90 04 09603 5
6. Aristotle's *De Anima* translated into Hebrew by Zeraḥyah ben Isaac ben Shealtiel Ḥen. Ed. by G. Bos. 1993. ISBN 90 04 09937 9
7. Lettinck, P. *Aristotle's* Physics *and its reception in the Arabic world.* With an edition of the unpublished parts of Ibn Bājja's *Commentary on the Physics.* 1994. ISBN 90 04 09960 3
8. Fontaine, R.. *Otot ha-Shamayim.* Samuel Ibn Tibbon's Hebrew version of Aristotle's *Meteorology.* A critical edition, with introduction, translation, and index. 1995. ISBN 90 04 10258 2
9. Aristoteles' *De Anima. Eine verlorene spätantike Paraphrase in arabischer und persischer Überlieferung.* Arabischer Text nebst Kommentar, quellengeschichtlichen Studien und Glossaren. Hrsg. von R. Arnzen. 1998. ISBN 90 04 10699 5
10. Lettinck P. *Aristotle's* Meteorology *and its reception in the Arab world.* With an Edition and Translation of Ibn Suwār's *Treatise on Meteorological Phenomena* and Ibn Bājja's *Commentary on the Meteorology.* 1999. ISBN 90 04 10933 1

11. Filius L.S. (ed.). *The Problemata Physica attributed to Aristotle.* The Arabic Version of Ḥunain ibn Isḥāq and the Hebrew Version of Moses ibn Tibbon. 1999. ISBN 90 04 11483 1
12. Schoonheim, P.L. *Aristotle's* Meteorology *in the Arabico-Latin Tradition.* A Critical Edition of the Texts, with Introduction and Indices. 2000. ISBN 90 04 11760 1
13. Poortman, E.L.J. *Petrus de Alvernia, Sententia super librum 'De vegetabilibus et plantis.* 2003. ISBN 90 04 11766 0
14. Gutman, O. *Pseudo-Avicenna, Liber Celi et Mundi.* A Critical Edition with Introduction. 2003. ISBN 90 04 13228 7
15. Takahashi, H. *Aristotelian Meteorology in Syriac.* Barhebraeus, *Butyrum Sapientiae,* Books of Mineralogy and Meteorology. 2004. ISBN 90 04 13031 4
16. Joosse, P. *A Syriac Encyclopaedia of Aristotelian Philosophy. Barhebraeus (13th c.),* Butyrum sapientiae, *Books of Ethics, Economy and Politics.* 2004. ISBN 90 04 14133 2
17. Akasoy, A.A. and A. Fidora. *The Arabic Version of The* Nicomachean Ethics. With an Introduction and Annotated Translation by Douglas M. Dunlop. 2005. ISBN 90 04 14647 4
18. Watt, J.W. with assistance of Daniel Isaac, Julian Faultless, and Ayman Shihadeh. *Aristotelian Rhetoric in Syriac.* Barhebraeus, *Butyrum Sapientiae,* Book of Rhetoric. 2005. ISBN 90 04 14517 6

In Preparation

Aristotle. *Historia Animalium. The Arabic translation commonly ascribed to Yaḥyā ibn al-Biṭrīq.* Ed. with introd. by L.S. Filius, J. den Heijer and J.N. Mattock.

Aristotle. *Poetica. The Syriac fragments.* Ed. by O. Schrier.

Aristotle. *Parva Naturalia. The Arabic translation.* Ed. by H. Daiber.

Aristoteles. *De Cælo. Die arabische Übersetzung.* Hrsg. von G. Endress.

Aristotle. *De Cælo. Gerard of Cremona's Arabic-Latin translation.* Ed. by A.M.I. van Oppenraaij.

Aristotle. *Physica. Gerard of Cremona's Arabic-Latin translation.* Ed. by D. Konstan.

Pedro Gallego. *De Animalibus. A Latin compendium of Aristotle's* De Animalibus. Ed. by A.M.I. van Oppenraaij.

Printed in the United States
By Bookmasters